America's
TEST KITCHEN

THE COOK'S ILLUSTRATED GUIDE
TO GRILLING AND BARBECUE

A BEST RECIPE CLASSIC

The Cook's Illustrated Guide to
Grilling and Barbecue

A BEST RECIPE CLASSIC

BY THE EDITORS OF

COOK'S ILLUSTRATED

PHOTOGRAPHY
CARL TREMBLAY
DANIEL J. VAN ACKERE

ILLUSTRATIONS
JOHN BURGOYNE

America's TEST KITCHEN

BROOKLINE, MASSACHUSETTS

America's Test Kitchen
17 Station Street
Brookline, MA 02445

ISBN-13: 978-0-936184-86-9
ISBN-10: 0-936184-86-8
Library of Congress Cataloging-in-Publication Data
The Editors of *Cook's Illustrated*

The Cook's Illustrated Guide to Grilling and Barbecue: A Practical Guide for the Outdoor Cook
We lit more than 6,000 fires to find the absolute best way to grill favorite foods. Here are more than 450 exhaustively tested recipes plus no-nonsense kitchen tests and tastings.

1st Edition

ISBN 0-936184-86-8 (hardcover): U.S. $35.00
I. Cooking. I. Title
2005

Manufactured in the United States of America

10 9 8

Distributed by America's Test Kitchen, 17 Station Street, Brookline, MA 02445.

Senior Editor: Lori Galvin
Editorial Assistant: Elizabeth Wray
Series Designer: Amy Klee
Jacket Designer: Richard Oriolo
Book Production Specialist: Ronald Bilodeau
Graphic Designer: Nina Madjid
Photographers: Carl Tremblay, Daniel J. van Ackere
Illustrator: John Burgoyne
Senior Production Manager: Jessica Lindheimer Quirk
Copyeditor: Cheryl Redmond
Proofreader: Holly Hartman
Indexer: Elizabeth Parson

Pictured on back of jacket: Barbecued Baby Back Ribs (page 108), Grilled Tuscan Steak with Olive Oil and Lemon (page 36), Grilled Chicken Breast with Barbecue Sauce (page 170) and Sesame-Lemon Cucumber Salad (page 351), Grilled Pizza with Fresh Tomatoes and Basil (page 335), Grill-Roasted Turkey (page 201), and Grilled Corn with Spicy Chili Butter (page 299).

CONTENTS

Welcome to America's Test Kitchen   x

Preface by Christopher Kimball   xi

Outdoor Cooking 101   1

Equipment and Tools for Outdoor Cooking   13

CHAPTER 1   Beef   27

CHAPTER 2   Pork   89

CHAPTER 3   Lamb   133

CHAPTER 4   Chicken   153

CHAPTER 5   Turkey and Other Birds   195

CHAPTER 6   Fish   221

CHAPTER 7   Shellfish   259

CHAPTER 8   Vegetables   293

CHAPTER 9   Pizza and Bruschetta   329

CHAPTER 10   Sides and Salads   347

CHAPTER 11   Rubs and Sauces   373

Index   401

A Note on Conversion   419

WELCOME TO
AMERICA'S TEST KITCHEN

THIS BOOK HAS BEEN TESTED, WRITTEN, AND edited by the folks at America's Test Kitchen, a very real 2,500-square-foot kitchen located just outside of Boston. It is the home of *Cook's Illustrated* magazine and *Cook's Country* magazine and is the Monday-through-Friday destination for more than three dozen test cooks, editors, food scientists, tasters, and cookware specialists. Our mission is to test recipes over and over again until we understand how and why they work and until we arrive at the "best" version.

We start the process of testing a recipe with a complete lack of conviction, which means that we accept no claim, no theory, no technique, and no recipe at face value. We simply assemble as many variations as possible, test a half-dozen of the most promising, and taste the results blind. We then construct our own hybrid recipe and continue to test it, varying ingredients, techniques, and cooking times until we reach a consensus. The result, we hope, is the best version of a particular recipe, but we realize that only you can be the final judge of our success (or failure). As we like to say in the test kitchen, "We make the mistakes, so you don't have to."

All of this would not be possible without a belief that good cooking, much like good music, is indeed based on a foundation of objective technique. Some people like spicy foods and others don't, but there is a right way to sauté, there is a best way to cook a pot roast, and there are measurable scientific principles involved in producing perfectly beaten, stable egg whites. This is our ultimate goal: to investigate the fundamental principles of cooking so that you become a better cook. It is as simple as that.

You can watch us work (in our actual test kitchen) by tuning in to *America's Test Kitchen* (www.americastestkitchentv.com) or *Cook's Country from America's Test Kitchen* (www.cookscountrytv.com) on public television, or by subscribing to *Cook's Illustrated* magazine (www.cooksillustrated.com) or *Cook's Country* magazine (www.cookscountry.com). We welcome you into our kitchen, where you can stand by our side as we test our way to the "best" recipes in America.

PREFACE

EVERY FOURTH OF JULY, OUR SMALL VERMONT town has a parade consisting of horses (I ride a paint named Concho), wagons pulled by Charlie Bentley's old teams, an ox that is hitched to a small breaking cart, and a tractor that pulls the bandwagon (hence the phrase, "getting on the bandwagon"). It's about as small town as you can get since the band knows only one song—"Grand Old Flag"—really well and so plays it over and over as we approach each new group of bystanders. The picnic afterward is a modest affair centered around an old, greasy, somewhat tipsy gas grill that probably predates the Carter administration. Last year, I brought a couple of barbecued pork butts and a vinegar moppin' sauce, a dish that was simple enough to make but a world apart from the usual Fourth of July hot dogs and hamburgers.

That got me thinking about grilling and barbecue. It's not just one thing—it encompasses a world of cookery, from a quick hot-grilled steak to a long and slow-cooked thick piece of meat such as the pork butt I made for the picnic. You can grill-roast a chicken on a beer can, you can flash-grill salmon fillets, and you can even grill pizzas that taste twice as good as those baked in an oven. And if you've had any experience at all with outdoor cooking, you know that there is a thin line between success and failure. Fish easily sticks to the grill. Chicken burns on the outside while remaining raw on the inside. Keeping a slow-cooking barbecue fire going for hours is no mean feat. And setting up a one-, two-, or three-level fire is part and parcel of good technique. In fact, grilling and barbecuing demand as much technique as making a great French sauce. There is little room for error when cooking over a hot fire.

I admit that the temptation of outdoor cooking is to go about it haphazardly. Which reminds me of the first time I tried to plant a field of corn. I had an old—really old—Ford seeder I had picked up at auction that consisted of two containers for the seed and one large box for the fertilizer. I hooked it up to my tractor—a huge and hard-to-turn International 404—and started off down the field. First, I found that the seeding discs at the bottom of the containers were too large for the seed (the discs turn much like the disc in the bottom of a bubblegum machine, releasing one seed at a time), so I was getting two seeds for every hole. Next, the field wasn't perfectly flat, so some rows were planted deeper than others. To top it off, I had a hard time adjusting the fertilizer, so I ran out halfway through the field. By August, it was clear to everyone in town that I had a most uneven crop, the field looking like it got hit by a particularly vicious plague. The next year, I asked a neighboring farmer to help. The whole field got planted in about an hour and the corn grew perfectly. It was just a matter of knowing how a seeder worked and how to plant.

Outdoor cooking may be easy enough for a grilling expert, but for the rest of us there really is a lot to learn. I hope that *The Cook's Illustrated Guide to Grilling and Barbecue* comes in handy not just for the recipes but for the techniques. These days, when I embark on yet another foolhardy farming project, I am smart enough to stop by and chat with a local "expert." And when I fire up my charcoal grill, I am humble enough to spend a few minutes with this book. A poorly planted field of corn and badly cooked barbecue are both easy enough to avoid as long as you know who to ask.

Christopher Kimball
Founder and Editor
Cook's Illustrated and *Cook's Country*
Host, *America's Test Kitchen* and
Cook's Country from America's Test Kitchen

OUTDOOR COOKING 101

Outdoor Cooking 101

MOST COOKS USE THE TERM "GRILLING" TO DESCRIBE ALL COOKING THAT TAKES PLACE outdoors. However, this book recognizes two basic cooking methods possible on a charcoal or gas grill. Grilling involves cooking food directly over heat, whether generated by charcoal or gas. The goal is to cook the food quickly with a lot of heat. Barbecuing (and a related technique called grill-roasting) employs the cover to turn the grill into a combination oven and smoker. The goal is to cook the food slowly so that it can absorb smoke flavor.

Grilling

THE MOST COMMON METHOD—GRILLING— refers to cooking foods completely or partially over direct heat. Thin cuts such as steaks, as well as delicate foods like seafood and vegetables, are grilled. Once the food is seared on both sides, it's probably done. This method is ideal for foods that are naturally tender. The cooking method has two goals—to heat the food through and brown the exterior.

To put a good crust on foods, especially grilled meats, you must use enough heat and you must be familiar with your source of heat: charcoal grill or gas grill.

CHARCOAL GRILLING You can use hardwood charcoal or charcoal briquettes, depending on what you're grilling. Our general rule of thumb is to use hardwood charcoal where we want a hot, fast-burning fire, such as when grilling steak. For long-cooking foods like ribs, briquettes, which burn at a slower rate, are preferred. (Read more about hardwood charcoal and charcoal briquettes on page 6.)

Once the coals are lit, there are several ways to arrange them in the grill. They can be spread out in a single layer across the bottom of the grill (see the illustration on page 4). A single-level fire delivers even heat across the cooking grate, usually at a moderate temperature, because the coals are fairly distant from the cooking grate. We often use this kind of fire to cook vegetables and fish. (You can make a more intense single-level fire by adding unlit coals to the grill once the lit coals have been turned out of the chimney starter. Wait about 10 minutes for these new coals to catch fire.)

A second option, one that we often employ when grilling meat, is to build a two-level fire (see the illustration on page 4). Once the coals are lit, some of them are spread out in a single layer over half of the grill. The remaining coals are piled up on the other side of the grill so that they are closer to the cooking grate. This arrangement creates two levels of heat intensity on the grill. The part of the cooking grate above the taller pile of coals is quite hot, perfect for searing foods. The heat above the single level of coals is less intense, making this an ideal spot to cook thicker foods through once they have been browned. This cooler fire also comes in handy if flames engulf the food. Simply drag the food to the cooler part of the grill, and the flames should subside.

We use a two-level fire for grilling thick steaks and chops. A standard single-level fire is not quite hot enough to sear meats properly. You could bulk up the fire with more coals, but then the exterior tends to burn before the meat is cooked through. The two-level fire is the best of both worlds—a hot fire that will sear foods and a cooler spot that will allow slow, thorough cooking.

In a few instances, we prefer to use a modified two-level fire (see the illustration on page 4). We pile up all of the lit coals in half of the grill and leave the other half empty. This arrangement works for bone-in chicken breasts and other delicate foods that can dry out easily. We sear them over the hot coals and then let them cook through over a cooler side of the grill by means of gentle, indirect heat.

No matter how we build a charcoal fire for grilling, we always leave the cover off. Over time, soot and resinous compounds can build up on the inside of a kettle grill lid, which can then impart an off flavor, reminiscent of stale smoke, to the food. This effect is most noticeable in fish and poultry. When we want to trap heat on an open charcoal grill to make sure food cooks through, we prefer to cover the food with a disposable aluminum roasting pan or pie plate. (Note that for grill-roasting and barbecuing, the grill cover must be kept on to trap heat. However, the use of wood chips and chunks overpowers the off flavor the lid can impart.)

GAS GRILLING requires slightly different (but similar) procedures. You can create a single-level fire by adjusting all the burners to the same temperature—keeping them at high for the hottest fire or turning them to medium for a moderate fire once the grill has been heated. For a two-level fire, simply leave one burner on high or medium-high once the grill is hot and turn the other burners to medium or medium-low. And for a modified two-level fire, leave one burner on high and turn the other burners off. The idea is the same here as with charcoal. Sear foods over the more intense heat, then slide foods to the cooler part of the grill to cook them through.

We find that gas grills work best with the lid down in all instances. Because they put out a lot less heat than a charcoal fire, foods won't brown properly if the lid is left open. Gas burns cleanly, so there's no build-up of soot on the inside of the lid and therefore no danger that foods cooked in a covered gas grill will pick up an off flavor.

With both charcoal and gas, it's imperative to use the right level of heat. To make our recipes easy to follow, we have devised a system that determines the heat level by measuring the amount of time you can comfortably hold your hand above the cooking grate (see page 4 for details).

GRILL-ROASTING AND BARBECUING

A THICK PORK ROAST OR TURKEY CANNOT BE grilled—the exterior would be charred and ashen well before the interior of such a large piece of meat could cook through. The solution is the second method of outdoor cooking: indirect cooking.

With indirect cooking, the lid of the grill is down (not up, as in grilling). This traps heat and creates a regulated cooking environment much like that of an oven. While grilling calls for filling the grill with charcoal or lighting all the gas burners, indirect cooking involves a smaller fire. The lit coals are banked on one side of the grill, or one of the gas burners is turned off. Foods cooked by indirect heat are placed over the cooler part of the grill. Since there is no direct heat, the food cooks evenly, without flare-ups. Indirect cooking is generally divided into two categories: grill-roasting, in which food is cooked relatively quickly at a fairly high heat, and barbecuing, in which food is cooked quite slowly at low temperatures.

GRILL-ROASTING is best for foods that are already tender and don't require prolonged cooking. Birds are especially well suited to grill-roasting (at lower temperatures the skin remains soft and flabby), as are tender cuts of meat (like beef tenderloin) that need to develop a crisp crust during their relatively short cooking time, usually an hour or less. Grill-roasting occurs between 300 and 400 degrees. (Grilling occurs at temperatures in excess of 500 degrees; in comparison, it's hard to sustain higher temperatures with indirect cooking.)

BARBECUING is the traditional low and slow cooking method used with ribs, pulled pork (shredded Boston butt), and brisket. The goal is to impart as much smoke flavor as possible—hence a long cooking time (usually several hours) over a fairly low fire. Barbecuing also provides ample time for fatty, tough cuts to give up (or render) their fat and become tender. Although there is much debate among barbecue experts as to the proper cooking temperature, we believe that barbecuing should take place between 250 and 300 degrees. While some chefs and pit masters argue that ribs are best barbecued at 180 degrees, we find it very difficult to maintain such a low fire. Also, such low temperatures increase the risk of food-borne illness and prolong cooking times to many, many hours.

One final note about barbecuing: Despite the name (barbecue), food is generally flavored with a spice rub, not barbecue sauce, as it cooks. Barbecue sauce applied to ribs before cooking will burn. If you want to use barbecue sauce, apply it during the last minutes of cooking or pass some at the table.

The Basics of Charcoal Grilling

CHOOSING A CHARCOAL GRILL

Nothing beats the design of the standard covered kettle grill. Inside the deep, bowl-shaped grill are two separate grates (or racks)—one for holding the lit charcoal, the other for cooking the food. There's plenty of room between these two grates (at least six inches), so you can build a hot fire with a lot of charcoal. The grill is covered with a domed lid that is tall enough to accommodate a large roast or turkey. Both the grill and lid have adjustable air vents that let you control the rate at which the fuel burns. Some charcoal grill grates have hinged sections that make it much easier to add coals during cooking. If you have a choice, buy a grill with this feature. For the results from our testing of charcoal grills, including recommended brands, see pages 14–15.

KETTLE GRILL

TAKING THE TEMPERATURE OF THE FIRE

Use the chart below to determine the intensity of the fire. The terms "hot fire," "medium-hot fire," "medium fire," and "medium-low fire" are used throughout this book. (When using a gas grill, ignore dial readings such as medium or medium-low in favor of actual measurements of the temperature, as described here.)

INTENSITY OF FIRE	TIME YOU CAN HOLD YOUR HAND 5 INCHES ABOVE GRATE
Hot	2 seconds
Medium-hot	3 to 4 seconds
Medium	5 to 6 seconds
Medium-low	7 seconds

Once the coals have been spread out in the bottom of the grill, put the cooking grate in place and put the cover on for five minutes to heat up the grate. (On gas grills, preheat with the lid down and all burners on high for 15 minutes.) Scrape the cooking grate clean and then take the temperature of the fire by holding your hand 5 inches above the cooking grate and counting how many seconds you can comfortably leave it in place.

BUILDING A CHARCOAL FIRE TO MEET YOUR NEEDS

While cooking with a conventional oven is akin to driving an automatic shift automobile, outdoor cooking is a lot like driving a standard shift—a little more work, but a lot more fun. So, instead of just turning dials and pressing buttons to manipulate heat as you would with an oven, it is necessary to arrange lit coals according to what types of food you are grilling.

SINGLE-LEVEL FIRE
Delivers direct, moderate heat. Use with fairly thin foods that cook quickly, such as fruits, vegetables, fish and shellfish, hamburgers, and kebabs.

TO PREPARE: Arrange all the lit charcoal in an even layer.

TWO-LEVEL FIRE
Allows the cook to sear foods over a very hot section of the grill and to finish the cooking over a cooler section so that the exterior doesn't char. Use for chops, steaks, turkey burgers, bone-in chicken legs and thighs, and thick fish steaks.

TO PREPARE: Arrange some lit coals in a single layer on half of the grill. Leave the remaining coals in a pile.

MODIFIED TWO-LEVEL FIRE
Ideal for foods that are susceptible to burning but require a long cooking time. A modified two-level fire can also be used to create an especially hot fire when grilling small, thin cuts of meat. Use for bone-in chicken breasts, boneless chicken breasts and thighs, sausages, flank steak, pork tenderloin, rack of lamb, and butterflied leg of lamb.

TO PREPARE: Pile all the lit coals onto one side of the grill, leaving the other side empty. We often cover foods on the cooler side of the grill with a disposable aluminum pan to trap the heat and create an oven-like cooking environment.

LIGHTING A CHARCOAL GRILL

USE A CHIMNEY STARTER

We find that a chimney starter (also called a flue starter) is the best way to light charcoal. (See the illustration at right.) A chimney starter is foolproof, and it eliminates the need for lighter fluid (which can impart harsh, acrid flavors to food). We strongly recommend that you visit a hardware store (or other shop that sells grilling equipment) and purchase this indispensable device. For what to look for when purchasing a chimney starter, see page 18.

To use a chimney starter, place several sheets of crumpled newspaper in the lower chamber and set the starter on the bottom grate of a kettle grill (where the charcoal will eventually go); the top cooking grate should not be in place. Fill the upper chamber with as much charcoal as directed. Light the newspaper through the holes in the side of the chimney starter and wait until the coals at the top of the pile are covered with fine gray ash. (This will take about 20 minutes.) Dump the lit charcoal in the bottom of the grill and arrange as directed. (For additional firepower, add more unlit charcoal and wait until it has caught fire before grilling.) You can then set the cooking grate in place, allow it to heat up, and then clean it. After that, you are ready to grill.

Note that after you empty the lit charcoal into the grill, the starter will still be very hot. Don't put it down on the lawn—it will burn the grass. Instead, set the starter on a concrete or stone surface away from any flammable objects and allow it to cool off for at least half an hour. Make sure you choose a spot away from children and pets.

MAKING YOUR OWN CHIMNEY STARTER

Although a chimney starter is relatively inexpensive (about $15 to $25), you may want to save money and improvise with an empty 39-ounce coffee can that has had both ends removed with a can opener. Note that there are two drawbacks to this method. Because the improvised starter has no handles, you must maneuver it with long-handled tongs. Also, because of its size, this improvised starter can't light enough charcoal for most grilling jobs; you will need to add unlit coals once the lit coals have been dumped onto the charcoal grate.

1. Using a church-key can opener, punch six holes along the lower circumference of the can.

2. Set the can on the charcoal grate with the triangular holes at the bottom. Load the can about one-half full with crumpled newspaper and top it off with charcoal.

3. Insert a long match through one of the triangular holes at the bottom to set the crumpled paper on fire.

4. When the coals are lit (after about 20 minutes), use tongs to grasp the top of the starter and dump its contents onto the charcoal grate. Place more coals loosely around and on top of the burning coals to build up a cooking fire.

FOUR TIPS FOR BETTER CHARCOAL GRILLING

1. Use enough charcoal. There's no sense spending $50 on steaks and then steaming them over an inadequate fire. The size of your grill, the amount of food being cooked, and the desired intensity of the fire are all factors in deciding how much charcoal to use. In the end, you want a fire that is slightly larger than the space on the cooking grate occupied by the food. The higher you pile the charcoal (and therefore the closer it is to the cooking grate), the more intense the fire will be.

2. Make sure the coals are covered with fine gray ash before you start to grill. Fine gray ash is a sign that the coals are fully lit and hot.

3. Once the coals are ready, set the cooking grate in place and let it heat up for five minutes. Once the grate is hot, scrape it clean with a grill brush.

4. Don't use the cover when grilling. It can impart an off flavor to foods. If you need to trap heat to cook something through, cover the food with a disposable aluminum roasting pan or pie plate.

LIGHTING A FIRE WITHOUT A STARTER

If you don't have access to a chimney starter and don't have an empty coffee can around, use this method as a last resort.

1. Place eight crumpled sheets of newspaper beneath the rack on which the charcoal sits.

2. With the bottom air vents open, pile the charcoal on the rack and light the paper. After about 20 minutes, the coals should be covered with fine gray ash and ready for cooking.

5

Charcoal 101

CHOOSING A TYPE OF CHARCOAL

Traditional charcoal has come back into vogue in the past decade. Irregularly shaped lumps of charred wood burn hotter and faster than the neat briquettes that became popular in the United States after World War II. Lump hardwood charcoal, also known as charwood, is more expensive than the ubiquitous briquettes but is our preferred product for most direct grilling chores because it puts out so much heat. We also like the fact that this product is 100 percent hardwood and contains no additives. Look for it in hardware stores, although it occasionally shows up in supermarkets.

But does charcoal type influence flavor? To find out, we grilled steaks and zucchini over three fires built with the following: hardwood charcoal, regular charcoal briquettes, and Match Light, a Kingsford product infused with lighter fluid to guarantee rapid ignition. The flavor differences in the steaks were nearly imperceptible, but the delicate zucchini was a different story; the zucchini grilled over Match Light tasted oddly bitter. In separate tests with delicate foods—chicken, fish, and vegetables—grilled over fires started with lighter fluid, tasters also detected harsh, acrid flavors. Consequently, we like to steer clear of both Match Light and lighter fluid. Hardwood charcoal is the best choice for grilling because it burns hot and fast, while slower-burning briquettes are optimal for grill-roasting and barbecuing.

THE BRANDS WE TESTED

COMPARING HARDWOOD LUMP CHARCOAL AND BRIQUETTES

Ounce for ounce, hardwood lump charcoal burns much hotter than briquettes. However, the differences are less dramatic when the coals are measured by volume. (Because of their regular shape, briquettes compact more easily so you can fit more coals into the same amount of space.) For all practical purposes, a heaping chimney of charcoal briquettes will make a fire that is as hot as a level chimney of hardwood lump charcoal. So if you need to substitute briquettes for hardwood, use slightly more briquettes to achieve the same heat level. The following chart is based on a 6-quart chimney. Because of its irregular shape, hardwood charcoal should be measured by volume or weight, not the number of pieces.

HOW FULL IS THE CHIMNEY?	VOLUME	HARDWOOD CHARCOAL	CHARCOAL BRIQUETTES
Half	3 qts	1¼ lbs	2¾ lbs (45 pieces)
Two thirds	4 qts	1¾ lbs	3¾ lbs (60 pieces)
Three quarters	4½ qts	2 lbs	4 lbs (65 pieces)
Full	6 qts	2½ lbs	5½ lbs (90 pieces)

ADDING MORE COALS TO A LIT CHARCOAL FIRE

We recommend that you buy a charcoal grill with a hinged cooking grate. This feature allows you to lift up the edge of the grate and add more unlit charcoal as needed. If your grill doesn't have this feature, you must transfer foods to a tray, lift up the grate with fireproof gloves, and then add coals. A hinged cooking grate allows foods to stay in place as you add coals.

MEASURING CHARCOAL

Many recipes call for a particular volume of charcoal, such as 4 quarts. An easy way to measure it is to use an empty half-gallon milk or juice carton. Just wash the carton thoroughly and store it with the charcoal. Each full carton equals roughly two quarts.

The Basics of Gas Grilling

CHOOSING A GAS GRILL

A gas grill is consistent, delivering the same results day in and day out. Gas grills can be roughly three times more expensive than charcoal grills, so it pays to shop carefully.

Several features and design elements separate a good gas grill from a poor one. A built-in thermometer that registers real numbers (not just low, medium, and hot) is essential. A gauge that tells you how much gas is left in the tank is also a plus. As you might expect, a large grill offers the cook more possibilities. In addition to size, the number of burners is critical. It's not possible to cook by indirect heat on a grill with only one burner because the burner is usually positioned in the center of the grill, so the cooler parts of the grill are too small to accommodate most foods. Indirect cooking requires a grill with at least two burners. With one burner on and one burner off, at least half of the grill will be cool enough for slow cooking.

The heat should be evenly distributed across the entire surface of the grill. We found that most gas grills are plenty hot. The problem is that gas grills are often unable to sustain temperatures low enough for barbecuing. For the results from our testing of gas grills, see pages 16–17.

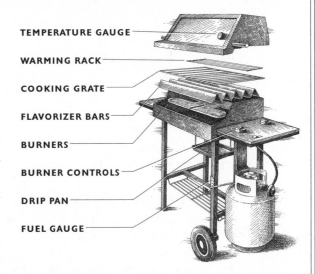

TEMPERATURE GAUGE

WARMING RACK

COOKING GRATE

FLAVORIZER BARS

BURNERS

BURNER CONTROLS

DRIP PAN

FUEL GAUGE

ADJUSTING A GAS GRILL TO MEET YOUR NEEDS

For information about which foods are appropriate for which fires, see page 4. It's quite simple to regulate the heat on a gas grill—just adjust the burners.

For a Single-Level Fire: Adjust all the burners to high for a hot fire, or turn the burners to medium after heating.

For a Two-Level Fire: Leave one burner on high or medium-high and turn the other(s) to medium or medium-low.

For a Modified Two-Level Fire: Leave one burner on high and turn the other burner(s) off.

LIGHTING A GAS GRILL

Lighting a gas grill is remarkably easy. Just make sure to read all the instructions in your owner's manual thoroughly and to follow directions regarding the order in which the burners must be lit. In most instances, an electric igniter will light the burners. We have found that electric igniters can fail occasionally, though, especially in windy conditions. Most models have a hole for lighting the burners with a match. Read all the directions carefully and make sure to wait several minutes (or as directed) between attempts at lighting the grill. This waiting time allows excess gas to dissipate and is an important safety measure.

CHECKING FUEL LEVEL IN A TANK

There's nothing worse than running out of fuel halfway through grilling. If your grill doesn't have a gas gauge, use this technique to estimate how much gas is left in the tank.

1. Bring a cup or so of water to a boil in a small saucepan or glass measuring cup (if using a microwave). Pour the water over the side of the tank.

2. Feel the metal with your hand. Where the water has succeeded in warming the tank, it is empty; where the tank remains cool to the touch, there is still propane inside.

THREE TIPS FOR BETTER GAS GRILLING

1. Remove the warming rack before lighting the grill unless you know you are going to need it. On most grills, the rack is very close to the cooking surface, and it can be hard to reach foods on the back of the grill without burning your hands on the hot metal.

2. Heat the grill with all the burners turned to high (even if you plan on cooking over low heat) and the lid down for at least 15 minutes. Once the grill is hot, scrape the grate clean with a grill brush and then adjust the burners as desired.

3. Whether cooking by direct or indirect heat, keep the lid down. With charcoal grills, residue from the briquettes can build up on the inside of the lid and give quickly cooked foods an off flavor, but this isn't a problem with gas grills because gas burns cleanly. Keeping the lid down concentrates the heat when searing and keeps the temperature steady when slow-cooking.

PROTECTING GRILL CONTROLS

The ignition and burner control knobs on some gas grills can be persnickety if they get wet or dirty from exposure to the elements, especially if the grill is kept outdoors in the snow during the winter. If your grill has no cover, try this impromptu solution.

Invert a disposable aluminum roasting pan over the control panel and tape it in place on either end with duct or electrical tape.

THE BASICS OF INDIRECT COOKING
ON A CHARCOAL GRILL

CHARCOAL GRILL GRILL-ROASTING AND BARBECUING

A KETTLE-STYLE GRILL WITH A COVER IS A must for grill-roasting or barbecuing with charcoal. The deep bowl shape allows air to circulate, and the high lid accommodates tall foods, such as a whole turkey. A large grill, with a cooking surface that measures 22 inches across, is best for indirect cooking. On smaller grills, the cooler part of the grill may be too small to hold large cuts of meat.

Before starting, empty the grill of any old ashes, which may block air circulation and prolong cooking times. In most cases, we prefer to bank all the coals on one side of the grill, leaving half of the grill free of coals and providing a large space for foods to cook without danger of burning. Because the lid is on, the heat is pretty well distributed. However, the side of the food closest to the fire will cook more quickly. For this reason, we found it necessary to flip foods (that is, turn them over) as well as rotate them (turn the side initially facing the lit coals 180 degrees on the grill so that it faces away from the lit coals). The one exception to this rule is a whole chicken, which is small enough to fit between piles of lit coals on either side of the grill. With heat attacking the bird from each side, there's no need to rotate.

You can control the heat level to some extent by adjusting the vents on the lid and base of the grill. Opening the vents gives the fire more oxygen and causes the coals to burn hotter at first, but then the fire cools down more quickly as the coals peter out. Closing the vents partially (don't close the vents all the way or the fire will die) lowers the heat but keeps the coals from burning up too fast and helps the fire last longer.

USING A CHARCOAL GRILL FOR INDIRECT COOKING

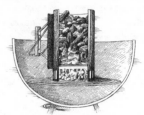

1. Light a chimney starter.

2. When the coals are well lit and covered with a layer of fine gray ash, dump them onto the charcoal grate, piling the coals up on one half of the grill and leaving the other half free of coals.

3. Place soaked and drained wood chunks or a foil packet filled with wood chips on top of the coals. Set the top grate in position, heat briefly, and then scrape the grate clean with a grill brush. You are now ready to cook over the cooler part of the grill. Put the food on the grill and set the lid in place. Open the air vents as directed in the recipe.

4. We like to have some idea of what the temperature is inside a kettle grill as food cooks. A grill thermometer (see page 21) inserted through the vents on the lid can tell you if the fire is too hot or if it is getting too cool and you need to add more charcoal. You will get different readings depending on where the lid vents—and therefore the thermometer—are in relation to the coals. Because you want to know what the temperature is where the food is being cooked, rotate the lid so that the thermometer is close to the food. Make sure, however, that the thermometer stem does not touch the food (this can be an issue when grill-roasting big foods, like a whole turkey).

THE BASICS OF INDIRECT COOKING ON A GAS GRILL

GAS GRILL GRILL-ROASTING AND BARBECUING

AS WITH A CHARCOAL GRILL, SIZE MATTERS when trying to grill-roast or barbecue many foods on a gas grill. For instance, the lid must be tall enough to accommodate a turkey. (A lid that rises less than 8 inches above the cooking grate will be a problem.) Likewise, the size of the cooking grate is important when preparing wide, flat cuts like brisket or ribs. Unless the cooking surface is at least 400 square inches, you might have trouble with such large cuts.

In addition to size, the number of burners is critical. It's not possible to cook indirectly on a grill with only one burner because the burner is usually positioned in the center of the grill; as a result, the cooler parts of the grill are too small to fit most foods. You must use a grill with at least two burners. With one burner on and one burner off, at least half of the grill will be cool enough for indirect cooking.

It is just as important to buy a gas grill with a thermometer. You can stick an oven thermometer on the cooking grate near the food, but then you have to open the lid to find out what the temperature is. Opening the lid causes heat to dissipate and prolongs the total cooking time. A gas gauge also comes in handy when grill-roasting or barbecuing. Many recipes require several hours of cooking, and there's nothing worse than unexpectedly running out of gas halfway through.

In our tests, we found it slightly easier to cook on a grill with left and right burners rather than front and back burners. The cooking grate on most gas grills is rectangular. When the grill is divided into front and back cooking zones, the cooler part of the grill will be a long, relatively narrow band. Although this shape is well suited to ribs and tenderloin, it can be a challenge when cooking a turkey, especially on a moderately sized grill. When the grill is divided into left and right cooking zones, each side is roughly a square, which we find to be a better shape for cooking birds. Foods that are long and thin, like beef tenderloin, can easily be curled into a C-shape over the cooler side of the grill.

To set up a gas grill for indirect cooking, remove all warming racks attached to the hood or the back of the grill. (Leave the racks in place when making ribs on a small grill.) Position the wood chips over the primary burner. With some gas grills, one burner must be turned on first. This is the primary burner. With other grills, you may designate a primary burner yourself.

USING A GAS GRILL FOR INDIRECT COOKING

Remove part or all of the cooking grate. Place a foil tray with soaked wood chips on top of the primary burner. Make sure the tray is resting securely on the burner so that it will not tip. Replace the cooking grate. Light all burners and cover the grill. When you see a lot of smoke (after about 20 minutes), turn off the burner (or burners) without chips and place the food over it (or them). If the chips start to flame, douse the fire with water from a squirt bottle. Cover the grill.

Wood Chips and Chunks 101

One of the best reasons to barbecue or grill-roast is to flavor foods with smoke. Charcoal itself has some flavor (gas adds none), but the real smoky flavor of good ribs or brisket comes from wood chunks or chips. Chips will work on either a charcoal or gas grill, but chunks are suited to charcoal fires only, since to work they must rest in a pile of lit coals. (If placed on the bottom of a gas grill they will not get hot enough to smoke.)

Chips and chunks come from the same source—trees. The only difference between them is size. Chunks are usually the size of lemons; chips are thinner shards, more like the fine wood chips you might spread over a garden bed. (That said, it's also the case that pieces from the same bag of chips or chunks can vary greatly in size.)

Wood chips and chunks are made from hardwoods because they burn more slowly than softer woods. The most common choices are hickory, mesquite, and alder, although some stores may carry cherry or oak. Resinous woods, like pine, are not used for grilling because they give foods an off flavor.

Using wood chunks is the easiest way to add smoke flavor when cooking over charcoal. You don't want the wood to catch fire and give up all its smoke at once. Ideally, the chunks should smolder slowly, releasing smoke for as long as possible. We found that soaking wood chunks in water adds enough moisture to prevent the wood from catching fire as soon as it is placed on the charcoal. Soak as many 3-inch chunks (each the size of a tennis ball) as directed in the recipe in cold water to cover for one hour. Drain the chunks and place them directly on the lit pile of charcoal.

If you can't find wood chunks, small wood chips may be used, but they must be protected in some fashion before using them on a charcoal or gas grill. (Chunks need only to be soaked in water for an hour or so.) To keep the chips from burning up too quickly, we devised the following strategies.

On a charcoal grill, we found it best to wrap the chips in a foil packet. (There's no need to soak the chips; the foil protects them from catching fire too quickly.)

On a gas grill, we found it best to place chips in an open foil tray. You can use a disposable aluminum pan or make a tray out of aluminum foil. Soak the chips in cold water for 30 minutes before adding them to the tray; this ensures that they smolder and don't burn out right away.

MAKING A FOIL PACKET FOR WOOD CHIPS ON A CHARCOAL GRILL

1. Place the amount of wood chips called for in the recipe in the center of an 18-inch square of heavy-duty aluminum foil. Fold in all four sides of the foil to encase the chips.

2. Turn the foil packet over. Tear about six large holes (each about the size of a quarter) through the top of the foil packet with a fork to allow smoke to escape. Place the packet, with holes facing up, directly on the pile of lit charcoal.

MAKING A FOIL TRAY FOR WOOD CHIPS ON A GAS GRILL

1. Start with a 12 by 18-inch piece of heavy-duty foil. Make a 1-inch fold on one long side. Repeat three more times, then turn the fold up to create a sturdy side that measures about an inch high. Repeat the process on the other long side.

2. With a short side facing you, fold in both corners as if wrapping a gift.

3. Turn up the inside inch or so of each triangular fold to match the rim on the long sides of the foil tray.

4. Lift the pointed end of the triangle over the rim of foil and fold down to seal. Repeat the process on the other short side. The tray can now be filled with soaked and drained wood chips.

The Top 10 Grilling Mistakes & How to Avoid Them

Many people assume that outdoor cooking is no more than lighting the grill and flipping burgers—or basting ribs. Not so. In fact, getting it right isn't so easy. Cooking outdoors on a grill, whether charcoal or gas, is less precise than cooking indoors with a calibrated oven. Successful results take practice, patience, and attention to detail. Mistakes are also common, and they're not just limited to the outdoor cooking novice—even grilling gurus (or test kitchen cooks) can make the occasional blunder. So before you fire up the grill, take a moment to read about the following problems (and their simple solutions) to ensure that your outdoor cooking remains rewarding, successful, and safe.

1. Grilling in a Dangerous Location Be mindful of where your charcoal grill is situated. Burning charcoal can sometimes fall out and burn wooden surfaces or ignite grass. Make sure the grill is located several feet from your home or garage and position the grill in an out-of-the-way spot, away from children and pets.

2. Running Out of Fuel Make sure you have enough fuel. There's nothing worse than firing up the grill only to have the gas peter out before the food is cooked. See page 7 for an easy way to check the fuel level on a gas grill. We also recommend keeping an extra tank on hand, especially if you grill frequently. As for hardwood charcoal and briquettes, avoid last-minute trips to the store by making sure before guests arrive that you have enough on hand. Most recipes require at least one chimney of charcoal—about six quarts.

3. Starting with a Dirty or Clogged Grill Check the drip pan of your gas grill. Dispose of any leftover grease, which can be a fire hazard, before turning on the grill. On a charcoal grill, dispose of any excess charcoal dust. A dirty grill can give foods, especially fish and vegetables, an off flavor.

4. Grilling on a Dirty Cooking Grate Make sure the cooking grate is clean. Foods will stick to a dirty grate and pick up off flavors. A functioning grill brush is key. We've found that most brushes are useless. See page 18 for the results of our tests of grill brushes. (Also, see page 250 for how we improvise a grill brush with tongs and foil.) As an added precaution for foods that tend to stick to the grate, such as burgers and fish, oil the cooking grate thoroughly (see the illustration on page 224).

5. Not Timing Your Cooking Appropriately Charcoal grills need about 30 minutes to achieve the proper temperature. Gas grills should preheat for 15 minutes. Plan ahead for grilled foods that require brining or marinating, which can take anywhere from 30 minutes to overnight.

6. Disregarding Food Safety Practices When cooking outdoors, observe the same food safety practices you employ when cooking indoors. Avoid cross-contamination by using separate platters for raw and cooked foods (or see our tip on page 152). When basting meat or poultry, pour what you'll need into a separate dish so as not to contaminate the extra sauce. Always dispose of leftover marinades. Leftover grilled foods should also be promptly refrigerated.

7. Misjudging When Food Is Done Food streaked with nice grill marks isn't necessarily done. Thick steaks or chicken parts can still be raw in the middle, even when the exterior is nicely colored. Remember to use an instant-read thermometer when checking the doneness of meat and poultry. Refer to individual recipes for doneness temperatures. See page 21 for our rating of instant-read thermometers.

8. Using Too Much Heat Bigger (and hotter) is not always better. Many meals can be ruined by excessive heat. Use the amount of charcoal specified in the recipe. On a gas grill, once the grate is preheated, make sure to adjust the heat level as directed. When using a charcoal grill, many recipes suggest building a two-level fire so that you have some place to drag food if it starts to burn.

9. Applying Barbecue Sauces Too Soon Unless you want a charred mess, wait till near the end of cooking before applying sweet, sticky barbecue sauces to foods. If added too early in the grilling process, the sauce is subjected to intense direct heat. Over a sustained period of time, the sugars in the sauce will burn and become unpalatable. It's best to apply these sauces during the last few minutes of cooking.

10. Neglecting to Make Adjustments for Inclement Weather Pay attention to weather conditions. If the weather is cool or windy, you may need to add more charcoal to the fire or adjust the burners on your grill. Cooking times for foods may also need to be increased in inclement weather.

CHARCOAL GRILLS VERSUS GAS GRILLS:

IS ONE BETTER THAN THE OTHER?

THE SHORT ANSWER IS NO. INSTEAD, WE RECOMMEND EXAMINING THE PROS AND CONS OF each grill to determine what strengths are most important to you (and what weaknesses you can tolerate). In other words, the choice of grill is up to you.

We have tested all the recipes in this book on both charcoal and gas grills and made plenty of general observations in the process. Here are our conclusions in the areas we feel are most important in outdoor cooking.

SEARING ABILITY AND SMOKE FLAVOR

CHARCOAL For foods like steaks and chops, where you want a good crust, the intense heat of a charcoal fire delivers an excellent sear and smoky wood flavor—but more so for long-cooking foods such as ribs or brisket. A charcoal fire also does a good job of burning wood chunks and chips.

Over time, however, soot and resinous compounds can build up on the inside of the grill cover. For this reason, we don't use the cover when grilling since we find that it often imparts a slightly sooty, off flavor to the food. We prefer to use a disposable aluminum roasting pan or pie plate to cover foods that require some buildup of heat to cook through. When barbecuing or grill-roasting, however, the lid must be used to trap heat. We find that the smoky flavor the food absorbs from wood chips or chunks, which are used in all recipes that call for indirect cooking, masks any off flavor the lid may impart.

GAS A gas fire doesn't get as hot as a charcoal fire, and therefore doesn't brown and sear as well, although it will work OK. As for flavor, gas adds no flavor on its own, and gas burners don't burn chips especially well. But for foods that require a moderate flame, such as vegetables, a gas grill works just as well as charcoal. Unlike on a charcoal grill, the inside of the cover stays fairly clean. Since there is no buildup of resinous smoke, the grill cover (rather than a disposable aluminum pan) can be used for recipes such as grilled chicken breasts, in which a cover is needed to cook foods through.

CONVENIENCE AND CONSISTENCY

CHARCOAL There's no way around it—a charcoal grill requires more effort than a gas grill. The fire must be built and maintained to ensure success. Inclement weather can also adversely affect a charcoal grill—more so than a gas grill.

GAS You can't beat a gas grill for convenience. You can grill in poor weather—even in the rain. While you need to keep an eye on the gas gauge to make sure you don't run out of fuel, a gas grill is predictable and nearly foolproof. The fire will always light.

Given constant weather conditions, a grill with both burners set to medium will always be about the same temperature. There's a learning curve with a gas grill. But with some practice, you will realize that a particular corner runs a bit hotter and is ideal for searing steaks, or that the middle area between the burners is the best spot to cook delicate vegetables. These quirks vary from grill to grill, so they are hard to detail. The point is that an experienced griller can depend on a gas grill to deliver the same results day in, day out, for better or for worse.

The one variable here is weather. All grills, gas or charcoal, will be more fickle in windy or cold weather. Fires may die out in extremely windy conditions. Wind and cold will lower the internal temperature of the grill, and food will take longer to cook. Under such adverse conditions, however, a gas grill is far more reliable than a charcoal grill.

EQUIPMENT AND TOOLS
FOR OUTDOOR COOKING

Equipment and Tools for Outdoor Cooking

WALKING PAST DISPLAYS OF GRILLING GEAR IN MOST KITCHENWARE STORES WOULD have you thinking you couldn't grill a hamburger without investing in a staggering assortment of equipment, tools, and gadgets. Not so. We have tested hundreds of pieces of grilling equipment over the years. Here are our findings about what works, what doesn't, and what you really need to cook outdoors. Thankfully, the list is fairly short.

Charcoal Grills

FLICKING A SWITCH TO LIGHT A GAS GRILL may be convenient, but for many die-hard grillers nothing beats cooking over a live charcoal fire. The pleasure is utterly visceral: the glowing, red-hot coals, the smoke, the intense sizzle, the interplay of food and flame, and the aroma of searing meat. And, of course, there is the flavor. Charcoal-fueled fires infuse food with characteristic notes of wood and smoke that no gas fire can match.

Yet deciding which charcoal grill to buy is not so straightforward. They come in different shapes and sizes, with different features and vastly different prices. The grills we tested—Weber One-Touch Silver, Weber Performer, Sunbeam Portable Charcoal Grill, Cajun Grill, and Thermos Kettle Grill—ran the gamut from round to rectangular, bare bones to fully loaded, smaller to larger, and $50 to more than 10 times that amount. A few weeks of grilling steaks, hamburgers, bone-in chicken breasts, and ribs led us to some useful observations and a couple of decent choices but not, alas, to a grill that is perfect in all respects.

Grilling a mountain of food over two weeks revealed very little difference in cooking performance in our grills. Each developed a fire hot enough to sear the food, which is what charcoal grilling is all about. Each also offers vents to control airflow—and thereby the intensity of the fire—but we were not able to detect any advantages or disadvantages based on the number or

position of the vents. It was possible, however, to identify two important design factors: the size of the grill and the depth of the grill cover.

Many of us in the test kitchen have had years of experience grilling at home on a small portable grill, so we can speak personally about the benefits of upsizing. (The cooking area on small grills is less than 350 square inches; the cooking area on the largest grill we tested was 468 square inches.) A large surface area is essential if you cook for large groups and useful even when you don't, because it affords the opportunity to easily grill some extra food for later alongside tonight's dinner. For instance, we rarely grill a meal without covering every available inch of grill space with vegetables to have on hand for tomorrow's antipasto, pizza, or pasta salad. It is also easier to build a two-level fire (hot on one side and cooler on the other) in a large grill. In short, size matters.

While we generally don't use the cover when grilling over high heat, it is necessary when grill-roasting large cuts, such as a turkey or prime rib, over lower heat. To trap heat and contain any flavorful smoke generated from wood chunks or chips, the grill cover must fit comfortably over the food and form a tight seal with the grill bottom. We recommend 12- to 14-pound turkeys for grill-roasting, and the Sunbeam grill was the only one with a cover that closed over a 14-pounder (set on a V-rack to promote even cooking). All of the grills in the group, except for the Thermos, swallowed the 12-pounder.

In some respects, charcoal grills are a little like cars. Any new car will get you from point A to point B, but extra features like traction control or anti-lock brakes make the car easier to drive. Likewise, all charcoal grills will cook your food, but several features can make the process easier and more enjoyable.

Though we never would have guessed it, the presence of an attached table made a huge difference. After years of precariously balancing platters on deck railings and chair arms, it was a welcome relief to have a secure, accessible place to put dishes and utensils. Among our group, only the Weber One-Touch Silver and the Thermos lacked tables of any kind.

If you plan to barbecue or grill-roast (both methods entail longer cooking than grilling), some means of easily adding charcoal to the fire is useful. The Webers offer specially designed cooking grates, which are either hinged or open at the ends so you can slip in the charcoal. If you have to add fuel to any of the other grills, you must endure the aggravation of removing the food and the cooking grate to get to the fire.

Another thoughtful feature is some means of adjusting the height of either the charcoal rack or the cooking grate. If given no respite from a hot fire, many foods, such as thick steaks, pork chops, and chicken breasts, will burn on the outside before cooking through on the inside. These foods must be finished over a cooler fire. This is easy to accomplish if you can adjust the charcoal rack down away from the cooking grate, as is the case with the Cajun and the Thermos. On the Sunbeam, the charcoal grate is fixed, but you can adjust the height of the cooking grate, so the effect is the same. Granted, the ability to adjust the charcoal rack or cooking grate is not essential. On the Webers, which do not offer such adjustability, you can build a two-level fire that is hot on one side and cooler on the other to achieve the same effect. This simply takes a little extra knowledge on the part of the griller. It is easier, though, if you can change the level of the fire with the shift of a lever or the turn of a dial.

Several other features fell into the nice but not necessary category. Notable among them was the gas ignition on the Weber Performer, which did its job well but added expense and weight. A chimney starter is so easy to use that we would happily forgo the gas ignition. An ash catcher—a container attached to the bottom of the grill to trap ashes—makes life easier when it comes time to clean out the grill. When you barbecue or grill-roast, a built-in thermometer is handy, though you can always put a grill thermometer through the lid vents.

In the end, value—which we define as the balance of size, features, and price—determined our recommendations. The one consideration you should make concerns price. The Weber Performer, which came out on top, is a costly $400. Another Weber model (one we didn't test), the One-Touch Platinum, which does not include a gas ignition system or thermometer but does include an ash catcher and a large attached table, is more affordable at $249. This grill strikes us as a better value than the Performer because it has all of the Performer's important features but none of the bells and whistles that add mightily to its price tag.

In the end, our general guideline is to buy the largest, best-outfitted grill your budget will allow. And whatever you do, make sure there is a table attached.

THE BEST CHARCOAL GRILL

The Weber Performer is the deluxe version of the classic kettle grill, but be prepared to pay a deluxe price ($400).

GAS GRILLS

ALTHOUGH COOKING OVER A LIVE FIRE on a charcoal grill may provide a vaguely primal thrill, gas grills deliver what 21st-century Americans prize most: ease. Turn on the gas, hit the ignition switch, and voilà—an instant fire of whatever intensity you need for tonight's recipe. It really is, or at least it really should be, a no-brainer.

Figuring out which gas grill to purchase, on the other hand, is a brain-bender. Discount and home improvement stores stock models as far as the eye can see, with burners of various number and type, overall sizes and cooking spaces from mini to maxi, and features ranging from automatic ignition to cup holders. And while no gas grill is cheap—prices start around $150—many constitute a substantial investment of several hundred, even several thousand, dollars.

We selected seven of the most promising models based on a combination of cooking area and price (which fell into three categories: less than $500, $500 to $1,000, and more than $1,000) and then performed a battery of cooking tests. The lineup included models in all three price categories: expensive Weber Summit Gold and Char-Broil Professional Series grills; midpriced, midsized Jenn-Air and Char-Broil grills; and lower-priced Weber Genesis Silver, Fiesta, and Great Outdoors grills. By grilling our way through almost $1,000 worth of groceries over high, medium, and low heat, we learned which designs and features affect performance the most.

Mention that you're firing up the grill and the first thing to pop into most people's minds is steak—sizzling, fragrant, grill marked, and caramelized to a rich red-brown hue. You'll need plenty of heat to bring that image to life, and on this count, all of the grills in our group delivered. Average high temperature readings were consistently in the range of roughly 600 to 800 degrees.

Our high-heat cooking tests, searing both steaks and chicken thighs, put these numbers in perspective. What did we find? That you don't need enough heat to launch a rocket to give steak or chicken a good sear. Despite registering

the third lowest average high-heat output in the group (596 degrees), one of our recommended models, the Jenn-Air, produced well-marked, heavily crusted steaks. If a grill was downgraded in the steak test, it was not due to lack of heat. We noted, in fact, that heat output was not necessarily related to price. The most expensive grill, the Weber Summit, scored first for heat output, generating 765 degrees. But the more modestly priced Weber Genesis Silver B took third place with 710 degrees.

Covering the entire grilling surface with 1-inch-thick planks of eggplant and cooking them over medium-high heat helped us to assess how the grills performed in the moderate heat range, as well as how evenly that heat was distributed. As with heat output, we found that evenness of heating was not necessarily related to price. Grills at all three price points—the Webers, the Jenn-Air, and the Fiesta—browned the eggplant evenly, indicating even heating. The remaining grills cooked the eggplant unevenly (the Great Outdoors grill most dramatically so).

Because gas grills allow precise heat control, they are especially well suited to barbecuing and grill-roasting. These techniques require low, indirect heat (in the range of 250 degrees to 350 degrees) for a long time to cook through

THE BEST GAS GRILLS

The Weber Genesis Silver A (left) at $375 and the Weber Genesis Silver B (right) at $450 trumped the competition with their strong designs and reasonable prices.

large cuts of meat, fish, or whole fowl. We grill-roasted whole, 3-pound sides of salmon to test the grills' abilities to maintain a low temperature—275 degrees was our target—for an extended period. Indeed, all but one of the grills performed acceptably, maintaining the temperature at or near the target, with minimal adjustment, for 1 hour and 15 minutes to 1 hour and 30 minutes. The exception was the Great Outdoors grill, which did not drop below 330 degrees at its lowest setting, well above our target. It is worth noting that the salmon, being a particularly fatty fish, was none the worse for wear. However, based on our experience, ribs cooked at this temperature will burn on the outside long before they become tender.

Melted fat that drips from hot food down onto the burners causes both excessive smoke and flare-ups that can give food an unwelcome, slightly burnt, off flavor. The fatty chicken thighs and steaks that we cooked were reliable indicators of which grills tended to flare. Effective design for fat drainage limits this problem, and the champs in this department were the Webers, which evidenced only minor flaring during testing. The keys to the Weber fat drainage system are so-called flavorizer bars. Their inverted V shape diverts the fat to a sloped pan that directs it out of the grill into a removable drip pan. We're not convinced that the flavorizer bars add discernible flavor, but they do divert fat.

Two grills, the Fiesta and the Char-Broil, produced moderate flare-ups, while the Great Outdoors had more serious problems. Ersatz briquettes, made of ceramic and meant to help distribute heat, were the problem with the Great Outdoors. They absorbed fat and continued to flame.

The grills to which we'd turn would be the Weber Genesis Silver models. Their performance proved strong, even, and reliable, their design for fat drainage effective, and their prices reasonable (both cost less than $500). If your budget allows, the larger, three-burner Genesis Silver B offers extra flexibility and cooking space; it would be our first choice. The two-burner Genesis Silver A provides the same great performance for $75 less, but the cooking area is 20 percent smaller.

PORTABLE GAS GRILLS

THE GREAT OUTDOORS AND GRILLED meats are an indisputable match. Unfortunately, owing to the immense bulk of today's grills, our grilling efforts are almost always confined to the back patio. A new line of portable, propane-powered grills addresses this issue.

There are dozens of portable gas grills on the market, ranging from the inexpensive (about $50) to the truly outrageous ($1,000 or more). We set our ceiling at $200 and gathered five prominent models to test. Our selection included two models that are truly portable and three whose size makes it difficult to venture very far from the back of the SUV. We quickly learned that the smaller models, though very convenient, offered little else of value. The Weber Gas Go Anywhere was extremely easy to carry, but its measly heat output caused us to question whether this model was meant to be a grill or a hand warmer. The gas Tool Box Grill, as the name implies, is the spitting image of your grandfather's toolbox, but its flimsy grates and inconsistent heat garnered poor marks from the testers. Overall, the portability of these two smaller grills could not make up for their lack of performance.

The three larger models were, predictably, stronger players. The Coleman Road Trip Sport, Weber Q Portable Propane Gas Grill, and Thermos Grill-2-Go all featured large, cast-iron grilling surfaces, high heat outputs, and sturdy

THE BEST PORTABLE GAS GRILL

With an even heating surface and a reasonable price, the Thermos Grill-2-Go ($140) took top honors in our testing.

designs. These characteristics not only increased the cooking ability of the grills but also added to their heft, and even the strongest among us found it difficult to carry these grills. Although their portability came into question, all three of these grills performed well. The Thermos Grill-2-Go came out on top during testing because of its consistent performance and low price. The Weber Q Portable Propane Gas Grill, a close second, was applauded for its even heating and sturdy construction.

CHIMNEY STARTERS

A CHIMNEY STARTERS IS CYLINDRICAL, WITH an attached heatproof handle. It resembles a huge beer mug. Inside the cylinder, just a few inches up from the bottom, a perforated metal plate separates the large upper chamber from the small lower chamber. Different models of chimney starters show very little variation. Some have wooden handles, some have plastic handles, but all do just about the same thing. One thing to keep in mind when buying a chimney is the charcoal capacity. We like a large chimney (one that holds about six quarts of charcoal briquettes and measures about 7½ inches across by 12 inches high) because it holds just the right amount for grilling most foods over medium-hot heat in a large kettle grill. Smaller chimneys necessitate extra heating time for the coals that cannot fit into the chimney. Expect to pay between $15 and $25 for a chimney starter—a very modest investment for such a useful tool.

ELECTRIC STARTERS

IF YOU KEEP YOUR CHARCOAL GRILL ON A deck or patio with a nearby source of electricity, you might consider using an electric starter to ignite charcoal. Most models have an oval heating coil that you nestle in a pile of coals. The starter is plugged in and after about half an hour the coals will be covered with fine gray ash.

As with the chimney starter, there is no need to use any lighter fluid, which is why we like this gadget. There is one minor drawback. We find that an electric starter takes longer to heat up coals than a chimney, especially if you are trying to ignite a large pile of coals. However, there's no need to find old newspaper or matches and the wind can never blow out the flames, which can happen on rare occasions with a chimney.

As with the chimney, an electric starter should be removed from the coals when they are covered with fine gray ash. It will be glowing red and extremely hot. Set it down on a fireproof surface away from foot traffic. As for cost, electric starters run between $10 and $25.

GRILL BRUSHES

ANYONE WHO HAS GRILLED A RACK OF sticky barbecued ribs has had to deal with the task of removing the sugary, burned-on mess that gets left behind. The ideal time to do this is soon after your food comes off the grill, but, if you're like most of us, you close the lid, walk away, and save the mess for the next time grill duty calls. We set out to find a grill brush that could make the tedious task of cleaning a gunked-up cooking grate more efficient. And we did not want to exert superhuman strength to get the job done.

To test the brushes, we concocted a "paint"—a mixture of honey, molasses, mustard, and barbecue sauce—that we could burn onto our grates. We coated the grates four times, baking them for one hour in the test kitchen ovens between coats.

THE BEST GRILL BRUSH

The Grill Wizard China Grill Brush at $19.99 was the most odd-looking of the bunch, with no bristles; instead, stainless steel "scrubbie" pads are held in place by stainless steel bars. The hardwood handle is very comfortable and smooth. The scrubbies can be removed and washed (or replaced for $2.50).

The result was a charred mess that would be sure to challenge even the hardiest of brushes. The grates were put back on the grills, which were then heated so that we could test the brushes under real-life conditions.

The seven brushes we tested were chosen based on the construction and design of the handle and the scrubbing head. The handle of the stainless steel model was decidedly the heaviest and looked to be the most durable, but it absorbed heat at an alarming rate. Plastic performed adequately if you didn't spend too much time in one place on the grill (melting occurred) and if the handle was long enough. One plastic-handled brush, the Grill Pro, with a skimpy 5-inch handle, didn't even make it through the first test. The handle was so short that we couldn't get the brush to the far side of the grill without getting burned. A combination plastic and aluminum brush handle was so flexible it caused burnt knuckles when pressed with any strength. The material of choice for grill brush handles is clearly wood, which is relatively comfortable and durable.

In terms of the scrubbing heads, six of the seven brushes tested had brass bristles. Among these six, those with stiffer bristles fared better than their softer counterparts, but none of them worked all that well. The bristles on most bent after a few strokes and trapped large quantities of gunk, thereby decreasing their efficiency.

In the end, only one brush was able to successfully clean our molten mess down to the cooking grate in a reasonable number of strokes. The unusual but incredibly effective Grill Wizard has no brass bristles to bend, break, or clog with unwanted grease and grime. Instead, this brush comes equipped with two large woven mesh stainless steel "scrubbie" pads. The pads are able to conform to any cooking grate's spacing, size, and material, including porcelain. Best of all, the pads are detachable, washable, and replaceable. The 14-inch handle, made of poplar, is smooth, with rounded edges (unlike its square-cut competitors) and has a hook for easy storage.

The one downside to this brush was the two-page instruction sheet that came affixed to the underside of the scrubbie head (yes, a grill brush

with instructions). Had we not seen a corner of the instructions sticking out, we would have used the brush and thereby burned the instructions. Not only do the instructions need better placement, but operating a grill brush should not be made to seem as difficult as programming a DVD player. Still, though the instructions were confusing, the process of replacing the scrubbies was fairly easy.

TONGS

A PAIR OF TONGS IS THE IDEAL TOOL FOR turning foods as they cook. A large fork pierces foods and causes some loss of fluids. A spatula is fine for small, flat foods, especially those prone to sticking, but it is useless with flank steak or chicken parts. A pair of tongs is the most useful and versatile turner of the lot, capable of flipping something as delicate as thin asparagus spears or as heavy as a rack of ribs.

Testing all manner of tongs, we groped and grabbed kebabs, asparagus, chicken drumsticks, and 3-pound slabs of ribs and found tong performance differed dramatically. Grill tongs by Progressive International, Charcoal, Lamson, Oxo Good Grips, and AMC Rosewood were heavy and difficult to maneuver, and their less delicate pincers couldn't get a grip on asparagus. Other problems included sharp, serrated edges that nicked the food, flimsy arms that bent under the strain of heavy food, and pincers whose spread could not even accommodate the girth of a chicken leg. The

THE BEST TONGS

A pair of 16-inch stainless steel kitchen tongs made by Amco ($8.95) outperformed tongs especially designed for use on the grill. Save money and use the same pair of tongs indoors and outdoors.

Lamson tongs had a spatula in place of one pincer, rendering its grasp almost useless.

The winner was a pair of 16-inch stainless steel kitchen tongs by Amco. Not only did they grip, turn, and move food around the grill easily, but they also were long enough to keep the cook a safe distance from the hot coals. So forget about all those flashy new grill utensils and simply bring your kitchen tongs outside.

SPATULAS

CERTAIN FOODS, ESPECIALLY THOSE PRONE to sticking, such as burgers and fish, are best turned with a spatula. Since grill heat is intense, a long-handled metal spatula is a must.

We tested a variety of grill spatulas against our favorite indoor spatula—called a dogleg, or offset, spatula. These names refer to the angle of the blade, which is on a plane that is different from that of the handle. Our favorite offset spatula has a blade that is 3 inches wide and 6 inches long.

In our testing of spatulas, size and strength turned out to be the most important variables. Larger spatulas did a better job turning burgers and fish fillets and made breakage far less likely. A stiff but thin blade got under foods easily and separated them from the cooking grate. None of these long-handled grill spatulas, however, could outperform our offset spatula. Yes, the extra handle length was nice, but you can flip burgers so easily and quickly with a large offset spatula that your hands don't spend enough time near the coals to

get hot. In addition, most of the grill spatulas were flimsy and much too flexible. Also, when turning large fish fillets, we really appreciated the large surface area of the offset spatula. Most grill spatulas are not even half as large, so foods hang off the edges of the turning blade and can break apart.

GRILL GRIDS

GRILL GRIDS, ALSO CALLED VEGETABLE GRIDS, are useful for cooking small pieces of food that might fall into the fire if placed on the cooking grate that comes with most grills. A grill grid goes on top of the grill's cooking grate, is allowed to heat up, and is then used as the cooking surface for the food. The grid is usually made out of wire, which is cross-hatched to prevent small pieces of food from falling through the holes; it can also be made out of any metal sheet perforated with holes to allow smoke and heat to directly hit the surface of the food.

While both designs work well for small, cut-up vegetables, we found that the perforated grill grids are more versatile. On these flat grids, you can cook delicate foods such as fish fillets and fish burgers and therefore avoid the problems of sticking and tearing. In contrast, the wire grids have an uneven surface that makes it difficult to turn and move these delicate items. It's hard to slip these spatulas under burgers on a grid because part of the meat actually drops into the squares of cross-hatched wire.

Perforated grill grids are available at cookware shops and many hardware stores. They range in price from about $15 to $25. We found the optimum size to be about half the size of a kettle grill or gas grill (depending on what you have), so that you can cook vegetables at the same time that you cook your main dish.

We also found that the type of material the grill grid is made out of makes a difference. We tried three grids made from three different materials: stainless steel, porcelain-coated steel, and nonstick-coated steel. While all the grill grids did fine with vegetables, when cooking delicate fish burgers, the porcelain-coated grid performed the

THE BEST SPATULA

There's no need to buy a separate spatula for the grill. Simply use the same offset metal spatula you use indoors. The offset design allows you to flip burgers easily and quickly while keeping your hand a safe distance from the heat of the grill.

best. The nonstick and stainless steel grids didn't allow the fish burgers to brown well (the stainless steel grid was worst of all). The porcelain-coated grill grid browned fish burgers the best, without any sticking.

In addition to these grids, we tried out a cast-iron grill grid, which has a parallel series of slats, just like the grill's cooking grate. While this is a nice gadget for those who like to grill steaks and chops with the heat of a cast-iron surface for better marking and searing, it really doesn't work well with vegetables and delicate items; it is not designed for cooking these foods.

SKEWERS

SKEWERS ARE GREAT TO HAVE FOR GRILLING white button mushrooms or sliced onions (the other option is a grill grid) and are essential when grilling kebabs. You basically have two choices: metal and wood. We prefer metal skewers, which can be used over and over again and do not burn on the grill. Wood skewers often do burn on the grill, even when soaked.

We have also seen some metal skewers at grilling stores with wood or plastic handles, supposedly for easy turning. These handles are not meant for use right above the fire but are supposed to hang over the side of the grill. Because of this design, not all the food on the skewer will have direct contact with the cooking grate, making even cooking impossible. For this reason, we do not recommend this type of skewer. Just use tongs to turn metal skewers on the grill.

A better option still is a double metal skewer shaped like a long U. Foods are threaded through the two prongs, which are joined by a loop of metal at one end. The advantage is that kebabs won't spin around the skewers when you try to turn them. You can achieve the same effect by threading foods through two separate skewers, held parallel to each other, at the same time (see the illustration on page 164). Expect to pay between $8 and $25 for a set of metal skewers.

FISH BASKETS

WE FOUND FISH BASKETS TO BE UNNECESSARY for the grill. Grilling both whole fish and fillets can be done easily if your grill is clean, hot, and well oiled. When testing fish baskets, we found that unless the basket is well oiled, it too will stick to the fish, making it hard to remove the fish from the basket. If you prefer to use a fish basket on the grill, make sure to oil the basket very well to prevent sticking. Fish baskets cost around $10.

SPRAYERS/MISTERS

NOTHING IS WORSE WHEN GRILLING THAN an uncontrolled fire that chars food. We recommend that you keep a plant mister or squirt bottle filled with water on hand to keep a grease fire from ruining your meal. At the first sign of flames, try to pull foods to a cooler part of the grill and douse the flames with water.

THERMOMETERS

WE RELY ON TWO KINDS OF THERMOMETERS when grilling. A grill thermometer will tell you what the temperature is inside a covered grill. Most gas grills come with this gauge. If you have a charcoal grill, you will need to buy a grill thermometer at a hardware store. This kind of thermometer has a dial face with numbers and a long stem. To use this device on a charcoal grill, simply insert it through the vents on the lid (see the illustration on page 8).

An instant-read thermometer is the best (and we would say, the only) way to determine when foods are properly cooked. If you want steaks cooked to medium-rare (not medium or rare) or a chicken that is cooked through but not dry, use an instant-read thermometer.

Unlike traditional meat thermometers, instant-read thermometers are not designed to be left in the foods as they cook. Prolonged exposure of the whole unit to heat will destroy the measuring mechanism. When you think foods might be done, simply insert the probe deep into the food

THE BEST INSTANT-READ DIGITAL THERMOMETER

The Thermapen ($80) is our top choice for its pinpoint accuracy and quick response time.

(away from any bones) and wait 10 seconds for the temperature to register.

There are two types of instant-read thermometers on the market: dial-face and digital. Though pocket-sized dial-face thermometers are less expensive than digitals, they are also less precise, and most read temperatures in a narrower range. (Although this is not an issue when grilling, it can be a problem when chilling custards for ice cream or making caramel sauce.) Our favorite digital thermometer registers temperatures from below 0 to 500 degrees.

Another important difference between digital and dial-face thermometers is the location of the temperature sensor. On a dial-face thermometer, the sensor is roughly 1½ inches from the tip of the stem. The sensor on a digital thermometer is usually located at the very tip of the stem. What this means is that the stem of the dial-face thermometer must be stuck deep into the meat or other food. A digital thermometer will deliver a more accurate reading in thin cutlets or chops.

While they both take accurate readings when used correctly, we prefer digital thermometers because they register temperatures faster and are easier to read. After testing a variety of digital thermometers, we preferred the Thermapen for its well-thought-out design (a long, folding probe and comfortable handle) and speed (just 10 seconds for a reading). If you don't want to spend so much money on a thermometer, at the very least purchase an inexpensive dial-face model. There's no sense ruining a $50 roast because you don't own even a $10 thermometer. Another good option is a timer/thermometer; read on for details.

TIMER/THERMOMETERS

A REGULAR TIMER IS FINE FOR REMINDING you that a certain period of time has elapsed. But it can't tell you precisely when your tenderloin or turkey is done. You still need to pull out an instant-read thermometer and check the meat. What if you could combine the timer and thermometer into one handy device? Several companies have done so in making the timer/thermometer, which allows you to use its timing and thermometer functions separately or at the same time. Here's how it works.

Attached to a standard timer-type base is a long wire that ends with a sensor probe that measures temperature. To use this device, you insert the sensor probe into foods before they go on the grill. You place the food on the grill and snake the long wire cord through the top vent on a charcoal grill or under the cover of a gas grill. The cord attaches to the base unit via a back-mounted magnet. You program the base unit with the desired internal temperature (say 125 degrees for a rare roast beef). Once the sensor probe determines that the meat has reached this temperature, the timer unit will beep. It also provides you with a constant display of the temperature of the food as it cooks.

We rounded up six timer/thermometers, ranging in price from $20 to $50, to see which model is the best option for the home cook. We tested each device in beef roasts and set the timer to beep at various temperatures. We doubled-checked

THE BEST TIMER/THERMOMETER

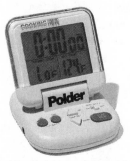

Features such as a 4-foot-long thermometer probe cord and a loud alarm brought the Polder Cooking Thermometer/Timer ($25) to the head of the pack in our testing.

these temperatures with a separate thermometer and found that all six models were accurate—they beeped right on cue.

The tests revealed some differences in ease of operation and features, however. Several models had short wire cords that made them harder to use. Also, the magnet on some timer/thermometers was not strong enough, and we worried that the units would come crashing down onto the ground. A few models were harder to program and read.

In the end, testers agreed that the Polder Cooking Thermometer/Timer was the best choice. It was the easiest and most intuitive to use. It also has a 4-foot-long cord and the loudest alarm of those tested, making it the best choice to use on the grill.

SMALL BRUSHES

A GOOD PASTRY BRUSH IS HARD TO maintain. Most quickly degrade into a stained, shaggy mess. Hoping to find one that could swab barbecue sauce, brush glazes, and other similar tasks and still clean up free of stains, lingering odors, or stiff greasy bristles, we ran eight brushes through a series of kitchen tests.

In terms of bristles, we found that no material can compete with the quality and feel of natural boar's hair. While often not labeled as such, most gold-colored bristles are made from boar's hair. These bristles are also available in black, a color that is easier to spot on food if a bristle falls out. Avoid brushes with nylon bristles, which are usually clear. We found that these bristles lack absorbency and tend to clump. Silicone bristles (which are usually very thick and black) are both

THE BEST SMALL BRUSH

The Oxo Good Grips ($6) combines traditional boar's hair bristles with a modern, dishwasher-safe handle.

nonabsorbent and overly flexible.

We preferred pastry brushes with handles and collars made of plastic or rubber. These brushes are dishwasher-safe and make swollen, cracked wooden handles a thing of the past. Traditional paintbrush-style brushes with wooden handles and metal collars tend to have pockets of space under the collar that trap oil and off flavors.

Only one brush, the Oxo Good Grips, successfully combined the tradition of boar's hair bristles with the more modern design of a dishwasher-safe plastic handle and a tight-fitting rubber collar that made no room for grease. It was the clear winner of our tests.

FOIL PANS, HEAVY-DUTY FOIL, BROWN PAPER BAGS, AND PAPER TOWELS

IT MAY SEEM UNNECESSARY TO INCLUDE this kind of equipment, but often a foil pan or a paper bag makes the difference between good food from the grill and great food from the grill. Here are some notes on these essential, if mundane, items.

Keep disposable aluminum pans in a variety of sizes on hand. You may want to use these pans to transfer foods from the kitchen to the grill. (Make sure to wash them before putting cooked foods back in them.) When grilling, we like to use these pans to cover certain foods to heat them through more quickly so that the exterior doesn't burn. For instance, an aluminum pan helps to heat up pizza toppings before the bottom crust has a chance to burn. Likewise, a pan placed over bone-in chicken breasts on the cooler part of the grill captures the available heat and cooks the meat through to the bone with little further browning of the skin.

Heavy-duty aluminum foil is the best material in which to wrap wood chips. Don't use regular foil. It's not nearly as thick, and chips will ignite more quickly. We found that wrapping barbecued foods such as brisket and pulled pork in foil when they come off the grill helps trap moisture and allows the juices in the meat to be redistributed as the meat rests. We place the wrapped meat in a brown paper bag (the kind you get at the supermarket), which helps trap heat and keeps the food from cooling off too much as it rests.

Paper towels serve several functions at the grill. We often dip a wad of towels in vegetable oil, grasp the oiled towels with tongs, and rub the oil over the cooking grate. This both cleans the grate and greases it, so that fish and other delicate foods won't stick. We also use wads of paper towels to turn whole birds on the grill.

PLASTIC WRAP

WE KEEP LOTS OF PLASTIC WRAP ON HAND for many tasks relating to outdoor cooking, such as covering bowls of marinating meat, forming compound butter for steak and fish, and wrapping pizza dough destined for the grill. Plastic wrap also helps us with less obvious tasks, such as helping to evenly season large roasts (see the illustration on page 74). To find out if all plastic wraps are created equal, we bought five wraps and put them through a series of tests.

Stretch-Tite, Saran Premium, Saran Cling Plus, Glad Cling Wrap, and Glad Press'n Seal all survived a microwave test and kept guacamole from turning brown for 72 hours. The real differences came when we tried using these wraps to cover bowls made of glass, metal, and plastic. The Glad Press'n Seal stuck to all three—but only if the bowls were perfectly dry. A glass bowl kept in a refrigerator for a few minutes gathered enough condensation to render the Press'n Seal useless. We consider this a fatal flaw.

The other four wraps performed equally well when used on metal or on glass. Plastic was another story. None of the wraps could cling to the plastic bowl. In every case we had to wind extra wrap around the first sheet. This is where Stretch-Tite, the stickiest of all the wraps we tested, really shines. Stretch-Tite is not as readily available as Saran or Glad products, but mail-ordering big 500-square-foot rolls (about $10 per roll) is an option. Also look for these rolls at warehouse clubs.

FOOD STORAGE CONTAINERS

ALTHOUGH YOU WOULDN'T WANT TO STORE leftover grilled hamburgers, there are foods from the grill that make great leftovers; vegetables, for example. We often throw a few extra vegetables onto the grill to use as pizza toppings or to add to pasta salads. And leftover barbecued chicken, shredded and mixed with a little mayonnaise, makes wonderful chicken salad. In short, food storage containers can come in handy. Circa 1950, leftovers went into Tupperware . . . period. Today, some 50 years later, you can store leftovers in any number of containers made from plastic, glass, or metal and including features such as vacuum sealing, stain resistance, locking lids, and special venting. We wanted to find out if any of the newer models offered a higher level of protection for your food, more useful features, or significantly better design.

"Food storage containers?" grimaced one test kitchen skeptic. "Just how do you rate those?" After much discussion, we came up with several reliable, if slightly unconventional, methods to test the seal between the container and its lid. The "sink test" was first. We filled each container with 2 pounds of pie weights topped with a layer of sugar and, with the lid in place, submerged the whole thing in water. Then we fished out the container, dried it, and inspected the sugar inside. To further assess the seal, we devised the "shake test." We filled each container with soup, fixed the lid in place, and shook vigorously. If we ended up wearing soup, the seal wasn't tight enough.

Preventing the transfer of food odors is also largely up to the seal between container and lid. After all, you don't want your last few bites of chocolate mousse to smell like the smoky ribs next to it in the fridge. To gauge odor protection, we conducted the "stink test" by loading slices of white sandwich bread into each container, positioning the lids, and storing them in the fridge with a huge, uncovered bowl of diced raw onions. Over the course of five days, we sniffed the bread daily to see if we could detect any "eau de allium."

We chose chili for the "stain test," refrigerating it in the containers for three days, microwaving it to serving temperature (about three minutes), and then immediately running the containers through the dishwasher. Last, to mimic the ravages of time, we ran the containers through 100 cycles in the dishwasher, and then repeated every test.

Our lineup of 12 containers included Tupperware, two Rubbermaid models (Seal'n Saver and Stain Shield), several competing plastic containers, two inexpensive disposable containers, two vacuum-sealing models, and models made from both ovensafe glass and metal. The Genius VakSet container, with its pump-operated vacuum seal, performed impressively in the sink, shake, and stink tests. Several other containers with tight-fitting lids, particularly the Tupperware, both Rubbermaid models, and the Tramontina stainless steel, held their own against the vice grip of the Genius.

The stink test produced no clear pattern among the odor control champs, including the Genius, GladWare, Tupperware, Tramontina, Betty Crocker, and Rubbermaid Seal'n Saver, which just edged out the Rubbermaid Stain Shield. The Pyrex glass container was a loser in both the stink and sink tests.

THE BEST FOOD STORAGE CONTAINERS

The Tupperware Rock 'N Serve Medium Deep Container (top, $12.99) boasted great design with performance to match. The more modestly priced (at $4.99) Rubbermaid Stain Shield Square Container (bottom) lives up to the marketing claims of stain resistance, although odor-control performance was not perfect.

The results of the stain test, on the other hand, did reveal a pattern. The winners were made of the hardest materials. The glass Pyrex and stainless steel Tramontina containers proved stain resistant, though the same cannot be said of the latter's plastic lid. Among the plastic containers, those made from hard, clear polycarbonate (the same stuff used for lightweight eyeglass lenses and compact disks), including the Tupperware, Rubbermaid Stain Shield, Genius, and Snapware, resisted stains best in our tests. The remaining plastic containers were made of polypropylene, a somewhat softer polymer that seems more susceptible to staining, as we observed in our tests.

To our surprise, several containers matched or surpassed the performance of the reigning king, Tupperware. Strictly speaking, the vacuum-sealed Genius VakSet edged out the Tupperware by one point in the performance tests. Yet despite stellar performance, we'd still hesitate to buy it because of its design. We fear that some cooks would lose the pump and therefore the containers would become useless. Also, no one in our test kitchen could figure out how to release the vacuum seal without first reading the instruction manual. Throwing leftovers in the fridge shouldn't be any hassle at all. That's why our nod goes to the Tupperware, followed closely by the Rubbermaid Stain Shield. Their performance was excellent, and you don't have to think twice to use them.

STAIN REMOVERS

MANY OF THE FOODS WE GRILL AND barbecue are, well, messy. Any food topped with ketchup or mustard or brushed with barbecue sauce is a stain waiting to happen. In the test kitchen, we've had more than our share of stained clothing cooking outdoors (as well as indoors). Tired of throwing out otherwise perfectly good shirts, we decided to get serious about laundry and put 16 supermarket stain removers to the test. These products fell into four categories: pretreaters, laundry additives, spot removers, and oxygen-based powders.

PRETREATERS

THESE PRODUCTS ARE APPLIED TO THE stained garment, which is then thrown into the wash. This group included Spray 'n Wash, Shout, Zout, Shout Ultra Gel, Shout Action Gel, Extra-Strength Spray 'n Wash, and Spray 'n Wash Stain Stick.

LAUNDRY ADDITIVES

THESE PRODUCTS GO RIGHT INTO THE machine with the wash to boost the stain-removing power of the detergent used. Both products in this group were made by Spray 'n Wash, one a liquid additive and one a concentrated tablet referred to as Actionball.

SPOT REMOVERS

THESE PRODUCTS ARE APPLIED TO CLOTHES, rubbed into the stains, and finally washed. Those tested included Gonzo Stain Remover, Amodex Premium Spot Remover, and Didi Seven Ultra Super Concentrated Cleaner.

OXYGEN-BASED POWDERS

THESE PRODUCTS ARE DILUTED WITH water to make a soaking solution for garments. Once the stains are gone, the clothes can be washed. This group included All Oxi-Active, Shout Oxy Power, Clorox Oxygen Action, and Oxi-Clean.

For our tests, we took plain 100 percent cotton T-shirts and dirtied them with the foods most infamous for leaving unrelenting stains: pureed blueberries, pureed beets, black coffee, red wine, ketchup and yellow mustard (to simulate a hot dog mishap), melted bittersweet chocolate, and chili (which also covered grease stains). Each cleaning product was applied according to the manufacturer's instructions for maximum stain removal.

THE BEST STAIN REMOVER

With very little work but considerable soaking time, Oxi-Clean ($5.99) removed the toughest food stains.

All of the products removed the coffee, wine, ketchup, and beet stains, but only the spot removers and oxygen-based powders managed to completely remove the tougher stains left by chili, blueberries, chocolate, and mustard. T-shirts tested with the pretreaters and laundry additives came out of the wash with several distinct, if muted, stains.

Spot removers call for brushing or blotting the stain until it is gone, and although this method is the most labor-intensive (in some cases up to seven applications were necessary), even the toughest stains were gone before the garment went into the washing machine. If time is a luxury you can afford and scrubbing and blotting are not your thing, then the oxygen-based powders are the way to go. T-shirts treated with these cleaners—used as concentrated soaking solutions, as per the manufacturers' instructions—needed only a light rubbing to remove the toughest stains. Although the T-shirts did need to soak for up to three hours (with Oxi-Clean working in the shortest amount of time), the process was mostly hands-off.

So if you can't part with that favorite blouse or pair of pants and you don't mind an investment of time and a little elbow grease, use an oxygen-based powder.

1

BEEF

BEEF

CHARCOAL-GRILLED STRIP OR RIB STEAKS 37
    Gas-Grilled Strip or Rib Steaks

CHARCOAL-GRILLED PORTERHOUSE OR T-BONE STEAKS 38
    Gas-Grilled Porterhouse or T-Bone Steaks
    Grilled Tuscan Steak with Olive Oil and Lemon (*Bistecca alla Fiorentina*)

CHARCOAL-GRILLED FILETS MIGNONS 41
    Gas-Grilled Filets Mignons

GRILLED PREMIUM STEAK AND POTATOES WITH BLUE CHEESE BUTTER . . . 42

CHARCOAL-GRILLED FREE-FORM BEEF WELLINGTON WITH PORT SYRUP . . 43
    Gas-Grilled Free-Form Beef Wellington with Port Syrup

CHARCOAL-GRILLED STEAK TIPS 47
    Gas-Grilled Steak Tips

SOUTHWESTERN MARINADE 47

GARLIC, GINGER, AND SOY MARINADE 48

CHARCOAL-GRILLED FLANK STEAK 49
    Gas-Grilled Flank Steak
    Grilled Flank Steak Rubbed with Latin Spices
    Grilled Flank Steak with Sweet-and-Sour Chipotle Sauce
    Grilled Flank Steak and Red Onion with Chimichurri

CLASSIC FAJITAS 51

CHARCOAL-GRILLED SKIRT STEAK TACOS WITH ROASTED POBLANOS 53
    Gas-Grilled Skirt Steak Tacos with Roasted Poblanos

CHARCOAL-GRILLED LONDON BROIL 55
    Gas-Grilled London Broil

CHARCOAL-GRILLED BEEF KEBABS 58
    Gas-Grilled Beef Kebabs
    Beef Kebabs with Asian Flavors
    Southwestern Beef Kebabs

CHARCOAL-GRILLED BEEF SATAY WITH SPICY PEANUT DIPPING SAUCE 60
    Gas-Grilled Beef Satay with Spicy Peanut Dipping Sauce

CHARCOAL-GRILLED HAMBURGERS 63
    Gas-Grilled Hamburgers
    Grilled Cheeseburgers
    Grilled Hamburgers with Garlic, Chipotle, and Scallions
    Grilled Hamburgers with Cognac, Mustard, and Chives
    Grilled Hamburgers with Porcini Mushrooms and Thyme
    Ultimate Grilled Hamburgers

GRILL-ROASTED PRIME RIB ON A CHARCOAL GRILL 67
    Grill-Roasted Prime Rib on a Gas Grill
    Grill-Roasted Prime Rib with Garlic and Rosemary Crust

GRILL-ROASTED BEEF TENDERLOIN ON A CHARCOAL GRILL 73
    Grill-Roasted Beef Tenderloin on a Gas Grill
    Grill-Roasted Beef Tenderloin with Mixed Peppercorn Crust
    Grill-Roasted Beef Tenderloin with Garlic and Rosemary

CHARCOAL-GRILLED RIB VEAL CHOPS 76
    Gas-Grilled Rib Veal Chops
    Grilled Veal Chops with Mediterranean Herb Paste
    Porcini-Rubbed Grilled Veal Chops
    Grilled Veal Chops on a Bed of Arugula

TEXAS-STYLE BARBECUED BEEF RIBS 80
    Texas-Style Barbecued Beef Ribs on a Gas Grill

BARBECUE SAUCE FOR TEXAS-STYLE BEEF RIBS 81

CHARCOAL-GRILLED BEEF SHORT RIBS 83
    Gas-Grilled Beef Short Ribs
    Grilled Beef Short Ribs, Korean Style
    Grilled Beef Short Ribs with Chipotle and Citrus Marinade

BARBECUED BEEF BRISKET ON A CHARCOAL GRILL 86
    Barbecued Beef Brisket on a Gas Grill

GRILLED BEEF, FROM BURGERS AND STEAKS to prime rib, is an American classic. And, beef (unlike poultry and pork) can be cooked to various levels of doneness: rare, medium-rare, medium, and so on. Great grilled beef is about achieving a balance between a dark, well-seared crust and an interior that is tender and juicy. Grilling beef also poses other challenges. Burgers can stubbornly stick to the grill; some steaks are better suited to grilling than others; and large cuts of beef, such as prime rib, require a grill-roast method (as opposed to a direct-heat method) to cook through without burning their exterior.

Before you choose a particular steak or roast, it helps to understand something about the anatomy of a cow. Eight different cuts of beef are sold at the wholesale level (see the illustration below). From this first series of cuts, known as primal cuts, a butcher will make the retail cuts that you bring home from the market. How you choose to cook a particular piece of beef depends on where the meat comes from on the cow and how it was butchered.

CHUCK/SHOULDER Starting at the front of the animal, the chuck (or shoulder) runs from the neck down to the fifth rib. There are four major muscles in this region, and meat from the chuck tends to be flavorful and fairly fatty, which is why ground chuck makes the best hamburgers. Chuck also contains a fair amount of connective tissue, so when the meat is not ground, it generally requires a long cooking time to become tender.

THE EIGHT PRIMAL CUTS OF BEEF

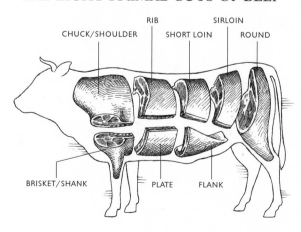

RIB Moving back from the chuck, the next primal cut along the top half of the animal is the rib section, which extends from the sixth to the twelfth rib. The prime rib comes from this area, as do rib-eye steaks. Rib cuts have excellent beefy flavor and are quite tender.

SHORT LOIN The short loin (also called the loin) extends from the last rib back through the midsection of the animal to the hip area. It contains two major muscles—the tenderloin and the shell. The tenderloin is extremely tender (it is positioned right under the spine) and has quite a mild flavor. This muscle may be sold whole as a roast or sliced crosswise into steaks, called filets mignons. The shell is a much larger muscle and has a more robust beef flavor as well as more fat. Strip steaks (also called shell steaks) come from this muscle and are our favorite. Two steaks from the short loin area contain portions of both the tenderloin and the shell muscles. These steaks are called the T-bone and porterhouse, and both are excellent choices.

SIRLOIN The next area is the sirloin, which contains relatively inexpensive cuts that are sold both as steaks and roasts. We find that sirloin cuts are fairly lean and tough. In general, we prefer other parts of the animal, although top sirloin makes a decent roast.

ROUND The back of the cow is called the round. Roasts and steaks cut from this area are usually sold boneless and are quite lean and can be tough. Again, we generally prefer cuts from other parts of the cow, although top round can be grill-roasted with some success.

BRISKET/SHANK, PLATE, AND FLANK The underside of the animal is divided into the brisket/shank (near the front of the animal), the plate, and the flank. Thick boneless cuts are removed from these three parts of the cow. The brisket is rather tough and contains a lot of connective tissue. The plate is rarely sold at the retail level (it is used to make pastrami). The flank is a leaner cut that makes an excellent steak when grilled.

HOW TO BUY BEEF STEAKS FOR THE GRILL

BEFORE YOU CHOOSE A STEAK FOR THE GRILL, it pays to know something about the many cuts available. Steaks generally come from many places on the cow, although most come from the tender midsections (see the illustration on the facing page). Steaks sport different names depending on locale. We've used industry names that we feel best describe where the steaks lie on the animal; you'll find some other common names also listed. We've rated steaks for tenderness and flavor (★★★★ being the best) and cost ($$$$ being the most expensive). Note that tenderness is an issue with steaks because they are best cooked quickly and there is not time to transform a tough cut into something more palatable.

WHAT TO LOOK FOR:

➤ For all cuts of steak, look for meat that has a bright, lively color. Beef normally ranges in color from pink to red, but dark meat probably indicates an older, tougher animal.

➤ The external fat as well as the fat that runs through the meat (called intramuscular fat) should be as white as possible. As a general rule, the more intramuscular fat (marbling), the more flavorful and juicy the steak will be. But the marbling should be smooth and fine, running all through the meat, rather than showing up in clumps; smooth marbling melts into the meat during cooking, while knots remain as fat pockets.

➤ Stay away from packaged steaks that show a lot of red juice (known as purge). The purge may indicate a bad job of freezing; as a result, the steak will be dry and cottony.

DOES BRANDING MATTER?

To guarantee quality, more and more people are looking beyond the confines of their local supermarket butcher case and buying their steaks through mail-order sources. These outlets promise all-star beef with a price tag to match. But do the mail-order steaks really outshine the ones you can get around the corner? And is there something you can buy locally that's better than your average supermarket steak?

We gathered seven widely available mail-order strip steaks and two from local supermarkets (Coleman Natural—hormone- and antibiotic-free—from our local Whole Foods Market and choice steak from the regular market). Our candidates included Niman Ranch, a high-end, all-natural, restaurant favorite; Peter Luger, a New York steakhouse that many consider to be the best in the country; Omaha, probably the most well-known mail-order steak company, with two steaks in the running (their "private reserve" as well as their standard); Allen Brothers, a Chicago-based company that supplies many of this country's steakhouses; and Lobel's, a New York butcher shop. In addition to Lobel's boneless strip steak we included Lobel's Wagyu, or Kobe-style, steak from Oakleigh Ranch in Australia. Kobe beef comes from Wagyu cattle raised to certain specifications in Kobe, Japan. Considered the foie gras of beef, the meat is extremely well marbled, tender, and rich. Wagyu is the more generic name for the same type of beef, but not from Japan. Although few of us could afford the hefty $68/per pound price tag for Wagyu beef, we wanted to see if it was really worth that much.

Well, it was. After pan-searing three dozen steaks (four of each type for perhaps the largest-ever tasting turnout in the test kitchen), we found that money can buy you happiness, if happiness for you is the best steak you ever ate.

"Wow," wrote one happy taster of our first-place Wagyu steak. "This is unlike any strip that I've had." Others deemed the Wagyu steak "tender like a filet" and "very rich and meaty." But the overwhelming richness—which one taster likened to "foie gras–infused beef"—was not everyone's cup of tea. A minority of tasters agreed with the one who wrote, "This doesn't taste like beef at all."

Three steaks shared the spot for second place: Niman Ranch ($22 per pound), praised for its "good flavor" and "nice texture"; Coleman Natural, deemed "very robust"; and Peter Luger, described as having "strong beef flavor" and "great juiciness."

Unfortunately, the brand most people turn to when ordering steak through the mail took the last two spots in our tasting. The Omaha strip steak had "off flavors" and was "grainy tasting," while the Omaha Private Reserve (at almost twice the price) finished last, with tasters finding it "a little chewy" and "very dry."

The good news is that you don't have to spend a small fortune (or pay for shipping) to get a great steak. Coleman Natural steak, available at all-natural supermarkets, tied for second place and was a comparative bargain at $14 per pound (just $4 more than the low-ranked Stop & Shop beef). If you want to sample true steak greatness, however, you may want to splurge on the Wagyu beef—at least once.

SHOULDER STEAK

Primal Cut: Chuck/Shoulder
Tenderness: ★★
Flavor: ★★
Cost: $
Alternate Names: Chuck Steak, London Broil

Often labeled London broil, steaks from the shoulder of the cow are boneless and consist of a single muscle. Buy a shoulder steak that is 1½ pounds to 2 pounds and slice it thin on the bias after cooking. We find that shoulder steaks offer the best value for cost-conscious shoppers.

TOP BLADE STEAK

Primal Cut: Chuck/Shoulder
Tenderness: ★★★
Flavor: ★★★
Cost: $
Alternate Names: Flat-iron Steak, Blade Steak

These small steaks are cut from the shoulder area of the cow. Top blade steaks are tender, but each has a line of gristle running down the center, which can be cut out when turning these steaks into kebabs.

RIB STEAK

Primal Cut: Rib
Tenderness: ★★★
Flavor: ★★★
Cost: $ $ $
Alternate Name: None

Imagine a prime rib roast at a hotel buffet or banquet. A rib steak is a steak cut from that rib roast, with the curved rib bone attached. Rib steaks are less prevalent than the boneless version, the rib eye.

RIB-EYE STEAK

Primal Cut: Rib
Tenderness: ★★★
Flavor: ★★★
Cost: $ $ $
Alternate Names:
Spencer Steak, Delmonico Steak

A rib-eye steak is a rib steak with the bone removed. The steak has an oval shape with a narrow strip of meat that curves around one end. Rib-eye steaks, like other steaks from the rib section, contain large pockets of fat and have a rich, smooth texture. Rib eye is often known as Spencer steak in the West and Delmonico steak in New York.

TOP LOIN STEAK

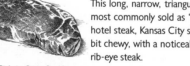

Primal Cut: Short Loin
Tenderness: ★★★
Flavor: ★★★
Cost: $ $ $
Alternate Names: Strip Steak, Shell Steak, Sirloin Strip Steak

This long, narrow, triangular steak may be sold bone-in or boneless. It is most commonly sold as "strip steak." Boneless top loin is also known as hotel steak, Kansas City strip, and New York strip. The top loin steak is a bit chewy, with a noticeable grain, and is slightly less fatty than the rib or rib-eye steak.

TENDERLOIN STEAK

Primal Cut: Short Loin
Tenderness: ★★★★
Flavor: ★
Cost: $ $ $ $
Alternate Names:
Filet Mignon,
Châteaubriand, Tournedo

The tenderloin, a long, cylindrical muscle that is the most tender meat on the cow, may be cut into a number of different steaks, each of which has its own name but all of which are very expensive, since Americans prize tenderness above all else in their steaks. Châteaubriand is a 3-inch-thick steak cut from the thickest part of the tenderloin, usually large enough to serve two. Filet, filet mignon, or tenderloin steak is typically 1 to 2 inches thick, cut from the narrow end of the tenderloin. Tournedos are the smallest tenderloin steaks, about an inch thick, cut toward the tip end. Tenderloin steaks are extremely tender but are not known for having much beefy flavor.

T-BONE STEAK

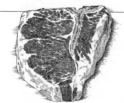

Primal Cut: Short Loin
Tenderness: ★★★
Flavor: ★★★
Cost: $ $ $
Alternate Name: None

The T-shaped bone in this steak separates the long, narrow strip of top loin and a small piece of tenderloin (on the right side of the bone in this drawing). Since it contains top loin and tenderloin meat, the T-bone is well balanced for texture and flavor.

PORTERHOUSE STEAK

Primal Cut: Short Loin
Tenderness: ★★★
Flavor: ★★★
Cost: $ $ $
Alternate Name: None

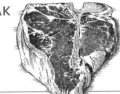

The porterhouse is really just a huge T-bone steak with a larger tenderloin section. It is cut farther back on the animal than the T-bone steak. Like the T-bone, the porterhouse, with both top loin and tenderloin sections, has well-balanced flavor and texture.

ROUND-BONE

Primal Cut: Sirloin
Tenderness: ★★
Flavor: ★★
Cost: $
Alternate Names:
New York Sirloin Steak,
Shell Sirloin Steak

Several steaks are cut from the sirloin, or hip, section; moving from the front to the rear of the animal, they are pin- or hipbone steak, flat-bone steak, round-bone steak, and wedge-bone steak. Of these, the round bone is best; the others are rarely found in supermarkets. Shell sirloin steak is simply a round-bone sirloin steak that has had the small piece of tenderloin removed. It is most commonly found in the Northeast and is sometimes called New York sirloin. Do not confuse sirloin steaks with the superior top loin steak, which is sometimes called sirloin strip steak or New York strip steak.

TOP SIRLOIN STEAK

Primal Cut: Sirloin
Tenderness: ★★
Flavor: ★★
Cost: $
Alternate Name:
Sirloin Butt Steak

This steak is merely a boneless round-bone steak. It is sometimes sold as boneless sirloin butt steak or top sirloin butt center-cut steak. Again, do not confuse this steak with top loin steak, which is sometimes called sirloin strip steak.

FLAP MEAT SIRLOIN STEAK TIP

Primal Cut: Sirloin
Tenderness: ★★
Flavor: ★★★
Cost: $ $
Alternate Names:
Sirloin Tips,
Flap Meat, Steak Tips

This thin rectangular steak weighs about 2½ pounds and is often sold in strips or cubes. To ensure that you are buying the real thing, buy the whole steak. The meat has a distinctive longitudinal grain and a rich, deep beefy flavor. This meat can range in thickness from ½ to 1½ inches. A relatively even steak will be easier to cook than a steak with both thin and thick portions. When serving, slice the steak thin across the grain or the meat will be tough.

SKIRT STEAK

Primal Cut: Plate
Tenderness: ★★
Flavor: ★★★
Cost: $ $ $
Alternate Names:
Fajita Steak, Philadelphia Steak

This thin steak from the underside of the animal has an especially beefy flavor. It was the original choice for fajitas, although most cooks now use easier-to-find flank steak. Although it can be cooked like flank steak, skirt steak is fattier and juicier. Look for it at better markets and butcher shops.

FLANK STEAK

Primal Cut: Flank
Tenderness: ★★
Flavor: ★★★
Cost: $ $ $
Alternate Name:
Jiffy Steak

Flank steak is a large, thin, flat cut with a distinct longitudinal grain. To minimize the stringy, chewy nature of flank steak, it should not be cooked past medium and should always be sliced thin across the grain. It is usually sold whole and weighs roughly two pounds, although some grocery stores package flank steaks cut into smaller portions.

HANGER STEAK

Primal Cut: Flank
Tenderness: ★
Flavor: ★★
Cost: $ $ $
Alternate Names:
Hanging Tenderloin,
Butcher's Steak, Hanging Tender

This bistro favorite is actually a thick muscle attached to the diaphragm on the underside of the cow. When a cow is butchered, this steak hangs down into the center of the carcass, thus its name. Hanger steak is much tougher than flank steak and not nearly as flavorful. Don't go out of your way to find this hard-to-come-by steak.

CHOOSING A GRADE OF BEEF

The U.S. Department of Agriculture (USDA) recognizes eight grades of beef, but most everything available to consumers falls into the top three: Prime, Choice, and Select. The grades classify meat according to fat marbling and age, which are relatively accurate predictors of palatability; they have nothing to do with freshness or purity. Grading is voluntary on the part of the meat packer. If the meat is graded, it should bear a USDA stamp indicating the grade, but it may not be visible. Ask the butcher when in doubt.

We pan-seared rib-eye steaks from all three grades and tasted them blind. Prime ranked first for its tender, buttery texture and rich beefy flavor; it was discernibly fattier. Choice came in second, with solid flavor and a little more chew. The Select steak was tough and stringy, with flavor that was only "acceptable." The lesson here is that you get what you pay for. Prime steaks are worth the extra money, but Choice steaks that exhibit a moderate amount of marbling are a fine and more affordable option.

PRIME

Prime meat is heavily marbled with intramuscular fat (seen as white streaks within the meat in this drawing), which makes for a tender, flavorful steak. A very small percentage (about 2 percent) of graded beef is considered Prime. Prime meats are most often served in restaurants or sold in high-end grocery stores or butcher shops.

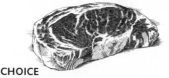

CHOICE

The majority of graded beef is graded Choice. While the levels of marbling in Choice beef can vary, it is generally moderately marbled with intramuscular fat.

SELECT

Select beef has little marbling. Because of the small amount of intramuscular fat, Select meats are drier, tougher, and less flavorful than the two higher grades.

EQUIPMENT: Steak Knives

If you've ever shopped for steak knives, you might have noticed that sets of four can range in price from as little as $30 to as much as $150. We wondered if price really makes a difference when it comes to the performance of these knives, so we bought five sets of knives and cooked up some steaks to find out.

Our favorites were pricey. A set of four Henckels Four Star Steak Knives or Wüsthof-Trident Classic Steak Knives fetches between $140 and $150. Manufactured in the same manner as the other kitchen knives in their high-quality lines, these knives justly demand a high price. Fresh from their boxes, they had razor-sharp blades that sliced effortlessly through crusts and glided through meat, and their handles made them comfortable to use (Henckels got top honors here). But if you are lax in the upkeep of your knives, beware—these knives require regular honing and sharpening to be kept in tiptop shape.

Right behind these big shots were Chicago Cutlery Steak Knives, Walnut Tradition. At $40 for a set of four, it's easy to overlook their slightly less comfortable handles and somewhat flimsier feel but rank them right in with the best. These knives also were sharp, and the gently curved angle of the blades made for simple and smooth slicing. And they look like they belong in a butcher shop—or in the fist of a serious steak eater. Don't forget to steel these knives as well to keep them sharp.

Our least favorite knife sets contained knives with serrated blades. Henckels Gourmet Steak Knives, $40 for a set of four, and Dexter Russell Steakhouse Steak Knives, $30 for a set of four, required a good deal of sawing to cut through a steak and produced rather ragged pieces (not that your taste buds care). The cheaper set of Henckels steak knives felt insubstantial in their construction, whereas the Dexter Russell knives were of mammoth proportions. Neither requires steeling for upkeep.

THE BEST STEAK KNIVES

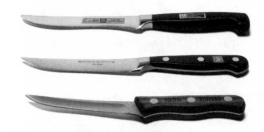

The Henckels Four Star Steak Knives (top) were the top choice of testers, followed closely by the Wüsthof-Trident Classic Steak Knives (middle). At a fraction of the cost, the Chicago Cutlery Steak Knives, Walnut Tradition (bottom), are a great value with good (if not great) performance in our kitchen tests.

GRILLING MEAT 101

THERE ARE A COUPLE OF ISSUES THAT APPLY TO MEAT COOKERY REGARDLESS OF WHETHER you choose to grill, grill-roast, or barbecue your meat. (See pages 2–3 for detailed explanations of each method.) The following three points are crucial to the success of most meat recipes:

BROWN IS GOOD

Meat with a browned exterior tastes better. So why does browned food taste so good?

When meat browns, something called the Maillard reaction occurs. This process is named after the French chemist who first described this reaction about one hundred years ago. When the amino acids (or protein components) and natural sugars in meat are subjected to intense heat, like that found over a hot fire (or in a hot skillet), they begin to combine and form new compounds. These compounds in turn break down and form yet more new flavor compounds, and so on and so on.

In order to encourage browning, use sufficient heat. Steaks cooked over a wimpy fire will not brown properly. (Just as many home cooks hesitate to preheat pans on the stovetop sufficiently.) As a result, meat steams rather than sizzles and does not brown and, as a consequence, does not taste very good.

KNOW WHEN FOOD IS DONE

Although professional cooks might rely on the feel of a steak to determine doneness, we find this method much too imprecise. An instant-read thermometer (see page 21) coupled with knowledge of how temperatures relate to desired doneness will ensure success. (The chart below lists these temperatures.)

Know that maximum juiciness and flavor often collides with maximum safety. Health officials generally suggest cooking all meat to 160 degrees in order to ensure that any bacteria or pathogens that may be present have been killed. This is sound advice if food safety is your top concern. However, the reality is that most people (including us) prefer their meat cooked to a lower internal temperature. The reason is simple. Heating causes meat fibers to contract and expel juices. A steak cooked to 160 degrees will be significantly drier than a steak cooked to 130 degrees. In most instances, we cook

Optimum Internal Temperatures for Meat

The chart below lists optimum internal temperatures, based on maximum juiciness and flavor. For optimum safety, all meat should be cooked until the internal temperature reaches 160 degrees.

To determine internal temperature, insert an instant-read thermometer deep into the meat away from any bone. Take two or three readings to make sure the entire piece of meat has reached the proper temperature.

Note that the temperatures that follow are at serving time. Since the internal temperature of most cuts will rise as the meat rests (the effect is called carryover cooking), you will want to remove meat from the grill before it hits these temperatures. For instance, a roast that registers 125 degrees on an instant-read thermometer when it comes out of the oven might reach 135 degrees by the time it has rested on the counter for 15 minutes.

Unfortunately, the significance of the carryover effect will vary from recipe to recipe based on the thickness of the cut (thicker cuts hold onto heat better than thinner cuts and will experience a greater rise in temperature as they rest) as well as the heat level used during the grilling process. For this reason, you should follow the temperatures in recipes, which have been designed to compensate for the carryover effect for that specific recipe. Recipes give temperatures at which the meat should be removed from the grill. The numbers below indicate how the temperature at serving time correlates with various levels of doneness.

	RARE	MEDIUM-RARE	MEDIUM	MEDIUM-WELL	WELL-DONE
Beef	125°F	130°F	140°F	150°F	160°F
Veal	125°F	135°F	140°F	150°F	160°F
Lamb	125°F	130°F	140°F	150°F	160°F
Pork	*	*	145°F	150°F	160°F

*(Not Recommended)

meat for maximum palatability. If safety is your top concern, you should cook all meat until it is well-done (and the internal temperature registers at least 160 degrees).

Note that these temperatures apply only to lean cuts and dry-heat cooking methods such as grilling and roasting.

LET MEAT REST AFTER COOKING

A final but very important step when cooking meat is allowing it to rest after it comes off the heat. This is common wisdom among cooks, but to be sure it was correct, we grilled several steaks, sliced several up immediately after they came off the fire, and allowed the second batch to rest for 10 minutes before slicing them. Not only did the first batch of steaks exude almost 40 percent more juice than the second batch when sliced, the meat also looked grayer and was not as tender. In this case, it is crucial to follow the conventional wisdom: Give your steaks a rest. (To read more about why meat should rest before being sliced, see page 103.)

GRILLED PREMIUM STEAKS

GRILLED PREMIUM STEAKS HAVE MANY attractive qualities: rich, beefy flavor; a thick, caramelized crust; and almost no prep or cleanup for the cook. But sometimes a small bonfire fueled by steak fat can leave expensive steaks charred and tasting of resinous smoke. Other times the coals burn down so low that the steaks end up with pale, wimpy grill marks and almost no flavor at all. In these cases, the steaks were likely left on the grill long enough to develop flavor, but they just overcooked.

So we went to work, promising ourselves we'd figure out how to use the grill to cook the entire steak perfectly: meat seared evenly on both sides so that the juices are concentrated into a powerfully flavored, dark brown, brittle coating of crust; the juicy inside cooked a little past rare; and the outside strip of rich, soft fat crisped and browned slightly on the edges.

We decided to focus on the steaks from the short loin and rib sections of the animal that we think are the best the cow has to offer—the T-bone and porterhouse as well as the strip and filet mignon (all from the short loin) and the rib eye (a rib steak without the bone, which is the most common way this cut is sold). We figured these steaks were bound to cook pretty much the same because they were all cut from the same general part of the cow.

Early on in our testing, we determined that we needed a very hot fire to get the crust we wanted without overcooking the steak. We could get that kind of heat by building the charcoal up to within 2 or 2½ inches of the grilling grate. But with this arrangement, we ran into problems with the fat dripping down onto the charcoal and flaming. We had already decided that a thick steak—at least 1¼ inches thick—was optimum, because at that thickness we achieved a tasty contrast between the charcoal flavoring on the outside of the steak and the beefy flavor on the inside. The problem was that we couldn't cook a thick steak over consistently high heat without burning it.

After considerable experimentation, we found the answer to this dilemma: We had to build a fire with two levels of heat. Once we realized that we needed a fire with a lot of coals on one side and far fewer coals on the other, we could sear the steak

GRILLING PORTERHOUSE AND T-BONE STEAKS

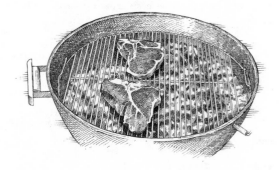

The delicate, buttery tenderloin portion must be protected when grilling porterhouse and T-bone steaks. Keep the tenderloin (the smaller portion of the left side of the bone on these steaks) over the cooler part of the fire.

properly at the beginning of cooking, then pull it onto the cooler half of the grill to finish cooking at a lower temperature. We could also use the dual heat levels to cook thin steaks as well as thick ones properly, and the system provided insurance against bonfires as well—if a steak flared up, we simply moved it off the high heat.

We gauged the level of heat on both sides of the fire by holding a hand about five inches over the cooking grate (as explained on page 4). When the medium-hot side of the grill was hot enough for searing, we could stand to hold a hand over the grill only for three or four seconds. For the cooler side of the grill, we could count seven seconds. (This is how we adapted our recipes for a gas grill, using burners set to high and medium.)

A two-level fire is also good for cooking porterhouse and T-bone, two of our favorite cuts, which are especially tricky to cook properly. Both consist of two muscles (strip and tenderloin) with a T-shaped bone in between. When grilled long enough to cook the strip section perfectly, the lean tenderloin is inevitably overcooked, dry, and flavorless. We found that if we grilled the steak with the tenderloin toward the cooler side of the fire, it cooked more slowly and reached proper doneness at the same time as the strip.

Common cooking wisdom suggests that bringing meat to room temperature before grilling will cause it to cook more evenly, and that letting it rest for five minutes after taking it off the grill will both preserve the juices and provide a more even color. We tested the first of these theories by simultaneously grilling two similar steaks, one straight from the refrigerator and a second that had stood at room temperature for one hour.

We noticed no difference in the cooked steaks except that the room temperature steak cooked a couple of minutes faster than the other. The second test was more conclusive. Letting a cooked steak rest for five minutes does indeed help the meat retain more juices when sliced and promotes a more even color throughout the meat.

We tried lightly oiling steaks before grilling to see if they browned better that way, and tried brushing them with butter halfway through grilling to see if the flavor improved. Although the oiled steaks browned a tiny bit better, the difference wasn't significant enough to merit the added ingredient. (The filet mignon cut was an exception; oiling improved browning in this leaner steak.) As for the butter, we couldn't taste any difference.

We did find that proper seasoning with salt and pepper before grilling is essential. Seasonings added after cooking sit on the surface and don't penetrate as well as salt and pepper added before cooking. Be liberal with the salt and pepper. A fair amount falls off during the cooking process. Finally, consider using coarse sea salt or kosher salt. In our tests, tasters consistently preferred steaks sprinkled with coarse salt before grilling compared with those sprinkled with table salt. The larger crystals are more easily absorbed by the meat and sprinkle more evenly.

Charcoal-Grilled Strip or Rib Steaks

SERVES 4

Strip and rib steaks, on or off the bone, are our first choice for individual steaks. A steak that's between 1¼ and 1½ inches thick gives you solid meat flavor as well as a little taste of the grill; any thicker and the steak becomes too much for one person to eat. If your guests are more likely to eat only an 8-ounce steak, grill two 1-pounders, slice them, and serve each person a half steak. Serve as is, or with one of the compound butters on pages 384–385.

4   strip or rib steaks, with or without the bone, 1¼ to 1½ inches thick (12 to 16 ounces each), patted dry with paper towels
     Salt and ground black pepper

1. Light a large chimney starter filled with hardwood charcoal (about 6 quarts) and allow to burn until all the charcoal is covered with a layer of fine gray ash. Build a two-level fire by stacking most of the coals on one side of the grill and arranging the remaining coals in a single layer on the other side of the grill. Set the cooking grate in place, cover the grill with the lid, and let the grate heat up, about 5 minutes. Use a grill brush to scrape the cooking grate clean. The grill is ready when the pile of coals is medium-hot and

BARBECUE 911

Steaks Are Overcooked

You spent $50 on prime porterhouse steaks, but then you overcooked them. You were using an instant-read thermometer, but something went wrong. It turns out that the sensor on most of these handy tools is located an inch or two up from the tip of the shaft. If you poke the thermometer straight down into a steak, you aren't going to get an accurate reading. Instead, use tongs to lift the steak off the grill and follow this method for taking the temperature of any steak or chop.

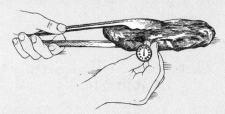

Insert the tip of an instant-read thermometer through the side of the steak until most of the shaft is embedded in the meat. Make sure the shaft is not touching any bone, which will throw off the reading. And make sure to check each steak—based on their thickness and location on the grill, some will cook faster than others.

the single layer of coals is medium-low. (See how to gauge heat level on page 4.)

2. Meanwhile, sprinkle both sides of the steaks with salt and pepper to taste. Grill the steaks, uncovered, over the hotter part of the fire until well browned on one side, 2 to 3 minutes. Turn the steaks; grill until well browned on the other side, 2 to 3 minutes. (If the steaks start to flame, pull them to the cooler part of the grill and/or extinguish the flames with a squirt bottle filled with water.)

3. Once the steaks are well browned on both sides, slide them to the cooler part of grill. Continue grilling, uncovered, to the desired doneness, 5 to 6 minutes more for rare (120 degrees on an instant-read thermometer), 6 to 7 minutes

for medium-rare on the rare side (125 degrees), 7 to 8 minutes for medium-rare on the medium side (130 degrees), or 8 to 9 minutes for medium (135 to 140 degrees).

4. Remove the steaks from the grill and let rest for 5 minutes. Serve immediately.

➤ VARIATION

Gas-Grilled Strip or Rib Steaks

Depending on the heat output of your gas grill, you may need to cook the steaks over the cooler part of the grill for an extra minute or two.

Turn on all the burners to high, close the lid, and heat the grill until very hot, about 15 minutes. Use a grill brush to scrape the cooking grate clean. Leave one burner on high and turn the other burner(s) to medium. Follow the recipe for Charcoal-Grilled Strip or Rib Steaks from step 2 and cook with the lid down.

Charcoal-Grilled Porterhouse or T-Bone Steaks

SERVES 4

How can you argue with a steak that gives you two different tastes and textures—from the strip and the tenderloin—in one cut, plus the bone? Since T-bone and porterhouse steaks are so large, it's best to have the butcher cut them thick (1½ inches) and let one steak serve two people. The key to keeping the delicate tenderloin from overcooking is to sear the steaks with the strip portions over the hottest coals and the tenderloin portions facing the cooler part of the fire. Serve as is or with one of the compound butters on pages 384–385.

2   porterhouse or T-bone steaks, 1½ inches thick (about 1¾ pounds each), patted dry with paper towels
Salt and ground black pepper

1. Light a large chimney starter filled with hardwood charcoal (about 6 quarts) and allow to burn until all the charcoal is covered with a layer of fine gray ash. Build a two-level fire by stacking most of the coals on one side of the grill and arranging the remaining coals in a single layer on the other side of the grill. Set the cooking grate

in place, cover the grill with the lid, and let the grate heat up, about 5 minutes. Use a grill brush to scrape the cooking grate clean. The grill is ready when the pile of coals is medium-hot and the single layer of coals is medium-low. (See how to gauge heat level on page 4.)

2. Meanwhile, sprinkle both sides of the steaks with salt and pepper to taste. Position the steaks on the grill so that the tenderloin pieces are over the cooler part of the fire and the strip pieces are over the hotter part of the fire (see the illustration on page 36). Grill the steaks, uncovered, until well browned on one side, 2 to 3 minutes. Turn the steaks; grill until well browned on the other side, 2 to 3 minutes. (If the steaks start to flame, pull them to the cooler part of the grill and/or extinguish the flames with a squirt bottle filled with water.)

3. Once the steaks are well browned on both sides, slide them completely to the cooler part of the grill. Continue grilling, uncovered, to the desired doneness, 5 to 6 minutes more for rare (120 degrees on an instant-read thermometer), 6 to 7 minutes for medium-rare on the rare side (125 degrees), 7 to 8 minutes for medium-rare on the medium side (130 degrees), or 8 to 9 minutes for medium (135 to 140 degrees).

4. Remove the steaks from the grill to a cutting board and let rest for 5 minutes. Cut the strip and filet pieces off the bones and slice each piece crosswise about ½ inch thick (see the illustrations at right). Serve immediately.

➤ VARIATIONS

Gas-Grilled Porterhouse or T-Bone Steaks
The key to preventing the delicate tenderloin portions of the steaks from overcooking is to sear the steaks with the strip portions over the burner turned to high and to keep the tenderloin facing the burner turned to medium.

Turn on all the burners to high, close the lid, and heat the grill until very hot, about 15 minutes. Use a grill brush to scrape the cooking grate clean. Leave one burner on high and turn the other burner(s) to medium. Follow the recipe for Charcoal-Grilled Porterhouse or T-Bone Steaks from step 2 and cook with the lid down.

CARVING PORTERHOUSE AND T-BONE STEAKS

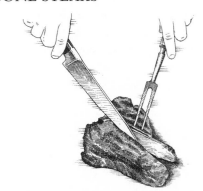

1. Once grilled, let a porterhouse or T-bone steak rest for 5 minutes before slicing. After the meat has rested, start by slicing close to the bone to remove the strip section.

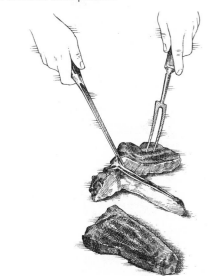

2. Turn the steak around and cut the tenderloin section off the bone.

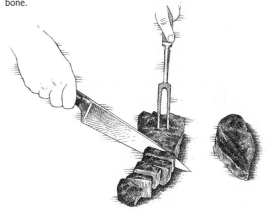

3. Slice each piece crosswise about ½ inch thick. Serve immediately.

Grilled Tuscan Steak with Olive Oil and Lemon (*Bistecca alla Fiorentina*)

Where the French use a compound butter to enhance the flavor of steak, the Italians use olive oil and lemon. Bistecca alla Fiorentina, as it is called in Tuscany, couldn't be simpler; a thick, juicy steak is grilled rare, sliced, and served with a drizzle of extra-virgin olive oil and a squeeze of lemon. The fruity, peppery olive oil amplifies the savory nature of the beef, while the lemon provides a bright counterpoint that cuts right through the richness to sharpen the other flavors. Make sure to use the finest quality oil in this recipe. You can also try rubbing a halved, peeled garlic clove over the bone and meat on each side of each steak before seasoning with salt and pepper.

Follow the recipe for Charcoal-Grilled or Gas–Grilled Porterhouse or T–Bone Steaks. Once

---

INGREDIENTS: Supermarket Extra-Virgin Olive Oils

When you purchase an artisanal oil in a high-end shop, certain informational perks are expected (and paid for). These typically include written explanations of the character and nuances of the particular oil as well as the assistance of knowledgeable staff. But in a supermarket, it's just you and a price tag (usually $8 to $10 per liter). How do you know which supermarket extra-virgin olive oil best suits your needs? To provide some guidance, we decided to hold a blind tasting of the nine best-selling extra-virgin olive oils typically available in American supermarkets.

The label extra-virgin denotes the highest quality of olive oil, with the most delicate and prized flavor. (The three other grades are virgin, pure, and olive pomace. Pure oil, often labeled simply olive oil, is the most commonly available.) To be tagged as extra-virgin, an oil must meet three basic criteria. First, it must contain less than 1 percent oleic free fatty acids per 100 grams of oil. Second, the oil must not have been treated with any solvents or heat. (Heat is used to reduce strong acidity in some nonvirgin olive oils to make them palatable.) This is where the term cold-pressed comes into play, meaning that the olives are pressed into a paste using mechanical wheels or hammers and are then kneaded to separate the oil from the fruit. Third, it must pass taste and aroma standards as defined by groups such as the International Olive Oil Council (IOOC), a Madrid-based intergovernmental olive oil regulatory committee that sets the bar for its member countries.

Tasting extra-virgin olive oil is much like tasting wine. The flavors of these oils range from citrusy to herbal, musty to floral, with every possibility in between. And what one taster finds particularly attractive—a slight briny flavor, for example—another might find unappealing. Also like wine, the flavor of a particular brand of olive oil can change from year to year, depending on the quality of the harvest and the olives' place of origin.

We chose to taste extra-virgin olive oil in its most pure and unadulterated state: raw. Tasters were given the option of sampling the oil from a spoon or on neutral-flavored French bread and were asked to eat a slice of green apple—for its acidity—to cleanse the palate between oils. The olive oils were evaluated for color, clarity, viscosity, bouquet, depth of flavor, and persistence of flavor.

The panel seemed to quickly divide itself into those who liked a gutsy olive oil with bold flavor and those who preferred a milder, more mellow approach. Tasters in the mild and delicate camp gave high scores to Pompeian and Whole Foods oils. Among tasters who preferred full-bodied, bold oils, Colavita and Filippo Berio earned high marks. Nonetheless, in both camps one oil clearly had more of a following than any other—the all-Italian-olive Da Vinci brand. Praised for its rounded and buttery flavor, it was the only olive oil we tasted that seemed to garner across-the-board approval with olive oil experts and in-house staff alike.

THE BEST OLIVE OILS
ALL-PURPOSE Da Vinci Extra-Virgin Olive Oil (left) was the favorite in our tasting of leading supermarket brands. It was described as "very ripe," "buttery," and "complex."

MILD Pompeian Extra-Virgin Olive Oil (center) was a favorite among tasters who preferred a milder, more delicate oil. It was described as "clean," "round," and "sunny."

FULL-BODIED Colavita Extra-Virgin Olive Oil (right) was a favorite among tasters who preferred a bolder, more full-bodied oil. It was described as "heavy," "complex," and "briny."

the slices are arranged on a platter, drizzle with 3 tablespoons extra-virgin olive oil and serve immediately with lemon wedges.

Charcoal-Grilled Filets Mignons

SERVES 4

Filets mignons are cut from the tenderloin, which is, as the name indicates, an especially tender portion of meat. Though tender, the steaks are not extremely rich. To prevent the steaks from drying out on the grill and to encourage browning, we found it helpful to rub each steak lightly with a little oil before grilling. To serve, we suggest that you drizzle the grilled steaks with olive oil and garnish them with lemon wedges; or serve them with one of the compound butters on pages 384–385. You can also season the filets prior to grilling with Cracked Peppercorn Rub or Rosemary Garlic Paste on page 381. If the filets are misshapen or unevenly cut, as supermarket steaks sometimes are, follow the illustration at right to tie each one before grilling.

> 4 center-cut filets mignons, 1½ to 2 inches thick (7 to 8 ounces each), patted dry with paper towels
>
> 4 teaspoons olive oil
>   Salt and ground black pepper

1. Light a large chimney starter filled with hardwood charcoal (about 6 quarts) and allow to burn until all the charcoal is covered with a layer of fine gray ash. Build a two-level fire by stacking most of the coals on one side of the grill and arranging the remaining coals in a single layer on the other side of the grill. Set the cooking grate in place, cover the grill with the lid, and let the grate heat up, about 5 minutes. Use a grill brush to scrape the cooking grate clean. The grill is ready when the pile of coals is medium-hot and the single layer of coals is medium-low. (See how to gauge heat level on page 4.)

2. Meanwhile, lightly rub the steaks with the oil and sprinkle both sides of the steaks with salt and pepper to taste. Grill the steaks, uncovered, over the hotter part of the fire until well browned on one side, 2 to 3 minutes. Turn the steaks; grill until well browned on the other side, 2 to 3 minutes.

3. Once the steaks are well browned on both sides, slide them to the cooler part of the grill. Continue grilling, uncovered, to the desired doneness, 6 minutes more for rare (120 degrees on an instant-read thermometer), 7 minutes for medium-rare on the rare side (125 degrees), 8 minutes for medium-rare on the medium side (130 degrees), or 9 to 10 minutes for medium (135 to 140 degrees).

4. Remove the steaks from the grill and let rest for 5 minutes. Serve immediately.

➤ VARIATION
Gas-Grilled Filets Mignons
Depending on the heat output of your gas grill, you may need to cook the steaks over the cooler part of the grill for an extra minute or two.

Turn on all the burners to high, close the lid, and heat the grill until very hot, about 15 minutes. Use a grill brush to scrape the cooking grate clean. Leave one burner on high and turn the other burner(s) to medium. Follow the recipe for Charcoal-Grilled Filets Mignons from step 2 and cook with the lid down.

DEALING WITH MISSHAPEN FILETS

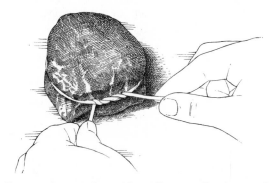

To correct for unevenly or oddly cut filets, tie a 12-inch piece of kitchen twine around each steak. Snip off the excess twine at the knot to make sure it does not ignite on the grill. Adjust the shape of the tied filet by gently rolling or patting it with your hand until it is more uniform in appearance and thickness.

Grilled Premium Steak and Potatoes with Blue Cheese Butter

SERVES 4

Watch the potatoes closely as they are blanching; it is important to take them out of the water before they are fully tender. Trying to grill potatoes that are already fully cooked is nearly impossible.

2	pounds medium red potatoes, scrubbed and cut crosswise into 1/2-inch-thick rounds
	Salt
2	tablespoons vegetable oil
	Ground black pepper
1	recipe Grilled Strip Steaks or Rib Steaks (page 37), Grilled Filets Mignons (page 41), or Grilled Porterhouse or T-Bone Steaks (page 38)
4	tablespoons (1/2 stick) unsalted butter, softened
3	tablespoons crumbled blue cheese
1	small shallot, minced (about 2 tablespoons)
1	teaspoon chopped fresh parsley leaves
1	small garlic clove, minced or pressed through a garlic press (about 1/2 teaspoon)

1. Place the potatoes in a large pot. Cover with 1½ quarts of cold water. Add 1 teaspoon salt and bring to a boil over high heat. Reduce the heat to medium and simmer until the potatoes are barely tender, about 6 minutes. Drain the potatoes in a colander, being careful not to break them. Transfer the potatoes to a baking sheet coated with 1 tablespoon of the oil. Drizzle the remaining 1 tablespoon oil over the potatoes and season with salt and pepper to taste.

2. While the potatoes are cooking, follow one of the premium steak recipes through step 2.

3. Once the steaks are moved to the cooler part of the grill, place the potatoes on the hotter part. Cook, turning once, until grill marks appear and the potato slices are cooked through, 6 to 8 minutes.

4. Meanwhile, beat the butter with a large fork in a medium bowl until light and fluffy. Add the cheese, shallot, parsley, garlic, ¼ teaspoon salt, and ⅛ teaspoon pepper.

5. To serve, place one steak and some of the potatoes on each plate. Top each steak with about 2 tablespoons of the butter mixture and serve immediately.

FREE-FORM BEEF WELLINGTON

BEEF WELLINGTON IS ONE OF THOSE DISHES we always envision being served on a silver platter by a waiter in a tuxedo and white gloves. This decadent beef tenderloin is topped with foie gras and mushrooms and then wrapped in pastry and baked. As such, beef Wellington isn't a dish

MINCING A SHALLOT

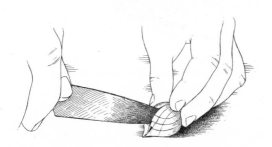

1. Place the peeled bulb flat-side down and make several slices parallel to the work surface, almost to (but not through) the root end. Then make a number of very closely spaced parallel cuts through the top of the shallot down to the work surface.

2. Finish the mincing by making very thin slices perpendicular to the lengthwise cuts.

that anyone would consider quick and simple—but, as the combination of flavors and textures is so appealing, we sought to update this classic and create our own version of beef Wellington on the grill.

Having made beef Wellington in the past, we wanted to avoid what we knew to be a common pitfall: failing to cook both the pastry and the beef properly. If the beef was well cooked, the pastry was soggy; if the pastry was light and flaky, the beef was overcooked. We found that by grilling the ingredients separately and assembling them afterward, we could avoid the problematic discrepancy in cooking times.

Traditionally, Wellington is made with filet mignon, a cut of beef that has little intramuscular fat, meaning it lacks the intense beefy flavor of a strip or rib-eye steak. We preferred it for a Wellington, however, because the milder steak allowed the other ingredients to show off. Grilling over a two-level fire was the best way to cook the steaks. This way, we were able to sear them over high heat for a flavorful crust and then move them to the cooler part of the grill to finish cooking. This arrangement was also perfect for the next part of our Wellington, the mushrooms.

Normally, Wellington contains mushroom duxelles, which are finely chopped mushrooms that have been slowly cooked in butter until they devolve into a paste. This method seemed impractical for our purposes, so we opted to grill portobello mushrooms instead. With the hot part of the fire free, we could grill the mushrooms quickly. We found that the portobellos are much tastier cooked over a hot fire than a cooler fire, where they tend to steam and won't brown.

The next step was preparing the foie gras—which we quickly decided not to do, mainly because it is so expensive but also because we were unsure how it would fare on the grill. Instead, we looked for alternative ingredients. We tried duck and chicken livers, but we found they were not meant for the grill due to their small size. Next, we tried several store-bought pâtés. Our innovative solution was to use duck liver pâté, which has a flavor similar to that of foie gras but is a lot less expensive and doesn't require cooking.

Spreading the pâté lightly on grilled bread (rather than pastry, which can't be grilled) and then topping it with slices of the portobellos and steak completed our free-form Wellington. When assembled, however, it seemed a little dry. Without the time to make a proper reduction sauce, which usually accompanies beef Wellington, we decided to abbreviate the process. By quickly reducing red wine and port with shallots and thyme until they reached a syrupy consistency, we made a sauce that enhanced the flavors of our Wellington and provided welcome moisture.

Charcoal-Grilled Free-Form Beef Wellington with Port Syrup
SERVES 4

This recipe calls for three steaks but feeds four people. We found that four 8-ounce steaks, when served with the pâté and mushrooms, was simply too rich.

1½	cups ruby port
1½	cups red wine
1	small shallot, minced (about 2 tablespoons)
1	teaspoon whole fresh thyme leaves
3	filets mignons, about 2 inches thick (8 ounces each), patted dry
2	tablespoons olive oil
	Salt and ground black pepper
4	large portobello mushroom caps (each 4 inches in diameter)
4	slices country bread (each 5 inches across and ½ inch thick)
4	ounces smooth duck liver pâté

1. Light a large chimney starter filled with hardwood charcoal (about 6 quarts) and allow it to burn until all the charcoal is covered with a layer of fine gray ash. Build a two-level fire by stacking most of the coals on one side of the grill and arranging the remaining coals in a single layer on the other side of the grill (see the illustration on page 4). Set the cooking grate in place, cover the grill with the lid, and let the grate heat up, about 5 minutes. Use a grill brush to scrape the cooking grate clean. The grill is ready when the temperature of the stacked

coals is medium-hot and that of the remaining coals is medium-low (see how to gauge heat level on page 4).

2. Meanwhile, bring the port, red wine, shallot, and thyme to a boil in a medium saucepan over high heat. Reduce the heat to medium and simmer until the mixture thickens and is reduced to ½ cup, about 15 minutes.

3. Lightly rub the steaks with 1 tablespoon of the oil and sprinkle with salt and pepper to taste. Brush the portobellos with the remaining 1 tablespoon oil and season with salt and pepper to taste.

4. Cook the steaks, uncovered, over the hotter part of the fire until well browned on one side, 2 to 3 minutes. Turn the steaks; grill until well browned on the other side, 2 to 3 minutes. Move the browned steaks to the cooler part of the grill. Continue grilling, uncovered, to the desired doneness, 6 minutes more for rare (120 degrees on an instant-read thermometer), 7 minutes for medium-rare on the rare side (125 degrees), 8 minutes for medium-rare on the medium side (130 degrees), or 9 to 10 minutes for medium (135 to 140 degrees).

5. Once the steaks are moved, set the mushrooms over the hotter coals. Grill, turning once, until tender and lightly browned, 8 to 10 minutes. Transfer the mushrooms to a platter and cover with foil. After both the steaks and the mushrooms are removed from the grill, set the bread over the cooler part of the grill and toast, turning once, until golden brown on both sides, 1 to 1½ minutes.

6. To assemble: Spread 1 ounce of pâté over each piece of grilled bread. Slice the mushrooms into wide strips and arrange them uniformly over the bread. Cut the beef into ¼-inch-thick strips and place some on top of the mushrooms. Drizzle with the port syrup and serve immediately.

➤ VARIATION

Gas-Grilled Free-Form Beef Wellington with Port Syrup

Turn on all the burners to high, close the lid, and heat the grill until very hot, about 15 minutes. Use a grill brush to scrape the cooking grate clean. Leave one burner on high and turn the other burner(s) to medium. Follow the recipe for Charcoal-Grilled Free-Form Beef Wellington with Port Syrup from step 2 and cook with the lid down, moving the mushrooms to the hotter part of the grill in step 5. Proceed as directed.

GRILLED STEAK TIPS

STEAK TIPS HAVE NEVER BEEN ON OUR list of favorite meats. It's not that we're premium steak snobs, but we were skeptical about a cut of meat that has long been the darling of all-you-can-eat restaurant chains, where quantity takes precedence over quality. There is also some confusion about what constitutes a steak tip. Some steak tips are sautéed and served with a sauce (these are often called pub-style steak tips), some are marinated and grilled (known as tailgate tips). We were drawn to grilling and so began by testing five such recipes.

The recipes differed in the ingredients used to marinate the meat and in the marinating time. The simplest recipe marinated the tips in a bottled Italian-style salad dressing for 24 hours. The most complex marinated the meat for three days in a mixture that included aromatics and herbs. Despite such variations in time and ingredients, none of these grilled tips was very good. Some were mushy, but most were tough and dry. At this point, steak tips still seemed like a cheap cut of meat, with promising beefy flavor but poor texture.

Thinking that the problem might be the cut of meat, we went to the supermarket only to discover a confusing array of meats—cubes, strips, and steaks—labeled "steak tips." Still more confusing, these cubes, strips, and steaks could be cut from a half-dozen different parts of the cow.

After grilling more than 50 pounds of tips, it became clear that the only cut worth grilling is one referred to by butchers as flap meat. (For more information on buying steak tips, see the facing page.) When we grilled whole flap meat steaks and then sliced them on the bias before serving, tasters were impressed. Although the meat was still a bit chewy, choosing the right cut was a start.

We now turned to marinades. Given the long-held belief that acidic marinades tenderize tough meat, we created four recipes using four popular acids: yogurt, wine, vinegar, and fruit juice. To determine optimal marinating time, we let the meat sit in each marinade for four hours and for 24 hours. Curious about marinade's other claim to fame—flavoring—we added aromatics, spices, and herbs.

The yogurt marinade was the least favorite, producing dry meat that was chewy and tough. Tasters also panned the wine-based marinade. The meat was tough and dry, while the flavors were either harsh or bland. Some tasters liked the complex flavor of the vinegar marinade, but everyone found the tips to be "overly chewy." The marinade prepared with pineapple juice was the favorite. Both the four-hour and 24-hour versions yielded juicy, tender, flavorful meat.

So what was it in our pineapple marinade that worked so well with our steak tips? Our first thought was the pineapple juice itself. Pineapple contains proteases, enzymes that help to break down proteins. Proteases are also found in papaya and other fruits. One of them, papain, from papayas, is the active component of meat tenderizers such as Adolph's. The juice we had been using was pasteurized, however, and the heat of pasteurization is thought to disable such enzymes. To see if proteases were in fact at work, we devised a test in which we made three more marinades: one with pasteurized pineapple juice from the supermarket; a second with pasteurized pineapple juice heated to the boiling point and then cooled; and a third with fresh pineapple pureed in a food processor.

The result? The fresh juice was a much more aggressive "tenderizer," so much so that it turned

INGREDIENTS: Steak Tips

Steak tips can come from two different parts of the cow. One type comes from tender, expensive cuts in the middle of the back of the cow, such as the tenderloin. These tips are a superior cut, but not what we consider to be a true steak tip, which should be a more pedestrian cut that is magically transformed into a desirable dish through marinating and cooking. If the steak tips at your market cost $8 to $10 per pound, the meat likely comes from the tenderloin.

True steak tips come from various muscles in the sirloin and round and cost about $5 per pound. After tasting 50 pounds of lower-priced cuts, tasters had a clear favorite: a single muscle that butchers call flap meat, with tips from this cut typically labeled "sirloin tips." A whole piece of flap meat weighs about $2\frac{1}{2}$ pounds. One piece can range in thickness from $\frac{1}{2}$ inch to $1\frac{1}{2}$ inches and may be sold as cubes, strips, or small steaks. It has a rich, deep beefy flavor and a distinctive longitudinal grain.

We found that it's best to buy flap meat in steak form rather than cut into cubes or strips, which are often taken from nearby muscles in the hip and butt that are neither as tasty nor as tender. Because meat labeling is so haphazard, you must visually identify flap meat; buying it in steak form makes this easy.

Steak tips can be cut from a half-dozen muscles and are sold in three basic forms: cubes, strips, and steaks. To make sure that you are buying the most flavorful cut—flap meat sirloin tips (pictured above left)—buy whole steaks.

the meat mushy on the inside and slimy on the outside. We had learned: Proteases do break down meat, but they don't make it any better (tasters universally disapproved of these overly tenderized tips); pasteurization does kill this enzyme (the fresh juice was much more powerful than the supermarket variety); and proteases were not responsible for the strong showing made by the original pineapple marinade. Why, then, did tasters prefer the pineapple marinade?

After rereading the ingredient list, we devised a new theory. The pineapple marinade included soy sauce, an ingredient that is packed with salt and that was not used in any of the other marinades. Was the soy sauce tenderizing the meat by acting like a brine? In the past, the test kitchen has demonstrated the beneficial effects of brining on lean poultry and pork.

To answer these questions, we ran another series of tests, trying various oil-based marinades made with salt or soy sauce (in earlier tests, we had determined that oil helped to keep the meat moist and promoted searing). To use salt in a marinade, we first had to dissolve it. Because salt doesn't dissolve in oil, we used water, but the liquid prevented the meat from browning properly. That said, brining did make these steak tips tender and juicy.

We concluded that soy sauce, not pineapple juice, was the secret ingredient in our tasters' favorite marinade. The salt in soy sauce was responsible for the improved texture of the steak tips, and the soy sauce also promoted browning. After experimenting with brining times, we determined that an hour was optimal. It allowed for the thicker parts of the meat to become tender while preventing the thinner sections from becoming too salty.

We then went to work on flavor variations, adding garlic, ginger, orange zest, hot pepper, brown sugar, and scallions for an Asian marinade and making a Southwest-inspired marinade that included garlic, chili powder, cumin, cayenne, brown sugar, and tomato paste. We found that a squeeze of fresh citrus served with the steak provided a bright acidic counterpoint.

Because this relatively thin cut cooks quickly, high heat is necessary to achieve a perfect crust. The uneven thickness of many tips presented a problem, though. The exterior would scorch by the time the thick portions were cooked, and the thin parts would be overcooked. A two-level fire, with more coals on one side of the grill to create hotter and cooler areas, solved the problem. We started the tips over high heat to sear them and then moved them to the cooler area to finish cooking.

We usually prefer steaks grilled rare, so we were surprised to find that when cooked rare, the tips were rubbery, whereas longer cooking gave them a tender chew—without drying out the meat. Even when cooked until well done, the tips were exceptionally juicy. We had the brine to

INGREDIENTS: Soy Sauce

Few condiments are as misunderstood as soy sauce, the pungent, fragrant, fermented flavoring that's a mainstay in Asian cooking. Its simple, straightforward composition—equal parts soybeans and a roasted grain, usually wheat, plus water and salt—belies the subtle, sophisticated contribution it makes as an all-purpose seasoning, flavor enhancer, tabletop condiment, and dipping sauce.

The three products consumers are likely to encounter are regular soy sauce, light soy sauce (made with a higher percentage of water and hence lower in sodium), and tamari (made with fermented soybeans, water, and salt—no wheat). Tamari generally has a stronger flavor and thicker consistency than soy sauce. It is traditionally used in Japanese cooking.

In a tasting of leading soy sauces, we found that products aged according to ancient customs were superior to synthetic sauces, such as La Choy's, which are made in a day and almost always contain hydrolyzed vegetable protein. Our favorite soy sauce, Eden Selected Shoyu Soy Sauce (*shoyu* is the Japanese word for soy sauce), is aged for three years. Tasters also liked products made by San-J and Kikkoman.

THE BEST SOY SAUCE
Eden Selected Shoyu Soy Sauce was described by tasters as "toasty," "caramel-y," and "complex." The saltiness was pronounced but not overwhelming. Among the 12 brands tested, it was the clear favorite.

thank again: The salty soy marinade helped the meat hold onto its moisture.

Conventional wisdom prompted one more test. We grilled two more batches of tips and sliced one immediately after it came off the grill and the other five minutes later. Sure enough, the rested tips were both more juicy and more tender. Finally, we had a recipe for steak tips as pleasing to the palate as it is to the pocketbook.

Charcoal-Grilled Steak Tips
SERVES 4 TO 6

A two-level fire allows you to brown the steak over the hot side of the grill, then move it to the cooler side if it is not yet cooked through. If your steak is thin, however, you may not need to use the cooler side of the grill. The times in the recipe below are for relatively even, 1-inch-thick steak tips. When grilling, bear in mind that even those tasters who usually prefer rare beef preferred steak tips cooked medium-rare to medium because the texture is firmer and not quite so chewy. Serve lime wedges with the Southwestern-marinated tips and orange wedges with the tips marinated in garlic, ginger, and soy sauce.

I	recipe marinade (recipes follow)
2	pounds flap meat sirloin steak tips, trimmed of excess fat
	Lime or orange wedges for serving

1. Combine the marinade and meat in a gallon-size zipper-lock bag; press out as much air as possible and seal the bag. Refrigerate for 1 hour, flipping the bag after 30 minutes to ensure that the meat marinates evenly.

2. About halfway through the marinating time, light a large chimney starter filled with hardwood charcoal (about 6 quarts) and allow to burn until all the charcoal is covered with a layer of fine gray ash. Build a two-level fire by stacking most of the coals on one side of the grill and arranging the remaining coals in a single layer on the other side of the grill. Set the cooking grate in place, cover the grill with the lid, and let the grate heat up, about 5 minutes. Use a grill brush to scrape the cooking grate clean. The grill is ready when the pile of coals is medium-hot and the single layer of coals is medium-low. (See how to gauge heat level on page 4.)

3. Remove the steak tips from the marinade and pat dry with paper towels. Grill, uncovered, over the hotter part of the fire, until well seared and dark brown on the first side, about 4 minutes. Using tongs, flip the steak tips and grill until the second side is well seared and the thickest part of the meat is slightly less done than desired, 4 to 5 minutes for medium-rare (about 130 degrees on an instant-read thermometer), 6 to 8 minutes for medium (about 135 degrees); if the exterior of the meat is browned but the steak is not yet cooked through, move the steak tips to the cooler side of the grill and continue to grill to the desired doneness.

4. Transfer the steak tips to a cutting board. Tent the tips loosely with foil and let rest for 5 minutes. Slice the steak tips very thin on the bias. Serve immediately with the lime or orange wedges.

> VARIATION
Gas-Grilled Steak Tips
Follow the recipe for Charcoal-Grilled Steak Tips through step 1. When about 15 minutes of marinating time remains, turn on all the burners to high, close the lid, and heat the grill until very hot, about 15 minutes. Use a grill brush to scrape the cooking grate clean. Leave one burner on high and turn the other burner(s) to medium. Continue with the recipe from step 3 and cook with the lid down.

Southwestern Marinade
MAKES ENOUGH FOR 2 POUNDS OF STEAK TIPS

1/3	cup soy sauce
1/3	cup vegetable oil
3	medium garlic cloves, minced or pressed through a garlic press (about I tablespoon)
I	tablespoon dark brown sugar
I	tablespoon tomato paste
I	tablespoon chili powder
2	teaspoons ground cumin
1/4	teaspoon cayenne pepper

Combine all of the ingredients in a small bowl.

Garlic, Ginger, and Soy Marinade

MAKES ENOUGH FOR 2 POUNDS OF STEAK TIPS

1/3	cup soy sauce
3	tablespoons vegetable oil
3	tablespoons toasted sesame oil
2	tablespoons dark brown sugar
3	medium garlic cloves, minced or pressed through a garlic press (about 1 tablespoon)
1	tablespoon minced fresh ginger
2	teaspoons grated zest from 1 orange
1/2	teaspoon red pepper flakes
1	medium scallion, sliced thin

Combine all of the ingredients in a small bowl.

GRILLED FLANK STEAK

THANKS TO FAJITAS, FLANK STEAK HAS become the darling of Tex-Mex fans from New York to California and everywhere in between. But there are good reasons for the popularity of flank steak in addition to mere culinary fashion. Like other steaks cut from the chest and side of the cow, flank has a rich, full, beefy flavor. Also, because it is thin, it cooks relatively quickly. Because flank steaks are typically too long to fit into a pan, grilling makes the most sense for this cut.

Although grilling flank steak appeared to be a pretty straightforward procedure, we still had some questions about exactly what was the best way to go about it. We had two very simple goals: creating a good sear on the outside of this thin cut before it overcooked on the inside, and tenderness. We wondered whether the meat should be marinated or rubbed with spices, how hot the fire should be, and how long the meat should be cooked.

Virtually every recipe we found for flank steak called for marinating it. Most sources championed the marinade as a means of tenderizing the meat as well as adding flavor. We found that marinades with a lot of acid eventually made this thin cut mushy and unappealing. If we omitted the acid,

we could flavor the meat, but this took at least 12 hours. As for tenderness, when the cooked steaks were sliced thin across the grain, there was virtually no difference between those that had been marinated and those that had not.

With marinades no longer in the running, we turned to spice rubs. We rubbed one steak with a spice rub eight hours before cooking, one an hour before, and one just before we put it over the flames. A fourth steak, with no spice rub at all, was cooked just like the others. The three spice-rubbed steaks all had about the same amount of flavor and all developed almost identical dark brown, very flavorful crusts. The plain steak did not develop nearly as nice a crust, but cooked in approximately the same amount of time. We noticed no difference in tenderness among the steaks.

While spice rubs create excellent crust with plenty of intense flavor, they are not necessarily a good choice for folks who like their flank steak cooked to medium, because if you leave the steak on for that long, the spices burn. (You have to be a bit careful to keep the spices from burning even if you like your steak medium-rare.) But if you don't mind exercising a small degree of attention while grilling, we highly recommend using spice rubs for flank steak. If you want to cook flank steak beyond medium, we suggest adding flavor by passing a sauce separately at the table.

Every source we checked was in the same camp when it came to cooking flank steak, and it is the right camp. Flank steak should be cooked over high heat for a short period of time. We tried lower heat and longer cooking times, but inevitably the meat ended up tough. Because flank steak is too thin to be checked with a meat thermometer, you must resort to a primitive method of checking for doneness: Cut into the meat to see if it is done to your liking. Remember that carryover heat will continue to cook the steak after it comes off the grill. So if you want the steak medium-rare, take it off the heat when it tests rare, and so on.

Most sources were also in agreement when it came to letting the steak rest after cooking. During cooking, the heat drives the juices to the center of the meat. This phenomenon is particularly noticeable with high-heat cooking. If you cut the meat right after it comes off the heat, much more of the juice spills out than if you allow the meat to rest, during which time the juices become evenly distributed throughout the meat once again. This is common wisdom among cooks, but to be sure it was correct, we cooked two more flank steaks, sliced one immediately after it came off the fire, and allowed the second steak to rest for five minutes before slicing it. Not only did the first steak exude almost twice as much juice when sliced as the second, it also looked grayer and was not as tender. So in this case, conventional wisdom prevails: Give your steak a rest.

Charcoal-Grilled Flank Steak

SERVES 4 TO 6

For this recipe, all the coals are banked on one side of the grill to create an especially hot fire. Because flank steak is so thin, there's no need to use the cooler part of the grill for cooking the meat through. Also, the thinness of the meat means you have to rely on timing, touch, and/or nick-and-peek, not an instant-read thermometer, to determine doneness.

I   **flank steak (about 2½ pounds)**
     Salt and ground black pepper

1. Light a large chimney starter filled with hardwood charcoal (about 6 quarts) and allow to burn until all the charcoal is covered with a layer of fine gray ash. Build a modified two-level fire by spreading the coals out over half the grill bottom, leaving the other half with no coals. Set the cooking grate in place, cover the grill with the lid, and let the grate heat up, about 5 minutes. Use a grill brush to scrape the cooking grate clean. The grill is ready when you have a hot fire. (See how to gauge heat level on page 4.)

2. Sprinkle both sides of the steak generously with salt and pepper to taste. Grill the steak over the coals until well seared and dark brown on one side, 5 to 7 minutes. Using tongs, flip the steak and grill until the interior of the meat is slightly less done than you want it to be when you eat it, 2 to 5 minutes more for rare or medium-rare (depending on the heat of the fire and thickness of the steak).

3. Transfer the steak to a cutting board. Tent loosely with foil and let rest for 5 minutes. Slice the steak thin on the bias across the grain. Season with additional salt and pepper to taste and serve immediately.

INGREDIENTS: Three Flat Steaks

When it comes to flat steaks, skirt and hanger steak are most similar to flank steak, and, like flank, have recently become fashionable. The similarities: All are long, relatively thin, quite tough, and grainy, but each has rich, deep, beefy flavor. Hanger and flank both come from the rear side of the animal, while skirt comes from the area between the abdomen and the chest cavity.

We soon came to realize that all flat steaks are not equal. Hanger, a thick muscle that is attached to the diaphragm of the cow, derives its name from the fact that when the animal is butchered, this steak hangs down into the center of the carcass. Because hanger steak is a classic French bistro dish, the cut is highly prized in restaurants and, therefore, difficult to find in butcher shops. We don't think this is a great loss, since the hanger steaks we sampled had the toughest texture and least flavor of these three cuts.

On the other hand, flank steak is easy to find in any supermarket. It has great beef flavor and is quite tender if cooked rare or medium-rare and sliced thin across the grain. Because of the

popularity of fajitas, flank steak has recently gone up steeply in price, often retailing for $7 a pound.

Last but not least, skirt steak, which was the cut originally used for fajitas, can also be difficult to find in supermarkets and even butcher shops. This is a real pity because skirt steak has more fat than flank steak, which makes it juicier and richer-tasting. At the same time, skirt has a deep, beefy flavor that outshines both hanger and flank steak. If you see skirt steak, buy it and cook it like flank.

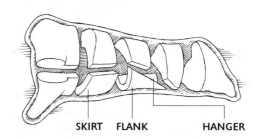

SKIRT   FLANK   HANGER

VARIATIONS
Gas-Grilled Flank Steak
Turn on all the burners to high, close the lid, and heat the grill until very hot, about 15 minutes. Use a grill brush to scrape the cooking grate clean. Leave all the burners on high. Follow the recipe for Charcoal-Grilled Flank Steak from step 2 and cook with the lid down.

Grilled Flank Steak Rubbed with Latin Spices
Watch the meat carefully as it cooks to ensure that the spice rub darkens but does not burn. If necessary, slide the steak to the cooler part of the charcoal grill (or reduce the heat on a gas grill) to keep the meat from charring. Flank steak can also be rubbed with Simple Spice Rub for Beef or Lamb on page 377.

- 2 tablespoons ground cumin
- 2 tablespoons chili powder
- I tablespoon ground coriander
- 2 teaspoons ground black pepper
- 1½ teaspoons salt
- ½ teaspoon ground cinnamon
- ½ teaspoon red pepper flakes
- I recipe Charcoal-Grilled or Gas-Grilled Flank Steak (page 49)

1. Combine all of the spices and the salt in a small bowl.

HANDLING HONEY

When measuring sticky ingredients like honey (or molasses), spray the measuring cup with nonstick cooking spray before filling it. When emptied, the liquid will slip right out of the cup.

BARBECUE 911
Flare-Ups from the Grill
Flare-ups from the grill are a not-so-rare occurrence, caused primarily by fats melting into the fire. Sometimes there's no way around this, but don't let a grease fire get out of control and ruin your meal. Take action with this method.

Keep a squirt bottle or plant mister filled with water near the grill. At the first sign of flames, try to pull foods to a cool part of the grill and douse the flames with water.

2. Follow the recipe for Charcoal-Grilled or Gas-Grilled Flank Steak, omitting the salt and pepper in step 2 and rubbing the steak on both sides with the spice mixture instead.

Grilled Flank Steak with Sweet-and-Sour Chipotle Sauce
Try serving this zesty variation with guacamole and warm flour tortillas.

- ½ cup juice from 8 limes
- ¼ cup honey
- 2 tablespoons vegetable oil
- 3 chipotle chiles in adobo sauce
- 2 tablespoons balsamic vinegar
- 2 tablespoons whole-grain mustard
- 2 medium garlic cloves, minced or pressed through a garlic press (about 2 teaspoons)
- I teaspoon ground cumin
- 2 tablespoons chopped fresh cilantro leaves
- ½ teaspoon salt

Ground black pepper

1 recipe Charcoal-Grilled or Gas-Grilled Flank Steak (page 49)

1. Combine the lime juice, honey, oil, chiles, vinegar, mustard, garlic, and cumin in a blender or food processor and puree or process until smooth. Transfer to a small bowl and stir in the cilantro, salt, and pepper to taste; set aside. (The sauce can be covered and refrigerated for up to 3 days.)

2. Follow the recipe for Charcoal-Grilled or Gas-Grilled Flank Steak. After you remove the steak from the grill, brush both sides generously with the chipotle sauce. Let the steak rest for 5 minutes. Pass the remaining sauce separately with the sliced steak.

Grilled Flank Steak and Red Onion with Chimichurri

Chimichurri is a sauce that often accompanies grilled beef. Similar to a pesto but looser in consistency and based on parsley rather than basil, chimichurri is a flavorful addition to grilled steak.

1 large red onion, peeled and sliced crosswise into 1/2-inch-thick rounds
1 tablespoon olive oil
Salt and ground black pepper
1 recipe Charcoal-Grilled or Gas-Grilled Flank Steak (page 49)
1 recipe Chimichurri (page 397)

1. Place the onion slices on a baking sheet; brush both sides lightly with the oil and season with salt and pepper to taste. Thread the onion slices onto skewers (see the illustration on page 314).

2. Follow the recipe for Charcoal-Grilled or Gas-Grilled Flank Steak, cooking the onion with the steak over the coals. Grill the onion, turning once, until streaked with dark grill marks, 10 to 12 minutes. Remove the onion slices from the skewers, separate the rings, and place them on a large platter, then arrange the meat over the onions. Serve immediately, passing the chimichurri at the table.

Classic Fajitas
SERVES 8

Although fajitas were originally made with skirt steak, the combination of flank steak and vegetables grilled and then wrapped in warm tortillas is the one that put flank steak on the culinary map in the United States. The ingredients should go on the grill in this order: the steak over a hot fire, the vegetables over a medium fire, and the tortillas around the edge of a medium-to-low fire just to warm them. The tortillas can also be stacked, wrapped in a clean, damp dish towel, and warmed in a microwave oven for 3 minutes; keep the tortillas wrapped until serving time. Cover the grilled but unsliced flank steak with foil for the 10 minutes or so it takes for the vegetables and tortillas to cook.

1 recipe Charcoal-Grilled or Gas-Grilled Flank Steak (page 49)
1/4 cup juice from 4 limes
Salt and ground black pepper
1 very large onion, peeled and sliced crosswise into 1/2-inch rounds
2 very large red or green bell peppers, cut according to the illustration below
16 flour tortillas (each 10 to 12 inches in diameter)
Fresh Tomato Salsa (page 390) and/or Chunky Guacamole (page 390)

CUTTING PEPPERS FOR THE GRILL

Remove and discard a 1/4-inch-thick slice from the top and bottom of each pepper. Reach into the pepper and pull out the seeds in a single bunch. Slice down one side of the pepper, then lay it flat, skin-side down, in a long strip. Slide a sharp knife along the inside of the pepper to remove the white ribs and any remaining seeds. The flattened and cleaned pepper is now ready for grilling.

1. Follow the recipe for either Charcoal-Grilled or Gas-Grilled Flank Steak, sprinkling the meat with the lime juice and salt and pepper to taste before grilling.

2. Remove the steak to a cutting board and tent loosely with foil. When the charcoal fire has died down to medium or the gas grill burners have been adjusted to medium, place the onion slices and peppers on the grill and grill them, turning occasionally, until the onion slices are lightly charred, about 6 minutes, and the peppers are streaked with dark grill marks, about 10 minutes. Remove the vegetables to a cutting board and slice them into thin strips; set aside. Arrange the tortillas around the edge of the grill and heat until just warmed, about 20 seconds per side. (Take care not to let the tortillas dry out or they will become brittle; wrap the tortillas in a dish towel to keep them warm, then place them in a basket.)

3. Slice the steak thin on the bias across the grain. Arrange the sliced meat and vegetables on a large platter. Serve immediately with the tortillas, passing the salsa and guacamole separately.

GRILLED SKIRT STEAK TACOS WITH ROASTED POBLANOS

CHEF RICK BAYLESS OF FRONTERA GRILL serves up our favorite grilled steak tacos. Unencumbered with competing flavors, these soft tacos are deliciously to the point: the grilled beef is rich and smoky, perfectly complemented by the sweet-hot peppers and piquant onions. Authentically South-of-the-Border, they are also easy to prepare—the perfect recipe with which the home cook can comfortably explore traditional Mexican cooking.

All told, the restaurant's recipe has few ingredients, some of which you may already have in your kitchen. Two of the ingredients, however, may be new to you: skirt steak and poblano peppers. If your market doesn't regularly stock skirt steak, it should be able to special-order it for you, or you may substitute another cut of meat, such

as flank steak. Flank steak has some of the same characteristics we like about skirt steak. Following the recipe, but replacing the skirt steak with a flank steak, we found that the cooking times and temperatures were virtually the same but that because flank steak is leaner than skirt steak, it ended up being slightly less flavorful and a little chewier. Flank steak is an acceptable substitution for skirt steak in this recipe, but skirt steak is preferred.

Poblano peppers are thin-skinned, glossy, forest green peppers quite common in Mexican cooking. They are sweeter and fuller tasting than green bell peppers, and while generally mild, they sometimes pack a punch. During testing, we found that most of the peppers we tasted were mellow, but a few were quite spicy. When roasted, peeled, seeded, and cut into strips, poblano chiles are called rajas. Rajas are used throughout Mexican cooking in tostadas, quesadillas, and grilled seafood dishes. In the tacos, the sweet-hot peppers amplify the meat's smoky, rich flavor.

As for cooking the tacos, everything is done over very hot coals on the grill. The peppers are grilled first, followed by the onions, and finally the meat. Roasting the peppers on the grill over a hot fire, as the restaurant's recipe recommends, proved a faultless method: The skin blistered and blackened quickly, leaving the flesh relatively unscathed. Do pay keen attention as you grill the peppers, checking them often to prevent burning—there's a fine line between blackened and burned. If you see any gray patches, the peppers have burned. Immediately place the peppers in a bowl and cover with aluminum foil so that the heat is contained. The resulting steam makes for easy peeling later on.

The original recipe called for marinating the meat before grilling in a combination of lime juice, garlic, cumin, and white onion. The marinade tasted good—sharp and piquant—but it proved problematic. Even after the recommended maximum eight hours of marinating, the grilled meat possessed little of the marinade's flavor. We decided to take a slightly different approach—one we have used often in other grilled meat recipes—and coat the meat with the marinade after grilling, while it rested (the time allotted post-cooking to allow the juices to recirculate throughout the meat). The marinade's flavors were much more apparent. Unconventional, yes, but successful in a case like this, in which the marinade does little to tenderize the meat. And it saves time; the marinade can be prepared just 30 minutes before dinner instead of eight hours ahead.

For the most tender texture, skirt steak must be cut across the grain. Granted, this is true for most meat, but with skirt steak it means slicing parallel to the long side. Considering that some of the steaks we cooked were upward of a foot long, this posed some problems. The best method we found was to cut the steaks into smaller (roughly four- to six-inch) lengths, and then slice them thin crosswise. The smaller strips were quite tender and easily fit into small tortillas.

For a hint of additional smokiness, we briefly warmed the tortillas over the grill before wrapping them in a damp towel as the recipe specified. In a matter of seconds, the tortillas picked up light grill markings and improved flavor. If left unwrapped, they dry out quickly, which leads to cracking.

Charcoal-Grilled Skirt Steak Tacos with Roasted Poblanos

SERVES 6

If you can't find skirt steak, substitute flank steak, although the meat will be a bit more chewy. This is at its best served family-style so that people can assemble their own tacos at the table. The tacos can also be served with sour cream. Leftovers make a great sandwich filling, with a spritz of lime and a little mayonnaise.

4	medium white onions, 3 sliced crosswise into 1/2-inch-thick rounds, 1 chopped coarse
1	tablespoon vegetable oil
	Salt and ground black pepper
6	tablespoons juice from 6 limes
3	medium garlic cloves, chopped coarse (about 1 tablespoon)
1/2	teaspoon ground cumin
1 1/2	pounds poblano chiles
2	pounds skirt steak, trimmed of excess fat
18–24	small corn tortillas
1	lime, cut into wedges

1. Adjust an oven rack to the middle position and heat the oven to 200 degrees. Following the illustration on page 314, skewer the onion slices. Brush both sides of each onion slice with the vegetable oil and season generously with salt and pepper. Set aside.

2. Process the chopped onion, lime juice, garlic, 1 teaspoon salt, and cumin in a food processor until smooth, about 30 seconds, scraping down the sides of the bowl with a rubber spatula as necessary. Transfer to a large, shallow baking dish and set aside.

3. Light a large chimney starter filled with hardwood charcoal (about 6 quarts) and allow to burn until all the charcoal is covered with a layer of fine gray ash. Build a modified two-level fire by spreading the coals out over half the grill bottom, leaving the other half with no coals. Set the cooking grate in place, cover the grill with the lid, and let the grate heat up, about 5 minutes. Use a grill brush to scrape the cooking grate clean. The grill is ready when you have a hot fire. (See how to gauge heat level on page 4.)

4. Place the poblano chiles in the center of the cooking grate and cook until the skin is blistered and blackened, but not gray, 3 to 4 minutes. Turn to blacken the next side. Repeat the process until all the chiles are blackened on all sides.

5. Meanwhile, place the onion slices around the chiles on the grill and cook until streaked with dark grill marks, about 6 minutes. Using tongs, turn and cook the second side until marked. Transfer to an oven-safe dish and slide the slices off the skewers. Separate the slices into individual rings and keep warm in the oven.

6. Transfer the chiles to a bowl and cover with aluminum foil for 5 minutes. Rub the blackened skin off the outside of the chiles, then remove the stems and seeds. Slice into thin strips and add to the baking dish with the onions. Cover and keep warm in the oven.

7. Grill the steak over the coals until well seared and browned on the first side, about 4 minutes. Flip the steak using tongs and grill until the interior of the meat is slightly less done than you want it to be when you eat it, 2 to 4 minutes more for rare or medium-rare (depending on the thickness

of the steak and the heat of the fire). Remove the steak from the grill and coat with the onion puree. Cover the dish with aluminum foil and let the meat rest for at least 5 minutes.

8. Spread out the tortillas on the cooking grate and grill until lightly marked, 15 to 30 seconds. Using tongs, flip the tortillas and grill on the second side until marked, 10 to 15 seconds longer. Wrap the tortillas in a clean, damp dish towel on a baking sheet and keep warm in the oven.

9. Remove the chiles and onions from the oven. Remove the steak from the marinade and slice the steak into 4- to 6-inch lengths. Slice the steak thin across the grain and place in a serving bowl. Serve immediately, accompanied by the poblano and onion mixture, tortillas, and lime wedges.

➤ VARIATION
Gas-Grilled Skirt Steak Tacos with Roasted Poblanos

Follow steps 1 and 2 of the recipe for Charcoal-Grilled Skirt Steak Tacos with Roasted Poblanos. Turn on all the burners to high, close the lid, and heat the grill until very hot, about 15 minutes. Use a grill brush to scrape the cooking grate clean. Leave all the burners on high and continue with the recipe for Charcoal-Grilled Skirt Steak Tacos with Roasted Poblanos from step 4, cooking with the lid down.

GRILLED LONDON BROIL

LONDON BROIL IS A RECIPE, NOT A PARTICULAR cut of meat. Steaks labeled London broil are usually taken from the shoulder or round and sometimes from the sirloin of the cow. Typically the steaks are thick and well suited for grilling. Slicing them thin on the bias across the grain makes the most of this often inexpensive beef.

It was in fact a thinner cut, flank steak, that set the stage for how London broil is best handled. (See pages 48 through 49 for more information on flank steak.) But now that it costs in the environs of $7 a pound, flank steak is not such an inexpensive cut—especially when some cuts from the

round or shoulder can cost just $2 or $3 a pound. We wanted, therefore, to figure out how to cook these less expensive cuts, which are quite lean and pose certain challenges for the cook.

Before figuring out which of the cheaper cuts would work best for London broil, we needed to determine cooking technique. We wanted a London broil with a nice crisp crust and a rare to medium-rare interior—lean cuts of meat become intolerably dry and tough if cooked to medium or beyond. We realized we would need a two-level fire that would allow the meat to sear on the hot side of the grill and cook through on the cooler, more moderate side.

To work as London broil, the cut of meat must be made of one muscle; otherwise it simply falls apart when sliced. There are only a few cuts of beef that meet this criterion. We eliminated one of them, the tri-tip cut, because it can be difficult for most consumers to find. We also put top sirloin, along with the flank steak, out of the running as they are both too expensive. Eye of round has the wrong shape for steaks, while bottom round is almost always used for roasts.

That left two possibilities—the top round and the shoulder. When we began investigating them, we quickly made an important discovery: Although supermarkets tend to sell top round and shoulder the same way—as thick steaks labeled London broil—the cuts are very different.

If you cook a thick cut of top round like a flank steak, you will be disappointed. The round is lean and tight-grained, with a liver-like flavor that is undesirable in quickly cooked muscle meat. If, however, you treat a 1- or 1½-inch-thick shoulder steak like flank steak, you get good results—a robust beef flavor and reasonably tender texture. It also has a little bit of fat, which you want. These qualities, along with the knowledge that it is the least expensive steak you can buy, made shoulder steak our top choice.

We prepared our London broil seasoned with just salt and pepper. Some tasters, however, appreciated the addition of a spice rub before grilling, or a pat of compound butter served over the steak. We leave the choice up to you.

Charcoal-Grilled London Broil

SERVES 4

Because the shoulder steak is so thick, it must be grilled over a two-level fire. Do not cook it past medium-rare or this lean cut will be unpalatably dry. London broil can be seasoned with just salt and pepper or be more boldly flavored by the addition of one of the spice rubs or sauces in Chapter 11. Because London broil is relatively lean, it is especially good when served with either of the compound butters on pages 384–385.

1   boneless shoulder steak, 1½ inches thick
     (1½ to 2 pounds)
     Salt and ground black pepper

1. Light a large chimney starter filled with hardwood charcoal (about 6 quarts) and allow to burn until all the charcoal is covered with a layer of fine gray ash. Build a two-level fire by stacking most of the coals on one side of the grill and arranging the remaining coals in a single layer on the other side of the grill. Set the cooking grate in place, cover the grill with the lid, and let the grate heat up, about 5 minutes. Use a grill brush to scrape the cooking grate clean. The grill is ready when the pile of coals is medium-hot and the single layer of coals is medium-low. (See how to gauge heat level on page 4.)

2. Meanwhile, sprinkle both sides of the steak with salt and pepper to taste. Grill the steak, uncovered, over the hotter part of the fire until well browned on one side, 2 to 3 minutes. Turn the steak; grill until well browned on the other side, 2 to 3 minutes.

3. Once the steak is well browned on both sides, slide it to the cooler part of the grill. Continue grilling, uncovered, to the desired doneness, 5 to 6 minutes more for rare (120 degrees on an instant-read thermometer), 6 to 7 minutes for medium-rare on the rare side (125 degrees), or 7 to 8 minutes for medium-rare on the medium side (130 degrees).

4. Remove the steak from the grill and let rest for 5 minutes. Slice the steak thin on the bias across the grain. Adjust the seasonings with additional salt and pepper and serve immediately.

➤ VARIATION
Gas-Grilled London Broil

As in charcoal grilling, London broil should be cooked over a two-level fire.

Turn on all the burners to high, close the lid, and heat the grill until very hot, about 15 minutes. Scrape the cooking grate clean with a grill brush. Leave one burner on high and turn the other burner(s) down to medium. Follow the recipe for Charcoal-Grilled London Broil from step 2 and cook with the lid down.

GRILLED BEEF KEBABS

OUR GOALS WHEN DEVELOPING A RECIPE FOR beef kebabs seemed simple. We wanted meat that was nicely seared but not overcooked and vegetables that were tender but not mushy. We also wanted to cook the meat and vegetables on the same skewer so that their flavors could meld. Finally, we didn't want to spend a fortune on meat. It makes little sense to buy a premium steak and then cut it up into chunks for kebabs.

The concept behind grilled beef and vegetable kebabs is ingenious. Cut beef into small pieces, skewer along with flavorful, aromatic vegetables, and grill over a live fire—the beef juices emitted during cooking flavor the vegetables, and the vegetables in turn add flavor to the pieces of beef, while both are seared by the intense heat and infused with the smoke of the grill. Unfortunately, the idea of a kebab is often more appealing than the kebab itself; the pitfalls of grilling on skewers are many. To begin with, it's very easy to pick the wrong cut of beef. There are dozens of choices. It's also not very hard to overcook the meat when it's cut into smaller pieces. Or you can grill the skewers over a heat that's too intense and end up with meat that's charred on the outside and raw on the inside, and vegetables that are just plain raw. When not seasoned carefully, kebabs can taste dull and bland.

We knew that choosing the right cut of beef was the most important decision we would make. Given that we didn't want to pay top price for a premium cut, we considered which cheaper cuts of meat would be tender enough to use for kebabs.

We also wanted a cut of meat that wasn't too hard to cut into small pieces. In some cuts of meat, fat and sinew are abundant, making it extremely hard to prepare evenly sized pieces for the skewer. We weren't about to spend hours trimming and cutting intramuscular fat and connective tissue to make kebabs. It had to be a simple, quick process.

So we began skewering and grilling less expensive cuts of meat. From the chuck, we tried the mock tender steak, clod steak, and top blade steak; we tested steaks cut from the top, bottom, and eye of round muscles; from the plate and the flank came the skirt and flank steak; and from the sirloin portion, we tried a top sirloin steak.

The cuts from the round portion of the cow were quite dry and chewy, with a weak, livery beef flavor. The skirt and flank steak were both flavorful and juicy, but their flat configuration and loose grain made them almost impossible to grill along with vegetables and even harder to cook to rare or medium-rare. They are much more appropriate for satay, in which long, thin strips of meat are skewered and cooked without vegetables.

Not surprisingly, all but one of the nonpremium cuts from the chuck were also too tough. We say it is not surprising because this part of the steer—the neck and shoulder—is known to be flavorful but quite tough, best suited for stewing and braising. This was definitely true of the mock tender steak and clod steak. But the top blade steak was a different matter entirely—well marbled, intensely beefy, and notably tender and suitable for grilling.

It was our first choice for skewers.

Our second choice was the top sirloin. This steak comes from the sirloin portion of the cow, just behind the short loin, which is the source of premium steaks such as porterhouse, filet mignon, and New York strip. The sirloin is made up of several muscles, the most tender of which is the top sirloin, from which this particular steak is cut.

Though the top sirloin and top blade steaks were relatively flavorful and tender on their own, we hoped that marinating the steaks would not only flavor the kebabs but also add some moisture. Thus far, we had approached the kebabs as we would a steak, seasoning with salt and pepper only. While the results were decent, the meat was a touch dry and bland. Most kebab recipes call for marinating the meat in an acidic marinade, which supposedly tenderizes it, before grilling. We tried both an acidic and a nonacidic (oil-based) marinade and left pieces of meat in each for one hour, two hours, and four hours.

In all three cases, the acidic marinade produced meat that was mushier on the surface but not noticeably more tender than the meat in the oil-based marinade. The oil-based marinade didn't really change the texture of the meat, but the olive oil in it kept the meat from drying out on the grill and served as a great flavor vehicle for garlic, salt, and pepper. The lime juice in the acidic marinade, however, did contribute a nice flavor. We decided that instead of marinating the meat in the acid, we would marinate the meat in an oil-based marinade

PREPARING BEEF FOR KEBABS

Steps 1 and 2 are necessary if using top blade steaks. If using top sirloin, trim away any gristle and cut into cubes as in step 3.

1. Halve each blade steak lengthwise, leaving the gristle attached to one half.

2. Cut away the gristle from the piece to which it is still attached.

3. Cut the meat into 1¼ inch cubes, then cut each cube almost through at the center to butterfly it.

and squeeze a little lime or lemon juice onto the kebabs after they came off the grill. We were pleased by the results. The meat was tender yet still firm, and the lime or lemon juice tasted fresher when added to the meat just before serving.

The next step was to figure out how best to cut the steaks for skewering. As many meat connoisseurs know, beef cooked past medium becomes dry and tough. We wanted the kebabs to be cooked to medium-rare or, at most, to medium. This meant that the cubes of beef would have to be relatively large. After a few rounds of grilling, we noticed that any beef cut into pieces smaller than an inch was very hard to keep from overcooking. On the other hand, pieces of beef cut this large took quite a bit of time to marinate fully. We tried marinating overnight, and the meat still tasted a little bland because the seasoning didn't penetrate the surface very much.

After researching a number of kebab recipes, we came upon one from Paula Wolfert's *The Cooking of the Eastern Mediterranean* (HarperCollins, 1994), in which cubes of lamb are butterflied (cut open and flattened) before being skewered for kebabs. This, we thought, might produce a more flavorful kebab. Because the pieces of meat would have more surface area, more marinade might penetrate the surface in a shorter period of time. We tested this theory and were pleased to find the meat more flavorful; it was also easier to eat and less chewy. Unfortunately, since the meat was also thinner after being butterflied, it was getting cooked to the well-done stage. To combat this problem, we simply butterflied the meat, marinated it, and then put it on the skewer as if it were still a cube. This technique worked perfectly. Now the meat was easier to eat and packed with flavor all the way through to the center, and it was also nicely caramelized without being overcooked at the interior.

As for vegetables to skewer with our beef, we settled on peppers and onions. They maintained a pleasant tender-crisp texture (like that of vegetables in a stir-fry), and we found this to be a nice contrast with the texture of the meat. The trick is to cut them to the right dimensions so that they don't come off the grill undercooked. Mushrooms and zucchini were deemed too soft to grill with beef—they work better with firmer and drier chicken and fish chunks. To add variety, we threaded chunks of pineapple onto the skewers; they grilled well and contributed a nice sweetness and fruitiness to the kebabs.

There were two options when it came to grilling the kebabs: cooking over a single-level fire or over a two-level fire. Thinking that simpler is better, we started cooking the kebabs over a single-level fire. Because we wanted the kebabs to cook quickly, so that the exterior would become nicely browned while the interior retained as much juice as possible, we started with a medium-

PREPARING ONIONS FOR KEBABS

1. Trim off the stem and root ends and cut the onion into quarters. Peel the three outer layers of the onion away from the core.

2. Working with the outer layers only, cut each quarter—from pole to pole—into three equal strips.

3. Cut each of the 12 strips crosswise into three pieces. You should have thirty-six 3-layer stacks of separate pieces of onion.

hot fire. While meat cooked this way came out relatively well browned, we thought it might be even better if cooked over a hotter fire. Instead of covering the entire grill with the hot charcoal, we used the same amount and covered only three quarters of the grill bottom. This produced a more intense fire when cooking directly over the charcoal, searing the outside of the kebabs more successfully. The meat was richly caramelized, with a perfectly cooked, juicy interior.

Charcoal-Grilled Beef Kebabs
SERVES 4 TO 6

Our favorite cut of beef for kebabs is top blade steak (known sometimes as blade or flat-iron steak), but you can also use top sirloin. If you do, ask the butcher to cut the top sirloin steak between 1 and 1¼ inches thick (most packaged sirloin steaks are thinner). If desired, add 2 teaspoons minced fresh rosemary, thyme, basil, or oregano leaves to the garlic and oil mixture for this marinade. For maximum efficiency, prepare the fruit and vegetables while the meat is marinating.

BEEF
- ¼ cup extra-virgin olive oil
- 3 medium garlic cloves, minced or pressed through a garlic press (about 1 tablespoon)
- ¾ teaspoon salt
- ½ teaspoon ground black pepper
- 2 pounds top blade steaks (4 to 5 steaks), trimmed of fat and prepared according to the illustrations on page 56

FRUIT AND VEGETABLES
- 1 pineapple (about 3½ pounds), peeled, cored, and cut into 1-inch chunks (see the illustrations on page 392)
- 1 medium red bell pepper, cored, seeded, and cut into 1-inch pieces (page 51)
- 1 medium yellow bell pepper, cored, seeded, and cut into 1-inch pieces (page 51)
- 2 tablespoons extra-virgin olive oil
  Salt and ground black pepper
- 1 large red onion, peeled and cut into ¾-inch pieces (see the illustrations on page 57)
  Lemon or lime wedges for serving (optional)

1. FOR THE BEEF: Combine the oil, garlic, salt, and pepper in a gallon-size zipper-lock plastic bag or a large bowl. Add the steak cubes and toss to coat evenly. Seal the bag or cover the bowl and refrigerate until fully seasoned, at least 1 hour or up to 24 hours.

2. Light a large chimney starter filled with hardwood charcoal (about 6 quarts) and allow to burn until all the charcoal is covered with a layer of fine gray ash. Build a modified two-level fire by spreading the coals over just three quarters of the grill bottom. Set the cooking grate in place, cover the grill with the lid, and let the grate heat up, about 5 minutes. Use a grill brush to scrape the cooking grate clean. The grill is ready when you have a hot fire. (See how to gauge heat level on page 4.)

3. FOR THE FRUIT AND VEGETABLES: Meanwhile, toss the pineapple and peppers with 1½ tablespoons of the oil in a medium bowl and season with salt and pepper to taste. Brush the onion with the remaining 1½ teaspoons oil and season with salt and pepper to taste. Using eight 12-inch wooden or metal skewers, thread each skewer with a pineapple chunk, an onion stack (with three layers), a cube of meat (skewering as if it were an uncut cube), and 1 piece of each kind of pepper, and then repeat this sequence two more times. Brush any oil remaining in the bowl over the skewers.

4. Grill the kebabs directly over the coals, uncovered, turning each kebab one-quarter turn every 1¾ minutes, until the meat is well browned, grill marked, and cooked to medium-rare, about 7 minutes (or about 8 minutes for medium). Transfer the kebabs to a serving platter and squeeze the lemon or lime wedges over the kebabs, if desired. Serve immediately.

➤ VARIATIONS
Gas-Grilled Beef Kebabs
Work quickly when opening the lid to turn the kebabs; you don't want too much heat to escape.

Follow the recipe for Charcoal-Grilled Beef Kebabs through step 1. Turn on all the burners to high, close the lid, and heat the grill until very hot, about 15 minutes. Scrape the cooking grate clean with a grill brush. Leave all the burners on high. Proceed with the recipe as directed from step 3 and cook with the lid down.

Beef Kebabs with Asian Flavors

Follow the recipe for Charcoal-Grilled or Gas-Grilled Beef Kebabs, substituting 3 tablespoons vegetable oil and 1 tablespoon toasted sesame oil for the olive oil in the garlic marinade, omitting the salt, and adding 2 tablespoons soy sauce, 1 teaspoon sugar, 1 teaspoon minced fresh ginger, ½ teaspoon red pepper flakes, and 2 minced scallions. Proceed with the recipe, substituting an equal amount of vegetable oil for the olive oil for coating the fruit and vegetables.

Southwestern Beef Kebabs

Follow the recipe for Charcoal-Grilled or Gas-Grilled Beef Kebabs, adding 2 tablespoons minced fresh cilantro leaves, 1 minced chipotle chile in adobo sauce, ½ teaspoon ground cumin, and ½ teaspoon chili powder to the oil and garlic marinade.

BEEF SATAY

SLENDER SLICES OF MARINATED BEEF WOVEN onto skewers and thrown briefly on the grill are a traditional Indonesian favorite known as satay or sate. The meat has a sweet yet salty flavor, and the skewers are served as an appetizer, snack, or light main course alongside a spicy peanut sauce. When done correctly, the tender meat is easily pulled apart into small bites right off the skewer. All too often, however, the beef is tough and sliced so thick that it doesn't pull apart, leaving you with an ungainly mouthful of meat. The peanut sauce can be graceless, with a glue-like consistency and muddy peanut flavor. Not only would finding the right cut of beef and slicing it correctly be key for a tender satay, but we wondered how to make the exotic-tasting marinade and accompanying peanut sauce.

Starting with the beef, we surveyed the local butcher counter for possibilities. Skipping over the expensive cuts such as top loin, rib eye, and tenderloin, we focused on the less expensive cuts

more appropriate for marinating and skewering—sirloin, sirloin flap, round, skirt, flank, and blade steaks. Bringing these cheaper cuts back to the test kitchen, we immediately noted that slicing the raw beef into thin strips is a difficult task. To make it easier, we found it best to firm the meat in the freezer for about 30 minutes. Sliced, skewered, and cooked, these various cheaper cuts of meat produced substantially different textures. Steaks from the round were the worst, with a tough, dry texture, followed closely by chewy sirloin and stringy sirloin flap (a cut from the bottom sirloin). The blade steaks tasted great and were fairly tender, but their small size made it difficult to slice them into long, elegant strips. Both the skirt and flank steak were easy to slice and tasted best. Since skirt steak can be difficult to find and is a bit more expensive, flank steak is the best option.

We found the key to tenderness hinges on slicing the meat perpendicular to its large, obvious grain (see the illustration on page 60). Using a small, 2-pound flank steak, we could make about 40 small or 20 large skewers, enough for 12 to 18 people as an appetizer or four to six as a main course.

Having found a tender cut of meat, we focused next on adding flavor with the marinade. Researching a variety of traditional Indonesian recipes, we noted that most were based on a combination of fish sauce and oil. Using vegetable oil, we tested various amounts of fish sauce, but tasters simply did not like its fermented fish flavor in combination with the beef. Replacing it with soy sauce, although not traditional, worked well, lending a salty, fermented flavor without any "fishiness."

We then tried adding other flavors such as coconut milk, lime juice, Tabasco, Asian chili sauce, brown sugar, and an array of fresh herbs. Coconut milk dulled the beef's natural flavor, while the tart, acidic flavor of lime juice tasted out of place. Asian chili sauce added a pleasant, spicy heat without the sour, vinegary flavor that Tabasco contributed. The sweet, molasses flavor of the brown sugar added a welcome balance to the hot chili sauce and salty soy, while enhancing the beef's ability to brown on the grill. Garlic and cilantro rounded out all of these flavors nicely.

Sliced scallions tasted old and soapy when mixed into the marinade, but tasters liked their fresh flavor and color when sprinkled over the cooked skewers. Marinating the beef for more than one hour turned the texture of the thin sliced beef mushy, while less time didn't give the meat long enough to pick up the marinade flavors. One hour of marinating was perfect.

Lastly, we focused on the peanut sauce. Using creamy peanut butter, we tried spicing it up with a variety of flavorings. In the end, the same ingredients used in the marinade also tasted good in the peanut sauce—soy sauce, Asian chili sauce, brown sugar, garlic, cilantro, and scallions. This time, however, lime juice added a welcome burst of tart acidity. We then stumbled on the obvious way to keep the sauce from being too thick or pasty: Thin it with hot water. Pairing perfectly with the flavor of the marinated beef, the peanut sauce turns these exotic-tasting skewers into an authentic satay.

Charcoal-Grilled Beef Satay with Spicy Peanut Dipping Sauce

SERVES 12 TO 18 AS AN APPETIZER
OR 4 TO 6 AS A MAIN COURSE

Meat that is partially frozen is easier to slice into thin strips. Asian chili sauce is available in most supermarkets under the name Sriracha. A chili-garlic sauce known as sambal could also be used; however, it is much spicier. About forty 6-inch-long wooden skewers or twenty 12-inch wooden or metal skewers are required for this recipe. If you would like to halve the recipe, buy a 1-pound flank steak and cut the remaining ingredients in half.

2	pounds flank steak
1/4	cup soy sauce
1/4	cup vegetable oil
1/4	cup packed dark brown sugar
1/4	cup minced fresh cilantro leaves
2	tablespoons Asian chili sauce, or more to taste
4	scallions, sliced thin
2	medium garlic cloves, minced or pressed through a garlic press (about 2 teaspoons)
1	recipe Spicy Peanut Dipping Sauce (page 400)

1. Cut the flank steak in half lengthwise and freeze for 30 minutes.

2. Following the illustration below, slice each piece across the grain into 1/4-inch-thick strips. Combine the soy sauce, oil, brown sugar, cilantro, chili sauce, scallions, and garlic in a gallon-size zipper-lock plastic bag or a large bowl. Add the steak strips and toss to coat evenly. Seal the bag or cover the bowl and refrigerate for 1 hour only. Weave the meat onto individual skewers—one strip of meat if you're using short skewers or two strips of meat for the longer ones—and lay them flat in a shallow container.

3. Light a large chimney starter filled with hardwood charcoal (about 6 quarts) and allow to burn until all the charcoal is covered with a layer of fine gray ash. Spread the coals evenly over the bottom of the grill. Set the cooking grate in place, cover the grill with the lid, and let the grate heat up, about 5 minutes. Use a grill brush to scrape the cooking grate clean. The grill is ready when you have a medium-hot fire. (See how to gauge heat level on page 4.)

4. Spread half the skewers over the hot cooking grate and grill, uncovered, until the meat has cooked through and lightly charred around the edges, about 7 minutes, flipping the skewers over halfway through the grilling time. Transfer to a serving platter and cover with foil to keep warm. Repeat with the remaining skewers. Serve immediately with the peanut sauce.

SLICING FLANK STEAK THIN FOR SATAY

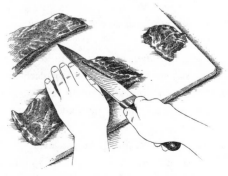

Using a chef's knife, cut the partially frozen flank steak across the grain into 1/4-inch-thick slices.

➤ VARIATION

Gas-Grilled Beef Satay with Spicy Peanut Dipping Sauce

Follow the recipe for Charcoal-Grilled Beef Satay with Spicy Peanut Dipping Sauce through step 2. Turn on all the burners to high, close the lid, and heat the grill until very hot, about 15 minutes. Scrape the cooking grate clean with a grill brush. Turn all the burners to medium high and proceed from step 4, cooking with the lid down.

HAMBURGERS

AMERICANS PROBABLY GRILL MORE HAMBURGERS than they do any other food. Despite all this practice, plenty of hamburgers seem merely to satisfy hunger rather than give pleasure. Too bad, because making an exceptional hamburger isn't that hard or time-consuming. If you have the right ground beef, the perfect hamburger can be ready in less than 15 minutes, assuming you season, form, and cook it properly. The biggest difficulty for many cooks, though, may be finding the right beef.

To test which cut or cuts of beef would cook up into the best burgers, we called a butcher and ordered chuck, round, rump, sirloin, and hanger steak, all ground to order with 20 percent fat. (Although we would question fat percentages in later testing, we needed a standard for these early tests. Based on experience, this percentage seemed right.) After a side-by-side taste test, we quickly concluded that most cuts of ground beef are pleasant but bland when compared with robust, beefy flavored ground chuck. Pricier ground sirloin, for example, cooked up into a particularly boring burger.

So pure ground chuck—the cut of beef that starts where the ribs end and travels up to the shoulder and neck, ending at the foreshank—was the clear winner. We were ready to race ahead to seasonings, but before moving on we stopped to ask ourselves whether cooks buying ground chuck from the grocery store would agree with our choice. Our efforts to determine whether grocery-store ground chuck and ground-to-order

chuck were even remotely similar took us along a culinary blue highway from kitchen to packing plant, butcher shop, and science lab.

According to the National Livestock and Meat Board, the percentage of fat in beef is checked and enforced at the retail level. If a package of beef is labeled 90 percent lean, then it must contain no more than 10 percent fat, give or take a point. Retail stores are required to test each batch of ground beef, make the necessary adjustments, and keep a log of the results. Local inspectors routinely pull ground beef from a store's meat case for a fat check. If the fat content is not within 1 percent of the package sticker, the store is fined.

Whether a package labeled ground chuck is, in fact, 100 percent ground chuck is a different story. First, we surveyed a number of grocery store meat department managers, who said that what was written on the label did match what was in the package. For instance, a package labeled "ground chuck" would have been made only from chuck trimmings. Same for sirloin and round. Only "ground beef" would be made from mixed beef trimmings.

We got a little closer to the truth, however, by interviewing a respected butcher in the Chicago area. At the several grocery stores and butcher shops where he had worked over the years, he had never known a store to segregate meat trimmings. In fact, at his present butcher shop, he sells only two kinds of ground beef: sirloin and chuck. He defines ground sirloin as ground beef (mostly but not exclusively sirloin) that's labeled 90 percent lean, and chuck as ground beef (including a lot of chuck trimmings) that's labeled 85 percent lean.

Only meat ground at federally inspected plants is guaranteed to match its label. At these plants, an inspector checks to make sure that labeled ground beef actually comes from the cut of beef named on the label and that the fat percentage is correct. Most retailers, though, cannot guarantee that their ground beef has been made from a specific cut; they can only guarantee fat percentages. Because the labeling of retail ground beef can be deceptive, we suggest that you buy a chuck roast and have the butcher grind it for you. Even at a local grocery store, we found that the butcher was willing to grind to order. Some meat always gets lost in the grinder, so count on losing a bit (2 to 3 percent).

Because commercially ground beef is at risk for contamination with the bacteria E. coli, we thought it made theoretical sense for home cooks to grind their beef at home, thereby reducing their odds of eating tainted beef. It doesn't make much practical sense, though. Not all cooks own a grinder. And even if they did, we thought home grinding demanded far too much setup, cleanup, and effort for a dish meant to be so simple.

To see if there was an easier way, we tried two other methods: chopping the meat by hand and grinding it in the food processor. The hibachi-style hand-chopping method was just as time-consuming and even more messy than the traditional grinder. In this method, you must slice the meat thin and then cut it into cubes before going at it with two chef's knives. The fat doesn't distribute evenly, meat flies everywhere, and, unless your knives are razor sharp, it's difficult to chop through the meat. What's worse, you can't efficiently chop more than two burgers at a time. In the end, the cooked burgers can be mistaken for chopped steak.

The food processor, however, did a surprisingly good job of grinding meat. We thought the steel blade would raggedly chew the meat, but the hamburger turned out evenly chopped and fluffy. (For more information, see Ultimate Grilled Hamburgers on page 65.)

We figured the average chuck roast to be about 80 percent lean. To check its leanness, we bought a chuck roast—not too fatty, not too lean—and ground it in the food processor. We then took our ground chuck back to the grocery store and asked the butcher to check its fat content in the Univex Fat Analyzer, a machine the store uses to check each batch of beef it grinds. A plug of our ground beef scored an almost perfect 21 percent fat when tested.

Up to this point, all of our ground beef had approximately 20 percent fat. A quick test of burgers with less and more fat helped us to decide that 20 percent fat, give or take a few percentage points, was good for burgers. Any more fat and the burgers are just too greasy. Any less starts to

BARBECUE 911

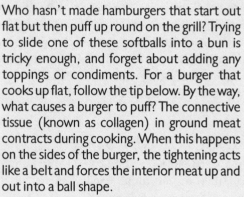

Preventing Puffy Burgers

Who hasn't made hamburgers that start out flat but then puff up round on the grill? Trying to slide one of these softballs into a bun is tricky enough, and forget about adding any toppings or condiments. For a burger that cooks up flat, follow the tip below. By the way, what causes a burger to puff? The connective tissue (known as collagen) in ground meat contracts during cooking. When this happens on the sides of the burger, the tightening acts like a belt and forces the interior meat up and out into a ball shape.

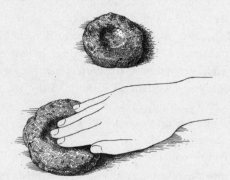

For burgers that cook up flat, press the center of each patty down with your fingertips before grilling. We like ¾-inch-thick patties that measure about 4½ inches across. The well in the center of the patty should measure just ½ inch thick.

compromise the beef's juicy, moist texture.

When to season the meat with salt and pepper may seem an insignificant detail, but when making a dish as simple as a hamburger, little things matter. We tried seasoning the meat at four different points in the process. Our first burger was seasoned before the meat was shaped, the second burger was seasoned right before cooking, the third after each side was seared, and the fourth after the burger had been fully cooked. Predictably, the burger that had been seasoned before shaping was our preference. All the surface-seasoned burgers were the same. Tasters got a hit of salt up front, then the burger went bland. The thin surface area was well seasoned while the interior of the burger was not.

Working with fresh-ground chuck seasoned with salt and pepper, we now moved on to shaping and cooking. To test the overpacking and overhandling warning you see in many recipes, we thoroughly worked a portion of ground beef before cooking it. The well-done burger exterior was nearly as dense as a meat pâté, and the less well-done interior was compact and pasty. It was time to take a gentle approach. Once the meat had been divided into portions, we found that tossing each portion from one hand to the other helped bring the meat together into a ball without overworking it.

We made one of our most interesting discoveries when we tested various shaping techniques for the patties. A well in the center of each burger ensured that they came off the grill with an even thickness instead of puffed up like a tennis ball. (See "Preventing Puffy Burgers" on the facing page.) To our taste, a 4-ounce burger seemed a little skimpy. A 6-ounce portion of meat patted into a nicely sized burger fit perfectly in a bun.

Now nearly done with our testing, we needed only to perfect our grilling method. Burgers require a real blast of heat if they are to form a crunchy, flavorful crust before the interior overcooks. While many of the recipes we looked at advise the cook to grill burgers over a hot fire, we suspected we'd have to adjust the heat because our patties were quite thin in the middle. Sure enough, a super-hot fire made it too easy to overcook the burgers. We found a medium-hot fire formed a crust quickly, while also providing a wider margin of error for properly cooking the center. Nonetheless, burgers cook quickly, needing only two to three minutes per side. Don't walk away from the grill when cooking burgers.

To keep the burgers from sticking to the cooking grate, we coated it with oil. All you need to do is dip a wad of paper towels in some vegetable oil, hold the wad with long-handled tongs, and rub it on the hot grate just before adding the burgers (see the illustration on page 224).

One last finding from our testing: Don't ever press down on burgers as they cook. Rather than speeding their cooking, pressing on the patties serves only to squeeze out their juices and make the burgers dry.

Charcoal-Grilled Hamburgers
SERVES 4

For those who like their burgers well done, we found that poking a small hole in the center of the patty before cooking helped the burger cook through to the center before the edges dried out. See the illustration on the facing page for tips on shaping burgers. See page 65 for details about grinding your own meat with a food processor.

1½   pounds 80 percent lean ground chuck
1   teaspoon salt
½   teaspoon ground black pepper
    Vegetable oil for the cooking grate
    Buns and desired toppings

1. Light a large chimney starter filled with hardwood charcoal (about 6 quarts) and allow to burn until all the charcoal is covered with a layer of fine gray ash. Spread the coals evenly over the bottom of the grill. Set the cooking grate in place, cover the grill with the lid, and let the grate heat up, about 5 minutes. Use a grill brush to scrape the cooking grate clean. The grill is ready when the coals are medium-hot. (See how to gauge heat level on page 4.)

2. Meanwhile, break up the chuck to increase the surface area for seasoning. Sprinkle the salt and pepper over the meat; toss lightly with your hands to distribute the seasonings. Divide the meat into 4 equal portions (6 ounces each); with cupped hands, toss one portion of meat back and forth to form a loose ball. Pat lightly to flatten the meat into a ¾-inch-thick burger that measures about 4½ inches across. Press the center of the patty down with your fingertips until it is about ½ inch thick, creating a well, or divot, in the center of the patty. Repeat with the remaining portions of meat.

3. Lightly dip a wad of paper towels in vegetable oil; holding the wad with tongs, wipe the cooking

grate. Grill the burgers, divot-side up, uncovered and without pressing down on them, until well seared on the first side, about 2½ minutes. Flip the burgers with a wide metal spatula. Continue grilling to the desired doneness, about 2 minutes for rare, 2½ minutes for medium-rare, 3 minutes for medium, and 4 minutes for well-done. Serve immediately in buns with desired toppings.

➤ VARIATIONS

Gas-Grilled Hamburgers

Turn on all the burners to high, close the lid, and heat the grill until very hot, about 15 minutes. Use a grill brush to scrape the cooking grate clean. Leave all the burners on high. Follow the recipe for Charcoal-Grilled Hamburgers from step 2 and cook with the lid down.

Grilled Cheeseburgers

We suggest grating cheese into the raw beef as opposed to melting it on top. Because the cheese is more evenly distributed, a little goes much further than a chunk on top. Also, there's no danger of overcooking the burgers while you wait for the cheese to melt.

Follow the recipe for Charcoal-Grilled or Gas-Grilled Hamburgers, mixing 3½ ounces cheddar, Swiss, Jack, or blue cheese, shredded or crumbled, into the meat along with the salt and pepper. Shape and cook the burgers as directed.

Grilled Hamburgers with Garlic, Chipotle, and Scallions

Toast 3 medium unpeeled garlic cloves in a small dry skillet over medium heat, shaking the pan occasionally, until the garlic is fragrant and the color deepens slightly, about 8 minutes. When cool enough to handle, skin and mince the garlic. Follow the recipe for Charcoal-Grilled or Gas-Grilled Hamburgers, mixing 2 tablespoons minced scallions, the garlic, and 1 tablespoon minced chipotle chile in adobo sauce into the meat along with the salt and pepper. Shape and cook the burgers as directed.

Grilled Hamburgers with Cognac, Mustard, and Chives

Mix 1½ tablespoons cognac, 1 tablespoon minced fresh chives, and 2 teaspoons Dijon mustard together in a small bowl. Follow the recipe for Charcoal-Grilled or Gas-Grilled Hamburgers,

INGREDIENTS: Ketchup

For many people, a burger isn't done until it has been coated liberally with ketchup. Ketchup is also an essential ingredient in many meat loaf recipes, including ours. This condiment originated in Asia as a salty, fermented medium for pickling or preserving ingredients, primarily fish. Early versions were made with anchovies and generally were highly spiced.

Tomato-based ketchup has its origins in 19th-century America. Americans now consume more than 600 million pints of ketchup every year, much of it landing on top of burgers. But as any ketchup connoisseur knows, not all brands are created equal. To find out which is the best, we tasted 13 different samples, including several fancy mail-order ketchups and one we made in our test kitchen.

For all tasters but one, Heinz ranked first or second; tasters described it with words like "classic" and "perfect." A tiny bit sweeter than Heinz, Del Monte took second place, while Hunt's (the other leading national brand, along with Heinz and Del Monte) rated third.

What about the mail-order, organic, fruit-sweetened, and homemade ketchups? Most tasters felt these samples were overly thick and not smooth enough. Some were too spicy, others too vinegary. Our homemade ketchup was too chunky, more like "tomato jam" than ketchup. In color, consistency, and flavor, none of these interlopers could match the archetypal ketchup, Heinz.

THE BEST KETCHUP
In a blind taste test, Heinz beat 12 other samples, including several high-priced boutique brands. Panelists described it as "glossy," "balanced," and "smooth."

mixing the cognac mixture into the meat along with the salt and pepper. Shape and cook the burgers as directed.

Grilled Hamburgers with Porcini Mushrooms and Thyme

Cover ½ ounce dried porcini mushroom pieces with ½ cup hot tap water in a small microwave-safe bowl; cover with plastic wrap, cut several steam vents with a paring knife, and microwave on high power for 30 seconds. Let stand until the mushrooms soften, about 5 minutes. Lift the mushrooms from the liquid with a fork and mince (you should have about 2 tablespoons). Follow the recipe for Charcoal-Grilled or Gas-Grilled Hamburgers, mixing the porcini mushrooms and 1 teaspoon minced fresh thyme leaves into the meat along with the salt and pepper. Shape and cook the burgers as directed.

Ultimate Grilled Hamburgers

When it comes to grinding chuck for hamburgers, the test kitchen found that a food processor does a respectable job, and it's much easier to use than a grinder. The key is to make sure the roast is cold, that it is cut into small chunks, and that it is processed in small batches.

Cut a well-chilled 2-pound chuck roast into 1-inch chunks. Divide the chunks into four equal portions. Place one portion of meat in a food processor fitted with a steel blade. Pulse the cubes until the meat is ground, 15 to 20 one-second pulses. Repeat with the remaining portions of beef. Follow the recipes for Charcoal-Grilled or Gas-Grilled Hamburgers on pages 63–64, using the homemade ground chuck.

GRILL-ROASTED PRIME RIB

PRIME RIB IS THE ULTIMATE MEAT DISH for entertaining—it's impressive and it feeds a crowd. But if you're making prime rib, you're probably making a lot of other food. We think it's worth considering the grill when cooking prime rib. Rather than tying up your oven for hours on end (and thus making the preparation of side dishes a real hassle), let the meat cook outside on the grill. Besides convenience, a grilled prime rib has two advantages over a roasted prime rib—a better crust and some smoky flavor. The end result should be slices that are rosy pink and meat

---

INGREDIENTS: Two Rib Roasts

A whole rib roast (aka prime rib) consists of ribs 6 through 12. Butchers tend to cut the roast in two. We prefer the cut that is further back on the cow, closer to the loin. This cut is referred to as the first cut, the loin end, or sometimes the small end because the meat and ribs get smaller toward the loin. The first cut can include anywhere from two to four ribs. Sometimes we like a large roast for the holidays; in this case, we prefer a roast with four ribs. At other times, a slightly smaller roast, with just three ribs, is fine. When ordering the former, be sure to specify the first four ribs from the loin end—ribs 9 through 12—to receive the first cut. When ordering a three-rib roast, ask for the first three ribs from the loin end—ribs 10 through 12.

Either way, the first cut is more desirable because it contains the large, single rib-eye muscle and is less fatty. The less desirable cut, which is still an excellent roast, is closer to the chuck (or shoulder) end and is sometimes called the second cut. The closer to the chuck, the less tender the roast will be.

FIRST CUT   SECOND CUT

that's juicy and tender.

We started our testing by examining the issues of trimming fat and tying the roast. We found that it is best to leave about a quarter inch of fat on the roast to prevent it from drying out on the grill. Most of this fat drips off of the rib roast as it cooks, basting the meat. Tying the meat before grilling is essential. Two pieces of twine keep the surrounding muscles from separating from the main part of the roast and thus improve the appearance of the grilled roast. In addition, these smaller, thin pieces of meat will overcook if they detach from the main muscle during grill-roasting.

We wondered just how few coals we could get away with. From our work in the past with prime rib cooked in the oven, we knew that a low oven temperature is kinder to prime rib, helping the meat to retain its juices and promoting even cooking. We figured the same would be true on the grill.

After much testing, we found about 45 briquettes to be optimum. This was the least amount of coals we could use to make it possible to cook the whole roast properly without adding more briquettes. With 45 briquettes (about three quarts), the fire reaches an initial temperature of about 375 degrees and eventually burns down to about 300 degrees by the time the roast is finished (the last 45 minutes or so). Using the indirect method, you still get a lovely surface caramelization, while the interior is almost entirely pink, except for the outer half inch or so.

We wanted to add some wood to the fire to flavor the meat, but not enough to overpower its own delicious flavor. We didn't want our prime rib to taste like barbecued ribs. Adding two cups of chips or two larger wood chunks to the fire creates a rib roast with a nice contrast between the smoky caramelized exterior and savory, beefy interior meat.

The next issue to examine was at what internal temperature the roast should be removed from the grill. We knew that the temperature inside the roast would continue to rise as the meat rested before carving. For the perfect medium-rare, we found it best to take the meat off the grill when it hit an internal temperature

of 125 degrees. When removed at 125 degrees and then allowed to rest for 20 minutes, the temperature jumped another 12 to 13 degrees. As with rack of lamb, it is imperative with prime rib to use an instant-read thermometer. There is no really good way of telling how cooked the meat is at the very center of a rib roast without one, and if you spend about $50 for a 7-pound roast, you don't want to mess up by over- or undercooking. Also, using a thermometer to determine doneness will keep you from cutting into the meat to check doneness before it's had a chance to rest; if you cut into the meat too soon (before it has rested off the grill for 20 minutes), you will lose a good amount of the juices. (During the rest period, the juices evenly redistribute themselves throughout the meat.)

CARVING PRIME RIB

1. Using a carving fork to hold the roast in place, cut along the rib bones to sever the meat from the bones.

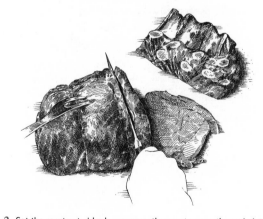

2. Set the roast cut-side down; carve the meat across the grain into thick slices.

Grill-Roasted Prime Rib on a Charcoal Grill

SERVES 6 TO 8

You may or may not have to trim some fat off your rib roast, depending on how well it was butchered at the store. Just be sure to leave about ¼ inch of fat on the side opposite the bones to keep the meat from drying out; the fat will slowly render, basting the meat as it melts. If you purchase the roast several days in advance, see page 68 to learn more about the benefits of aging the roast in the refrigerator before cooking it.

1	(3- or 4-rib) standing rib roast (preferably first cut; see page 65) about 7 pounds, aged up to 4 days (if desired), and tied with kitchen twine at both ends, twine running parallel to the bone (see the illustration at right)
2	(3-inch) wood chunks
1	tablespoon vegetable oil
	Salt and ground black pepper

1. An hour before cooking, remove the roast from the refrigerator to bring it to room temperature.

2. Meanwhile, soak the wood chunks in cold water to cover for 1 hour and drain.

3. Light a large chimney starter filled halfway with 45 charcoal briquettes (about 3 quarts) and allow to burn until all the charcoal is covered with a layer of fine gray ash. Build a modified two-level fire by piling the charcoal on one side of the grill in a mound 2 or 3 briquettes high. Keep the bottom vents completely open. Lay the wood chunks on top of the charcoal. Put the cooking grate in place, open the grill lid vents completely, and cover, turning the lid so that the vents are opposite the wood chunks to draw smoke through the grill. Let the grate heat for 5 minutes. Use a grill brush to scrape the cooking grate clean.

4. Rub the rib roast with the oil. Season generously with salt and pepper to taste.

5. Position the rib roast, bone-side down, on the side of the grate opposite the fire, with the meaty eye of the roast closest to the fire. Cover the grill, turning the lid so that the vents are opposite the fire to draw smoke through the grill.

Grill-roast without removing the lid for 1 hour. (The initial temperature inside the grill will be about 375 degrees.) Remove the lid and turn the roast so that the bone side of the roast is facing up. Replace the lid and continue grill-roasting until an instant-read thermometer inserted into the center of the roast registers 125 degrees (for medium-rare), 30 to 60 minutes. (The temperature inside the grill will gradually fall to about 300 degrees by the time the roast is done.)

6. Transfer the roast to a cutting board and tent loosely with foil. Let stand for 20 minutes to allow the juices to redistribute themselves evenly throughout the roast.

7. To carve (see the illustrations on the facing page), remove the twine and set the roast on a cutting board with the rib bones perpendicular to the board. Using a carving fork to hold the roast in place, cut along the rib bones to sever the meat from the bones. Set the roast cut-side down; carve the meat across the grain into thick slices. Serve immediately.

➤ VARIATIONS

Grill-Roasted Prime Rib on a Gas Grill

Use wood chips, not chunks, on a gas grill. To make sure the wood chips begin to smoke, the grill is quite hot—550 degrees—when you first put the meat on the fire. Once you turn off all but the primary burner (which is left on

---

TYING PRIME RIB

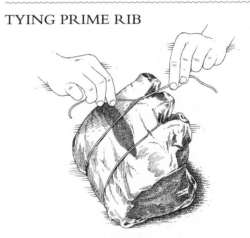

It is imperative to tie prime rib before roasting. If left untied, the outer layer of meat will pull away from the rib-eye muscle and over-cook. To prevent this problem, tie the roast at both ends, running the string parallel to the bone.

medium-high), the temperature of the grill averages out to about 350 degrees. The roast cooks at this heat level for 1 hour. The primary burner is then turned down once again to medium heat, and the average temperature of the grill hovers around 300 degrees for the rest of the cooking time, which should be between 1 hour and 1 hour and 15 minutes, until the internal temperature of the roast is 125 degrees. Be sure not to open the lid of the gas grill too often during cooking; the temperature of the grill will drop significantly each time you open it, and then take some time to come back up to temperature. If you prefer a roast with a less smoky flavor, gas grilling is the right option (as opposed to charcoal grilling). In fact, if you are simply cooking on the grill to save oven space and don't care to taste the smoky flavor of the grill, omit the use of wood chips altogether.

Follow the recipe for Grill-Roasted Prime Rib on a Charcoal Grill, letting the roast come to room

temperature, rubbing it with oil, and seasoning it with salt and pepper as directed in steps 1 and 4. Meanwhile, soak 2 cups wood chips (instead of the wood chunks) in cold water to cover for 30 minutes. Drain the chips, then place them in a foil tray (see the illustrations on page 10). Place the pan with the soaked wood chips on top of the primary burner (see the illustration on page 9) and replace the cooking grate. Turn on all the burners to high and heat with the lid down until the chips are smoking heavily, about 15 minutes. Carefully open the grill (there may be some smoke), use a grill brush to scrape the cooking grate clean, and turn the primary burner down to medium-high; turn the other burner(s) off. Place the rib roast over the cooler side of the grill, bone-side down. Cover and cook until an instant-read thermometer inserted into the center of the roast reads between

SCIENCE: Why Aging Tenderizes Beef

Meat is aged to develop its flavor and improve its texture. This process depends on certain enzymes, whose function while the animal is alive is to digest proteins. After the animal is slaughtered, the cells that contain these enzymes start to break down and release the enzymes into the meat, where they attack the cell proteins and break them down into amino acids, which add more flavor. The enzymes also break down the muscles, so that the tissue becomes softer. This process can take a few days or a few weeks. (For the sake of safety, meat should not be aged for more than four days at home; beyond that time it must be done under carefully controlled conditions.)

Traditionally, butchers have hung carcasses in the meat locker to age their beef. Today, some beef is still aged on hooks (this process is called dry aging), but for the most part beef is wet-aged in vacuum-sealed packets. We wondered if it was worth it to the home cook to go the extra mile for dry-aged beef, so we ordered both a dry-aged and wet-aged prime rib roast from a restaurant supplier in Manhattan. The differences between the two roasts were clear.

Like a good, young red wine, wet-aged beef tasted pleasant and fresh on its own. When compared with the dry-aged beef, though, we realized its flavors were less concentrated. The meat tasted washed out. The dry-aged beef, on the other hand, engaged the mouth. It was stronger, richer, and gamier-tasting, with a pleasant tang. The dry-aged and wet-aged beef were equally

tender, but the dry-aged beef had an added buttery texture.

Unfortunately, most butchers don't dry-age beef anymore because hanging the quarters of beef uses valuable refrigerator space. Dry-aged beef also dehydrates (loses weight) and requires trimming (losing more weight). That weight loss means less beef costs more money. Wet-aged beef loses virtually no weight during the aging process, and it comes prebutchered, packaged, and ready to sell. Because beef is expensive to begin with, most customers opt for the less expensive wet-aged beef. Why does dry aging work better than wet aging? The answer is simple: air. Encased in plastic, wet-aged beef is shut off from oxygen—the key to flavor development and concentration.

Because availability and price pose problems, you may simply want to age beef yourself. It's just a matter of making room in the refrigerator and remembering to buy the roast ahead of time, up to four days before you plan on roasting it. When you get the roast home, pat it dry and place it on a wire rack set over a paper towel–lined cake pan or plate. Set the racked roast in the refrigerator and let it age until you are ready to roast it, up to four days. (Aging begins to have a dramatic effect on the roast after three days, but we also detected some improvement in flavor and texture after just one day of aging.) Before roasting, shave off any exterior meat that has completely dehydrated. Between the trimming and dehydration, count on a 7-pound roast losing at least half a pound during aging.

80 and 85 degrees, about 1 hour. (During this hour the temperature inside the grill will initially be very hot, 550 degrees, and then it will drop off to about 350 degrees.) Turn the primary burner down to medium and continue cooking, covered, until the instant-read thermometer inserted into the center of the roast reads 125 degrees (for medium-rare), about 60 to 75 minutes longer. (During this period of time, the average temperature of the grill should be about 300 degrees.) Transfer the roast to a cutting board and proceed as directed in steps 6 and 7.

Grill-Roasted Prime Rib with Garlic and Rosemary Crust

Rosemary and garlic are a simple embellishment for the roast and won't overwhelm the beefy flavor of the meat.

Combine 6 medium garlic cloves, minced or pressed through a garlic press (about 2 tablespoons), 2 tablespoons chopped fresh rosemary, 2 teaspoons ground black pepper, and 1 teaspoon salt in a small bowl. Follow the recipe for Grill-Roasted Prime Rib (charcoal or gas), oiling the roast as directed in step 4. Instead of sprinkling the oiled roast with salt and pepper, rub it with the garlic and rosemary mixture. Proceed as directed.

GRILL-ROASTED BEEF TENDERLOIN

WE DON'T PART EASILY WITH MONEY, BUT we will on occasion break the bank to buy a beef tenderloin. The tender, buttery interior is the big draw, and the combination of a healthy dose of seasoning and the flavor from the charcoal grill is a perfect solution to a rather mild-tasting (boring) piece of meat. Recently, we ordered a whole beef tenderloin from a local supermarket. Six pounds of perfectly trimmed tenderloin later, we had shelled out a jaw-dropping $167.94 (that's $27.99 per pound).

We heated up the grill and gingerly placed our new, most valuable possession over the hot coals. Even though we watched it like a hawk, we couldn't get the tenderloin to cook evenly. The exterior was charred and tough; the interior of the fat butt end was pink, and the thinner tail end was

BARBECUE 911

Unevenly Cooked Tenderloin

You splurged on an expensive tenderloin to grill for your guests, only to find that the tip (the portion of the roast where it narrows) is well overcooked by the time the rest of the roast is perfect. Short of a magic wand, there's nothing you can do now. But next time you are faced with a tenderloin that narrows at one end, here's what to do.

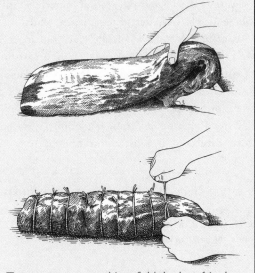

To ensure even cooking, fold the last 6 inches of the thin tip end under the roast, then tie 12-inch lengths of kitchen twine crosswise along the length of the roast, spacing the ties about 1½ to 2 inches apart.

beyond well-done. Worst of all, because we were able to season only the exterior of the tenderloin, the interior was bland.

We wondered if there was a way to take this mammoth and insanely expensive cut of beef and grill it to absolute perfection. And, after having spent nearly $170 on a complete flop, we were determined to find a cheaper alternative to supermarket shopping.

Great tenderloin begins at the market. At local supermarkets, we learned, whole beef tenderloin isn't a meat case–ready item. Most butchers we talked to said they keep the tenderloins in the back to be cut for filets, so if you want one, you've got to ask for it. When you do ask for a whole tenderloin, it will usually come "peeled," which means the outer membrane of fat and sinew has been removed. A peeled tenderloin runs anywhere from $13.99 per pound for Choice grade meat to an even more astounding $32.99 per pound for Prime grade at a high-end butcher—that's nearly $200 dollars for a 6-pound roast. At that price, we expect the butcher to come to our house, grill the meat for us, wash the dishes, and throw in a back rub as well.

A few days later, we found ourselves in a wholesale club. No longer just a place to buy giant cans of beans, most wholesale clubs sell meat as well. We soon stood eye-to-eye with a case full of vacuum-sealed, Choice grade, whole tenderloins. If the mountain of meat hadn't caught our attention, the price sure would have. Weighing in at about $9 per pound, these tenderloins were one third the cost of the roast we had bought from our butcher. We grabbed as many as we could stuff into the giant shopping cart and headed back to the kitchen.

We soon discovered the one downside of using the wholesale club tenderloins. They came "unpeeled," so a fair amount of trimming, tugging, and prying was necessary to rid the meat of its fat, sinew, and silver skin. And we had to be judicious, as we found the trimmings could weigh more than 1½ pounds, including the loss of some valuable meat. The best way to trim one of these tenderloins was to first peel off as much fat as possible with our hands; the fat came away clean and took very little of the pricey meat with it (see the illustrations below). Next, we used a flexible boning knife (a sharp paring knife works well in a pinch) to remove the silver skin, the muscle sheath that would otherwise cause the tenderloin to curl up on the grill. Last, we took the advice of many cookbooks and tucked the narrow tip end of the tenderloin under and tied it securely. This tuck-and-tie step gave the tenderloin a more consistent

TRIMMING A BEEF TENDERLOIN

Although wholesale clubs offer whole beef tenderloins at an affordable price, most come unpeeled, with the fat and silver skin (a tough membrane) intact. Here's how to trim a tenderloin for the grill. Expect to lose between 1 and 1½ pounds during the trimming process. A boning knife is the best tool for this job.

1. Pull away the outer layer of fat to expose the fatty chain in the meat.

2. Pull the chain of fat away from the roast, cut it off, and discard the chain.

3. Scrape the silver skin at the creases in the thick end to expose the lobes.

4. Trim the silver skin by slicing under it and cutting upward.

5. Remove the remaining silver skin in the creases at the thick end.

6. Turn the tenderloin over and remove the fat from the underside.

thickness that would allow it to grill more evenly.

Was this extra 20 minutes of preparatory work worth the effort? We got out our calculator and crunched the numbers. Let's see . . . with a loss of about a pound of trimmings, our $54 roast was now divided by the 5 pounds of remaining meat . . . and that came to around $10.80 per pound. You better believe it was worth it! It still was by no means a "cheap" piece of meat, but it didn't empty our wallet.

While some love beef tenderloin for its "mild" beef flavor, others scoff at it for exactly the same reason. We found ourselves in the latter camp and felt that the tenderloin could use a flavor boost. Many recipes suggested marinades, spice rubs, or herb crusts. Tasters rejected the marinated tenderloins for their weird, spongy texture. Spice rubs made the beef taste too much like barbecue (if we wanted barbecue, we'd buy a cheap rack of ribs), while herb crusts were too powerful for such a tame cut of meat. We were looking for a way to enhance the beef flavor, not to mask it.

Then a colleague suggested a recently heralded technique in which the tenderloin is salted and left to sit overnight in the fridge. The theory goes that the salt penetrates the meat all the way to the center, seasoning the tenderloin throughout. Sure enough, the salted-overnight beef was seasoned through and through, but at quite a cost. The meat had turned a sickly brown-gray (even when the center was cooked to medium-rare), and the texture was webby, like that of an overcooked pot roast. We played around a bit with amounts of salt, going up to ¼ cup of kosher salt and down to 1 tablespoon. But it seemed that time was the villain here—an overnight salting was just too much.

For the next round, we went back to the original 1½ tablespoons of kosher salt and rubbed a couple of tenderloins. We wrapped both in plastic and refrigerated one for four hours and the other for one hour. Although both were markedly better than the overnight-salted tenderloin, the winner was the beef that had been salted for only one hour. With just enough time for the salt to season the meat without compromising the texture, the salt brought out a decidedly beefier flavor, one that we greatly appreciated. Even better was

letting the salted tenderloin sit on the countertop rather than refrigerating it. The tenderloin lost some of its chill, and it grilled at a more even rate. We were ready to take our well-seasoned tenderloin in hand and head for the nearest grill.

Up to this point, we had been grilling the

SCIENCE: When Should You Salt Meat?

Salting meat is nothing new; it was used centuries before refrigeration as a method of preservation. Recently, though, there has been a renewed chorus of voices singing the praises of the simple salt rub, sometimes applied the night before. One might understand why salt could make a tough cut more palatable, but would this technique improve pricey tenderloin?

We found that salting the meat an hour before cooking gave the roast a beefier flavor. A four-hour salt produced much the same results, but salting the roast the night before cooking was a disaster. The roast turned brown. But why?

Anyone who lives in a cold climate knows that the salting of roadways causes cars to rust. This is due to salt's ability to promote oxidation in iron. Salt can also help to oxidize myoglobin, an iron-containing protein that gives meat its red color. The brown-as-pot-roast color of the tenderloin that had been salted overnight indicated that much of the myoglobin had been oxidized and thus most of its red color lost.

Perhaps the poor color could be excused if the procedure had produced phenomenal flavor. In fact, the opposite was true; the meat was stringy and the flavor was tired. In addition to oxidizing the myoglobin, the salt had drawn water from the meat, causing it to look thready, as if it had been overcooked. Moreover, little of the mild but juicy beef flavor normally associated with tenderloin was present; instead it tasted dull. In the case of tenderloin, which is beautifully textured and delicately flavored out of the package, there is really no good reason to salt for extended periods—unless, of course, you want to pay at least $9 a pound for pot roast.

OVERNIGHT SALTING
Looks like overcooked pot roast.

ONE-HOUR SALTING
A tender, juicy, and flavorful roast.

tenderloin directly over the hot fire, an approach that burned the outer crust before the interior had a chance to cook properly. We tried a more moderate heat. Now the exterior was no longer scorched, but the outer inch-thick perimeter of the meat was approaching the well-done mark before the interior was cooked.

In a forehead-slapping moment, it struck us that we were treating (and grilling) the tenderloin as a steak and not as what it was—a roast. For our next test, we set up the grill for grill-roasting, in which indirect heat is used to cook the meat. We piled the coals up on one side of the grill, leaving the other side empty, then placed the tenderloin over the empty side (opposite the coals), covered the grill, and left it alone. About 45 minutes later, we knew that we were onto something. The indirect

heat had cooked the tenderloin evenly from tip to tip (OK, so the very ends were more well-done), and the meat had taken on a mild, smoky flavor from spending so much time exposed to the hot coals. But we missed the crust that came with searing the meat. The solution was to first sear the tenderloin over the hot coals on all sides before switching to the cooler (coal-free) side to finish grilling. This was it: a remarkable, well-browned crust and a rosy pink interior. We tried adding a couple of soaked wood chunks to the pile of hot coals, in hopes of imparting even more smoky flavor to the meat. And smoky was just what we got; there was no denying that this cut of meat had been cooked on the grill. (Although some in the test kitchen thought the smoke flavor was too strong for the mild beef, others loved it. For those

INGREDIENTS: Beef Tenderloin

When it comes to buying a special cut of beef like tenderloin, more and more cooks are bypassing the supermarket and either seeking bargain prices at wholesale clubs or paying a premium for the "specialty" beef available through mail-order sources. Is there a difference between roasts that cost $9 and $55 per pound?

In a blind tasting, we evaluated a broad selection of tenderloins—one from a local supermarket, three from warehouse clubs, and three from well-known mail-order sources. This last group included several Prime roasts; the roasts from the supermarket and warehouse clubs were either Choice or Select, the next two grades down the quality chain and those commonly found in supermarkets. Given the price differential as well as the various grades of beef in the tasting, we were shocked by the results.

As a whole, our panel found only subtle differences in flavor and texture among the seven tenderloins. None of the mail-order tenderloins managed to stand out from the crowd. The top choice came from the supermarket. And our panel's second choice was a Select roast from a warehouse club. Only the previously frozen Omaha Steaks tenderloin failed to please tasters and is not recommended. So when it comes to tenderloin, you don't have to pay a king's ransom for a princely roast.

The chart at right indicates the price we paid per pound for our tenderloin. But some tenderloins required much more trimming than others. The figures indicate the edible portion (as a percentage of the initial weight) we obtained once trimming was

complete. We then recalculated the prices to indicate what each pound of edible meat really cost us.

So what did we learn? All of the tenderloins purchased at the supermarket and warehouse clubs required more trimming than the mail-order samples, but not enough to really affect overall prices. Even taking into account the extra waste on the tenderloins we purchased at warehouse clubs, they averaged just $13 per pound, compared with $23 per pound for our supermarket sample, and from $41 to $57 per pound for the mail-order samples. Note that the tenderloin from Lobel's required no trimming at all, making this expensive mail-order sample the best choice for lazy cooks with money to burn.

The brands of tenderloins below are listed in order of preference based on their scores in our tasting.

	EDIBLE PORTION (after trimming)	ACTUAL COST (per pound)
Stop & Shop	64%	$23.34
BJ's	67%	$13.24
Lobel's	100%	$54.84
Niman Ranch	76%	$57.50
Costco	70%	$12.60
Sam's Club	64%	$13.87
Omaha	80%	$40.94

in this camp, just omit the wood chunks.)

When we cut into a tenderloin right off the grill, it gave off a lot of juice—not a good idea with such a lean piece of meat. The easy solution was to let the meat rest for 10 to 15 minutes before cutting, but during this rest period the meat rose from medium-rare (about 135 degrees) to medium-well (over 150 degrees). We next removed the tenderloin from the grill when the meat was still rare. After resting, the roast was incredibly juicy, with a rosy pink interior, a beautiful dark brown crust, and a smoky, seasoned flavor—all of which made it worth every cent we had paid.

Grill-Roasted Beef Tenderloin on a Charcoal Grill

SERVES 10 TO 12

Beef tenderloin purchased from wholesale clubs requires a good amount of trimming before cooking. At the grocery store, however, you may have the option of having the butcher trim it for you. Once trimmed, and with the butt tenderloin still attached (the butt tenderloin is the lobe attached to the large end of the roast), the roast should weigh 4½ to 5 pounds. If you purchase an already-trimmed tenderloin without the butt tenderloin attached, begin checking for doneness about 5 minutes early. If you prefer your tenderloin without a smoky flavor, omit the wood chips or chunks. Serve as is or with Salsa Verde (page 397), Romesco Sauce (page 398), or Cilantro-Parsley Sauce with Pickled Jalapenos (page 398).

I	beef tenderloin (about 6 pounds), trimmed of fat and silver skin (according to the illustrations on page 70), tail end tucked and tied at 2-inch intervals
1½	tablespoons kosher salt
2	(3-inch) wood chunks
2	tablespoons olive oil
I	tablespoon ground black pepper

1. About 1 hour before grilling, set the tenderloin on a cutting board or rimmed baking sheet and rub with the salt. Cover loosely with plastic wrap and let stand at room temperature. Cover the wood chunks with cold water and soak 1 hour; drain.

2. About 25 minutes before grilling, open the bottom grill vents. Light a large chimney starter filled with charcoal briquettes (about 6 quarts) and allow to burn until all the charcoal is covered with a layer of fine gray ash. Build a modified two-level fire by spreading the coals onto one side of the grill in a mound about 3 briquettes high. Set the wood chunks on the coals. Position the cooking grate over the coals, cover the grill, and heat the grate, about 10 minutes (the grill should be medium-hot; see how to gauge heat level on page 4). Use a grill brush to scrape the cooking grate clean.

3. Uncover the tenderloin, coat it with the olive oil, and sprinkle all sides with the pepper, using the plastic wrap to help evenly coat the tenderloin (see illustration on page 74). Place the tenderloin on the hot side of the grill directly over the coals. Cook until well browned, about 2 minutes, then rotate one quarter turn and repeat until all sides are well browned, a total of 8 minutes. Move the tenderloin to the cooler side of the grill and cover, positioning the lid vents over the tenderloin. Cook until an instant-read thermometer inserted into the thickest part of the tenderloin registers 120 degrees for rare, 16 to 20 minutes, or 125 degrees for medium-rare, 20 to 25 minutes.

4. Transfer the tenderloin to a cutting board, tent loosely with foil, and let rest 10 to 15 minutes. Cut into ½-inch-thick slices and serve.

VARIATIONS

Grill-Roasted Beef Tenderloin on a Gas Grill

Use wood chips, not wood chunks, on a gas grill.

1. Follow step 1 of the recipe for Grill-Roasted Beef Tenderloin, substituting 2 cups wood chips for the wood chunks and soaking the chips for 30 minutes. Drain the chips, then place them in a foil tray (see the illustrations on page 10).

2. About 20 minutes before grilling, place the wood chip pan on the primary burner (the burner that will remain on during grilling); position the cooking grate. Turn on all the burners to high, close the lid, and heat the grill until the chips smoke heavily, about 20 minutes (if the chips ignite, extinguish the flames with a water-filled squirt bottle). Scrape the cooking grate clean with a grill brush.

3. Uncover the tenderloin, coat it with the olive

oil, and sprinkle all sides with the pepper. Place the tenderloin on the side of the grate opposite the primary burner. Grill the tenderloin over the burner(s) without the wood chips until well browned, 2 to 3 minutes, then rotate one quarter turn and repeat until all sides are well browned, for a total of 8 to 12 minutes. Turn off all the burners except the primary burner (the tenderloin should be positioned over the extinguished burner[s]). Cover and cook until an instant-read thermometer inserted into the thickest part of the tenderloin registers 120 degrees for rare, 16 to 20 minutes, or 125 degrees for medium-rare, 20 to 25 minutes.

4. Transfer the tenderloin to a cutting board, tent loosely with foil, and let rest 10 to 15 minutes. Cut into ½-inch-thick slices and serve.

Grill-Roasted Beef Tenderloin with Mixed Peppercorn Crust

Buy a mixture of peppercorns at the supermarket or create your own mixture at home. Black and white peppercorns are much stronger than the pink and green varieties, so adjust the blend to suit your personal taste.

Coarsely crush 6 tablespoons black, white, pink, and green peppercorns with a mortar and pestle or with a heavy-bottomed saucepan or skillet (see page 189). Follow the recipe for Grill-Roasted Beef Tenderloin (charcoal or gas), replacing the coarsely ground black pepper with the peppercorn mixture. Proceed as directed.

Grill-Roasted Beef Tenderloin with Garlic and Rosemary

Studding the tenderloin with slivered garlic and fresh rosemary gives it an Italian flavor.

Follow the recipe for Grill-Roasted Beef Tenderloin (charcoal or gas), making the following changes: After tying the roast, use a paring knife to make several dozen shallow incisions around the surface of the roast. Stuff a few fresh rosemary needles and 1 thin sliver of garlic into each incision. (Use a total of 1 tablespoon rosemary and 3 large garlic cloves, peeled and slivered.) Oil the roast as directed. Sprinkle with salt, pepper, and an additional 2 tablespoons minced fresh rosemary, pressing the herb into the meat with the plastic wrap. Proceed as directed.

PREPARING A BEEF TENDERLOIN

To keep the meat from bowing as it cooks, slide a knife under the silver skin and flick the blade upward to cut through the silver skin at five or six spots along the length of the roast.

EVENLY COATING A BEEF TENDERLOIN

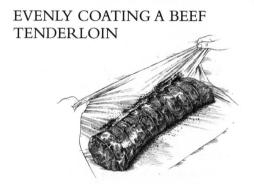

Set the tenderloin on a sheet of plastic wrap and rub it all over with oil. Sprinkle with the pepper, then lift the plastic wrap up and around the meat to press on the excess. This last step guarantees even coverage.

GRILLED VEAL CHOPS

VEAL CHOPS ARE NOT AS POPULAR AS PORK chops or even lamb chops. One reason is certainly price. Another reason may be flavor. Veal chops can be a bit bland, especially if you try to broil or sauté them. At upward of $13 per pound, bland veal chops can be an expensive disappointment. Yet another reason is the way in which some of the calves used for veal are raised (see Milk-Fed versus Natural Veal, below).

We think that if you're going to spend the money for veal chops, you must grill them. The combination of smoky flavor and intense browning does these expensive chops justice. That said, you need the right grilling technique. Should the chops be cooked over direct heat, or do they need a two-level fire? And what about the various choices at the market? There are chops from the shoulder, loin, and rib, as well as the choice between milk-fed and natural veal.

We began by testing various types of veal chops on the grill. We quickly dismissed inexpensive shoulder chops. They were tough and chewy and seemed better suited to braising or cutting up for stews.

Both the loin and rib chops were exceptionally tender and expensive; $13 to $14 per pound in our local markets. The rib chops were a touch juicier and richer in flavor than the loin chops, so they are our first choice. However, if your market carries only loin chops, don't worry. These chops are also quite good and can be grilled just like rib chops.

With our type of chops chosen, we focused on size. We found that thin chops are hard to cook correctly because they dry out before you can get any color on the exterior. Likewise, superthick chops can overbrown by the time the meat near the bone is done. We had the best luck with chops about 1¼ inches thick. Slightly thicker chops (up to 1½ inches) are fine, and will take just an extra minute or so to grill.

It was then time to perfect our grilling technique. It quickly became clear that veal chops did not fare well when cooked solely over hot coals. The exterior burned before the center was done. Cooking over a two-level fire produced chops that were evenly cooked and nicely caramelized on the exterior. Our tasters preferred chops pulled off the grill when the internal temperature reached 130 degrees. At this stage, the chops have just a tinge of pink in the center. Do not cook veal chops past this point or they will be tough and dry.

We did have problems with flare-ups. When we trimmed away excess fat, flare-ups were reduced but not eliminated. We decided not to oil these chops to further reduce the risk of flare-ups. Keep the squirt bottle close at hand while grilling to tame any flare-ups that might occur.

Grilled veal chops are delicious with a simple seasoning of salt and pepper. If you choose to add more flavor, we suggest herbs or something fairly mild. There's no sense masking the delicate veal flavor with too many spices or seasonings.

INGREDIENTS: Milk-Fed Versus Natural Veal

Many people are opposed to milk-fed veal because the calves are confined to small stalls before being butchered. "Natural" is the term used to inform the consumer that the calves are allowed to move freely, without the confines of the stalls. Natural veal is also generally raised on grass (the calves can graze) and without hormones or antibiotics.

Moral issues aside, the differences in how the calves are raised create differences in the texture and flavor of the veal. Natural veal is darker, meatier, and more like beef. Milk-fed veal is paler in color, more tender, and milder in flavor. When we grilled both types of chops in the test kitchen, each had its supporters.

Several tasters preferred the meatier, more intense flavor of the natural veal. They thought the milk-fed veal seemed bland in comparison. Other tasters preferred the softer texture and milder flavor of the milk-fed veal. They felt that the natural veal tasted like "wimpy" beef and that the milk-fed veal chops had the mild, sweet flavor they expected from veal.

Both natural and milk-fed veal chops grill well, so the choice is really a personal one. Milk-fed veal is sold in most grocery stores, while natural veal is available at butcher shops, specialty markets, and natural food stores. When shopping, read labels and check the color of the meat. If the meat is red (rather than pale pink), it most likely came from an animal raised on grass rather than milk.

Charcoal-Grilled Rib Veal Chops

SERVES 4

Be sure to trim the veal chops of any excess fat to prevent flare-ups. Keep a squirt bottle filled with water on hand to spray on flare-ups that may still occur. Veal chops need to be cooked over a two-level fire to achieve a nicely caramelized crust and a center perfectly cooked to medium. Use an instant-read thermometer to ensure that the chops don't overcook.

4   bone-in rib veal chops, 1¼ inches thick (about 10 ounces each), trimmed of excess fat
Salt and ground black pepper

1. Light a large chimney starter filled with hardwood charcoal (about 6 quarts) and allow to burn until all the charcoal is covered with a layer of fine gray ash. Build a two-level fire by stacking most of the coals on one side of the grill and arranging the remaining coals in a single layer on the other side of the grill. Set the cooking grate in place, cover the grill with the lid, and let the grate heat up, about 5 minutes. Use a grill brush to scrape the cooking grate clean. The grill is ready when the pile of coals is medium-hot and the single layer of coals is medium-low. (See how to gauge heat level on page 4.)

2. Sprinkle the chops with salt and pepper to taste.

3. Grill the chops, uncovered, over the hotter part of the fire until browned, about 2 minutes on each side. (If the chops start to flame, drag them to the cooler part of the grill for a moment and/or extinguish the flames with a squirt bottle filled with water.) Move the chops to the cooler part of the grill. Continue grilling, turning once, until the meat is rosy pink at the center and an instant-read thermometer inserted through the side of the chop and away from the bone registers 130 degrees, 10 to 11 minutes.

4. Remove the chops from the grill and let rest for 5 minutes. Serve immediately.

VARIATIONS
Gas-Grilled Rib Veal Chops

Be sure to trim the veal chops of any excess fat to prevent flare-ups. Keep a squirt bottle filled with water on hand to spray on flare-ups that may still occur. Use an instant-read thermometer to ensure that the chops don't overcook.

Turn on all the burners to high, close the lid, and heat the grill until very hot, about 15 minutes. Use a grill brush to scrape the cooking grate clean. Leave one burner on high and turn the other burner(s) to medium. Follow the recipe for Charcoal-Grilled Rib Veal Chops from step 2 and cook with the lid down.

Grilled Veal Chops with Mediterranean Herb Paste

These herb- and garlic-infused chops go very well with mashed potatoes. Because of the oil in the herb paste, these chops are prone to flare-ups, so be vigilant when grilling.

Combine ¼ cup extra-virgin olive oil, 3 medium garlic cloves, minced or pressed through a garlic press, 1 tablespoon chopped fresh parsley leaves, and 2 teaspoons each chopped fresh sage leaves, thyme leaves, rosemary, and oregano leaves in a small bowl. Follow the recipe for Charcoal-Grilled or Gas-Grilled Rib Veal Chops, rubbing the chops with the herb paste and then sprinkling them with salt and pepper to taste. Grill as directed and serve with lemon wedges.

Porcini-Rubbed Grilled Veal Chops

Dried porcini mushrooms can be ground to a powder and then moistened with oil to form a thick paste. When spread on veal chops, the porcini paste gives the chops an especially meaty flavor. If you don't have a spice grinder, use a blender to grind the mushrooms into a powder. You can substitute dried shiitake or oyster mushrooms for the porcini.

Grind ½ ounce dried porcini to a powder in a spice grinder. Mix the ground mushrooms with 6 tablespoons extra-virgin olive oil, 2 medium garlic cloves, minced or pressed through a garlic press, 1 teaspoon salt, and ¼ teaspoon ground black pepper in a small bowl. Follow the recipe for Charcoal-Grilled or Gas-Grilled Rib Veal Chops, rubbing the chops with the mushroom paste. Do not sprinkle the chops with salt and pepper before grilling. Grill as directed.

Grilled Veal Chops on a Bed of Arugula

The clean, peppery flavor of the arugula pairs well with the rich, mildly sweet veal in this Italian-style dish. The heat of the chops wilts the arugula, rendering it toothsome and just slightly soft.

I	recipe Charcoal-Grilled or Gas-Grilled Rib Veal Chops
5	tablespoons extra-virgin olive oil
I¹/₂	tablespoons balsamic vinegar
I	small garlic clove, minced or pressed through a garlic press (about ¹/₂ teaspoon) Salt and ground black pepper
8	cups lightly packed, stemmed arugula, washed and thoroughly dried

1. Grill the chops as directed.

2. While the chops are cooking, whisk together the oil, vinegar, and garlic in a small bowl. Season with salt and pepper to taste. Toss the arugula and dressing in a large bowl. Transfer the arugula to a platter or divide it among individual plates.

3. As soon as the chops are done, arrange them on the arugula. Let rest for 5 minutes. Serve immediately.

TEXAS BEEF RIBS

IN TEXAS, GOOD BEEF RIBS ARE THE SECRET handshake between experienced grillers. With a price tag of roughly $2 a pound and availability at nearly every butcher counter (they are the scrap bones from trimming rib-eye steaks), beef ribs manage to maintain a cool, cult-like obscurity only because their more popular porky brethren hog all the attention. Cost and anonymity aside, it is their huge meaty flavor—combined with spice, smoke, and fire—that epitomizes beef barbecue for many Texans. We set out to find a way to re-create authentic Texas barbecued ribs—with their intense beef flavor—at home.

Reckoning that we'd better get a sense of what authentic Texas beef ribs really taste like before we fired up the grill, we flew to Texas and spent a hot day driving around Austin and neighboring towns to check out some of the country's best rib joints and roadside stands. Sampling plates of beef ribs throughout the day, we were repeatedly surprised by how much they weren't like what we thought of as barbecued ribs. The meat was not fall-off-the-bone tender but actually required a small toothy tug, and the immense, meaty flavor of the ribs was relatively unadorned by spice rubs and sticky sauces. In fact, if we hadn't been looking for evidence of a spice rub, we might have missed it all together. Served dry with a vinegary dipping sauce on the side, the ribs did not boast a lot of smoke flavor, either; instead, the smoke served as a backdrop for the incredible beefy taste.

How were these surprisingly flavorful ribs—basically bones lined with juicy steak trimmings—produced? That became our problem. The various barbecue chefs we talked to at each stop simply set dials and pushed buttons on gargantuan, electric smokers outfitted with automated temperature controls. We flew home having learned nothing of value in terms of backyard cooking in a simple kettle-style grill, but at least we knew exactly what we were looking for: potent meat flavor with a bit of honest Texas chew.

Back in Boston, our first task was to track down beef ribs at the local supermarket. Known to butchers as beef back ribs (not to be confused with beef short ribs), they were in fact widely available; we probably had been reaching over them for years. Because these ribs are often considered scrap bones (especially by Yankee butchers), the real challenge is finding any with a decent amount of meat (see "Choosing Beef Ribs" on page 79), and we learned the hard way that skimpy ribs are simply not worth cooking.

There is a membrane with a fair amount of fat that runs along the backside of the bones, and we tested the effects of removing it, scoring it, and leaving it alone. A number of the recipes we had looked at provided detailed instructions on how to remove the membrane using a screwdriver (no joke), but we found this step to be wholly unnecessary, as it resulted in drier meat. Scoring the membrane with a sharp knife also failed to wow tasters; now the ribs presented relatively dry meat as well as a shaggy appearance. The best results—

the juiciest meat with the most flavor—were had by means of the easiest route: simply leaving the membrane in place. The fat not only bastes the ribs as they cook but also renders to a crisp, bacon-like texture, which one old local told us is called candy—and a real Texan never trims away the candy.

Moving on to the rub, we remembered the comments of one Austin cook, who said, "It's not about what you put on beef ribs that makes the difference, it's what you leave off." Using a simple mixture of salt, pepper, cayenne, and chili powder, we found that a mere 2 teaspoons rubbed into each rack were all that it took to bring out the flavor of the meat. We then tested the effects of rubbing the slabs and refrigerating them, both wrapped in plastic and unwrapped, on wire racks for two days, one day, and one hour versus the effects of rubbing a slab and cooking it straight away. Surprisingly, we found that the differences in flavor were not the result of the rub's having infiltrated the meat but rather the result of the aging of the beef. Here in the test kitchen, we have generally found that aged beef roasts take on a pleasant hearty flavor. In this case, however, the aged ribs were a bust. They tasted sour and smelled tallowy. We did make one useful discovery, though: Ribs left at room temperature for an

SCIENCE: Best Fire for a Barbecue

Barbecue experts have plenty of theories as to exactly what goes on inside a covered grill, but agreement is hard to come by. In search of wisdom rather than witchcraft, we wanted to see if we could scientifically determine the best way to lay a fire. What, once and for all, really is the best way to arrange the coals to ensure evenly, thoroughly barbecued meat?

To answer this question, we outfitted a Weber kettle grill with five temperature probes, four around the edges of the grill and one in the center. Through holes drilled in the lid, we attached these probes, or thermocouples, to a computer data recorder that would measure the temperature inside the grill every minute for up to two hours. After running more than a dozen tests over a six-week period, we arrived at some answers.

Because barbecue is by definition slow cooking over low heat, the high temperatures produced by so-called direct heat (cooking directly over a pile of coals) are unacceptable. What's wanted is indirect heat, and, in a kettle grill, you can produce indirect heat in one of two ways: by banking two piles of coals on opposite sides of the grill or by banking one pile on one side.

The computer data showed that splitting the coals between two sides produced worrisome temperature spikes. This was unacceptable if the goal was to maintain a near-constant temperature. Moreover, the temperature at different sites in the grill showed significant variation.

If anything, we expected the variation in heat distribution with the single-banked coals to be even worse. With the exception of the probe placed directly over the fire, however, the probes in this case produced temperature readings that were within a few degrees of each other. This was surprising, considering that one probe was about twice as far from the fire as the other three. This was also good news, as it meant that a large part of the cooking area was being held at a pretty constant temperature. The single-banked method also showed almost no heat spikes and held the temperature between the ideal (for barbecue) 250 and 300 degrees for the longest period of time.

The results of these tests, then, seemed clear: It's best to have a single pile of coals rather than two piles, because one source of heat produced steady, evenly distributed heat, while two sources produced greater temperature variation.

But this wasn't the only thing we learned. Barbecue experts often recommend placing the lid vent (or vents) away from the fire, so this is what we'd been doing during testing. Was it really part of the reason why the pile of banked coals was providing even, steady heat? Sure enough, when we placed the open vent directly over the fire, the fire burned hotter and faster. With the vent in this position, a direct convection current was formed inside the egg-shaped Weber kettle. When the vent was placed away from the fire, a more diffuse convection current ensured a more even distribution of heat. Also important was the degree to which we opened the lid vent. When the vent was opened up completely, the fire burned much hotter, and the heat was less even throughout the grill. The vent is best kept partially cracked. (Close the vent completely, of course, and you risk snuffing out the fire.)

The final, and most important, thing we learned was also probably the most obvious: When you open the lid to check on the progress of your barbecue, you lose all of the even heat distribution that you have worked so hard to establish. Above all, resist the temptation to peek.

hour cooked through more evenly.

The next question was how to turn a kettle grill into a backyard smoker. The first step was choosing the correct fuel. Hardwood charcoal was out; briquettes burn cooler and longer, making them perfect for barbecue. We had already discovered that cooking the ribs directly over the briquettes didn't work—the ribs burned long before they had cooked through and become tender. We needed indirect heat, and there were two ways to get it. We could bank all of the coals on one side of the grill, or we could create two piles on opposite sides. A single pile on one side of the grill proved best, providing a slow, even fire that was easy to stoke with fresh coals and left more room for the ribs.

In Texas, barbecue fanatics can be particular about the kind of wood they use to create smoke, so we tested the three most popular varieties: hickory, mesquite, and green oak. The green oak had a clean, gentle smoke that was mild and pleasant, but this wood was hard to find. Dried hickory chunks offered a similar flavor profile and were easy to locate at a hardware store. Mesquite, on the other hand, had a fake, pungent flavor that tasters universally hated. We then wondered if chips (rather than chunks) wrapped in a foil packet were as good. No, they reduced the heat of the charcoal (the aluminum foil acted as a shield), whereas the chunks extended its burning power, acting as a fuel source.

Not wanting the meat to taste too smoky, we then tested the difference among using one, two, and three medium-size (about 2 ounces each) chunks (all soaked in water, as dry chunks burn rather than smoke). We determined that two chunks were just right. We tried adding both chunks to the fire right at the beginning versus adding just one and letting it burn out before adding the second. Tasters favored the ribs smoked steadily during the entire cooking time, which is how an electric smoker works. These ribs had a more complex flavor than those that were bombarded with lots of smoke at the beginning.

Inspired by the temperature-controlled smokers we saw in Texas, we decided to use an indoor oven to test various cooking temperatures. We would then go back outside to the grill to apply what we'd learned. We tested more than 15 combinations of time and temperature until we got it right. The first thing we learned was that the cooking temperature should never exceed 300 degrees. Higher temperatures render too much fat and turn the meat dry and stringy. Yet the temperature should not dip below 250 degrees. At that temperature, the fat won't render, the meat stays tough, and the ribs never achieve that signature roasted beefy flavor. The ideal temperature, then, was a range of 250 to 300 degrees, and the ideal time was about 2 hours and 30 minutes, which causes some, but not all, of the fat to render and makes the ribs juicy, tender, and slightly toothy. When cooked any longer, as is the case with pork ribs, the meat disintegrates into messy shreds, taking on

CHOOSING BEEF RIBS

Be careful when shopping for beef ribs—some ribs will yield poor results when barbecued. We prefer partial slabs (with three or four bones) that are very meaty.

TOO SKIMPY
The butcher trimmed too much meat from this slab; you can see the bones.

TOO SMALL
"Shorties" are cut in half and don't offer much meat.

TOO BIG
A whole slab (with seven ribs) is hard to maneuver on the grill.

JUST RIGHT
This partial slab has a thick layer of meat that covers the bones.

a sticky, pot-roasted sort of texture that any real Texan would immediately reject.

Now we were ready to go back to the grill and add the finishing touches. The first problem was maintaining a constant temperature. The solution was to count out exactly 30 briquettes (and one wood chunk) to start, which brought the grill up to 300 degrees. Over the next hour, the grill cooled to 250 degrees, and it became necessary to add another 20 briquettes along with the second wood chunk. We also found that the top vents should be open two thirds of the way and positioned at the side of the grill opposite the wood chunk, so that the smoke is drawn across the grill, not straight up and out.

So, yes, you can make authentic Texas ribs at home, with big beef flavor, great chew, and just a hint of smoke and spice. The secret handshake? Confidence. Let the wood and smoke do their work without constant peeking and checking. Don't mess with Texas ribs.

Texas-Style Barbecued Beef Ribs

SERVES 4

It is important to use beef ribs with a decent amount of meat, not bony scraps; otherwise, the rewards of making this recipe are few. For more information about what to look for when buying ribs, see the photos on page 79. Because the ribs cook slowly and for an extended period of time, charcoal briquettes, not hardwood charcoal (which burns hot and fast), make a better fuel. That said, do not use Match Light charcoal, which contains lighter fluid for easy ignition. For the wood chunks, use any type of wood but mesquite, as its smoke flavor is too strong for this recipe. It's a good idea to monitor the grill heat; if you don't own a reliable grill thermometer, insert an instant-read thermometer through the lid vent to spot-check the temperature. Except when adding coals, do not lift the grill lid, which will allow both smoke and heat to escape. When barbecuing, we prefer to use a Weber 22-inch kettle grill.

4	teaspoons chili powder
2	teaspoons salt
1½	teaspoons ground black pepper
½	teaspoon cayenne
3–4	beef rib slabs (3 to 4 ribs per slab, about 5 pounds total)
2	(3-inch) wood chunks
1	recipe Barbecue Sauce for Texas-Style Beef Ribs (facing page)

1. Mix the chili powder, salt, pepper, and cayenne in a small bowl; rub the ribs evenly with the spice mixture. Let the ribs stand at room temperature for 1 hour.

2. Meanwhile, cover the wood chunks (see headnote) with cold water and soak 1 hour; drain. About 20 minutes before grilling, open the bottom grill vents. Light a chimney starter filled about one third with charcoal briquettes (about 2 quarts) and burn until all the charcoal is covered with a layer of fine gray ash. Build a modified two-level fire by spreading the charcoal onto one side of the grill, 2 to 3 briquettes high; place 1 soaked wood chunk on top of the coals. Position the cooking grate over the coals, cover the grill, and adjust the lid vents two-thirds open. Let the grate heat 5 minutes, then use a grill brush to scrape the cooking grate clean.

3. Position the ribs, meat-side down, on the cooler side of the grill (the ribs may overlap slightly); cover, positioning the lid so that the vents are directly above the ribs. (The temperature on an instant-read thermometer inserted through the vents should register about 300 degrees.) Cook until the grill temperature drops to about 250 degrees, about 1 hour. (On cold, windy days, the temperature may drop more quickly, so spot-check the temperature. If necessary, add 5 additional briquettes to maintain the temperature above 250 degrees during the first hour of cooking.)

4. After 1 hour, add 20 more briquettes and the remaining wood chunk to the coals. Using tongs, flip the ribs meat-side up and rotate them so that the edges that were closest to the coals are now farthest away. Cover the grill, positioning the lid so that the vents are opposite the wood chunk. Continue to cook until a dinner fork can be inserted into and removed from the meat with

little resistance, the meat pulls away from the bones when the rack is gently twisted, and the meat shrinks ½ to 1 inch up the rib bones, 1¼ to 1¾ hours longer. Transfer the ribs to a cutting board and let rest 5 minutes. Using a chef's knife, slice between the bones to separate into individual ribs. Serve, passing the sauce separately.

 VARIATION

Texas-Style Barbecued Beef Ribs on a Gas Grill

On a gas grill, leaving one burner on and turning the other(s) off simulates the indirect heat method on a charcoal grill. Use wood chips instead of wood chunks and a disposable aluminum pan to hold them. On a gas grill, it is important to monitor the temperature closely; use an oven thermometer set on the grate next to the ribs and check the temperature every 15 minutes. Maintain a 250- to 300-degree grill temperature by adjusting the setting of the lit burner.

1. Follow the recipe for Texas-Style Barbecued Beef Ribs through step 1.

2. Cover 3 cups wood chips with cold water; soak 30 minutes. Drain the chips, then place them in a foil tray (see the illustrations on page 10); set the pan on the burner that will remain on during grilling. Turn on all the burners to high, close the lid, and heat the grill until the chips smoke heavily, about 20 minutes (if the chips ignite, extinguish the flames with a water-filled squirt bottle). Use a grill brush to scrape the cooking grate clean; turn off the burner(s) without wood chips. Position an oven thermometer and the ribs, meat-side down, on the cooler side of the grill. Cover and cook 1¼ hours, checking the grill temperature every 15 minutes and adjusting the lit burner as needed to maintain a temperature of 250 to 300 degrees.

3. Using tongs, flip the ribs meat-side up and rotate them so that the edges that were closest to the lit burner are now farthest away. Cover and continue to cook and check/adjust grill temperature until a dinner fork can be inserted into and removed from the meat with little resistance, the meat pulls away from the bones when the rack is gently twisted, and the meat shrinks ½ to 1 inch up the rib bones, 1 to 1½ hours longer. Transfer the ribs to a cutting board and let rest 5 minutes.

Using a chef's knife, slice between the bones to separate into individual ribs. Serve, passing the sauce separately.

Barbecue Sauce for Texas-Style Beef Ribs
MAKES 1¾ CUPS

Every plate of beef ribs we tasted in Texas was accompanied by a simple, vinegary dipping sauce quite unlike the sweet, thick barbecue sauces found in the supermarket. After more than 30 tries, we figured out that the light flavor of tomato juice was the key.

2	tablespoons unsalted butter
¼	cup minced onion
1½	teaspoons chili powder
1	medium garlic clove, minced or pressed through a garlic press (about 1 teaspoon)
2	cups tomato juice
¾	cup distilled white vinegar
2	tablespoons Worcestershire sauce
2	tablespoons mild or dark (not blackstrap) molasses
½	teaspoon dry mustard mixed with 1 tablespoon water
1½	teaspoons salt
1	teaspoon minced chipotle chile in adobo sauce
¼	teaspoon ground black pepper

Heat the butter in a small nonreactive saucepan over medium heat until foaming. Add the onion and cook, stirring occasionally, until softened, 2 to 3 minutes. Add the chili powder and garlic and cook, stirring constantly, until fragrant, about 20 seconds. Add the tomato juice, ½ cup of the vinegar, the Worcestershire sauce, molasses, mustard, salt, and chipotle. Increase the heat to high and bring to a simmer, then reduce the heat to medium and continue to simmer, stirring occasionally, until the sauce is slightly thickened and reduced to about 1½ cups, 30 to 40 minutes. Off the heat, stir in the pepper and the remaining ¼ cup vinegar. Cool to room temperature before serving. (The sauce can be refrigerated in an airtight container for up to 4 days; bring it to room temperature before serving.)

SHORT RIBS

SHORT RIBS ARE JUST WHAT THEIR NAME says they are: "short ribs" cut from any location along the length of the cow's ribs. They can come from the lower belly section or higher up toward the back, from the shoulder (or chuck) area or the forward midsection. There is no way to know, either by appearance or labeling, from where short ribs have been cut.

No matter what part of the rib section they come from, short ribs can be butchered in one of two ways. In most supermarkets, you will see English-style short ribs, in which each rib bone has been separated, with the thick chunk of meat attached, and the bone and the meat cut into manageable, rectangular chunks. In the other style of butchering, called flanken-style, the short ribs are cut into thin cross sections that contain two or three pieces of bone surrounded by pieces of meat.

Both styles of short ribs are fairly fatty, making them ideal candidates for the grill. Most cooks braise this cheap cut, which becomes yielding and tender in a stew. However, the cook must jump through several hoops—trimming the excess fat before cooking, draining off fat from the browned ribs, degreasing the stew liquid before serving—to keep the braise from tasting greasy. On the grill, the fat melts into the fire. Flare-ups can be an issue, however, so keep a squirt bottle handy to douse any flames.

Although short ribs are similar to beef ribs in that each contains meat and bone, our research indicates that most cooks prefer to grill short ribs rather quickly. Given their diminutive size, this makes sense. If you gave a short rib enough time on the grill to truly barbecue it, it would shrink up to a tiny speck of meat.

Since English-style short ribs are more widely available, we started our tests with them. Our first efforts produced terrible results. At first, we burned the exterior before the thick middle portion of the meat was cooked through. We lowered the temperature and still found the interior to be tough by the time the exterior was charred. We figured maybe all the experts were wrong and that we should grill-roast English-style short ribs

PREPARING ENGLISH-STYLE RIBS

Flanken-style short ribs are thin enough to marinate and cook as is. Thicker English-style short ribs must be opened up into a flatter piece of meat before being marinated.

1. With a paring or boning knife, trim off the surface fat and silver skin from each rib.

2. Right above the bone, make a cut into the meat. Continue cutting almost, but not quite all the way, through the meat.

3. Open the meat onto a cutting board, as you would open a book. Make another cut into the meat, parallel to the board, making the lower half of the section of meat that you are slicing about 1/4 inch thick, cutting almost, but not all the way, through to the end of the meat. Open the meat again, like a book.

4. Repeat step 3 as needed, 1 or 2 more times, until the meat is about 1/4 inch thick throughout. You should have a bone connected to a long strip of meat about 1/4 inch thick.

in a kind of compromise between barbecuing and grilling (see page 3 for a definition of grill-roasting). Although this method worked better, the meat became dry and stringy after half an hour of grill-roasting. Worse, there were several layers of unrendered fat throughout each rib that were flabby and unappealing.

Next, we tried simmering the ribs on the stovetop and finishing them on the grill. This method is tedious. First, you have to make a flavorful liquid for the meat to stew in, and then you have to cook the ribs down in the liquid for a few hours to make them tender. Finally, you have to finish by grilling the ribs until crisped and browned, which takes only eight minutes or so—not enough time to give them much smoke flavor. We'd rather spend all that time making braised short ribs, where you end up not only with tender meat but a great, satisfying, rich sauce that becomes a complete meal with mashed potatoes or noodles. It seemed like a waste to have to fire up the grill just to brown the ribs, after you'd spent three hours braising them. It made more sense to brown the ribs on the stovetop before braising them.

At this point, we decided to follow some Asian recipes in which short ribs are butchered further before being cooked. In effect, the meat is slit crosswise several times and opened up like a book until it is quite thin (between one quarter and one half inch thick), which makes it eligible for straightforward grilling. (See the illustrations on page 82.) While this method worked well—the meat cooked quickly, it became tender, and the fat was easily rendered—there was a drawback: the need to butcher each short rib at home.

You can avoid this hassle by asking the butcher for flanken-style ribs. Because the meat is already cut thin and across the grain, flanken-style ribs are much easier to cook on the grill. While these ribs are not as tender as the more familiar pork ribs (you have to work a little at eating them), they are juicy, rich, and packed with beefy flavor, especially near the bones, which are great to gnaw on. Furthermore, these ribs have a large surface area for caramelization, which makes for better flavor. When marinated, the ribs are infused with lots of good flavor because the meat is so thin.

When purchasing the ribs, try to get thinly sliced flanken-style ribs, which should be, on average, about one quarter inch thick. If you end up having to buy English-style ribs, be sure that you get meaty ones. We've seen ribs that are mostly bone. The meat should extend at least one inch above the rib bones. Also, in addition to butchering the ribs Asian-style, you will need to trim off the silver skin and fat on the surface of the ribs.

Grilling the ribs is extremely easy, but you must have a fire that is hot enough to sear the meat. The meat is thin and cooks extremely quickly, making it impossible to go for medium-rare or even medium meat. You just want to have good caramelization to add a layer of sweet flavor on the surface of the ribs. We found that a medium-hot fire (a full chimney starter of hardwood charcoal) sears the meat in about five minutes.

Charcoal-Grilled Beef Short Ribs

SERVES 4

If you are using English-style ribs, purchase only ribs with a good amount of meat on the bones; there should be at least 1 inch of meat above the bone. Keep a squirt bottle handy to douse any flare-ups caused by this fatty cut of meat. Short ribs are delicious enough to eat when seasoned with just salt and pepper. The variations that follow offer more complex flavors. Note that because of the higher cooking temperature, these ribs are actually grilled rather than barbecued. Also, the higher cooking temperature means that wood chunks or chips, which would ignite very quickly, are not a practical option in this recipe. Rely on hardwood charcoal (rather than briquettes) to supply some smoky flavor.

2½   pounds flanken-style short ribs, about ¼ inch thick, or 3 pounds English-style short ribs, prepared according to the illustrations on the facing page
       Salt and ground black pepper

1. Light a large chimney starter full of hardwood charcoal (about 6 quarts) and allow to burn until all the charcoal is covered with a layer of

fine gray ash, about 15 minutes. Spread the coals evenly over the bottom of the grill. Set the cooking grate in place, cover the grill with the lid, and let the grate heat up, about 5 minutes. Use a grill brush to scrape the cooking grate clean. The fire is ready when the coals are medium-hot. (See how to gauge heat level on page 4.)

2. Season the ribs with salt and pepper to taste. Grill half of the ribs, uncovered and turning once, until richly browned on both sides, about 4½ minutes total. Transfer the ribs to a serving platter and cover with foil. Repeat with the second batch of ribs. Serve immediately.

➤ VARIATIONS
Gas-Grilled Beef Short Ribs
Turn on all the burners to high, close the lid, and heat the grill until very hot, about 15 minutes. Use a grill brush to scrape the cooking grate clean. Follow step 2 of the recipe for Charcoal-Grilled Beef Short Ribs and cook with the lid down.

Grilled Beef Short Ribs, Korean Style
This recipe is based on kalbi, a standard barbecued short rib dish from Korea. The sweet, salty marinade promotes excellent browning on the grill. Be sure to marinate the ribs for at least 4 hours or, preferably, overnight. If you like, add ½ teaspoon or more red pepper flakes to the marinade. Serve with steamed rice and kimchee (spicy Korean pickled vegetables, available in Asian markets and some supermarkets).

I	medium, ripe pear, halved, cored, peeled, and cut into ½-inch pieces
½	cup soy sauce
6	medium garlic cloves, chopped (about 2 tablespoons)
2	teaspoons chopped fresh ginger
6	tablespoons sugar
2	tablespoons toasted sesame oil
3	medium scallions, green and white parts sliced thin
I	tablespoon rice vinegar
I	recipe Charcoal-Grilled or Gas-Grilled Beef Short Ribs (omit the salt and pepper in step 2)

1. Place the pear, soy sauce, garlic, and ginger in a food processor. Pulse until smooth, scraping down the sides of the bowl as necessary. Transfer the mixture to a medium bowl and stir in the sugar, sesame oil, scallions, and vinegar.

2. Place the ribs in a gallon-size, zipper-lock plastic bag and pour the soy sauce mixture over them. Seal the bag. Place the bag in the refrigerator and marinate the ribs for at least 4 hours or overnight.

3. Remove the ribs from the marinade and grill as directed.

Grilled Beef Short Ribs with Chipotle and Citrus Marinade
This marinade has some heat, smoky flavor, and acidity.

2	chipotle chiles in adobo sauce, minced, with 1½ teaspoons adobo sauce
6	tablespoons olive oil
6	tablespoons chopped fresh cilantro leaves
3	tablespoons juice from 3 limes
4	medium garlic cloves, minced or pressed through a garlic press (about 4 teaspoons)
I	tablespoon honey
1½	teaspoons chili powder
1½	teaspoons ground cumin
1½	teaspoons salt
1½	teaspoons ground black pepper
I	recipe Charcoal-Grilled or Gas-Grilled Beef Short Ribs (omit the salt and pepper in step 2)
I	lime, cut into wedges

1. Mix the chiles and adobo sauce, olive oil, cilantro, lime juice, garlic, honey, chili powder, cumin, salt, and pepper together in a medium bowl.

2. Place the ribs in a gallon-size, zipper-lock plastic bag and pour the chile mixture over them. Seal the bag. Place the bag in the refrigerator and marinate the ribs for at least 4 hours or overnight.

3. Grill the ribs as directed, serving them with the lime wedges.

BARBECUED BRISKET

OUR FAVORITE WAY TO COOK BRISKET IS to barbecue it. When prepared correctly, the meat picks up a great smoky flavor and becomes fork-tender. Unfortunately, many a barbecued brisket ends up burnt, tough, or chewy. This is because brisket is so tough to begin with. Unless it is fully cooked, the meat is very chewy and practically inedible. Because brisket is so large (a full cut can weigh 13 pounds), getting the meat "fully cooked" can take many hours. Our goal was to make the meat as tender as possible as quickly as possible.

What does "fully cooked" mean when talking about brisket? To find out, we roasted four small pieces to various internal temperatures. The pieces cooked to 160 and 180 degrees were dry and quite tough. A piece cooked to 200 degrees was slightly less tough, although quite dry. A final piece cooked to 210 degrees had the most appealing texture and the most pleasant chew, despite the fact that it was the driest.

So what's going on here? Heat causes muscle proteins to uncoil and then rejoin in a different formation, which drives out juices in the same way that wringing removes moisture from a wet cloth. This process starts in earnest at around 140 degrees, and by the time the meat reaches 180 degrees, most of its juices have been expelled. This explains why a medium-rare steak (cooked to 130 degrees) is much juicier than a well-done steak (cooked to 160 degrees).

With tender cuts, like steak, the lower the internal temperature of the meat, the juicier and less tough the meat will be. However, with cuts that start out tough, like brisket, another process is also at work. Brisket is loaded with waxy-looking connective tissue called collagen, which makes the meat chewy and tough. Only when the collagen has been transformed into gelatin will the meat be tender. Collagen begins to convert to gelatin at 130 to 140 degrees, but the conversion process occurs most rapidly at temperatures above 180 degrees.

When cooking brisket, the gelatinization of collagen must be the priority. Thus, the meat should be cooked as fully as possible, or to an internal temperature of 210 degrees. The muscle juices will be long gone (that's why the sliced meat is served with barbecue sauce), but the meat will be extremely tender because all the collagen will have been converted to gelatin.

It is important to point out that moist-heat cooking methods (such as braising) are appropriate for cooking meats to such high internal temperatures because water is a more efficient conductor of heat than air. Meats cooked in a moist environment heat up faster and can be held at high internal temperatures without burning or drying out.

Given the fact that brisket must be fully cooked and that it can be so big, the meat needs 10 or 12 hours of barbecuing to reach the fork-tender stage. Even when butchers separate the brisket into smaller pieces, as is often the case, the cooking time is astronomical. Most cooks are not prepared to keep a fire going that long. To get around this tending-the-fire-all-day-long problem, we found it necessary to commit barbecue heresy. After much testing, we decided to start the meat on the grill but finish it in the oven, where it could be left to cook unattended.

We wondered how long the meat would have to stay on the grill to pick up enough smoke flavor. In our testing, we found that two hours allows the meat to absorb plenty of smoke flavor and creates a dark brown, crusty exterior. At this point, the meat is ready for the oven. We found it best to wrap the meat in foil to create a moist environment. (Unwrapped briskets cooked up drier, and the exterior was prone to burning.) After barbecuing, a whole brisket requires three hours or so in a 300-degree oven to become fork-tender. Barbecue purists might object to our use of the oven, but this method works, and it doesn't require a tremendous commitment of hands-on cooking time.

Some further notes about our testing. Although many experts recommend basting a brisket regularly as it cooks on the grill to ensure moistness, we disagree. Taking the lid off wreaked havoc with our charcoal fire, and the meat didn't taste any different despite frequent basting with sauce. Likewise, we don't recommend placing a pan filled with water (we also tried beer) on the grill. Some barbecue masters believe that the liquid adds moisture and flavor to the meat, but we couldn't tell any difference between brisket cooked with and without the pan of liquid.

Brisket comes with a thick layer of fat on one side. We tried turning the brisket as it cooked, thinking this might promote even cooking, but we had better results when we barbecued the brisket fat-side up the entire time. This way, the fat slowly melts, lubricating the meat underneath.

Barbecued Beef Brisket on a Charcoal Grill

SERVES 18 TO 24

Cooking a whole brisket, which weighs about 10 pounds, may seem like overkill. However, the process is easy, and the leftovers keep well in the refrigerator for up to 4 days. (Leave leftover brisket unsliced, and reheat the foil-wrapped meat in a 300-degree oven until warm.) Still, if you don't want to bother with a big piece of meat or if your grill has fewer than 400 square inches of cooking space, barbecuing brisket for less than a crowd is easy to do. Simply ask your butcher for either the point or flat portion of the brisket (we prefer the point cut; see the illustration at right), each of which weighs about half as much as a whole brisket. Then follow this recipe, reducing the spice rub by half and barbecuing for just 1 hour and thirty minutes. Wrap the meat tightly in foil and reduce the time in the oven to 2 hours. No matter how large or small a piece you cook, it's a good idea to save the juices the meat gives off while in the oven to enrich the barbecue sauce. Hickory and mesquite are both traditional wood choices with brisket.

    1   cup Dry Rub for Barbecue (page 376)
    1   whole beef brisket (9 to 11 pounds),
            fat trimmed to ¼-inch thickness
    2   (3-inch) wood chunks
    3   cups barbecue sauce (see pages 386–388)

1. Apply the dry rub liberally to all sides of the meat, patting it on firmly to make sure the spices adhere and completely obscure the meat. Wrap the brisket tightly in plastic wrap and refrigerate for 2 hours. (For stronger flavor, refrigerate for up to 2 days.)

2. About 1 hour prior to cooking, remove the brisket from the refrigerator, unwrap, and let it come up to room temperature. Soak the wood chunks in cold water to cover for 1 hour and drain.

3. Meanwhile, light a large chimney starter filled a bit less than halfway with charcoal briquettes (about 2½ quarts) and allow to burn until all the charcoal is covered with a layer of fine gray ash. Empty the coals into one side of the grill, piling them up in a mound 2 or 3 briquettes high. Keep the bottom vents completely open. Place the wood chunks on top of the charcoal. Put the cooking grate in place, open the grill lid vents completely, and cover, turning the lid so that the vents are opposite the wood chunks to draw smoke through the grill. Let the grate heat up for 5 minutes and then use a grill brush to scrape it clean.

4. Position the brisket, fat-side up, on the side of the grill opposite the fire. Barbecue, without removing the lid, for 2 hours. (The initial

LOCATING THE BRISKET

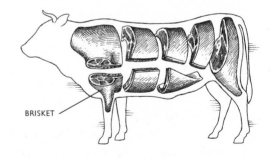

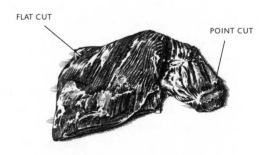

Butchers often separate the whole brisket into two parts, the flat cut (left portion) and the point cut (right portion). The point cut is a bit thicker and contains more fat. It is more tender than the flat cut and is our first choice.

temperature will be about 350 degrees and will drop to 250 degrees after 2 hours.)

5. Adjust an oven rack to the middle position and heat the oven to 300 degrees. Attach 2 pieces of heavy-duty foil, 4 feet long, by folding the long edges together 2 or 3 times, crimping tightly to seal well, to form an approximately 4 by 3 foot rectangle. Position the brisket lengthwise in the center of the foil. Bring the short edges over the brisket and fold down, crimping tightly to seal. Repeat with the long sides of the foil to seal the brisket completely. (See illustrations 1 and 2 below.) Place the brisket on a rimmed baking sheet. Bake until the meat is fork-tender, 3 to 3½ hours.

6. Remove the brisket from the oven, loosen the foil at one end to release steam, and let rest for 30 minutes. If you like, drain the juices into a bowl (see illustration 3 below) and defat the juices in a gravy skimmer.

7. Unwrap the brisket and place it on a cutting board. Separate the meat into two sections and carve it on the bias across the grain into long, thin slices (see illustrations 4 and 5 below). Serve with plain barbecue sauce or with barbecue sauce that has been flavored with up to 1 cup of the defatted brisket juices.

➤ VARIATION

Barbecued Beef Brisket on a Gas Grill

You will need a pretty large grill to cook a whole brisket. If your grill has fewer than 400 square inches of cooking space, barbecue either the point or flat end, each of which weighs about half as much as a whole brisket. Follow the directions in the note on page 86 for cooking a smaller piece of brisket.

Follow the recipe for Barbecued Beef Brisket on a Charcoal Grill through step 2, substituting 2 cups wood chips for the wood chunks and soaking

KEY STEPS TO BARBECUED BRISKET

1. After barbecuing, place the brisket on two 4-foot sections of heavy-duty aluminum foil that have been sealed together to make a 4 by 3-foot rectangle. Bring the short ends of the foil up over the brisket and crimp tightly to seal.

2. Seal the long sides of the foil packet tightly up against the sides of the meat. Put the brisket on a rimmed baking sheet and put the sheet in the oven.

3. After the brisket comes out of the oven, use oven mitts to hold the rimmed baking sheet and carefully pour the juices into a bowl. If you like, reserve the juices and defat. They make a delicious addition to barbecue sauce.

4. Since the grain on the two sections of the brisket goes in opposite directions, separate the cuts before slicing.

5. Carve the brisket on the bias across the grain into long, thin slices.

them for 30 minutes in cold water to cover. Drain the chips and place them in a foil tray (see the illustrations on page 10). Place the pan on top of the primary burner (see the illustration on page 9). Turn all the burners to high and heat with the lid down until the chips are smoking heavily, about 20 minutes. Use a grill brush to scrape the cooking grate clean. Turn the primary burner down to medium and turn off the other burner(s). Position the brisket, fat-side up, over the cooler part of the grill. Cover and barbecue for 2 hours. (The temperature inside the grill should be a constant 275 degrees; adjust the lit burner as necessary.) Proceed as directed from step 5.

EQUIPMENT: Santoku Knives

The santoku has long been the Japanese equivalent of a chef's knife—an all-purpose blade capable of performing any task in the kitchen. But only recently has this knife gained America's attention, as the darling of celebrity chefs such as Ming Tsai and Rachel Ray.

What is a santoku knife? Compared with a classic chef's knife, the santoku, sometimes labeled in stores as an Asian or oriental chef's knife, is typically shorter and has a thinner blade, a stubbier tip, and a straighter edge. The santoku's slight size, believed to have evolved from the narrow, rectangular Japanese vegetable knife, means a great amount of blade control.

To fully evaluate the santoku, we bought 10 models, ranging in price from $30 to $100, with blades made from a variety of materials, from the conventional high-carbon stainless steel to the exotic, including ceramic and a titanium silver alloy. To be as thorough as possible, we ran them through a series of tests, using the Forschner (Victorinox) chef's knife (the winning model from an earlier test of chef's knives) for comparison. The tests included preparing onions, garlic, carrots, tomatoes, and boneless chicken breasts. We assessed each knife for precision, control, sharpness of blade, efficiency, comfort, price, and finally size, which proved to be very significant in these tests.

During the first test we conducted, mincing and chopping onions, the size of the santoku blade came into play. All of the santoku blades ranged in size from 6 to 7 inches, but the larger blades significantly outperformed their smaller counterparts. The 6-inch blade was so short that most of the testers ended up knuckle-deep in onions after just a few strokes. The larger-bladed santokus, on the other hand, performed very well during the onion test, with the Kershaw Shun ($99.95) taking home top honors over the Forschner chef's knife.

Where the santoku really excelled was in more precise or delicate tasks. Julienned carrots rifled off the blade, and chicken breasts practically butterflied themselves under the accurate blade of the santoku. Most testers found the santoku superior in these situations because its thin, short blade reduced friction and felt more exact against the dense flesh of the carrots and the chicken.

During mincing evaluations, the curve of the blade was the main factor mentioned by our testers. Because of the rocking motion used during mincing, the santokus with straighter edges tended to feel more jarring than those with more rounded edges. The straight-edged santokus seemed to be geared more toward slicing, and, in fact, they performed very well while slicing tomatoes. A very telling test, slicing tomatoes calls for only the sharpest of blades. High-carbon stainless steel knives performed best in this test, followed by the ceramic-bladed Kyocera Ming Tsai ($99.95) that was adequately sharp, but not weighty enough to take top honors. Bringing up the rear in the tomato test was the titanium silver alloy Boker Cera-Titan I ($63.95) that was at once too thin, overly flexible, and disappointingly dull.

While most of the testers appreciated the performance and quality of many of the santoku knives, only two knives—the MAC Superior ($55) and the Kershaw Shun Classic—were consistently preferred to the Forschner chef's knife in the tests. Now, although this fact speaks highly of santoku knives in general, it could be argued that the tests we performed were geared toward the lightweight santokus. In preliminary tests, we attempted tasks such as butchering a whole chicken or halving acorn squash. In most cases, the santokus were deemed too small or lightweight for these operations, while the chef's knife tackled them with ease.

Our conclusions: The santoku would certainly be a reliable addition to any kitchen. However, due to its smaller size and delicate blade, the santoku comes up short in its ability to function as an all-purpose blade. A good santoku can complement (but not replace) a trusted chef's knife.

THE BEST SANTOKU KNIFE
Admired for being the most sharp, responsive, and easy to use, the MAC Superior Santoku ($55) is the knife to use for delicate tasks such as julienning carrots and butterflying chicken breasts.

2

PORK

PORK

CHARCOAL-GRILLED PORK CHOPS 93
    Gas-Grilled Pork Chops
    Grilled Pork Chops with Peaches, Radicchio, and Balsamic Vinaigrette

GRILL-SMOKED PORK CHOPS WITH APPLE CHUTNEY 96
    Gas Grill–Smoked Pork Chops with Apple Chutney

CHARCOAL-GRILLED PORK KEBABS. 98
    Gas-Grilled Pork Kebabs
    Grilled Pork Kebabs with West Indian Flavors
    Grilled Pork Kebabs with Southeast Asian Flavors

CHARCOAL-GRILLED ITALIAN SAUSAGES 101
    Gas-Grilled Italian Sausages

GRILL-ROASTED PORK LOIN ON A CHARCOAL GRILL 102
    Grill-Roasted Pork Loin on a Gas Grill
    Grill-Roasted Pork Loin with Garlic and Rosemary
    Grill-Roasted Pork Loin with Barbecue Rub and Fruit Salsa
    Grill-Roasted Pork Loin with Maple-Mustard Glaze

CHARCOAL-GRILLED PORK TENDERLOIN 106
    Gas-Grilled Pork Tenderloin

BARBECUED SPARERIBS ON A CHARCOAL GRILL 108
    Barbecued Spareribs on a Gas Grill
    Barbecued Spareribs with Hoisin, Honey, and Ginger Glaze
    Barbecued Spareribs with Mexican Flavors

BARBECUED BABY BACK RIBS ON A CHARCOAL GRILL 111
    Barbecued Baby Back Ribs on a Gas Grill

BARBECUED PULLED PORK ON A CHARCOAL GRILL 114
    Barbecued Pulled Pork on a Gas Grill
    Cuban-Style Barbecued Pulled Pork with Mojo Sauce

FROM QUICK-COOKING PORK CHOPS TO all-day barbecued ribs, the leanness of pork poses a challenge to the outdoor cook. This is particularly true with cuts from the especially lean center, or loin, of the animal. This hasn't always been the case with pork.

In 1985, amid growing concerns about saturated fat in the American diet, Congress created the National Pork Board with the goal of helping producers provide consumers with the leaner meat they desired. Working with the board, producers developed new breeding techniques and feeding systems aimed at slimming down pigs. As a result, pigs are now much leaner and more heavily muscled than they were 20 years ago, with an average of 31 percent less fat. This is good news for our waistlines, but much of the meaty flavor, moisture, and tenderness disappeared along with the fat, causing some cuts of pork to taste like diet food. For this reason, choosing the right cut and the right cooking method makes a big difference when preparing today's pork.

A pig is butchered into four primal cuts. The term primal cuts refers to the basic cuts made to an animal when it is initially butchered. Butchers turn primal cuts into the chops, roasts, and other cuts sold at the retail level. Retail cuts from the same primal cut generally share similar traits, so when shopping it helps to understand the characteristics of the four primal cuts of pork.

THE FOUR PRIMAL CUTS OF PORK

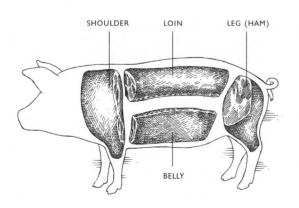

SHOULDER   LOIN   LEG (HAM)

BELLY

SHOULDER Cuts from the upper portion of the well-exercised front legs (called the blade shoulder) tend to be tough, with a fair amount of fat. The economical arm, or picnic (or ham) shoulder, has characteristics similar to the blade shoulder. Shoulder hocks (used primarily as a flavoring agent for soups, slow-cooked greens, and stews) also come from this part of the pig, while ham hocks come from the hind legs of the animal. All shoulder cuts require long, slow cooking to become fork-tender.

LOIN Butchers divide this area between the shoulder and the leg into some of the most popular cuts of pork, including pork chops, tenderloin, roasts, and ribs. Because the loin area is so lean, these cuts are prone to dryness.

LEG The leg is sometimes referred to as the ham. Ham can be wet- or dry-cured or sold fresh, as a roast.

BELLY The belly, or side, of the pig is, not surprisingly, the fattiest part, home to spareribs and bacon.

GRILLED PORK CHOPS

WE LOVE A JUICY, FLAVORFUL PORK CHOP. Too bad most pork chops are dry and bland. The pork industry has reduced the fat in pigs by 50 percent since the 1950s. Yes, pork is now the "other white meat," nearly as lean as chicken. But along with all that fat went flavor and juiciness.

The reality of many a grilled pork chop is a burnt exterior, raw interior, tough meat, nary a hint of flavor—the list goes on. We were looking for perfection: a plump, Rubenesque chop with a seared, richly brown crust and an interior that would be juicy and flavorful all the way to the bone. We wanted a chop that looked and tasted so good that it transcended the far reaches of backyard grilling and became art.

Thick pork chops usually come from the loin of the pig, which runs from the shoulder to the hip. To determine which cut would be best, we conducted a blind taste test with four different chops, starting with the blade chop, which is from the shoulder end, or front, of the loin. Because the shoulder region of the loin has the most fat and is riddled with connective tissue, tasters found the blade chops to be full of flavor but also tough and chewy. At the hip end of the loin are the sirloin chops. These were dry, somewhat tasteless, and a bit tough. Moving on to the center of the loin, we tested the center-cut chop and the rib chop. Although both were tender and flavorful, tasters preferred the rib chops, which were juicy and well marbled with fat.

Although rib chops are flavorful on their own, we wanted to see if we could boost their flavor by using a spice rub, marinade, or brine. We tested two types of rub: wet and dry. The wet rubs, made with spices and a liquid, gave the chops good flavor but also caused their exterior to turn syrupy. Tasters preferred the dry rubs, which combine potent dried spices with sugar to create big flavor and a crisp crust.

Next, we tried marinating the chops in an acidic oil mixture flavored with herbs and garlic. While the marinade succeeded in flavoring the exterior of the chops, it did little for the interior. Moreover, the meat took on a slimy texture that prohibited formation of a good crust.

Finally, we tried brining, a method we often turn to in the test kitchen, in which lean cuts of meat (usually pork or poultry) are soaked in a solution of water and salt and sometimes sugar. (Brining yields moist, well-seasoned meat and poultry that are hard to overcook, an important factor when grilling.) The brined chops were well seasoned throughout, not just on the surface. They were also extremely juicy—each bite was full of moist, seasoned pork flavor, complemented by the warm crunch of the spice rub.

It was now time to grill. As a preliminary test, we pitted hardwood charcoal against the more traditional charcoal briquettes. After grilling a few chops over each, we found we preferred the hardwood for its intensely hot fire and slightly smoky flavor. As for the fire itself, we always begin testing with a single-level fire—that is, a fire of even and generally high heat made by spreading coals evenly across the grill. We threw the chops over the fire and watched as they browned to a beautiful bronze within minutes. But when we pulled the chops off the grill and cut into one, it was rare at the bone. Moderating the temperature of the fire only drew out the cooking time and sacrificed the deep, caramelized crust we had achieved over high heat.

Moving next to a two-level fire, which is

INGREDIENTS: Modern Versus Old-Fashioned Pork

A few farmers are raising fattier pigs, yielding chops and roasts that are similar to the pork enjoyed by our grandparents. We wondered how this pork would taste to modern cooks raised on leaner modern pork. To find out, we purchased center-cut pork chops from New York farmers who raise heritage breeds the old-fashioned way (the animals are free roaming and are fed natural diets) and tasted them alongside supermarket chops.

Tasters had an interesting response to the farm-raised pork, noting that while it was juicy, with significantly more fat than the supermarket chops, it had unusual "mineral" and "iron" flavors. Some tasters also found that the extra fat in the old-fashioned pork left behind an unpleasant coating in their mouths. Surprisingly, most tasters favored the more familiar supermarket meat. A few tasters thought that the old-fashioned pork was delicious but definitely an acquired taste.

We wondered just how fatty this old-fashioned pork was and so sent a sample pork butt to a food laboratory to be ground and analyzed for fat content. For comparison, we also sent a supermarket sample of the same cut. As we expected, the old-fashioned pork butt had significantly more fat—50 percent more—than the supermarket butt. Old-fashioned pork chops had 210 percent more fat than the supermarket samples, but this sky-high fat level was probably due to differences in the way the two kinds of pork were trimmed; supermarkets tend to remove most external fat, while pork farmers who raise heritage breeds do not.

So is it worth the effort and money to search for a local or mail-order source for old-fashioned pork? The answer may have something to do with your age. If you were raised on old-fashioned pork, you will appreciate its flavor and extra fat. If your palate is accustomed to leaner pork, you are better off shopping at the supermarket.

achieved by banking more hot coals on one side of the grill than on the other, we tried a multitude of temperature combinations, each time starting the chops over high heat to develop a nicely browned crust. Moving the chops from high to medium, high to low, and high to no heat were all tested, but none of these combinations produced a thoroughly cooked interior in a reasonable amount of time. Throwing the grill lid back on after the initial sear cooked the chops all the way through—a breakthrough to be sure—but the flavor of the meat was adversely affected. (The inside of most charcoal grill covers is coated with a charcoal residue that can impart bitter, spent flavors to foods.) Seizing on the notion of covering the chops for part of the cooking time, we turned to a handy disposable aluminum roasting pan to solve the problem. We threw the pan over the chops after searing them over high heat and moving them to the cooler part of the grill. This time we had a crisp crust, juicy meat, and no off flavors.

In our eagerness to serve these perfect chops, we cut into them right off the grill and watched as the juices ran out onto the plate. We allowed the next round of chops to sit covered under the foil pan for five minutes. When we cut into the chops this time, only a little of the juice escaped. We were surprised, however, to find that these chops were slightly tougher than the chops that did not rest. We took the internal temperature and found that it was now nearly 165 degrees—overcooked in our book. We cooked one more batch of chops and this time took them off the grill earlier, once they had reached an internal temperature of 135 degrees, and let them sit under the foil pan for a good five minutes. Thanks to the residual heat left in the bone, the temperature shot up an average of 10 to 15 degrees, bringing the meat into a desirable range of 145 to 150. Magic.

Some tasters found the chops flavorful enough from the spice rub, but others appreciated the extra moisture from a fruit salsa or chutney served alongside, especially the Peach Salsa on page 393 or the Curried Fruit Chutney with Lime and Ginger on page 396.

Charcoal-Grilled Pork Chops
SERVES 4

Rib loin chops are our top choice for their big flavor and juiciness. Dry rubs add a lot of flavor for very little effort, but the chops can also be seasoned with pepper alone just before grilling. To use kosher salt in the brine, see page 172 for conversion information. You will need a large disposable aluminum roasting pan to cover the chops and help them finish cooking through to the bone. Consider serving the chops with a fruit salsa (see pages 392 through 393) for added moisture.

6	tablespoons table salt (see note)
6	tablespoons sugar
4	bone-in pork loin rib chops or center-cut loin chops, 1½ inches thick (about 12 ounces each)
1	recipe Basic Spice Rub for Pork (page 377) or ground black pepper

1. Dissolve the salt and sugar in 3 quarts of cold water in a 2-gallon zipper-lock plastic bag. Add the chops and seal the bag, pressing out as much air as possible. (Alternatively, divide the brine and chops evenly between two 1-gallon zipper-lock bags.) Refrigerate, turning the bag once, until fully seasoned, about 1 hour. Remove the chops from the brine and pat thoroughly dry with paper towels. Coat the chops with the dry rub or season generously with pepper.

2. Light a large chimney starter filled with hardwood charcoal (about 6 quarts) and allow to burn until all the charcoal is covered with a layer of fine gray ash. Build a two-level fire by stacking most of the coals on one side of the grill and arranging the remaining coals in a single layer on the other side of the grill. Set the cooking grate in place, cover the grill with the lid, and let the grate heat up, about 5 minutes. Use a grill brush to scrape the cooking grate clean. The grill is ready when the pile of coals is medium-hot and the single layer of coals is medium-low. (See how to gauge heat level on page 4.)

3. Grill the chops, uncovered, over the hotter part of the fire until browned on each side, 2½ to 3 minutes per side. Move the chops to the cooler

part of the grill and cover with a disposable aluminum roasting pan (see the illustration on page 167). Continue grilling, turning once, until an instant-read thermometer inserted through the side of a chop away from the bone registers 135 degrees, 7 to 9 minutes longer. Transfer the chops to a platter, cover with the foil pan, and let rest for 5 minutes. (The internal temperature should rise to 145 to 150 degrees.) Serve immediately.

➤ VARIATIONS
Gas-Grilled Pork Chops
Because gas grill lids don't build up a residue that can impart an off flavor to foods (as charcoal grills do), they can be used to concentrate heat to cook the pork chops through; there's no need, therefore, for a disposable roasting pan.

Follow step 1 of the recipe for Charcoal-Grilled Pork Chops. Turn on all the burners to high, close the lid, and heat the grill until very hot, about 15 minutes. Scrape the cooking grate clean with a grill brush. Leave one burner on high and turn the other burner(s) to medium-low. Cook the chops as directed in step 3 with the lid down.

Grilled Pork Chops with Peaches, Radicchio, and Balsamic Vinaigrette
Use ripe but not mushy peaches in this recipe. Don't bother grilling hard peaches; they will be mealy and unappetizing. Nectarines may be substituted for the peaches.

6   tablespoons extra-virgin olive oil
1   tablespoon balsamic vinegar
1   small shallot, minced (about 2 tablespoons)
    Salt and ground black pepper
1   recipe Charcoal-Grilled or Gas-Grilled Pork Chops, without the dry rub (page 93)
2   small peaches, halved and pitted
2   small heads radicchio, cut into quarters with core intact (see the illustration at right)

1. Whisk together 4 tablespoons of the oil, the vinegar, shallot, ¼ teaspoon salt, and a pinch of pepper in a small bowl until smooth. Brush the peaches with 2 teaspoons more of the oil and season with salt and pepper to taste. Brush the radicchio with the remaining 4 teaspoons oil and

THE BEST CHOP FOR GRILLING
Pork chops come from the loin of the pig. A whole pork loin weighs 14 to 17 pounds and can be cut into blade chops, rib chops, center-cut chops, and sirloin chops. The loin muscle runs the entire length of the backbone. Starting midway back, the tenderloin muscle runs along the opposite side of the backbone. Center-cut and sirloin chops contain both kinds of muscle. We found that the tenderloin cooks more quickly than the loin and can dry out on the grill. Following are tasters' impressions after sampling four different chops cut from the loin. Rib chops were the tasters' top choice, followed by center-cut chops.

BLADE CHOP
Fatty, toughest, juiciest, most flavor

RIB CHOP
Some fat, relatively tender, juicy, great flavor

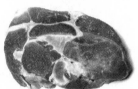

CENTER-CUT CHOP
Little fat, relatively tender, less juicy, good flavor

SIRLOIN CHOP
Quite fatty, tough, dry, little flavor

PREPARING RADICCHIO

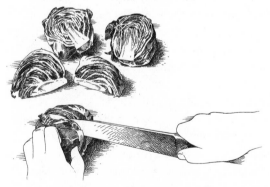

Remove any brown leaves. Cut the radicchio in half through the core. Cut each half again through the core so that you have four wedges. Since each piece has a bit of the core, the layers of leaves will remain together on the grill.

season with salt and pepper to taste.

2. Follow the recipe for Charcoal-Grilled or Gas-Grilled Pork Chops, seasoning the chops with pepper, through step 3. Transfer the grilled chops to a platter, cover with an aluminum roasting pan, and let rest while you prepare the peaches and radicchio.

3. Place the peach halves, skin-side up, on the hotter part of the grill. Cook until well caramelized, 3 to 4 minutes. Turn and continue to cook until slightly softened, about 3 minutes more. Transfer the peaches to the platter with the chops.

4. Place the radicchio on the hotter part of the grill. Cook, turning every 1½ minutes, until the edges are browned and wilted but the center remains slightly firm, about 4½ minutes total. Transfer the radicchio to the platter with the pork and peaches.

5. Rewhisk the balsamic vinaigrette and drizzle it over the pork, peaches, and radicchio. Serve immediately.

GRILL-SMOKED PORK CHOPS

GRILL-SMOKING IS ANOTHER EXCELLENT WAY to prepare pork chops. And we especially like the method used to prepare the signature dish, smoked pork chops with apple chutney, from the restaurant at Wente Vineyards in California. The restaurant's recipe yields incredibly tender chops with a delicately perfumed smoke flavor that, when paired with the spicy-sweet chutney, had us drooling in the test kitchen.

The key to this dish's success is the grilling technique. The theory behind the technique is to cook the 14-ounce center-cut pork chops slowly on the cooler side of the grill (opposite the fire), thus maximizing their exposure to the flavorful smoke. Getting the temperature of the grill just right is therefore crucial. If you start with a grill that is too cool, the pork chops will take too long to cook through and will wind up incredibly dry and overly smoky. Yet at the other extreme, a grill that is too hot will cook the chops too quickly,

denying them exposure to the smoke. The restaurant's recipe uses a smoker or kettle-type grill to cook the chops. Realizing that most people don't own a smoker, we wanted to figure out how to produce tender, flavorful pork chops using either a charcoal or gas grill.

Starting with a charcoal grill, we fiddled with various amounts of fuel and determined that half a large chimney full of hardwood charcoal (about 3 quarts), banked to one side of the grill, was just right, bringing the initial temperature of the grill to roughly 350 degrees. Moving over to the gas grill, we found it necessary to heat up the grill initially by turning all the burners to high, but then turn off all but one to cook the chops. For good smoky flavor, it is necessary to add to the grill wood chunks or chips that have been soaked in water. If not soaked, they will only burn rather than "smoke." Soaked wood chunks can be tossed onto the hot coals of a charcoal grill, but wood chips require a foil packet or foil tray before being added to a charcoal or gas grill (see the illustrations on page 10).

The restaurant's recipe recommends that the chops be brought to room temperature before being grilled. We found this small step helped them cook more evenly, and they came off the grill tender and juicy. Placing the pork chops on the grill correctly is another crucial step. They should be placed on the side opposite the fire, bone-side down so that they stand upright.

MEASURING THE INTERNAL TEMPERATURE OF A PORK CHOP

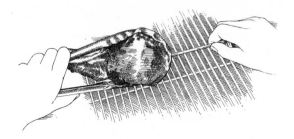

When you think a chop might be done, use a pair of tongs to hold the chop and then slide an instant-read thermometer through the edge of the chop and deep into the meat, making sure to avoid the bone.

This ensures that the meat of each chop has full exposure to the flavoring smoke. Last, we noted it was important to cover the grill with the lid vents opposite the fire (over the chops) to help draw the smoke through the grill. The chops took roughly 35 minutes to reach 145 degrees, at which point we removed them from the grill. The meat will have a slightly pink tinge, but it will be far juicier than chops cooked to an internal temperature just 10 degrees higher. (However, the U.S. Department of Agriculture recommends cooking all meat to an internal temperature of 160 degrees to kill bacteria such as salmonella. If safety is your primary concern, follow the USDA's guidelines.)

While the pork chops are grilling, there is plenty of time to make the apple chutney. The base of the chutney is a quickly simmered brown sugar and cider vinegar mixture flavored with onion, garlic, ginger, red bell pepper, and several spices, including cayenne. The apples are sautéed separately in a skillet, then added to the sugar-vinegar base after it has cooled off a bit. This dual-pot method ensures that the chutney is well seasoned and has the correct consistency, yet the apples retain just a little of their crunch.

Grill-Smoked Pork Chops with Apple Chutney

SERVES 6

Cooking the chops slowly on the cooler side of the grill (opposite the fire) maximizes their exposure to the flavorful smoke. For good smoky flavor, it is necessary to add to the grill wood chunks that have been soaked in water. If not soaked, they will only burn rather than "smoke." This recipe is best made with chops about 2 inches thick; thinner chops will cook through too quickly, before the meat has had time to absorb the smoke flavor. The chutney can be made a day ahead, kept refrigerated, and reheated in a small heavy-bottomed saucepan over low heat.

PORK CHOPS

2	(3-inch) wood chunks
6	center-cut pork chops, about 2 inches thick (14 ounces each)
	Salt and ground black pepper

CHUTNEY

3	tablespoons vegetable oil
1	medium red bell pepper, cored, seeded, and cut into 1/2-inch dice
1/2	small onion, minced (about 1/4 cup)
2	tablespoons minced fresh ginger
2	medium garlic cloves, minced or pressed through a garlic press (about 2 teaspoons)
1	cup apple cider vinegar
1	cup packed light brown sugar
1	tablespoon mustard seeds
1/2	teaspoon ground allspice
1/8	teaspoon cayenne pepper
3	Granny Smith apples, peeled, cored, and cut into 1/2-inch dice

1. FOR THE PORK CHOPS: Soak the wood chunks in cold water to cover for 1 hour and drain. Meanwhile, allow the pork chops to come to room temperature, about 1 hour.

2. Open the bottom vents on the grill. Light a large chimney starter filled halfway with hardwood charcoal (about 3 quarts) and allow to burn until all the charcoal is covered with a layer of fine gray ash. Build a modified two-level fire by spreading the coals out over half the grill bottom, leaving the other half with no coals. Place the soaked wood chunks on top of the coals. Set the cooking grate in place and let it heat up for 5 minutes. Use a grill brush to scrape the cooking grate clean. Cover the grill and open the lid vents two thirds of the way.

3. Season the chops generously with salt and pepper. Arrange them bone-side down (see the

BUY THE RIGHT PORK CHOP

Supermarket chops are often cut thick at the bone and thinner at the outer edge, like the one on the left. With such chops, the thinner edge will overcook before the thicker meat near the bone is finished. Make sure you buy chops that are of even thickness, like the one on the right.

illustration below) on the cooler side of the grill. Cover the grill, positioning the lid so that the vents are opposite the wood chunks to draw the smoke through the grill (the grill temperature should register about 350 degrees on a grill thermometer, but will soon start dropping). Cook until an instant-read thermometer inserted into the side of a chop away from the bone registers 145 degrees, 30 to 45 minutes.

4. FOR THE CHUTNEY: While the pork chops are on the grill, heat 1 tablespoon of the vegetable oil in a medium saucepan over medium-high heat until shimmering. Add the bell pepper, onion, ginger, and garlic. Cover, reduce the heat to medium, and cook until the vegetables have softened, about 5 minutes. Stir in the vinegar, brown sugar, mustard seeds, allspice, and cayenne and bring to a simmer over medium-high heat. Cook, adjusting the heat as necessary to maintain a simmer, until the mixture is thick and syrupy and has reduced to 1¼ cups, about 10 minutes. Remove from the heat, transfer to a medium bowl, and cool.

5. Heat 1 tablespoon of the remaining vegetable oil in a 12-inch nonstick skillet over medium-high heat until just smoking. Add half of the apples and cook, stirring frequently, until golden brown on all sides, about 4 minutes. Transfer to the bowl with the syrupy vinegar reduction. Repeat with the remaining 1 tablespoon vegetable oil and the remaining apples. Toss the chutney gently to combine. Serve with the pork chops.

GRILL-SMOKING PORK CHOPS

To ensure that the smoke evenly surrounds the pork chops, place them bone-side down on the grill, about 2 inches apart.

VARIATION
Gas Grill–Smoked Pork Chops with Apple Chutney
If you're using a gas grill, leaving one burner on and turning off the other(s) mimics the indirect-heat method on a charcoal grill. Use wood chips instead of wood chunks and an aluminum foil pan to hold them (see the illustrations on page 10).

Follow the recipe for Grill-Smoked Pork Chops with Apple Chutney, making the following changes: Cover 2 cups wood chips with water and soak for 30 minutes, then drain. Meanwhile, make a tray out of aluminum foil following the illustrations on page 10. Place the soaked wood chips in the aluminum tray and set the tray over the burner that will remain on. Turn on all the burners to high, close the lid, and heat the grill until the chips smoke heavily, about 20 minutes. (If the chips ignite, extinguish the flames with water from a squirt bottle.) Turn off the burner(s) without the wood chips. Arrange the pork chops bone-side down (see the illustration at left) on the cooler side of grill and cover (the grill temperature should register about 275 degrees on a grill thermometer). Cook until an instant-read thermometer inserted in the side of a chop away from the bone registers 145 degrees, 30 to 45 minutes.

GRILLED PORK KEBABS
ONE MAJOR ISSUE THAT MUST BE DEALT with when making kebabs with pork is its tendency to dry out on the grill. We wanted to develop a method that delivers moist, tender meat. The other major issue is flavor. Unlike beef and lamb, pork can be fairly bland—especially the tender cuts from the loin that, because they cook quickly, we expected would work best for kebabs. We needed to figure out a way to boost the flavor.

We focused on two tender cuts—the loin and the tenderloin. As its name indicates, the tenderloin is plenty tender, but tasters felt it cooked up a bit mushy. We found the pork loin more appealing. It has a slightly fuller flavor and, while still tender, it has an appealing resistance when you bite into it. A moderate degree of chew is pleasing and works well on a kebab.

Unfortunately, as expected, the loin meat dried out easily. As we often recommend when cooking meat or poultry that tends to dry out, we tried brining the loin. In addition to brining, we tested marinating the meat in an oil-based marinade to see if it would combat dryness. Side-by-side taste tests showed that the marinated kebabs were tastier and just as moist and juicy as the brined meat. The marinade not only moistened the meat but also added richness of flavor that was lacking in the lean pork loin. The oil in the marinade lubricated the meat and improved its texture. The marinade also made a great vehicle for adding other flavors to the meat.

Whether marinated or not, pork that is overcooked will be dry. We found that pork kebabs should be cooked until barely pink at the center—an internal temperature of 145 degrees is ideal.

To cook the pork through at the center and get a good caramelization on the outside without singeing, we found that we needed to use a more moderate level of heat than with beef or lamb. A medium-hot fire worked like a charm. The outside of the pork was well marked, and the meat cooked through to the center. The meat also cooked through quickly, giving the moisture little time to escape from the meat and resulting in a tasty, moist kebab.

Because pork loin is neutral-tasting (some would say bland), with little fat, we wanted to infuse as much flavor and seasoning as possible

BUTTERFLYING PORK FOR KEBABS

Cut the boneless pork chops into 1¼-inch cubes, then cut each cube almost through at the center to butterfly before marinating.

into the meat before grilling. We decided to cube the meat and then butterfly each cube, as we did for the lamb and beef kebabs, to expose the most surface area possible to the marinade.

Charcoal-Grilled Pork Kebabs
SERVES 4 TO 6

Be sure not to overcook the pork, since this meat is prone to drying out. To make sure that the pork is done, peek into the cut that was made in the meat before skewering. It should appear opaque and just barely pink.

PORK

¼   cup extra-virgin olive oil
3   medium garlic cloves, minced or pressed through a garlic press (about 1 tablespoon)
¾   teaspoon salt
½   teaspoon ground black pepper
1¾   pounds boneless center-cut pork chops, 1¼ inches thick (4 to 5 chops), cut into 1¼-inch cubes and butterflied (see the illustration at left)

FRUIT AND VEGETABLES

1   pineapple (about 3½ pounds), peeled, cored, and cut into 1-inch chunks (see the illustrations on page 392)
1   medium red bell pepper, cored, seeded, and cut into 1-inch pieces (see page 51)
1   medium yellow bell pepper, cored, seeded, and cut into 1-inch pieces (see page 51)
2   tablespoons extra-virgin olive oil
      Salt and ground black pepper
1   large red onion, peeled and cut into ¾-inch pieces (see the illustrations on page 57)
      Lemon or lime wedges for serving (optional)

1. FOR THE PORK: Combine the oil, garlic, salt, and pepper in a gallon-size zipper-lock plastic bag or a large bowl. Add the pork cubes and toss to coat evenly. Seal the bag or cover the bowl and refrigerate until fully seasoned, at least 1 hour or up to 24 hours.

2. Light a large chimney starter filled with hardwood charcoal (about 6 quarts) and allow

to burn until all the charcoal is covered with a layer of fine gray ash. Build a single-level fire by spreading the coals over the grill bottom. Set the cooking grate in place, cover the grill with the lid, and let the grate heat up, about 5 minutes. Use a grill brush to scrape the cooking grate clean. The grill is ready when you have a medium-hot fire. (See how to gauge heat level on page 4.)

3. FOR THE FRUIT AND VEGETABLES: Meanwhile, toss the pineapple and peppers with 1½ tablespoons of the oil in a medium bowl and season with salt and pepper to taste. Brush the onion with the remaining 1½ teaspoons oil and season with salt and pepper to taste. Using eight 12-inch metal skewers, thread each skewer with a pineapple chunk, an onion stack (with 3 layers), a cube of meat (skewering as if it were an uncut cube), and one piece of each kind of pepper, and then repeat this sequence two more times. Brush any oil remaining in the bowl over the skewers.

4. Grill the kebabs, uncovered, turning each kebab one-quarter turn every 2½ minutes, until the meat is well browned, grill marked, and cooked to medium-rare, 9 to 10 minutes. Transfer the kebabs to a large serving platter and squeeze the lemon or lime wedges over the kebabs, if desired. Serve immediately.

➤ VARIATIONS

Gas-Grilled Pork Kebabs

Work quickly when opening the lid to turn the kebabs; you don't want too much heat to escape.

Follow the recipe for Charcoal-Grilled Pork Kebabs through step 1. Turn on all the burners to high, close the lid, and heat the grill until very hot, about 15 minutes. Use a grill brush to scrape the cooking grate clean. Leave all the burners on high. Proceed with the recipe as directed from step 3 and cook with the lid down.

Grilled Pork Kebabs with West Indian Flavors

Be extremely careful handling the habañero chile pepper: Wash your hands immediately after chopping, and keep your hands away from your eyes. You may want to use disposable gloves when working with these explosively hot peppers.

¼	cup juice from 4 limes
¼	cup vegetable oil
3	medium scallions, sliced thin
3	medium garlic cloves, chopped rough (about 1 tablespoon)
½	medium habañero chile, stemmed, seeded, and chopped rough
1	tablespoon plus 2 teaspoons brown sugar
1	teaspoon minced fresh thyme leaves
1	teaspoon salt
	Pinch ground allspice
1	recipe Charcoal-Grilled or Gas-Grilled Pork Kebabs, without the marinade (page 98)

1. Place the lime juice, oil, scallions, garlic, chile, brown sugar, thyme, salt, and allspice in a food processor and process until smooth.

2. Place the pork and the lime juice mixture in a large nonreactive bowl and toss to coat evenly. Cover and refrigerate until fully seasoned, at least 3 hours or up to 24 hours. Proceed with the recipe, substituting an equal amount of vegetable oil for the olive oil when coating the fruit and vegetables.

Grilled Pork Kebabs with Southeast Asian Flavors

Thai fish sauce has a more authentic Asian flavor, but if it's unavailable, soy sauce may be used in its place.

¼	cup fish sauce or soy sauce
¼	cup sugar
¼	cup vegetable oil
¼	cup juice from 4 limes
2	medium scallions, sliced thin
2	tablespoons minced fresh cilantro leaves
3	medium garlic cloves, minced or pressed through a garlic press (about 1 tablespoon)
2	teaspoons minced fresh ginger
1	recipe Charcoal-Grilled or Gas-Grilled Pork Kebabs without the marinade (page 98)

1. Combine the fish sauce, sugar, oil, lime juice, scallions, cilantro, garlic, and ginger in a large nonreactive bowl, stirring to dissolve to the sugar.

2. Add the pork and toss to coat evenly. Cover and refrigerate until fully seasoned, at least 1 hour or up to 8 hours. Proceed with the recipe, substituting an equal amount of vegetable oil for the olive oil when coating the fruit and vegetables.

TRADITIONAL PORK SAUSAGES

FRESH LINK SAUSAGES ARE NOTHING MORE than ground meat (usually pork) with seasonings and fat added for lubrication. Traditional Italian sausages—the kind sold in supermarkets in sweet and hot versions—contain a lot of fat, making flare-ups the biggest cooking challenge. We wanted the links to cook through in the center while developing a crisp exterior that was nicely browned but not charred.

We started our testing by cooking the links over a medium-hot fire. By the time the center had cooked through, the sausages were too dark. A medium fire proved easier to work with. The sausages were evenly browned and had a moist, juicy interior that was cooked through. Over a cooler fire, the links simply took longer to brown and dried out a bit in the center.

Although we had fewer problems with flare-ups when cooking the links over a medium fire, we still recommend that you keep a squirt bottle filled with water ready to douse any flames. Building a modified two-level fire, with half the grill free of coals, is also a good idea. If flames become too intense, just roll the links to the cooler part of the grill and wait until the fire is back under control to continue grilling.

Several sources we consulted suggested precooking the links, either by poaching or microwaving. We poached links for five minutes and then grilled them over a medium fire. The links were slightly waterlogged and less caramelized. Tasters deemed the results acceptable but by no means better than the sausages cooked directly over a medium fire without any precooking. Microwaving—we cooked the links in a covered dish filled with half an inch of water for

PEPPERS AND ONIONS
FOR MANY COOKS, GRILLED ONIONS and peppers are a nonnegotiable accompaniment to grilled sausages. Onions and peppers are best cooked over a medium-hot fire (see the onion recipe on page 313 and the pepper recipe on page 316.) Therefore, you should start the vegetables as soon the cooking grate is hot. By the time the vegetables are done (this takes about 10 minutes), the coals will have cooled down enough to cook the sausage. To keep the grilled vegetables warm, simply cover them with foil or throw them back on the grill for a minute or two once the sausages are nearly done.

INGREDIENTS: Coiled Sausage

Some markets fill a single casing that is several feet long and then shape the filled sausage into a coil. We find that this type of sausage is harder to cook than links for several reasons. First of all, it's harder to get the casing nicely browned, especially on the inner rings of the coil. Second, the outer rings of the coil tend to cook faster than the inner rings. If you have a choice, buy link sausage, which browns better and cooks more evenly. If you do cook coiled fresh pork sausage, we suggest that you try the following technique. It will promote (but cannot guarantee) more even cooking.

Lay the coiled sausage on a baking sheet and pull apart the rings so that there is a space of $1/2$ inch between each ring. Insert a metal skewer, parallel to the tray, through the center of all the rings. Use another large metal skewer inserted perpendicular through all the rings so that the skewers are at right angles to one another. Grill as directed, turning only once, and increasing the cooking time on charcoal or gas by several minutes.

two minutes—caused the sausages to be slightly shrunken and a bit tough when grilled, although browning was better than with links that had been poached. Here, too, the results were acceptable but no better than just throwing the sausages on the grill from the start.

We had noticed during our testing that the casing would occasionally burst or split open on the grill. Poking the sausages as they cooked prevented this but also caused the loss of juices and fat, which encouraged flare-ups and made the links a bit dry. In the end, we decided to live with the occasional link that split open. We did notice that links that were overstuffed tended to burst more often than links with a little headspace at the knotted end, so try to shop accordingly.

Charcoal-Grilled Italian Sausages
SERVES 4

Flare-ups can occur when grilling high-fat links. Don't walk away when grilling these sausages, and keep a squirt bottle filled with water on hand to douse flames. We tested this recipe using supermarket Italian sausage links that measured about 1 inch thick. If your sausages are thicker, simply leave them on the grill a few minutes longer. Serve the sausages as is or with grilled onions and peppers (see page 100) in toasted buns.

2   pounds fresh pork sausage (8 links)

1. Light a large chimney starter filled halfway with hardwood charcoal (about 3 quarts) and allow to burn until all the charcoal is covered with a layer of fine gray ash. Build a modified two-level fire by spreading the coals out over half of the grill bottom. Set the cooking grate in place. Cover the grill with the lid and let the grate heat up, about 5 minutes. Use a grill brush to scrape the cooking grate clean. Let the coals burn down to a medium fire, about 10 minutes. (See how to gauge heat level on page 4.)

2. Grill the sausages, uncovered, directly over the coals, turning them every minute or two so that all sides are evenly browned, until the casings are richly caramelized and the centers are cooked through, 9 to 11 minutes. (To check for doneness, cut one of the sausages down the center with a knife; the interior should no longer be pink. Alternatively, insert an instant-read thermometer through one end of the link; the center of the link should register about 170 degrees.) Serve immediately.

INGREDIENTS: Smoked Sausage

Italian sausages start with fresh (uncooked) pork. Pork is also used to make smoked, fully cooked sausages, such as kielbasa. The packaging on these sausages usually indicates that they are fully cooked. Grilling these sausages requires only that you brown them and heat them through.

As with fresh pork sausages, we found that smoked links are best cooked over a medium fire. Since you don't need to worry about bringing the center of the links up to temperature, simply grill smoked sausages until nicely browned. Follow the recipes on this page, shaving a minute or two off the cooking times.

> VARIATION
Gas-Grilled Italian Sausages
Be sure to stay near the grill as you cook these sausages. They are very high in fat, so flare-ups are common. Be ready to move the sausages around the grill to prevent them from scorching.

Turn on all the burners to high, close the lid, and heat the grill until very hot, about 15 minutes. Use a grill brush to scrape the cooking grate clean. Keep one burner on high and turn the other(s) to medium low. Follow the recipe for Charcoal-Grilled Sausages from step 2 and cook with the lid down.

GRILL-ROASTED PORK LOIN

A BONELESS PORK LOIN IS AN IDEAL CANDIDATE for grill-roasting. As opposed to barbecued pulled pork (see page 114), which starts out with a very fatty cut from the shoulder or leg, lean loin roasts are the best choice for relatively quick grill-roasting since they are already tender. However, unlike a thin pork tenderloin, the loin is too thick to cook over direct heat. The exterior chars long before the interior comes up to temperature.

Unlike a beef tenderloin, a pork center loin has a fairly even thickness from end to end, so there is no need to tuck up one side or the other. To make the meat perfectly even and ensure proper cooking, we found it helpful to tie the roast at regular intervals.

A pork loin can be grill-roasted much like a beef tenderloin, although it does not need an initial searing period over direct heat. (The meat stays on the grill longer because it must be cooked to a higher internal temperature, so there's plenty of time for a nice crust to form when the roast is cooked strictly over indirect heat.)

The biggest challenge when grill-roasting pork loin is keeping the meat moist. Beef tenderloin can be pulled from the grill at 125 degrees and eaten medium-rare. Pork must be cooked to a higher temperature to make the meat palatable (rare pork has an unappealing texture).

Using the kettle grill, we tried a couple of different setups for indirect cooking. We tried putting the roast in the center of the grill, with two piles of charcoal on opposite sides. This worked reasonably well, but the crust was a bit weak. Banking a full chimney of coals on one side of the grill and placing the roast over the other side worked better. To get the best crust, put the roast close to, but not directly over, the coals.

After testing various temperatures, we found that center loin roasts should be taken off the grill when the internal temperature registers 135 degrees on an instant-read thermometer. After the meat rests for 15 minutes, the temperature will rise to about 150 degrees. The meat will have a slight pink tinge, but it will be far juicier than roasts cooked to an internal temperature that is just 10 degrees higher. (However, the U.S. Department of Agriculture recommends cooking all meat to an internal temperature of 160 degrees to kill bacteria such as salmonella. If safety is your primary concern, follow the USDA's guidelines.) Because the diameter of a pork loin can vary from one roast to another, allow a window of 30 to 45 minutes to cook the roast through.

While we had little trouble getting the meat properly cooked on the grill, we found pork loin to be a bit bland and not as moist as we might have liked. Both problems stem from the fact that most of the internal fat has been bred out of the pig in recent years. We hit upon several strategies for making the meat taste better and juicier when cooked.

Like poultry, lean pork responds well to brining. A brined pork roast will cook up juicier

and more flavorful than a regular roast. Aggressive seasoning is also a good idea. A potent spice rub or a heady mixture of garlic and rosemary will improve the flavor of the meat. A rich mustard-maple glaze, applied when the roast is nearly cooked through, is another option.

Grill-Roasted Pork Loin on a Charcoal Grill

SERVES 4 TO 6

We find that the blade-end roast is a bit more flavorful than the center-cut roast, but either works well in this recipe. To make sure the roast doesn't dry out during cooking, look for one covered with a layer of fat on one side that is at least 1/8 inch thick. To use kosher salt in the brine, see page 172 for conversion information. Because the diameter of pork loins varies significantly from one to another, check the internal temperature of the loin with an instant-read thermometer at 30 minutes, then every 5 minutes or so thereafter, to make sure that your pork cooks to the optimum temperature of 135 degrees on an instant-read thermometer. Do not overcook the pork, as it dries out easily. Let the roast rest for at least 15 minutes in order for its internal temperature to rise to a safe level—about 150 degrees. Serve the pork loin as is or with a fruit salsa (pages 392–393) or Mojo Sauce (page 399). Use leftover meat for sandwiches.

6	tablespoons table salt (see note)
I	boneless blade-end or center-cut pork loin roast (2¹/₂ to 3 pounds), tied with twine at I¹/₂-inch intervals
2	(3-inch) wood chunks
2	tablespoons olive oil
I¹/₂	tablespoons coarsely ground black pepper

1. At least 8 hours before grill-roasting, dissolve the salt in 3 quarts of cold water in a large container. Place the pork loin in the saltwater mixture, cover, and refrigerate for at least 8 hours or overnight.

2. An hour before cooking, remove the roast from the brine, rinse, and pat dry; let the roast come to room temperature.

3. Meanwhile, soak the wood chunks in cold water to cover for 1 hour and drain.

4. Set the roast on a sheet of plastic wrap and rub it all over with the oil. Sprinkle with the pepper and then lift the plastic wrap and use it to press the excess seasoning into the meat (see the illustration on page 74).

5. Light a large chimney starter filled with charcoal briquettes (about 6 quarts) and allow to burn until all the charcoal is covered with a thin layer of gray ash. Build a modified two-level fire by spreading the coals out over half the grill bottom, piling them up in a mound 3 briquettes high, leaving the other half with no coals. Keep the bottom vents completely open. Lay the soaked wood chunks on top of the charcoal. Put the cooking grate in place and open the grill lid vents halfway. Let the grate heat for 5 minutes. Use a grill brush to scrape the cooking grate clean.

6. Roll the pork loin off the plastic wrap and onto the grate opposite, but close to the fire; the long side of the loin should be perpendicular to the grill rods. Cover with the lid, turning the lid so that the vents are opposite the fire to draw smoke through the grill. (The initial temperature inside the grill will be about 425 degrees.) Grill-roast the pork loin, covered, until an instant-read thermometer inserted into the thickest part of the roast registers about 135 degrees, 30 to 45 minutes, depending on the thickness of the loin.

7. Transfer the loin to a cutting board. Tent loosely with foil and let stand for about 15 minutes. (The internal temperature should rise to about 150 degrees.) Cut the roast into ½-inch-thick slices and serve.

➤ VARIATIONS
Grill-Roasted Pork Loin on a Gas Grill
When using the gas grill for this recipe, the meat must be seared over direct heat. This is because the gas grill's maximum temperature using indirect heat is about 400 degrees, which is not quite hot enough to give the loin a deep crust in the amount of time it takes to cook through over indirect heat.

Follow the recipe for Grill-Roasted Pork Loin on a Charcoal Grill, brining the roast, letting it come to room temperature, rubbing it with oil, and seasoning it with salt and pepper as directed in steps 1, 2, and 4. Meanwhile, soak 2 cups wood chips in

BARBECUE 911

Giving Meat a Rest

If you slice meat straight from the grill, say goodbye to its juicy flavor, which will have ended up in a puddle of juice on the cutting board. There's nothing you can do now, but next time take this precaution.

Allow the meat to rest before you slice it. Here's why: As meat cooks, its proteins coagulate, or uncoil and reconfigure themselves, squeezing out the moisture that was trapped inside their coiled structure. The heat from the grill drives these freed liquids toward the cooler center of the meat. As the meat returns to a lower temperature after cooking, this process partially reverses, and the protein molecules reabsorb some of the liquid. When you let the meat rest, it loses less juice when you cut into it, which in turn makes for much juicier and more tender meat. Also, when slicing meat, avoid using a fork to steady it. Tongs are more stable and less likely to puncture the meat.

a bowl of cold water for 30 minutes. Drain the chips and place them in a foil tray (see the illustrations on page 10). Place the foil tray with the soaked wood chips on top of the primary burner (see the illustration on page 9) and replace the cooking grate on the gas grill. Turn on all the burners to high and heat with the lid down until very hot, about 15 minutes. Carefully open the heated grill (there may be some smoke), use a grill brush to scrape the cooking grate clean, and place the roast, fat-side down, on the side opposite the primary burner. Cover and grill-roast until the meat is grill marked, about 4 minutes. Turn the roast over, cover again, and grill for another 4 minutes. Leave the primary burner on high, but turn off all the other burners. Cover with the lid and grill-roast until an instant-read thermometer reads 135 degrees at the thickest part of the roast, 30 to 45 minutes. (The temperature inside the grill should average between 375 and 400 degrees; adjust the lit burner as necessary). Transfer the loin to a cutting board and proceed as directed in step 7.

Grill-Roasted Pork Loin with Garlic and Rosemary

Other fresh herbs, especially sage or thyme, can be used in place of the rosemary.

Follow the recipe for Grill-Roasted Pork Loin (charcoal or gas), making the following changes: After tying the roast, use a paring knife to make several dozen shallow incisions around the surface of the roast. Stuff a few fresh rosemary needles and 1 thin sliver of garlic into each incision. (Use a total of 1 tablespoon rosemary and 3 large garlic cloves, peeled and slivered.) Oil the roast as directed. Sprinkle with salt, pepper, and an additional 2 tablespoons minced fresh rosemary, pressing the excess seasoning into the meat with the plastic wrap. Proceed as directed.

Grill-Roasted Pork Loin with Barbecue Rub and Fruit Salsa

Because of its mild flavor, pork loin benefits greatly from spice rubs. Fruit salsa adds both moisture and a sweetness that is naturally compatible with pork.

Follow the recipe for Grill-Roasted Pork Loin (charcoal or gas), replacing the pepper with 2 tablespoons Dry Rub for Barbecue (page 376). Proceed as directed, serving the sliced meat with Peach Salsa (page 393) or Mango Salsa (page 392).

Grill-Roasted Pork Loin with Maple-Mustard Glaze

This glaze can be prepared in less than a minute.

Mix ½ cup pure maple syrup, ½ cup whole-grain mustard, and 1 teaspoon soy sauce together in a medium bowl. Reserve half of the glaze in a separate bowl. Follow the recipe for Grill-Roasted Pork Loin (charcoal or gas), brushing the loin with half of the glaze about 5 minutes before it reaches the

BARBECUE 911

Roast Becomes Soggy While Resting

You've spent time and effort getting a wonderfully crusty exterior on your grilled roast and you know to let meat rest before carving, but the bottom of the roast often gets soggy while it sits, softened by the juices that accumulate in the platter. For many of us, the crispy brown crust that forms is the most sought after morsel and a soggy bottom simply won't do.

Let your roast rest on a wire rack. Elevating the meat over the puddle of juice will keep your roast crust dry and sog-free. Use this tip with any crusty roast from ham (pictured above) and pork to beef and lamb.

designated internal temperature. Slice the pork and serve it with the remaining glaze passed at the table.

TYING A PORK LOIN

Straight from the supermarket packaging, most pork loins will lie flat and cook unevenly (left). Tying the roast not only yields more attractive slices but ensures that the roast will have the same thickness from end to end so that it cooks evenly (right).

GRILLED PORK TENDERLOIN

ALTHOUGH A PORK TENDERLOIN IS TOO small to grill-roast, it is a roast and it can be grilled. In fact, grilling is a terrific way to cook pork tenderloin, a sublimely tender cut that benefits especially from the flavor boost provided by fire. But grilling a tenderloin does have its challenges. The chief problem is how to achieve a rich, golden, caramelized crust without destroying the delicate texture of the meat by overcooking it. What level of heat is best, and exactly how long should a tenderloin cook? Will grilling alone adequately flavor the meat, or should you pull another flavor-building trick from your culinary magic hat?

As the name suggests, tenderness is the tenderloin's main appeal. Anatomically speaking, the tenderloin is a small, cylindrical muscle located against the inside of the pig's rib cage. (In a human being, the equivalent muscle is in the midback area.) Because this muscle doesn't get much use, it remains very tender. Also, because the tenderloin is small, usually weighing 12 to 16 ounces, it cooks very quickly. This makes it great for fast, easy weeknight dinners.

Another reason for the tenderloin's popularity is its natural leanness. Though this is good news for diners concerned about fat intake, it can cause problems for the cook. The cut has almost no marbling, the threads of intramuscular fat that contribute a great deal of flavor to meat. Marbling also helps ensure juiciness, since the fat between the muscle fibers melts during cooking. Without that extra measure of protection, the long, slender, quick-cooking tenderloin can overcook and dry out much faster than fattier cuts.

To guard against this possibility, the tenderloin should be cooked to medium so that it will retain a slightly rosy hue in the center. The internal temperature should be 145 to 150 degrees, which is just short of the 160 degrees recommended by the U.S. Department of Agriculture. In the time it takes this cut to reach 160 degrees, the meat becomes dry, chewy, grayish white, and unappetizing. (For information on safe internal temperatures for cooking pork, see page 35.)

Before setting match to charcoal, we reviewed numerous grilled tenderloin recipes and found most to be more confusing than enlightening. Many recipes were vague, offering ambiguous directions such as "grill the tenderloins for 10 to 12 minutes, turning." Those that did provide details disagreed on almost every point, from method (direct or indirect heat, open or covered grill) to heat level (hot, medium-hot, medium, or medium-low), timing (anywhere from 12 to 60 minutes), and internal temperature (from 145 to 160 degrees).

Direct grilling over hot, medium-hot, medium, and medium-low fires constituted our first series of tests. While the meat certainly cooked over all of these fires, it didn't cook perfectly over any of them. The medium-low fire failed to produce the essential crust. Each of the other fires produced more of a crust than we wanted by the time the internal temperature of the tenderloins had reached 145 degrees. Even the medium fire, which took 16 minutes to cook the tenderloin to 145 degrees, charred the crust a little too much by the time the meat had cooked through. The more intense medium-hot and hot fires cooked the meat a little faster, which meant less time on the grill, but the crust was still overly blackened in some spots.

It was clear at this point that building a modified two-level fire and some indirect cooking on a cooler area of the grill would be necessary to allow the tenderloin to cook through without becoming charred. Cooking over a medium-hot fire seared the meat steadily and evenly in 2½ minutes on each of four sides, but the internal temperature at this point usually hovered around 125 degrees. To finish cooking, we moved the tenderloin to the cooler part of the grill and waited for the internal temperature to climb. And we waited, and waited some more. About 10 seemingly endless minutes and countless temperature checks later, the meat arrived at 145 degrees. Since this took so long, we tried speeding up the process up by covering the tenderloin with a disposable aluminum roasting pan.

We seared the meat directly over medium-hot coals for 2½ minutes per side, then moved it to a cooler part of the grill and covered it with a pan. In just 2½ minutes under the pan, the tenderloin reached an internal temperature of 145 degrees without picking up additional char on the crust.

The well-developed crust did the tenderloin a world of good, but we knew there were other flavor development methods to try, including marinating, dry and wet flavor rubs, and brining. Marinating, which required at least 2 to 3 hours and often up to 24, simply took too long, especially for an impromptu weeknight meal. Next we tried both dry and wet flavor rubs. Our tasters' favorite dry spice rubs for pork were quick to throw together and gave the tenderloin a fantastic, flavorful crust. We also had good luck with wet rubs. They are also easy to make, have strong flavors, and give the pork a lovely, crusty, glazed effect.

As good as these methods are, though, the meat still lacked seasoning at its center. So we tried brining. Since it takes close to an hour to make a rub and any side dishes, prepare the fire, and heat the cooking grate, we reasoned that the tenderloins could spend that time—but no more—sitting in a brine. We started out with a simple saltwater brine, which seasoned the meat nicely throughout. Then, picking up on the subtle sweetness we liked in the dry and wet rubs, we added some sugar to the brine. The results were spectacular. The sweetness enhanced the flavor of the pork, and the brine ensured robust flavor in every bite of every slice of meat.

REMOVING THE SILVER SKIN FROM PORK TENDERLOIN

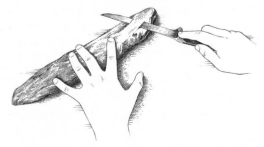

Slip a knife under the silver skin, angle it slightly upward, and use a gentle back and forth motion to remove the silver skin. Discard the skin.

Charcoal-Grilled Pork Tenderloin

SERVES 6 TO 8

Pork tenderloins are often sold two to a package, each piece usually weighing 12 to 16 ounces. The cooking times below are for two average 12-ounce tenderloins; if necessary, adjust the cooking times to suit the size of the cuts you are cooking. For maximum efficiency, while the pork is brining, make the flavor rub and then light the fire. (To use kosher salt in the brine, see page 172 for conversion information.) If you opt not to brine, bypass step 1 in the recipe below and sprinkle the tenderloins generously with salt before grilling. Use a spice rub whether or not the pork has been brined—it adds extra flavor and forms a nice crust on the meat. If rubbing tenderloins with dry spices, consider serving them with a fruit salsa (pages 392 to 393) for added moisture and flavor. You will need a disposable aluminum roasting pan for this recipe.

- **⅓ cup sugar**
- **1½ tablespoons table salt (see note)**
- **2 pork tenderloins (1½ to 2 pounds total), trimmed of silver skin (see the illustration at left)**
- **1 recipe wet rub for pork (pages 378–379) or 2 tablespoons olive oil and 1 recipe dry spice rub for pork (pages 377–378)**

1. Dissolve the sugar and salt in 1 quart of cold water in a medium bowl. Add the tenderloins, cover the bowl with plastic wrap, and refrigerate until fully seasoned, about 1 hour. Remove the tenderloins from the brine, rinse well, and dry thoroughly with paper towels. Set aside.

2. Light a large chimney starter filled with hardwood charcoal (about 6 quarts) and allow to burn until all the charcoal is covered with a layer of fine gray ash. Build a modified two-level fire by spreading the coals out over half of the grill bottom, leaving the other half with no coals. Set the cooking grate in place, cover the grill with the lid, and let the grate heat up, about 5 minutes. Use a grill brush to scrape the cooking grate clean. The grill is ready when the coals are medium-hot. (See how to gauge heat level on page 4.)

3. If using a wet spice rub, rub the tenderloins

with the mixture. If using a dry spice rub, coat the tenderloins with the oil and then rub with the spice mixture.

4. Cook the tenderloins, uncovered, over the hotter part of the grill until browned on all four sides, about 2½ minutes on each side. Move the tenderloins to the cooler part of the grill and cover with a disposable aluminum roasting pan. Grill, turning once, until an instant-read thermometer inserted into the thickest part of the tenderloin registers 145 degrees or until the meat is slightly pink at the center when cut with a paring knife, 2 to 3 minutes longer. Transfer the tenderloins to a cutting board, cover with the disposable aluminum pan, and let rest about 5 minutes. Slice crosswise into 1-inch-thick pieces and serve.

➤ VARIATION

Gas-Grilled Pork Tenderloin

A gas grill runs slightly cooler than a charcoal fire so the tenderloins can be cooked over direct heat for the entire time.

Follow step 1 of Charcoal-Grilled Pork Tenderloin. Turn on all the burners to high,

INGREDIENTS:
Enhanced or Unenhanced Pork?

Because modern pork is remarkably lean and therefore somewhat bland and prone to dryness if overcooked, a product called enhanced pork has overtaken the market. In fact, it can be hard to find unenhanced pork in some areas. Enhanced pork has been injected with a solution of water, salt, sodium phosphates, sodium lactate, potassium lactate, sodium diacetate, and varying flavor agents to bolster flavor and juiciness, with the total amount of enhancing ingredients adding 7 percent to 15 percent extra weight. Pork containing additives must be so labeled, with a list of the ingredients.

After several taste tests, we have concluded that while enhanced pork is indeed juicier and more tender than unenhanced pork, the latter has more genuine pork flavor. Some tasters picked up unappealing artificial, salty flavors in enhanced pork. Enhanced pork can also leach juices that, once reduced, will result in overly salty pan sauces. If you want to add moisture and flavor to a dry cut while maintaining complete control of flavor and salt levels, we recommend that you buy unenhanced pork and brine it at home (that is, soak the meat in a saltwater solution).

close the lid, and heat the grill until very hot, about 15 minutes. Use a grill brush to scrape the cooking grate clean. Coat the tenderloins with the spice rub of choice and grill, with the lid down, until browned on all four sides, about 3 minutes per side.

BARBECUED SPARERIBS

WHEN PEOPLE USE THE WORDS "RIBS" and "barbecue" in the same sentence, they are usually talking about pork spareribs. We wanted to know whether it is possible to produce authentic ribs (the kind you get at a barbecue joint) at home.

We started our tests by cooking one slab of ribs over indirect heat (the ribs on one side of the grill, the coals on the other), parboiling and then grilling another slab over direct heat, and cooking a third on our grill's rotisserie attachment (although reluctant to use this unusual bit of equipment, we thought, in the name of science, that we should give it a shot). All three tests were conducted over charcoal briquettes with hickory chips in a covered grill.

The ribs cooked over indirect heat were the hands-down favorite. Those cooked on the rotisserie were not nearly as tender, and the parboiled ribs retained the unappealing flavor of boiled meat. While the indirect method needed some refinement, we were convinced that it is the best way to cook ribs at home. It also comes closest to replicating the method used by barbecue-pit masters.

We tested a number of popular techniques for barbecuing ribs. Some experts swear by placing a source of moisture in the grill, most often an aluminum pan filled with water or beer. We filled a pan with water and put it next to the coals to create some steam. We couldn't taste the difference between the ribs cooked with and without the water. Next, we tested turning and basting. We found that for an even melting of the fat, it is best to turn ribs every half hour. Turning also ensures even cooking. It's important, though, to work as quickly as possible when turning the ribs to conserve heat in the grill. Basting proved to be a bust. Tomato-based sauces burned over the long cooking time, and we didn't find the basted meat any more moist than meat that wasn't basted.

Under warm weather conditions, we found the ribs were done in two to three hours. Signs of doneness include the meat starting to pull away from the ribs (if you grab one end of an individual rib bone and twist it, the bone will actually turn a bit and separate from the meat) and a distinct rosy glow on the exterior. Because the ribs do not require an extended cooking time, there is no need to replenish the coals. A fire that starts out at 350 degrees will drop to around 250 degrees at the end of two hours.

At this point in our testing, we had produced good ribs, but they were not quite as moist and tender as some restaurant ribs. We spoke with several pit masters, and they suggested wrapping the ribs when they came off the grill. We wrapped the ribs in foil and then placed them in a brown paper bag to trap any escaping steam. After an hour, we unwrapped the ribs and couldn't believe the difference. The flavor, which was great straight off the grill, was the same, but the texture was markedly improved. The meat on the wrapped ribs literally fell off the bone.

We spoke with several food scientists, who explained that as the ribs rest, the juices redistribute throughout the meat, making the ribs more moist and tender. In fact, these ribs are so flavorful and tender that we consider sauce optional.

Barbecued Spareribs on a Charcoal Grill

SERVES 4

Hickory is the traditional wood choice with ribs, but some of our tasters liked mesquite as well. If you like, serve the ribs with barbecue sauce, but they are delicious as is. You will need a fair amount of heavy-duty aluminum foil and a brown paper grocery bag for this recipe.

2 full racks spareribs (about 6 pounds total)
¾ cup Dry Rub for Barbecue (page 376)
2 (3-inch) wood chunks
2 cups barbecue sauce (see pages 386–388) (optional)

1. Rub both sides of the ribs with the dry rub and let stand at room temperature for 1 hour. (For stronger flavor, wrap the rubbed ribs in a double layer of plastic wrap and refrigerate for up to 1 day.)

2. Soak the wood chunks in cold water to cover for 1 hour and drain.

3. Meanwhile, light a large chimney starter filled a bit less than halfway with charcoal briquettes (about 2½ quarts) and allow to burn until all the charcoal is covered with a thin layer of gray ash. Build a modified two-level fire by spreading the coals over half the grill bottom, piling them in a mound 2 or 3 briquettes high, leaving the other half with no coals. Keep the bottom vents completely open. Place the wood chunks on top of the charcoal. Put the cooking grate in place, open the grill lid vents completely, and cover, turning the lid so that the vents are opposite the wood chunks or chips to draw smoke through the grill. Let the grate heat for 5 minutes, then use a grill brush to scrape the cooking grate clean.

4. Position the ribs over the cooler part of the grill. Barbecue, turning the ribs every 30 minutes, until the meat starts to pull away from the bones and has a rosy glow on the exterior, 2 to 3 hours. (The initial temperature inside the grill will be about 350 degrees; it will drop to 250 degrees after 2 hours.)

5. Remove the ribs from the grill and wrap each slab completely in aluminum foil. Put the foil-wrapped slabs in a brown paper bag and crimp the top of the bag to seal tightly. Allow to rest at room temperature for 1 hour.

6. Unwrap the ribs and brush with the barbecue sauce, if desired (or serve with the sauce on the side). Cut the ribs between the bones and serve immediately.

➤ VARIATIONS
Barbecued Spareribs on a Gas Grill
If working with a small grill, cook the second slab of ribs on the warming rack.

Follow the recipe for Barbecued Spareribs on a Charcoal Grill through step 1. Soak 2 cups wood chips for 30 minutes in cold water to cover. Place the wood chips in a foil tray (see the illustrations on page 10). Place the foil tray with the soaked wood chips on top of the primary burner (see the illustration on page 9). Turn on all the burners to high and heat with the lid down until the chips are smoking heavily, about 20 minutes. Use a grill brush to scrape the cooking grate clean. Turn the primary burner down to medium and turn off the other burner(s). Position the ribs over the cool part of the grill and close the lid. Barbecue, turning the ribs every 30 minutes, until the meat starts to pull away from the bones and has a rosy glow on the exterior, 2 to 3 hours. (The temperature inside the grill should be a constant 275 degrees; adjust the lit burner as necessary.) Proceed with the recipe from step 5, wrapping and resting the ribs as directed.

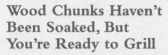

BARBECUE 911

Wood Chunks Haven't Been Soaked, But You're Ready to Grill

The spontaneous cookout can be fun, but you like to smoke your ribs over wood chunks, and they have to be soaked an hour ahead of time. Here's a way to make sure those wood chunks are always at the ready when you are motivated to fire up the grill.

Soak as many chunks as you like at the same time. Drain the chunks, seal them in a zipper-lock bag, and store them in the freezer. When you're ready to grill, place the frozen chunks on the grill. They defrost quickly and impart as much flavor as freshly soaked chunks.

Barbecued Spareribs with Hoisin, Honey, and Ginger Glaze

A combination of ground Szechuan and white peppercorns and coriander gives these ribs a complex peppery flavor. Use a spice grinder or dedicated coffee grinder to grind the peppercorns.

Mix 1½ tablespoons ground Szechuan peppercorns, 4 teaspoons ground white peppercorns, and 1½ teaspoons ground coriander together in a small bowl. Follow the recipe for Barbecued Spareribs (charcoal or gas), replacing the Dry Rub for Barbecue with the Szechuan peppercorn mixture. Grill as directed. When the meat starts to pull away from the bones, brush the ribs with ½ cup Hoisin, Honey, and Ginger Glaze (page 389) and barbecue for another 15 minutes. Wrap and let the ribs rest as directed. Serve with the remaining glaze passed separately at the table. (Omit the barbecue sauce.)

Barbecued Spareribs with Mexican Flavors

Barbecue Sauce with Mexican Flavors (page 386) is ideal to serve with this recipe, although any barbecue sauce will taste fine.

Mix 2 tablespoons chili powder, 2 tablespoons ground cumin, 2 tablespoons dried oregano, 4 teaspoons ground coriander, 1 tablespoon salt, 2 teaspoons ground cinnamon, 2 teaspoons brown sugar, 2 teaspoons ground black pepper, and ¼ teaspoon ground cloves together in a medium bowl. Follow the recipe for Barbecued Spareribs (charcoal or gas), replacing the Dry Rub for Barbecue with the chili powder mixture. Grill, wrap, and rest the ribs as directed. Serve with a barbecue sauce of your choice.

BARBECUED BABY BACK RIBS

BABY BACK RIBS FROM MOST BARBECUE joints are hard to beat. But more often than not, baby back ribs cooked at home come out tasting like dry shoe leather on a bone. Given the expense (two slabs, enough to feed four people, run about $24) and time commitment (many recipes require half a day), bad ribs are a true culinary disaster. Our goal was to produce flavorful, juicy, tender ribs that would be well worth the time, money, and effort.

Great baby back ribs start at the meat counter. We quickly learned that you have to shop carefully. Unfortunately, labeling of pork ribs can be confusing. Some slabs are labeled "baby back ribs," while other, seemingly identical ribs are labeled "loin back ribs." After a bit of detective work, we learned that the only difference is weight. Both types of ribs are taken from the upper portion of a young hog's rib cage near the backbone (see the illustration at right) and should have 11 to 13 bones. A slab (or rack) of loin back ribs generally comes from a larger pig and weighs more than 1¾ pounds; a slab of ribs weighing less is referred to as baby back ribs. (That said, most restaurants don't follow this rule, using the term "baby back" no matter what they've got because it sounds better.) During testing, we came to prefer loin back ribs because they are meatier.

There is one other shopping issue to consider. Beware of racks with bare bone peeking through the meat (along the center of the bones). This means that the butcher took off more meat than necessary, robbing you and your guests of full, meaty portions. Once you've purchased the ribs, there remains the question of whether the skin-like membrane located on the "bone side" of the ribs should be left on during cooking. One theory holds that it prevents smoke and spice from penetrating the meat, while some rib experts say that removing it robs the ribs of flavor and moisture. We found that the skin did not interfere with flavor; in fact, it helped to form a spicy, crispy crust.

It was time to start cooking. Our first step was to research the range of grilling times and techniques called for in other recipes. Most recommend a total cooking time of one hour and 30 minutes to three hours. Some use a very hot grill, while others use a moderate grill. We tested all of these recipes and found the resulting ribs to be extremely tough. High-heat cooking was particularly troublesome, as it quickly dried out the meat. Ribs cooked over moderate heat for three hours were better, but they were still too tough.

We realized that the only way to go was the classic "low-and-slow" method. We built a modified two-level fire, in which only half of the grill is covered with charcoal, thinking it would be best to smoke the ribs indirectly—on the coal-less side of the grill—to prevent overcooking. (Two full racks of ribs fit on one side of a 22-inch grill.) To add flavor, we placed soaked wood chunks on the bed of coals and then put the cooking grate in place and laid down the spice-rubbed ribs. Finally, we put the grill cover in place, with the vent holes over the ribs to help draw heat and smoke past the meat.

We found that maintaining a temperature between 275 and 300 degrees for four hours produced ribs that were tasty and tender, with meat that fell off the bone. Decent ribs could be had in less time, but they weren't as tender as those cooked for a full four hours. It's easy to tell when the ribs are ready—the meat pulls away from the bone when the ribs are gently twisted.

The problem was that the dry heat of the grill produced ribs that were not as moist as we would have liked. Our next test, then, was to cook the ribs halfway in an oven, using steam, and to finish them on the grill. These ribs were more moist, but now flavor was the problem; these ribs lacked the intense smokiness of ribs cooked entirely on the

THREE KINDS OF PORK RIBS

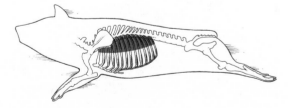

Baby back ribs (sometimes called back ribs or loin back ribs) come from the section of the rib cage closest to the backbone (the shaded area). Lean center-cut roasts and chops come from the same part of the pig, which explains why baby back ribs can be expensive and are prone to drying out when cooked. Spareribs are closer to the belly (just below the shaded area), which is also where bacon comes from. Spareribs are larger and fattier than baby back ribs. Meaty country-style ribs are cut from various parts of the pig and are usually cut into individual pieces before being packaged. Since these ribs are generally not sold in slabs, we do not barbecue them.

grill. Hoping to find another way to add moisture, we simmered the ribs in water for two hours. This robbed them of valuable pork flavor.

It then occurred to us that brining the ribs prior to cooking them might be the solution. We used our standard brining formula, which when applied to two 2-pound racks of ribs amounted to a two-hour immersion in four quarts of cold water mixed with 1 cup of table salt and 1 cup of sugar. This method produced two very highly seasoned, in fact overseasoned, racks of ribs. Why? Ribs pack much more bone per pound than other cuts of meat, and all of the meat is right there on the exterior, so the brine doesn't have very far to go. We figured that a 2-pound rack of ribs must soak up the brine much more quickly than an equal-size roast. We cut the salt, sugar, and brining time by half, and the results were better, but the meat was still too sweet. We cut the sugar by half once more, and this time the meat was both moist and perfectly seasoned.

These ribs are so good that they don't even need barbecue sauce, although you certainly could add some if you like. A quick rub with an easy-to-mix spice blend before going on the grill gives them just the right warm and savory touch.

Barbecued Baby Back Ribs on a Charcoal Grill

SERVES 4

For a potent spice flavor, brine and dry the ribs as directed, then coat them with the spice rub, wrap tightly in plastic, and refrigerate overnight before grilling. (To use kosher salt in the brine, see page 172 for conversion information.) Serve with barbecue sauce (pages 386 through 388) if you like.

¹⁄₂	**cup table salt (see note)**
¹⁄₄	**cup sugar**
2	**full racks baby back or loin back ribs (about 4 pounds total)**
¹⁄₄	**cup Dry Rub for Barbecue (page 376)**
2	**(3-inch) wood chunks**

1. Dissolve the salt and sugar in 4 quarts of cold water in a large container. Submerge the ribs in

GRILLING RIBS FOR A CROWD

A standard kettle grill has only enough space to hold two racks of ribs at a time. For those times when you're grilling for a crowd, try using a rib rack, which makes it possible to grill twice as many ribs at once.

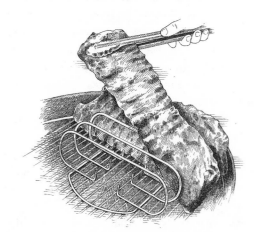

A. A rib rack rests directly on the cooking grate. Four slots neatly hold four slabs of ribs.

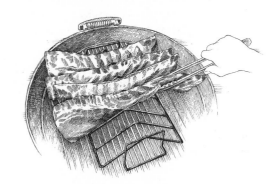

B. If you don't already own a rib rack, improvise with a fixed V-rack (used for grilling or roasting poultry). A fixed V-rack placed upside down on the cooking grate can hold up to six slabs of baby back ribs.

the brine and refrigerate 1 hour until fully seasoned. Remove the ribs from the brine and thoroughly pat dry with paper towels. Rub each side of the racks with 1 tablespoon of the dry rub and refrigerate the racks for 30 minutes.

2. While the ribs are being brined, soak the wood chunks in cold water to cover for 1 hour and drain.

3. Meanwhile, light a large chimney starter filled three quarters with charcoal briquettes (about 4½ quarts) and allow to burn until all the charcoal is covered with a layer of fine gray ash. Build a modified two-level fire by spreading the

coals into one side of the grill, piling them up in a mound 2 or 3 briquettes high, leaving the other half with no coals. Keep the bottom vents completely open. Place the wood chunks on top of the charcoal. Put the cooking grate in place, open the grill lid vents completely, and cover, turning the lid so that the vents are opposite the wood chunks to draw smoke through the grill. Let the grate heat for 5 minutes and use a grill brush to scrape the cooking grate clean.

4. Place the ribs on the cooler side of grill. Cover, positioning the lid so that the vents are opposite the wood chunks to draw smoke through the grill (the temperature inside the grill should register about 350 degrees but will soon start dropping). Cook for 2 hours, until the grill temperature drops to about 250 degrees, flipping the rib racks, switching their position so that the rack that was nearest the fire is on the outside, and turning the racks 180 degrees every 30 minutes. Add 10 fresh briquettes to the pile of coals. Continue to cook (the temperature should register 275 to 300 degrees), flipping, switching, and rotating the ribs every 30 minutes, until the meat easily pulls away from the bone, 1½ to 2 hours longer. Transfer the ribs to a cutting board, cut between the bones, and serve.

➤ VARIATION

Barbecued Baby Back Ribs on a Gas Grill
If you're using a gas grill, leaving one burner on and the other(s) off mimics the indirect heat method on a charcoal grill.

Follow the recipe for Barbecued Spareribs on a Charcoal Grill through step 1. Soak 2 cups wood chips for 30 minutes in cold water to cover, then drain. Place the wood chips in a foil tray (see the illustrations on page 10). Place the foil tray with the soaked wood chips on top of the primary burner (see the illustration on page 9). Turn on all the burners to high and heat with the lid down until the chips are smoking heavily, about 20 minutes. Use a grill brush to scrape the cooking grate clean. Turn the primary burner down to medium and turn off the other burner(s). Position the ribs over the cooler part of the grill and close the lid.

Cook, turning the ribs every 30 minutes, until the meat easily pulls away from the bones, about 4 hours. (The temperature inside the grill should be a constant 275 degrees; adjust the lit burner as necessary.) Cut the ribs as directed and serve.

BARBECUE 911

Handling Cumbersome Charcoal

Hoisting a huge bag of charcoal to pour some into a chimney starter can be messy and difficult, especially when you are dressed nicely for a summer party. Some advance preparation streamlines the process.

1. When you bring home the sack from the store, divide the briquettes into smaller bags, about 4 quarts (50 briquettes) to a bag.

2. When you need to build a fire, just cut a large hole in the bottom of one of the smaller bags. The charcoal will flow right into the chimney without making a mess or straining your back.

PULLED PORK

PULLED PORK, ALSO CALLED PULLED PIG OR sometimes just plain barbecue, is slow-cooked pork roast that is shredded, seasoned, and then served on a hamburger bun (or sliced white bread) with just enough of your favorite barbecue sauce, a couple of dill pickle chips, and a topping of coleslaw.

Our goal was to devise a procedure for cooking this classic Southern dish that was both doable and delicious. The meat should be tender, not tough, and moist but not too fatty. Most barbecue joints use a special smoker. We wanted to adapt the technique for the grill. We also set out to reduce the hands-on cooking time, which in some recipes can stretch to eight hours of constant fire tending.

There are two pork roasts commonly associated with pulled pork sandwiches: the shoulder roast and the fresh ham. In their whole state, both are massive roasts, anywhere from 14 to 20 pounds. Because they are so large, most butchers and supermarket meat departments cut both the front and back leg roasts into more manageable sizes. The part of the front leg containing the shoulder blade is usually sold as either a pork shoulder roast or a Boston butt and runs from 6 to 8 pounds. The meat from the upper portion of the front leg is marketed as a picnic roast and runs about the same size. The meat from the rear leg is often segmented into three or four separate boneless roasts called a fresh ham or boneless fresh ham roast.

For barbecue, we find it best to choose a cut of meat with a fair amount of fat, which helps keep

KEY STEPS TO PULLED PORK

1. If using a fresh ham or picnic roast (shown here), cut through the skin with the tip of a chef's knife. Slide the knife blade just under the skin and work around to loosen the skin while pulling it off with your other hand. Boston butt, or shoulder roast, does not need to be trimmed.

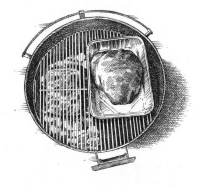

2. Set the unwrapped roast, which has been placed in a disposable aluminum pan barely larger than the meat itself, on the cooking grate opposite the coals and the wood.

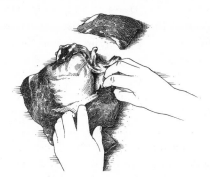

3. After cooking, as soon as the meat is cool enough to handle, remove the meat from the bones and separate the major muscle sections with your hands.

4. Remove as much fat as desired and tear the meat into thin shreds.

the meat moist and succulent during long cooking and adds considerably to the flavor. For this reason, we think the pork shoulder roast, or Boston butt, is the best choice. We found that picnic roasts and fresh hams will also produce excellent results, but they are our second choice.

To set our benchmark for quality, we first cooked a Boston butt using the traditional low-and-slow barbecue method. Using a standard 22-inch kettle grill, we lit about two quarts of coals, and cooked the roast over indirect heat (with the coals on one side of the grill and the roast on the other), adding about eight coals every half-hour or so. It took seven hours to cook a 7-pound roast. While the meat was delicious, tending a grill fire for seven hours is not something many people want to do.

In our next test we tried a much bigger initial fire, with about six quarts of charcoal. After the coals were lit, we placed the pork in a disposable aluminum pan and set it on the grate. The trick to this more intense method is not to remove the lid for any reason until the fire is out three hours later. Because you start with so many coals, it is not necessary to add charcoal during the cooking time.

Unfortunately, the high initial heat charred the exterior of the roast, while the interior was still tough and not nearly fork-tender when we took it off the grill. So we tried a combination approach: a moderate amount of charcoal (more than in the low-and-slow method but less than in the no-peek procedure), cooking the pork roast for three hours on the grill and adding more charcoal four times. We then finished the roast in a 325-degree oven for two hours. This method produced almost the same results as the traditional barbecue, but in considerably less time and with nine fewer additions of charcoal.

We find it helpful to let the finished roast rest wrapped in foil in a sealed paper bag for an hour to allow the meat to reabsorb the flavorful juices. In addition, the sealed bag produces a steaming effect that helps break down any remaining tough collagen. The result is a much more savory and succulent roast. Don't omit this step; it's the difference between good pulled pork and great pulled pork.

As with most barbecue, pork roast benefits from being rubbed with a ground spice mixture.

However, because the roast is so thick, we find it best to let the rubbed roast "marinate" in the refrigerator for at least three hours and preferably overnight. The salt in the rub is slowly absorbed by the meat and carries some of the spices with it. The result is a more evenly flavored piece of meat.

Barbecued Pulled Pork on a Charcoal Grill

SERVES 8

Pulled pork can be made with a fresh ham or picnic roast, although our preference is for Boston butt. If using a fresh ham or picnic roast, remove the skin (see illustration 1 on page 113). Preparing pulled pork requires little effort but lots of time. Plan on 9 hours from start to finish: 3 hours with the spice rub, 3 hours on the grill, 2 hours in the oven, and 1 hour to rest. Hickory is the traditional choice with pork, although mesquite can be used if desired. Serve the pulled pork on plain white bread or warmed buns with the classic accompaniments of dill pickle chips and coleslaw. You will need a disposable aluminum roasting pan that measures about 10 inches by 8 inches as well as heavy-duty aluminum foil and a brown paper grocery bag.

1	bone-in pork roast, preferably Boston butt (6 to 8 pounds)
3/4	cup Dry Rub for Barbecue (page 376)
4	(3-inch) wood chunks
2	cups barbecue sauce (see pages 386–388)

1. Massage the dry rub into the meat. Wrap the meat tightly in a double layer of plastic wrap and refrigerate for at least 3 hours. (For stronger flavor, the roast can be refrigerated for up to 3 days.)

2. At least 1 hour prior to cooking, remove the roast from the refrigerator, unwrap, and let it come to room temperature. Soak the wood chunks in cold water to cover for 1 hour and drain.

3. Meanwhile, light a large chimney starter filled a bit less than halfway with charcoal briquettes (about 2½ quarts) and allow to burn until all the charcoal is covered with a layer of fine gray ash. Build a modified two-level fire by spreading the coals onto one side of the grill, piling them up in a mound 2 or 3 briquettes high, leaving the other half with no coals. Open the bottom vents

BARBECUE 911

Dealing with Messy Ashes

You want to get a fire going but the grill is clogged with old ashes and bits of half-burned charcoal. Guests are arriving any minute and you don't want to make a mess while cleaning out the grill. Here's how to create your own ash scoop to make this job less messy.

1. Cut off a bottom corner of a plastic milk jug to form a scoop.

2. The plastic conforms to the curve of the grill bottom, which makes it easy to collect ashes with a single sweep.

completely. Place the wood chunks on top of the charcoal.

4. Set the unwrapped roast in the disposable aluminum pan and place it on the grate opposite the fire (see illustration 2 on page 113). Open the grill lid vents three quarters of the way and cover, turning the lid so that the vents are opposite the wood chunks to draw smoke through the grill. Cook, adding about 8 briquettes every hour or so to maintain an average temperature of 275 degrees, for 3 hours.

5. Adjust an oven rack to the middle position and heat the oven to 325 degrees. Wrap the pan holding the roast with heavy-duty foil to cover

completely. Place the pan in the oven and cook until the meat is fork-tender, about 2 hours.

6. Slide the foil-wrapped pan with the roast into a brown paper bag. Crimp the end shut. Let the roast rest for 1 hour.

7. Transfer the roast to a cutting board and unwrap. When cool enough to handle, "pull" the pork by separating the roast into muscle sections, removing the fat, if desired, and tearing the meat into thin shreds with your fingers (see illustrations 3 and 4). Place the shredded meat in a large bowl. Toss with 1 cup of the barbecue sauce, adding more to taste. Serve, passing the remaining sauce separately.

➤ VARIATIONS

Barbecued Pulled Pork on a Gas Grill

Follow the recipe for Barbecued Pulled Pork on a Charcoal Grill through step 2. Soak 4 cups wood chips for 30 minutes in cold water to cover, then drain. Place the wood chips in a foil tray (see the illustrations on page 10). Place the foil tray with the soaked wood chips on top of the primary burner (see the illustration on page 9). Turn on all the burners to high and heat with the lid down until the chips are smoking heavily, about 20 minutes. Turn the primary burner down to medium and turn off the other burner(s). Set the unwrapped roast in the disposable pan, position the pan over the cooler part of the grill, and close the lid. Barbecue for 3 hours. (The temperature inside the grill should be a constant 275 degrees; adjust the lit burner as necessary.) Proceed as directed from step 5 of the recipe.

Cuban-Style Barbecued Pulled Pork with Mojo Sauce

Mojo sauce (page 399) is a citrus-flavored Cuban sauce served with pork. Rice with black beans is an excellent accompaniment to this dish. The use of wood for flavoring is not traditional in this dish and can be omitted if you prefer to keep the emphasis on the pork and seasonings.

Mix 9 medium garlic cloves, minced or pressed through a garlic press (about 3 tablespoons), 3 tablespoons extra-virgin olive oil, 1 tablespoon ground cumin, 1 tablespoon dried oregano, 1 tablespoon salt, 2 teaspoons brown sugar, and 1½ teaspoons ground black pepper together in a small bowl. Follow the recipe for Barbecued Pulled Pork (charcoal or gas), replacing the Dry Rub for Barbecue with the garlic mixture. Proceed with the recipe, omitting the barbecue sauce. To serve, pass Mojo Sauce (page 399) separately with the pulled pork.

EQUIPMENT: Chef's Knives

A good chef's knife is probably the most useful tool any cook owns. So what separates a good knife from an inferior one? To understand the answer to this question, it helps to know something about how knives are constructed.

The first pieces of cutlery were made about 4,000 years ago with the discovery that iron ore could be melted and shaped into tools. The creation of steel, which is 80 percent iron and 20 percent other elements, led to the development of carbon steel knives (the standard for 3,000 years). Although this kind of steel takes and holds an edge easily, it also stains and rusts. Something as simple as cutting an acidic tomato or living in the salt air of the seacoast can corrode carbon steel.

Today, new alloys have given cooks better options. Stainless steel, made with at least 4 percent chromium and/or nickel, will never rust. Used for many cheap knives, stainless steel is also very difficult to sharpen. The compromise between durable but dull stainless steel and sharp but corrodible carbon steel is a material called high-carbon stainless steel. Used by most knife manufacturers, this blend combines durability and sharpness.

Until recently, all knives were hot drop forged—that is, the steel was heated to 2000°F, dropped into a mold, given four or five shots with a hammer, and then tempered (cooled and heated several times to build strength). This process is labor intensive (many steps must be done by hand), which explains why many chef's knives cost almost $100.

A second manufacturing process feeds long sheets of steel through a press that punches out knife after knife, much like a cookie cutter slicing through dough. Called stamped blades, these knives require some hand finishing but are much cheaper to produce because a machine does most of the work.

While experts have long argued that forged knives are better than stamped ones, our testing did not fully support this position. We liked some forged knives and did not like others. Likewise, we liked some stamped knives and did not like others. The weight and shape of the handle (it must be comfortable to hold and substantial but not too heavy), the ability of the blade to take an edge, and the shape of the blade (we like a slightly curved blade, which is better suited to the rocking motion often used to mince herbs or garlic than a straight blade) are all key factors in choosing a knife.

When shopping, pick up the knife and see how it feels in your hand. Is it easy to grip? Does the weight seem properly distributed between the handle and blade? In our testing, we liked knives made by Henckels and Wüsthof. An inexpensive knife by Forschner, with a stamped blade, also scored well.

Buying a good knife is only half the challenge. You must keep the edge sharp. To that end, we recommend buying an electric knife sharpener. Steels are best for modest corrections, but all knives will require more substantial sharpening at least several times a year, if not more often if you cook a lot. Stones are difficult to use because they require that you maintain a perfect 20-degree angle between the stone and blade. An electric knife sharpener (we like models made by Chef's Choice) takes the guesswork out of sharpening and allows you to keep edges sharp and effective.

THE BEST CHEF'S KNIVES
The Henckels Four Star (top) and Wüsthof-Trident Grand Prix (center) are top choices, but expect to spend about $80 for one of these knives. The Forschner (Victorinox) Fibrox (bottom) is lighter but still solid and costs just $30.

GRILLED TUSCAN STEAK WITH OLIVE OIL AND LEMON (*BISTECCA ALLA FIORENTINA*) **PAGE 40**

GRILLED FILET MIGNON WITH ASPARAGUS **PAGES 41 AND 296**

118

TEXAS-STYLE BARBECUED BEEF RIBS **PAGE 80**

STEAK TIPS WITH SOUTHWESTERN MARINADE **PAGE 47**

GRILLED HAMBURGER **PAGE 63**

GRILLED BEEF KEBABS **PAGE 58**

CLASSIC FAJITAS AND GRILLED CORN **PAGES 51 AND 299**

123

GRILLED VEAL CHOPS ON A BED OF ARUGULA **PAGE 77**

124

BARBECUED BABY BACK RIBS **PAGE 111**

GRILLED PORK TENDERLOIN **PAGE 106**

GRILLED PORK CHOP **PAGE 93**

BARBECUED PULLED PORK **PAGE 114**

GRILLED SHISH KEBAB **PAGE 141**

GRILL-ROASTED TURKEY **PAGE 201**

GRILLED TURKEY BURGER WITH ISRAELI TOMATO AND CUCUMBER SALAD **PAGES 198 AND 352**

131

GRILLED QUAIL **PAGE 216**

132

3

LAMB

LAMB

CHARCOAL-GRILLED SHOULDER LAMB CHOPS 136
    Gas-Grilled Shoulder Lamb Chops
    Grilled Shoulder Lamb Chops with Garlic-Rosemary Marinade
    Grilled Shoulder Lamb Chops with Soy-Shallot Marinade
    Spiced Grilled Shoulder Lamb Chops with Quick Onion and Parsley Relish
    Grilled Shoulder Lamb Chops with Near East Red Pepper Paste

CHARCOAL-GRILLED LOIN OR RIB LAMB CHOPS 138
    Gas-Grilled Loin or Rib Lamb Chops
    Grilled Loin or Rib Lamb Chops with Mediterranean Herb and Garlic Paste
    Grilled Loin or Rib Lamb Chops and Zucchini with Mint Sauce

CHARCOAL-GRILLED SHISH KEBAB 141
    Gas-Grilled Shish Kebab
    Lamb and Fig Kebabs with Garlic-Parsley Marinade

MARINADES FOR SHISH KEBAB 142
    Garlic and Cilantro Marinade with Garam Masala
    Warm-Spiced Parsley Marinade with Ginger
    Sweet Curry Marinade with Buttermilk
    Rosemary-Mint Marinade with Garlic and Lemon

CHARCOAL-GRILLED RACK OF LAMB. 145
    Gas-Grilled Rack of Lamb
    Grilled Rack of Lamb with Garlic and Herbs
    Grilled Rack of Lamb with Turkish Spice Rub

CHARCOAL-GRILLED BUTTERFLIED LEG OF LAMB 148
    Gas-Grilled Butterflied Leg of Lamb

MARINADES FOR GRILLED LEG OF LAMB. 150
    Tandoori Marinade
    Lemon Marinade with Greek Flavorings
    Garlic and Rosemary Marinade
    Soy-Honey Marinade with Thyme

CLASSIC MINT SAUCE. 152

LIKE BEEF, LAMB HAS A RICH RED COLOR, but the meat is generally stronger-tasting. This is because the muscle itself is quite tasty and because lamb fat has a particularly strong flavor.

Most lamb sold in the supermarket has been slaughtered when 6 to 12 months old. (When the animal is slaughtered past the first year, the meat

~~~~~~

INGREDIENTS: Lamb

Lamb is a hard sell in the United States. According to the American Meat Institute, we eat less than 1½ pounds of lamb per person each year. Lamb gets a much more favorable reception abroad. We wondered why. Is imported grass-fed lamb that much more tender and less "lamby" than domestic grain-fed lamb?

To find out, we held a blind taste test of imported lamb legs from New Zealand, Australia, and Iceland, along with domestic lamb. Our tasters included both lamb enthusiasts and the lamb-averse.

Tasters didn't find any of the roasts "gamey" or overly tough, and they found all of them to be juicy. The Australian lamb had the strongest lamb flavor. The meat was chewy and dark, indicating older lamb, a trait not offensive to the lamb lovers in our group. The New Zealand lamb had a bold lamb flavor, but some tasters disliked the texture, finding it "stringy" and "more like ham." The domestic lamb was milder in taste; many thought it more reminiscent of roast beef than lamb. Tasters thought that the domestic lamb's texture was a bit chewy, but not unpleasantly so. The lamb from Iceland was the smallest lamb by far. It also had the most delicate flavor—too delicate for those tasters who enjoyed a stronger lamb flavor (one referred to the Icelandic lamb as "lamb lite"). All found the texture of the Icelandic lamb to be the most tender. As one taster noted, it "cut like butter."

~~~~~~

THE FIVE PRIMAL CUTS OF LAMB

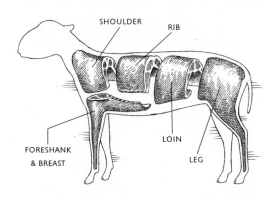

must be labeled mutton.) Generally, younger lamb has a milder flavor that most people prefer. The only indication of slaughter age at the supermarket is size. A whole leg of lamb weighing 9 pounds is likely to have come from an older animal than a whole leg weighing just 6 pounds. Lamb is initially divided into five primal (or major) cuts. With the exception of cuts from the loin, lamb tends to be quite chewy. This is exacerbated when lamb is overcooked to the 'gray stage,' where mint jelly, usually intended as a pleasant flavor counterbalance to lamb, becomes more of a lubricant to aid in the swallowing of the tough meat. For the best balance of moisture, flavor, and texture, we prefer to cook lamb to the same doneness temperatures as we do beef, which is 130 degrees for medium rare and 140 degrees for medium.

SHOULDER This area extends from the neck through the fourth rib. Meat from this area is flavorful, although it contains a fair amount of connective tissue and can be tough. Chops, roasts, and boneless stew meat all come from the shoulder.

RIB The rib area is directly behind the shoulder and extends from the fifth to the twelfth rib. The rack (all eight ribs from this section) is cut from the rib. When cut into individual chops, the meat is called rib chops. Meat from this area has a fine, tender grain and a mild flavor.

LOIN The loin extends from the last rib down to the hip area. The loin chop is the most familiar cut from this part of the lamb. Like the rib chop, it is tender and has a mild, sweet flavor.

LEG The leg area runs from the hip down to the hoof. It may be sold whole or broken into smaller roasts and shanks (one comes from each hind leg). These roasts may be sold with the bones in, or they may be butterflied and sold boneless.

FORESHANK & BREAST The final primal cut is from the underside of the animal and is called the foreshank and breast. This area includes the two front legs (each yields a shank) as well as the breast, which is rarely sold in supermarkets.

INGREDIENTS: Shoulder Lamb Chops

Lamb shoulder is sliced into two different cuts, blade and round-bone chops. You'll find them sold in a range of thicknesses (from about half an inch to more than an inch thick), depending on who's doing the butchering. (In our experience, supermarkets tend to cut them thinner, while independent butchers cut them thicker.) Blade chops are roughly rectangular in shape, and some are thickly striated with fat. Each blade chop includes a piece of the chine bone (the backbone of the animal) and a thin piece of the blade bone (the shoulder blade of the animal).

Round-bone chops, also called arm chops, are more oval in shape and as a rule are substantially leaner than blade chops. Each contains a round cross section of the arm bone so that the chop looks a bit like a mini ham steak. In addition to the arm bone, there's also a tiny line of riblets on the side of each chop.

As to which chop is better, we didn't find any difference in taste or texture between the two types except that the blade chops generally have more fat. We grill both blade and round-bone chops. We like the way the fat in the blade chop melts on the grill, flavoring and moistening the meat, and we love the grilled riblets from the round-bone chop.

THE BLADE CHOP

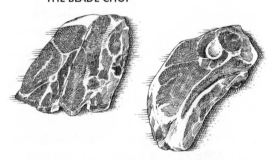

ROUND-BONE CHOP

The blade chop (left) is roughly rectangular in shape and contains a piece of the chine bone and a thin piece of the blade bone. The arm, or round-bone, chop (right) is leaner and contains a round cross section of the arm bone. Both are great on the grill.

GRILLED LAMB CHOPS

LAMB CHOPS DON'T HAVE TO BE A RARE and expensive treat. True, loin and rib chops (together, the eight rib chops form the cut known as rack of lamb) can cost upward of $15 a pound. But we love the meaty flavor and chewy (but not tough) texture of shoulder chops. We also like the

fact that they cost only about $4 per pound.

In a side-by-side taste test, we grilled rib, loin, and shoulder chops to medium-rare and let them stand about 5 minutes before tasting. The rib chop was the most refined of the three, with a mild, almost sweet flavor and tender texture. The loin chop had a slightly stronger flavor, and the texture was a bit firmer (but not chewier) than the rib chop. The shoulder chop had a distinctly gutsier flavor than the other two. While it was not at all tough, it was chewier. If you like the flavor of lamb (and we do) and are trying to keep within a budget, then try shoulder chops.

We also tried a second test in which we grilled the chops to medium, a stage at which many people prefer lamb. Both the rib and loin chops were dry and less flavorful and juicy than they were at medium-rare. But the shoulder chop held its own in both taste and texture when cooked to medium, displaying another advantage besides price.

Shoulder chops can range in thickness from half an inch to an inch. We prefer the thicker chops; you should ask your butcher to cut them for you if necessary. Loin and rib chops are usually thicker, often close to one and a half inches.

In our testing, we found that all of these chops should be cooked over a two-level fire to allow the interior to cook sufficiently without charring the exterior. A two-level fire also makes sense because lamb tends to flame; the cooler part of the grill is the perfect place to move the chops to let the flames die down. Even when cooking thinner chops, we found that the flames often became too intense on a single-level fire. A squirt bottle filled with water can be a handy item to have near the grill; use it to douse any flare-ups that may occur.

Charcoal-Grilled Shoulder Lamb Chops
SERVES 4

Try to get shoulder lamb chops that are at least ¾ inch thick, since they are less likely to overcook. If you can only find chops that are ½ inch thick, reduce the cooking time over the medium-low fire by about 30 seconds on each side. For information about the different kinds of shoulder chops, see the box at left.

4   shoulder lamb chops (blade or round bone),
    ¾ to 1 inch thick
2   tablespoons extra-virgin olive oil
    Salt and ground black pepper

1. Light a large chimney starter filled with hardwood charcoal (about 6 quarts) and allow to burn until all the charcoal is covered with a layer of fine gray ash. Build a two-level fire by stacking most of the coals on one side of the grill and arranging the remaining coals in a single layer on the other side of the grill. Set the cooking grate in place, cover the grill with the lid, and let the grate heat up, about 5 minutes. Use a grill brush to scrape the cooking grate clean. The grill is ready when the pile of coals is medium-hot and the single layer of coals is medium-low. (See how to gauge heat level on page 4.)

2. Rub the chops with the oil and sprinkle with salt and pepper to taste.

3. Grill the chops, uncovered, over the hotter part of the grill, turning them once, until well browned, about 4 minutes. (If the chops start to flame, drag them to the cooler part of the grill and/or extinguish the flames with a squirt bottle filled with water.) Move the chops to the cooler part of the grill and continue grilling, turning once, to the desired doneness, about 5 minutes for rare (about 120 degrees on an instant-read thermometer), about 7 minutes for medium (about 130 degrees), or about 9 minutes for well-done (140 to 150 degrees).

4. Remove the chops from the grill and let rest for 5 minutes. Serve immediately.

➤ VARIATIONS

Gas-Grilled Shoulder Lamb Chops

To make sure the lamb chops aren't flaming under the grill cover, watch for any substantial amount of smoke coming through the vents. This indicates that flare-ups are occurring and need to be extinguished.

Turn on all the burners to high, close the lid, and heat the grill until very hot, about 15 minutes. Use a grill brush to scrape the cooking grate clean. Leave one burner on high and turn the other burner(s) to medium. Follow the recipe for Charcoal-Grilled Shoulder Lamb Chops from step 2 and cook with the lid down.

Grilled Shoulder Lamb Chops with Garlic-Rosemary Marinade

Garlic and rosemary are classic accompaniments with lamb.

Combine 2 tablespoons extra-virgin olive oil, 2 large garlic cloves, minced or pressed through a garlic press, 1 tablespoon minced fresh rosemary, and a pinch of cayenne pepper in a small bowl. Follow the recipe for Charcoal-Grilled or Gas-Grilled Lamb Chops, rubbing the chops with the garlic-rosemary marinade instead of the olive oil. Marinate, covered, in the refrigerator for at least 20 minutes or up to 1 day. Sprinkle the chops with salt and pepper to taste before grilling, then grill as directed.

Grilled Shoulder Lamb Chops with Soy-Shallot Marinade

Soy sauce works well with the gutsy flavor of shoulder chops.

Combine ¼ cup minced shallots or scallions, 3 tablespoons juice from 2 lemons, 2 tablespoons each minced fresh thyme and parsley leaves, 2 tablespoons canola oil, 2 tablespoons soy sauce, and ground black pepper to taste in a shallow dish. Follow the recipe for Charcoal-Grilled or Gas-Grilled Lamb Chops, omitting step 2 and marinating the chops in the soy marinade, covered, in the refrigerator for at least 20 minutes or up to 1 hour. (Do not marinate longer.)

Spiced Grilled Shoulder Lamb Chops with Quick Onion and Parsley Relish

You can prepare the relish a day ahead of time if you like and store it in the refrigerator. The combination of onion and parsley makes a cool and refreshing foil for savory lamb chops.

Prepare Quick Onion and Parsley Relish (page 394). Follow the recipe for Charcoal-Grilled or Gas-Grilled Lamb Chops, rubbing each chop with the oil as directed and then with 1½ teaspoons Simple Spice Rub for Beef or Lamb (page 377). Sprinkle with salt to taste but omit the pepper. Grill as directed and serve with the relish.

Grilled Shoulder Lamb Chops with Near East Red Pepper Paste

This paste of fresh peppers and exotic spices lends sweet spiciness and deep color to grilled lamb.

3	tablespoons extra-virgin olive oil
$1/2$	medium red bell pepper, cored, seeded, and roughly chopped
$1/2$	medium serrano or jalapeño chile, seeds and ribs removed, then minced
2	teaspoons juice from I lemon
I	medium garlic clove, minced or pressed through a garlic press (about I teaspoon)
$1/2$	teaspoon ground cumin
$1/2$	teaspoon dried summer savory
$1/2$	teaspoon dried mint or $1^{1}/2$ teaspoons chopped fresh mint leaves
$1/4$	teaspoon ground cinnamon
I	recipe Charcoal-Grilled or Gas-Grilled Shoulder Lamb Chops (page 136)

1. Heat 1 tablespoon of the oil in a small skillet over medium-high heat until shimmering. Add the bell pepper and chile and sauté until they start

---

RIB AND LOIN LAMB CHOPS

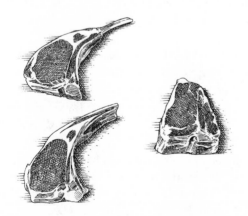

A rib chop (bottom left) often contains a lot of fat on the bone. Have your butcher french the chop (top left) by scraping away this fat. Like a T-bone steak, a loin chop (right) has meat on both sides of the bone. The small piece of meat on the right side of the bone on this chop is very tender and fine-grained. The larger piece of meat on the other side of the bone is chewier. The rib chop has a slightly milder, more tender texture than a loin chop, which is a bit firmer (but not chewy). We found that both rib and loin chops do well on the grill.

to soften, about 2 minutes. Reduce the heat to medium-low and continue to cook until thoroughly softened, about 5 minutes.

2. Transfer the mixture to a food processor. Add the lemon juice, garlic, cumin, summer savory, mint, cinnamon, and the remaining 2 tablespoons oil and process until almost smooth (there should still be some chunky pieces of pepper).

3. Follow the recipe for Charcoal-Grilled or Gas-Grilled Shoulder Lamb Chops, rubbing the chops with the red pepper paste instead of the oil and marinating them, covered, in the refrigerator for at least 20 minutes or up to 1 day. Sprinkle the chops with the salt and pepper to taste before grilling.

Charcoal-Grilled Loin or Rib Lamb Chops

SERVES 4

While loin and rib chops are especially tender cuts of lamb, they tend to dry out if cooked past medium since they have less intramuscular fat than shoulder chops. To make these chops worth their high price, keep an eye on the grill to make sure the meat does not overcook. These chops are smaller than shoulder chops, so you will need two for each serving. Their flavor is more delicate and refined, so season lightly with just salt and pepper, or perhaps herbs (as in the variation that follows). Aggressive spices can be overpowering with these rarefied chops.

8	loin or rib lamb chops, $1^{1}/4$ to $1^{1}/2$ inches thick
2	tablespoons extra-virgin olive oil
	Salt and ground black pepper

1. Light a large chimney starter filled with hardwood charcoal (about 6 quarts) and allow to burn until all the charcoal is covered with a layer of fine gray ash. Build a two-level fire by stacking most of the coals on one side of the grill and arranging the remaining coals in a single layer on the other side of the grill. Set the cooking grate in place, cover the grill with the lid, and let the grate heat up, about 5 minutes. Use a grill brush to scrape the cooking grate clean. The grill is ready when the pile of coals is medium-hot and the single layer of coals is medium-low. (See how to gauge heat level on page 4.)

2. Rub the chops with the oil and sprinkle with salt and pepper to taste.

3. Grill the chops, uncovered, over the hotter part of the grill, turning them once, until well browned, about 4 minutes. (If the chops start to flame, drag them to the cooler part of the grill for a moment and/or extinguish the flames with a squirt bottle filled with water.) Move the chops to the cooler part of the grill and continue grilling, turning once, to the desired doneness, about 6 minutes for rare (about 120 degrees on an instant-read thermometer) or about 8 minutes for medium (about 130 degrees).

4. Remove the chops from the grill and let rest for 5 minutes. Serve immediately.

➤ VARIATIONS

Gas-Grilled Loin or Rib Lamb Chops
Turn on all the burners to high, close the lid, and heat the grill until very hot, about 15 minutes. Use a grill brush to scrape the cooking grate clean. Leave one burner on high and turn the other burner(s) to medium-low. Follow the recipe for Charcoal-Grilled Loin or Rib Lamb Chops from step 2 and cook with the lid down.

Grilled Loin or Rib Lamb Chops with Mediterranean Herb and Garlic Paste
The delicate flavor of loin or rib lamb chops is enhanced—not overwhelmed—by this spirited Mediterranean-inspired paste.

Combine ¼ cup extra-virgin olive oil, 3 medium garlic cloves, minced or pressed through a garlic press (about 1 tablespoon), 1 tablespoon chopped fresh parsley leaves, and 2 teaspoons each chopped fresh sage leaves, thyme leaves, rosemary, and oregano leaves in a small bowl. Follow the recipe for Charcoal-Grilled or Gas-Grilled Loin or Rib Lamb Chops, rubbing the chops with the herb paste instead of the oil. Marinate in the refrigerator, covered, for at least 20 minutes or up to 1 day. Sprinkle with the salt and pepper to taste before grilling.

Grilled Loin or Rib Lamb Chops and Zucchini with Mint Sauce
For bold mint flavor, we found it best to have a small amount of a concentrated sauce rather than a thin, less

intense but voluminous sauce. To make this a meal, tasters agreed zucchini was the vegetable of choice. Its mild flavor let the lamb and mint take center stage. Eggplant was a close second in our testing and can be used if you prefer; simply replace the zucchini with 3 small eggplants sliced the same way.

½ cup plus 2 tablespoons extra-virgin olive oil
½ cup minced fresh mint leaves
2 tablespoons minced fresh chives
1 small shallot, minced (about 2 tablespoons)
2 tablespoons juice from 1 lemon
   Salt and ground black pepper
3 medium zucchini (1¼ to 1½ pounds), trimmed and sliced lengthwise (see the illustrations on page 325)
1 recipe Charcoal-Grilled or Gas-Grilled Loin or Rib Lamb Chops

Follow the recipe for Charcoal-Grilled or Gas-Grilled Loin or Rib Lamb Chops. While the grill is heating up, stir together ½ cup of the oil, the mint, chives, shallot, lemon juice, and salt and pepper to taste in a medium bowl. Lay the zucchini on a baking sheet and brush both sides of each slice with the remaining 2 tablespoons oil and season with salt and pepper to taste. Once the chops are removed from the grill, place the zucchini over the hotter side of the grill. Grill, turning once, until streaked with dark grill marks, 8 to 10 minutes. Transfer the zucchini to the platter with the lamb. Spoon the mint sauce over the lamb and zucchini and serve immediately.

GRILLED SHISH KEBAB

SHISH KEBAB, SKEWERS OF LAMB AND vegetables, is perhaps the greatest "barbecue" dish from Turkey and the Middle East. When done right, the lamb is well browned but not overcooked and the vegetables are crisp and tender. Everything is perfumed with the flavor of smoke.

Shish kebab's components cook at different rates—either the vegetables are still raw when the meat is cooked perfectly to medium-rare, or the lamb is long overdone by the time the vegetables have been cooked properly. Our efforts to resolve this dilemma led us to explore which cut of lamb and which vegetables serve the kebab best. Getting the grill temperature just right was another challenge. Too hot, and the kebabs charred on the outside without being fully cooked; too cool, and they cooked without the benefit of flavorful browning.

Lamb can be expensive, so we searched for a cut that would give us tender, flavorful kebabs without breaking the bank. We immediately ruled out high-end cuts like loin and rib chops, which fetch upward of $15 per pound. These chops are just too pricey to cut up for a skewer, and they yield little meat. We had better luck with sirloin and shoulder chops, which are meatier and far more reasonable at around $4 per pound. Each of these, however, requires cutting the meat off the bone before trimming and cubing. The best cut turned out to be the shank end of a boneless leg of lamb. It requires little trimming, yields the perfect amount of meat for four to six people, and can be purchased for about $7 per pound.

Lamb has a supple, chewy texture and yields the best results when cut into fairly small pieces. We found 1-inch pieces of lamb to be the optimal size for kebabs. With the meat cut and ready to go, we could now focus on the vegetables.

Many vegetables don't cook through by the time the lamb reaches the right temperature. We tried precooking the vegetables, but they turned slimy and were difficult to skewer. We thought about cooking them separately alongside the lamb on the grill, but that's just not shish kebab. Some vegetables, such as cherry tomatoes, initially looked great on the skewer but had a hard time staying put once cooked.

As we worked our way through various vegetables, we came up with two that work well within the constraints of this particular cooking method. Red onions and bell peppers have a similar texture and cook through at about the same rate. When cut fairly small, these two vegetables were the perfect accompaniments to the lamb, adding flavor and color to the kebab without demanding any special attention.

What these handsome kebabs needed now was seasoning, so we tried a variety of spices, dry rubs, and marinades on the meat. Spice rubs tasted good but left the surface of the meat chalky and dry; kebabs just aren't on the fire long enough for their juices to mix with the dried spices and form a glaze. Marinades, on the other hand, added a layer of moisture that kept the kebabs from drying out on the grill while their flavors penetrated the meat. Two hours in the marinade was sufficient time to achieve some flavor, but it took a good eight hours for these flavors to really sink in. Marinating for 12 hours, or overnight, was even better.

PREPARING LAMB FOR KEBABS

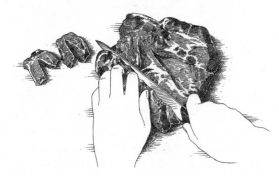

1. Cut the meat into 1¼-inch cubes, then cut each cube almost through at the center to butterfly the cube.

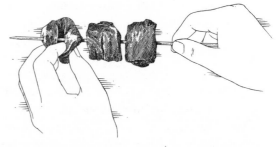

2. For areas of the boned leg of lamb that are thinner than 1¼ inches, cut the lamb into pieces that are approximately 2½ by 1¼-inch rectangles. Skewer thinner pieces of meat by folding the pieces in half and skewering them through the center to imitate a 1¼-inch cube.

Charcoal-Grilled Shish Kebab

SERVES 6

Shish kebab benefits from a long marinating time, up to 24 hours, so plan ahead.

 1   recipe marinade (recipes follow)
2¼ pounds boneless leg of lamb (shank end),
     trimmed of fat and silver skin and prepared
     according to the illustrations on page 140
 1   large red onion, cut into ¾-inch pieces (see the
     illustration on page 57)
 3   medium bell peppers, I red, I yellow, and
     I orange, cored, seeded, and cut into 1-inch
     pieces (see the illustrations on page 51)
     Lemon or lime wedges for serving (optional)

1. Toss the marinade and lamb in a gallon-size zipper-lock plastic bag or large nonreactive bowl. Seal the bag or cover the bowl and refrigerate until fully seasoned, at least 2 hours and up to 24 hours.

2. Light a large chimney starter filled with hardwood charcoal (about 6 quarts) and allow to burn until all the charcoal is covered with a layer of fine gray ash. Build a modified two-level fire by spreading the coals over just three quarters of the grill bottom. Set the cooking grate in place, cover the grill with the lid, and let the grate heat up, about 5 minutes. Use a grill brush to scrape the cooking grate clean. The grill is ready when you have a hot fire. (See how to gauge heat level on page 4.)

3. Meanwhile, using twelve 12-inch metal skewers, thread each skewer with one piece of meat, an onion stack (with three layers), and 2 pieces of pepper (of different colors) and then repeat this sequence two more times. Place a piece of meat on the end of each skewer.

4. Grill the kebabs, uncovered, until the meat is well browned all over, grill-marked, and cooked to medium-rare, about 7 minutes, or medium, about 8 minutes, turning each kebab one-quarter turn every 1¾ minutes to brown all sides. Transfer the kebabs to a serving platter, squeeze the lemon or lime wedges over the kebabs, if desired, and serve immediately.

INGREDIENTS: Garam Masala

Garam masala, which means "hot mixture," is a northern Indian combination of dry-roasted, ground spices used in a wide range of dishes. Often used as a base to which other spices are added, the exact composition of the mixture varies with the tastes of the cook. The most common ingredients include black peppercorns, cinnamon, cloves, cardamom, coriander, cumin, dried chiles, fennel, mace, nutmeg, and bay leaves. Ginger and caraway seeds also make frequent appearances, and we have encountered recipes that call for saffron, sesame seed, and ajowan. As evidence that the proportions of the spices vary from cook to cook, Monisha Bharadwaj says in her book *The Indian Pantry* (Kyle Cathie Limited, 1996) that "there are as many recipes for [garam masala] as there are households in India." All of the spice merchants, Indian cooks, and cookbook authors we contacted agreed. Our sources agreed further that commercial mixtures tend to be less aromatic and more mellow than a batch you toast and grind fresh at home.

➤ VARIATIONS

Gas-Grilled Shish Kebab

Work quickly when opening the lid to turn the kebabs; you don't want too much heat to escape.

Follow the recipe for Charcoal-Grilled Shish Kebab through step 1. Turn on all the burners to high, close the lid, and heat the grill until very hot, about 15 minutes. Use a grill brush to scrape the cooking grate clean. Leave all the burners on high. Proceed with the recipe as directed from step 3 and cook with the lid down.

Lamb and Fig Kebabs with Garlic-Parsley Marinade

Sweet fresh figs soften beautifully on the grill in this variation.

Follow the recipe for Garlic and Cilantro Marinade with Garam Masala (page 142), substituting parsley for the cilantro. Set aside. Follow the recipe for Charcoal-Grilled or Gas-Grilled Shish Kebab, marinating the meat in the reserved marinade. Continue as directed, substituting 18 fresh figs (about 2 pints), halved, for the bell pepper.

MARINADES FOR SHISH KEBAB

Garlic and Cilantro Marinade with Garam Masala

ENOUGH FOR I RECIPE OF SHISH KEBAB

Garam masala, which means "hot mixture," is a northern Indian combination of dry-roasted, ground spices used in a wide range of dishes. See page 141 for more information.

1/2	cup packed fresh cilantro leaves
1/2	cup olive oil
1/4	cup dark raisins
1 1/2	tablespoons juice from 1 lemon
3	medium garlic cloves, peeled (see the illustration on the facing page)
1	teaspoon salt
1/2	teaspoon garam masala
1/8	teaspoon ground black pepper

Process all of the ingredients in a food processor until smooth, about 1 minute, stopping to scrape the sides of the workbowl with a rubber spatula as needed.

Sweet Curry Marinade with Buttermilk

ENOUGH FOR I RECIPE OF SHISH KEBAB

3/4	cup buttermilk
1	tablespoon juice from 1 lemon
3	medium garlic cloves, minced or pressed through a garlic press (about 1 tablespoon)
1	tablespoon brown sugar
1	tablespoon curry powder
1	teaspoon red pepper flakes
1	teaspoon ground coriander
1	teaspoon chili powder
1	teaspoon salt
1/8	teaspoon ground black pepper

Combine all of the ingredients in the gallon-size zipper-lock plastic bag or large nonreactive bowl in which the meat will marinate.

Warm-Spiced Parsley Marinade with Ginger

ENOUGH FOR I RECIPE OF SHISH KEBAB

We find that the edge of a teaspoon is the best tool to scrape the peel from ginger.

1/2	cup packed fresh parsley leaves
1/2	cup olive oil
1	(2-inch) piece fresh ginger, peeled and chopped coarse
1	jalapeño chile, seeds and ribs removed, then minced
3	medium garlic cloves, peeled (see the illustration on the facing page)
1	teaspoon ground cumin
1	teaspoon ground cardamom
1	teaspoon ground cinnamon
1	teaspoon salt
1/8	teaspoon ground black pepper

Process all of the ingredients in a food processor until smooth, about 1 minute, stopping to scrape the sides of the workbowl with a rubber spatula as needed.

Rosemary-Mint Marinade with Garlic and Lemon

ENOUGH FOR I RECIPE OF SHISH KEBAB

1/2	cup olive oil
2	tablespoons juice and 1/2 tablespoon grated zest from 1 lemon
3	medium garlic cloves, peeled (see the illustration on the facing page)
10	large fresh mint leaves
1 1/2	teaspoons chopped fresh rosemary
1	teaspoon salt
1/8	teaspoon ground black pepper

Process all of the ingredients in a food processor until smooth, about 1 minute, stopping to scrape the sides of the workbowl with a rubber spatula as needed.

GRILLED RACK OF LAMB

A RACK OF LAMB IS A PERFECT CANDIDATE FOR grilling. This fatty cut is actually easier to cook outdoors and the meat develops an excellent crust.

We started our tests by focusing on trimming the racks. Rack of lamb has a lot of excess fat, and we wondered how much would have to be removed before grilling. We found that racks sold at butcher shops and high-end grocery stores tend to be frenched—that is, the butcher has removed the fat and gristle between each chop to expose the ends of the bones. The chine bone had been removed from most racks that we purchased at butcher shops. At many supermarkets, however, we found racks that were not frenched and still had the chine bone attached. If the chine bone is left on, it is very hard to separate the grilled rack into individual chops. Since it is quite difficult to remove the chine bone at home, ask the butcher to do this. (Also, why pay $17 a pound for useless bone?) We found that most frenched racks with the chine bone removed weigh in at about 1½ pounds or so, and that racks weighing 2 pounds or more usually need more butchering. If you are about to purchase a rack that is this heavy, ask the butcher to make sure that the chine bone has been removed.

Even if you buy a frenched rack with the chine bone removed, you will still have some work to do. A typical rack is thicker at one end. At the thicker end, there is a layer of fat covering a thin

PEELING GARLIC

Unless whole cloves are needed, we crush garlic cloves with the side of a large chef's knife to loosen their skins and make them easier to remove.

layer of meat, called the cap. Another thin layer of fat rests underneath the cap. Trying to save as much meat as we could on the rack, we trimmed off only the first layer of fat. Unfortunately, however, the thin layer of meat was not really worth saving—the extra layer of fat underneath caused flare-ups on the grill, and we found the meat hard to eat because there was just too much fat surrounding it. We also found that leaving on the extra layer of meat and fat made the rack cook unevenly—the small end was overdone by the time the thicker end cooked to medium-rare. So we trimmed the cap and all the fat underneath it, leaving only a minimal amount of fat at the top of the rack and covering the bones to give the cut its characteristic rounded shape.

With our trimming tests completed, we turned to grilling. Our research uncovered three options: grilling the racks directly over the coals, searing the racks over hot coals and then sliding them to a cooler part of the grill to cook by indirect heat, or cooking the racks completely over indirect heat.

Direct heat was unsuccessful when cooking the racks over a medium-hot fire as well as over a medium fire. We found that the racks charred on the outside, while the inside was still raw. Grilling over direct heat using a cooler fire just doesn't make sense; there are too few coals, which will burn out too quickly.

A combination of direct and indirect heat worked better. First, we seared the racks directly over a hot fire and then moved the meat to indirect heat on the other side of the grill. The racks were satisfactorily cooked to medium-rare at the center. However, the outer layers of meat were a tad overdone.

We were surprised to find that cooking completely by indirect heat worked best. The racks slowly developed a rich crust, and the interior was more evenly cooked to medium-rare than by the direct/indirect method. On charcoal, we had to use disposable aluminum pie plates to cover each of the racks to prevent the meat from drying out (the total grill time was 17 to 18 minutes) and to speed up grilling time. The racks must also be placed quite close to, but not directly over, the pile of coals. To ensure even cooking, the racks must be rotated 180 degrees on each side in addition to being flipped over. Some sources suggest covering the protruding bones with foil to keep them from charring. We didn't have a problem with bones burning, so we feel that this extra step is not necessary.

Our final tests concerned flavoring. Rack of lamb is so tasty (that's why we are willing to pay so dearly for it) that it doesn't need much help, just a little salt and pepper to heighten its natural flavor. For variety, though, we found that both dry rubs and pastes work equally well to flavor the exterior of the meat. Rack of lamb has a tendency to be soft and mushy, and we found that marinades only exacerbated this problem.

One final note. We strongly recommend using an instant-read thermometer when grilling rack of lamb. There is no other reliable way to tell if the rack is properly cooked. No one wants to ruin $50 worth of meat because they overcooked it.

Simply slide an instant-read thermometer through the end of the meat, toward the center but away from any bones, to gauge the temperature at the center of the rack.

We found that cooking the meat to 125 degrees is perfect for medium-rare, as long as the meat is allowed to rest, tented with foil, after coming off the grill. Carryover cooking brings the temperature of the meat up to about 135 degrees after 10 minutes. For those who like their rack cooked further, 130 degrees is right for medium. After resting, the meat will reach 140 to 145 degrees. Keep in mind that the chops closer to the ends of the rack will cook somewhat ahead of the chops at the center. For example, when the chops are medium-rare at the center, you can expect those toward the ends to be cooked to medium, and for racks where the center chop is medium, the chops at the end will be medium-well to well-done.

EQUIPMENT: Boning Knives

The slim, flexible blade of a boning knife may look eccentric, but it is perfectly designed to slide nimbly through joints and between bones. It is an essential tool for such tasks as removing cutlets from a whole chicken breast and can also be used to remove fat and silver skin from a beef tenderloin or rack of lamb. The slim blade creates less drag through the meat, and the slices made are neater than those possible with the wider blade on a chef's knife.

Because most home cooks are likely to use a boning knife infrequently, we wondered if a cheaper knife would do. To find out, we tested six leading knives with blades between 5 and 7 inches long and prices between $9 and $71. Both large- and small-handed testers used each knife to butcher a whole chicken and to trim beef ribs of fat and silver skin. Each knife was evaluated for handle comfort, slipperiness (hands become very greasy when butchering), agility (including flexibility), and sharpness.

The winning Forschner (Victorinox) Fibrox boning knife, priced at $17.90, received high marks for its uniquely designed ergonomic handle as well as its slim, highly maneuverable blade and razor-sharp edge. The plastic handle nestled comfortably into both large and small hands, and it stayed there even when our hands became slick with fat. The blade was the narrowest of the lot, which made it very agile. And while all the knives arrived with razor-sharp edges, the Forschner seemed exceptionally

keen, gliding effortlessly through tough tendon and thick skin.

The J.A. Henckels Professional S boning knife ($49.99) finished a close second. Its blade was nearly as agile as the Forschner, but the handle was somewhat slippery. The Wüsthof-Trident Grand Prix boning knife ($54) was "fiendishly sharp," but the wide blade was not as agile as the top models and the handle became slippery when coated with chicken fat. The textured metal handle of the Global boning knife ($70.99) received mixed reviews, and testers did not like the boxy handle on the Chicago Cutlery boning knife ($14.99) or the flimsy blade on the Farberware Professional boning knife ($8.99).

THE BEST BONING KNIFE
The Forschner (Victorinox) Fibrox knife boasts a handle that testers found "easy to grip" and a narrow blade that shows "great flexibility around bones." Everyone raved about the "amazing" sharpness of this knife straight out of the box.

Charcoal-Grilled Rack of Lamb

SERVES 4

Have your butcher french the racks of lamb for you (this means that part of each rib bone will be exposed). If the racks are available already frenched, chances are there is still a good deal of fat on one side. Be sure to trim this excess fat away (according to the illustrations at right) to prevent flare-ups on the grill. Also, make sure that the chine bone (the bone running along the bottom of the rack) has been removed to ensure that it will be easy to cut between the ribs after cooking. Ask the butcher to do it; it's very hard to cut the chine bone off at home. You will need two 9-inch disposable pie plates for this recipe.

2   racks of lamb (about 1½ pounds each),
     trimmed according to the illustrations
     at right
     Salt and ground black pepper

1. Light a large chimney starter three-quarters full with hardwood charcoal (about 4½ quarts) and allow to burn until all the charcoal is covered with a layer of fine gray ash. Build a modified two-level fire by spreading the coals over half the grill bottom. Set the cooking grate in place, cover the grill with the lid, and let the grate heat up, about 5 minutes. Use a grill brush to scrape the cooking grate clean. The grill is ready when the coals are medium-hot. (See how to gauge heat level on page 4.)

2. Meanwhile, sprinkle both sides of the trimmed racks with a generous amount of salt and pepper to taste.

3. Place the racks of lamb, bone-side up, on the grill, with the meaty side of the racks very close to, but not quite over, the hot coals. Cover with the pie plates and grill until a deeply colored crust develops, about 8½ minutes, rotating the racks halfway through the cooking time so that the protruding bones are closer to the coals. Turn the racks over, bone-side down, and cover with the pie plates. Grill, rotating the racks halfway through for even cooking, until an instant-read thermometer inserted from the side of the rack through to the center, but

away from any bone, reads 125 degrees for medium-rare, about 10 minutes, or 130 degrees for medium, about 15 minutes.

4. Remove the racks from the grill to a cutting board and allow to rest, tented with foil, for 10 minutes (the racks will continue to cook while resting). Cut between each rib to separate chops and serve immediately.

➤ VARIATIONS

Gas-Grilled Rack of Lamb
Turn on all the burners to high, close the lid, and heat the grill until very hot, about 15 minutes. Use a grill brush to scrape the cooking grate clean. Leave one burner on high and turn the other

PREPARING A RACK OF LAMB

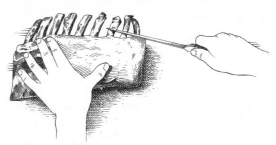

1. Using a boning or paring knife, scrape the ribs clean of any scraps of meat or fat.

2. Trim off the outer layer of fat, the flap of meat underneath it, and the fat underneath that flap.

3. Remove the silver skin by sliding the boning knife between the silver skin and the flesh.

burner(s) to medium-low. Follow the recipe for Charcoal-Grilled Rack of Lamb, seasoning the racks as directed in step 2 and cooking the racks with the lid down as directed in step 3. Let rest as directed in step 4 before serving.

Grilled Rack of Lamb with Garlic and Herbs

Mix 4 teaspoons extra-virgin olive oil, 4 teaspoons chopped fresh rosemary, 2 teaspoons chopped fresh thyme leaves, and 2 medium garlic cloves, minced or pressed through a garlic press, together in a small bowl. Follow the recipe for Charcoal-Grilled or Gas-Grilled Rack of Lamb, rubbing the herb/garlic mixture over the lamb after seasoning it with salt and pepper.

Grilled Rack of Lamb with Turkish Spice Rub

Pickling spice is a spice blend sold in many supermarkets.

Grind 1 tablespoon pickling spice in a spice grinder. Mix the ground pickling spice, 1 teaspoon dried summer savory, ¾ teaspoon salt, ½ teaspoon ground black pepper, ½ teaspoon ground cumin, ¼ teaspoon grated nutmeg, and ¼ teaspoon ground cinnamon together in a small bowl. Follow the recipe for Charcoal-Grilled or Gas-Grilled Rack of Lamb, rubbing the meat with the pickling spice rub instead of sprinkling it with salt and pepper in step 2. Proceed with the recipe.

GRILLED BUTTERFLIED LEG OF LAMB

A LEG OF LAMB CAN BE GRILLED IF THE leg is boned and then butterflied, a technique in which several cuts are made in the boned flesh to open and flatten the leg so that its uneven topography is smoothed to an even thickness. A butterflied leg of lamb is a large, unwieldy piece of meat, about three quarters of an inch thick and covered with a thin layer of fat. You can butterfly a leg of lamb yourself or buy a butterflied leg of lamb at the supermarket (see pages 147 to 151 for more detailed information on both of these options).

For our first test, we used a kettle grill and our preferred fuel—hardwood charcoal—to build a two-level fire. We seasoned the butterflied meat with salt and pepper and, wary of flaming, used no oil. We placed the meat fat-side down over the coals, intending to brown it quickly over direct heat and then finish it over indirect heat.

The results dismayed us. The leg flamed and blackened. It was difficult to maneuver on the grill because of its size. The connective tissue in the shank retracted and curled so badly that eventually we had to cut the tissue off and cook it longer. The rest of the leg cooked unevenly and tasted oily as well as scorched from the flame. Because it was so thin, it was difficult to carve into attractive slices.

We made up our minds to start from scratch and find the best way to grill a butterflied leg of

BUYING A LEG OF LAMB

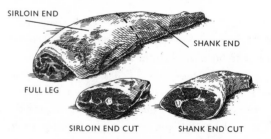

When you go to the supermarket, you will probably be able to buy either a whole leg or a half leg. When buying a half, you can get either the sirloin (the upper half) or the shank (the lower half). Of the two, we prefer the sirloin end because it is slightly more tender.

LEG OF LAMB: THE BONES

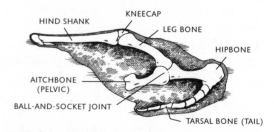

When boning a leg of lamb (see the illustrations on page 149), it is helpful to know the inner skeletal structure. In particular, note where all the bones come together in the center of the leg, at the large ball-and-socket joint.

lamb. We had several questions: What's the best way to butterfly a leg of lamb? Is there a way to grill the shank attached to the leg, or must we always cut it off? Direct heat chars the leg more than we like, but how else can we grill it? Do we need to cover the grill to control the flaming? And is it necessary to carve a leg of lamb across the grain for the sake of tenderness?

Our goal was to come up with a butchering technique that would yield an easy-to-manage piece of meat that was thick enough to carve into attractive slices. And, as always when grilling, we wanted a crust that was caramelized but not blackened and a moist, tender interior.

To start, it helps to understand the structure of the leg, which consists of six different muscles: the meaty, dome-shaped top and smaller bottom rounds; the small cylindrical eye of round; the flat trapezoidal hip; the round knuckle; and the oblong shank. Restaurant chefs sometimes separate the muscles from one another (they pull apart very easily) and then cook and carve each separately because that allows each muscle to be cooked perfectly and carved across the grain into large slices for optimum tenderness. (After the meat is butterflied, the grain runs every which way, so it's impossible to carve against the grain.)

Cooking the muscles separately doesn't make sense for a home cook, particularly since people tend to turn to this cut when planning for a crowd. But we tried to adapt this technique by boning the leg and cooking it as is—with all the muscles intact and unbutterflied—planning to cut the muscles apart after cooking and carve each one separately. This time, to solve the flaming problem, we cooked the lamb entirely over indirect heat. It browned beautifully and didn't flame, but after 40 minutes it was clear that there wasn't enough heat to cook through the larger muscles (the top round and knuckle). We then turned our thoughts to butchering the leg to allow for more even cooking.

We were familiar with two methods of butterflying. One calls for cutting straight down into the meat and then spreading the meat open on either side of the cut. The second technique is to cut into the meat horizontally and then open it

SIMPLIFIED BUTTERFLIED LEG OF LAMB

SO YOU DON'T WANT TO BUTTERFLY your own leg of lamb and just want to buy something straight from the meat case that can be seasoned and grilled? Here's how to adapt our recipe. The cooking times are the same, but note that you will probably have more gradations in the meat, with some parts more well-done and other parts more rare since a leg of lamb that is butterflied according to the traditional method usually has an uneven thickness.

Buy a 4½- to 5-pound butterflied leg of lamb that has been divided into two equal pieces (this makes turning the lamb easier). The butterflied lamb should be about one inch thick throughout. If you cannot find this at your supermarket, we suggest that you buy a bone-in whole leg of lamb that weighs between 6½ and 7 pounds and ask to have it boned and butterflied. Be sure to indicate that you want the meat to be about one inch thick throughout, and ask the butcher to divide the lamb into two pieces after butterflying. You may also find a boneless whole leg of lamb roast that has been rolled and tied. This roast simply needs to be butterflied. Again, you can ask your butcher to do this for you.

Because this recipe feeds a crowd (between 8 and 10 people), you may want to grill only half a leg of lamb. Supermarkets usually sell half legs of lamb, either the shank end or the sirloin end. Once again, you can purchase this cut of meat with the bone in and have it boned and butterflied by your butcher, again about one inch thick throughout. Also remember to cut the ingredients in a marinade by half (if you are using one).

out like a book. We tried both and found that a combination of the two techniques worked best (see page 151). What we were after was a single piece of meat about one inch thick. Traditional butterflying, as done by most butchers, produces

147

a flat piece of meat, but it can be uneven in thickness. The butterflying method we adopted produces the evenness we wanted.

The butterflied leg was very large, however, so we cut it in half along a natural separation between the muscles. This enabled us to turn each piece with a single pair of tongs rather than struggle with a pair of tongs in each hand. This also made it more practical to buy, since you can freeze half if you are cooking for only four.

Satisfied with our butchering technique, we returned to the cooking. Working again over indirect heat, we grilled the butterflied leg pieces, cut-side up, for 5 minutes. Then we turned them 180 degrees and cooked them 5 more minutes to ensure that the meat cooked evenly all around. After 10 minutes the leg was well browned on the skin side, so we turned the pieces over and repeated the procedure, cooking the meat another 10 minutes, until it registered 130 degrees on an instant-read thermometer. We let the meat rest 10 minutes and then sliced into it. The outside crust was perfect, but inside we still had problems. While the meat in the center was a beautiful medium-rare, the perimeter of the leg was still pale because it needed more time to rest. And the shank meat was still undercooked.

The problem with the shank was easy enough to solve; we decided to cut it off and save it for another use. (Some supermarkets also sell the leg without the shank.) Then we tested resting times, letting the meat rest 15, 20, and 25 minutes, and found that 20 minutes was ample time for the juices to be redistributed throughout the leg.

Finally, we experimented with carving to test for tenderness. We carved the meat into thin slices on the bias (for slices as large as possible) and actively disregarded slicing across the grain. As it turned out, this was a good decision. Although the different muscles varied in taste and texture, they were all plenty tender.

Although the lamb tastes great as is, we also recommend using one of the marinades on page 150 for a boost of flavor.

Charcoal-Grilled Butterflied Leg of Lamb
SERVES 8 TO 10

Be sure to have a squirt bottle filled with water ready to douse the flames, if necessary. See page 150 for marinades that work well with this recipe.

| 1 | leg of lamb (about 7 pounds), boned, butterflied, and halved between the eye and the bottom round (see the illustrations on pages 149 and 151) |
| 1½ | tablespoons extra-virgin olive oil Salt and ground black pepper |

1. Light a large chimney starter filled with hardwood charcoal (about 6 quarts) and allow to burn until all the charcoal is covered with a layer of fine gray ash. Build a modified two-level fire by spreading the coals over half the grill bottom. Set the cooking grate in place, cover the grill with the lid, and let the grate heat up, about 5 minutes. Use a grill brush to scrape the cooking grate clean. The grill is ready when the coals are hot. (See how to gauge heat level on page 4.)

2. Rub both sides of the lamb pieces with the oil and sprinkle generously with salt and pepper to taste.

3. Place the lamb pieces, fat-side down, on the side of the grate that is not directly over the coals but close to the fire. Grill the lamb, uncovered, for 5 minutes. Rotate the meat so that the outside edges are now closest to the fire. Grill until the fat side of the lamb is a rich dark brown, 5 minutes longer. With tongs or a large meat fork, turn both pieces over. Cook, fat-side up, for 5 minutes, then move the meat directly over the coals (they will have partially burned out by this point, putting out less heat), and cook until an instant-read thermometer inserted into the thickest part of each piece registers 125 to 130 degrees for medium-rare, about 6 minutes or 135 degrees for medium, about 10 minutes.

4. Transfer the meat to a large platter or cutting board, tent loosely with foil, and let rest for 20 minutes. Slice thin on the bias and serve.

BONING A LEG OF LAMB

1. Using the tip of a boning knife, make the first cut at the top of the shank, cutting around the kneecap, and continuing down one side of the leg bone.

2. Cut straight down to the leg bone with the tip of the knife, and, using the bone as a guide, cut until you reach the hipbone and must stop. Repeat on the other side.

3. Cut under and around the kneecap and along the side of the leg bone, loosening the meat from the bone as you go.

4. Cut around the hipbone to loosen the meat from the bone.

5. Using the tip of the knife, cut the meat away from the aitchbone (or pelvic bone). Use the tip of the knife to scrape the meat away from the bone.

6. At this point, the meat should be free from the leg bone (center), the aitchbone (lower left center), and the hipbone (lower right). The ball-and-socket joint is in the center.

7. Cut beneath the tarsal bone (tailbone), keeping the knife right along the bone.

8. Lift the tarsal bone and continue scraping the meat away from the bone until you reach the ball-and-socket joint.

9. With the tip of the knife, scrape along and beneath the ball-and-socket joint to loosen it from the meat, and cut between ball and socket to loosen.

10. Snap the ball and socket apart and pull the tail-, hip-, and aitchbones away from the leg bone (save this piece for stock or discard).

11. Continue to cut beneath the leg bone, lifting it from the meat as you cut.

12. Lift the leg bone and cartilage around the kneecap to totally separate the leg and shank portion (if the leg came with the shank attached) and remove (save it for stock or discard).

MARINADES FOR GRILLED LEG OF LAMB

LEG OF LAMB HAS A RICH FLAVOR THAT STANDS UP WELL TO A VARIETY OF MARINADES. To use any of these marinades, butcher the lamb as directed, place the lamb in a nonreactive large shallow pan or baking dish, and rub the marinade into all parts of the meat. Cover the pan with plastic wrap and refrigerate it at least 8 hours and up to 24 hours. Except for the Soy-Honey Marinade with Thyme, which is salty enough, season the marinated lamb with salt and pepper just before grilling, but do not oil the lamb.

Tandoori Marinade

ENOUGH FOR I BUTTERFLIED LEG OF LAMB

The yogurt forms an especially thick, browned crust when the lamb is grilled.

1/3	cup plain yogurt
2	tablespoons juice from I lemon
5	medium garlic cloves, minced or pressed through a garlic press (about 5 teaspoons)
I	tablespoon grated fresh ginger
2	teaspoons ground cumin
2	teaspoons ground coriander
I	teaspoon ground turmeric
I	teaspoon cayenne pepper
1/2	teaspoon ground cinnamon

Combine all of the ingredients in a small bowl.

Garlic and Rosemary Marinade

ENOUGH FOR I BUTTERFLIED LEG OF LAMB

A leg of lamb will be nicely flavored after just 3 hours in this marinade, but can be marinated longer if you like.

1/4	cup extra-virgin olive oil
6	medium garlic cloves, minced or pressed through a garlic press (about 2 tablespoons)
1 1/2	tablespoons minced fresh rosemary

Combine all of the ingredients in a small bowl.

Lemon Marinade with Greek Flavorings

ENOUGH FOR I BUTTERFLIED LEG OF LAMB

If you like, use fresh oregano and thyme leaves, doubling their amounts, in this marinade.

1/4	cup extra-virgin olive oil
2	tablespoons juice from I lemon
3	medium garlic cloves, minced or pressed through a garlic press (about I tablespoon)
I	tablespoon dried oregano
I	tablespoon dried thyme
	Pinch sweet paprika

Combine all of the ingredients in a small bowl.

Soy-Honey Marinade with Thyme

ENOUGH FOR I BUTTERFLIED LEG OF LAMB

Minced fresh chile or red pepper flakes make a good addition to this marinade.

1/3	cup soy sauce
1/3	cup honey
I	tablespoon grated fresh ginger
2	medium garlic cloves, minced or pressed through a garlic press (about 2 teaspoons)
I	teaspoon minced fresh thyme leaves
	Pinch cayenne pepper

Combine all of the ingredients in a small bowl.

➤ VARIATIONS
Gas-Grilled Butterflied Leg of Lamb

Watch for flare-ups on the grill; have a squirt bottle filled with water ready to dampen the flames as necessary.

1	leg of lamb (about 7 pounds), boned, butterflied, and halved between the eye and the bottom round (see the illustrations on pages 149 and below)
1½	tablespoons extra-virgin olive oil Salt and ground black pepper

1. Turn on all the burners to high, close the lid, and heat the grill until very hot, about 15 minutes. Use a grill brush to scrape the cooking grate clean. Leave one burner on high and turn the other burner(s) down to medium.

2. Rub both sides of the lamb pieces with the oil and sprinkle generously with salt and pepper to taste.

3. Place the lamb pieces, fat-side down, over the burner(s) set to medium. Grill the lamb, covered, for 5 minutes. Rotate the meat so that the

BUTTERFLYING A LEG OF LAMB

1. To butterfly, lay a large chef's knife flat on the center of the meat, at the thinnest part, parallel to the top round.

2. Keeping the knife blade parallel to the board, begin slicing through the muscle. Cut horizontally about 1 inch.

3. Begin to unroll the meat (it's like unrolling a carpet) with your other hand as you continue to cut into the muscle, always keeping the knife blade parallel to the board, cutting about 1 inch at a time, and unrolling as you cut.

4. Stopping about 1 inch from the end, unfold the edge of the meat and flatten it.

5. The butterflied muscle should be even in thickness.

6. Turn the board around and cut the knuckle muscle on the other side using the same method as in steps 1 through 4.

7. Near the center of the bottom round, locate a hard thick section of fat. Using the tip of the boning knife, cut into the fat to locate the lymph node (a ½-inch round, grayish flat nodule). Carefully remove and discard.

8. Divide the butterflied meat in half by cutting between the eye and the bottom round.

9. Turn the pieces of meat over and use a boning knife to cut away the thick pieces of fat, leaving about ⅛-inch thickness for self-basting during grilling.

outside edges are now facing the hotter burner. Grill, covered, until the fat side of the lamb is a rich dark brown, 5 minutes longer. With tongs or a large meat fork, turn both pieces over. Cook, fat-side up, for 5 minutes, then rotate the meat 180 degrees to ensure even cooking. Continue grilling, covered, until an instant-read thermometer inserted into the thickest part of each piece registers 125 degrees for medium-rare, about 10 minutes in all, or 130 to 135 degrees for medium, 10 to 12 minutes longer.

4. Transfer the meat to a large platter or cutting board, tent with foil, and let rest 20 minutes. Slice thin on this bias and serve.

Classic Mint Sauce

MAKES ENOUGH TO ACCOMPANY I LEG OF LAMB

This sauce has a refreshing mint flavor without the cloying sweetness of mint jelly. The texture is much thinner than jelly, similar to maple syrup. This sauce is remarkably easy to make and does not require any bones since no stock is necessary. Mince the mint right before adding it to the sauce to preserve its fresh flavor.

I	cup white wine vinegar
6	tablespoons sugar
1/4	cup minced fresh mint leaves

1. Bring the vinegar and sugar to a simmer in a nonreactive medium saucepan over medium heat and cook until slightly syrupy, 8 to 10 minutes. (The liquid should be reduced to about ½ cup.)

2. Remove the pan from the heat, let cool for 5 minutes, and stir in the mint. Pour the sauce into a bowl and cover with plastic wrap. Set aside

BARBECUE 911

Raw Meat Precaution

Grilled meat, poultry, and fish should not be returned to the same platter that was used to carry the raw food to the grill. Instead of last-minute fumbling for a clean platter, this method uses a single platter for both jobs and saves on cleanup time.

I. Cover the platter with foil before placing the raw food on it.

2. While the food is grilling, remove the foil so that you can use the same platter when the food comes off the grill.

for at least 1 hour. (The sauce can be set aside for several hours.) Serve at room temperature with the lamb.

4
CHICKEN

CHICKEN

CHARCOAL-GRILLED CHICKEN CUTLETS 159
    Gas-Grilled Chicken Cutlets

CUCUMBER AND MANGO RELISH WITH YOGURT. 160

SPICY TOMATILLO AND PINEAPPLE SALSA. 160

GRILLED CHICKEN SALAD WITH SESAME-MISO DRESSING 160

CHARCOAL-GRILLED CHICKEN KEBABS 163
    Gas-Grilled Chicken Kebabs
    Caribbean Chicken Kebabs with Black Bean and Mango Salsa
    Thai Chicken Satay with Spicy Peanut Sauce
    Curried Chicken Kebabs and Cucumber Salad with Yogurt and Mint
    Southwestern Kebabs with Red Pepper–Jicama Relish

MARINADES FOR CHICKEN KEBABS 165
    Garlic and Herb Marinade
    Middle Eastern Marinade
    Southwestern Marinade
    Curry Marinade
    Caribbean Marinade
    Asian Marinade

CHARCOAL-GRILLED POULTRY SAUSAGES 166
    Gas-Grilled Poultry Sausages

CHARCOAL-GRILLED BONE-IN CHICKEN THIGHS OR LEGS 169
    Gas-Grilled Bone-In Chicken Thighs or Legs
    Hoisin-Glazed Grilled Chicken Thighs or Legs with Napa Cabbage Slaw

CHARCOAL-GRILLED BONE-IN CHICKEN BREASTS 170
    Gas-Grilled Bone-In Chicken Breasts

CHARCOAL-GRILLED TANDOORI-STYLE CHICKEN BREASTS WITH RAITA . . . 174
    Gas-Grilled Tandoori-Style Chicken Breasts with Raita

THAI GRILLED CHICKEN BREASTS WITH SPICY, SWEET,
AND SOUR DIPPING SAUCE 177
    Thai-Grilled Chicken Breasts on a Gas Grill

CHARCOAL-GRILLED MIXED CHICKEN PARTS 179
    Gas-Grilled Mixed Chicken Parts

SAUCES FOR CHICKEN WINGS 182
    Hoisin-Sesame Sauce
    Spicy Sauce for Buffalo Wings
    Blue Cheese Dressing

CHARCOAL-GRILLED CHICKEN WINGS 183
    Gas-Grilled Chicken Wings

CHARCOAL-GRILLED BUTTERFLIED CHICKEN 185
    Gas-Grilled Butterflied Chicken
    Butterflied Chicken with Pesto
    Butterflied Chicken with Barbecue Sauce
    Butterflied Chicken with Green Olive Tapenade
    Butterflied Chicken with Chipotle, Honey, and Lime
    Butterflied Chicken with Lemon and Rosemary

CHICKEN ALLA DIAVOLA ON A CHARCOAL GRILL 188
    Chicken alla Diavola on a Gas Grill

GRILL-ROASTED WHOLE CHICKEN ON A CHARCOAL GRILL 191
    Grill-Roasted Whole Chicken on a Gas Grill
    Grill-Roasted Whole Chicken with Barbecue Sauce

GRILL-ROASTED BEER CAN CHICKEN 194

CHICKEN IS ONE OF THE MOST POPULAR items for grilling. Because it takes well to numerous seasonings, it need never taste or appear to be quite the same from one meal to another. The fact that chicken can be served in so many forms—parts, whole birds, and cutlets—adds to its appeal.

The challenge in grilling chicken is twofold. The first consideration is what type of chicken to use. Broiler/fryers are the standard supermarket chicken—and our favorite. They generally weigh between 3 and 4½ pounds and will serve four people. All the recipes in this book using whole birds are developed with broiler/fryers.

We tasted 3½- to 4-pound chickens from nine widely available producers. Supermarket chickens range from budget birds raised on factory farms to pricier fowl with ambiguous labels—"organic," "free range," "all natural"—proclaiming the virtues of their diet and lifestyle. These terms mean different things to different producers, and, as our tasting demonstrated, they are not reliable indicators of flavor or texture. Neither is price.

Tyson, a mass-produced bird, came in third, ahead of birds costing twice as much. Perdue, the other mass-produced brand in our tasting, came in dead last. The best-tasting chicken was a kosher bird from Empire. Tasters found it to be the most juicy and well seasoned of the bunch. During the koshering process, a chicken is covered with salt to draw out impurities. This leads to a moister, more flavorful bird that never needs to be brined to pump up taste or juiciness. If your supermarket doesn't carry kosher chickens, brining can improve the quality of just about any chicken, even last-place Perdue. To read more about brining, see page 172.

The second point to take into consideration when grilling chicken is the type of chicken part, whether it's white meat vs. dark, chicken parts vs. whole chicken, or whole butterflied chicken—each pose different challenges and require different cooking methods. The one challenge they all share, however, is chicken's tendency to dry out on the grill. For example, where a thin chicken cutlet can be grilled directly and quickly over a hot fire, a bone-in chicken breast must first be started over a hot fire, then moved to less intense heat and covered to finish cooking. Both recipes ensure a moist, juicy bird, hot off the grill.

GRILLED CHICKEN CUTLETS

CUT FROM THE BREAST AND STRIPPED OF bones and skin, chicken cutlets are the essence of convenience. Unfortunately, that convenience comes at a price. With no skin or bones to protect and flavor the meat, chicken cutlets can cook up into tasteless, dry pieces of leather in no time flat. Throwing the cutlets on the grill only compounds the problem. In the time it takes to say "briquette," the cutlets can overcook into a carbon-flavored nightmare. Then there's the shape of the chicken breast: thick at one end, thin at the other. The meat never seems to cook evenly. But during hot summer days we like to avoid turning on the oven, so we set out to find a trouble-free way to grill cutlets that are tasty and tender, with plump, juicy meat and an attractive seared exterior.

Just about every cookbook offers a way to grill boneless chicken breasts, and we tried them all. Our tests fell into three categories: single-level fires, in which the grill cooks at one constant temperature; two-level fires, in which the grill is set up to cook at two different temperatures; and covered cooking, in which the meat is cooked under the cover of the grill or tented with an aluminum pan.

From the start we had very good luck with single-level fires, especially at high heat. Medium and low heat did not provide a good sear; without any fat from the skin, the interior overcooked in the time necessary to color the exterior. High heat produced the most attractive chicken breasts, turning them a deep golden brown. At this temperature the chicken cooked up in only three minutes per side and produced the least dry meat. Unfortunately, the breasts did not cook evenly; the thin tapered end was almost inedible. We wanted to find a way to cook the breasts evenly, but grilling the unevenly shaped pieces at any temperature was bound to produce uneven results.

Handling Chicken 101

When grilling chicken parts, start with a whole chicken. Whole birds taste better than packaged parts and cost less, so it makes sense to cut up chicken at home. Here's all you need to know to master this basic skill.

CUTTING UP A WHOLE CHICKEN

Even when a recipe calls for chicken parts, there are many advantages to purchasing a whole chicken and cutting it up yourself. Packaged chicken parts are generally mass-produced and are of a lower quality, so buying a whole chicken gives you the chance to buy a better bird. In addition, packages of chicken parts often come from different chickens of different sizes; as a result, the pieces may cook unevenly. To top it off, whole chickens generally cost less per pound and provide trimmings that are perfect for freezing to make homemade stock.

THE LEGS

  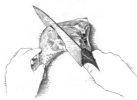

1. Cut through the skin around the leg where it attaches to the breast. Using both hands, bend the leg back to pop the leg joint out of its socket.

2. Cut through the broken joint to separate the leg. Cut very close to the back so that the tender, meaty "oyster" is removed along with the leg.

3. Note the line of fat separating the thigh and drumstick. Cut through the joint at this line.

THE WINGS

1. Bend the wing out from the breast and cut through the joint to separate.

2. Cut through the cartilage around the wingtip to remove it. Freeze the tips and use them to make your next batch of homemade chicken stock.

3. A triangular flap of skin connecting the two halves of the chicken wing can make it awkward to eat. Cut straight through the center joint; the two smaller pieces will cook up crispier and be easier to eat.

THE BREAST

1. To separate the whole breast from the backbone, cut through the ribs with kitchen shears, following the vertical line of fat from the tapered end of the breast up to the socket where the wing was attached.

2. With the whole breast skin-side down on the cutting board, center the knife on the breastbone, then apply pressure to cut through and separate the breast into halves.

3. If you purchase one whole, bone-in chicken breast, you may need to trim the rib sections with kitchen shears.

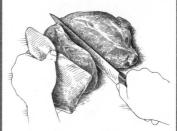

Playing around with different grilling times provided no relief.

We decided to remove the tenderloins and then pound the breasts to an even thickness. Once again, we threw the chicken breasts on the hot grill, this time pounded to within half an inch of their lives. These cutlets cooked evenly, and now the grilling time was reduced to two minutes per side. Another benefit of the cutlets' now-flat surface was that they browned evenly. The interior was relatively juicy—we were headed in the right direction.

Grilled or not, chicken breasts are decidedly mild-tasting. Our next round of tests included methods to add flavor—marinating, basting, using spice rubs and pastes, and brining.

Marinating proved the most disappointing. Although the meat was pounded relatively thin, it took several hours of soaking in an oil and lemon juice marinade to make any flavor difference. We tried poking holes in the chicken breasts, but this caused no appreciable improvement in flavor. In addition, the appearance of the marinated chicken

suffered greatly from the frequent flare-ups caused by the dripping oil. Basting the chicken breasts with flavored oils and vinaigrettes was inconvenient; in the four minutes it took to grill the cutlets, little flavor was imparted, but flames again leaped up from the coals. We had high hopes for the spice rubs and pastes but these, too, disappointed. Though well suited to more robust cuts of meat and poultry, the rubs and pastes all but decimated the flavor of the cutlets.

Finally, we tested brining, a method used often in the test kitchen, in which poultry is soaked in a saltwater solution to promote flavor and juiciness. In conjunction with the quick, high-heat fire, this turned out to be the key to perfect grilled chicken breasts. After experimenting with different salt ratios and soaking times, we found that a high concentration of salt penetrates the thin cutlets in a short amount of time—30 minutes, to be exact, about the same amount of time it takes to fire up the grill. These cutlets were well seasoned, juicy, and very tender. We added sugar to the brine, which not only improved the

INGREDIENTS: **Chicken Cutlets**

In a world of low-fat fanaticism and a society obsessed with weight, it is not surprising that boneless, skinless chicken breasts are a standard in many home kitchens. No fat, no fuss, and, unfortunately, no flavor. We've come up with countless recipes to add zip to these otherwise boring pieces of meat, but we never stopped to look at the chicken itself. Was there a difference in flavor among the popular brands? Do terms like "organic," "free range," "natural," or "kosher" have any real bearing on the quality of the meat?

To find out, we gathered six brands of boneless, skinless chicken breasts, broiled them without seasoning, and had 20 tasters sample the chickens side by side. Among the contenders were one kosher bird, two "natural," and one "free range." The remaining two were just "chicken."

The U.S. Department of Agriculture defines "natural" as "a product containing no artificial ingredients or added color and [that] is only minimally processed (a process which does not fundamentally alter the raw product) . . ." In the case of the chicken, it means there are no antibiotics or hormones, and the birds are fed a vegetarian diet. "Free range" means exactly what

it says: The birds are not confined to small cages but allowed to roam freely. Some people feel that this excess motion yields tougher meat, but our tasters did not find this to be the case.

As in our last tasting of whole chickens, Empire Kosher topped the charts, this time tying for first place with all-natural Bell & Evans. The only kosher bird, Empire won points with tasters for its superior flavor: namely, salt. The koshering process involves coating the chicken with salt to draw out any impurities; this process, similar to brining, results in moist, salted meat (for this reason, we do not recommend brining kosher birds). Springer Farms All-Natural and Eberly's Free Range chickens also scored well.

Last place finishers (and lowest priced) Perdue and White Gem (our local supermarket brand) were downgraded for poor texture and unnatural flavor. Tasters were also put off by the brash yellow color of the birds.

In the end, it seems that more money can buy you better chicken and, many would argue, a better-for-you bird. (Kosher chickens are also all-natural and contain no hormones or antibiotics.) As for lower-priced supermarket staples and store brands, a cheaper price does indicate a cheaper product.

flavor of the cutlets but also their appearance as the sugar caramelized on the exterior, adding more color. These cutlets were ready to step up to the plate as the basis for quick, satisfying salads and sandwiches or to be served with a salsa, relish, or chutney accompaniment.

Charcoal-Grilled Chicken Cutlets

SERVES 6 TO 8

To save time, the chicken cutlets are brined while the fire gets going. To use kosher salt in the brine, see page 172 for conversion information. Try the cutlets in our salad recipe or with our relish or salsa (recipes follow). They're also great served simply with lemon or lime wedges.

8	boneless, skinless chicken breasts (about 6 ounces each), trimmed of excess fat, tenderloins removed (see the illustrations at right) and reserved for another use
¼	cup sugar
¼	cup table salt (see note)
	Ground black pepper
	Vegetable oil

1. Pound the chicken breasts to an even ½-inch thickness (see the illustration at right).

2. In a gallon-size zipper-lock plastic bag, dissolve the sugar and salt in 1 quart of cold water. Add the chicken and seal the bag, pressing out as much air as possible; refrigerate 30 minutes. Remove from the brine, dry thoroughly with paper towels, and sprinkle with pepper.

3. While the chicken is brining, light a large chimney starter filled with hardwood charcoal (6 quarts) and burn until all the charcoal is covered with a layer of fine gray ash. Spread the coals evenly over the grill bottom, then spread an additional 6 quarts unlit charcoal over the lit coals. Position the grill grate over the coals and heat until very hot, about 15 minutes. (See how to gauge heat level on page 4.) Use a grill brush to scrape the cooking grate clean.

4. Lightly brush both sides of the chicken breasts with vegetable oil. Grill uncovered until light brown, 2 to 3 minutes on each side.

TRIMMING CUTLETS

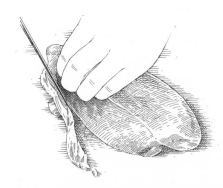

Most cutlets have a little yellow or white fat still attached to the breast meat. Lay each cutlet tenderloin-side down and smooth the top with your fingers. Any fat will slide to the edge of the cutlet, where it can be trimmed with a knife.

REMOVING THE TENDERLOIN

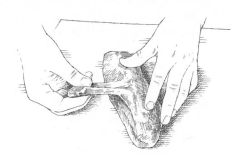

The tenderloin (the long narrow piece of meat attached to each cutlet) tends to fall off during pounding, so it is best removed and reserved for another use, such as a stir-fry.

POUNDING CUTLETS

Place the cutlets, smooth-side down, on a large sheet of plastic wrap. Cover with a second sheet of plastic wrap and pound gently. The cutlets should already be thin; you simply want to make sure that they have the same thickness from end to end.

> VARIATION
Gas-Grilled Chicken Cutlets

Follow steps 1 and 2 of Charcoal-Grilled Chicken Cutlets. While the chicken is brining, turn on all the burners to high, close the lid, and heat until hot, 10 to 15 minutes. Use a grill brush to scrape the cooking grate clean. Continue with the recipe from step 4, grilling the chicken breasts uncovered, 3 to 4 minutes on each side.

Cucumber and Mango Relish with Yogurt
MAKES 1 3/4 CUPS

1	large cucumber, peeled, seeded, and cut into 1/4-inch cubes
1	large mango (about 1 pound), peeled and cut into 1/4-inch cubes
1	medium jalapeño chile, seeds and ribs removed, then minced
1/4	cup plain yogurt
1	tablespoon chopped fresh mint leaves
1/2	teaspoon sugar
1/4	teaspoon ground cardamom
	Salt

In a small bowl, combine all of the ingredients, including salt to taste. Cover and refrigerate at least 30 minutes to blend the flavors.

INGREDIENTS: Peanut Oil

You may think all peanut oils are the same. Think again. Highly refined oils, such as Planters, are basically tasteless. They are indistinguishable from safflower, corn, or vegetable oil. In contrast, unrefined peanut oils (also labeled roasted or cold-pressed peanut oil) have a rich nut fragrance straight from the bottle. When heated, these oils smell like freshly roasted peanuts.

In the test kitchen, we find that unrefined, or roasted, peanut oil is a real plus in simple stir-fries. Like good olive oil, good peanut oil makes many dishes taste better. Three brands that we particularly like are Loriva, Hollywood, and Spectrum.

Spicy Tomatillo and Pineapple Salsa
MAKES 3 CUPS

Be sure to use a ripe pineapple. Tomatillos are very tart—blanching softens their texture and their sour edge.

6	small tomatillos, husked
1/2	large pineapple, cut into 1/2-inch cubes (about 3 cups)
1	chipotle chile in adobo sauce, minced
1	teaspoon juice from 1 lime
	Salt

1. Bring 1 quart of water to a boil in a small saucepan over high heat; boil the tomatillos until the skins start to pucker, about 5 minutes. With a slotted spoon, remove the tomatillos to a bowl of ice water to stop the cooking process. When cool enough to handle, core the tomatillos and cut into 1/2-inch cubes.

2. Toss the tomatillos, pineapple, chipotle chile, lime juice, and salt to taste in a medium bowl. Cover and refrigerate at least 30 minutes to blend the flavors.

Grilled Chicken Salad with Sesame-Miso Dressing
SERVES 4 TO 6

This recipe uses a half recipe of the grilled chicken cutlets. Halve the brine ingredients, but brine for the same length of time.

2	tablespoons white miso
2	tablespoons water
1	tablespoon honey
1	tablespoon soy sauce
2	tablespoons peanut oil
2	tablespoons sesame seeds, toasted in a small dry skillet until golden, 7 to 10 minutes, and then crushed
1	scallion, sliced thin
1/2	recipe Charcoal-Grilled or Gas-Grilled Chicken Cutlets, cut crosswise into 1/2-inch wide strips
10	cups mesclun, washed and dried

Whisk together the miso, water, honey, and soy sauce in a medium bowl; gradually whisk in the peanut oil, then stir in the sesame seeds and scallion. Toss the chicken with 2 tablespoons of the dressing in a large bowl. Add the mesclun and remaining dressing; toss to combine. Divide the salad among individual plates; serve immediately.

CHICKEN KEBABS

CHICKEN AND FRESH VEGETABLE KEBABS grilled to juicy perfection make great summer fare, either as appetizers or as the main course. The best grilled chicken kebabs are succulent, well-seasoned, and really taste like they've been cooked over an open fire. They are complemented by fruits and vegetables that are equally satisfying—grill-marked but juicy, cooked all the way through but neither shrunken nor incinerated.

When we started our testing, we figured it would be simple. After all, skewered chicken is simple food, a standby of every street-corner grill cook from here to China. But after some early attempts, we ran into a few difficulties. When we simply threaded the chicken and veggies on skewers, brushed them with a little oil, and sprinkled them with salt and pepper, we were always disappointed. Sometimes the components cooked at different rates, resulting in dry meat and undercooked vegetables. Even when nicely grilled, quick-cooking kebabs didn't absorb much flavor from the fire and were bland. White meat seemed to lose moisture as it cooked, so that by the time it had reached a temperature zone that made it safe to eat, it was also too dry to enjoy. With its extra fat, dark meat was invariably juicier than white meat, but still needed a considerable flavor boost before it could be called perfect. Sticking with dark meat, we decided to attack the flavor problem first, reasoning that once we could produce well-seasoned, juicy chicken chunks, we'd work out the kinks of cooking fruits and vegetables at the same time.

Always thinking that simpler is better, we decided to go with the simplest solution, a spice rub. We'd had success with rubs on grilled chicken parts, and we saw no reason why rubs wouldn't lend flavor to kebabs as well. Intrigued by a suggestion in a recent cookbook that the rub might be sprinkled on the cooked meat immediately after grilling rather than worked into it beforehand, we decided to try this, too. The spice rub was disappointing all around. The chicken pieces looked and tasted dry. Because chicken chunks consist mostly of surface area, the flavors of the rub were much more prominent than with chicken parts, obscuring any grilled flavor. Furthermore, because the chunks are skinless, there was no fat to dissolve the spices and help form a crispy crust. The surface of the chunks looked and tasted dry, and the spices were a little powdery and raw-tasting, especially when sprinkled on after cooking.

Wanting to add a little moisture, we turned to wet preparations, or marinades. We mixed together a simple marinade of lemon juice, olive oil, garlic, and herbs and soaked the chicken in it for three hours, the recommended time for skin-on chicken parts. We liked the glossy, slightly moist grilled crust that the marinade produced and the way the garlic and herb flavors had penetrated the meat. But we found the flavor of the lemon juice to be overpowering on these small chunks. More of a problem, however, was the way the acid-based marinade "tenderized" the chicken. When chicken parts are bathed in this solution, the skin protects the meat, which grills up juicy and firm. Even with shorter marinating times (we tried one hour and half an hour), the skinless chunks were mushy after cooking.

Was there a way to season the chicken all the way through and keep it moist on the grill without the acid? We ruled out brining because it would make the small skinless chicken chunks much too salty. But we wanted to get the juiciness and flavor that brining imparts. Figuring that soaking the chicken in a lightly salted marinade (rather than the large quantities of water and salt called for in brining) might work, we prepared two batches of acid-free olive oil marinade, one with salt and one without, and let the chunks sit in the marinade for three hours before grilling. The results were what we hoped for. The salted marinade produced plump, well-seasoned chunks of chicken. The chicken marinated without salt was drier and seemed to have absorbed less flavor from the garlic and herbs.

One small problem remained. What if we wanted a little bit of lemon flavor on our chicken without sacrificing texture? We made up a batch of our marinade and added just a teaspoon of lemon juice to see what would happen. After just half an hour with such a small amount of juice, the chicken chunks had turned white, indicating that they had been partially cooked by the acid. When cooked, they exhibited the same softening as chicken marinated for a longer time in a much more acidic solution. Our suggestion for people who like their chicken kebabs lemony, then, is to squirt the kebabs with a wedge of lemon after they come off the grill instead of adding lemon juice to the marinade (just as we suggest for beef kebabs).

After fine-tuning the method, we settled on 1 teaspoon salt (this quantity seasons the chicken without making it overly salty) for 1½ pounds of chicken and a marinating time of at least three hours (during testing, chicken marinated for less time did not absorb enough flavor). Because there is no acid in the marinade and thus no danger of it breaking down the texture of the meat, it can be combined with the chicken up to 24 hours before cooking.

It was clear early on that cooking chicken and vegetables together enhances the flavor of both. Therefore, we needed to figure out how to prepare the vegetables so that they would cook at the same rate as the chicken. Precooking seemed like a hassle, so we eliminated items like potatoes and yams, which take more time to cook through on the grill than chicken. Because the chicken was so highly flavored from the marinade, and because we did not like the way some vegetables and fruits began to lose their characteristic flavor after just a short dip, we decided against marinating them. We found that simply tossing the fruits and vegetables with a little olive oil, salt, and pepper produced the best-textured and best-flavored chunks.

In general, resilient (but not rock-hard) vegetables fared well. When cut in proper sizes, zucchini, eggplant, mushrooms, and bell peppers cook thoroughly but stay moist and lend good flavor and crunch to chicken skewers. Cherry tomatoes, on the other hand, cook too quickly and tend to disintegrate by the time the chicken is done.

Preparing Vegetables and Fruits for Skewering

If prepared according to these directions, the following vegetables and fruits will cook through at the same rate as the chicken chunks. We found that the tendency of chicken to be bland and dry permits a wider range of vegetable and fruit selections than other meat. Use ripe fruit that is still fairly firm. Mushy fruit will fall apart on the grill. We have suggested marinades for the chicken (page 165) that work well with each vegetable, keeping in mind cultural traditions as well as the flavor and texture of the vegetable or fruit.

VEGETABLE OR FRUIT	PREPARATION	MARINADE FOR CHICKEN
Mushrooms, button (small)	Slice off stems and wipe clean	Garlic and Herb, Southwestern, Asian
Onions	Peel and cut into ½-inch-thick wedges	Any
Peppers, bell	Stem, seed, and cut into 1-inch-wide wedges	Any
Shallots (small)	Peel and skewer whole	Any
Zucchini	Remove ends; slice into ½-inch-thick rounds	Garlic and Herb, Middle Eastern, Curry, Asian
Apples	Core and cut into 1-inch cubes	Garlic and Herb, Middle Eastern, Curry, Asian
Peaches	Halve, pit, and cut each half into thirds	Garlic and Herb, Southwestern, Curry, Caribbean
Pears	Core and cut into 1-inch cubes	Garlic and Herb, Middle Eastern, Curry, Asian
Pineapples	Peel, core, and cut into 1-inch cubes	Southwestern, Curry, Caribbean

Firm-textured fruits like apples, pears, and pineapples grill beautifully, holding their shape while cooking all the way through. Fruits that tend toward softness when overripe, like peaches and nectarines, work fine if still firm. Softer fruits like mangoes or grapes turn to mush after 10 minutes over the fire, no matter what their size. Certain fruits and vegetables are obvious matches for certain marinades. With curry-marinated chicken, we like pineapple cubes and slices of onion. With Middle Eastern flavors, zucchini and eggplant are good choices. See the chart on the facing page for information on preparing individual fruits and vegetables for chicken skewers and matching them with marinades.

As for the fire, we found medium-hot to be best. A hotter fire chars the outside before the inside is done; a cooler fire won't give you those appetizing grill marks and may dry out the chicken as it cooks. For the juiciest chicken with the strongest grilled flavor, skewers should be cooked for eight to 10 minutes. Check for doneness by cutting into one of the pieces with a small knife as soon as the chicken looks opaque on all sides. Remove it from the grill as soon as there is no sign of pink at the center.

After experimenting with various sizes and shapes, we chose 1½-inch chunks, small enough for easy eating but big enough to get some good grilled flavor before they have to come off the fire. With smaller chunks and thin strips, there's no margin for error; a few seconds too long on the grill and you'll wind up with a dry-as-dust dinner.

A final note on skewering. Chicken pieces simply skewered through the center may spin around when you lift them from the grill, inhibiting even cooking. (For some reason, this is less of a problem with other meat, probably because chicken is just slippery by nature.) We tried out some heavy-gauge twisted metal skewers designed to prevent this problem, but in the end found that threading the ingredients through two thinner skewers at once (see the illustration on page 164) was more effective. We prefer thin but sturdy metal skewers that can fit two at a time through the kebabs but won't bend under the weight of the food.

Charcoal-Grilled Chicken Kebabs

SERVES 4 AS A MAIN COURSE
OR 8 AS AN APPETIZER

Although white breast meat can be used, we prefer the juicier, more flavorful dark thigh meat for these kebabs. Whichever you choose, do not mix white and dark meat on the same skewer, since they cook at different rates.

1	recipe marinade of choice (see page 165)
1½	pounds skinless boneless chicken thighs, cut into 1½-inch chunks
3	cups vegetables and/or fruit, prepared according to the instructions on page 162
2	tablespoons extra-virgin olive oil
	Salt and ground black pepper
	Lemon wedges for serving (optional)

1. Mix the marinade and the chicken in a gallon-size zipper-lock plastic bag; seal the bag and refrigerate, turning once or twice, until the chicken has marinated fully, at least 3 and up to 24 hours.

2. Light a large chimney starter filled with hardwood charcoal (about 6 quarts) and allow to burn until all the charcoal is covered with a layer of fine gray ash. Build a single-level fire by spreading the coals evenly out over the bottom of the grill. Set the cooking grate in place, cover the grill with the lid, and let the grate heat up, about 5 minutes. Use a grill brush to scrape the cooking grate clean. The grill is ready when you have a medium-hot fire. (See how to gauge heat level on page 4.)

3. Meanwhile, lightly coat the vegetables and/or fruit by tossing them in a medium bowl with the oil and salt and pepper to taste.

4. Remove the chicken chunks from the bag; discard the marinade. Use one hand to hold two skewers about ½ inch apart, then thread a portion of the chicken and vegetables on both skewers at once for easy turning on the grill (see the illustration on page 164). Repeat with the remaining chicken and vegetables to make eight sets of double skewers.

5. Grill the kebabs, uncovered, turning each

BARBECUE 911

Spinning Chicken Kebabs

Who hasn't fumbled when trying to thread raw chicken onto skewers for kebabs? Raw chicken is slippery and even more so with the addition of marinade. This can cause the meat to spin around on a skewer, resulting in unevenly cooked kebabs. How can you ensure that your chicken stays in place?

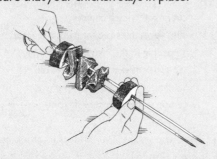

Simply thread the chicken onto two skewers held side by side (rather than one) to keep it stable. Use one hand to hold two skewers about ½ inch apart, then thread boneless chunks of chicken and vegetables, if desired, onto both skewers simultaneously.

---

kebab one-quarter turn every 2 minutes, until the chicken and vegetables and/or fruit are lightly browned and the meat is fully cooked, about 9 minutes (or 8 minutes if you are cooking white meat). Check for doneness by cutting into one piece when it looks opaque on all sides. Remove the kebabs from the grill when there is no pink at the center. Serve immediately.

➤ VARIATIONS
Gas-Grilled Chicken Kebabs

Heat the grill until very hot to burn off any residue from your last meal, but then turn the burners down to medium-high to avoid singeing the kebabs.

Follow the recipe for Charcoal-Grilled Chicken Kebabs through step 1. Turn on all the burners to high, close the lid, and heat the grill until very hot, about 15 minutes. Use a grill brush to scrape the cooking grate clean. Turn the burners down to

medium-high. Proceed with the recipe as directed from Step 3.

Caribbean Chicken Kebabs with Black Bean and Mango Salsa

Mango salsa works especially well with Caribbean flavors.

Follow the recipe for Charcoal-Grilled or Gas-Grilled Chicken Skewers, using Caribbean Marinade (page 165) and 2 medium onions, peeled and cut into ½-inch-thick wedges (about 3 cups), for the vegetable. Serve with Black Bean and Mango Salsa (page 392).

Thai Chicken Satay with Spicy Peanut Sauce

Grilled chicken skewers are paired with peanut sauce for a Thai-influenced satay.

Follow the recipe for Charcoal-Grilled or Gas-Grilled Chicken Skewers, using Asian Marinade (page 165) and 2 medium red bell peppers, cored, seeded, and cut into 1-inch-pieces (about 3 cups), for the vegetable. Toss the peppers with peanut oil in place of olive oil. Serve with Spicy Peanut Dipping Sauce (page 400).

Curried Chicken Kebabs and Yogurt-Mint Cucumber Salad

The flavor of this cucumber salad is similar to that of raita, a yogurt-based condiment from India that tames the heat of spicy food.

Follow the recipe for Charcoal-Grilled or Gas-Grilled Chicken Skewers, using Curry Marinade and 1 small pineapple, peeled, cored, and cut into 1-inch cubes (about 3 cups), for the fruit. Serve with Yogurt-Mint Cucumber Salad with (page 351).

Southwestern Kebabs with Red Pepper–Jicama Relish

The relish is an excellent foil to the spicy kebabs.

Follow the recipe for Charcoal-Grilled or Gas-Grilled Chicken Skewers, using Southwestern Marinade (page 165) and 1 medium onion, cut into ½-inch-thick wedges, and 1 medium green bell pepper, cored, seeded, and cut into 1½-inch pieces (about 3 cups total), for the vegetables. Serve with Red Pepper–Jicama Relish (page 395).

MARINADES FOR CHICKEN KEBABS

Garlic and Herb Marinade

MAKES A SCANT ¾ CUP, ENOUGH TO COAT
1½ POUNDS OF CHICKEN CHUNKS

½   cup extra-virgin olive oil
¼   cup minced fresh basil, parsley, tarragon,
     oregano, mint, or snipped chives or
     2 tablespoons minced fresh thyme or
     rosemary
2   medium garlic cloves, minced or pressed
     through a garlic press (about 2 teaspoons)
1   teaspoon salt
     Ground black pepper

Whisk the ingredients, including pepper to
taste, together in a small bowl.

➤ VARIATIONS

Middle Eastern Marinade

Follow the recipe for Garlic and Herb Marinade,
using ¼ cup minced fresh mint or parsley leaves,
alone or in combination, and adding ½ teaspoon
ground cinnamon, ½ teaspoon ground allspice,
and ¼ teaspoon cayenne.

Southwestern Marinade

Follow the recipe for Garlic and Herb Marinade,
using ¼ cup minced fresh cilantro leaves,
decreasing the salt to ½ teaspoon, and adding 1
teaspoon ground cumin, 1 teaspoon chili powder, 1 teaspoon ground turmeric, and 1 seeded
and minced small fresh chile, such as a jalapeño.

Curry Marinade

Follow the recipe for Garlic and Herb
Marinade, using ¼ cup minced fresh mint or
cilantro leaves and adding 1 teaspoon curry
powder.

Caribbean Marinade

Follow the recipe for Garlic and Herb
Marinade, using ¼ cup minced fresh parsley
leaves and adding 1 teaspoon ground cumin,
1 teaspoon chili powder, ½ teaspoon ground
allspice, ½ teaspoon pepper, and ¼ teaspoon
ground cinnamon.

Asian Marinade

MAKES ¾ CUP, ENOUGH TO COAT
1½ POUNDS OF CHICKEN CHUNKS

6   tablespoons vegetable oil
¼   cup soy sauce
¼   cup minced fresh cilantro leaves
6   medium garlic cloves, minced or
     pressed through a garlic press
     (about 2 tablespoons)
2   tablespoons toasted sesame oil
1   tablespoon minced fresh ginger
2   medium scallions, sliced thin
     Ground black pepper

Whisk the ingredients, including pepper to
taste, together in a small bowl.

POULTRY SAUSAGE

OUR GOALS FOR GRILLING LOWER-FAT
poultry sausage were essentially the same as for
the traditional higher-fat pork sausages. We
wanted sausages that were moist inside (although
we knew they would be drier than the higher-
fat sausages), with nicely caramelized casings. Of
course, we also wanted to ensure that the sausages
were thoroughly cooked.

Because of their lower fat content, poultry

sausages have a tendency to dry out on the grill.
We figured that the best way to grill them would
be quickly, to better retain the juices. We began
by using direct heat but found the sausages a bit
dry. We tried various heat levels, cooking them as
quickly as possible over a hot fire and more gently
over a moderate fire. In every case, the sausages
were acceptable but not great.

At this point, we turned our attention to precooking the links. By shortening the grilling time,

we hoped to reduce moisture loss. We microwaved the links in a glass pie plate filled with ½ inch of water and covered tightly with plastic wrap for 1½ minutes. As with pork sausage, we found that microwaved poultry links looked shrunken after grilling and were slightly tough. We also noticed that the sausages seemed to have released a lot of juices and fat into the steaming water in the pie plate.

We next tried poaching the sausages in simmering water for five minutes and then grilling. This method resulted in the best poultry sausages, more moist and juicy than links that were just cooked over direct heat and much better than links that were microwaved before grilling. (As an aside, the sausages released minimal amounts of fat and juices into the poaching water.) Once grilled, these links were slightly less caramelized than those simply grilled over direct heat. Overall, though, we felt that they had as good a flavor and a far better mouthfeel and texture than links grilled without any precooking.

Charcoal-Grilled Poultry Sausages
SERVES 4
This recipe was developed for 1-inch-thick links; make adjustments as necessary when cooking thinner or thicker links.

2 pounds lean poultry sausage (8 links)

1. Light a large chimney starter filled halfway with hardwood charcoal (about 3 quarts) and allow to burn until all the charcoal is covered with a layer of fine gray ash. Build a modified two-level fire by spreading the coals out over half of the grill bottom. Set the cooking grate in place. Cover the grill with the lid and let the grate heat up, about 5 minutes. Use a grill brush to scrape the cooking grate clean. Let the coals burn down to a medium fire, about 10 minutes. (See how to gauge heat level on page 4.)

2. Meanwhile, fill a large saucepan with approximately 2 inches of water; bring to a boil over high heat. Add the sausages, reduce the heat to low, and cover. Simmer the sausages for 4 minutes. Transfer the sausages to a plate.

3. Grill the sausages, uncovered, directly over the coals, turning them every minute or two so that all sides are evenly browned, until the casings are richly caramelized and the centers are cooked through, 6 to 7 minutes. (To check for doneness, cut one of the sausages down the center with a knife; the interior should no longer be pink. Alternatively, insert an instant-read thermometer through one end of the link; the center of the link should register at least 170 degrees.) Serve immediately.

➤ VARIATION
Gas-Grilled Poultry Sausages
Make sure to turn the sausages frequently to promote even browning, but work quickly so that too much heat doesn't escape when the lid is opened.

1. Turn on all the burners to high, close the lid, and heat the grill until very hot, about 15 minutes. Use a grill brush to scrape the cooking grate clean. Turn all the burners to medium.

2. Follow the recipe for Charcoal-Grilled Poultry Sausages from step 2 and cook with the lid down.

GRILLED BONE-IN CHICKEN PARTS

GRILLED CHICKEN PARTS SHOULD HAVE richly caramelized, golden brown (not burnt) skin and moist, juicy meat. As soon as our testing started, we realized we needed to develop slightly different methods for dark and white meat parts. The higher fat content in thighs and legs makes flare-ups a greater problem, while the breasts have a tendency to dry out.

We started with dark meat and divided our tests into two sets. The first set involved particular ways of moving the chicken around on the grill surface, as well as using the grill cover for part of the cooking time, and the second set involved various ways of treating the chicken before it cooked, both to add flavor and to improve texture. We began our tests by examining grilling methods. Each method involved some variation on the two-level fire—that is, a fire in which one area is hotter than the other. The idea in every case was to get the sear from the hotter fire and cook the chicken evenly all the way through over the cooler fire.

The first of these methods seemed illogical, but a friend had insisted that it worked, so we gave it a try. In this method, the chicken was to be cooked on a low fire first, then finished up on a hot fire. However, this backward approach resulted in dry meat—a lame result for a method that saved no time or energy.

Next we tried the method that intuitively seemed most likely to succeed: searing the chicken over a medium-hot fire and then moving it to a medium-low fire to finish cooking. This approach proved to be a winner. The interior was evenly cooked, moist, and tender, and the skin dark and crisp. We found that we could use this method to cook whole legs with thighs attached or just the thighs alone with only one difference—timing. With thighs alone, you take about four to eight minutes off the cooking time.

It was now time to consider ways of adding flavor to the chicken. Options included marinating, spice rubs and pastes, barbecue sauces, salsas, and brining (soaking the chicken in a solution of saltwater, sometimes with added sugar).

Marinating the chicken was disappointing. Even several hours in a classic oil-and-acid marinade added only a small amount of flavor to the finished chicken, and oil dripping off the marinated chicken caused constant flare-ups during the initial searing period.

Rubbing the chicken with a spice rub prior to grilling proved far more satisfactory. Because rubs and pastes are composed almost entirely of spices, they have enough flavor intensity to stand up to the smoky grilled flavor and, as a result, come through much more clearly. Wet pastes and barbecue sauces often contain some sweetener and can burn if brushed on the chicken before cooking. We found it best to brush them on just before taking the chicken off the grill and then to serve extra sauce at the table.

If serving salsa or chutney at the table with the chicken, you don't need to add special flavors to the chicken before or during cooking. You should, however, still season the raw chicken

BARBECUE 911

Off-Flavored Grilled Chicken Breast

Because chicken breasts are thick and unevenly shaped, it's impossible to grill them uncovered, as you would chicken parts such as legs and thighs. Putting the grill lid down creates an oven-like effect that ensures thorough cooking, but the built-up soot on the inside of a charcoal grill cover gives the chicken an off flavor—much like soot. We found a way around this problem.

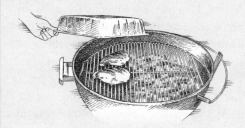

Cover the chicken breasts with a disposable aluminum roasting pan while they cook on a charcoal grill. This creates an oven-like effect that speeds up grilling but still allows air to circulate.

with salt and pepper.

As a final test, we tried brining the chicken before grilling it. Admittedly, we didn't approach this test with a lot of enthusiasm—it seemed like too much bother for what should be a simple cooking process. This just goes to show how preconceptions can be faulty, though, because it turned out to be an excellent idea.

We tried brining for various amounts of time and found that by using a brine with a high concentration of salt and sugar, we could achieve the result we wanted in only about one and a half hours. The brine penetrated the chicken, seasoning it and slightly firming up its texture before grilling. On a molecular level, the salt caused the strands of protein in the chicken meat to unwind and get tangled up with one another, forming a matrix that then served to trap water. When the chicken was grilled, this matrix created a sort of

CHICKEN PARTS WITH
BARBECUE SAUCE

ANY OF THE TOMATO-BASED BARBECUE
sauces on pages 386–387 will taste great
on grilled chicken. To use barbecue sauce,
grill the chicken following the instructions
in the appropriate recipe. During the last
two minutes of cooking, brush with some
of the sauce, cook about one minute, turn
over, brush again, and cook one minute
more. Transfer the chicken to a serving platter, brush with additional sauce to taste, and
serve, with more sauce passed at the table, if
desired. Plan on using about half a cup of barbecue sauce for a single chicken recipe, more
if you serve barbecue sauce at the table.

barrier that kept water from leaking out of the
bird. As a result, the finished chicken was juicier
and more tender. (For more information, see
"Why Brining Works," page 172.)

The sugar in the brine had one very good
effect that carried with it the potential for a minor
problem. The traces of sugar left on the exterior
of the chicken, while not enough to affect the flavor, did cause the chicken to brown more quickly
and thoroughly. Since browning adds rich, deep
flavor to any food, this was a decided advantage.
However, the browning also took place more
quickly than with nonbrined chicken, so on our
first try we managed to burn the skin on some
pieces. When grilling brined chicken, be sure to
watch it very carefully during the initial browning
period to prevent charring.

If you don't have time to brine your chicken,
you can still get excellent results with the two-
level fire method by adding deep flavor with a
spice rub or paste. If you choose not to brine,
make sure to sprinkle the chicken with salt before
heading to the grill.

Having conducted all of the above tests with
legs, we now turned to breasts, which proved even
more challenging. Bone-in chicken breasts can be
especially tricky to grill because they're thick and
unevenly shaped. Grilling thighs, legs, or boneless

breasts is much easier. But when properly grilled,
bone-in, skin-on breasts can be particularly tasty.
As with dark meat parts, we found starting the
chicken over a low fire, then moving the meat to a
hotter part of the grill to finish cooking unsatisfac-
tory. And, because the breast is leaner than the dark
meat parts, the meat was unbearably dry.

Like legs, we found that breasts are best started
over a medium-hot fire and then moved to a
cooler part of the grill. Because bone-in breasts
are thicker than thighs or legs, cooking times were
significantly longer. The breasts refused to cook
through to the bone in less than half an hour. By
this time, the skin was burning and the outer layers
of meat were dry. We tried using the grill cover,
but detected some off flavors from the burnt-on
ashes on the inside of the cover.

We did notice, however, that cooking with the
cover cut the grilling time back to 20 minutes,
about the same amount of time needed for legs and
thighs. And this shorter cooking time translated
into skin that was not black and meat that was
still juicy. We decided to improvise a cover, using
an old restaurant trick—a disposable aluminum
roasting pan—to build up heat around the breasts
and help speed along the cooking. After searing
for five minutes, we moved the breasts to a cooler
part of the fire, covered them with a disposable
pan, and continued grilling for another 15 minutes
or so. This allowed the breasts to cook through
without burning.

Like legs and thighs, breasts respond well to
brining before grilling. The same collection of
rubs, pastes, sauces, and salsas work as well with
breasts as they do with legs. You can grill dark
and white meat parts together, if you like. Set up
a three-level fire with most of the coals on one
side of the grill, some coals in the middle, and
no coals on the opposite side. Sear all the chicken
parts over the hottest part of the fire, finish cooking the legs and thighs over the medium-low heat
in the middle, and move the seared breasts to the
coolest part of the grill and cover with a disposable pan. Sounds complicated, but it makes perfect
sense once you try it and taste the results. For more
information on grilling mixed chicken parts, see
page 179.

Charcoal-Grilled Bone-In Chicken Thighs or Legs

SERVES 4

Brining improves the chicken's flavor, but if you're short on time, skip step 1 and season the chicken generously with salt and pepper before cooking. To use kosher salt in the brine, see page 172 for conversion information. Add flavorings before or during cooking: Rub the chicken parts with a spice rub or paste before putting them on the grill. If you'd prefer to season the chicken with barbecue sauce, brush the sauce on during the final 2 minutes of cooking (see page 168 for details). If the fire flares because of dripping fat, move the chicken to a cooler area.

8   bone-in, skin-on chicken thighs or 4 whole chicken legs
6   tablespoons table salt (see note)
6   tablespoons sugar
    Ground black pepper or 1 recipe spice rub or paste (see pages 382–384)

1. To prevent burning, trim overhanging fat and skin from the chicken pieces. Dissolve the salt and sugar in 1 quart of cold water in a gallon-size zipper-lock plastic bag. Add the chicken; press out as much air as possible from the bag and seal. Refrigerate about 1½ hours.

2. Light a large chimney starter filled with hardwood charcoal (about 6 quarts) and allow to burn until all the charcoal is covered with a layer of fine gray ash. Build a two-level fire by stacking most of the coals on one side of the grill and arranging the remaining coals in a single layer on the other side of the grill. Set the cooking grate in place, cover the grill with the lid, and let the grate heat up, about 5 minutes. Use a grill brush to scrape the cooking grate clean. The grill is ready when the temperature of the stacked coals is medium-hot and that of the remaining coals is medium-low. (See how to gauge heat level on page 4.)

3. Meanwhile, remove the chicken from the brine, rinse well, dry thoroughly with paper towels, and season with pepper to taste or a spice rub or paste.

4. Cook the chicken, uncovered, over the hotter part of the grill until seared, 1 to 2 minutes on each side. Move the chicken to the cooler part of the grill; continue to grill, uncovered and turning occasionally, until dark and fully cooked, 12 to 16 minutes for thighs, 16 to 20 minutes for whole legs. To test for doneness, either peek into the thickest part of the chicken with the tip of a small knife (you should see no redness near the bone) or check the internal temperature at the thickest part with an instant-read thermometer, which should register 165 degrees. Transfer to a serving platter. Serve warm or at room temperature.

➤ VARIATIONS

Gas-Grilled Bone-In Chicken Thighs or Legs

Brining improves the chicken's flavor, but if you're short on time, skip step 1 and season the chicken generously with salt and pepper before cooking. Add flavorings before or during cooking: Rub the chicken parts with a spice rub or paste before putting them on the grill, or brush them with barbecue sauce during the final 2 minutes of cooking (see page 168 for details). Initial high heat is crucial in order to produce crisp skin. The chicken is then moved to a cooler part of the grill to cook through.

Follow the recipe for Charcoal-Grilled Bone-In Chicken Thighs or Legs through step 1. Turn on all the burners to high, close the lid, and heat the grill until very hot, about 15 minutes. Use a grill brush to scrape the cooking grate clean. Leave one burner on high and turn the other burner(s) down to medium-low. Meanwhile, remove the chicken from the brine, rinse well, dry thoroughly with paper towels, and season with pepper or one of the spice rubs or pastes on pages 382–384. Cook the chicken, covered, over the hotter part of the grill until seared, 1 to 2 minutes on each side. Move the chicken to the cooler part of the grill; continue to grill, covered and turning occasionally, until dark and fully cooked, 12 to 16 minutes for thighs, 16 to 20 minutes for whole legs. To test for doneness, either peek into the thickest part of the chicken with the tip of a small knife (you should see no redness near the bone) or check the internal temperature at the thickest part with an instant-read thermometer, which should register 165 degrees. Transfer to a serving platter. Serve warm or at room temperature.

Hoisin-Glazed Grilled Chicken Thighs or Legs with Napa Cabbage Slaw

This sweet and spicy Asian spin on barbecued chicken makes a fairly complete meal. Five-spice powder, which lends this dish its distinctive flavor, can be found in the Asian foods or spice aisle of most well-stocked supermarkets.

½	small head napa cabbage (about ¾ pound), halved through the core end, tough core removed, and cut crosswise into ⅛-inch strips (about 4 cups)
I	medium red bell pepper, cored, seeded, and cut into thin strips
¼	cup vegetable oil
4	tablespoons rice vinegar
2	tablespoons soy sauce
3	teaspoons minced fresh ginger
⅓	cup hoisin sauce
I	tablespoon Asian chili paste
¼	teaspoon five-spice powder
I	recipe Grilled Bone-In Chicken Thighs or Legs (charcoal or gas)

1. Mix the cabbage and bell pepper in a large bowl and set aside. For the dressing, whisk together the oil, 2 tablespoons of the vinegar, 1½ tablespoons of the soy sauce, and 1½ teaspoons of the ginger in a medium bowl until smooth.

2. For the hoisin glaze, mix the remaining 2 tablespoons vinegar, ½ tablespoon soy sauce, and 1½ teaspoons ginger in a small bowl with the hoisin sauce, chili paste, and five-spice powder.

3. Meanwhile, follow the recipe for Grilled Bone-In Chicken Thighs or Legs (charcoal or gas). During the last 2 minutes of cooking, brush the chicken with the hoisin glaze. Cook about 1 minute, turn the chicken over, brush it again, and cook 1 minute more. Transfer the chicken to a serving platter. Rewhisk the dressing and toss with the cabbage mixture. Serve the chicken immediately, with the slaw passed separately at the table.

Charcoal-Grilled Bone-In Chicken Breasts

SERVES 4

We recommend splitting whole breasts at home, rather than purchasing already split breasts (see below). Brining improves the chicken's flavor, but if you're short on time, skip step 1 and season the chicken generously with salt and pepper before cooking. To use kosher salt in the brine, see page 172 for conversion information. Add flavorings

SPLITTING A CHICKEN BREAST

Store-bought split chicken breasts are highly problematic, and we do not recommend that you buy them. Some are so sloppily cut that the tenderloins are often missing, some retain only tattered shreds of skin, and some packages contain wildly divergent sizes. You're better off buying whole breasts and splitting them yourself.

The basic method for splitting a chicken breast is to simply push a chef's knife through the skin, flesh, and bone. While this method is straightforward, sometimes the split breasts are lopsided or both lobes are marred by unruly bits of bone and cartilage around which the knife and fork must eventually navigate. Enter a classic technique to split a chicken breast. It involves the removal of the keel bone and the cartilage that divide the breast, thereby making the chicken easier to eat. This method takes a few extra minutes, but we think it's time well spent.

Begin by trimming the rib sections off the split breast (kitchen shears work particularly well for this task). Then, with the breast turned skin-side down on a cutting board, use a chef's knife to score the membrane down the center along the length of the breast. Pick up the breast and, using both hands and some force, bend back the breast lobes, forcing the keel bone to pop free. Put the chicken back on the board, grasp the keel bone, and pull it free. (On occasion, the cartilage breaks—if it does, just dig in with your fingers, grip the remaining piece, and pull it out.) Finally, use the chef's knife to halve the breast down the center at the seam, applying force near the top to cut through the wishbone.

  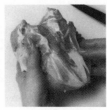  

1. Trim rib sections.　**2.** Score membrane.　**3.** Pop out keel bone.　**4.** Pull out keel bone.　**5.** Halve breast.

before or during cooking. Rub the chicken parts with a spice rub or paste before they go on the grill. Or, if you wish to season your chicken with barbecue sauce, brush the sauce on during the final 2 minutes of cooking (see page 168 for details). If the fire flares because of dripping fat, move the chicken to a cooler area.

    6   tablespoons table salt (see note)
    6   tablespoons sugar
    2   whole chicken breasts, bone-in, skin-on, split
        to make 4 halves (10 to 12 ounces each)
        Ground black pepper or 1 recipe spice rub or
        paste (see pages 382–384)
        Disposable aluminum roasting pan

1. Dissolve the salt and sugar in 1 quart of cold water in a gallon-size zipper-lock plastic bag. Add the chicken; press out as much air as possible from the bag and seal. Refrigerate until fully seasoned, about 1½ hours.

2. Light a large chimney starter filled with hardwood charcoal (about 6 quarts) and allow to burn until all the charcoal is covered with a layer of fine gray ash. Build a modified two-level fire by stacking all of the coals on one side of the grill. Set the cooking grate in place, cover the grill with the lid, and let the grate heat up, about 5 minutes. Use a grill brush to scrape the cooking grate clean. The grill is ready when you have a medium-hot fire. (See how to gauge heat level on page 4.)

3. Meanwhile, remove the chicken from the brine, rinse well, dry thoroughly with paper towels, and season with pepper to taste or a spice rub or paste.

4. Cook the chicken, uncovered, over the hotter part of the grill until well browned, 2 to 3 minutes per side. Move the chicken to the cooler part of the grill and cover with a disposable aluminum roasting pan; continue to cook, skin-side up, for 10 minutes. Turn and cook for 5 minutes more or until done. To test for doneness, either peek into the thickest part of the chicken with the tip of a small knife (you should see no redness near the bone) or check the internal temperature at the thickest part with an instant-read thermometer, which should register 160 degrees. Transfer to a serving platter. Serve warm or at room temperature.

➤ VARIATION
Gas-Grilled Bone-In Chicken Breasts
With the lid down on a gas grill, there's no need to cook the chicken under a disposable roasting pan. If the fire flares because of dripping fat or a gust of wind, move the chicken to the cooler area of the grill until the flames die down.

Follow the recipe for Charcoal-Grilled Bone-In Chicken Breasts through step 1. Turn on all the burners to high, close the lid, and heat the grill until very hot, about 15 minutes. Scrape the cooking grate clean with a grill brush. Leave one burner on high and turn the other burner(s) down to medium-low. Meanwhile, remove the chicken from the brine, rinse well, dry thoroughly with paper towels, and season with one of the spice rubs or pastes on pages 382–384. Cook the chicken, covered, over the hotter part of the grill until well browned, 2 to 3 minutes per side. Move the chicken to the cooler part of the grill; continue to cook, skin-side up and covered, for 10 minutes. Turn and cook for 5 minutes more or until done. To test for doneness, either peek into the thickest part of the chicken with the tip of a small knife (you should see no redness near the bone) or check the internal temperature at the thickest part with an instant-read thermometer, which should register 160 degrees. Transfer to a serving platter. Serve warm or at room temperature.

APPLYING BARBECUE SAUCE WITH A SQUEEZE BOTTLE

Instead of brushing barbecue sauce onto foods and dirtying both the brush and bowl, recycle a pull-top water bottle by filling it with sauce and keeping it in the refrigerator until needed. When the chicken, pork chop, or other food is almost done, squirt a little sauce onto the food, taking care not to let the bottle touch the food. Wipe the bottle clean and store it in the refrigerator until needed again.

Brining Poultry 101

Chicken, turkey, and pork have a tendency to dry out on the grill. For meat that turns out firm, juicy, and well-seasoned, we recommend brining. Soaking a chicken or turkey (or pork) in a brine—a solution of salt (and often sugar) and a liquid (usually water)—provides it with a plump cushion of seasoned moisture that will sustain it throughout cooking. The bird will actually gain a bit of weight—call it, for lack of a better phrase, water retention—that stays with it through the cooking process. This weight gain translates into moist meat; the salt and sometimes sugar in the brine translate into seasoned, flavorful meat. For a complete explanation of the process, read on.

SCIENCE: WHY BRINING WORKS

Many have attributed the added juiciness of brined chicken to osmosis—the flow of water across a barrier from a place with a higher water concentration (the brine) to a place with a lower one (the chicken). We decided to test this explanation. If osmosis is, in fact, the source of the added juiciness of brined meat, we reasoned, then a bucket of pure unsalted water should add moisture at least as well as a brine, because water alone has the highest water concentration possible: 100 percent. After soaking one chicken in brine and another in water for the same amount of time, we found that both had gained moisture, about 6 percent by weight. Satisfied that osmosis was indeed the force driving the addition of moisture to meat during brining, we roasted the two birds, along with a third straight out of the package. We would soon discover that osmosis was not the only reason why brined meat cooked up juicy.

During roasting, the chicken taken straight from the package lost 18 percent of its original weight, and the chicken soaked in water lost 12 percent of its presoaking weight. Remarkably, the brined bird shed a mere 7 percent of its starting weight. Looking at the test results, we realized that the benefit of brining could not be explained by osmosis alone. Salt, too, was playing a crucial role by aiding in the retention of water.

Table salt is made up of two ions, sodium and chloride, that are oppositely charged. Proteins, such as those in meat, are large molecules that contain a mosaic of charges, negative and positive. When proteins are placed in a solution containing salt, they readjust their shape to accommodate the opposing charges. This rearrangement of the protein molecules compromises the structural integrity of the meat, reducing its overall toughness. It also creates gaps that fill up with water. The added salt makes the water less likely to evaporate during cooking, and the result is meat that is both juicy and tender.

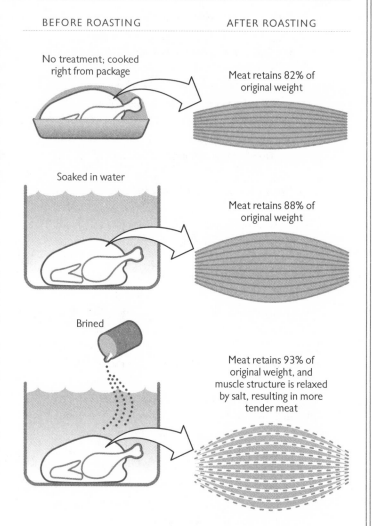

BEFORE ROASTING | AFTER ROASTING

No treatment; cooked right from package

Meat retains 82% of original weight

Soaked in water

Meat retains 88% of original weight

Brined

Meat retains 93% of original weight, and muscle structure is relaxed by salt, resulting in more tender meat

TWO TYPES OF SALT FOR BRINING

You can use either kosher or regular table salt for brining. Kosher salt is ideal because its large, airy crystals dissolve so quickly in water. Unfortunately, the salt crystals of the two major brands of kosher salt—Morton and Diamond Crystal—are not equally airy, and therefore measure differently. This inconsistency between the two brands makes precise recipe writing a challenge. Because there's no way to tell which brand of kosher salt you might have on hand, we list table salt in our brining recipes. If you use kosher salt in your brine, keep the following in mind when making the conversions from table salt in our brining recipes:

¼ cup table salt =
½ cup Diamond Crystal Kosher Salt
—or—
¼ cup plus 2 tablespoons Morton Kosher Salt

TABLE SALT   KOSHER SALT

TOOLS OF THE TRADE

From zipper-lock plastic bags that fit on the shelf of the refrigerator to a self-contained cooler chilled with ice packs and stored in a cool garage or cellar, brining vessels come in all shapes and sizes. When brining in coolers or large containers, it may be necessary to weight the food with a wide, heavy object such as a dinner plate or soup bowl. This helps keep the food fully immersed in the brine.

ZIPPER-LOCK PLASTIC BAGS
Use for: Chicken or turkey parts

COOLER OR WASHTUB
Use for: Turkey

LARGE BOWL, SOUP POT, OR DUTCH OVEN
Use for: Cornish hen (whole or butterflied), chicken (whole or butterflied)

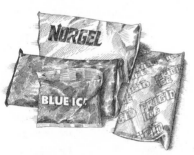

ICE PACKS
The refrigerator keeps a brine at the ideal temperature of 40 degrees. Ice packs keep the temperature down when refrigerator space is at a premium or the brining vessel is especially large.

TWO WAYS TO RINSE BRINED POULTRY

Some recipes call for rinsing brined chicken or turkey of the excess salt on its surface. This step can make a mess of your countertop. Using your sink to contain the mess and a wire rack or colander to hold the meat will streamline the process.

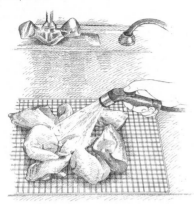

Place the chicken or turkey on a wire rack or in a colander. Set the rack or colander in an empty sink and use the sink sprayer or tap to wash off the meat. Then blot the meat dry with paper towels.

HANGING IT OUT TO DRY

Brining does have one negative effect on chicken and turkey: Adding moisture to the skin as well as the flesh can prevent the skin from crisping when cooked. We found that air-drying, a technique used in many Chinese recipes for roast duck, solves this problem. Letting brined chicken and turkey dry uncovered in the refrigerator allows surface moisture to evaporate, making the skin visibly more dry and taut, thereby promoting crispness when cooked. Although this step is optional, if crisp skin is a goal, it's worth the extra time. For best results, air-dry whole brined birds overnight. Brined chicken parts can be air-dried for several hours.

Transfer the brined bird to a heavy-duty wire rack set over a rimmed baking sheet, pat the bird dry with paper towels, and refrigerate. The rack lifts the bird off the baking sheet, allowing air to circulate freely under the bird.

GRILLED TANDOORI-STYLE CHICKEN

TO MOST PEOPLE, TANDOORI CONJURES AN image of pieces of unnaturally red dyed chicken from local Indian restaurants. What they often don't realize is that tandoori is not a dish per se but a cooking method. A tandoor oven is a beehive-shaped structure that cooks both meats and breads at a very high temperature in a very short time. While not exactly a tandoor oven, the grill works on the same principles: high temperatures and short cooking times. Our goal was to replicate the flavors of tandoori chicken on the grill.

We were hoping to avoid the dry and flavorless chicken that arrives when you order tandoori chicken in many restaurants. We also wanted to flavor the chicken in the time that it took for the grill to heat, and we didn't want to use any exotic spices. During our research, we ran across many recipes that called for marinating the chicken in spiced yogurt from six to 24 hours. Marinating seemed like a lengthy proposition, so we choose to forgo it in favor of a dry spice rub.

Consulting the recipes we had gathered, we compiled a list of spices to try in our rub. The three flavors that topped the list were ginger, coriander, and cumin. Our initial attempt combined equal amounts of all three, but we found that the cumin was too aggressive and masked the other flavors. Reducing the cumin by half took care of this problem. Beyond these three spices, the combinations were endless. After much testing, we chose turmeric for color and pungency, a small amount of cinnamon for sweetness, and a pinch of cayenne pepper for heat.

Once we had determined the makeup of the spice rub, we had to decide what type of chicken part we wanted to use. Chicken legs and thighs worked well, but tasters felt that while the chicken meat was moist, it did not absorb enough flavor from the rub. Our next test was with boneless, skinless breasts. The result was the exact opposite of the legs: The breasts were well flavored but dry. Seeking the middle ground, we tried bone-in, skin-on chicken breasts, which turned out to be the answer. The skin protected the meat from drying out, and direct contact between the meat and

rub was enough to give the chicken good flavor.

Tasters noticed that the tanginess normally associated with tandoori chicken was missing in our version. This was because we didn't marinate our chicken in yogurt. We decided instead to introduce the yogurt in the form of raita. A common Indian condiment, raita is a yogurt-based sauce served with a variety of foods. Mixing yogurt with garlic and cilantro provided a fresh and flavorful sauce that complemented the flavors in the spice rub.

Charcoal-Grilled Tandoori-Style Chicken Breasts with Raita
SERVES 4

We found the raita tastes much better made with whole-milk yogurt, although low-fat yogurt can be used. Do not use nonfat yogurt; the sauce will taste hollow and bland.

1	cup whole-milk yogurt
2	tablespoons chopped fresh cilantro leaves
1	medium garlic clove, minced or pressed through a garlic press (about 1 teaspoon)
	Salt and cayenne pepper
1	tablespoon minced fresh ginger
1	tablespoon ground coriander
1½	teaspoons ground cumin
1	teaspoon ground turmeric
½	teaspoon ground cinnamon
2	whole chicken breasts, bone-in, skin-on, split to make 4 halves (10 to 12 ounces each) (see page 170)

1. Light a large chimney starter filled with hardwood charcoal (about 6 quarts) and allow it to burn until all the charcoal is covered with a layer of fine gray ash. Build a modified two-level fire by spreading the coals over half of the grill (see the illustration on page 4). Set the cooking grate in place, cover the grill with the lid, and let the grate heat up, about 5 minutes. Use a grill brush to scrape the cooking grate clean. The grill is ready when the coals are hot. (See how to gauge heat level on page 4.)

2. Meanwhile, mix the yogurt, cilantro, and

garlic together in a medium bowl. Season with salt and cayenne pepper to taste and refrigerate until needed. Mix the ginger, coriander, cumin, turmeric, cinnamon, ½ teaspoon salt, and ¼ teaspoon cayenne together in a small bowl.

3. Coat both sides of the chicken breasts with the spice mixture. Cook the chicken, uncovered, over the hotter part of the grill until well browned, 2 to 3 minutes per side. Move the chicken, skin-side up, to the cooler side of the grill and cover with a disposable aluminum roasting pan (see the illustration on page 167); continue to cook for 10 minutes. Turn and cook for 5 minutes more or until done. To test for doneness, either peek into the thickest part of the chicken with the tip of a small knife (you should see no redness near the bone) or check the internal temperature at the thickest part with an instant-read thermometer, which should register 160 degrees. Transfer to a serving platter. Serve immediately with the yogurt mixture.

➤ VARIATION

Gas-Grilled Tandoori-Style Chicken Breasts with Raita

With the lid down on a gas grill, there's no need to cook the chicken under a disposable roasting pan. If the fire flares because of dripping fat or a gust of wind, move the chicken to the cooler area of the grill until the flames die down.

Turn on all the burners to high, close the lid, and heat the grill until very hot, about 15 minutes. Use a grill brush to scrape the cooking grate clean. Leave one burner on high and turn the other burner(s) down to medium-low. Follow the recipe for Charcoal-Grilled Tandoori Breast with Raita from step 2. Cook the chicken, skin-side up, covered, over the hotter part of the grill until well browned, 2 to 3 minutes per side. Move the chicken to the cooler side of the grill and continue to cook, covered, for 10 minutes. Turn and cook for 5 minutes more or until done. To test for doneness, either peek into the thickest part of the chicken with the tip of a small knife (you should see no redness near the bone) or check the internal temperature at the thickest part with an instant-read thermometer, which should register 160 degrees. Transfer to a serving platter. Serve immediately with the yogurt mixture.

THAI GRILLED CHICKEN

THAI GRILLED CHICKEN, OR GAI YANG, IS classic street fare. This herb- and spice-rubbed chicken is served in small pieces and eaten as finger food, along with a sweet and spicy dipping sauce. Thai flavors are wonderfully aromatic and complex, making this dish a refreshing change of pace from typical barbecue fare. But is it possible to bring the flavors of Thailand into the American kitchen (or backyard) without using an ingredient list as long as your arm and making several trips to Asian specialty stores?

An initial sampling of recipes made us wonder if this dish ought to remain as indigenous street food. Among the hard-to-find ingredients were cilantro root and lemongrass, and there was a profusion of odd mixtures, including an unlikely marriage of peanut butter and brown sugar. In the end, the simplest version won out: a rub made only with cilantro, black pepper, lime juice, and garlic. We would use this as our working recipe.

Because tasters preferred white meat, we decided to go with bone-in breasts. Brined chicken was vastly preferred to unbrined, and tasters liked the addition of sugar along with salt, which complemented the sweetness of the sauce. We settled on ½ cup of each in 2 quarts of water.

Tasters liked the working rub recipe, but they wanted more complexity of flavor. Our first step was to reduce the amount of cilantro, as it had been overpowering the other ingredients. Curry powder made the chicken taste too much like Indian food, and coconut milk turned the chicken milky and soggy, with flabby skin. The earthy flavor of coriander was welcome, and fresh ginger worked well to balance the garlic. Tasters praised this blend as more complex but still lacking bite, so we added more garlic.

The skin on the chicken was now crisp and flavorful, but not much rub was getting through to the meat. Test cooks offered suggestions ranging from slicing pockets in the meat and stuffing them with the rub to butterflying the breasts and placing the rub inside. In the end, the best alternative proved to be the easiest: We took some of the rub and placed it in a thick layer under the skin as well as on top of it. Now not only the crisp skin was flavorful but the moist flesh beneath it as well.

Most recipes call for grilling the chicken over a single-level fire, but this resulted in a charred exterior and an uncooked interior. We tried a modified two-level fire (one side of the grill holds all of the coals; the other side is empty) and, voilà, partial success! We first browned the chicken directly over the coals and then moved it to the cooler side of the grill to finish cooking. This was a big improvement, but the chicken still wasn't cooking through to the middle. Covering the grill—to make it more like an oven—was an obvious solution, but better yet was using a disposable foil pan, which creates a "mini oven." (Charcoal grill covers are home to deposits of smoke, ash, and debris that lend off flavors to foods.)

The true Thai flavors of this dish come through in the sauce, a classic combination of sweet and spicy. Most recipes suffered from one extreme or the other. In our working recipe, we had tried to create a balance of flavors: 2 teaspoons of red pepper flakes, ⅓ cup of sugar, ¼ cup of lime juice, ¼ cup of white vinegar, and 3 tablespoons of fish sauce. But tasters found even this sauce to be overwhelmingly sweet and spicy.

Reducing the red pepper flakes was a step in the right direction, as it allowed the other flavors to come through. Everyone liked garlic, but not too much; there was already a lot of garlic on the chicken. A decrease in the amount of fish sauce was welcomed, reducing the fishy flavor of the sauce but not its salty complexity. We found it best to mix the sauce right after the chicken goes into the brine, which gives the flavors time to meld.

Traditionally, gai yang is cut into small pieces and eaten as finger food. But our version is just as

SCIENCE: Cutting Boards and Bacteria

In 1994, a research report was published that proved to be the opening salvo in a long battle over which material was more sanitary for cutting boards, wood or plastic. The researchers found that fewer bacteria could be recovered from wooden boards infected with live cultures than from plastic boards treated the same way. These results caused the researchers to question the prevailing view that plastic was more sanitary than wood; some have further interpreted the data to mean that wood is, in fact, a safer material for cutting boards. In a report that followed, researchers at a U.S. Department of Agriculture lab concluded that beef bacteria on polyethylene and wooden cutting boards had statistically similar patterns of attachment and removal. Even so, the idea that wood is more sanitary than plastic persists.

We wanted to get our own perspective on the problem and so asked four staff members to donate their used boards, two wooden and two plastic. We found very little bacteria growing on these boards when we sampled them, so we took the boards to a local lab to have them artificially inoculated with bacteria. The procedure worked as follows: A drop of the medium was placed on the boards, the boards were left to sit for 40 minutes to allow for absorption of the bacteria, and an attempt was then made to remove the bacteria. In repeated tests, between 6.0 percent and 8.1 percent of the bacteria were recovered from the plastic and between 1.3 percent and

6.2 percent from the wood. Given that the number of bacteria recovered from each type of board was well into the hundreds of thousands, there was little to assure us that one material was much safer than the other.

Scrubbing the boards with hot soapy water was a different story. Once the contaminated boards were cleaned, we recovered an average of 0.00015 percent from the plastic and 0.00037 percent from the wood—or fewer than 100 bacteria from each board. In a related test, we were also able to transfer bacteria from contaminated, unwashed boards made from both wood and plastic to a Petri dish using potatoes and onions. But our most surprising discovery by far was that the bacteria could persist on unwashed boards of both types for up to 60 hours!

What, then, is the truth about cutting boards? Both plastic and wooden boards can hold on to bacteria for long periods of time. Both plastic and wooden boards allow for easy transference of bacteria to other foods. Luckily, we found that scrubbing with hot soapy water was quite an effective (though not perfect) way of cleaning both kinds of boards; the USDA also recommends the regular application of a solution of 1 teaspoon bleach per quart of water and then allowing the board to air-dry. Simply put, maintenance, not material, provides the greatest margin of safety.

good (and a whole lot neater) when served whole with a knife and fork. Is this an Americanized dish? Yes. But the flavors are true to its Thai roots, and the ingredients can be found in most supermarkets.

Thai Grilled Chicken Breasts with Spicy, Sweet, and Sour Dipping Sauce
SERVES 4

For even cooking, the chicken breasts should be of comparable size. The best way to ensure this is to buy whole breasts and split them yourself (see the instructions on page 170). If you prefer to skip this step, try to purchase split bone-in, skin-on breasts that weigh about 12 ounces each. To use kosher salt in the brine, see page 172 for conversion information. If using a charcoal grill, you will need a disposable aluminum roasting pan to cover the chicken (the lid on a charcoal grill can give the chicken resinous off flavors). Some of the rub is inevitably lost to the grill, but the chicken will still be flavorful.

CHICKEN AND BRINE
- 1/2 cup sugar
- 1/2 cup table salt (see note)
- 2 whole chicken breasts, bone-in, skin-on, split to make 4 halves (10 to 12 ounces each)

DIPPING SAUCE
- 1/3 cup sugar
- 1/4 cup distilled white vinegar
- 1/4 cup juice from 4 limes
- 2 tablespoons fish sauce
- 3 small garlic cloves, minced or pressed through a garlic press (about 1 1/2 teaspoons)
- 1 teaspoon red pepper flakes

RUB
- 2/3 cup chopped fresh cilantro leaves
- 1/4 cup juice from 4 limes
- 12 medium garlic cloves, minced or pressed through a garlic press (about 1/4 cup)
- 2 tablespoons minced fresh ginger
- 2 tablespoons ground black pepper
- 2 tablespoons ground coriander
- 2 tablespoons vegetable oil, plus more for the cooking grate

INGREDIENTS: Fish Sauce

Fish sauce is a potent Asian condiment based on the liquid from salted, fermented fish—and smells as such. It has a very concentrated flavor and, like anchovy paste, when used in appropriately small amounts it lends foods a salty complexity that is impossible to replicate. We gathered six brands from the local supermarket, natural food store, and Asian market. Tasters had the option of tasting the fish sauce straight up (which few could stomach) or in a modified version of the Thai grilled chicken dipping sauce.

Our most interesting finding was that color correlates with flavor; the lighter the sauce, the lighter the flavor. That said, all six brands are recommended. There was in fact only one point (out of 10) separating all six sauces. With such a limited ingredient list—most brands contained some combination of fish extract, water, salt, and sugar—it makes sense that the differences in the sauces were nominal. And because fish sauce is used in such small amounts, minute flavor differences get lost among the other flavors of a dish. Our advice: Purchase whatever is available.

1. TO BRINE THE CHICKEN: Dissolve the sugar and salt in 2 quarts of cold water in a large container. Submerge the chicken in the brine, cover, and refrigerate at least 30 minutes but not longer than 1 hour. Rinse the chicken under cool running water and pat dry with paper towels.

2. FOR THE DIPPING SAUCE: Whisk the ingredients in a small bowl until the sugar dissolves. Let stand 1 hour at room temperature to allow the flavors to meld.

3. TO MAKE AND APPLY THE RUB: Combine all the rub ingredients in a small bowl; work the mixture with your fingers to thoroughly combine. Slide your fingers between the skin and meat of one chicken piece to loosen the skin, taking care not to detach the skin. Rub about 2 tablespoons of the mixture under the skin. Thoroughly rub an even layer of the mixture onto all exterior surfaces, including the bottom and sides. Repeat with the remaining chicken pieces. Place the chicken in a medium bowl, cover with plastic wrap, and refrigerate while preparing the grill.

4. TO GRILL THE CHICKEN: Light a large chimney starter filled with charcoal briquettes (6 quarts) and burn until all the charcoal is covered with a layer of

fine gray ash, about 15 minutes. Build a modified two-level fire by arranging the coals to cover one half of the grill, piling them about 3 briquettes high. Position the cooking grate over the coals, cover the grill, and let the grate heat up, about 5 minutes.

Use a grill brush to scrape the cooking grate clean. The grill is ready when you have a medium-hot fire. (See how to gauge heat level on page 4.) Using long-handled grill tongs, dip a wad of paper towels in vegetable oil and wipe the cooking grate.

EQUIPMENT: Garlic Presses

Most cooks dislike the chore of mincing garlic, and many turn to garlic presses. We know that many professional cooks sneer at this tool, but we have a different opinion. In hundreds of hours of use in our test kitchen, we have found that this little tool delivers speed, ease, and a comfortable separation of garlic from fingers.

The garlic press offers other advantages. First is flavor, which changes perceptibly depending on how the cloves are broken down. The finer a clove of garlic is cut, the more flavor is released from its broken cells. Fine mincing or pureeing, therefore, results in a fuller, more pungent garlic flavor. A good garlic press breaks down the cloves more than the average cook would with a knife. Second, a good garlic press ensures a consistently fine texture, which in turn means better distribution of the garlic throughout the dish.

The question for us, then, was not whether garlic presses work but which of the many available presses work best. Armed with 10 popular models, we pressed our way through a mountain of garlic cloves to find out.

Garlic press prices vary by a shocking 700 percent, from about $3 up to $25. Some are made from metal and others from plastic. Some offer devices to ease cleaning, and most show subtle differences in handle and hopper design.

Most garlic presses share a common design consisting of two handles connected by a hinge. At the end of one handle is a small, perforated hopper; at the end of the other is a plunger that fits snugly inside the hopper. The garlic cloves in the hopper get crushed by the descending plunger when the handles are squeezed together, and the puree is extruded through the perforations in the bottom of the hopper.

Some presses employ a completely different design—a relatively large cylindrical container with a tight-fitting screw-down plunger. These presses are designed for large capacity, but the unusual design failed to impress us. The screw-type plungers required both pressure and significant repetitive motion, which contributed to hand fatigue. This seemed like a lot of work just to press garlic. Matters did not improve when the hoppers were loaded with multiple garlic cloves. Even greater effort was required to twist down the plungers, and the texture of the garlic puree produced was coarse and uneven.

A good garlic press should not only produce a smooth, even-textured puree but also be easy to use. To us, this meant that different users should be able to operate it without straining their hands. With some notable exceptions, all of our presses performed reasonably well in this regard.

Several of our test cooks wondered if we could make an easy task even easier by putting the garlic cloves through the presses without first removing their skins. Instructions on the packaging of the Zyliss and Bodum presses specified that it was OK to press unpeeled cloves, and our tests bore out this assertion. Though the directions for several other presses did not address this issue specifically, we found that the Oxo and the Endurance also handled unpeeled garlic with ease. We did note, however, that the yield of garlic puree was greater across the board when we pressed peeled cloves. While we were at it, we also tried pressing chunks of peeled fresh ginger. The Zyliss, Kuhn Rikon, and Oxo were the only three to excel in this department, and we found that smaller chunks, about 1/2 inch, were crushed much more easily than larger, 1-inch pieces.

When all was said and pressed, the traditionally designed, moderately priced Zyliss turned out to be comfortable and consistent, and it produced the finest, most even garlic puree. In addition, it handled unpeeled garlic and small chunks of fresh ginger without incident. While other presses got the job done, the Zyliss just edged out the field in terms of both performance and design.

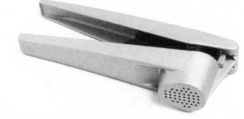

THE BEST GARLIC PRESS
We found that this Zyliss press can handle two cloves at once, producing very finely pureed garlic in a flash.

5. Place the chicken, skin-side down, on the hotter side of the grill and cook until browned, about 3 minutes. Using tongs, flip the chicken breasts and cook until browned on the second side, about 3 minutes longer. Move the chicken, skin-side up, to the cooler side of the grill and cover with a disposable aluminum roasting pan; continue to cook until an instant-read thermometer inserted into the thickest part of the breast (not touching the bone) registers 160 degrees, 10 to 15 minutes longer. Transfer the chicken to a platter and let rest 10 minutes. Serve, passing the sauce separately.

➤ VARIATION

Thai Grilled Chicken Breasts on a Gas Grill

1. Follow the recipe for Thai Grilled Chicken Breasts with Spicy, Sweet, and Sour Dipping Sauce through step 3.

2. Turn on all the burners to high, close the lid, and heat until the grill is very hot, about 15 minutes. Use a grill brush to scrape the cooking grate clean. Using long-handled grill tongs, lightly dip a wad of paper towels in vegetable oil and wipe the grill grate. Turn all but one burner to low. Place the chicken, skin-side down, on the hotter side of the grill and cook until browned, 4 to 5 minutes. Using tongs, flip the chicken breasts and cook until browned on the second side, 4 to 5 minutes longer. Move the chicken, skin-side up, to the cooler side of the grill and close the lid;

CLEANING A GARLIC PRESS

Garlic presses make quick work of garlic but are notoriously hard to clean. Recycle an old toothbrush with worn bristles for this job. The bristles will clear bits of garlic from the press and are easy to rinse clean.

cook until an instant-read thermometer inserted into the thickest part of the breast (not touching the bone) registers 160 degrees, 12 to 15 minutes more. Transfer the chicken to a platter and let rest 10 minutes. Serve, passing the sauce separately.

Charcoal-Grilled Mixed Chicken Parts
SERVES 8

Although dark meat and white meat require different grilling techniques, you can cook legs, thighs, and breasts together if you follow this method. Basically, you need to build a three-level fire, with most of the coals on one side of the grill, some coals in the middle, and no coals on the opposite side. Sear all the chicken parts over the hottest part of the fire, finish cooking the legs or thighs in the middle of the grill, and moved the seared breasts to the coolest part of the grill and cover with a disposable pan. As always, brining improves the chicken's flavor, but if you're short on time, skip step 1 and season the chicken generously with salt and pepper before cooking. To use kosher salt in the brine, see page 172 for conversion information. Add flavorings before or during cooking: Rub the chicken parts with a spice rub or paste before they go on the grill or brush them with barbecue sauce during the final 2 minutes of cooking. (See pages 382–384 for spice rub and paste recipes.)

- 3/4 cup sugar
- 3/4 cup table salt (see note)
- 8 bone-in, skin-on chicken thighs or 4 whole chicken legs
- 2 whole chicken breasts, bone-in, skin-on, split to make 4 halves (10 to 12 ounces each)
  Ground black pepper

1. Dissolve half the sugar and salt in 1 quart of cold water in a gallon-sized zipper-lock plastic bag. Add the chicken thighs or legs; press out as much air as possible from the bag and seal. Repeat the process in a second bag with the remaining salt, sugar, 1 quart of cold water, and chicken breasts. Refrigerate both bags until the chicken is fully seasoned, about 1½ hours.

2. Light a large chimney starter filled with hardwood charcoal (about 6 quarts) and allow

to burn until all the charcoal is covered with a layer of fine gray ash. Build a three-level fire by stacking most of the coals on one side of the grill, arranging the remaining coals in a single layer in the middle of the grill, and leaving the other side empty of coals. Set the cooking grate in place, cover the grill with the lid, and let the grate heat up, about 5 minutes. Use a grill brush to scrape the cooking grate clean. The grill is ready when the temperature of the stacked coals is medium-hot and that of the single layer of coals is medium-low. (See how to gauge heat level on page 4.)

3. Meanwhile, remove the chicken from the brine, rinse well, dry thoroughly with paper towels, and season with pepper to taste or one of the spice rubs or pastes on pages 382–384.

4. Cook the chicken, uncovered, over the hottest part of the grill until well browned, 2 to 3 minutes per side. Move the chicken thighs or legs to the middle part of the grill and move the chicken breasts to the area with no fire and cover with a disposable aluminum roasting pan. Continue to grill the thighs or legs, uncovered, turning occasionally, until dark and fully cooked, 12 to 16 minutes for thighs, 16 to 20 minutes for whole legs. Continue to grill the breasts, skin-side up, for 10 minutes. Turn and cook for 5 minutes more or until done. To test for doneness, either peek into the thickest part of the chicken with the tip of a small knife (you should see no redness near the bone) or check the internal temperature at the thickest part with an instant-read thermometer, which should register 165 degrees for dark meat and 160 degrees for breasts. Transfer to a serving platter. Serve warm or at room temperature.

➤ VARIATION

Gas-Grilled Mixed Chicken Parts

Since the grilling technique for light and dark meat parts is basically the same when using gas, there's not much need to adapt your cooking technique. As always, brining improves the chicken's flavor, but if you're short on time, skip step 1 and season the chicken generously with salt and pepper before cooking. (To use kosher salt in the brine, see page 172 for conversion information.) Add flavorings before or during cooking: Rub the

chicken parts with a spice rub or paste (see Chapter 11) before they go on the grill or brush them with barbecue sauce during the final 2 minutes of cooking (see page 168 for details).

1. Follow the recipe for Charcoal-Grilled Mixed Chicken Parts through step 1. Turn on all the burners to high, close the lid, and heat the grill until very hot, about 15 minutes. Use a grill brush to scrape the cooking grate clean. Leave one burner on high and turn the other burner(s) down to medium-low.

2. Proceed with the recipe for Charcoal-Grilled Chicken Parts from step 3, cooking the chicken parts, covered, over the hotter part of the grill until seared, 1 to 2 minutes on each side for dark meat and 2 to 3 minutes per side for breasts. Move the chicken to the cooler part of the grill; continue to grill, covered and turning occasionally, until dark and fully cooked, 12 to 16 minutes for thighs, 16 to 20 minutes for whole legs. Cook the breasts, skin-side up and covered, for 10 minutes, then turn and cook for 5 minutes more or until done. To test the parts for doneness, either peek into the thickest part of the chicken with the tip of a small knife (you should see no redness near the bone) or check the internal temperature at the thickest part with an instant-read thermometer, which should register 165 degrees for dark meat and 160 degrees for breasts. Transfer to a serving platter. Serve warm or at room temperature.

CHICKEN WINGS

CHICKEN WINGS ARE BEST COOKED ON THE grill so that their fat is rendered and falls away onto the coals. Cooked in the oven, the wings rest in their own fat and turn out flabby. But grill wings incorrectly and you get greasy meat, surrounded by a charred, rubbery, thick coating of skin that is hardly appealing. We wanted to develop a grilling technique that was foolproof, that would produce wings with crisp, thin, caramelized skin, tender and moist meat, and smoky grilled flavor that was well seasoned throughout. Furthermore, we wanted the wings to be eater-friendly; eating them should not be a chore.

Wings are made up of three parts: the meaty, drumstick-like portion that is closest to the breast section of the bird; the two-boned center portion that is surrounded by a band of meat and skin; and the small, almost meatless wingtip. After cutting and grilling wings several different ways, we concluded that wingtips are not worth grilling. They offer almost no meat and char long before the other two parts are even close to being cooked through.

Wingtips discarded, we pushed the meat up the bones of the remaining, meatier parts to replicate the lollipop-shaped wings favored by traditional chefs. This took too much time and effort. We then decided that the best method for preparing wings is to separate the two usable portions at the joint. The pieces are small enough to be eaten as finger food and are less awkward to eat than a whole wing.

Our first round of tests was disappointing.

Grilling the wings directly over the coals at temperatures ranging from high heat to low heat produced wings that were mediocre at best. Those cooked over medium-high and high heat charred quickly, and the skin remained thick and tough. Grilling the wings over medium and medium-low heat produced better wings; the skin was crispier and thinner, but the wings still lacked the great caramelized crust that we desired.

It was at this point that we tried a modified two-level fire, banking all of the coals on one side of the grill and leaving the other side empty. We then cooked the wings, covered, over the empty side of the grill, until cooked through. The result was a nicely moist interior, but the skin was flaccid and had a very unappealing grayish tint.

Gathering information from these initial tests, we concluded that a more sophisticated grilling technique was necessary and that perhaps even a

CUTTING WINGS

1. With a chef's knife, cut into the skin between the two larger sections of the wing until you hit the joint.

2. Bend back the two sections to pop and break the joint.

3. Cut through the skin and flesh to completely separate the two meaty portions.

4. Hack off the wingtip and discard.

SAUCES FOR CHICKEN WINGS

SERVE GRILLED WINGS WITH ONE OF THE FOLLOWING SAUCES OR WITH store-bought or homemade barbecue sauce (any of the tomato-based sauces on pages 386–387). A few of these sauces (as indicated) can be brushed on just before the wings come off the grill for a light glaze. All can be served at the table as dipping sauces.

Hoisin-Sesame Sauce

MAKES ENOUGH FOR 12 WINGS

Use as a light glaze while the wings are still on the grill or at the table as a dipping sauce.

2	tablespoons hoisin sauce
2	tablespoons water
I	tablespoon rice vinegar
I	tablespoon soy sauce
I	teaspoon toasted sesame oil
I	tablespoon vegetable oil
2	tablespoons minced fresh ginger
2	medium garlic cloves, minced or pressed through a garlic press (about 2 teaspoons)
2	tablespoons minced fresh cilantro leaves

1. Mix the hoisin sauce, water, vinegar, soy sauce, and sesame oil together in a small bowl.

2. Heat the vegetable oil in a small saucepan over medium heat. Add the ginger and garlic and sauté until fragrant but not browned, about 30 seconds. Add the hoisin mixture and cook until thickened, 1 to 2 minutes. Off the heat, stir in the cilantro.

Spicy Sauce for Buffalo Wings

MAKES ENOUGH FOR 12 WINGS

This is the classic spicy sauce for wings. Serve with Blue Cheese Dressing (this page) if desired.

I½	tablespoons unsalted butter, melted
I½	tablespoons Tabasco sauce

Mix the butter and Tabasco sauce together in a large bowl. When the chicken wings are cooked through, immediately toss them in the bowl with the Tabasco mixture.

Blue Cheese Dressing

MAKES ENOUGH FOR 12 WINGS

This is the classic accompaniment to buffalo wings. Serve as a dipping sauce at the table.

2½	ounces crumbled blue cheese (about ½ cup)
3	tablespoons buttermilk
3	tablespoons sour cream
2	tablespoons mayonnaise
2	teaspoons white wine vinegar
¼	teaspoon sugar
⅛	teaspoon garlic powder
	Salt and ground black pepper

Mash the blue cheese and buttermilk in a small bowl with a fork until the mixture resembles cottage cheese with small curds. Stir in the sour cream, mayonnaise, vinegar, sugar, and garlic powder. Taste and adjust the seasonings with salt and pepper. (The dressing can be refrigerated in an airtight container up to 1 week.)

second method of cooking was in order. We tried blanching the wings for various amounts of time before throwing them on the grill for crisping and browning, but this technique, while producing thinner, crispier skin, yielded wings with less flavor and drier meat. It was also time-consuming and added extra clean-up—not what we wanted.

So far, the best wings were those cooked directly over the coals at a medium-low heat level (a single layer of charcoal). Although they were acceptable, we felt that the texture and flavor would be greatly improved with a crispier, darker exterior. At this point we decided to try a two-level fire (not modified), in which the coals are stacked on one side of the grill (for a medium-hot fire) and placed in a single layer on the other side (for a medium-low fire). We grilled the chicken wings using two different methods. One batch was browned over medium-high heat and then moved to the cooler side of the grill to continue cooking slowly, while the other was started on medium-low heat to cook low and slow and then moved to medium-high heat to get a final quick crisping and browning. While both methods worked well, the wings cooked first over medium-low heat and then moved to medium-high heat were superior, rendering more fat from the skin and thereby producing a thin, delicate crust.

Prompted by past experience, we felt that brining might improve the flavor as well as the texture of our chicken wings. We used a brining solution in which equal amounts of sugar and kosher salt are added to water. Tasting the wings as they came off the grill, we happily discovered that the brined chicken wings were not only tasty and well seasoned throughout but that brining had produced some unexpected bonuses. The brined chicken meat was noticeably plumper before grilling and more tender after, and the wings developed a crispier, more caramelized skin than those that had not been brined.

Charcoal-Grilled Chicken Wings

SERVES 4 TO 6 AS AN APPETIZER

Make sure your grill is large enough to hold all the wings over roughly one half of the rack surface. To save time, brine the wings while the grill heats up. (To use kosher salt in the brine, see page 172 for conversion information.) Serve the wings as is, with a squeeze of lemon or lime, or with one of the sauce recipes on page 182.

 6 tablespoons table salt (see note)
 6 tablespoons sugar
 12 whole chicken wings (about 2¹/₂ pounds), separated into sections following the illustrations on page 181, wingtips discarded
  Ground black pepper

1. Dissolve the salt and sugar in 1 quart of cold water in a gallon-size zipper-lock plastic bag. Add the chicken, press out as much air as possible from the bag and seal, then refrigerate until fully seasoned, 30 minutes.

2. Light a large chimney starter filled with hardwood charcoal (about 6 quarts) and allow to burn until all the charcoal is covered with a layer of fine gray ash. Build a two-level fire by stacking most of the coals on one side of the grill and arranging the remaining coals in a single layer on the other side. Set the cooking grate in place, cover the grill with the lid, and let the grate heat up, about 5 minutes. Use a grill brush to scrape the cooking grate clean. Using long-handled grill tongs, lightly dip a wad of paper towels in vegetable oil and wipe the cooking grate. The grill is ready when the temperature of the stacked coals is medium-hot and that of the remaining coals is medium-low. (See how to gauge heat level on page 4.)

3. Meanwhile, remove the chicken from the brine, rinse well, dry thoroughly with paper towels, and season with pepper to taste.

4. Cook the chicken, uncovered, over the cooler part of the grill, turning once, until the color is spotty light brown, the skin has thinned, and the fat has rendered, 8 to 10 minutes. Move the chicken pieces to the hotter part of the grill; continue to grill, turning often to prevent charring, until the wings are spotty dark brown and the skin has crisped, 2 to 3 minutes longer. Transfer to a serving platter and serve immediately.

➤ VARIATION
Gas-Grilled Chicken Wings
Chicken wings require a lot of space on the grill. Rather than regulating the burners to create two heat levels, both burners are turned to medium heat for the initial phase of cooking and then turned to high to finish the process.

Follow the recipe for Charcoal-Grilled Chicken Wings through step 1. Turn on all the burners to high, close the lid, and heat until the grill is very hot, about 15 minutes. Use a grill brush to scrape the cooking grate clean. Using long-handled grill tongs, lightly dip a wad of paper towels in vegetable oil and wipe the cooking grate. Turn all the burners down to medium. Proceed with step 3 of Charcoal-Grilled Chicken Wings. In step 4, cook the chicken, larger drumettes toward the back of the grill (where the heat is usually more intense), covered, turning once, until the color is spotty light brown, the skin has thinned, and the fat has rendered, 12 to 14 minutes. Turn all the burners up to high; continue to grill, covered, turning often to prevent charring, until the wings are spotty dark brown and the skin has crisped, 3 to 4 minutes longer. Transfer to a serving platter and serve immediately.

BUTTERFLIED CHICKEN

REMOVING THE BACKBONE FROM A WHOLE chicken—a process known as butterflying—may seem like an unnecessary and time-consuming process. But we have found that this relatively quick and simple procedure provides many benefits, because it leaves the bird with a more even thickness. Basically, butterflying lets you grill a whole chicken in much the same way that you grill parts.

A flattened 3-pound chicken cooks in half an hour or less, whereas a whole grill-roasted bird requires one hour and 30 minutes of cooking. In addition, because the breast isn't sticking out exposed to the heat while the legs are tucked under and away from the heat, all the parts of a flattened bird get done at the same time. Finally, unlike a whole roasted chicken, the butterfly cut is a breeze to separate into sections when carving. One cut down the breast with the kitchen shears, a quick snip of the skin holding the legs, and the job is done. (See more about butterflying chicken on the facing page.)

Most recipes for butterflied chicken call for weighting the bird on the grill to promote fast, even cooking. The chicken is covered with a baking sheet and weighed down with heavy cans or bricks. We grilled butterflied chicken with and without weights and found that the weighted bird cooked more quickly and looked more attractive.

We still had a number of questions about the butterflying and cooking. Was it necessary to

cut slits on either side of the breast so that we could tuck in each leg? And did we really need to pound the chicken after we butterflied it, or was it enough to just flatten it with our hands? Finally, we wanted to know if we could season the chicken with herbs and garlic without having them burn on the grill.

We quickly discovered that tucking the chicken legs under was worth the effort, if only for visual appeal. Chickens cooked with untucked legs tended to bow and warp. Tucking the legs into the breast takes just seconds and is recommended.

We thought pounding the chicken might decrease cooking time, but it made no noticeable difference. However, it was easier to weight a chicken that had been pounded to a uniform thickness. We also liked the look of the really flattened chicken. We used a mallet with a flat side for this purpose, but whatever tool you use, make sure it has a smooth face. A rough-textured mallet will tear the chicken and give it a pockmarked appearance.

Seasoning the outside of the chicken with herbs or garlic proved to be pointless—the herbs charred and the garlic burned. But a butterflied chicken is especially easy to season under the skin. Since the back is removed, access to the legs and thighs is simple. Barbecue sauces and glazes can be brushed onto the skin once the chicken is nearly done. After just two or three minutes on the grill,

WEIGHTING A BUTTERFLIED CHICKEN

To weight a butterflied chicken while it grills, find an old rimmed baking sheet and set it on top of the chicken. Put two bricks on the pan.

the glaze will caramelize nicely and give the skin excellent flavor.

Many recipes call for turning the chicken several times on the grill. Since it is weighted, this is cumbersome. If possible, we wanted to turn the bird just once. We found that one turn was fine as long as the chicken was started skin-side up on charcoal. When we started the chicken skin-side down, the skin burned because the grill was too hot. The opposite was true on a gas grill. We found it best to start the chicken skin-side down for the best coloring. If we started the bird skin-side up, the grill surface had cooled by the time the bird was flipped, and the skin looked a bit anemic.

Charcoal-Grilled Butterflied Chicken

SERVES 4

We tested this recipe several times with a 3-pound chicken. Although grilling conditions vary, each time we cooked the chicken, it was done in less than 30 minutes—12 minutes on one side and 12 to 15 minutes on the other. For chickens that weigh closer to 3½ pounds, plan on the full 15 minutes once the chicken has been turned. To use kosher salt in the brine, see page 172 for conversion information.

- 6 tablespoons table salt (see note)
- 6 tablespoons sugar
- I whole chicken (3 to 3¹/₂ pounds), butterflied (see illustrations below)
     Ground black pepper

1. Dissolve the salt and sugar in 1 quart of cold water in a large bowl, stockpot, or Dutch oven. Immerse the chicken in the brine, cover, and refrigerate, at least 2 hours or up to 4 hours.

2. Light a large chimney starter filled three-quarters full with hardwood charcoal (about 4½ quarts) and allow to burn until all the charcoal is covered with a layer of fine gray ash. Build a single-level fire by spreading the coals evenly over the bottom of the grill. Set the cooking grate in place, cover the grill with the lid, and let the grate heat up, about 5 minutes. Use a grill brush to

BUTTERFLYING A CHICKEN

1. With the breast side down and the tail of the chicken facing you, use poultry shears to cut along one side of the backbone down its entire length.

2. With the breast side still down, turn the neck end to face you. Cut along the other side of the backbone and remove it.

3. Turn the chicken breast-side up; open the chicken out on the work surface. Use the palm of your hand to flatten it.

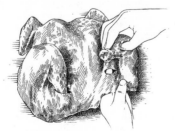

4. Make ¹/₂-inch slits on either side of each breast about I inch from the tip; tuck the legs into these openings.

5. Use the smooth face of a mallet to pound the chicken to a fairly even thickness.

185

scrape the cooking grate clean. The grill is ready when you have a medium fire. (See how to gauge heat level on page 4.)

3. Meanwhile, remove the chicken from the brine, rinse well, dry thoroughly with paper towels, and season with pepper to taste. Reposition the chicken parts if necessary.

4. Place the chicken skin-side up on the grill rack. Set a rimmed baking sheet or other flat pan on top of the chicken; put 2 bricks on the baking sheet (see the illustration on page 184). Grill until the chicken is deep brown, about 12 minutes. Turn the chicken with tongs and replace the pan and bricks. Cook until the chicken juices run clear and an instant-read thermometer inserted deep into the thigh registers 165 degrees, 12 to 15 minutes more.

5. Remove the chicken from the grill, then cover with foil and let rest for 10 to 15 minutes. Carve and serve.

➤ VARIATIONS

Gas-Grilled Butterflied Chicken
Because the chicken is cooked skin-side down first, we found it best not to replace the bricks on top of the crisp skin.

Follow the recipe for Charcoal-Grilled Butterflied Chicken through step 1. Turn on all the burners to high, close the lid, and heat until the grill is very hot, about 15 minutes. Use a grill brush to scrape the cooking grate clean. Turn all the burners down to medium. Proceed with the recipe through step 3. In step 4, place the chicken skin-side down on the cooking grate. Set a rimmed baking sheet or other flat pan on top of the chicken; put 2 bricks on the baking sheet (see the illustration on page 184). Cover and grill until the chicken skin is deeply browned and shows grill marks, 12 to 15 minutes. Turn the chicken with tongs. Do not replace the pan and bricks. Continue cooking until the chicken juices run clear and an instant-read thermometer inserted deep into the thigh registers 165 degrees, about 15 more minutes. Remove the chicken from the grill, then cover with foil and let rest for 10 to 15 minutes. Carve (see below) and serve.

Butterflied Chicken with Pesto
Classic Pesto (page 399), made with basil, is delicious, but feel free to use almost any herb paste, including pesto made with cilantro, arugula, or mint. Store-bought pesto also works well in this recipe.

Follow the recipe for Charcoal-Grilled or Gas-Grilled Butterflied Chicken, brining, rinsing, and drying the chicken as directed. Rub ½ cup pesto under the skin of the breasts, thighs, and legs. Reposition the chicken parts and season with pepper. Grill as directed.

CARVING A BUTTERFLIED CHICKEN

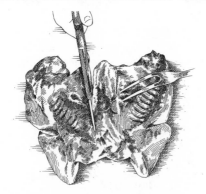

1. Place the chicken skin-side down and use kitchen shears to cut through the breastbone. (Since the breastbone is broken and the meat is flattened during pounding, this should be easy.)

2. Once the breast has been split, only the skin holds the portions together. Separate each leg and thigh from each breast and wing.

Butterflied Chicken with Barbecue Sauce

Use one of the tomato-based barbecue sauces on pages 386–387 or store-bought sauce if you like.

Follow the recipe for Charcoal-Grilled or Gas-Grilled Butterflied Chicken, brushing both sides of the chicken with ⅓ cup barbecue sauce during the last 2 minutes of the cooking time.

Butterflied Chicken with Green Olive Tapenade

The tapenade is pretty salty, so make sure to rinse the chicken thoroughly after brining.

Pulse 10 large pitted Spanish green olives, 3 tablespoons extra-virgin olive oil, 1 garlic clove, chopped, 2 anchovy fillets, and 1 teaspoon rinsed capers in a food processor until the mixture resembles a slightly chunky paste (do not overprocess). Follow the recipe for Charcoal-Grilled or Gas-Grilled Butterflied Chicken, brining, rinsing, and drying the chicken as directed. Rub the olive mixture under the skin of the breasts, thighs, and legs. Reposition the chicken parts and season with pepper. Grill as directed.

Butterflied Chicken with Chipotle, Honey, and Lime

A spicy paste made with smoky chipotle chiles is rubbed under the chicken skin before cooking, and a sweet honey–lime juice glaze is applied once the chicken is almost done.

Mix 3 chipotle chiles in adobo sauce, minced, 2 teaspoons minced fresh cilantro leaves, and ½ teaspoon lime zest together in a small bowl. Whisk 3 tablespoons lime juice and 2 tablespoons honey together in another small bowl. Follow the recipe for Charcoal-Grilled or Gas-Grilled Butterflied Chicken, brining, rinsing, and drying the chicken as directed. Rub the chile mixture under the skin of the breasts, thighs, and legs. Reposition the chicken parts and season with pepper. Grill as directed, brushing both sides of the chicken with the honey–lime juice glaze during the last 2 minutes of cooking time.

Butterflied Chicken with Lemon and Rosemary

An Italian classic. Try other herbs, including oregano, sage, thyme, or marjoram, in place of the rosemary.

Mix 2 teaspoons lemon zest, 2 medium garlic cloves, minced or pressed through a garlic press, and 1 teaspoon minced fresh rosemary together in a small bowl. Whisk 3 tablespoons lemon juice and 3 tablespoons extra-virgin olive oil together in another small bowl. Follow the recipe for Charcoal-Grilled or Gas-Grilled Butterflied Chicken, brining, rinsing, and drying the bird as directed. Rub the lemon zest mixture under the skin of the breasts, thighs, and legs. Reposition the chicken parts and season with pepper. Grill as directed, brushing both sides of the chicken with the lemon juice–oil mixture during the last 2 minutes of cooking time.

EQUIPMENT: Kitchen Shears

A pair of kitchen shears is not an essential kitchen implement. But when you need to butterfly or trim chicken, there is no tool better suited than kitchen shears. To test their versatility, we also used kitchen shears to cut lengths of kitchen twine, trim pie dough, and cut out parchment paper rounds. We found two pairs to recommend.

Wüsthof Kitchen Shears ($28) made easy, smooth cuts even through small chicken bones and completed all tasks flawlessly. The size and proportion of the shears felt ideal—the blades could open wide for large jobs and to achieve more forceful cutting, but the shears were also suited to smaller, more detailed tasks such as snipping pieces of twine. These shears boasted heft, solid construction, and textured handles that were comfortable, even when wet and greasy. They were also suitable and comfortable for left-handed users.

Messermeister Take Apart Kitchen Shears ($17) were also great performers, though the blades didn't have quite the spread of those on the Wüsthof. These shears, too, made clean, easy cuts and accomplished all tasks without hesitation. The soft, rubber-like handles proved extremely comfortable, but lefties take note: These scissors were clearly designed for right-handed users.

THE BEST KITCHEN SHEARS
Wüsthof Kitchen Shears ($28) easily cut through bones and performed all tasks flawlessly.

CHICKEN ALLA DIAVOLA

THERE ARE MANY THEORIES ON HOW THIS "chicken of the devil" got its name. Some say it is in reference to the fiery coals over which the chicken is grilled; others claim it is for the diabolical amount of black pepper or red pepper flakes that are used. But name aside, most recipes for this classic grilled chicken are quite similar; the chicken is butterflied and grilled with a heavy dousing of either black pepper or red pepper flakes and lots of lemon. As simple as it sounds, we found that grilling a whole butterflied chicken is tricky, and it is difficult to get the lemon and pepper seasonings to shine through.

Saving the issue of flavor for later, we first focused on the obvious problem of how to grill a butterflied chicken. Most recipes call for weights to be placed on top of the bird as it is grilled, to promote fast and even cooking. Covered with a cast-iron pan or old baking sheet, the flattened chicken is then weighted down with bricks or heavy cans. After cooking two chickens, with and without weights, it became obvious why the weights were necessary. When pounded, then weighted flat, the chicken not only cooked more quickly and evenly but also achieved beautiful grill marks. The unweighted chicken, by comparison, had a less evenly colored skin and took longer to cook through.

We found the chicken skin was quick to tear when overhandled, and we wanted to find a cooking method that involved a minimum of flipping. When cooked over a single level medium-hot grill, the chicken cooked in about 30 minutes, flipped once halfway through. Interestingly, we found cooking on a charcoal grill required a different method from a gas grill. On charcoal, it is important to cook the chicken skin-side up first, or else the bright, hot coals will burn the skin. For a gas grill, the bird must be grilled skin-side down first, or else the grill will cool, making it difficult to get decent grill marks on the skin.

Moving on to flavor, we tested several ways to make the chicken taste robust and spicy. Immediately, we found that marinating the chicken before grilling was essential. Although marinating does little to enhance the texture of the meat, it does a lot in terms of flavor. Marinating in lemon juice, black pepper, and olive oil offered a good base, but we wanted more flavor. In an effort to bring out the black pepper, we found it better to rub the chicken vigorously first before dousing it with the lemon juice and olive oil. To make the chicken a bit spicier, we added red pepper flakes and smashed garlic cloves to the marinade.

Although our recipe was coming along, we still had problems getting the lemon to shine through. Lemon has an ethereal flavor that can disappear quickly when cooked. Adding zest to the marinade helped the lemon flavor permeate the meat, yet we still wanted more. Basting the chicken with marinade helped a little, but the smoke from the grill dulled the lemon flavor as it continued to cook. To prevent the grill from stealing our flavor, we discovered that a last-minute brush of fresh marinade and a quick revisit to the coals to fuse the marinade to the skin was the key. The result is a perfectly grilled butterflied chicken with potent lemon and pepper flavor.

Chicken alla Diavola on a Charcoal Grill

SERVES 4

You will need at least four lemons for this recipe.

1	whole chicken (3 to 3½ pounds), butterflied (see the illustrations on page 185)
1½	tablespoons coarsely ground black pepper
¾	cup juice and 1 teaspoon grated zest from 4 to 6 lemons
½	cup extra-virgin olive oil
3	medium garlic cloves, skins left on, smashed
¼	teaspoon red pepper flakes
1¼	teaspoons salt

1. Rub the chicken all over with 1 tablespoon of the black pepper. Place the chicken in a gallon-size zipper-lock plastic bag and add ½ cup of the lemon juice, the zest, oil, garlic, red pepper flakes, and 1 teaspoon of the salt. Press out as much air as possible and seal the bag. Gently massage the bag to

mix the marinade around the chicken and refrigerate for 2 hours. Mix the remaining ½ tablespoon black pepper, ¼ cup lemon juice, and ¼ teaspoon salt together in a small bowl and set aside.

2. Light a large chimney starter filled three-quarters full with hardwood charcoal (about 4½ quarts) and allow to burn until all the charcoal is covered with a layer of fine gray ash. Build a single-level fire by spreading the coals evenly over the bottom of the grill. Set the cooking grate in place, cover with the lid, and let the grate heat up, about 5 minutes. Use a grill brush to scrape the cooking grate clean. The grill is ready when the coals are medium-hot. (See how to gauge heat level on page 4.)

3. Remove the chicken from the marinade and discard the marinade. Place the chicken, skin-side up, on the cooking grate. Set a rimmed baking sheet (or other flat pan) on top of the chicken and put two bricks in the pan (see the illustration on page 184). Grill until the chicken is deep brown, about 12 minutes. Turn the chicken skin-side down with tongs. Replace the baking sheet and bricks and continue cooking until the chicken juices run clear and an instant-read thermometer inserted deep into the thigh registers 165 degrees, 12 to 15 minutes longer.

4. Remove the bricks and pan, turn the chicken skin-side up, and brush the skin with the reserved lemon mixture. Carefully flip the chicken skin-side down and allow the skin to crisp, 1 to 2 minutes. Transfer the chicken to a cutting board, cover with foil, and let rest for 10 minutes. Carve according to the illustrations on page 186 and serve hot.

➤ VARIATION

Chicken alla Diavola on a Gas Grill

Because this chicken is cooked skin-side down first, we found it best not to replace the bricks on top of the crisp skin.

Follow the recipe for Chicken alla Diavola through step 1. Turn on all the burners to high, close the lid, and heat until the grill is very hot, about 15 minutes. Use a grill brush to scrape the cooking grate clean. Turn all the burners to medium. Place the chicken skin-side down on the cooking grate. Set a rimmed baking sheet (or other flat pan) on top of the chicken and put two bricks in the pan (see the illustration on page 184). Cover and grill until the chicken skin is deep brown and shows grill marks, 12 to 15 minutes. Turn the chicken skin-side up with tongs and continue to cook (without replacing the pan or the bricks on top) until the chicken juices run clear and an instant-read thermometer inserted deep into the thigh registers 165 degrees, about 15 minutes more. Brush the skin with the reserved lemon mixture. Carefully flip the chicken skin-side down and allow the skin to crisp, 1 to 2 minutes. Transfer the chicken to a cutting board, cover with foil, and let rest for 10 minutes. Carve according to the illustrations on page 186 and serve.

COARSELY GROUND PEPPERCORNS

For coarsely ground peppercorns, grind or crush whole peppercorns (left) to a very coarse texture (right).

SHORTCUT FOR SQUEEZING LEMON JUICE

Squeeze a large amount of juice from lemons (or other citrus fruit) quickly by placing two or three quartered lemons in the hopper of a potato ricer and squeezing the handles together.

GRILL-ROASTED WHOLE CHICKEN

EVERY YEAR MILLIONS OF COOKS GRILL ALL manner of chicken parts, from breasts and thighs to drumsticks. If you're one of them, you can follow the recipes for chicken parts in this chapter. There's only one problem with this scenario: Chicken parts don't spend enough time on the grill to pick up much smoke flavor. Since the smoky taste is one of the main reasons we like to grill, we often grill a whole chicken rather than parts. When grilled over indirect heat (coals banked to the side, with the chicken over the cool part of a covered grill), the bird cooks in about an hour, giving it plenty of time to pick up a good hit of smoke.

Grill-roasting a whole chicken turns out to be a fairly straightforward matter. On reading through various recipes while researching this topic, however, we did notice some variations in technique. Wanting to determine the very best technique, we decided to test the important variables, including how to arrange the coals, whether or not to use a V-rack, when and how to turn the bird, and how to flavor it.

When grill-roasting large birds (such as turkeys) or big cuts of meat (such as prime rib), the standard setup is to fill half of a kettle grill with charcoal and to leave the other half empty. The food is placed on the cooler side of the grill, and the kettle is covered. Because one side of the food faces the lit coals, the bird or meat will cook unevenly unless it is rotated at least once. Rotating is simple enough, but the heat dissipates when the lid is removed, and you often have to add more coals, which is a pain.

Since a chicken is so much smaller than a turkey or prime rib, we wondered if the lit coals could be banked on either side of the kettle grill and the chicken cooked in the middle. After several tests, we concluded that this arrangement works fine, with some caveats.

First, the coals must be piled fairly high on either side to form relatively tall but narrow piles. We split the coals between either side of the grill and ended up piling the lit briquettes three or four levels high. If the coals are arranged in wider, shorter piles, the cool spot in the middle of the grill won't be large enough to protect the bird from direct heat.

Second, don't use too much charcoal. When we split 70 briquettes into two piles, we burned the chicken. Reducing the number of coals to just 50 kept the temperature inside the grill between 325 and 375 degrees, the ideal range for grill-roasting.

Third, you must use a relatively small chicken. We found that the skin on a large roaster scorches

MEASURING THE INTERNAL TEMPERATURE OF A CHICKEN

The most accurate way to tell if a chicken is done is to use an instant-read thermometer. Be sure to put the thermometer into the thickest part of the bird and avoid all bones, which can throw off your reading.

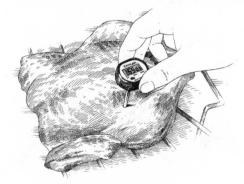

1. To take the temperature of the thigh, insert the thermometer at an angle into the area between the drumstick and breast. Dark meat should be cooked to 165 or 170 degrees.

2. To take the temperature of the breast, insert the thermometer from the neck end, holding it parallel to the bird. The breast meat is done at 160 degrees and will begin to dry out at higher temperatures.

long before the meat cooks through.

Last, keep the vents in the lid halfway open so that the fire burns at a fairly even pace. If the vents are open all the way, the fire burns too hot at the outset—thereby scorching the bird's skin—and then peters out before the chicken has cooked through.

With the heat attacking the chicken from two sides, the bird cooks evenly, so there's no need to rotate it. (On gas grills, where just one lit burner is used to cook by indirect heat, you will need to rotate the bird.) After our initial tests, however, we did conclude that it was necessary to flip the bird over once during the hour-long cooking process. The skin on top of the bird cooks faster than the skin touching the grate. (Although this seems counterintuitive, repeated tests confirmed this observation.) Because the side of the bird that finishes right-side up tends to look better (grill marks fade and the skin bronzes more evenly), we decided to start the chicken breast-side down.

When we cook a turkey on the grill, we always cradle it in a V-rack, which keeps the skin from scorching and promotes even cooking. We prepared several chickens with and without V-racks and found that those placed right on the cooking grate browned better and cooked just fine. Again, because a chicken is small, the bird spends much less time on the grill than a turkey, and the skin is less likely to burn.

With our technique perfected, we focused on the flavoring options. As expected, we found that brining the chicken helps it retain moisture while cooking and is recommended. The one exception is a kosher bird, which is salted during processing and cooks up moist—and perfectly seasoned—without brining.

During the course of our testing, we tried brushing the chicken with melted butter and olive oil before and during grilling. Although a buttered bird browned marginally better than an oiled one, we don't recommend using either. Birds coated with a spice rub cooked up more crisp and were better looking than greased birds.

Grill-Roasted Whole Chicken on a Charcoal Grill

SERVES 4

If you choose not to brine, skip that part of step 1 and season the bird generously with salt inside and out before rubbing with spices. To use kosher salt in the brine, see page 172 for conversion information. For added accuracy, place an instant-read thermometer in the lid vents as the chicken cooks. The temperature inside the grill should be about 375 degrees at the outset and will fall to about 325 degrees by the time the chicken is done.

1/2	cup table salt (see note)
1/2	cup sugar
1	whole chicken (about 3 1/2 pounds)
3	tablespoons spice rub (pages 382–383)
4	(3-inch) wood chunks or 4 cups wood chips

1. Dissolve the salt and sugar in 2 quarts of cold water in a large bowl, stockpot, or Dutch oven. Immerse the chicken in the salted water, cover, and refrigerate, about 1 hour. Remove the chicken from the brine and rinse inside and out with cool running water; pat dry with paper towels. Massage the spice rub all over the chicken, inside and out. Lift up the skin over the breast and rub the spice mixture directly onto the meat.

2. Soak the wood chunks in cold water to cover for 1 hour and drain. If using wood chips, divide them between two 18-inch squares of aluminum foil, seal to make two packets, and use a fork to create about six holes in each packet (see the illustrations on page 10).

3. Light a large chimney starter filled a little more than halfway with charcoal briquettes (about 3½ quarts) and allow to burn until all the charcoal is covered with a layer of fine gray ash. Empty the coals into the grill. Divide the coals in half to form two piles on either side of the grill; use long-handled tongs to move any stray coals into the piles. Nestle 2 soaked wood chunks or one foil packet with chips on top of each pile. Position the cooking grate over the coals and cover the grill. Heat the grate for 5 minutes, then use a grill brush to scrape it clean.

4. Position the bird breast-side down in the middle of the grate, over a portion of the grill without any coals. Cover, opening the grill lid vents halfway. Turn the lid so that the vents are between the two piles of coals. Grill-roast for 30 minutes.

5. Working quickly to prevent excessive heat loss, remove the lid and, using two large wads of paper towels, turn the chicken breast-side up. Cover and grill-roast until an instant-read thermometer inserted into the thickest part of the thigh registers 170 to 175 degrees, 25 to 35 minutes longer.

6. Transfer the chicken to a cutting board, tent loosely with foil, and let rest 15 minutes. Carve and serve.

➤ VARIATIONS

Grill-Roasted Whole Chicken on a Gas Grill

If you choose not to brine, skip that part of step 1 and season the bird generously with salt inside and out before rubbing with spices. (To use kosher salt in the brine,

see page 172 for conversion information.) While grill-roasting, adjust the lit burner as necessary to maintain a temperature of 350 to 375 degrees inside the grill.

Follow the recipe for Grill-Roasted Whole Chicken on a Charcoal Grill through step 1. Soak 4 cups wood chips for 30 minutes in cold water to cover. Place the wood chips in a foil tray (see the illustration on page 10). Place the foil tray with the soaked wood chips on top of the primary burner (see the illustration on page 9). Turn on all the burners to high and heat with the lid down until the chips are smoking heavily, about 20 minutes. Open the grill and turn off all but one burner. (Leave the primary burner on high.) Scrape the cooking grate clean with a grill brush. Place the chicken breast-side down over the cooler part of the grill. Cover and grill-roast for 35 minutes. Turn the chicken breast-side up so that the leg and wing that were facing away from the lit burner are now facing toward it. Close the lid and continue grill-roasting until an instant-read thermometer inserted into the thickest part

---

INGREDIENTS: **Bottled Barbecue Sauce**

Despite the best of intentions, there's not always time to make barbecue sauce. It's no surprise that many cooks turn to bottled sauces.

We wondered if some brands of bottled barbecue sauce were much better than others. Are the "gourmet" brands worth the extra money, or will a supermarket brand suffice? We tasted 12 samples to find out. We limited the tasting to tomato-based sauces because they are far and away the most popular and represent what most Americans picture when they think "barbecue sauce."

In general, tasters were not overly impressed with these bottled sauces. Most were much too sweet and had an overly thick, gummy texture. The ingredients responsible were high-fructose corn syrup and food starch. We did find one sauce that everyone agreed was quite good and another three sauces worth considering. Three of these four sauces were more expensive "gourmet," organic offerings, so, at least when it comes to barbecue sauce, more money does buy a better product.

Our favorite sauce is Mad Dog, a boutique brand from Boston. Although the ingredient list is mercifully short (many other sauces have long lists of hard-to-pronounce ingredients), tasters thought this sauce was more complex and balanced than

the rest of the pack. It also contained less sugar than most brands and no corn syrup, an ingredient found in all but three of the sauces tested.

Bull's Eye, Sweet Baby Ray's, and Muir Glen received decent scores and mixed comments. Like most supermarket offerings, Bull's Eye is very sweet and has a thick, glossy consistency, but it also delivers a decent hit of smoke, something missing from other mass-market sauces. Tasters liked the strong molasses flavor in the Sweet Baby Ray's and Muir Glen sauces, although neither was an overwhelming favorite. The rest of the sauces were so bad that tasters felt they harmed rather than improved the flavor of plain broiled chicken. With one exception then, this tasting did not uncover products about which we could get enthused.

As with homemade barbecue sauce, bottled sauces are finishing sauces, not basting sauces. They all contain sweeteners and tomatoes, which will cause foods to burn within minutes after application. Foods destined for the grill should not be marinated in barbecue sauce. The food will burn and taste awful. Just brush a little sauce on during the last two or three minutes of the cooking time, and then brush again just before serving.

of the thigh registers 170 to 175 degrees, 30 to 40 minutes longer. Transfer the chicken to a cutting board, tent loosely with foil, and let rest 15 minutes. Carve and serve.

Grill-Roasted Whole Chicken with Barbecue Sauce

If you like, you can use barbecue sauce along with Pantry Spice Rub for Chicken (page 383). See our tasting of supermarket barbecue sauces on the facing page. Wait until the bird is almost done to brush on the barbecue sauce, so that it does not scorch.

Follow the recipe for Grill-Roasted Whole Chicken (charcoal or gas), making the following changes: After rotating the chicken breast-side up, roast only until an instant-read thermometer inserted into the thickest part of the thigh registers 160 degrees, 15 to 30 minutes longer. Working quickly to prevent excessive heat loss, brush the outside and inside of the chicken with ½ cup of any tomato-based barbecue sauce on pages 386–387. Cover and continue grill-roasting until an instant-read thermometer inserted into the thickest part of the thigh registers 170 to 175 degrees, 10 to 15 minutes longer. Tent with foil, carve, and serve.

BEER CAN CHICKEN

AS WE WERE DEVELOPING OUR GRILL-roasted chicken recipes, a friend who spends many weekends at barbecue cook-offs raved to us about beer can chicken. On the barbecue circuit, she said, this is how beer can chicken is done: The bird is rubbed with spices, and then an open, partially filled beer can is inserted into the main cavity of the chicken. The chicken is grill-roasted as it "sits" on the can, which functions as a vertical roaster.

We decided to try this wacky idea, convinced we would have something silly to write about. We culled a half-dozen recipes for beer can chicken (sometimes called drunken chicken) from the Internet, and they all followed the same basic formula, with some variation in the spice rub and the liquid inside the can. We decided to stick with our favorite dry rub and a can of cheap beer for our first test.

We should have had more confidence in our friend's opinion. The bird came off the grill looking beautiful, with a deeply tanned, crisp skin. And the flavor was fantastic. Although we had a hard time tasting the beer, the spices had penetrated deep into the meat.

Beer can chicken has a number of things going for it. The beer in the open can creates steam as the chicken roasts. This steam keeps the meat incredibly juicy. The moist heat also gives the meat an unctuous, rich quality. If you have ever steamed or braised a chicken, you know what we mean. Some people may not like this texture (the meat is a bit slippery), but we found this moist meat preferable to the dry, shredded quality of chicken cooked by dry heat.

The beer can chicken also tasted better seasoned with spices—almost right down to the bone—than any chicken we have ever eaten. For the best flavor, we found it imperative to rub the spices inside the cavity (where the steam is generated) and under the breast skin.

Because our first test was such a success, we wondered about some of the variables we had uncovered in our research. We focused on the liquid in the can first, adding some barbecue sauce to the beer in one test, adding chopped aromatic vegetables to the beer in another, and using Guinness, a rich, dark beer, in a third test. In all cases, we couldn't detect much difference from the first bird steamed over a can of cheap beer without any additions.

We then replaced the beer with lemonade in one test and white wine in another. Tasters were able to detect a lightly sweet, lemon flavor in the bird cooked over lemonade. With the white wine, we rubbed a garlic, rosemary, and olive oil paste into the bird. This bird was a dud. The skin was not nearly as crisp and the flavor of the garlic and rosemary was confined to the surface. Furthermore, tasters thought the wine had not done much for the bird.

For one last test, we emptied a soda can and filled it with water, then rubbed the bird with spices as before. Although the differences were not dramatic, the flavor was a bit washed out and less

193

appealing. Evidently, the beer was contributing something to the bird in addition to steam.

One last note: Chickens that weigh about 3½ pounds are ideal for this recipe. The cavity in smaller birds is too narrow to hold a beer can, and larger birds won't fit upright in most grills.

Grill-Roasted Beer Can Chicken

SERVES 4

To use kosher salt in the brine, see page 172 for conversion information. If you prefer, use lemonade instead of beer. Fill an empty 12-ounce soda or beer can with 10 ounces (1¼ cups) of lemonade and proceed as directed.

½	cup table salt (see note)
½	cup sugar
I	whole chicken (about 3½ pounds)
3	tablespoons spice rub (see recipes in Chapter 11)
4	(3-inch) wood chunks or 4 cups wood chips
I	(12-ounce) can beer

1. Follow the recipe for Grill-Roasted Whole Chicken (charcoal or gas), brining the chicken and applying the spice rub as directed. Light the charcoal or gas grill and prepare the wood chunks or chips as directed.

2. Open the beer can and pour out (or drink) about ¼ cup. With a church key can opener, punch two more large holes in the top of the can (for a total of three). Slide the chicken over the can so that the drumsticks reach down to the bottom of the can and the chicken stands upright (see the illustration at right).

3. Place the chicken and beer can on the cooler part of the grill, using the ends of the drumsticks to help steady the bird. Cover and grill-roast, rotating the bird and can 180 degrees at the halfway mark to ensure even cooking, until an instant-read thermometer inserted into the thickest part of the thigh registers 170 to 175 degrees, 70 to 90 minutes.

4. With a large wad of paper towels in each hand, transfer the chicken and can to a platter or tray, making sure to keep the can upright. Tent with foil and let rest for 15 minutes. Using wads of paper towels, carefully lift the chicken off the can and onto a platter or cutting board. Discard the can and remaining beer. Carve the chicken and serve.

SETTING UP BEER CAN CHICKEN

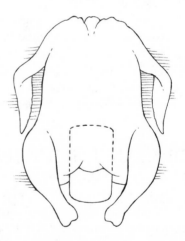

With the legs pointing down, slide the chicken over the open beer can. The two legs and the beer can form a tripod that steadies the chicken on the grill.

5

TURKEY AND OTHER BIRDS

TURKEY AND OTHER BIRDS

CHARCOAL-GRILLED TURKEY BURGERS 198
    Gas-Grilled Turkey Burgers
    Turkey Burgers with Porcini Mushrooms
    Turkey Burgers with Miso
    Ultimate Turkey Burgers

GRILL-ROASTED TURKEY ON A CHARCOAL GRILL 201
    Grill-Roasted Turkey on a Gas Grill
    Grill-Roasted Turkey with Aromatic Spice Rub
    Grill-Roasted Turkey with Cranberry–Red Pepper Relish

GRILL-ROASTED TURKEY BREAST ON A CHARCOAL GRILL 206
    Grill-Roasted Turkey Breast on a Gas Grill
    Grill-Roasted Turkey Breast with Cumin Spice Rub

GRILL-ROASTED CORNISH HENS ON A CHARCOAL GRILL 209
    Grill-Roasted Cornish Hens on a Gas Grill

GRILL-ROASTED DUCK ON A CHARCOAL GRILL 211
    Grill-Roasted Duck on a Gas Grill
    Grill-Roasted Five-Spice Duck with Soy Glaze

CHARCOAL-GRILLED DUCK BREASTS 214
    Gas-Grilled Duck Breasts
    Curried Grilled Duck Breasts
    Grilled Duck Breasts with Peach-Habanero Chutney
    Grilled Duck Breasts with Pickled Ginger Relish
    Grilled Duck Breasts with Tapenade

CHARCOAL-GRILLED QUAIL 216
    Gas-Grilled Quail
    Grilled Quail with Sage, Mustard, and Honey
    Grilled Quail with Chili-Lime Glaze
    Grilled Quail with Cherry-Port Sauce

CHARCOAL-GRILLED SQUAB 218
    Gas-Grilled Squab
    Asian-Style Grilled Squab on Salad with Grilled Shiitake Mushrooms
    Grilled Squab with Greek Flavors

ALTHOUGH THERE'S A REASON WHY CHICKEN is so popular—the combination of crisp, well-browned skin and tender, juicy meat holds plenty of attraction—there are many occasions when you may not want to serve "plain old chicken." The birds covered in this chapter offer a nice alternative.

Turkey, for example. Although we love the traditional roasted holiday turkey, grill-roasting the bird transforms the dish into something truly special. Likewise, whole breasts can be grilled with excellent results. Even turkey burgers, once thought of as unpalatable, pick up a smoky distinctiveness from a hot fire.

Small birds, too, can be grilled, such as whole quail, squab, and Cornish hens. A whole duck is an ideal candidate for grill-roasting, and boneless breasts—an item made popular by restaurant chefs but increasingly available at butcher shops—are thin enough to grill much as you would chicken breasts.

A note about the recipes in this chapter. The basic recipes call for very simple seasoning. The variations, however, are more complex (and sophisticated) than most of the other recipes in this book, reflecting the way we think people will want to prepare these fancy birds.

Duck, quail, and squab are prone to flare-ups, so stick close by the grill and be ready to slide foods to a cooler part of the grill or douse flames with water from a squirt bottle.

TURKEY BURGERS

A LEAN, FULLY COOKED TURKEY BURGER, seasoned with salt and pepper, is typically a weak stand-in for an all-beef burger. Simply put, it is often dry, tasteless, and colorless. We wanted a turkey burger with beef burger qualities—dark and crusty on the outside and full-flavored and juicy with every bite.

Finding the right meat was crucial to developing the best turkey burger. According to the National Turkey Federation, there are three options: white meat (with 1 percent to 2 percent fat), dark meat (more than 15 percent fat), and a blend of the two (ranging from 7 percent to 15 percent fat).

At the grocery store, we found multiple variations on the white meat/dark meat theme, including fresh or frozen preformed lean patties, higher-fat ground fresh turkey on Styrofoam trays or frozen in tubes like bulk sausage, and lower-fat ground turkey breasts. There were also individual turkey parts that we could grind up ourselves. We bought them all, took them back to the test kitchen, and fired up the grill.

We first tested the preformed lean patties—refrigerated and frozen—and found them mediocre. To varying degrees, the frozen ones had a week-old-roast-turkey taste. A few bites from one of the refrigerated varieties turned up significant turkey debris: tendon, ground-up gristle, and bone-like chips. We moved on to bulk ground turkey.

The higher-fat (15 percent) ground turkey turned out to be flavorful and reasonably juicy, with a decent, burger-like crust. Frankly, these burgers didn't need too much help. On the other hand, we didn't see much point in eating them, either. Given that a great beef burger contains only 20 percent fat, a mere 5 percent fat savings didn't seem worth it.

At the other extreme, with only 1 or 2 percent fat, was ground turkey breast. As we were mixing and forming these patties, we knew our chances of success would be slim. They needed a binder to keep them from falling apart. They needed extra fat to keep them from parching and sticking to the grill. And they needed flavor to save them from blandness.

With 7 percent fat, 93 percent lean ground turkey was the most popular variety at all the grocery stores we checked. Burgers made from this mix were dry, rubbery textured, and mild flavored. With a little help, however, these leaner patties were meaty enough to have real burger potential.

Most flavorful of all were the boned and skinless turkey thighs we ground ourselves in the food processor. We first tried grinding the skin with the meat but found that it ground inconsistently, and we had to pick it out. In the next batch we left it out and found the result to be equally flavorful and much lower in calories. As a matter of fact, our butcher declared our home-ground skinless turkey almost 90 percent lean when he tested it in his Univex Fat Analyzer.

For all the obvious reasons, we had sworn that even if we liked the outcome we weren't going to make grind-your-own-turkey part of the recipe, but these burgers—meaty flavored with a beef-like chew—were far superior to any we made with the commercially ground turkey. If you are willing to take the time, turkey thighs ground in the food processor cook up into low-fat turkey burgers with great flavor and texture.

For those not inclined to grind their own meat, we decided to see what we could do to improve the lean commercially ground turkey (with 7 percent fat). To improve texture and juiciness, we started with milk-soaked bread. For comparison, we also made burgers with buttermilk- and yogurt-soaked bread. All these additions made the burgers seem too much like meat loaf and destroyed whatever meaty flavor there had been, since turkey is mild to start with. The bread and milk lightened the meat's color unpleasantly, while the sugar in both ingredients caused the burgers to burn easily and made it impossible to develop a good thick crust.

We tried other fillers to improve the texture, including cornmeal mush, mashed pinto beans, and minced tempeh, but their flavors were too distinct. Minced, rehydrated, dried mushrooms added a moist, chewy texture that the burgers desperately needed. They also offered an earthy, meaty, yet not overly distinct flavor. However, the real winner—for flavor, texture, and easy availability—was ricotta cheese. Moist and chewy, it gave the burgers the texture boost they needed and required very little effort.

Finally, we decided to experiment a bit with added flavorings. We wanted only those that would enhance the flavor of the burgers without drawing attention to themselves. We tried more than 25 different flavorings—from fermented black beans to olive paste to teriyaki marinade—and found only two that we liked: Worcestershire sauce and Dijon mustard.

Next we turned to the cooking method. Since turkey burgers must be well-done for safety reasons, cooking them can be a bit tricky. If the heat is too high, they burn before they're done; too

low, and they look pale and steamed. A two-level fire proved to be the right solution. The burgers are seared over high heat and then moved to the cooler part of the grill where they can cook through. With charcoal grilling, we recommend that you place an aluminum roasting pan over the burgers to contain the heat and ensure even cooking.

Although our generous cooking times should ensure a fully cooked burger, as an extra precaution you may want to test for doneness by sticking an instant-read thermometer through the side and into the center of one of them. The burgers are done at 160 degrees.

A final note about shaping turkey burgers. Unlike beef, ground turkey does not contain a high percentage of collagen. You can make evenly shaped patties (without forming a well in the center, as for beef burgers) and they won't puff up on the grill.

Charcoal-Grilled Turkey Burgers
SERVES 4

Ricotta cheese keeps ground turkey moist as it cooks. Unlike other kinds of burgers, turkey burgers must be thoroughly cooked for the sake of safety and flavor. You will need a disposable aluminum roasting pan for this recipe.

1¼	pounds 93 percent lean ground turkey
½	cup ricotta cheese
2	teaspoons Worcestershire sauce
2	teaspoons Dijon mustard
½	teaspoon salt
½	teaspoon ground black pepper
	Vegetable oil for the cooking grate

1. Light a large chimney starter filled a little less than halfway with hardwood charcoal (about 2½ quarts) and allow to burn until all the charcoal is covered with a layer of fine gray ash. Build a two-level fire by stacking most of the coals on one side of the grill and arranging the remaining coals in a single layer on the other side of the grill. Set the cooking grate in place, cover the grill with the lid, and let the grate heat up, about 5 minutes. Use a

grill brush to scrape the cooking grate clean. The grill is ready when the temperature of the stacked coals is medium-hot and that of the remaining coals is medium-low. (See how to gauge heat level on page 4.)

2. Meanwhile, combine the ground turkey, ricotta, Worcestershire sauce, mustard, salt, and pepper in a medium bowl until blended. Divide the meat into 4 portions. Lightly toss one portion from hand to hand to form a ball, then lightly flatten the ball with your fingertips into a 1-inch-thick patty. Repeat with the remaining portions of meat.

3. Lightly dip a small wad of paper towels in vegetable oil; holding the wad with tongs, wipe the cooking grate. Grill the burgers, uncovered, over the hotter part of the grill, turning once, until well browned on both sides, 6 to 8 minutes. Slide the burgers to the cooler part of the grill, cover them with a disposable aluminum roasting pan, and continue grilling until cooked through, another 5 to 7 minutes. To test for doneness, either peek into the thickest part of the burgers with the tip of a small knife (you should see no redness at the center) or insert an instant-read thermometer from the side of the burger into the center (it should register 160 degrees). Serve immediately.

➤ VARIATIONS
Gas-Grilled Turkey Burgers
To ensure that your burgers are cooked through, use an instant-read thermometer inserted through the side of the burger toward the center; it should read 160 degrees. Because the heat is less intense on a gas grill, the cooking times are slightly longer than for a charcoal grill.

Turn on all the burners to high, close the lid, and heat the grill until very hot, about 15 minutes. Use a grill brush to scrape the cooking grate clean. Leave one burner on high and turn the other burner(s) down to medium-low. Follow the recipe for Charcoal Grilled Turkey Burgers from step 2, with the following change. In step 3, grill the burgers, turning once, until well browned on both sides, 8 to 10 minutes. Slide the burgers to the cooler part of the grill and proceed as directed.

Turkey Burgers with Porcini Mushrooms
Reconstituted dried porcini mushrooms give turkey burgers a particularly meaty flavor. Dried shiitakes also work well in this recipe.

Follow the recipe for Charcoal-Grilled or Gas-Grilled Turkey Burgers, replacing the Worcestershire sauce and mustard with 1 ounce dried porcini mushrooms that have been rehydrated in 1 cup of hot water for 15 minutes, squeezed dry, and minced fine.

Turkey Burgers with Miso
Miso is a fermented soybean paste with a pungent, robust flavor. It is sold in Asian markets as well as natural food stores. It comes in several colors, any of which can be used in this recipe.

Follow the recipe for Charcoal-Grilled or Gas-Grilled Turkey Burgers, replacing the Worcestershire sauce and mustard with 2 teaspoons miso thinned with 2 teaspoons water.

Ultimate Turkey Burgers
We found that the extra step of grinding fresh turkey thighs ourselves made the most flavorful, best-textured burgers. If you can, buy boneless turkey thighs.

Cut 1½ pounds skinless, boneless thighs into 1-inch chunks and arrange in a single layer on a baking sheet. Freeze until somewhat firm, about 30 minutes. Working in three batches, place the semifrozen turkey chunks in a food processor; pulse until the largest pieces are no bigger than ⅛ inch, 12 to 14 one-second pulses. Follow the recipe for Charcoal-Grilled or Gas-Grilled Turkey Burgers, using homemade ground turkey and omitting the ricotta cheese.

GRILL–ROASTED TURKEY

WE CAN STILL REMEMBER THE FIRST TIME WE cooked a whole turkey in a covered grill. We lit the charcoal, banked the coals to one side, added some wood chips, and placed a small turkey over the cooler part of the grill. Two hours later, we had the best-looking and best-tasting turkey ever—the crispiest skin imaginable coupled with moist meat that had been perfumed with smoke.

Unfortunately, we can also remember the second time we tried this feat. We must have built the fire a little too hot; when we checked the bird after the first hour, the skin had burned. We nonetheless continued grilling, and, before serving, removed the charred skin from the blackened bird. We also served some juicy mango salsa to camouflage the dryness of the overcooked breast.

We have continued to grill-roast turkeys over the years, not only because the bird sometimes turns out to be fantastic but also because using the grill for the turkey frees up the oven for all the other components of a holiday meal. But the results have been inconsistent.

Part of the problem is the inherent unpredictability of grill-roasting over charcoal. Sometimes the fire can be too hot, other times it can be too cool. If the day is particularly windy, the fire will cool down faster than on a hot, sultry night. Because you are cooking with the cover down to conserve fuel (frequent peeking will cause the fire to die down and is a no-no), it's hard to know what's happening inside the grill.

We decided to get serious and figure out what the variables are when grill-roasting a turkey and then devise a method for controlling these variables. Our goal was simple: We wanted a bird with crisp, browned skin, moist meat, and a good smoky flavor—every time.

Because gas grilling involves fewer variables than charcoal grilling, we decided to start with gas. We quickly learned that a small turkey (fewer than 14 pounds) works best when grill-roasting. Even on a really large gas grill, we found that the skin on a large bird burns by the time the meat comes up to temperature. For the same reason, you can't cook a stuffed turkey on the grill. A stuffed bird takes longer to cook through, and this added time almost guarantees that the skin will blacken.

Following the lead of previous turkey recipes developed in the test kitchen, we also confirmed that brining the turkey is a must for a tender, juicy bird. Grilling is even more punishing on delicate breast meat than oven roasting. The bird's proximity to the heat source, coupled with all that smoke

(which tends to dehydrate foods), makes brining an essential step when grill-roasting turkey. If you can't be bothered with brining, buy a kosher bird (the bird is soaked in saltwater during processing, which acts much like brining) or season a regular bird liberally with salt just before grilling and be prepared to serve the white meat with plenty of cranberry sauce.

Next we turned to the issue of trussing. Our test kitchen staff generally ties the legs of the turkey together to keep them from splaying open as they roast. When we tried this, we noticed that the inner thigh cooked more slowly than the rest of the bird. Trussed birds needed an extra 10 to 15 minutes on the grill to get the shielded portion of the thigh up to the correct internal temperature. While this may not sound like much extra time, it translated into overcooked breast meat. Even worse, the skin burned. When we abandoned any trussing or tying of the legs, the temperature in the thighs and breasts was equalized and the skin was extremely crisp and dark brown, but not black.

Our next set of experiments centered on turning the bird. As with oven roasting, we found it best to start the bird breast-side down. After an hour, we flipped the bird breast-side up for the remainder of the cooking time. We noticed that the side (wing and leg) closest to the fire was cooking faster than the other side of the bird. To eliminate this problem, we found it necessary to rotate the bird twice—once when it is turned breast-side up, and once when the cooking is almost completed. Each time, we turned the bird so that the opposite wing and leg faced the heat source.

We next focused on whether to cook the bird right on the cooking grate or on a rack. We found that a turkey placed in a nonadjustable V-rack cooked more evenly and with less scorching of the skin than a bird placed right on the grate. But a rack with a sturdy metal base is essential. If the V-rack rests on just two little legs, those legs can fall through the cooking grate and the turkey can topple over.

Our last area of investigation on the gas grill was its temperature. Clearly, we needed to grill-roast the bird over indirect heat, with one burner lit and the other burner(s) turned off. Our question was how high to keep the heat on the lit burner. We tested this recipe on three grills—two models with two burners and one model with three burners. We found it best to leave the lit burner turned to high in each case. At lower settings, there was not enough heat to cook the bird properly. The temperature gauges on the three grills we worked with ranged from 300 to 350 degrees during the entire cooking time. Total cooking time for a 12- to 14-pound bird varied from 2 to 2½ hours. (Count on the longer time if the weather is cool or windy.)

Turkey cooked on a gas grill is delicious. The recipe is foolproof, and the skin becomes especially crisp and richly colored. But getting smoke flavor into a gas-grilled bird is not so easy. While adding wood chips before lighting the grill helped some, the resulting smoke flavor was mild. And, the problem with gas grills is that there's no way to add chips once the fire is going. We concluded that removing the turkey, trying to lift off the hot, heavy cooking grate, and then placing more chips over the lit burner was much too dangerous.

Charcoal is another matter. We quickly realized that because we had to add fuel to the fire at the halfway point anyway, we could add more wood at the same time. We came to this conclusion after producing yet another blackened bird. We foolishly thought we could build a really big fire on one side of the grill, put the turkey on the cool side, throw on the cover, and come back two hours later. While it's possible to get the meat up to temperature with this method, the intense initial heat (upward of 425 degrees) causes the skin to burn.

We found it far better to build a moderate fire, bank the coals to one side of the grill, and cook the turkey breast-side down for one hour, just as we had on the gas grill. After an hour, the temperature inside the grill drops from a high of 350 to 375 degrees to somewhere around 275 degrees. At this point, the grill needs more fuel to finish cooking the turkey. Since we were removing the cooking grate anyway, we decided to add more wood along with a dozen unlit briquettes. (Unlike the very heavy gas grate, you can lift a charcoal grate with

heavy-duty tongs. You can also simply toss wood into a pile of charcoal; for gas, you must position the foil tray over the burner, an impossible task when the grill is hot.)

At this point we began experimenting with chunks of wood versus wood chips. We found that chunks, although not suitable for use with a gas grill, were far superior (they gave off a lot more smoke) and easy to use with a charcoal grill.

So would we cook our next turkey over gas or charcoal? Gas is certainly more convenient and more reliable if the weather is especially cold or windy. However, the extra smoky flavor that only charcoal and wood chunks can deliver makes the kettle grill our first choice for grill-roasting a turkey.

Grill-Roasted Turkey on a Charcoal Grill

SERVES 10 TO 12

See page 204 for information about buying a turkey. If you'd like to use kosher salt in the brine, see page 172 for conversion information. Charcoal grilling gives you the opportunity to add wood twice—at the outset of grilling and when the bird is turned breast-side up at the 1-hour mark—for a stronger smoke flavor. Hardwood charcoal burns faster and hotter than briquettes, so be sure to use briquettes when grill-roasting turkey. The total cooking time is 2 to 2½ hours, depending on the size of the bird, the ambient conditions, and the intensity of the fire. Check the internal temperature in the thigh when rotating the bird at the 1-hour-and-45-minute mark. If the thigh is nearly up to temperature (the final temperature should be 175 to 180 degrees), check the temperature again after about 15 minutes. If the thigh is still well below temperature (145 degrees or cooler), don't bother checking the bird again for at least another 30 minutes.

I	cup table salt (see note)
I	turkey (12 to 14 pounds), giblets and tail removed, rinsed thoroughly, and wings tucked (see the illustration on page 204)
6	(3-inch) wood chunks or 3 cups wood chips Nonstick cooking spray
2	tablespoons unsalted butter, melted

1. Dissolve the salt in 2 gallons of cold water in a large (at least 16-quart) stockpot or clean bucket. Add the turkey, cover, and refrigerate or set in a very cool spot (between 32 and 40 degrees), 12 hours or overnight. (Or try the shorter, more intense brine described on page 204.)

2. Toward the end of the brining time, soak the wood chunks in cold water to cover for 1 hour and drain. Or, if using wood chips, divide the unsoaked chips between two 18-inch squares of aluminum foil, seal to make two packets, and use a fork to create about six holes in each packet to allow smoke to escape (see the illustrations on page 10).

3. Light a large chimney starter filled three-quarters full with charcoal briquettes (about 4½ quarts) and allow to burn until all the charcoal is covered with a layer of fine gray ash.

4. Meanwhile, spray a V-rack with nonstick cooking spray. Remove the turkey from the brine and rinse inside and out under cool running water to remove all traces of salt. Pat the turkey dry with paper towels; brush both sides with the melted butter. Set the turkey, breast-side down, in the V-rack.

5. Empty the coals into the grill and pile onto one side. Place 3 soaked wood chunks or one wood chip packet on top of the coals. Position the cooking grate over the coals, and place the V-rack with the turkey over the cooler part of the grill; open the grill lid vents halfway and cover, positioning the vents over the turkey. Cover and grill-roast for 1 hour.

6. Remove the lid from the grill. Using very thick potholders, transfer the V-rack with the turkey to a rimmed baking sheet or roasting pan. Remove the cooking grate and place 12 new briquettes and the 3 remaining soaked wood chunks or remaining wood chip packet on top of the coals; replace the cooking grate. With a wad of paper towels in each hand, flip the turkey breast-side up in the rack. Return the V-rack with the turkey to the cooler part of the grill. Cover and grill-roast for 45 minutes.

7. Using very thick potholders, carefully turn the V-rack with the turkey (the breast remains up) so that the leg and wing that were facing the

coals are now facing away from the coals. Insert an instant-read thermometer into each thigh to check the temperature and gauge how much longer the turkey must cook (see the note on page 201).

8. Cover and continue grill-roasting until a thermometer inserted into the thigh registers 175 to 180 degrees, 15 to 45 minutes more.

9. Remove the turkey from the grill, tent loosely with foil, and let rest 20 to 30 minutes. Carve and serve.

➤ VARIATIONS
Grill-Roasted Turkey on a Gas Grill
See page 206 for information about buying a turkey. Because it's not possible to add more wood during the cooking process, a turkey grill-roasted over a gas fire will not taste as smoky as one roasted over charcoal. The total cooking time is 2 to 2½ hours, depending on the size of the bird, the ambient conditions (the bird will require more time on a cool, windy day), and the intensity of the fire. Check the internal temperature in the thigh when rotating the bird at the 1-hour-and-45-minute mark. If the thigh is nearly up to temperature (the final temperature should be 175 to 180 degrees), check the temperature again after about 15 minutes. If the thigh is still well below temperature (145 degrees or cooler), don't bother checking the bird again for at least another 30 minutes.

1. Follow the recipe for Grill-Roasted Turkey on a Charcoal Grill through step 1. In step 2, follow the instructions using the wood chips, with the following changes. Instead of making a foil packet for the chips, soak the wood chips in cold water for 30 minutes, drain, and place the wood chips in a foil tray (see the illustrations on page 10). Place the foil tray with the soaked wood chips on top of the primary burner (see illustration on page 9). Turn on all the burners to high and heat with the lid down until the chips are smoking heavily, about 20 minutes.

2. Meanwhile, spray a V-rack with nonstick cooking spray. Remove the turkey from the brine and rinse inside and out under cool running water to remove all traces of salt. Pat the turkey dry with paper towels; brush both sides with the melted butter. Set the turkey, breast-side down, in the V-rack.

3. Turn off all burners but one. Leave the

primary burner on high. Place the V-rack with the turkey over the cooler part of grill. Cover and grill-roast, regulating the lit burner as necessary to maintain a temperature between 300 and 350 degrees, for 1 hour.

4. Open the lid. With a wad of paper towels in each hand, flip the turkey breast-side up. Close the lid and continue grill-roasting for 45 minutes.

5. Using very thick potholders, carefully turn the rack with the turkey (the breast remains up) so that the leg and wing that were facing the lit burner are now facing away from it. Insert an instant-read thermometer into each thigh to check the temperature and gauge how much longer the turkey must cook. (See the note on page 202.)

6. Close the lid and continue grill-roasting until a thermometer inserted into the thigh registers 175 to 180 degrees, 15 to 45 minutes more.

7. Remove the turkey from the grill, tent loosely with foil, and let rest for 20 to 30 minutes. Carve and serve.

Grill-Roasted Turkey with Aromatic Spice Rub

Adding a spice rub makes turkey more appropriate for summer barbecue meals, with salsas and salads, than for a traditional Thanksgiving dinner. See chapter 11 for fruit salsas to serve with the turkey.

Follow the recipe for Grill-Roasted Turkey (charcoal or gas), replacing the butter with ½ cup Aromatic Rub for Poultry (page 382), rubbing the spices inside and out as well as under the skin on the breast. Proceed as directed.

Grill-Roasted Turkey with Cranberry–Red Pepper Relish

This relish works best with the spice-rub turkey above.

4	medium red bell peppers, cored, seeded, and cut into small dice
4	cups cranberries, picked through and chopped coarse
2	medium onions, chopped fine
1½	cups sugar
1	cup cider vinegar
2	medium jalapeño chiles, seeds and ribs removed, then minced
½	teaspoon salt
½	teaspoon red pepper flakes
1	recipe Grill-Roasted Turkey (charcoal or gas)

1. While the turkey is brining or grilling, mix the peppers, cranberries, onions, sugar, vinegar, chiles, salt, and red pepper flakes together in a medium saucepan. Bring to a boil, reduce the heat, and simmer, stirring occasionally, until the mixture thickens to a jam-like consistency, about 30 minutes. Cool to room temperature. (The relish can be refrigerated in an airtight container for up to 2 weeks.)

2. Prepare the turkey as directed. Serve the carved turkey with the relish passed separately at the table.

TURKEY BREAST

GRILL-ROASTING A WHOLE, BONE-IN TURKEY breast has plenty of appeal. Many families prefer white meat to dark meat. In addition, a whole turkey is just too much food for a small gathering. We figured that the cooking method would be similar to that used to grill-roast a whole turkey. This proved to be the case, with a couple of adjustments.

As long as you don't buy a huge turkey breast, it can be cooked through without having to add more coals to the fire at the halfway point. A full chimney's worth of coals will cook a breast that weighs less than seven pounds in less than two hours. Larger breasts will need more charcoal after one hour, and, given the hassle associated with removing the bird from the grill and lifting up the cooking grate, we strongly recommend that you shop for a breast that weighs between 5½ and seven pounds.

As with a whole turkey, brining is essential. In fact, because white meat is especially prone to drying out, brining is even more important when grill-roasting a breast. As an added precaution, make sure to remove the breast from the grill once the internal temperature reaches 165 degrees. While dark meat needs to reach a higher temperature to become palatable, white

Grill-Roasted Turkey 101

Give your holiday bird a new twist this year by grill-roasting your turkey. The steps are not difficult and the smoky flavor you'll achieve with our method will be well worth the effort. And, by using the grill for the turkey, you'll free up oven space to comfortably prepare as many side dishes as you choose.

INGREDIENTS: TURKEY

Many people purchase a turkey just once during the year. Thanksgiving, of course, would be that occasion. When the moment of purchase arrives, however, the buyer may be somewhat befuddled. The options are many—this brand or that brand, fresh or frozen, flavor-enhanced or not. Then there is the growing number of product disclaimers to plow through—no antibiotics, no animal byproducts, minimal processing, and on and on it goes.

Everyone has priorities and standards when it comes to purchasing turkey. But what it all reduces to for most every cook is whether friends or relatives drive away after the big meal murmuring "That was the best turkey I've ever had" or "Thank goodness there was plenty of gravy and cranberry sauce."

To try to ensure the former response, we decided to do some testing to answer the following questions: What is the difference between basted, kosher, and natural turkeys, and which tastes best?

Self-basting, kosher, and natural turkeys are the types most often available to consumers. Traditionally processed frozen turkey is labeled "basted" or "self-basting." This means that it has been injected with a solution intended to make it more flavorful and tender. The components of this solution, which vary from company to company, are listed on the labels of these turkeys. Expect to see ingredients as innocent as turkey broth and as dubious as emulsifiers and artificial flavors. While tasters liked the texture and extreme juiciness of these birds, they also noted many off and unnatural flavors.

Kosher turkeys are processed mostly by hand and according to kosher law. Tasters generally preferred the juiciness of a brined, natural bird to the drier texture of a kosher turkey.

"Natural" turkeys are untreated fresh turkeys. This broad category includes free-range birds raised on small organic farms as well as birds raised for large commercial enterprises that are neither organic nor free-range. We tasted two "natural" birds: a Butterball Fresh Young Turkey and a Plainville Farms Young Turkey, a regionally available "veggie grown" bird. We brined these turkeys to level the playing field with the koshered and injected birds. While the Butterball had a juicy texture, its flavor paled next to that of the Plainville Farms turkey. (A Plainville Farms turkey that was not brined, however, was very bland. Locally grown, "all-natural" turkeys almost always need the moisture that brining provides.)

PROTECTING THE WINGS

Tucking the wings under the bird will prevent them from burning.

TESTING A TURKEY FOR DONENESS

The outside of a turkey will look done well before the inside is cooked. To avoid any unpleasant surprises come carving time, use an instant-read thermometer to accurately gauge doneness. When using an instant-read thermometer, measure the temperature of the thickest part of the thigh away from any bone. This cutaway drawing shows the depth at which the thermometer should be inserted. The temperature of the breast should reach 160 to 165 degrees and dark meat should reach between 170 and 175 degrees.

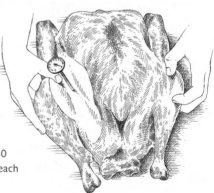

QUICK-BRINING TURKEY

Soaking a turkey in a saltwater bath—a process called brining—before cooking produces an exceptionally moist and well-seasoned bird. The problem is where to keep the turkey as it brines. A stockpot or clean bucket large enough to hold a turkey, 2 gallons of cold water, and salt simply won't fit in most refrigerators. You could use a cold basement or garage, but when those options are not available, try this method.

Line a large stockpot or clean bucket with a turkey-sized oven bag. Place several large, clean, frozen ice-gel packs in the brine with the turkey. Tie the bag shut, cover the container, and place in a cool spot for four hours. Because of the short brining time, you must use a lot of salt—either 2 cups of table salt or 4 cups of kosher salt. Once the turkey is brined, remember to rinse the bird well under cool running water and pat it dry with paper towels.

CARVING A TURKEY

1. Start by slicing the skin between the meat of the breast and the leg.

2. Continue to cut down to the joint, using a fork to pull the leg away from the bird while the tip of the knife severs the joint between the leg and breast.

3. Place the leg/thigh piece skin-side down on a cutting board. Use the blade to locate the joint between the thigh and leg. It's right where the thigh and leg form their sharpest angle. Cut through the joint. If you have properly located it, this should be easy since you are not cutting through bone.

4. Slice medallions from the leg, turning it so that you can cut off all of the meat.

5. Remove the large pieces of meat from either side of the thighbone.

6. Slice these large thigh pieces, leaving a bit of skin attached to each slice.

7. Use a fork to pull the wing away from the body. Cut through the joint between the wing and the breast to separate the wing from the bird.

8. Cut the wing in half for easier eating.

9. With the tip of your knife, cut along the length of the breastbone.

10. Angle the blade of the knife, and slice along the line of the rib cage to remove the entire breast half. Use a fork to pull the breast half away from the cage in a single piece.

11. Cut thin slices from the breast, slicing across the grain of the meat.

STABILIZING TURKEY ON THE GRILL

We like to use a V-rack to elevate turkey while it roasts on the grill. The problem is that the base of some V-racks may slip through the bars of the cooking grate. As an extra precaution, we cover the cooking grate with a wire cooling rack for baking so that its bars run perpendicular to the bars on the cooking grate. The cooling rack provides a stable surface on which the base of the V-rack can rest.

DEFROSTING A FROZEN TURKEY

Although we prefer fresh turkeys, they are not always available. For those times when you must buy a frozen turkey, be sure to allow sufficient time for defrosting, because this iceberg of a bird can sink your Thanksgiving dinner faster than you can say "Titanic." It's best to defrost the turkey in the refrigerator, figuring one day of defrosting for every 4 pounds of turkey. That means a frozen 20-pound turkey should go into the refrigerator on Saturday morning if it's to be ready by Thursday, Thanksgiving Day.

There is a faster (and more tedious) means of defrosting the turkey if you find yourself on Wednesday morning with a frozen bird. Place the turkey, still in its original wrapper, in a bucket of cold water for about 10 hours (or 30 minutes per pound) and change the water every half hour. Yes, every 30 minutes you will be handling this gargantuan bird, a step necessary to guard against bacterial growth.

meat is fully cooked (and safe) at this temperature. Cooked any more, the breast dries out and begins to taste like sawdust.

Unlike a whole bird, which has wings and legs that can dangle dangerously close to the fire, a breast is a single piece of meat. It can be cooked right on the cooking grate, without the use of a V-rack.

Grill-Roasted Turkey Breast on a Charcoal Grill

SERVES 6 TO 8

When brining, be sure to use a container that rises at least 4 inches above the turkey breast once it is placed inside. This way, the brine can completely cover the turkey. (To use kosher salt in the brine, see page 172 for conversion information.) If you are buying a frozen turkey breast, be sure to buy the turkey 3 days ahead; it takes 2 days to defrost in the refrigerator and should be brined overnight before grill-roasting.

¹/₂	cup table salt (see note)
I	whole, bone-in turkey breast (5¹/₂ to 7 pounds), prepared according to the illustrations on the facing page and rinsed
3	(3-inch) wood chunks or 3 cups wood chips
2	tablespoons unsalted butter, melted

1. Dissolve the salt in 1 gallon of cold water in a large stockpot or clean bucket. Add the turkey breast, cover, and refrigerate or set in a very cool spot (between 32 and 40 degrees), 12 hours or overnight. (Or try the shorter, more intense brine described on page 204, but for this recipe use just 1 gallon of water with 1 cup of table salt.)

2. Toward the end of the brining time, soak the wood chunks in cold water to cover for 1 hour and drain. Or, if using wood chips, divide the unsoaked chips between two 18-inch squares of aluminum foil, seal to make two packets, and use a fork to create about six holes in each packet to allow smoke to escape (see the illustrations on page 10).

3. Light a large chimney starter filled three-quarters full with charcoal briquettes (about 4½ quarts) and allow to burn until all the charcoal is covered with a layer of fine gray ash.

4. Meanwhile, remove the turkey breast from the brine and rinse inside and out under cool running water to remove all traces of salt. Pat the turkey dry with paper towels; brush with the melted butter.

5. Empty the coals into the grill and pile onto one side. Place the soaked wood chunks or the wood chip packet on top of the coals. Position the cooking grate over the coals and place the turkey breast, meaty-side down, over the cooler part of the grill. Open the grill lid vents halfway and cover, positioning the vents over the turkey. Cover and grill-roast for 1 hour.

6. Remove the lid from the grill. Using a

INGREDIENTS: Turkey Breast

Supermarkets generally offer two slightly different cuts of turkey breast. Regular, or "true cut," is the most readily available, either fresh or frozen. It is a whole turkey breast, bone in, with skin and usually with ribs, a portion of wing meat, and a portion of back and neck skin. The best ones are U.S. Department of Agriculture Grade A and are minimally processed. Although a true-cut breast is excellent carved at the table, it lacks the wings, neck, and giblets, which you will want if you plan to make gravy or stock. If this is the case, try to buy a hotel or country-style turkey breast, which usually comes with wings, neck, and giblets. These breasts, which are more expensive than true-cut breasts, are usually sold fresh but not frozen.

Try to avoid turkey breasts that have been injected with a saline solution, often called "self-basters," as the solution masks the natural flavor of the turkey. (If these are the only turkey breasts available, omit the brining step; these birds are already quite salty.) Also best avoided are those turkey breasts sold with a pop-up timer; it won't pop until the turkey breast is overcooked. If removed before cooking, it breaks the skin and juices can escape during cooking. If you have no choice but to purchase a pop-up, leave the timer in place until the turkey breast is fully cooked—according to internal temperature, not the timer—and pull it out just before carving the breast.

wad of paper towels in each hand, flip the breast meaty-side up, with the side that was facing the coals now facing away from the coals. Cover and grill-roast until an instant-read thermometer inserted into the thickest part of the breast registers 165 degrees, 40 to 60 minutes more.

7. Remove the turkey breast from the grill, tent loosely with foil, and let rest 20 minutes. Carve and serve.

➤ VARIATIONS

Grill-Roasted Turkey Breast on a Gas Grill

1. Follow the recipe for Grill-Roasted Turkey Breast on a Charcoal Grill through step 1. In step 2, follow the instructions using the wood chips, with the following changes. Instead of making a foil packet for the chips, soak the wood chips in cold water for 30 minutes, drain, and place the wood chips in a foil tray (see the illustrations on page 10). Place the foil tray with the soaked wood chips on top of the primary burner. Turn on all the burners to high and heat with the lid down until the chips are smoking heavily, about 20 minutes.

2. Meanwhile, remove the turkey breast from the brine and rinse inside and out under cool running water to remove all traces of salt. Pat the turkey dry with paper towels; brush with the melted butter.

3. Turn off the burner(s) without the chips. Leave the primary burner on high. Use a grill brush to scrape the cooking grate clean. Place the turkey breast, meaty-side down, over the cooler part of the grill. Cover and grill-roast, regulating the lit burner as necessary to maintain a temperature between 325 and 350 degrees for 1 hour.

4. Open the lid. Using a wad of paper towels in each hand, flip the breast meaty-side up so that the side that was facing the fire is now facing away from the lit burner. Cover and grill-roast until an instant-read thermometer inserted into the thickest part of the breast registers 165 degrees, about 40 minutes more.

5. Remove the turkey breast from the grill, tent loosely with foil, and let rest 20 minutes. Carve and serve.

PREPARING TURKEY BREAST FOR THE GRILL

1. Use a boning knife to cut out the remaining portion of the neck. (You can reserve this piece to make stock.)

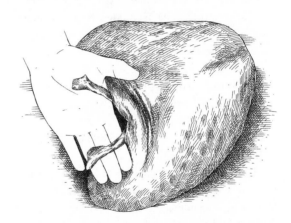

2. To facilitate carving, scrape the meat away from the wishbone with the boning knife to expose it. Pull the wishbone out with your hands.

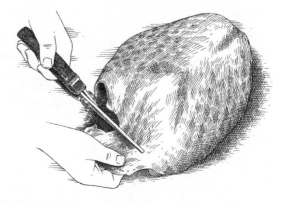

3. Cut off any extra skin that hangs off the neck end.

Grill-Roasted Turkey Breast with Cumin Spice Rub

Serve slices of this cumin-flavored turkey breast with any fruit salsa (see chapter 11 for recipes). The smoky and spicy flavors of the turkey go well with the sweetness of the fruit.

Mix together 1 tablespoon ground cumin, 1 tablespoon curry powder, 1 tablespoon chili powder, 1½ teaspoons ground black pepper, ½ teaspoon ground allspice, and ½ teaspoon ground cinnamon. Follow the recipe for Grill-Roasted Turkey Breast (charcoal or gas), rubbing the brined bird with the spice mixture instead of the melted butter. Proceed as directed.

CORNISH HENS

CORNISH HENS ARE ANOTHER GOOD CANDIDATE for grill-roasting. The technique is pretty much the same as for chicken. In fact, we found that the cooking time for two Cornish hens is almost the same as the cooking time for one chicken. How can it be that two 1½-pound hens take 50 to 60 minutes to grill-roast, while a 3½-pound chicken is done in 55 to 65 minutes?

One reason is that the hens are best trussed before grilling. Cornish hens have a looser frame than chickens, and the legs dangle from the bird. When the birds were not trussed, we occasionally had problems with a leg falling off as we tried to remove the finished bird from the grill. A quick truss—just tie the two legs together with a length of twine—keeps the legs in place and yields a better-looking hen.

With the legs tucked against the body, the thighs cook more slowly. In addition, a hen isn't all that much thinner than a chicken. The thickness of the bird—rather than its weight—is the main factor affecting cooking time. Finally, two hens cool down the grill as much as a single chicken. If you grill-roast just a single Cornish hen (to serve two), the cooking time will be five or 10 minutes shorter because there's less food to absorb the heat of the grill.

In addition to trussing the legs, we found it best to tuck the wings behind the hen. These small appendages tended to flop down between the bars of the cooking grate and burn. One final note: The juices in a hen can build up between the breast meat and skin, causing the skin to balloon and then burst. To prevent this problem, prick the skin carefully with the tip of a knife before cooking.

With our grill-roasting technique perfected, we moved on to flavor issues. After a few rounds of roasting, we realized that these birds didn't taste superb. Because most Cornish hens are mass-produced and not of premium quality, we were faced with the added challenge of trying to deepen their flavor. Having roasted the first few birds without brining, we wondered if they tasted good enough to even bother writing about. Although our local grocery store sells premium-quality poussins (baby chickens), all of its Cornish hens are mass-produced (see page 209 for more information). We found brining to be essential—it transforms mediocre-tasting birds into something worth eating. A spice rub (use one of the poultry rubs in Chapter 11) adds another layer of flavor.

PREPARING HENS FOR THE GRILL

 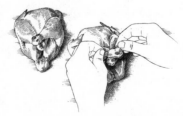 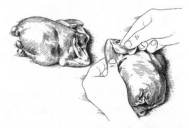

1. To prevent the skin from ballooning when juices build up, carefully prick the skin (but not the meat) on the breast and leg of each Cornish hen with the tip of a knife.

2. To keep the legs close to the body and prevent them from flopping around on the grill, tie the legs together with a short piece of twine.

3. To keep the wings close to the body and prevent them from burning or falling off, tuck the wingtips behind the back.

Grill-Roasted Cornish Hens on a Charcoal Grill

SERVES 4

We highly recommend you take the time to brine, since most Cornish hens are quite bland tasting. (To use kosher salt in the brine, see page 172 for conversion information.) If you choose not to brine, skip that part of step 1 and season the birds generously with salt inside and out before rubbing with spices. The temperature inside the grill should be about 375 degrees at the outset and will fall to about 325 degrees by the time the hens are done.

- ½   cup table salt (see note)
- 2   Cornish hens (each about 1½ pounds), trimmed of extra fat, giblets removed, and rinsed well
- 3   tablespoons poultry rub (see poultry rubs on pages 382–384)
- 4   (3-inch) wood chunks (or 4 cups wood chips)

1. Dissolve the salt in 2 quarts of cold water in a large container. Immerse the hens in the salted water, cover, and refrigerate, about 1 hour. Remove the hens from the brine and rinse inside and out with cool running water; pat dry with paper towels. Massage the spice rub all over the hens, inside and out. Lift up the skin over the breast and rub the spice mixture directly onto the meat.

2. Soak the wood chunks in cold water to cover for 1 hour and drain. Or, if using wood chips, divide the unsoaked chips between two 18-inch squares of aluminum foil, seal to make two packets, and use a fork to create about six holes in each packet to allow smoke to escape (see the illustrations on page 10).

3. Light a large chimney starter filled a little more than halfway with charcoal briquettes (about 3½ quarts) and allow to burn until all the charcoal is covered with a layer of fine gray ash. Pour the charcoal out onto the bottom of the grill and separate into two piles on opposite sides of the grill using long-handled tongs. Nestle 2 soaked wood chunks or one foil packet with chips on top of each pile. Position the cooking grate over the coals and cover the grill. Heat the grate for 5 minutes, then use a grill brush to scrape the cooking grate clean.

INGREDIENTS:
Cornish Hens and Poussins

These days, it is becoming more and more difficult to find small Cornish hens. Not long ago, these dwarfed birds hovered at around a pound, but for economic reasons, producers have started growing them bigger. Now the consumer is lucky to find one under 1½ pounds.

This larger size is perfect for two people, but for individual presentation, seek out the smaller hens, or look for poussins, baby chickens sold at many butcher shops. Though a little more expensive, these baby chickens usually weigh about one pound and are perfect for one person. Poussins are likely to come from a smaller farm and generally taste better than mass-produced hens.

4. Position the birds, breast-side down, in the middle of the rack, over the portion of the grill without any coals. Cover, opening the grill lid vents halfway. Turn the lid so that the vents are between the two piles of coals. Grill-roast for 25 minutes.

5. Working quickly to prevent excessive heat loss, remove the lid and, with a wad of paper towels in each hand, turn the hens breast-side up. Cover and grill-roast until an instant-read thermometer inserted into the thickest part of the thigh registers 170 to 175 degrees, 25 to 35 minutes longer.

6. Transfer the hens to a cutting board, tent loosely with foil, and let rest 15 minutes. Carve and serve.

VARIATION
Grill-Roasted Cornish Hens on a Gas Grill
While grill-roasting, adjust the lit burner as necessary to maintain a temperature of 350 to 375 degrees inside the grill.

1. Follow the recipe for Grill-Roasted Cornish Hens on a Charcoal Grill through step 1. In step 2, follow the instructions using the wood chips, with the following changes. Instead of making a foil packet for the chips, soak the wood chips in cold water to cover for 30 minutes, drain, and place the wood chips in a foil tray (see the illustrations on page 10). Place the foil tray with the soaked wood chips on top of the primary burner (see the illustration on page 9). Turn on all the burners to

high and heat with the lid down until the chips are smoking heavily, about 20 minutes.

2. Open the grill and turn off all but one burner. Leave the primary burner on high. Use a grill brush to scrape the cooking grate clean. Place the hens, breast-side down, over the cooler part of the grill. Cover and grill-roast for 30 minutes. Turn the hens breast-side up so that the legs and wings that were facing away from the lit burner are now facing toward it. Close the lid and continue grill-roasting until an instant-read thermometer inserted into the thickest part of the thigh registers 170 to 175 degrees, 20 to 30 minutes longer.

3. Transfer the hens to a cutting board, tent loosely with foil, and let rest 15 minutes. Carve and serve.

DUCK

THE MAJOR PROBLEM THAT WE USUALLY encounter when cooking duck is the excessive amount of fat that must be rendered to attain crisp, thin, crackling-like skin. We found that grill-roasting is a great way to remedy this problem. Because the duck is cooked outdoors, we don't have to worry about smoke from dripping fat filling the kitchen. The fat drips away bit by bit, falling harmlessly into an aluminum pan set in the bottom of the grill.

We started our tests by examining two basic methods for grill-roasting duck. Some sources suggest grill-roasting a duck as we would a chicken or turkey—season and then cook over indirect heat until done. Other sources suggest steaming the duck first to render as much fat as possible and to partially cook the duck (which is how we treat duck we plan to roast in the oven). The steamed bird is then seasoned and grilled just to finish the cooking process and crisp up the skin.

We tried the first method, hoping to make this simpler process succeed. We pricked the skin with a fork before cooking to help the fat escape during grilling. We had decent results with this method but were frustrated by two aspects of the procedure. First, the skin was not as crisp as we liked, especially on the breast. We tried salting and

air-drying the duck overnight in the refrigerator and then grill-roasting. The duck was improved but not great. Second, the cooking time was about two hours and 30 minutes, and we found it necessary to add more coals to the fire to get the duck up to temperature. We then switched gears and tried steaming. Although not without problems, our first attempt at steaming then grill-roasting yielded a duck with skin that was much more thin and crisp. The meat, however, was dried out and stringy. Clearly, we had steamed the bird too long in order to get rid of all the fat. We would have to cut back on the steaming time and then let the heat of the grill render the remaining fat.

We cut the steaming time from 60 to 30 minutes and then grill-roasted the bird for one hour. This duck was the best of all, with very thin, crackling-like skin and meat that was still moist.

In addition to steaming the duck before grill-roasting, we found it important to prick the skin to help render the fat and thereby produce the wonderful, crispy skin that we desired. Although most recipes recommended using a fork, we found it hard to puncture the skin with the dull tines. We ended up using the tip of a sharp paring knife to make small holes in the skin (but without cutting into the flesh). We also found it important to make sure that we pricked the underside of the duck between the legs and breast to avoid trapping the melting fat.

After several tests, we concluded that grill-roasting a duck is best done between two piles of coals on opposite sides of the grill. The duck is placed in the center for a few reasons. First of all, a drip pan is necessary to catch the excess fat that drips from the duck; if placed in the center of a kettle grill, the pan will not block the air vents at the bottom of the grill. Without a drip pan, the rendered fat can cause a grease fire. If you do not have a disposable aluminum pan, you can fashion a grease pan out of heavy-duty aluminum foil. In addition to preventing a grease fire, placement of the duck between two piles of coals allows it to cook more evenly. With the heat attacking the bird from both sides, it is unnecessary to rotate the bird at all during cooking.

Because the duck has been steamed, it is possible

to grill-roast at the relatively high temperature of 425 degrees. This level of heat is easily attained on the charcoal grill by using a full chimney of charcoal (about 6 quarts). Because this level of heat can't be reached on a gas grill, we thought the cooking time would be longer. We found, however, that longer cooking with the indirect heat of grill-roasting just dried out the duck and did a poor job of browning it. To get the temperature inside the grill over 400 degrees (and thus to brown and crisp the skin), we would need to use a combination of direct and indirect cooking.

In the end, we steamed the bird for 30 minutes, then grill-roasted it on the gas grill with the primary burner on high and the secondary burner(s) turned off for another 30 minutes. (More fat renders during this time on the grill.) Once all of the fat was gone, we turned the secondary burner(s)—just below the duck—to low to boost the temperature inside the grill above 400 degrees. We cooked the bird for another 40 to 50 minutes at this temperature to brown and crisp the skin. Although we were afraid that the bottom of the bird would dry out from the direct heat at the end of cooking, we found that the meat was still moist. Best of all, the skin was crisp and brown.

We also learned that a sweet glaze elevates the flavor of the duck. To get the glaze to caramelize a bit, apply it during the last few minutes of cooking. If applied any earlier, the glaze will burn. The sweetness not only complements the richness of the duck but also gives the skin a nice color and finish.

Grill-Roasted Duck on a Charcoal Grill

SERVES 3 TO 4

Use a sharp knife to trim away any skin that is not directly above meat or bone. Pull back any remaining skin in the neck cavity and cut away pieces of fat on the underside of the skin to expose the backs of the wing joints. The excessive amount of fat under the skin of the duck is rendered through two cooking processes: steaming and then grill-roasting. This method produces very thin, crisp skin and meat that is cooked through but still moist.

If you don't have an aluminum pan to catch the dripping fat on the grill, fashion one out of heavy-duty aluminum foil. But, even with a pan to catch the drips, there may still be flare-ups, so it's best to keep a squirt bottle handy to douse any flames.

2   (3-inch) wood chunks or 2 cups wood chips
1   whole Pekin duck (about 4½ pounds), neck and giblets discarded, excess skin and fat removed
     Salt and ground black pepper
1   cup orange juice
2   tablespoons juice from 2 limes
2   tablespoons honey

1. Soak the wood chunks in cold water to cover for 1 hour and drain. Or, if using wood chips, divide the unsoaked chips between two 18-inch squares of aluminum foil, seal to make two packets, and use a fork to create about six holes in each packet to allow smoke to escape (see the illustrations on page 10).

2. Meanwhile, using the tip of a paring knife, make several pricks in the skin over the entire body of the duck, making sure not to cut into the meat. Set a V-rack inside a large roasting pan (you can also set a round rack inside a wok large enough to contain the entire duck). Place the duck, breast-side up, onto the rack. Place the roasting pan over two burners (or one burner if using a wok) and add enough water to come just below the bottom of the duck. Bring the water to a boil over high heat, cover tightly with aluminum foil (or the pan cover, if available), and adjust the heat to medium. Steam, adding more hot water to maintain the water level, if necessary, until the fat beads on the pores of the duck and the bird is partially cooked through, 30 minutes. Lift the duck from the rack, pat the skin gently, so as not to break it, with paper towels to remove excess fat and moisture. Season the bird with salt and pepper to taste.

3. Light a large chimney starter filled with charcoal briquettes (about 6 quarts) and allow to burn until all the charcoal is covered with a layer of fine gray ash. Pour the charcoal out onto the

bottom of the grill and separate into two piles on opposite sides of the grill using long-handled tongs. Place a drip pan in the center between the two piles. Add 1 soaked wood chunk to each of the piles, or place the chip packet on one of the piles. Replace the cooking grate, open the grill lid vents halfway, and place the lid on the grill. Let the grate heat for 5 minutes; use a grill brush to scrape the cooking grate clean.

4. Position the duck, breast-side up, in the middle of the cooking grate between the two piles of charcoal. Cover the grill, turning the lid so that the vents are between the two piles of coals. Grill-roast until the skin is crisp, thin, and richly browned, about 1 hour. (The initial temperature inside the grill should be about 425 degrees. It will drop to about 375 degrees by the time the duck is done.)

5. Meanwhile, bring the orange juice, lime juice, and honey to a boil in a small saucepan. Reduce the heat to medium-low and simmer until slightly thickened and reduced to ¼ cup, 25 to 30 minutes.

6. Brush the duck generously with the orange glaze. Cover the grill and cook until the glaze heats through, 3 to 5 minutes. (Make sure the glaze does not burn.)

7. Transfer the duck to a cutting board, tent with foil, and let rest for 10 minutes. Carve and serve.

➤ VARIATIONS
Grill-Roasted Duck on a Gas Grill
The meat on a duck that is grill-roasted on a gas grill will be more moist than meat cooked on a charcoal grill, but the skin on the gas grill–roasted bird will be a touch less crisp. Make sure that you use a drip pan under the bird to prevent a grease fire in the grill, as an excessive amount of fat will render from the duck. If you don't have an aluminum pan, fashion one out of heavy-duty aluminum foil. Even so, keep a squirt bottle handy in case of flare-ups.

1. Follow steps 1 and 2 of Grill-Roasted Duck on a Charcoal Grill, using wood chips in step 1 and making the following change. Instead of making a foil packet for the chips, soak the chips in cold water to cover for 30 minutes, drain, and place the wood chips in a foil tray (see the illustrations on page 10). Place the foil tray with the soaked wood chips on top of the primary burner (see illustration on page 9). Turn on all the burners to high and heat with the lid down until the chips are smoking heavily, about 20 minutes.

2. Open the grill and turn off all but the primary burner, which should be left on high. Use a grill brush to scrape the cooking grate clean. Position the duck, breast-side up, directly over the drip pan. Cover and grill-roast, allowing the fat to render, until the duck just begins to brown, about 30 minutes. The average temperature should be

---

INGREDIENTS: Types of Duck

The ducks sold in supermarkets are Pekin, or Long Island, ducks. Once raised on Long Island, these birds are now grown on farms around the country, and the largest producer is located in Indiana, not New York. These birds weigh about 4½ pounds, perhaps 5 pounds at the most. Don't be fooled into thinking that one can serve five or six people. A smaller chicken feeds more people. Ducks have a larger, heavier bone structure, and they contain a lot more fat, much of which melts away during cooking. A 4½-pound duck feeds three or maybe four people if you have a lot of side dishes. Ducks are almost always sold frozen.

Other duck species are available if you are willing to order by mail or can shop at a specialty butcher. The Muscovy is a South American bird that is less fatty than the Pekin and has a stronger game flavor. The Moulard is the sterile offspring of a Muscovy and

a Pekin duck and is popular in France. These birds are often bred for the production of foie gras. Both the Muscovy and Moulard ducks weigh more than Pekins, often as much as 8 pounds. Because these birds are so much leaner, they require a different cooking method. Since the Pekin duck is the breed found in supermarkets, we decided to stick with this variety when developing our recipe for grill-roasted whole duck.

Although whole Muscovy and Moulard ducks are hard to find, their breasts are often sold separately at better supermarkets and butcher shops. This meat is usually quite plump and lean. Most duck breasts are sold whole, with the skin on but without the bones. They can be split nicely into two halves, each weighing about 6 ounces. For information on grilling boneless duck breasts, see the facing page.

between 325 and 350 degrees. Turn the secondary burner(s) to low and grill-roast until the skin is dark brown and crisp, 40 to 50 minutes. (The average temperature will be between 425 and 450 degrees during this period.)

3. Proceed with the recipe for Grill-Roasted Duck on a Charcoal Grill from step 5.

Grill-Roasted Five-Spice Duck with Soy Glaze

Mix 1½ tablespoons soy sauce, 2 teaspoons five-spice powder, and 1 teaspoon toasted sesame oil together in a small bowl. Follow the recipe for Grill-Roasted Duck (charcoal or gas) but do not season with salt and pepper. Instead, brush the five-spice mixture onto all sides of the duck, being careful not to tear the skin. Place 3 large scallions, ends trimmed off and cut into thirds, and 1½ inches of unpeeled ginger, cut into thin coins, into the cavity of the duck. Grill as directed. Replace the orange glaze with an uncooked mixture of 2 tablespoons honey, 2 tablespoons rice vinegar, and 1 tablespoon soy sauce.

DUCK BREASTS

THE DEMAND FOR DUCK BREASTS HAS BEEN fueled by their popularity with chefs. In response to restaurant patrons who want to re-create these dishes at home, boneless duck breasts have become a standard item in a number of supermarkets and most butcher shops. Unfortunately, restaurant recipes rarely work for home cooks (professional equipment for cooking meat, such as an indoor grill or a salamander [a high-powered broiler], is completely different from home options), and few duck breast recipes have been published in cookbooks. With little good information to begin with, we wanted to figure out how to grill this special cut.

Depending on the variety of duck, an entire breast can weigh anywhere from 12 to 20 ounces. The most commonly available size is 12 ounces, which splits neatly into two breast halves, each weighing about six ounces—an ideal serving for one person.

Duck breast meat is firm and flavorful and tastes best when cooked to medium-rare, 140

degrees measured on an instant-read thermometer. Although health experts recommend cooking all poultry, including duck, to at least 160 degrees, we find that duck breast cooked to this stage is akin to a well-done steak. If you are concerned about eating medium-rare duck breast, roast a whole duck, which should be cooked to an internal temperature well above 160 degrees in order to render the fat.

Speaking of fat, the skin on a duck breast adds flavor and a pleasantly crisp texture when prepared correctly. However, when we prepared many recipes in the past, the skin has been flabby or chewy and there has been way too much of it. We knew the skin was going to be a focus in our testing.

At first, we simply seasoned a duck breast with a little salt and pepper and grilled it. As might be expected, the flare-ups were soon out of control. We tried to rescue the meat, but by the time we contained the inferno the duck breasts were charred. This failure clearly illustrated the need to remove some of the fat.

When we removed the excess fat (bits hanging off the meat itself), the results were better. The skin that remained became fairly crisp and there were no flare-ups. Several sources suggest scoring the skin with a sharp knife to help render more fat. When we tried this, we found that the skin cooked up crisper and with very little chewiness. Some of our testers, though, still thought the skin was overpowering the meat; it was delicious, but the meat seemed like an afterthought. When we removed all but a 2-inch-wide strip of skin at the center of the duck breast, everyone reacted positively. The balance between skin and meat was just right.

With the skin issue settled, we next focused on the heat level. We wondered if duck breasts would respond best to high heat or if indirect or medium heat might render more fat and cook the breasts more evenly. Indirect heat did not work because the skin did not crisp up. The same thing happened over a medium-low fire. Clearly, we needed a fairly hot (but not scorching) fire to crisp the skin and cook the breasts quickly before they had time to dry out. A medium-hot fire crisped the skin and cooked the meat perfectly.

With our testing almost done, we stumbled upon one last trick. We let one batch go skin-side down too long. Thinking that we had ruined the breasts, we turned them back over and finished cooking for a few minutes. To our surprise, the meat was perfectly cooked and the skin was even crisper than before. Upon reflection, we realized that it makes sense to cook the duck breast longer on the skin side. The extra cooking time renders more fat, and, because the skin protects the meat from the heat, the meat is less likely to dry out.

A final set of tests revolved around flavoring the duck before grilling. We tried several marinades but were unimpressed. Unlike chicken, duck has so much intrinsic flavor that it does not need a big boost. Salt and pepper are adequate, although a spice rub or simple paste (such as the tapenade on page 216) is certainly appropriate as well.

It's best to let the cooked duck breasts rest several minutes under foil before carving. As with beef, the juices redistribute within the meat and are less likely to leak out if the meat is allowed to rest. As for carving, we like to cut the breast on the diagonal into half-inch slices and then fan the slices out over a plate. Of course, you can serve the duck breast halves whole (like chicken cutlets) and let diners cut their own meat, but the sliced presentation is attractive and works especially well with sauces or chutneys.

Charcoal-Grilled Duck Breasts
SERVES 4

Trimmed and scored duck breasts may be rubbed with a mixture of spices (see the curry variation) or simply sprinkled with salt and pepper before being placed on the grill. It's a good idea to keep a squirt bottle handy in case of flare-ups.

2   whole boneless duck breasts (about 12 ounces each), split and trimmed of excess skin and fat, remaining skin scored 3 or 4 times diagonally (see the illustrations below)
    Salt and ground black pepper

1. Light a large chimney starter filled a little less than halfway with hardwood charcoal (about 2½ quarts) and allow to burn until all the charcoal is covered with a layer of fine gray ash. Build a single-level fire by spreading the coals evenly over the bottom of the grill. Set the cooking grate in place, cover the grill with the lid, and let the grate heat up, about 5 minutes. Use a grill brush to scrape the cooking grate clean. The grill is ready when the coals are medium-hot. (See how to gauge heat level on page 4.)

2. Sprinkle the duck breasts with salt and pepper to taste. Place the duck breasts, skin-side down, on the grill. Grill the duck breasts, uncovered,

PREPARING DUCK BREASTS

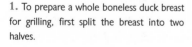

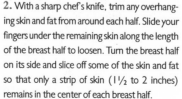

1. To prepare a whole boneless duck breast for grilling, first split the breast into two halves.

2. With a sharp chef's knife, trim any overhanging skin and fat from around each half. Slide your fingers under the remaining skin along the length of the breast half to loosen. Turn the breast half on its side and slice off some of the skin and fat so that only a strip of skin (1½ to 2 inches) remains in the center of each breast half.

3. Using a paring knife, score the skin on each breast half diagonally 3 or 4 times to allow the fat to melt during cooking.

until the skin is nicely browned, about 8 minutes. Turn the duck breasts and continue grilling until medium-rare (an instant-read thermometer inserted into the thickest part of the breast will read 140 degrees), 3 to 4 minutes more.

3. Remove the breasts from the grill, tent with foil, and let rest for 5 minutes. Slice each breast half diagonally into eight slices, ½ inch thick, and fan a sliced breast half on each dinner plate. Serve immediately.

➤ VARIATIONS

Gas-Grilled Duck Breasts

Duck breasts tend to cause flare-ups on a gas grill. Be ready to move the duck breasts to another part of the grill if flare-ups occur in the first half of the cooking time. It's also a good idea to keep a squirt bottle handy to douse any flames.

1. Turn on all the burners to high, close the lid, and heat the grill until very hot, about 15 minutes. Use a grill brush to scrape the cooking grate clean. Turn the burners down to medium-high.

2. Proceed with the recipe for Charcoal-Grilled Duck Breasts from step 2, grilling with the cover down.

Curried Grilled Duck Breasts

Serve with Yogurt-Mint Cucumber Salad (page 351) or Mango Salsa (page 392).

Combine 2 tablespoons curry powder, ½ teaspoon salt, and ¼ teaspoon ground black pepper in a small bowl. Follow the recipe for Charcoal-Grilled or Gas-Grilled Duck Breasts, rubbing the breasts with the curry mixture instead of salt and pepper. Proceed as directed.

Grilled Duck Breasts with Peach-Habanero Chutney

If you cannot find a habanero, substitute one whole serrano or jalapeño chile. Leave the seeds and ribs in if you like it spicy; omit them for a milder sauce.

1½	tablespoons vegetable oil
1	medium red onion, chopped fine
2	medium ripe but firm peaches, halved, pitted, and chopped
½	medium habanero chile, seeds and ribs removed and set aside (see note), flesh minced
¼	teaspoon ground ginger
	Pinch ground allspice
	Pinch ground cloves
¼	cup packed light brown sugar
¼	cup red wine vinegar
1	tablespoon thinly slivered fresh mint leaves
1	recipe Charcoal-Grilled or Gas-Grilled Duck Breasts

1. Heat the oil in a medium saucepan over medium heat until shimmering. Add the onion and cook until soft, about 7 minutes. Add the peaches and cook until they are soft but still intact, about 4 minutes longer. Add the chile, ginger, allspice, and cloves and cook until fragrant, about 1 minute longer. Stir in the brown sugar and vinegar and bring to a simmer. Reduce the heat to low and simmer until the liquid is very thick and syrupy, about 9 minutes. Transfer the mixture to a heatproof bowl and cool to room temperature. Stir in the mint and set the chutney aside. (The chutney can be refrigerated in an airtight container for several days.)

2. Grill and slice the duck breasts as directed. Serve with the chutney on the side.

Grilled Duck Breasts with Pickled Ginger Relish

Simple, fresh-tasting pickled ginger relish offsets the richness of duck breast. You can usually find pickled ginger in the Asian section of the supermarket or at Asian food stores. Serve with steamed rice.

¼	cup vegetable oil
¼	cup rice vinegar
¼	cup finely chopped pickled ginger
2	medium scallions, sliced thin
2	tablespoons sugar
1	tablespoon minced fresh cilantro leaves
2	teaspoons toasted sesame oil
1	recipe Charcoal-Grilled or Gas-Grilled Duck Breasts

1. Mix together the oil, vinegar, ginger, scallions, sugar, cilantro, and sesame oil in a medium bowl.

2. Grill and slice the duck breasts as directed. Drizzle some ginger relish over the duck slices and serve immediately.

Grilled Duck Breasts with Tapenade

Tapenade is a Provençal spread, or condiment, consisting of olives, capers, garlic, and anchovies. Here, half of the tapenade is rubbed onto the duck breast before it is grilled (do not be alarmed if some of it sticks to the cooking grate; its flavor will still infuse the meat), and the other half can be eaten alongside the sliced meat. Grilled bread is a great accompaniment to the duck. (Try Bruschetta with Fresh Herbs on page 344.) The tapenade can be spread on top of the bread as well.

1	cup kalamata olives, pitted
4	anchovy fillets, chopped
2	teaspoons drained capers
2	small garlic cloves, peeled and chopped (about 1 teaspoon)
1/4	cup extra-virgin olive oil
1	recipe Charcoal-Grilled or Gas-Grilled Duck Breasts (without salt and pepper)

1. Place the olives, anchovies, capers, and garlic in a food processor and pulse one or two times. With the motor running, drizzle the oil into the olive mixture and process until the oil is incorporated. (The mixture should still be slightly chunky.) Transfer the tapenade to a small bowl and cover.

2. Follow the recipe for Charcoal-Grilled or Gas-Grilled Duck Breasts, rubbing each breast with a little tapenade before grilling. Proceed as directed, serving extra tapenade at the table with the sliced duck.

QUAIL

QUAIL HAVE A RICH, MEATY FLAVOR THAT IS well suited to grilling. Grilling also crisps the skin on these small birds.

Quail meat is uniformly dark, both on the breasts and legs. Although bobwhite quail are native to this country (they are what hunters shoot), most commercial operations raise an Asian variety called Coturnix. These quail range in size from 4 to 6 ounces each, depending on where they were raised and their age at slaughter. We prefer larger quail, at least 5 ounces, since they are less bony and easier to eat.

Once you get quail home, you may need to remove the feet and pluck out a few remaining feathers. A thorough rinsing and drying with paper towels is also required. We tried boning quail and found that they are too small to survive this procedure. Be prepared to gnaw on tiny bones.

We found it best to split the quail along the backbone in a procedure called butterflying that lets the birds lie flat on the grill. Butterflying the quail also reduces grilling time, which keeps them from drying out. A medium-hot fire gets the skin as crisp as possible.

We found that cooking the meat just until it is no longer pink is best; it will be juicier and more flavorful than when cooked further. Although it is hard to measure the temperature in the tiny thighs and breasts of these birds, we found that an internal temperature of 160 to 165 degrees was ideal. Higher temperatures will produce meat that is dry and tough.

Charcoal-Grilled Quail
SERVES 4

Cook the quail over a medium-hot fire, taking care to douse any flames with a squirt bottle and/or move the quail to another part of the grill if flare-ups occur.

8	quail (about 5 ounces each), rinsed and patted dry, and prepared according to the illustrations on the facing page
2	tablespoons extra-virgin olive oil
	Salt and ground black pepper

1. Light a large chimney starter filled almost halfway with hardwood charcoal (about 2½ quarts) and allow to burn until all the charcoal is covered with a layer of fine gray ash. Build a single-level fire by spreading the coals evenly over the bottom of the grill. Set the cooking grate in place, cover the grill with the lid, and let the grate heat up, about 5 minutes. Use a grill brush to scrape the cooking grate clean. The grill is ready when the coals are medium-hot. (See how to gauge heat level on page 4.)

2. Meanwhile, brush the quail with the oil and sprinkle with salt and pepper to taste.

3. Place the quail, skin-side down, on the grill. Grill the quail, uncovered, until well browned, 5 to 6 minutes. Turn and cook the quail until the juices run clear when the thighs are pierced with a fork, about 5 minutes, or check the internal temperature with an instant-read thermometer, which should register 160 to 165 degrees. Serve immediately.

➤ VARIATIONS

Gas-Grilled Quail
Quail are small enough to grill over a hot gas fire. Just watch the birds carefully to make sure they are not burning, and keep an eye out for flare-ups.

Turn on all the burners to high, close the lid, and heat the grill until very hot, about 15 minutes. Use a grill brush to scrape the cooking grate clean. Leave the burners on high. Follow the recipe for Charcoal-Grilled Quail from step 2 with the following change. In step 3, grill the quail, covered, until well browned, 6 to 7 minutes (instead of 5 to 6 minutes) on the first side. Proceed as directed.

Grilled Quail with Sage, Mustard, and Honey
A whole leaf of sage is tucked under the skin of each side of the breast. The quail is grilled, then glazed with mustard and honey.

Mix 3 tablespoons Dijon mustard and 3 tablespoons honey together in a bowl. Follow the recipe for Charcoal-Grilled or Gas-Grilled Quail, using your fingertips to separate the skin from the breast meat and then inserting a flat sage leaf under the skin of each side of the breastbone. (You will need a total of 16 sage leaves for 8 quail.) Oil and season the quail as directed. Grill, brushing the mustard-honey mixture over the birds during the last 2 minutes of cooking time.

Grilled Quail with Chili-Lime Glaze
This sweet, spicy glaze is delicious with quail.

½	cup juice from 8 limes
3	tablespoons brown sugar
1	tablespoon chili powder
2	medium garlic cloves, minced or pressed through a garlic press (about 2 teaspoons)
1	teaspoon ground cumin
1	recipe Charcoal-Grilled or Gas-Grilled Quail

1. Mix the lime juice, brown sugar, chili powder, garlic, and cumin together in a small bowl.

2. Oil, season, and grill the birds as directed, brushing the chili-lime glaze over the birds during the last 2 minutes of cooking time.

PREPARING QUAIL

1. The tiny wingtips will singe on the grill. Use poultry scissors or a chef's knife to remove the tip from each wing.

2. Butterflied quail will cook more evenly on the grill. To butterfly, insert poultry or kitchen shears into the cavity and cut along one side of the backbone. The backbone is so small that there is no need to cut along the other side of the bone to remove it, as is necessary when butterflying a chicken.

3. Turn the butterflied bird skin-side up and flatten it by pressing down with your hands.

Grilled Quail with Cherry-Port Sauce

Savory grilled quail goes well with a sweet-and-sour pan sauce made with port and dried cherries. Other dried fruit, such as figs (cut into slices), raisins, or cranberries can be substituted for the cherries. Do not buy expensive port for this dish; less costly bottles will work fine. The sauce is made ahead and then finished at the last minute with the addition of butter, which enriches and binds the ingredients, and some fresh thyme.

1½	cups ruby port
½	cup dry red wine
½	cup dried tart cherries
4	medium shallots, chopped fine
2	tablespoons red wine vinegar
1	recipe Charcoal-Grilled or Gas-Grilled Quail
2	tablespoons chilled unsalted butter, cut into ¼-inch cubes
2	teaspoons minced fresh thyme leaves
	Salt and ground black pepper

1. Bring the port, red wine, cherries, shallots, and vinegar to a boil in a large skillet. Simmer over medium-high heat until syrupy, 12 to 15 minutes. Remove the pan from the heat.

2. Oil, season, and grill the birds as directed in the recipe. Transfer the grilled quail to a serving platter and cover with foil.

3. Bring the port sauce back up to a simmer over medium-high heat. Reduce the heat to low and add the butter and thyme. Swirl the pan to incorporate the butter into the sauce. Remove the pan from the heat and season the sauce with salt and pepper to taste. Remove the foil from the platter and spoon the sauce over and around the quail. Serve immediately.

SQUAB

A SQUAB IS A YOUNG PIGEON THAT CANNOT fly because its feathers have not developed fully. It bears little resemblance to other birds. The flesh is rich and gamy, more like venison or beef than chicken. Squabs are meatier than quail, weighing about a pound each.

Given the strong flavor of squab, it's no surprise that we found strong seasonings—such as chiles and garlic—work best with this bird. Unlike other whole birds, squabs are best cooked to medium-rare. The meat will be pink, and an instant-read thermometer will register about 145 degrees. If you can't stand the notion of pink poultry, you can cook squab a few minutes longer to an internal temperature of 160 degrees. The meat will be far less juicy and will resemble well-done beef in texture.

We tested grilling whole squabs and found that they are difficult to cook properly. When grilled over direct heat, the skin burned before the meat was cooked. A two-level fire worked better, but we discovered an option that is easier in terms of both cooking and eating.

Semiboneless squabs are available at most butcher shops and they cook much more evenly. The wings and legs still contain bones, but the birds have been freed from back, breast, and thigh bones. Without these major bones, squabs are much thinner and can be cooked over direct heat. Needless to say, squabs with fewer bones are also easier to eat.

In our initial tests, boneless squab cooked fairly evenly, except for the back portion of the breast. The wings were preventing the breast from lying flat against the grill. Since there's no meat on the wings, we decided to clip them before cooking. With the wings gone, the breast cooked flat against the grill.

Charcoal-Grilled Squab
SERVES 4 AS A MAIN COURSE
OR 8 AS AN APPETIZER

We find that semiboneless squabs (the leg and wing bones are still in place) are essential when grilling. You could bone the squabs yourself, but we strongly recommend buying squabs that have been boned during processing. Squab is pretty fatty, so keep a close eye on the grill and be ready to douse any flames with a squirt bottle filled with water. We feel that squab is best eaten medium-rare; cooked to a higher temperature, it becomes tough and dry. For eight appetizer portions, use kitchen shears to split the squabs in half lengthwise after grilling. Serve with a fruit salsa (see chapter 11) or Curried Fruit Chutney with Lime and Ginger (page 396).

4 boneless squabs (about 10 ounces each),
rinsed and patted dry, wings removed
(see the illustration on page 220)

1 tablespoon extra-virgin olive oil
Salt and ground black pepper

1. Light a large chimney starter filled a little less than halfway with hardwood charcoal (about 2½ quarts) and allow to burn until all the charcoal is covered with a layer of fine gray ash. Build a single-level fire by spreading the coals evenly over the bottom of the grill. Set the cooking grate in place, cover the grill with the lid, and let the grate heat up, about 5 minutes. Use a grill brush to scrape the cooking grate clean. The grill is ready when the coals are medium-hot. (See how to gauge heat level on page 4.)

2. Meanwhile, brush the squabs with oil and sprinkle liberally with salt and pepper to taste.

3. Place the squabs, breast-side down, on the grill. Grill the squabs, uncovered, until well browned, 5 to 7 minutes. Turn the squabs and cook until medium-rare, about 4 minutes. To test for doneness, either peek into the thickest part of the breast with the tip of a small knife (it should be a dark rosy red toward the center) or insert an instant-read thermometer into the thickest part of the breast (it should register 145 degrees).

4. Transfer the squabs to a serving platter and serve immediately.

➤ VARIATIONS

Gas-Grilled Squab

Turn on all the burners to high, close the lid, and heat the grill until very hot, about 15 minutes. Use a grill brush to scrape the cooking grate clean. Leave all the burners on high. Follow the recipe for Charcoal-Grilled Squab from step 2, grilling with the cover down.

Asian-Style Grilled Squab on Salad with Grilled Shiitake Mushrooms

Gamy and full-flavored, squab takes well to strong flavors. Here it is paired with a soy sauce, ginger, garlic, and scallion marinade and balanced with a light green salad and grilled mushrooms. If you cut the grilled squabs in half, this salad can be eaten as a light meal or as a first course salad for a special occasion. For a more refined presentation, slice the squab meat off the remaining bones and then fan the slices out over the salad.

½ cup soy sauce

4 small scallions, sliced thin

6 tablespoons rice vinegar

2½ tablespoons honey

1½ tablespoons minced fresh ginger

3 medium garlic cloves, minced or pressed through a garlic press (about 1 tablespoon)

4 boneless squabs (about 10 ounces each), rinsed and patted dry, wings removed (see the illustration on page 220)

8 ounces shiitake mushrooms, stems discarded, caps wiped clean

1 small carrot, cut into chunks

¼ cup peanut oil

4 red radishes, ends trimmed and cut into thin circles

8 cups lightly packed mesclun or other tender salad greens, washed and thoroughly dried

1. Whisk together the soy sauce, scallions, vinegar, honey, ginger, and garlic in a medium bowl; measure out ⅓ cup of this mixture and set it aside. Place the squabs and mushroom caps in a gallon-size zipper-lock plastic bag and pour the remaining soy sauce marinade over them. Press out as much air as possible and seal the bag. Marinate the squabs and mushrooms in the refrigerator for 1 hour.

2. Prepare the grill according to the instructions in the recipe for Charcoal-Grilled or Gas-Grilled Squab.

3. Meanwhile, place the carrot in a food processor. Pulse until chopped fine, scraping down the sides of the bowl if necessary. Add the reserved soy mixture and process until blended, about 10 seconds. With the motor running, drizzle in the oil until smooth. Transfer the dressing to a clean bowl.

4. Remove the squabs and mushrooms from the marinade and discard the marinade. Place the mushrooms and the squabs, breast-side down, on the grill. Grill the squabs, uncovered, until well browned, 5 to 7 minutes. Turn and cook the squabs until medium-rare, about 4 minutes. To test for doneness, either peek into the thickest part

of the breast with the tip of a small knife (it should be a dark rosy red toward the center) or insert an instant-read thermometer into the thickest part of the breast (it should register 145 degrees). At the same time, grill the mushrooms, turning them once, being careful that they don't fall through the cooking grate, until streaked with dark grill marks, about 6 minutes total. Transfer the squabs to a platter when done; cover with foil. Transfer the mushrooms to a cutting board when done.

5. Cut the grilled mushrooms in half. Toss the mushrooms, radishes, mesclun, and carrot dressing in a large bowl. Divide the salad among 4 dinner plates or 8 salad plates. Place one squab (or a half, if serving as an appetizer) on each plate and serve immediately.

Grilled Squab with Greek Flavors

For this recipe, squab is marinated in a mixture of lemon juice, oregano, garlic, and olive oil, grilled, then served over slices of tomato that have been sprinkled with feta cheese. The acidity of the lemon juice balances the rich meaty flavor of the squab. To prevent major flare-ups, be sure to shake off any excess marinade before grilling. Be ready to move the birds to another part of the grill if flare-ups occur and keep a squirt bottle handy to douse any flames. If fresh oregano is unavailable, substitute 1¼ teaspoons dried oregano.

6	tablespoons juice from 3 lemons
2	tablespoons chopped fresh oregano leaves
3	medium garlic cloves, minced or pressed through a garlic press (about 1 tablespoon)
1½	teaspoons salt
	Ground black pepper
¾	cup extra-virgin olive oil
4	boneless squabs (about 10 ounces each), rinsed and patted dry, wings removed (see illustration at right)
4	large tomatoes, cored and cut crosswise into ¼-inch-thick slices
4	ounces feta cheese, crumbled

1. Whisk together the lemon juice, oregano, garlic, salt, and pepper to taste in a small bowl.

Whisk in the oil. Measure out ½ cup of the mixture; cover and refrigerate the remaining dressing.

2. Place the squabs in a gallon-size zipper-lock plastic bag and pour the ½ cup lemon marinade over them. Press out as much air as possible and seal the bag. Marinate the squabs in the refrigerator for 30 to 60 minutes.

3. Ready the grill according to the instructions in the recipe for Charcoal-Grilled or Gas-Grilled Squab.

4. Remove the squabs from the marinade, making sure to shake off any excess marinade. Place the squabs, breast-side down, on the grill. Grill the squabs, uncovered, until well browned, 5 to 7 minutes. Turn and cook the squabs until medium-rare, about 4 minutes. To test for doneness, either peek into the thickest part of the breast with the tip of a small knife (it should be a dark rosy red toward the center) or insert an instant-read thermometer into the thickest part of the breast (it should register 145 degrees).

5. While the squabs are on the grill, fan the tomato slices out on a large serving platter or on individual plates. Sprinkle with the crumbled feta cheese.

6. Place the grilled squabs on top of the tomatoes and drizzle with the reserved dressing. Serve immediately.

PREPARING SQUAB

The wings of a squab are not very meaty and can prevent the nearby breast meat from cooking properly. Use a chef's knife or kitchen shears to remove the wings before grilling squab.

6
FISH

FISH

CHARCOAL-GRILLED BLUEFISH FILLETS 225
   Gas-Grilled Bluefish Fillets
   Cumin-Crusted Bluefish Fillets with Avocado-Corn Relish

CHARCOAL-GRILLED HALIBUT STEAKS 227
   Gas-Grilled Halibut Steaks
   Grilled Halibut Steaks with Chipotle-Lime Butter

CHARCOAL-GRILLED MAHI-MAHI FILLETS 228
   Gas-Grilled Mahi-Mahi Fillets
   Grilled Mahi-Mahi with Fillets Shallots, Lime, and Cilantro

CHARCOAL-GRILLED RED SNAPPER FILLETS 230
   Gas-Grilled Red Snapper Fillets
   Grilled Red Snapper Fillets with Spicy Yellow Pepper and Tomato Salsa

CHARCOAL-GRILLED SWORDFISH STEAKS 231
   Gas-Grilled Swordfish Steaks
   Grilled Swordfish Steaks with Lemon-Parsley Sauce
   Grilled Swordfish Steaks with Salsa Verde
   Grilled Swordfish Steaks with Chermoula

CHARCOAL-GRILLED SWORDFISH KEBABS 232
   Gas-Grilled Swordfish Kebabs
   Southeast Asian–Style Swordfish Kebabs
   Swordfish Kebabs with Salmoriglio Sauce

CHARCOAL-GRILLED SALMON FILLETS 234
   Gas-Grilled Salmon Fillets
   Grilled Salmon Fillets and Fennel with Orange Vinaigrette
   Grilled Salmon Fillets with Aromatic Spice Rub

GRILLED GLAZED SALMON FILLETS ON A CHARCOAL GRILL 236
   Grilled Glazed Salmon Fillets on a Gas Grill

GLAZES 237
   Maple-Chipotle Glaze
   Maple-Soy Glaze
   Honey-Mustard Glaze

BARBECUED SALMON ON A CHARCOAL GRILL 239
   Barbecued Salmon on a Gas Grill

SAUCES 240
   Horseradish Cream Sauce
   Mustard-Dill Sauce

CHARCOAL-GRILLED TUNA STEAKS 241
    Gas-Grilled Tuna Steaks
    Thin-Cut Grilled Tuna Steaks
    Grilled Tuna Steaks with Herb-Infused Oil
    Grilled Tuna Steaks with Peppercorn Crust
    Grilled Rare Tuna Steaks with Soy, Ginger, and Wasabi
    Grilled Tuna Steaks with Watercress, Parsley, and Spiced Vinaigrette
    Grilled Tuna Steaks and Bok Choy with Soy-Ginger Glaze
    Grilled Tuna Steaks with Tarragon-Lime Butter or Tapenade Butter

CHARCOAL-GRILLED SALMON BURGERS 245
    Gas-Grilled Salmon Burgers

CHARCOAL-GRILLED TUNA BURGERS 246
    Gas-Grilled Tuna Burgers

SAUCES FOR FISH BURGERS 248
    Creamy Chipotle-Lime Sauce
    Wasabi Mayonnaise
    Creamy Lemon-Herb Sauce
    Creamy Ginger-Cilantro Sauce

CHARCOAL-GRILLED WHOLE BLUEFISH 249
    Gas-Grilled Whole Bluefish

CHARCOAL-GRILLED WHOLE MACKEREL 252
    Gas-Grilled Whole Mackerel
    Spicy Grilled Mackerel with Garlic, Ginger, and Sesame Oil

CHARCOAL-GRILLED WHOLE RED SNAPPER OR STRIPED BASS 253
    Gas-Grilled Whole Red Snapper or Striped Bass
    Grilled Whole Red Snapper or Striped Bass with Orange, Lime, and Cilantro Vinaigrette
    Grilled Whole Red Snapper or Striped Bass with Parsley-Lemons Butter
    Grilled Whole Red Snapper or Striped Bass with Fresh Tomato-Basil Relish

CHARCOAL-GRILLED WHOLE POMPANO 255
    Gas-Grilled Whole Pompano
    Grilled Whole Pompano with Tarragon Butter Sauce

CHARCOAL-GRILLED WHOLE FRESHWATER TROUT 256
    Gas-Grilled Whole Freshwater Trout
    Grilled Whole Freshwater Trout with Bacon and Horseradish-Peppercorn Sauce

FISH IS IN SOME WAYS EASY TO COOK. THE actual cooking time for most of the recipes in this chapter is under 10 minutes. That said, keeping seafood moist is a constant challenge. The most important thing you can do to ensure good results is not to overcook fish. While we like most fish cooked through (salmon and tuna are exceptions), fish that is overcooked becomes dry and overly flaky.

A few general points about fish. You must buy from a trusted source, preferably one with a high volume to ensure freshness. Although cooking can hide imperfections in meat and poultry, there is little the cook can do to salvage a tired piece of salmon or tuna.

So what should you look for at the seafood shop? Fish should smell like the sea, not fishy or sour. The flesh should look bright, shiny, and firm, not dull or mushy. When possible, try to get your fishmonger to slice steaks and fillets to order, rather than buying precut pieces that may have been sitting for some time and thereby lost some fluids. Avoid fish that is shrink-wrapped, since the packaging makes it difficult to examine and smell the fish. No matter how you buy fish, make sure it has been kept chilled until the minute you buy it; then get fish home and into the refrigerator quickly.

This chapter is divided into two sections: the first on cooking fillets and steaks, the second on cooking whole fish. We have included only those fish you are likely to see in most fish shops and that are good candidates for grilling. Thin, flaky fish, such as flounder, are better cooked indoors. Meaty, dense, thicker fish, especially those that are a bit oily, are better suited to grilling.

FISH FILLETS AND STEAKS

FILLETS ARE BONELESS PIECES OF FISH cut along the length of the fish from head to tail. They may be sold with or without the skin attached. Steaks usually come from larger fish and are cut across the belly of the fish. Some steaks (such as salmon or halibut steaks) have bones.

Cooking fish fillets and steaks is easy. Because

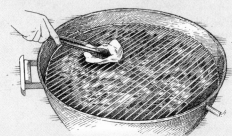

BARBECUE 911

Fish Sticks to the Grill

Fish sticks to the cooking grate. It seems like a fact of life for the avid griller. But must you resign yourself to always losing some fish to the grill? The answer is no. Preheat the grill, scrape it clean with a grill brush, and then use this trick.

Dip a wad of paper towels in vegetable oil, grasp the oiled towels with a pair of long-handled tongs, and rub the oil over the hot cooking grate. Place your fish on the oiled grate and leave it alone until it is time to flip the fish.

the pieces are generally thin (between ½ and 1½ inches thick), the fish is done by the time it is seared. The biggest issue is sticking. Many times we've put perfect, gleaming fillets on the grill only to have them stick and tear when we tried to turn them; this ruins the presentation of the fish, making it look like something the cat dragged in.

In developing recipes for this section, we found it useful to rub the heated cooking grate with a wad of paper towels dipped lightly in vegetable oil and held by long-handled tongs. (The paper doesn't catch fire.) This extra step not only lubricates the grate but cleans off lingering residue as well, which is important given the delicate flavor and light color of most fish.

We conducted several tests cooking fillets in a fish basket. A fish basket is a long-handled wire contraption that's shaped something like a sandwich press. The two rectangular halves (each half is a wire grid) sandwich the food between them. The fish is cooked in the basket on top of the cooking grate. Our first attempt was a bust; the fillets browned well but stuck to the basket. We oiled the basket for the next test; this method worked better. On the downside, we found that fillets cooked in a basket did not develop as nice a crust as fillets cooked right on the grill. Also, the basket does not allow the cook to compensate for thinner or thicker fillets, or for hotter or cooler spots on the grill, since everything must be turned at the same time. We prefer to move fish around gently with a metal spatula (see the illustration on page 228). If you decide to use a fish basket, remove the fish immediately from the basket once it is cooked. The skin will stick to the wire as it cools.

The other key to keeping fish from sticking is the use of a moderately hot fire. Fish grilled over a superhot fire will burn. However, if the fire is too cool, the fish will stick. In most cases, a medium-hot fire works best.

BLUEFISH FILLETS

BLUEFISH IS IN SEASON ON THE EASTERN seaboard from late spring until early fall. The fillets are gray-brown in color with a bluish tinge. Some fillets may contain a darker brown streak, which is the bloodline running down the center of the fillet.

Bluefish has a reputation for tasting fishy and oily. While this reputation is deserved, we find the flavor delicious, especially when the fish has been seasoned aggressively. In our testing, we found that lemon and a bit of mustard combat the oiliness of the bluefish. That said, bluefish will always taste somewhat oily, but we like to think of this as an asset. Bluefish doesn't dry out on the grill as easily as leaner fish such as tuna or swordfish.

Cooking bluefish is easy. We didn't have any problems with it sticking as long as the grill was hot, scraped clean, and well oiled. We tried cooking the fish in a basket but found that a basket just made the process harder. The fish actually stuck to the basket, and it didn't develop as nice a crust as it did when placed directly on the cooking grate.

Like other thinner fish fillets, bluefish will flake, so exercise caution when turning it on the grill. Slide a metal spatula under the fillets to turn them.

Bluefish does not keep well; that "fishy" flavor becomes pronounced the longer the fish sits on ice. Make sure to buy from a reputable fishmonger with access to fresh bluefish.

Charcoal-Grilled Bluefish Fillets
SERVES 4

Acidic ingredients marry very well with oily, strong-flavored bluefish. Be sure to get bluefish as close to the catch as possible and store it over ice; this fish quickly loses its freshness. The gray-brown flesh turns white once it is cooked through.

3	tablespoons extra-virgin olive oil
1½	tablespoons juice from 1 lemon
1	teaspoon Dijon mustard
1	medium garlic clove, minced or pressed through a garlic press (about 1 teaspoon)
¼	teaspoon salt
	Ground black pepper
4	skinless bluefish fillets (6½ to 7 ounces each)
	Vegetable oil for the cooking grate
	Lemon wedges for serving

1. Mix the olive oil, lemon juice, mustard, garlic, salt, and pepper to taste together in a small bowl. Place the bluefish in a single layer in a large baking dish and pour the lemon-oil mixture over the fillets. Rub the mixture all over the fillets to coat evenly. Cover and refrigerate for 30 minutes.

2. Light a large chimney starter filled with hardwood charcoal (about 6 quarts) and allow to burn until all the charcoal is covered with a layer of fine gray ash. Build a single-level fire by spreading the coals evenly over the bottom of the grill. Set the cooking grate in place, cover the grill with the lid, and let the grate heat up, about 5 minutes. Use a grill brush to scrape the cooking grate clean. The grill is ready when the coals are medium-hot. (See how to gauge heat level on page 4.)

3. Lightly dip a small wad of paper towels in vegetable oil; holding the wad with long-handled tongs, wipe the cooking grate (see the facing page). Remove the bluefish fillets from the marinade and

place them on the grill. Grill, uncovered, turning once (using a metal spatula), until the fish is no longer gray-brown in the center, about 7 minutes. Serve immediately with the lemon wedges.

➤ VARIATIONS
Gas-Grilled Bluefish Fillets

Because the heat of a gas grill is less intense than that of a charcoal grill, the cooking time is slightly increased.

Follow step 1 of Charcoal-Grilled Bluefish Fillets. Turn on all the burners to high, cover, and heat the grill until very hot, about 15 minutes. Use a grill brush to scrape the cooking grate clean. Leave all the burners on high. Proceed with the recipe from step 3, grilling the fish covered, turning once (using a metal spatula), until the fish is no longer gray-brown in the center, about 8 minutes. Serve immediately with the lemon wedges.

Cumin-Crusted Bluefish Fillets with Avocado-Corn Relish

Bluefish stands up nicely to the strong flavors of spice rubs. Here we have paired the fish with cumin, cayenne, and chili powder. This fish would also taste great coated with the Simple Spice Rub for Fish (page 379). If you like, pass warmed corn tortillas with the fish and relish and let everyone make their own fish tacos.

4	teaspoons ground cumin
1	teaspoon chili powder
1/4	teaspoon cayenne pepper
1/4	teaspoon salt
1/4	teaspoon ground black pepper
4	skinless bluefish fillets (6 1/2 to 7 ounces each)
3	tablespoons extra-virgin olive oil
	Vegetable oil for the cooking grate
	Lime wedges for serving
2	cups Avocado-Corn Relish (page 393)

1. Mix the cumin, chili powder, cayenne, salt, and pepper together in a small bowl. Rub the bluefish fillets with the olive oil, then rub the spice mixture onto the fillets until evenly coated. Cover and refrigerate for 30 minutes.

2. Prepare the grill as directed in either the Charcoal-Grilled or Gas-Grilled Bluefish Fillets recipe. Use a grill brush to scrape the cooking grate clean. Lightly dip a small of paper towels in vegetable oil; holding the wad with long-handled tongs, wipe the cooking grate (see page 224).

3. Grill the fillets as directed. Remove the fish from the grill and serve immediately, with the lime wedges and relish passed separately at the table.

HALIBUT STEAKS

HALIBUT IS A MILD-FLAVORED, LEAN, WHITE fish with firm flesh, making it a perfect choice for those who like other mild-flavored, steak-like fish such as swordfish or tuna. It is an easy fish to grill as long as you don't get a steak that is too thin and you don't allow it to overcook on the grill. Halibut can dry out if overcooked, so remove steaks from the grill once the center is just barely translucent.

We found halibut steaks in various forms at markets around town. Some were boneless, others had two sections of flesh separated by a bone, and others had four sections of meat separated by bone and membrane. Because you are most likely to see boneless steaks, we have written our halibut recipes for this cut. (In case you can find only bone-in steaks at the market, we provide instructions for boning below.)

Halibut is best simply prepared. No marinades are necessary, just a brush of oil, which keeps it from

PREPARING HALIBUT STEAKS

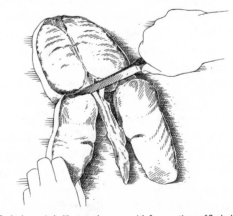

Whole, bone-in halibut steaks come with four sections of flesh divided by a long bone that runs down the center, crossed by a thin membrane. To remove the bone and separate the four boneless steaks, simply run a knife along the sides of the bone, then follow the line of the thin membrane with the knife to separate it from the flesh.

sticking to the grill, and some salt and pepper. Like swordfish, however (and like beefsteak), halibut takes well to flavorings such as butters and sauces.

Charcoal-Grilled Halibut Steaks

SERVES 4

In this recipe, we use boneless, skin-on halibut steaks. If the only kind of halibut steaks you can find have a bone running down the center, see the facing page for instructions on how to remove it. If your market carries only half steaks, which consist of two sections of flesh separated by a long, thin bone, you will need two steaks, about 1 pound each and 1 inch thick, for this recipe. If your market carries only whole halibut steaks (they have four sections of flesh divided by a bone and a membrane), you will need only one 2-pound steak, about 1 inch thick. If desired, serve the steaks with one of the compound butters on pages 384–385.

4	boneless, skin-on halibut steaks, 1 inch thick (7 to 8 ounces each)
2	tablespoons extra-virgin olive oil
	Salt and ground black pepper
	Vegetable oil for the cooking grate
	Lemon wedges for serving

1. Light a large chimney starter filled with hardwood charcoal (about 6 quarts) and allow to burn until all the charcoal is covered with a layer of fine gray ash. Build a single-level fire by spreading the coals evenly over the bottom of the grill. Set the cooking grate in place, cover the grill with the lid, and let the grate heat up, about 5 minutes. Use a grill brush to scrape the cooking grate clean. The grill is ready when the coals are medium-hot. (See how to gauge heat level on page 4.)

2. Brush the halibut with the olive oil and season well with salt and pepper to taste.

3. Lightly dip a small wad of paper towels in vegetable oil; holding the wad with long-handled tongs, wipe the cooking grate (see page 224). Grill the halibut, uncovered and turning once (using a metal spatula), until barely translucent at the very center of the steak, 7 to 8 minutes. Serve immediately with the lemon wedges.

➤ VARIATIONS

Gas-Grilled Halibut Steaks

Note that the grilling times are slightly longer when using a gas grill.

Turn on all the burners to high, cover, and heat the grill until very hot, about 15 minutes. Use a grill brush to scrape the cooking grate clean. Leave all the burners on high. Follow the recipe for Charcoal-Grilled Halibut Steaks from step 2, grilling the halibut, covered, and turning once (using a metal spatula), until barely translucent at the very center of the steak, 8 to 9 minutes.

Grilled Halibut Steaks with Chipotle-Lime Butter

Chipotles are actually dried, smoked jalapeño chiles. Small amounts of chipotle add gentle heat to the butter in this recipe. Here, we've used a chipotle chile in adobo sauce (a dark red sauce made with herbs, vinegar, and ground chiles), available in small cans in the ethnic food aisle of most supermarkets. Refrigerate or freeze any leftover peppers and sauce for future use. If you like, you can substitute Tarragon-Lime Butter or Tapenade Butter (see page 385).

4	tablespoons (½ stick) unsalted butter, softened
1	tablespoon roughly chopped fresh cilantro leaves
2	teaspoons juice from 1 lime
1	chipotle chile in adobo sauce, chopped fine
1	medium garlic clove, minced or pressed through a garlic press (about 1 teaspoon)
¼	teaspoon salt
1	recipe Charcoal-Grilled or Gas-Grilled Halibut Steaks (without the lemon wedges)

1. Beat the butter with a large fork in a medium bowl until light and fluffy. Add the cilantro, lime juice, chile, garlic, and salt and mix to combine. Following the illustration on page 384, roll the butter into a log about 3 inches long and 1½ inches in diameter. Refrigerate until firm, at least 2 hours and up to 3 days. (The butter can be frozen for 2 months. When ready to use, let soften just until the butter can be cut, about 15 minutes).

2. Follow the recipe for Charcoal-Grilled or Gas-Grilled Halibut Steaks. Transfer the steaks to

individual plates and set a slice of chipotle butter on top of each hot steak. Serve immediately.

MAHI-MAHI FILLETS

MAHI-MAHI WAS A LITTLE MORE DIFFICULT to grill than we had imagined. Its texture is similar to swordfish, but the flesh is actually a little oilier and fishier tasting. Despite the extra oil, we found that mahi-mahi still has a tendency to dry out on the grill.

We asked the fishmonger to cut a side of mahi-mahi (also known as dolphinfish—not to be confused with the mammal) into 8-ounce portions, just as you would cut a side of salmon into fillets. The fillets cut from the center of the side are thicker and more desirable than thinner fillets cut from the ends. Buy mahi-mahi fillets that have a bright coral-pink tinge and a slightly darker line running through the middle. This indicates freshness. Do not buy fillets that are streaked with a very dark (brown) line through the middle—they are probably past their prime. When cooked, mahi-mahi turns the color of swordfish.

Our mahi-mahi steaks were quite thick, so we cooked them over a two-level fire. Mahi-mahi needs to be cooked to between medium and medium-well, with no translucence left in the center of the meat. Even when cooked over a two-level fire and to medium, however, the fish was still a little dry and sawdusty, just as tuna becomes when it's cooked that far. We tried presoaking it

TURNING FISH FILLETS AND STEAKS

Use a metal spatula (pancake turner) for flipping fish. Always slide the spatula under the fish parallel to the bars of the cooking grate.

in extra-virgin olive oil, which helps keep thinner cuts of tuna from drying out, but this didn't help all that much on such thick, large fillets.

Next, we tried brining the fish in a salt and sugar water solution. The fish was much, much better, both juicier and tastier. Since mahi-mahi can be a little fishy, the sugar and salt in the brine helped to balance the flavors. The sugar also encouraged the formation of a caramelized crust on the fillet.

Charcoal-Grilled Mahi-Mahi Fillets

SERVES 4

We brine the mahi-mahi because, much like chicken breasts, mahi-mahi fillets tend to dry out quickly when grilled. Brining seasons the fish beautifully, adding a balance of saltiness and sweetness. (To use kosher salt in the brine, see page 172 for conversion information.)

6	tablespoons sugar
6	tablespoons table salt (see note)
4	skinless mahi-mahi fillets, center cut, if possible (7 to 8 ounces each)
3	tablespoons extra-virgin olive oil
	Ground black pepper
	Vegetable oil for the cooking grate
	Lemon wedges for serving

1. Dissolve the sugar and salt in 1 quart of cold water in a gallon-sized zipper-lock plastic bag. Add the fish; press out as much air as possible from the bag and seal. Refrigerate, about 40 minutes.

2. Meanwhile, light a large chimney starter filled with hardwood charcoal (about 6 quarts) and allow to burn until all the charcoal is covered with a layer of fine gray ash. Build a two-level fire by stacking most of the coals on one side of the grill and arranging the remaining coals in a single layer on the other side of the grill. Set the cooking grate in place, cover the grill with the lid, and let the grate heat up, about 5 minutes. Use a grill brush to scrape the cooking grate clean. The grill is ready when the temperature of the stacked coals is medium-hot and that of the remaining coals is medium-low. (See how to gauge heat level on page 4.)

3. Remove the fish from the brine and rinse well. Pat dry the fillets with paper towels. Brush the fish fillets with the olive oil and season to taste with pepper.

4. Lightly dip a small wad of paper towels in vegetable oil; holding the wad with long-handled tongs, wipe the cooking grate (see page 224). Grill the mahi-mahi, uncovered, turning once (using a metal spatula), over the hotter part of the grill until dark grill marks appear, about 5 minutes total. Move the fillets to the cooler part of the grill and cook, turning once, until the fish is no longer translucent at the center, 3 to 4 minutes. Serve immediately with the lemon wedges.

➢ VARIATIONS
Gas-Grilled Mahi-Mahi Fillets
To cook the mahi-mahi over a gas fire, grill with all burners set to high for several minutes, then turn the burners down to medium to cook the fish through and prevent it from browning too much.

Follow step 1 of the recipe for Charcoal-Grilled Mahi-Mahi Fillets. Turn on all the burners to high, cover, and heat the grill until very hot, about 15 minutes. Use a grill brush to scrape the cooking grate clean. Leave all the burners on high. Proceed with the recipe for Charcoal-Grilled Mahi-Mahi Fillets from step 3, grilling the mahi-mahi, covered, turning once (using a metal spatula), until dark grill marks appear, about 6 minutes total. Turn all the burners down to medium. Cover and continue grilling, turning once, until the fish is no longer translucent at the center, about 4 to 5 minutes. Serve immediately with the lemon wedges.

Grilled Mahi-Mahi Fillets with Shallots, Lime, and Cilantro
Mahi-mahi goes very well with assertive flavors such as acidic lime juice, cooling cilantro, and pungent shallots, ginger, and garlic. If shallots are unavailable, use ⅓ cup minced red onion instead.

1	recipe Charcoal-Grilled or Gas-Grilled Mahi-Mahi Fillets (without the olive oil, pepper, and lemon wedges)
4	tablespoons extra-virgin olive oil
4	medium shallots, chopped fine
4	medium garlic cloves, minced or pressed through a garlic press (about 1 heaping tablespoon)
2	teaspoons minced fresh ginger
2	teaspoons brown sugar
1½	teaspoons ground cumin
3	tablespoons juice from 3 limes
2	tablespoons chopped fresh cilantro leaves
2	teaspoons hot sauce, plus more to pass at the table
¼	teaspoon salt
	Ground black pepper
	Lime wedges for serving

1. Brine the fish as directed in the recipe for Charcoal-Grilled or Gas-Grilled Mahi-Mahi Fillets.

2. Meanwhile, heat the olive oil in a large skillet over medium-high heat until shimmering. Reduce the heat to medium and add the shallots; cook until soft, about 4 minutes. Add the garlic, ginger, brown sugar, and cumin and cook until fragrant, about 1 minute longer. Remove the pan from the heat and stir in the lime juice, cilantro, hot sauce, and salt. Transfer the mixture to a heatproof bowl and refrigerate until cool.

3. Prepare the grill as directed.

4. While the grill heats, rinse and dry the fillets as directed. Place them in a large dish or pie plate and pour the cooled shallot-lime mixture over them. Season the fish with ground black pepper. Cover the dish and marinate in the refrigerator for 20 minutes.

5. Lightly dip a small wad of paper towels in vegetable oil; holding the wad with long-handled tongs, wipe the cooking grate (see page 224). Remove the fish from the marinade and grill as directed. Serve with the lime wedges and hot sauce.

RED SNAPPER FILLETS
RED SNAPPER IS EASY TO GRILL. THE FILLETS are pretty thin—½ inch to ¾ inch at the thickest part—so they cook through in about five minutes. Red snapper is less dense and more flaky than steak-like fish such as tuna or mahi-mahi, so it cooks more quickly than you might think. The main challenge for the cook is to prevent the delicate fillets from falling apart. We found it wise to

oil both the grill and the fish. When turning, slide a metal spatula under the fish and flip carefully.

We like the flavor of red snapper, so we took a purist's approach to seasoning the fillets—salt and pepper before cooking, lemon wedges at the table. We found that spices and marinades detract from the delicate, almost sweet flavor of this fish, but you might add a salsa for more flavor and moisture.

When buying red snapper, look for fillets with gleaming reddish-pink flesh that smells fresh and doesn't look dried out.

Charcoal-Grilled Red Snapper Fillets
SERVES 4

Skinless red snapper fillets are quick and easy to grill, but they do require a gentle hand. Carefully turn these fillets over with a metal spatula and be sure that both the fish and the grill are well oiled. Because these fillets are so thin, they only take about 5 minutes to cook through.

4   skinless red snapper fillets (7 to 8 ounces each)
2   tablespoons extra-virgin olive oil
     Salt and ground black pepper
     Vegetable oil for the cooking grate
     Lemon wedges for serving

1. Light a large chimney starter filled with hardwood charcoal (about 6 quarts) and allow to burn until all the charcoal is covered with a layer of fine gray ash. Build a single-level fire by spreading the coals evenly over the bottom of the grill. Set the cooking grate in place, cover the grill with the lid, and let the grate heat up, about 5 minutes. Use a grill brush to scrape the cooking grate clean. The grill is ready when the coals are medium-hot. (See how to gauge heat level on page 4.)

2. Brush the red snapper fillets with the olive oil and season with salt and pepper to taste.

3. Lightly dip a small wad of paper towels in vegetable oil; holding the wad with long-handled tongs, wipe the cooking grate (see page 224). Grill the fillets, uncovered, turning once (using a metal spatula), until the snapper flakes at the center but is still moist, 5 to 5½ minutes total. Serve immediately with the lemon wedges.

> VARIATIONS
Gas-Grilled Red Snapper Fillets
Note that the fish takes slightly longer to cook on a gas grill.

1. Turn on all the burners to high, cover, and heat the grill until very hot, about 15 minutes. Use a grill brush to scrape the cooking grate clean. Leave all the burners on high.

2. Follow the recipe for Charcoal-Grilled Red Snapper from step 2, grilling the fillets, covered, turning once (using a metal spatula), until the snapper flakes at the center but is still moist, 6 to 6½ minutes total. Serve immediately with the lemon wedges.

Grilled Red Snapper Fillets with Spicy Yellow Pepper and Tomato Salsa
You can also serve warm corn tortillas and salsa alongside the fish for fish tacos.

Follow the recipe for Charcoal-Grilled or Gas-Grilled Red Snapper Fillets, serving the grilled fish with 2 cups Spicy Yellow Pepper and Tomato Salsa (page 391) and lime wedges instead of the lemon wedges.

SWORDFISH STEAKS
THICK SWORDFISH STEAKS ARE A FAVORITE on the grill. Their dense, meaty flesh keeps the steaks from falling apart on the grill, and their smooth surface reduces the risk of sticking.

After testing various steaks, we found that thicker steaks (close to 1¼ inches) were best because they can remain on the grill long enough to pick up some smoky flavor without drying out. Thinner steaks were either poorly seared or overcooked in the middle. Thicker pieces also retained moisture better and were easier to handle on the grill.

When grilling all fish (but especially swordfish), leave it in place long enough so that it develops good grill marks before moving it. Unlike salmon and tuna, we find that swordfish should be cooked until medium—no more, no less. A two-level fire is necessary; the fish sears over a hot fire and then cooks through on the cooler part of the grill.

Charcoal-Grilled Swordfish Steaks

SERVES 4

Because of the shape and size of swordfish, individual steaks are quite large. This recipe serves four—or more, if you want to cut the steaks into smaller pieces.

2	swordfish steaks, 1 to 1½ inches thick (about 1 pound each)
2	tablespoons extra-virgin olive oil
	Salt and ground black pepper
	Vegetable oil for the cooking grate
	Lemon wedges for serving

1. Light a large chimney starter filled with hardwood charcoal (about 6 quarts) and allow to burn until all the charcoal is covered with a layer of fine gray ash. Build a two-level fire by stacking most of the coals on one side of the grill and arranging the remaining coals in a single layer on the other side of the grill. Set the cooking grate in place, cover the grill with the lid, and let the grate heat up, about 5 minutes. Use a grill brush to scrape the cooking grate clean. The grill is ready when the heat level of the stacked coals is medium-hot and that of the remaining coals is medium-low. (See how to gauge heat level on page 4.)

2. Cut the swordfish steaks in half to make four equal pieces. Brush the fish with the olive oil and sprinkle generously with salt and pepper.

3. Lightly dip a small wad of paper towels in vegetable oil; holding the wad with long-handled tongs, wipe the cooking grate (see page 224). Grill the swordfish, uncovered, turning once (using a metal spatula), over the hotter part of the grill until the steaks are streaked with dark grill marks, 6 to 7 minutes. Move the fish to the cooler part of the grill and cook, uncovered, turning once, until the center is no longer translucent, 3 to 5 minutes. Serve immediately with the lemon wedges.

➤ VARIATIONS

Gas-Grilled Swordfish Steaks

Note that the grilling times are slightly longer when using a gas grill.

Turn on all the burners to high, cover, and heat the grill until very hot, about 15 minutes. Use a grill brush to scrape the cooking grate clean. Leave all the burners on high. Follow the recipe for Charcoal-Grilled Swordfish Steaks from step 2, grilling the swordfish, covered, and turning once (using a metal spatula), over high heat until the steaks are streaked with dark grill marks, 7 to 9 minutes. Turn the heat down to medium and cook, covered and turning once, until the center is no longer translucent, 4 to 6 minutes. Serve immediately with the lemon wedges.

Grilled Swordfish Steaks with Lemon-Parsley Sauce

¼	cup extra-virgin olive oil
2	tablespoons minced fresh parsley leaves
1½	tablespoons juice from 1 lemon
	Salt and ground black pepper
1	recipe Charcoal-Grilled or Gas-Grilled Swordfish Steaks

1. Combine the oil, parsley, lemon juice, and salt and pepper to taste in a small bowl. Set the sauce aside.

2. Follow the recipe for Charcoal-Grilled or Gas-Grilled Swordfish Steaks. Spoon the lemon-parsley sauce over the grilled fish just before serving.

Grilled Swordfish Steaks with Salsa Verde

This piquant Italian sauce is perfect with grilled swordfish.

Follow the recipe for Charcoal-Grilled or Gas-Grilled Swordfish Steaks, topping each portion of grilled fish with a generous tablespoon of Salsa Verde (page 397).

Grilled Swordfish Steaks with Chermoula

Chermoula is a zesty sauce popular in Morocco. Serve with sliced tomatoes and couscous to make a North African–inspired dinner.

Follow the recipe for Charcoal-Grilled or Gas-Grilled Swordfish Steaks, topping each portion of grilled fish with a generous tablespoon of Chermoula (page 397).

SWORDFISH KEBABS

SWORDFISH IS IDEAL FOR KEBABS BECAUSE the flesh is firm and has a steak-like quality. Because this fish is cut into small pieces, it cooks very quickly and does not dry out. (Coating the fish with some olive oil helps keep it moist, too.) In fact, we almost like the kebabs better than the steaks because there is more surface area for caramelization. Because swordfish kebabs cook so quickly, we found that vegetables must be cooked on separate skewers, giving them the extra time they need to cook through. While thick swordfish steaks are best grilled over a two-level fire (see page 4), we found that kebabs can be cooked over a medium-hot, single level fire.

Charcoal-Grilled Swordfish Kebabs

SERVES 4

You should grill vegetable kebabs alongside the swordfish on separate skewers, since the vegetables take a few minutes longer to cook through. See the chart on page 162 for directions on preparing the vegetables for skewers, tossing the vegetables with some oil and seasoning with salt and pepper before cooking but omitting the marinades, which are designed for chicken. Grill the vegetable skewers until tender and nicely browned, 8 to 10 minutes.

  2   swordfish steaks, 1 inch thick (about 2 pounds total), skin removed, cut into 1-inch cubes
  3   tablespoons extra-virgin olive oil
      Salt and ground black pepper
      Vegetable oil for the cooking grate
      Lemon or lime wedges for serving (optional)

1. Toss the swordfish cubes and oil in a large bowl. Season with salt and pepper to taste.

2. Light a large chimney starter filled with hardwood charcoal (about 6 quarts) and allow to burn until all the charcoal is covered with a layer of fine gray ash. Build a single-level fire by spreading the coals evenly over the bottom of the grill. Set the cooking grate in place, cover the grill with the lid, and let the grate heat up, about 5 minutes. Use a grill brush to scrape the cooking grate clean. The grill is ready when the coals are medium-hot.

(See how to gauge heat level on page 4.)

3. Thread the swordfish onto skewers. Lightly dip a small wad of paper towels in vegetable oil; holding the wad with long-handled tongs, wipe the cooking grate (see page 224).

4. Grill the kebabs, uncovered, giving each kebab a one-quarter turn every 1¾ minutes, until the center of the swordfish is no longer translucent, about 7 minutes. Transfer the kebabs to a serving platter and squeeze the lemon or lime wedges over the kebabs, if desired. Serve immediately.

➤ VARIATIONS

Gas-Grilled Swordfish Kebabs

Work quickly when you open the lid to turn the kebabs to keep the heat from dissipating.

Follow step 1 of the recipe for Charcoal-Grilled Swordfish Kebabs. Turn on all the burners to high, cover, and heat the grill until very hot, about 15 minutes. Use a grill brush to scrape the cooking grate clean. Leave all the burners on high. Proceed with the recipe from step 3. In step 4, grill the kebabs, covered, turning each a one-quarter turn every 2 minutes, until the center of swordfish is no longer translucent, about 8 minutes. Transfer the kebabs to a serving platter and squeeze the lemon or lime wedges over the kebabs, if desired. Serve immediately.

Southeast Asian–Style Swordfish Kebabs

The sugar in the marinade creates a wonderful deep caramelization on the grilled swordfish. If you wish, you can serve these with Spicy Peanut Dipping Sauce (page 400).

  4   tablespoons fish sauce or soy sauce
  4   tablespoons vegetable oil
  2   tablespoons juice from 2 limes
  4   teaspoons sugar
  3   medium garlic cloves, minced or pressed through a garlic press (about 1 tablespoon)
  2   swordfish steaks, 1 inch thick (about 2 pounds total), skin removed and cut into 1-inch cubes
      Vegetable oil for the cooking grate
      Lime wedges for serving

1. Mix the fish sauce, vegetable oil, lime juice, sugar, and garlic together in a small bowl. Place the swordfish cubes in a gallon-size zipper-lock plastic bag. Pour the fish sauce mixture over the fish, press out as much air as possible from the bag, and seal. Toss gently to coat the fish with the marinade. Refrigerate, 15 to 30 minutes, or up to 2 hours.

2. Prepare the grill as directed in either the Charcoal-Grilled or Gas-Grilled Swordfish Kebabs recipe. Use a grill brush to scrape the cooking grate clean.

3. Skewer the kebabs as directed. Lightly dip a small wad of paper towels in vegetable oil; holding the wad with long-handled tongs, wipe the cooking grate (see page 224).

4. Grill the kebabs as directed, serving them with the lime wedges.

Swordfish Kebabs with Salmoriglio Sauce

Considered one of the essential sauces of Sicilian cookery, salmoriglio is a potent dressing composed of extra-virgin olive oil, lemon juice, and abundant amounts of fresh oregano. As soon as the fish is removed from the grill, liberally brush this sauce over it. The heat "cooks" the sauce, releasing a heady aroma that is hard to resist. If you have extra sauce, pass it at the table.

Follow the recipe for Charcoal-Grilled or Gas-Grilled Swordfish Kebabs. Transfer the grilled swordfish skewers to a serving platter and liberally brush them with Salmoriglio Sauce (page 398). Serve immediately, passing any extra sauce at the table.

SALMON FILLETS

SALMON IS OUR FAVORITE FISH TO GRILL. Not only does it taste great, but it's firm enough to hold together better than many other fish. With its abundant natural fats and oils, salmon is also less prone to drying out than most other fish. While leaner fish like tuna, swordfish, and halibut benefit from a brush with oil before being grilled to help retain moisture, salmon needs no such treatment.

The cut of salmon we used for our tests was boneless, individual-portion farmed salmon fillets,

skin on, weighing about six ounces each. Salmon can be purchased as fillets or as steaks. We prefer fillets to steaks because fillets are boneless and thus easier to eat. Whenever possible, we buy center-cut fillets because in farmed salmon the center cut is often almost exactly 1½ inches thick and cooks consistently from one piece to the next. Cuts from the tail end are thinner and easier to overcook, while cuts from the head end are thicker and tend to take too long to cook through. Several tests proved that a medium-hot fire browned the salmon fillets without burning them and conveniently created a crust that made for fairly easy turning on the grill, after some initial prodding with long-handled tongs or a metal spatula. (We thus also found that oiling the salmon for easier turning was unnecessary.)

While the center cut cooked well over the direct heat of a single-level fire, we thought we would try a two-level fire, browning the fillets over the higher heat and then letting them cook through over the lower heat. We found no difference in taste or texture between the fillets grilled entirely over direct heat and those finished over indirect heat. Because direct heat cooks faster, we opted for that. That said, we found the direct/indirect method to be an excellent way to cook thin tail pieces; by the time the flesh had seared enough to turn, the fish was almost cooked through and needed just a minute or so of gentle heat to finish it without overcooking.

As we grilled the salmon, we remained alert for clues to tell us when it was properly cooked. We like salmon that is medium-rare in the center, or still slightly translucent. Mostly we found that by the time 1½-inch-thick fillets were well browned on both sides, the center was perfect—slightly undercooked, but close enough to finish cooking the last little bit on the plate. We also developed a tactile test. As the salmon cooked, we pulled it off the grill every now and then and squeezed the sides of the fillet gently between our fingertips. Raw salmon feels squishy; medium-rare salmon is firm but not hard. Of course, if you're stumped and want to be really sure, just cut into the fillet with a paring knife and take a look.

Charcoal-Grilled
Salmon Fillets

SERVES 4

If your fillets are less than 1½ inches thick, decrease the grilling time by roughly 30 seconds per side. To test fillets for doneness, either peek into the salmon with the tip of a small knife or remove the salmon from the grill and squeeze both sides of the fillet gently with your fingertips (raw salmon is squishy; medium-rare salmon is firm but not hard).

    4   center-cut salmon fillets, about 1½ inches
        thick (6 to 7 ounces each), pinbones removed
        (see illustration 1 on page 246)
        Salt and ground black pepper
        Vegetable oil for the cooking grate

1. Light a large chimney starter filled with hardwood charcoal (about 6 quarts) and allow to burn until all the charcoal is covered with a layer of fine gray ash. Build a single-level fire by spreading the coals evenly over the bottom of the grill. Set the cooking grate in place, cover the grill with the lid, and let the grate heat up, about 5 minutes. Use a grill brush to scrape the cooking grate clean. The grill is ready when the coals are medium-hot. (See how to gauge heat level on page 4.)

2. Generously sprinkle each side of the salmon fillets with salt and pepper.

3. Lightly dip a small wad of paper towels in vegetable oil; holding the wad with long-handled tongs, wipe the cooking grate (see page 224). Place the fillets skin-side down on the grill. Grill, uncovered, until the skin shrinks, separates from the flesh, and turns black, 2 to 3 minutes. Gently flip the fillets with a metal spatula. Grill, uncovered, until the fillets are opaque throughout, yet translucent at the very center, 3 to 4 minutes. Serve immediately.

➤ VARIATIONS
Gas-Grilled Salmon Fillets

If your fillets are less than 1½ inches thick, decrease the grilling time by roughly 30 seconds per side. To test fillets for doneness, either peek into the salmon with the tip of a small knife or remove the salmon from the grill and squeeze both sides of the fillet gently with your fingertips (raw salmon is squishy; medium-rare salmon is firm but not hard). Note that the grilling times are slightly longer when using a gas grill.

Turn on all the burners to high, cover, and heat the grill until very hot, about 15 minutes. Use a grill brush to scrape the cooking grate clean. Leave all the burners on high. Follow the recipe for Charcoal-Grilled Salmon Fillets from step 2, with the following change. In step 3, grill the fillets, covered, until the skin shrinks, separates from the flesh, and blackens, 3 to 4 minutes. Gently flip the fillets with a metal spatula. Grill, covered, until the fillets are opaque almost throughout, yet translucent at the very center, 4 to 5 minutes. Serve immediately.

Grilled Salmon Fillets and Fennel
with Orange Vinaigrette
You will need a spice grinder (or dedicated coffee grinder) for this variation.

    2   teaspoons fennel seeds
    1   teaspoon red pepper flakes
    1   tablespoon grated zest and ¼ cup juice
        from 1 orange
    2   teaspoons light brown sugar
        Salt
    6   tablespoons extra-virgin olive oil
    1   small shallot, minced (about 2 tablespoons)
    1   tablespoon juice from 1 lemon
    1   medium garlic clove, minced or pressed
        through a garlic press (about 1 teaspoon)
        Ground black pepper
    4   center-cut salmon fillets, about 1½ inches
        thick (6 to 7 ounces each), pinbones removed
        (see illustration 1 on page 246)
    2   medium fennel bulbs, prepared according to
        the illustrations on page 306
        Vegetable oil for the cooking grate

1. Light the grill as directed in the recipe for Charcoal-Grilled or Gas-Grilled Salmon Fillets.

2. Meanwhile, place the fennel seeds and pepper flakes in a spice grinder or dedicated coffee grinder and process until finely ground but not powdery. Transfer the spices to a small bowl and

combine with the orange zest, brown sugar, and ¼ teaspoon salt; set the spice mixture aside. Whisk together the orange juice, 4 tablespoons of the olive oil, the shallot, lemon juice, garlic, and salt and pepper to taste in another small bowl; set the vinaigrette aside.

3. Generously sprinkle the flesh of the salmon with the spice mixture. Toss the fennel with the remaining 2 tablespoons olive oil in a large bowl and season with salt and pepper to taste.

4. Lightly dip a small wad of paper towels in vegetable oil; holding the wad with long-handled tongs, wipe the cooking grate (see page 224). Continue with step 3 of the recipe, with the following exception: Place the fennel on the grill at the same time as the salmon and grill, turning once, until tender and streaked with dark grill marks, 8 to 10 minutes. Divide the salmon and fennel among the plates. Rewhisk the vinaigrette and drizzle a little over each piece of salmon and the fennel. Serve immediately.

Grilled Salmon Fillets with Aromatic Spice Rub

Serve this spice-rubbed salmon with lime or lemon wedges.

Follow the recipe for Charcoal-Grilled or Gas-Grilled Salmon Fillets, rubbing 1 tablespoon vegetable oil into the fillets and then coating the fillets with 1 tablespoon Simple Spice Rub for Fish (page 379). Grill as directed.

GRILLED GLAZED SALMON

WE HAVE ALWAYS FELT CONFIDENT IN OUR ability to produce great grilled salmon. With its firm, meaty texture and rich, buttery interior, the salmon on our grill had at least a chance of coming off that hot grate moist and in one piece. Then one day we tried grilled glazed salmon and watched as our dinner (as well as our bravado) went up in smoke. "Sticky" was the operative word here as the glazed salmon gripped the cooking grate for dear life and could only be torn off in many tiny pieces. Not that it was actually worth getting off the grill, mind you, because each of those tiny pieces was charred beyond recognition. When it comes to grilled glazed salmon, you can call us chicken.

So why glaze (and inevitably ruin) an otherwise perfect piece of fish? Well, because truly great glazed salmon off the grill is a thing of beauty, both inside and out. Working double duty, the sweet glaze not only forms a glossy, deeply caramelized crust but also permeates the flesh, making the last bite of fish every bit as good as the first. This was the salmon that we wanted to re-create—sweet, crisp, moist, and oh-so-flavorful—and we were willing to ruin a few more fish to get there.

We knew we needed all the help we could get, and we went straight to cookbooks in hopes of direction. The first choice was easy. When confronted with fillets, steaks, and whole sides, we went with the fillets for ease of grilling (ever try flipping a whole side?) and ease of eating (who wants to eat around all those salmon steak bones, anyway?). The next choice was glazing method, and here things were less clear. We could try using a marinade to flavor the fish. We could try brushing the fish with a thick glaze before throwing it on the grill. Finally, we could simply grill the fish plain and apply the glaze afterward. We fired up the grill and got to work.

After testing, there was no doubt that marinating gave the salmon flavor. Soy sauce was chosen for its ability to season the fish through and through, while vinegar (another standard marinade ingredient) was omitted, as it broke down the salmon until it was too fragile to hold its shape on the grill. In a perfect world, the marinade would also work as a glaze of sorts, with the sugars caramelizing once they hit the hot grill. In fact, tests demonstrated that the marinated salmon failed to produce any kind of crust. Increasing the amount of sugar only served to make the salmon too sweet. Taking a cue from some brush-on glaze recipes, we tested more viscous sweeteners, such as maple syrup, honey, and molasses. While the molasses was rejected for its bitter flavor, the maple syrup and honey worked like a dream. With a thicker marinade, the sweet flavors clung to the salmon rather than dripping through the bars of the grate, and a crust (however thin) was beginning to form.

Using a marinade alone wasn't going to

produce the thick crust we wanted, however. The next step was to brush the marinated salmon with a much thicker glaze—a winning combination of soy sauce and maple syrup—very similar to the marinade. Yep, here was a crust—a burnt, stuck-to-the-grill crust; not what we were after. Instead, we basted the salmon with this glaze a few moments after it hit the hot grill. Better. Not as charred, not as sticky, but still not acceptable. Not sure where else to turn at this point, we thought it might be time to examine the fire.

Up to this point, we had been cooking the salmon in a pretty traditional way. We were searing the fish skin-side down, then skin-side up over a hot fire; the superhot cooking grate helped to keep the fish from sticking. The problem now was that the hot fire was causing the sweet glazed salmon to burn.

After trying more temperate medium and low fires (both of which failed), we tried a two-level fire. Piling two thirds of the hot coals on one side of the grill and arranging the remaining coals in a single layer on the other side, we seared the marinated salmon over the high heat. We then brushed the salmon with some of the glaze and pulled it to the cooler side of the grill to cook through. This was a big improvement, with a decent crust.

But we were still having a problem. When started skin-side down, the fillet buckled, causing the other side to cook unevenly. The solution was to start the salmon skin-side up, flip it to sear the skin side, brush on some glaze, and then flip it again to finish cooking on the cooler side of the grill. The downside of this approach was that the grill had to be well oiled to prevent sticking, a step that is not optional. The good news was that we had an incredible crust, built in two layers, that was both sweet and substantial. All that was left to do was to brush the grilled salmon with more glaze before serving. Gilding the lily, perhaps, but with a high-gloss shine and potent flavor within, this fish never looked (or tasted) so good.

Grilled Glazed Salmon Fillets on a Charcoal Grill

SERVES 4

Be sure to oil the grate just before placing the fillets on the grill.

1	recipe glaze (recipes follow)
1/3	cup soy sauce
1/3	cup maple syrup
4	salmon fillets, about 1 1/2 inches at the thickest part (about 8 ounces each), pinbones removed (see illustration 1 on page 246)
	Ground black pepper
	Vegetable oil for the cooking grate
	Lemon wedges for serving

1. Measure 2 tablespoons of the glaze into a small bowl and set aside.

2. Whisk the soy sauce and maple syrup in a 13 by 9-inch baking dish until combined. Carefully place the fillets flesh-side down in a single layer in the marinade (do not coat the salmon skin with the marinade). Refrigerate while preparing the grill.

3. Light a large chimney starter filled with hardwood charcoal (about 6 quarts) and allow to burn until all the charcoal is covered with a layer of fine gray ash. Empty the coals into the grill and build a two-level fire by stacking two thirds of the coals

GLAZED SALMON: THE SOFT, THE STICKY, AND THE GOOD

TOO SOFT
Salmon that was marinated for more than 30 minutes became mushy and fell apart on the grill.

TOO STICKY
When we skipped the step of oiling the cooking grate, the salmon stuck terribly.

JUST RIGHT
With a short marinating time and a thorough oiling of the cooking grate, our salmon came off the fire intact.

in one half of the grill and arranging the remaining coals in a single layer in the other half. Position the cooking grate over the coals, cover the grill, and heat until the grate is hot, about 5 minutes. (See how to gauge heat level on page 4). Use a grill brush to scrape the cooking grate clean.

4. Remove the salmon from the marinade and sprinkle the flesh liberally with pepper. Using long-handled tongs, dip a wad of paper towels in vegetable oil and wipe the hotter side of the cooking grate (see page 224). Place the fillets flesh-side down on the hotter side of the grill (at a 45-degree angle to the bars) and cook until grill-marked, about 1 minute. Using tongs, flip the fillets skin-side down, still on the hotter side of the grill. Brush the flesh with the glaze and cook until the salmon is opaque about halfway up the thickness of the fillets, 3 to 4 minutes.

5. Again using long-handled tongs, dip another wad of paper towels in vegetable oil and wipe the cooler side of the cooking grate. Brush the flesh again with the glaze, then turn the fillets flesh-side down onto the cooler side of the grill. Cook until a deeply browned crust has formed and the center of the fillet is still translucent when cut into with a paring knife, about 1½ minutes. Transfer the fillets to a platter, brush with the reserved 2 tablespoons glaze, and serve with the lemon wedges.

➤ VARIATIONS
Grilled Glazed Salmon Fillets on a Gas Grill

1. Follow the recipe for Grilled Glazed Salmon Fillets on a Charcoal Grill through step 2.

2. Turn on all the burners to high, cover, and heat the grill until very hot, about 15 minutes. Scrape the cooking grate clean with a grill brush. Turn all but one burner to medium-low. Remove the salmon from the marinade and sprinkle the flesh liberally with pepper. Lightly dip a small wad of paper towels in vegetable oil; holding the wad with long-handled tongs, wipe the hotter side of the cooking grate (see page 224). Place the fillets flesh-side down on the hotter side of the grill (at a 45-degree angle to the bars) and cook until grill-marked, 1 to 2 minutes. Using tongs, flip the fillets skin-side down, still on the hotter side of the grill.

Brush the flesh with the glaze, cover the grill, and cook until the salmon is opaque about halfway up the thickness of the fillets, 3 to 4 minutes.

3. Again using long-handled tongs, dip another wad of paper towels in vegetable oil and wipe the cooler side of the cooking grate. Brush the flesh again with the glaze, then turn the fillets flesh-side down onto the cooler side of the grill. Cook until a deeply browned crust has formed and the center of the thickest part of the fillet is still translucent when cut into with a paring knife, about 2 minutes. Transfer the fillets to a platter, brush with the reserved 2 tablespoons glaze, and serve immediately with the lemon wedges.

Maple-Chipotle Glaze
Offer lime wedges instead of lemon wedges when serving.

Stir together ¼ cup maple syrup, 2 tablespoons soy sauce, and 1 teaspoon minced chipotle chile in adobo sauce in a small saucepan. Bring to a simmer over medium-high heat and cook until slightly thickened, 3 to 4 minutes. Off the heat, whisk in 2 tablespoons lime juice.

Maple-Soy Glaze

Stir together ¼ cup maple syrup and 2 tablespoons soy sauce in a small saucepan. Bring to a simmer over medium-high heat and cook until slightly thickened, 3 to 4 minutes.

Honey-Mustard Glaze

Stir together ¼ cup honey and 2 tablespoons soy sauce in a small saucepan. Bring to a simmer over medium-high heat and cook until slightly thickened, 3 to 4 minutes. Off the heat, whisk in 3 tablespoons Dijon mustard.

BARBECUED SALMON

IS IT POSSIBLE TO MAKE SMOKED SALMON AT home without a smoker? We thought it was worth a try and started off by attempting to make a covered grill act like a cold smoker, which cooks foods in a range of 75 to 110 degrees. We used very few coals, adding them as we went along, often putting out the fire with handfuls of wet smoking chips. The results were disappointing; the salmon was lacking in flavor, and the texture was a bit too wet to be palatable.

Patience is supposed to be a virtue, but in this case impatience turned out to be the key to success. We simply got tired of messing with the process of cold-smoking. In fact, at this point we realized that cold smoking, which is used by commercial smokers to make smoked salmon, is simply not practical for home cooks. It takes a very long time, requires both skill and patience, and, because of the low cooking temperatures involved, can be disastrous if health precautions are not followed carefully. We decided to use more briquettes in the initial fire. This eliminated the need to add more coals during the smoking process, and the larger fire was less likely to go out when we added wet wood chunks. This time the results were gratifying. The hotter fire cooked the fish more, giving it a more pleasing and flaky texture.

We continued to refine this method over many months of trial and error. Eventually, we perfected a procedure that yields a salmon that has many of the attributes of good smoked salmon but that is crustier and a whole lot easier to make. In fact, the technique is similar to traditional barbecue. The difference between barbecued salmon and cold-smoked salmon is largely one of texture: Cold-smoked salmon is more silky, like lox, whereas barbecued salmon will actually flake.

But the drawback of this method—and the reason why salmon is usually cold-smoked—is that it dries out the fish. We figured that brining might help the fish hold moisture as it cooked and

experimented with various brining times, eventually settling on three to four hours for a fillet weighing 2½ to 3 pounds. Any longer and the flavor of the brine was too intense; any shorter and it didn't produce the desired results as far as texture was concerned. This brined, barbecued salmon definitely had the moist texture we had been longing for, but we still wanted more flavor to complement its smokiness.

To improve the flavor, we added some sugar to the brine. We also experimented with various salt/sugar/water ratios; with different brining times (from two to 24 hours); and with all manner of smoking woods. We eventually settled on the recipe on the facing page, which calls for three hours of brining in a solution of ½ cup each of sugar and salt to 7 cups of water and which favors alder wood chunks for the distinctive flavor they give the fish. The salmon this recipe produces has a moist but flaky texture and is just smoky enough, with the natural flavors of the salmon getting a boost from the brining process.

Barbecued salmon can be served warm off the grill as well as chilled, and it works as both a traditional hors d'oeuvre and, somewhat surprisingly, an entrée. For hors d'oeuvres, it is absolutely delicious as is or accompanied by melba toast (or any other flat bread or cracker), finely chopped white onion, capers, and lemon wedges. If you serve the salmon as an entrée, simple wedges of lemon will suffice, or you might try one of the two sauces we've developed.

KEY STEPS FOR BARBECUED SALMON

1. Slide the salmon off the foil and onto the grill. To make it easier to remove the salmon from the grill once it is done, position the fillet so that the long side is perpendicular to the grill bars.

2. Use two metal spatulas to transfer the cooked fish from the grill to a rimmed baking sheet or cutting board.

3. To serve, cut through the pink flesh, but not the skin, to divide into individual portions.

4. Slide a spatula between the fillet and the skin to remove individual pieces, leaving the skin behind.

Barbecued Salmon on a Charcoal Grill

SERVES 4 TO 6

The cooking grate must be hot and thoroughly clean before you place the salmon on it; otherwise the fish might stick. Use foil (see illustration 1 on the facing page) or the back of a large rimmed baking sheet to get the fish onto the grill. Alder wood is our first choice for this recipe but hickory is fine, too. (Read more about wood chunks on page 10). To use kosher salt in the brine, see page 172 for conversion information.

½	cup sugar
½	cup table salt (see note)
1	skin-on salmon fillet (about 2½ pounds), pinbones removed (see the illustration below)
2	(3-inch) wood chunks
2	tablespoons vegetable oil, plus more for the cooking grate
1½	teaspoons sweet paprika
1	teaspoon ground white pepper

1. Dissolve the sugar and salt in 2 cups of hot water in a large bowl. Add 5 cups of cold water and the salmon, cover the bowl with plastic wrap, and refrigerate, about 3 hours.

2. Meanwhile, soak the wood chunks in cold water to cover for 1 hour, then drain and set aside.

3. Remove the salmon from the brine and blot dry completely with paper towels. Place the fillet, skin-side down, on a 30-inch sheet of heavy-duty foil. Rub both sides of the fillet, especially the skin side, with 2 tablespoons oil. Dust the flesh side of the fillet with the paprika and pepper.

4. Meanwhile, open the bottom vents on the grill. Light a large chimney starter filled halfway with charcoal briquettes (about 3 quarts) and burn until all the charcoal is covered with a layer of fine gray ash. Empty the coals into one side of the grill, piling them up in a mound two or three briquettes high. Place the wood chunks on top of the charcoal. Put the cooking grate in place, open the grill lid vents completely, and cover. Let the grate heat for 5 minutes and use a grill brush to scrape it clean. Lightly dip a small

wad of paper towels in vegetable oil; holding the wad with long-handled tongs, wipe the cooking grate (see page 224).

5. Following illustration 1 on the facing page, slide the salmon off the foil, skin-side down, and onto the cooking grate opposite the fire so that the long side of the fillet is perpendicular to the grill bars. Cover, positioning the lid so that the vents are opposite the wood chunks to draw smoke through the grill. Barbecue until cooked through and heavily flavored with smoke, 1½ hours. (The initial temperature will be about 350 degrees but will drop to about 250 degrees by the time the salmon is done.)

6. Following illustration 2 on the facing page, use two metal spatulas to remove the salmon from the grill. Serve either hot or at room temperature, cutting through the flesh but not the skin to divide the salmon into individual portions and sliding a spatula between the flesh and skin to remove individual pieces, leaving the skin behind (see illustrations 3 and 4 on the facing page). Serve as is or with one of the sauces that follow.

➤ VARIATIONS

Barbecued Salmon on a Gas Grill

Leaving one burner on and turning the other(s) off mimics the indirect heat method on a charcoal grill. Use wood chips instead of wood chunks and a foil tray (see page

REMOVING PINBONES FROM A SIDE OF SALMON

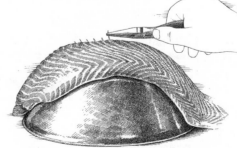

Locating and removing the pinbones from a side of salmon can be tricky. Running your fingers along the flesh is one way to locate them, but with a very large piece of salmon such as a side, we like to drape the salmon over an inverted mixing bowl. The curvature of the bowl forces the pinbones to stick up and out, so they are easier to spot. Grasp them with needle-nose pliers or tweezers and remove.

10) or disposable aluminum pan to hold them. *Keep a close eye on the grill thermometer to make sure that the temperature remains around 275 degrees.*

Follow the recipe for Barbecued Salmon on a Charcoal Grill through step 3, making the following changes. Cover 2 cups wood chips with cold water and soak 30 minutes, then drain. Place the soaked wood chips in a foil tray (see page 10) or small disposable aluminum pan; set the tray on the burner that will remain on. Turn on all the burners to high, close the lid, and heat the grill until the chips smoke heavily, about 20 minutes. (If the chips ignite, extinguish the flames with water from a squirt bottle.) Use a grill brush to scrape the cooking grate clean; turn off the burner(s) without the wood chips. Slide the salmon onto the grill as directed in step 5 and proceed with the recipe.

Horseradish Cream Sauce
MAKES ABOUT 1 CUP
Horseradish and crème fraîche are natural partners to the smoky salmon. They also make the fish seem a bit more moist, as does the sauce in the next variation.

- 1 cup crème fraîche or sour cream
- 2 tablespoons prepared horseradish, or more to taste
- 2 tablespoons minced fresh chives
  Pinch salt

Combine all the ingredients in a small bowl. (The sauce can be refrigerated in an airtight container overnight.)

Mustard-Dill Sauce
MAKES ABOUT 1 CUP
Use Dijon, honey, or grainy mustard, as desired. Depending on your choice of mustard, this sauce can be fairly hot.

- 1 cup mustard
- 1/4 cup minced fresh dill

Combine the mustard and dill in a small bowl. (The sauce can be refrigerated in an airtight container overnight.)

TUNA STEAKS

GRILLED TUNA HAS BECOME SUCH A FAMILIAR dish on the American home-cooking scene that it never occurred to us that it might also be a bear to cook. We had assumed that we could get a perfect tuna steak—beautifully seared on the outside, moist and tender on the inside—the same way we get a perfect beef or salmon steak: a quick sear over direct heat to brown and then, if the steak is really thick, a final few minutes over indirect heat to finish it. We knew that tuna, lacking the fat of salmon, would be particularly susceptible to overcooking, so we would probably need to undercook it.

But a few days of testing proved tuna to be a tougher customer than we'd imagined. No matter what thickness we sliced it or how we cooked it—medium-rare or rare, direct or indirect heat—we were startled to find that steak after steak was almost inedible. Each one was tough and dry and tasted off-puttingly strong and fishy. Clearly, more experimenting was in order.

For purposes of experimentation, we decided to work with steaks 3/4 to 1 inch thick, as these are the cuts usually available at supermarket fish counters. First we tried grilling over direct heat, starting with an oiled and salted steak, for 3½ minutes on each side over a medium fire. The outside of the tuna was paler than we liked and the inside was overcooked. In successive tests we determined that a hotter fire seared better, particularly since the tuna needed to cook only three minutes total for medium and four minutes for well-done.

While the hotter fire was an improvement, the fish was still drier than we liked, particularly when it was cooked past medium-rare. So we experimented with a two-level fire that would give us a source of indirect heat. We tried searing the tuna 1½ minutes on each side over direct heat, then moving it to the other side of the grill to finish cooking over indirect heat. The tuna came off the grill with the same texture it had when grilled entirely over direct heat, but it was less well seared, so we gave up on the two-level heat approach.

We thought it was time to test steaks of different thicknesses over direct heat and learned that if we wanted the tuna both well seared and rare, it would have to be cut thicker than the standard supermarket steak, about 1½ inches instead of ¾ to 1 inch. Thinner steaks had already cooked to at least medium-rare after the initial searing on both sides. But while we preferred the moistness of thick, rare steaks, we were concerned that some folks would not like to eat their tuna rare. In addition, we knew that many consumers would have difficulty locating thick steaks.

Clearly, the problem wasn't going to be solved in the actual cooking. Something had to be done to the tuna before it hit the grill. Our next inspiration was to test a marinade.

We talked to several restaurant chefs (after all, grilled tuna has become a restaurant classic), and they suggested marinating the tuna in olive oil and herbs. We marinated one 1½-inch-thick steak and one ½-inch-thick steak in herb-flavored oil for three hours, turning every now and then. We then grilled the thick steak to rare, and the thin steak to medium. The results were amazing. Both steaks were subtly flavored with olive oil and herbs, and their texture was moist and luscious. Perhaps most surprising, we liked the medium-cooked tuna as much as the rare.

We next ran tests to determine whether the type of oil made a difference. Comparing extra-virgin and pure olive oils with canola oil, we found that after one hour, only the extra-virgin olive oil made a noticeable difference in the tuna. The pure olive oil seemed to catch up after another hour, but it didn't flavor the tuna appreciably until after three hours. The canola oil never affected the taste or the texture of the tuna.

We learned that an oil marinade tenderizes tuna in much the same way that marbling tenderizes beef. The oil coats the strands of protein, allowing a tuna steak to feel moist in the mouth even after most of the moisture has been cooked out of it. The extra-virgin olive oil penetrates the fish more quickly than the other two oils because it is much richer in emulsifiers.

Finally, we learned that the 1½-inch-thick steak, when cooked to rare or medium-rare, needed only brushing with the oil; soaking it in

the oil actually made it a bit too moist. We liked the herbs in the marinade but found that the oil alone was still quite good. The basic recipes have just extra-virgin olive oil, salt, pepper, and tuna; see the many variations if you are interested in something a bit different.

Charcoal-Grilled Tuna Steaks

SERVES 4

If you like your tuna rare, you must buy steaks cut about 1½ inches thick. This will allow you to sear them well without overcooking the inside. To serve four people, you'll need two steaks (they run about 1 pound each). Cut each in half before grilling. If you prefer more well-done tuna, see the recipe for thin-cut tuna on page 242. If desired, serve the steaks with one of the compound butters on pages 384–385.

2   tuna steaks, about 1½ inches thick
     (about 1 pound each)
2   tablespoons extra-virgin olive oil
     Salt and ground black pepper
     Vegetable oil for the cooking grate

1. Light a large chimney starter filled with hardwood charcoal (about 6 quarts) and allow to burn until all the charcoal is covered with a layer of fine gray ash. Build a single-level fire by spreading the coals evenly over the bottom of the grill. Set the cooking grate in place, cover the grill with the lid, and let the grate heat up, about 5 minutes. Use a grill brush to scrape the cooking grate clean. The grill is ready when the coals are medium-hot. (See how to gauge heat level on page 4.)

2. Cut the tuna steaks in half to make four equal pieces. Brush the tuna with the olive oil and sprinkle generously with salt and pepper.

3. Lightly dip a small wad of paper towels in vegetable oil; holding the wad with long-handled tongs, wipe the cooking grate (see page 224). Grill the tuna, uncovered and turning once (using a metal spatula), to the desired doneness, 4 to 5 minutes for rare or 6 to 7 minutes for medium-rare. Serve immediately.

➤ VARIATIONS

Gas-Grilled Tuna Steaks

Note that the grilling times are slightly longer when using a gas grill.

Turn on all the burners to high, close the lid, and heat the grill until very hot, about 15 minutes. Use a grill brush to scrape the cooking grate clean. Leave the burners on high. Follow the recipe for Charcoal-Grilled Tuna Steaks, grilling the tuna, covered and turning once (using a metal spatula), to the desired doneness, 5 to 6 minutes for rare or 7 to 8 minutes for medium-rare. Serve immediately.

Thin-Cut Grilled Tuna Steaks

This recipe is for those who like their tuna cooked medium to well-done but still moist inside. The steaks are cut thinner for quicker cooking and marinated in extra-virgin olive oil, both of which prevent dryness. If using a gas grill, cook over high heat, keep the lid down, and increase the cooking times by a minute or so.

4	tuna steaks, about 3/4 inch thick (about 8 ounces each)
1/4	cup extra-virgin olive oil
	Salt and ground black pepper
	Vegetable oil for the cooking grate

1. Combine the tuna steaks and olive oil in a gallon-size zipper-lock plastic bag. Marinate in the refrigerator, turning several times, for at least 2 hours or overnight.

2. Light a large chimney starter filled with hardwood charcoal (about 6 quarts) and allow to

Substituting Different Types of Fish Fillets for Flavor Variations

The following table contains suggestions for substituting various kinds of fish fillets and steaks with the flavor variations included in this chapter. Always grill the substituted fish according to its respective charcoal or gas recipe directions. For example, if you substitute salmon fillets for bluefish fillets when making Cumin-Crusted Bluefish Fillets with Avocado-Corn Relish, prepare the salmon as you would the bluefish in the variation, but grill it according to the recipe for either Charcoal-Grilled or Gas-Grilled Salmon Fillets.

RECIPE	OTHER FISH THAT GO WITH THESE FLAVORS
Cumin-Crusted Bluefish Fillets with Avocado-Corn Relish	Mahi-Mahi, Red Snapper, Salmon, Swordfish, Tuna
Halibut Steaks with Chipotle-Lime Butter	Bluefish, Mahi-Mahi, Red Snapper, Swordfish, Tuna
Mahi-Mahi Fillets with Shallots, Lime, and Cilantro	Bluefish (do not brine)
Red Snapper Fillets with Spicy Yellow Pepper and Tomato Salsa	Mahi-Mahi, Red Snapper, Salmon, Swordfish
Salmon Fillets with Honey-Mustard Glaze	Bluefish, Mahi-Mahi
Salmon Fillets with Aromatic Spice Rub	Bluefish, Mahi-Mahi
Salmon Fillets with Maple-Soy Glaze	Bluefish, Mahi-Mahi, Swordfish, Tuna
Swordfish Steaks with Lemon-Parsley Sauce	Bluefish, Mahi-Mahi, Red Snapper, Tuna
Swordfish Steaks with Salsa Verde	Halibut, Mahi-Mahi, Tuna
Tuna Steaks with Herb-Infused Oil	Mahi-Mahi, Red Snapper, Swordfish
Tuna Steaks with Peppercorn Crust	Swordfish
Tuna Steaks with Tarragon-Lime Butter	Bluefish, Mahi-Mahi, Red Snapper, Swordfish
Tuna Steaks with Tapenade Butter	Mahi-Mahi, Salmon, Swordfish
Tuna Steaks with Watercress, Parsley, and Spiced Vinaigrette	Mahi-Mahi, Red Snapper, Swordfish

burn until all the charcoal is covered with a layer of fine gray ash. Build a single-level fire by spreading the coals out evenly over the bottom of the grill. Set the cooking grate in place, cover the grill with the lid, and let the grate heat up, about 5 minutes. Use a grill brush to scrape the cooking grate clean. The grill is ready when the coals are medium-hot. (See how to gauge heat level on page 4.)

3. Remove the tuna from the bag and sprinkle with salt and pepper to taste.

4. Lightly dip a small wad of paper towels in vegetable oil; holding the wad with long-handled tongs, wipe the cooking grate (see page 224). Grill the tuna, uncovered and turning once (using a metal spatula), to the desired doneness, about 3 minutes total for rare or about 4 minutes total for well-done. Serve immediately.

Grilled Tuna Steaks with Herb-Infused Oil

If cooking thin-cut tuna, use the herb oil as a marinade.

1/4	cup extra-virgin olive oil
1 1/2	teaspoons grated zest from 1 lemon
1 1/2	teaspoons chopped fresh thyme leaves
1	medium garlic clove, minced or pressed through a garlic press (about 1 teaspoon)
1/4	teaspoon red pepper flakes
1	recipe Charcoal-Grilled or Gas-Grilled Tuna Steaks (without the olive oil)

1. Heat the oil, lemon zest, thyme, garlic, and red pepper flakes in a small saucepan over medium-high heat until hot. Remove the pan from the heat and cool the oil mixture to room temperature.

2. Follow the recipe for Charcoal-Grilled or Gas-Grilled Tuna Steaks, brushing the fish with the herb oil instead of the plain olive oil in step 2. Proceed as directed.

Grilled Tuna Steaks with Peppercorn Crust

You can buy a whole-peppercorn mix in well-stocked grocery stores or at specialty markets. These mixes may include white, black, green, pink, and/or red peppercorns. Although somewhat less complex in flavor, whole black

peppercorns will do in place of the mix. Season the fish with kosher salt if possible. Serve as is or with one of the compound butters on page 384–385.

1	tablespoon whole-peppercorn mix
1	recipe Charcoal-Grilled or Gas-Grilled Tuna Steaks (without the ground black pepper)

1. Place the whole-peppercorn mix in the hopper of a spice grinder or dedicated coffee grinder and pulse until the peppercorns are coarsely ground, about six 1-second pulses.

2. Follow the recipe for Charcoal-Grilled or Gas-Grilled Tuna Steaks, pressing the peppercorn mixture into the tuna after it has been brushed with oil and sprinkled with salt in step 2. Proceed as directed.

Grilled Rare Tuna Steaks with Soy, Ginger, and Wasabi

SERVES 4 AS A MAIN COURSE OR 8 AS AN APPETIZER

Since this tuna is served very rare, use only the freshest, highest-quality tuna you can find. It is served with a soy and pickled ginger sauce and wasabi paste. Wasabi, or Japanese horseradish, is the pungent green condiment served with sushi and sashimi. Use the paste sparingly; it packs a spicy punch.

6	tablespoons soy sauce
2	tablespoons minced pickled ginger
2	medium scallions, thinly sliced
4	teaspoons juice from 1 or 2 limes
2	teaspoons toasted sesame oil
4	teaspoons wasabi powder
2	teaspoons water
1	recipe Charcoal-Grilled or Gas-Grilled Tuna Steaks

1. Mix the soy sauce, pickled ginger, scallions, lime juice, and sesame oil together in a small bowl. Set aside. Mix the wasabi and water together in a small bowl to form a thick paste. Cover and set aside.

2. Follow the recipe for Charcoal-Grilled or Gas-Grilled Tuna Steaks, grilling the fish just until rare. Cut the tuna into 1/4-inch-thick slices

and fan the tuna out over individual plates. Drizzle a little of the soy mixture over each plate and place a dollop of the wasabi paste on each plate. Serve immediately.

Grilled Tuna Steaks with Watercress, Parsley, and Spiced Vinaigrette

The hot tuna wilts the watercress and parsley slightly, while the spiced vinaigrette adds tons of flavor and moisture.

2½ tablespoons juice from 1 lemon
2 tablespoons chopped fresh cilantro leaves
2 small garlic cloves, minced or pressed through a garlic press (about 1 teaspoon)
½ teaspoon salt
½ teaspoon ground cumin
¼ teaspoon sweet paprika
⅛ teaspoon cayenne pepper
½ cup extra-virgin olive oil
   Ground black pepper
1 recipe Charcoal-Grilled or Gas-Grilled Tuna Steaks
1 bunch watercress, washed, dried thoroughly, and trimmed of tough stems
1 bunch flat-leaf parsley, washed and dried thoroughly

1. Whisk the lemon juice, cilantro, garlic, salt, cumin, paprika, and cayenne together in a small bowl. Add the oil in a slow, steady stream, whisking constantly until smooth; season with black pepper to taste. Set the dressing aside.

2. Follow the recipe for Charcoal-Grilled or Gas-Grilled Tuna Steaks. While the tuna is on the grill, place the watercress and parsley in a medium bowl. Drizzle half of the dressing over the greens and toss well. Divide the greens among 4 individual plates.

3. Place one grilled tuna steak on each plate over the salad greens. Drizzle the remaining dressing over the fish and serve immediately.

Grilled Tuna Steaks and Bok Choy with Soy-Ginger Glaze

When grilling the bok choy, mist the leaves lightly with water to prevent them from drying out and becoming too crisp. For those who prefer tuna cooked medium to well-done, we recommend buying thinner steaks.

6 tablespoons soy sauce
¼ cup packed light brown sugar
2 tablespoons minced fresh ginger
2 tablespoons rice vinegar
2 tablespoons mirin
4 heads baby bok choy (about 1¼ pounds), cut in half through the stem and rinsed but not dried
1 tablespoon vegetable oil, plus more for the cooking grate
   Salt and ground black pepper
2 tuna steaks, 1½ inches thick (about 1 pound each)
2 medium scallions, sliced thin on the bias

1. Mix the soy sauce, brown sugar, ginger, vinegar, and mirin in a small bowl; set aside ¼ cup of the glaze to dress the finished dish. Brush the bok choy with 1 tablespoon vegetable oil and season with salt and pepper to taste.

2. Prepare the grill as directed in either the Charcoal-Grilled or Gas-Grilled Tuna Steaks recipe. Lightly dip a small wad of paper towels in oil; holding the wad with long-handled tongs, wipe the cooking grate (see page 224). Brush one side of the tuna liberally with the glaze and put the tuna, glaze-side down, on the grill. Grill, uncovered, for 3 minutes, brush with more glaze, and turn with a metal spatula. Grill for 2 minutes, brush with more glaze, turn the fish, and cook for 1 minute more for rare or 2 to 3 minutes more for medium-rare.

3. While the tuna is grilling, place the bok choy around the outside edge of the grill. Grill, turning once, until crisp-tender, 6 to 7 minutes. Serve the tuna steaks and the bok choy immediately, topped with the reserved glaze and sprinkled with scallions.

Grilled Tuna Steaks with Tarragon-Lime Butter or Tapenade Butter

Like beef, a tuna steak can be embellished with a slice of compound butter. The zesty flavors in these butters work well with the richness of the tuna.

Follow the recipe for Charcoal-Grilled or Gas-Grilled Tuna Steaks, topping each grilled tuna steak with a slice of Tarragon-Lime Butter or Tapenade Butter (page 385).

Salmon and Tuna Burgers

LIKE TURKEY BURGERS, SALMON AND TUNA burgers can be dry. They don't have a lot of fat and can taste awful if overcooked. After some initial tests, we concluded that burgers made with fresh fish must be undercooked. Tuna burgers should be medium-rare (pink in the center). If cooked much further, the texture resembles canned tuna. Given the high price of tuna, this is an expensive mistake. Salmon has more fat than tuna so it is a tad more forgiving. However, salmon burgers cooked until the flesh is completely opaque will be dry and disappointing.

While undercooking helped, we wondered if there was an additional way to ensure moistness. We quickly realized that salmon and tuna are fundamentally different from ground turkey. Turkey is bland, so adding miso, porcini mushrooms, or ricotta cheese gives the meat a flavor boost as well as more moisture. However, salmon and tuna are delicious on their own. We needed something subtler in flavor than ricotta cheese to help keep these burgers moist.

We tried adding melted butter and vegetable oil, but these burgers were greasy. Egg yolks worked better, but tasters felt the egg flavor was too noticeable. We hit upon the right solution when we added some mayonnaise to salmon burgers. Just 2 tablespoons for four burgers added some creaminess and moisture. When we tried adding more mayonnaise, the burgers became greasy.

The subtle tang of mayonnaise worked well in salmon burgers, but tasters did not like the flavor of the mayonnaise in tuna burgers. In the end, we decided to leave the tuna burgers alone. Tuna has a more delicate flavor than salmon, and we didn't want to overwhelm it with mayonnaise or any other moisture-rich ingredients. We did find that the tuna burgers benefited from the addition of some garlic and ginger. However, to keep these burgers moist you simply must cook them right.

Most sources we consulted suggest chopping skinless salmon or tuna with a knife until finely ground. We wondered if the food processor could save some time here. After several attempts, we concluded that the knife is essential. There's no margin of error with a food processor. More often than not, we ended up with fish pureed to a mousse-like texture. For the best results, salmon and tuna should be chopped to resemble the texture of ground meat. Pieces that measure about ⅛ inch are ideal.

Our tests also revealed another problem when making salmon and tuna burgers—sticking. We lost many burgers in our early tests. Heating the grill thoroughly and then rubbing the surface with an oil-soaked paper towel helped, but these steps did not guarantee that the burgers could be flipped or removed from the grill. In the end, we turned to a grill grid, which we coated with oil for added protection. Coating the spatula with non-stick cooking spray also helps loosen the burger from the grill grid.

Charcoal-Grilled Salmon Burgers
SERVES 4

Be sure that your salmon burgers are refrigerated for at least 15 minutes before being grilled. Chilled burgers are more likely to hold their shape when grilled. Use a grill grid (see page 20) to prevent the burgers from falling apart and into the coals, and coat a metal spatula with nonstick cooking spray so that the burgers slide easily onto the grill. Serve the burgers with one of the sauces on page 248.

1¼	pounds salmon fillets
¼	cup chopped fresh parsley leaves
2	tablespoons mayonnaise
2	tablespoons finely grated onion
1	tablespoon juice from 1 lemon
½	teaspoon salt
	Ground black pepper
	Vegetable oil for the grill grid

1. Remove any pinbones from the salmon flesh using tweezers or needle-nose pliers (see illustration 1 on page 246). Separate the flesh from the skin (see illustration 2 on page 246), discarding the skin. Chop the salmon into ¼-inch pieces. Using a rocking motion with the knife, continue

to chop the salmon until it is coarsely ground into pieces roughly ⅛ inch each.

2. Place the salmon in a bowl and mix with the parsley, mayonnaise, onion, lemon juice, salt, and pepper to taste. Divide the mixture into 4 equal portions (about 5 ounces each) and use your hands to press each into a compact patty about 1 inch thick. Place the patties on a parchment-lined baking sheet and refrigerate for at least 15 minutes.

3. Meanwhile, light a large chimney starter filled with hardwood charcoal (about 6 quarts) and allow to burn until all the charcoal is covered with a layer of fine gray ash. Build a single-level fire by spreading the coals evenly over the bottom of the grill. Set the cooking grate in place and use a grill brush to scrape the cooking grate clean. Place the grill grid on top of the cooking grate,

cover the grill with the lid, and let the grate heat up, about 5 minutes. The grill is ready when the coals are medium-hot. (See how to gauge heat level on page 4.)

4. Lightly dip a small wad of paper towels in vegetable oil; holding the wad with long-handled tongs, wipe the grill grid (see page 224). Grill the salmon burgers, uncovered, until well browned on one side, 3 to 4 minutes. Flip the burgers with a greased metal spatula. Continue grilling, uncovered, until the other side is well browned and the burgers are barely translucent at the center, about 3 minutes. Serve immediately.

➤ VARIATION

Gas-Grilled Salmon Burgers

Set the grill grid (see page 20) on the cleaned cooking grate before you light the grill. This way the grid can be heated along with the grill itself.

Follow step 1 and 2 of the recipe for Charcoal-Grilled Salmon Burgers. Place the grill grid on top of the cooking grate. Turn on all the burners to high, close the lid, and heat the grill until very hot, about 15 minutes. Leave the burners on high. Continue as directed from step 4, grilling the salmon burgers, covered, until well browned on one side, 4 to 5 minutes. Flip the burgers with a greased metal spatula. Continue grilling, covered, until the other side is well browned and the burgers are barely translucent at the center, about 4 minutes. Serve immediately.

PREPARING SALMON FOR BURGERS

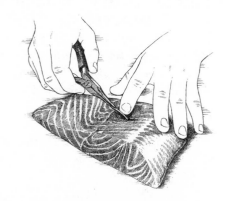

1. Rub your fingers over the surface of the fillet to feel for pinbones. Remove them using tweezers or needle-nose pliers.

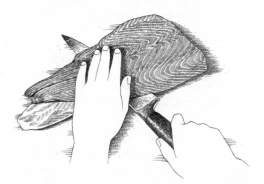

2. Place the fillet skin-side down on a cutting board. Holding a sharp knife parallel to the board, slice just above the skin to separate it from the flesh.

Charcoal-Grilled Tuna Burgers

SERVES 4

Do not let these burgers overcook; tuna tends to get very dry when cooked for too long. Because we recommend that you serve the burgers medium-rare to medium, we suggest that you use the highest quality tuna you can find. We use a grill grid (see page 20) to prevent the tuna from falling through the cooking grate during grilling. The garlic and ginger are subtle additions that we strongly recommend, although they can be omitted if you prefer. These lean burgers are greatly enhanced by one of the sauces on page 248. We particularly like the tuna paired with the Wasabi Mayonnaise.

1¼ pounds high-quality tuna steaks
1 medium garlic clove, minced or pressed
     through a garlic press (about 1 teaspoon)
1 teaspoon minced fresh ginger
½ teaspoon salt
     Ground black pepper
     Vegetable oil for the grill grid

1. Chop the tuna into ¼- to ⅓-inch pieces. Using a rocking motion with the knife, continue to chop the tuna until it is coarsely ground into pieces roughly ⅛ inch each. Mix with the garlic, ginger, salt, and pepper to taste. Divide the mixture into 4 equal portions (about 5 ounces each) and use your hands to press into a compact patty about 1 inch thick. Place the patties on a parchment-lined baking sheet and refrigerate for at least 15 minutes.

2. Meanwhile, light a large chimney starter filled with hardwood charcoal (about 6 quarts) and allow to burn until all the charcoal is covered with a layer of fine gray ash. Build a single-level fire by spreading the coals evenly over the bottom of the grill. Set the cooking grate in place and use a grill brush to scrape the cooking grate clean. Place the grill grid on top of the cooking grate, cover the grill with the lid, and let the grate heat up, about 5 minutes. The grill is ready when the coals are medium-hot. (See

how to gauge heat level on page 4.)

3. Lightly dip a small wad of paper towels in vegetable oil; holding the wad with long-handled tongs, wipe the grill grid (see page 224). Grill the tuna burgers, uncovered, until browned on one side, about 3 minutes. Flip the burgers with a greased metal spatula. Continue grilling, uncovered, to the desired doneness, about 2 minutes for medium-rare or 3 minutes for medium. Serve immediately.

➤ VARIATION
Gas-Grilled Tuna Burgers
Set the grill grid (see page 20) on the cleaned cooking grate before lighting the grill. Cook the burgers with the lid down over the highest possible heat.

Follow step 1 of the recipe for Charcoal-Grilled Tuna Burgers. Place the grill grid on top of the cooking grate. Turn on all the burners to high, close the lid, and heat the grill until very hot, about 15 minutes. Leave all the burners on high. Continue as directed from step 3, grilling the tuna burgers, covered, until well browned on one side, about 3 minutes. Flip the burgers with a greased metal spatula. Continue grilling, covered, to the desired doneness, about 3 minutes for medium-rare or 4 minutes for medium. Serve immediately.

PEELING AND MINCING GINGER
Ginger is highly fibrous, which makes it tricky to mince. Removing the skin with the edge of a teaspoon and using a sharp knife to mince the ginger make quick work of this task.

1. Slice the peeled knob of ginger into thin rounds, then fan the rounds out and cut them into matchsticks.

2. Chop the matchsticks into a fine mince.

IN GENERAL, ANY SAUCE THAT WILL TASTE GOOD WITH A PIECE OF GRILLED SALMON OR tuna will work with grilled salmon or tuna burgers. We often omit the bun and serve fish burgers over lightly dressed greens. Salsas are also good with fish burgers, especially Black Bean and Mango Salsa (page 392) with the salmon burgers.

If you want to slide these burgers onto a bun, you need some sort of sauce. The following sauces are designed to spread on buns and will work with tuna or salmon. Also, see our traditional Tartar Sauce on page 276. Each recipe yields enough sauce for four fish burgers.

Creamy Chipotle-Lime Sauce

MAKES ABOUT 1/3 CUP

This sauce lends a southwestern flair to burgers. Serve with sliced avocados and tomatoes.

2 small garlic cloves, unpeeled
1/4 cup mayonnaise
1 1/2 teaspoons juice from 1 lime
1/2 chipotle chile in adobo sauce, minced (about 1 teaspoon), with 1/2 teaspoon adobo sauce

1. Place the garlic cloves in a small, heavy-bottomed skillet over medium heat. Toast, turning the cloves occasionally, until they are fragrant and the skins have browned, 10 to 12 minutes. Cool, peel, and mince. (You should have about 1 teaspoon.)

2. Mix the garlic, mayonnaise, lime juice, chile, and adobo sauce together in a small bowl. Cover with plastic wrap and chill until the flavors blend, at least 30 minutes.

Wasabi Mayonnaise

MAKES ABOUT 1/4 CUP

This mayonnaise is particularly delicious with the tuna burgers.

1/4 cup mayonnaise
1 teaspoon soy sauce
1 teaspoon wasabi powder

Mix all the ingredients together in a small bowl. Cover with plastic wrap and chill until the flavors blend, at least 10 minutes.

Creamy Lemon-Herb Sauce

MAKES ABOUT 1/3 CUP

Other fresh herbs, such as basil, cilantro, mint, or tarragon, can be used in place of the parsley and thyme.

1/4 cup mayonnaise
1 small scallion, minced
1 tablespoon juice from 1 lemon
1 1/2 teaspoons minced fresh parsley leaves
1 1/2 teaspoons minced fresh thyme leaves
1/4 teaspoon salt
Ground black pepper

Mix all the ingredients, including pepper to taste, together in a small bowl. Cover with plastic wrap and chill until the flavors blend, at least 30 minutes.

Creamy Ginger-Cilantro Sauce

MAKES ABOUT 1/3 CUP

1/4 cup mayonnaise
1 tablespoon minced cilantro leaves
2 teaspoons minced fresh ginger
1 teaspoon juice from 1 lime
1 small garlic clove, minced or pressed through a garlic press (about 1/2 teaspoon)
1/4 teaspoon salt
Ground black pepper

Mix all the ingredients, including pepper to taste, together in a small bowl. Cover with plastic wrap and chill until the flavors blend, at least 30 minutes.

WHOLE BLUEFISH

BLUEFISH IS GREAT FOR GRILLING WHOLE because its oils keep it nice and moist; it won't dry out as quickly as red snapper or striped bass. We did notice that bluefish took slightly longer to cook through than red snapper at exactly the same weight, perhaps because of the oiliness. We marinated the bluefish in lemon juice to help cut the oiliness of the fish and to balance its strong flavor.

Ideally, whole bluefish for grilling should be about 1½ pounds before gutting and scaling. Any larger and it's better to fillet the fish and cook the fillets individually on the grill (see the recipes on page 225). Larger fish will char before cooking through on the grill, not to mention the fact that they are very hard to maneuver.

As a precaution against charring this oily fish, we found it best to build a moderate fire, with the chimney only three-quarters full with charcoal.

Charcoal-Grilled Whole Bluefish

SERVES 4

Because bluefish is somewhat fatty, flare-ups occur when grilling. Be ready to spray the flames with water or to move the fish to another part of the grill when this happens.

3	tablespoons extra-virgin olive oil
3	tablespoons juice from I to 2 lemons
³/₄	teaspoon salt
	Ground black pepper
2	whole bluefish (about 1½ pounds each), gutted, scaled, and skin slashed on both sides (see the illustrations on page 250)
	Vegetable oil for the cooking grate
	Lemon wedges for serving

1. Light a large chimney starter filled three-quarters full with hardwood charcoal (about 4½ quarts) and allow to burn until all the charcoal is covered with a layer of fine gray ash. Build a single-level fire by spreading the coals evenly over the bottom of the grill. Set the cooking grate in place, cover the grill with the lid, and let the grate heat up, about 10 minutes. Use a grill brush to scrape the cooking grate clean. The grill is ready when the heat level of the coals is medium. (See how to gauge heat level on page 4.)

2. Meanwhile, mix the olive oil, lemon juice, salt, and pepper to taste together in a small bowl. Place the bluefish in a large shallow baking dish and pour the lemon juice mixture over them. Turn the fish to ensure that the lemon juice mixture coats both sides as well as the inside of each fish. Cover and refrigerate until ready to grill.

3. Lightly dip a small wad of paper towels in vegetable oil; holding the wad with long-handled tongs, wipe the cooking grate (see page 224). Remove the fish from the marinade and place them on the grill. Grill, uncovered, until the side of the fish facing the charcoal is browned and crisp, about 7 minutes. Gently turn the fish over using two metal spatulas and cook until the flesh is no longer translucent at the center and the skin on both sides of each fish is blistered and crisp, 7 to 8 minutes more. (To check for doneness, peek into the slashed flesh or into the interior through the opened bottom area of the fish to see that the flesh is no longer translucent.) Use the two metal spatulas to transfer the fish to a platter (see the illustration on page 251).

4. Fillet the fish according to the illustrations on page 251 and serve with the lemon wedges.

➤ VARIATION

Gas-Grilled Whole Bluefish

Since the cover is down, be vigilant for signs of flare-ups, such as excessive smoking. Be ready to spray the flames with water or to move the fish to a cooler part of the grill.

1. Turn on all the burners to high, close the lid, and heat the grill until very hot, about 15 minutes. Use a grill brush to scrape the cooking grate clean. Turn all the burners down to medium-high.

2. Follow the recipe for Charcoal-Grilled Whole Bluefish from step 2. In step 3, grill the fish, covered, until the side of the fish facing the fire is browned and crisp, 7 to 8 minutes. Gently turn the fish over using two metal spatulas and cook until the flesh is no longer translucent at the center and the skin on both sides of each fish is

Grilling Whole Fish 101

Grilling a whole fish is one of those dazzling acts that looks harder than it really is. Most cooks don't want to bother with whole fish, but the rewards are ample. When cooked on the bone, the flesh is especially flavorful and juicy. This method also makes sense when you have caught the fish yourself. In our testing, we discovered a number of general techniques that make grilling whole fish much easier.

SCALING AND GUTTING WHOLE FISH

We recommend asking your fishmonger to scale and gut the fish. If you have caught your own fish, here's how to do this at home. Scaling is a messy job—try to do it outside or in a large, deep sink. It's also a good idea to wear rubber gloves.

1. Hold the fish by the tail with a kitchen towel. Using the back of a knife, a metal spoon, or a scaler, move from the tail toward the head, making short, firm strokes, until all scales are removed. You can tell if any scales remain by running your fingers along the fish in the same direction as you scale.

2. Using a very sharp knife, make an incision at the anal opening and continue cutting up the belly of the fish toward the head until the knife is just below the gills.

3. Using your fingers, pull out the innards of the fish, being sure to remove all viscera from the cavity; rinse with water. Use a spoon to scrape out any remaining innards.

SLASHING THE SKIN

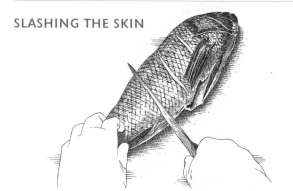

Once a fish is scaled and gutted, use a sharp knife to make shallow diagonal slashes every 2 inches along both sides of the fish from top to bottom, beginning just behind the dorsal fin. This helps to ensure even cooking and also allows the cook to peek into the flesh to see if it is done.

BRUSHLESS GRATE CLEANING

Oiling your cooking grate is a must for preventing fish from sticking (see the illustration on page 224). But first, you need to start with a clean cooking grate. If you don't have a grill brush, this method works just as well.

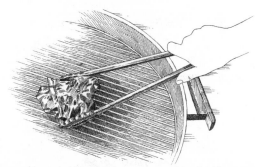

Once your cooking grate is hot, fashion your own grill brush with a crumpled wad of aluminum foil and long-handled tongs.

GRILLED FISH TROUBLESHOOTING

➤ **Preventing sticking.** Make sure your cooking grate is very hot before placing the fish on the grill. If using charcoal, we found it best to heat the cooking grate for 10 minutes rather than the standard five minutes. We found that oiling the fish as well as the grate also helped prevent sticking. (See the illustration on page 224.)

➤ **Controlling flare-ups.** Many whole fish are fairly oily, making flare-ups a major concern. Any oil rubbed into the skin to keep it from sticking only makes matters worse. Be prepared to move the fish to another part of the grill if flare-ups occur. Better yet, keep a squirt bottle filled with water

nearby. Whole fish can tear and fall apart if moved too much on the grill. Dousing the flames with a spritz of water makes more sense.

➤ **Keeping the whole fish intact.** Turning a whole fish can be tricky. Try to position the fish on the grill initially so that it can be turned by rolling. When turning the fish, lift it gently at first to make sure that it is not sticking to the grill. If the fish is sticking, gently pull it from the cooking grate, working the sticking skin off the grate. The skin may still break, but at least you won't split the fish in half. (Also, see our idea for using cheesecloth to turn and remove whole fish from the grill.)

TWO WAYS TO MOVE GRILLED WHOLE FISH

A grilled large fillet or whole fish can make an impressive presentation, but it can be a challenge to remove the fish from the grill without it falling apart. Is there a way to keep grilled fish intact when moving it? We have two solutions to this problem.

A1. Before grilling, place the fish on a length of cheesecloth that is about 4 to 6 inches longer than the fish.

A2. Wrap the fish carefully, then tie the cheesecloth shut at both ends with string; grill as directed.

A3. Though the cheesecloth will turn brown, the overhang creates handles that extend over the edges of the grill, making turning or lifting the fish risk-free.

B. Once the fish is done, slide two metal spatulas under the belly to give it proper support, lifting gently to make sure the skin is not sticking to the grill. Quickly lift the fish and place it on a nearby platter.

KEEPING FISH EXTRA-FRESH

Whether whole or filleted, fresh fish (and shellfish) is best purchased and served on the same day. If fish must be stored, even briefly, it is best kept on ice. Instead of keeping seafood in a messy container of melting ice, try this cleaner method:

Place a layer of sealed frozen ice bricks (the kind used in picnic coolers) along the bottom of the meat drawer in the refrigerator. Place the wrapped fish on top of the ice bricks. For firm-fleshed fish and shellfish, place additional ice bricks on top. Replace melted ice bricks with fully frozen bricks as necessary.

FILLETING GRILLED WHOLE FISH

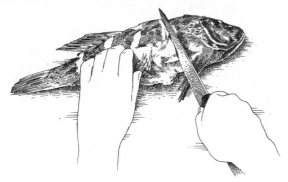 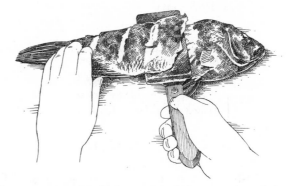

1. Using a sharp knife, make a vertical cut just behind the head from the top of the fish to the belly. Make another cut along the top of the fish from the head to the tail.

2. Use a metal spatula to lift the meat from the bones, starting at the head end and running the spatula over the bones to lift out the fillet. Repeat on the other side of the fish. Discard the fish head and skeleton.

blistered and crisp, 7 to 8 minutes more. (To check for doneness, peek into the slashed flesh or into the interior through the opened bottom area of the fish to see that the flesh is no longer translucent.) Use the two metal spatulas to transfer the fish to a platter (see the illustration on page 251). Fillet and serve as directed.

WHOLE MACKEREL

THERE ARE MANY TYPES OF MACKEREL, BUT common mackerel is usually under two pounds and has silvery blue-green skin with an attractive vertical pattern on the top of the fish. Mackerel are long and lean in appearance but are actually extremely oily fish that are well paired with the smoky flavor of the grill and with acidic or strongly flavored sauces. Mackerel do not need scaling, just gutting, which is easily done at home. These fish are easy to grill.

≈≈

Charcoal-Grilled Whole Mackerel

SERVES 2 TO 4

Most whole mackerel weigh between 1 and 1¼ pounds, more than enough for one person but not enough for two. If you can find larger mackerel (closer to 2 pounds), you can squeeze two servings out of one whole fish. Mackerel is high in fat; briefly marinating the fish in lemon juice tames some of this richness.

2	tablespoons extra-virgin olive oil
2	tablespoons juice from 1 lemon
½	teaspoon salt
	Ground black pepper
2	whole mackerel (1 to 2 pounds each), gutted and skin slashed on both sides (see the illustrations on page 250)
	Vegetable oil for the cooking grate
	Lemon wedges for serving

1. Light a large chimney starter filled with hardwood charcoal (about 6 quarts) and allow to burn until all the charcoal is covered with a layer of fine gray ash. Build a single-level fire by spreading the coals evenly over the bottom of the grill. Set the cooking grate in place, cover the grill with the lid, and let the grate heat up, about 10 minutes. Use a grill brush to scrape the cooking grate clean. The grill is ready when the coals are medium-hot. (See how to gauge heat level on page 4.)

2. Meanwhile, mix the olive oil, lemon juice, salt, and pepper to taste together in a small bowl. Place the mackerel in a large shallow baking dish and pour the lemon juice mixture over the fish. Turn the mackerel to ensure that the lemon juice mixture coats both sides as well as the inside of each fish. Cover and refrigerate until ready to grill.

3. Lightly dip a small wad of paper towels in vegetable oil; holding the wad with long-handled tongs, wipe the cooking grate (see page 224). Remove the fish from the marinade and place them on the grill. Grill, uncovered, until the side of the fish facing the charcoal is browned and crisp, 5 to 7 minutes. Gently turn the fish over using two metal spatulas and cook until the flesh is no longer translucent at the center and the skin on both sides of the fish is blistered and crisp, 5 to 7 minutes more. (To check for doneness, peek into the slashed flesh or into the interior through the opened bottom area of the fish to see that the flesh is no longer translucent.) Use the two metal spatulas to transfer the fish to a platter (see the illustration on page 251).

4. Fillet the fish according to the illustrations on page 251 and serve with the lemon wedges.

➤ VARIATIONS
Gas-Grilled Whole Mackerel
Note that the fish needs about 1 minute more of cooking time on a gas grill.

1. Turn on all the burners to high, close the lid, and heat the grill until very hot, about 15 minutes. Use a grill brush to scrape the cooking grate clean. Leave all the burners on high.

2. Follow the recipe for Charcoal-Grilled Whole Mackerel from step 2. In step 3, grill the fish, covered, until the side of the fish facing the fire is browned and crisp, about 6 minutes. Gently turn the fish over using two metal spatulas and cook until the flesh is no longer translucent at the center and the skin on both sides of the fish

is blistered and crisp, 6 to 8 minutes more. (To check for doneness, peek into the slashed flesh or into the interior through the opened bottom area of the fish to see that the flesh is no longer translucent.) Use the two metal spatulas to transfer the fish to a platter (see the illustration on page 251). Fillet and serve as directed.

Spicy Grilled Mackerel with Garlic, Ginger, and Sesame Oil

Here, strong-flavored mackerel is matched with garlic, chile, ginger, soy sauce, and sesame oil. Serve with plain steamed rice, which will act as a neutral foil for the intensely flavored fish. Have all the ingredients ready for the sauce so that it can be made quickly right after the fish come off the grill.

I	recipe Charcoal-Grilled or Gas-Grilled Whole Mackerel
2	tablespoons vegetable or peanut oil
I	medium scallion, minced
1/2	medium jalapeño chile, seeds and ribs removed, then minced
2	medium garlic cloves, minced or pressed through a garlic press (about 2 teaspoons)
1/2	teaspoon finely grated fresh ginger
I	tablespoon soy sauce
I	teaspoon toasted sesame oil

1. Follow the recipe for Charcoal-Grilled or Gas-Grilled Whole Mackerel; tent foil over the platter with the grilled fish to keep them warm.

2. Heat the oil in a small skillet over medium-high heat until it shimmers. Add the scallion and jalapeño and cook until softened, about 30 seconds. Add the garlic and ginger and cook until fragrant, about 30 seconds longer. Remove the pan from the heat and stir in the soy sauce and sesame oil. Spoon the sauce over the fish and serve immediately with the lemon wedges.

WHOLE RED SNAPPER AND STRIPED BASS

WE HAVE GROUPED THESE FISH TOGETHER because they are both fairly lean, white-fleshed fish that grill beautifully using the same level of heat for the same amount of time. They can also be served with the same sauces.

Red snapper is white-fleshed, firm, and lean, and when purchased the skin should be bright silvery red. Its flavor is mild and clean, and its skin crisps up nicely. We found that fish weighing from 1½ to 1¾ pounds are best for grilling. Fish any larger than 2 pounds are hard to grill because they are difficult to turn and to remove from the grill. Larger fish take a long time to cook through, and the skin is more likely to char. A 1½-pound red snapper will feed two people. (The same is true for striped bass.) If you have to scale the fish yourself, be careful of the sharp spines on the fins (they can easily prick your hands). The scales are rather large and tough, so we recommend that you have a fishmonger remove them.

Most small striped bass are from fish farms and are actually hybrid striped bass. They are a cross between wild striped bass (which lives in both freshwater and saltwater) and white bass (a freshwater variety). Striped bass is more full-flavored than red snapper, but it has the same firm texture and is fairly lean. Striped bass is grayish in color with long horizontal black stripes running along each side. Like snapper, striped bass needs to be scaled.

Charcoal-Grilled Whole Red Snapper or Striped Bass

SERVES 4

If your fish are a little larger (between 1½ and 2 pounds), simply grill them a minute or two longer on each side. Fish weighing more than 2 pounds will be hard to maneuver on the grill and should be avoided.

2	whole red snapper or striped bass (about 1½ pounds each), scaled, gutted, and skin slashed on both sides (see the illustrations on page 250)
3	tablespoons extra-virgin olive oil
	Salt and ground black pepper
	Vegetable oil for the cooking grate
	Lemon wedges for serving

1. Light a large chimney starter filled with hardwood charcoal (about 6 quarts) and allow to burn until all the charcoal is covered with a layer

of fine gray ash. Build a single-level fire by spreading the coals evenly over the bottom of the grill. Set the cooking grate in place, cover the grill with the lid, and let the grate heat up, about 10 minutes. Use a grill brush to scrape the cooking grate clean. The grill is ready when the coals are medium-hot. (See how to gauge heat level on page 4.)

2. Rub the fish with the olive oil and season generously with salt and pepper on the outside as well as the inside of each fish.

3. Lightly dip a small wad of paper towels in vegetable oil; holding the wad with long-handled tongs, wipe the cooking grate (see page 224). Place the fish on the grill. Grill, uncovered, until the side of the fish facing the charcoal is browned and crisp, 6 to 7 minutes. Gently turn the fish over using two metal spatulas and cook until the flesh is no longer translucent at the center and the skin on both sides of each fish is blistered and crisp, 6 to 8 minutes more. (To check for doneness, peek into the slashed flesh or into the interior through the opened bottom area of each fish to see that the flesh is no longer translucent.) Use the two metal spatulas to transfer the fish to a platter (see the illustration on page 251).

4. Fillet the fish according to the illustrations on page 251 and serve with the lemon wedges.

➤ VARIATIONS
Gas-Grilled Whole Red Snapper or Striped Bass
Make sure the grill is as hot and clean as possible.

1. Turn on all the burners to high, cover, and heat the grill until very hot, about 15 minutes. Use a grill brush to scrape the cooking grate clean. Leave all the burners on high.

2. Follow the recipe for Charcoal-Grilled Whole Red Snapper or Striped Bass from step 2. In step 3, grill, covered, until the side of the fish facing the fire is browned and crisp, 7 to 8 minutes. Gently turn the fish over using two metal spatulas and cook until the flesh is no longer translucent at the center and the skin on both sides of each fish is blistered and crisp, 6 to 8 minutes more. (To check for doneness, peek into the slashed flesh or into the interior through the opened bottom area of each fish to see that the flesh is no longer

translucent.) Use the two metal spatulas to transfer the fish to a platter (see the illustration on page 251). Fillet and serve as directed.

Grilled Whole Red Snapper or Striped Bass with Orange, Lime, and Cilantro Vinaigrette
This vinaigrette lends a light acidic counterpoint to the smoky grilled fish.

¼	cup orange juice
I	tablespoon juice from I lime
2	teaspoons sugar
I	medium garlic clove, minced or pressed through a garlic press (about I teaspoon)
½	teaspoon salt
	Ground black pepper
6	tablespoons vegetable oil
I	tablespoon chopped fresh cilantro leaves
I	recipe Charcoal-Grilled or Gas-Grilled Whole Red Snapper or Striped Bass (without the lemon wedges)
	Lime wedges for serving

1. Whisk the juices, sugar, garlic, salt, and pepper to taste together in a medium bowl. Whisk in the oil until the dressing is smooth. Whisk in the cilantro and adjust the seasonings.

2. Follow the recipe for Charcoal-Grilled or Gas-Grilled Whole Red Snapper or Striped Bass. Drizzle the filleted fish with the vinaigrette and serve with the lime wedges.

Grilled Whole Red Snapper or Striped Bass with Parsley-Lemon Butter
Compound butters are an easy and convenient way to flavor grilled whole fish.

Follow the recipe for Charcoal-Grilled or Gas-Grilled Whole Red Snapper or Striped Bass. Cut Parsley-Lemon Butter (page 385) into four slices and top each fillet with one piece of butter. Serve immediately with the lemon wedges.

Grilled Whole Red Snapper or Striped Bass with Fresh Tomato-Basil Relish

Fresh relishes are good on grilled fish. Use this recipe in the summer when tomatoes are at their peak.

1	pound fresh ripe tomatoes, cored, seeded, and cut into ¼-inch dice
1	medium shallot, minced
2	tablespoons chopped fresh basil leaves
2	tablespoons extra-virgin olive oil
1	teaspoon red wine vinegar
1	medium garlic clove, minced or pressed through a garlic press (about 1 teaspoon) Salt and ground black pepper
1	recipe Charcoal-Grilled or Gas-Grilled Whole Red Snapper or Striped Bass (without the lemon wedges)

1. Mix the tomatoes, shallot, basil, oil, vinegar, garlic, and salt and pepper to taste together in a medium bowl. (The relish can be covered and refrigerated for a day or two.)

2. Follow the recipe for Charcoal-Grilled or Gas-Grilled Whole Red Snapper or Striped Bass; serve the filleted fish with the relish.

WHOLE POMPANO

POMPANO IS A THIN, SILVERY FISH. IT HAS rich, full-flavored, slightly oily flesh. Because the flesh is somewhat oily, flare-ups are a real concern. We found it helpful to reduce the amount of charcoal from the standard full chimney to three quarters of a chimney. Still, be prepared to move the fish to another part of the grill or to douse the flames with a squirt bottle if flare-ups occur.

When grilling whole pompano, be sure to buy fish caught in waters off the Gulf Coast and Florida. This variety is much larger than Pacific pompano (also called butterfish) and is better suited to grilling whole.

As with grilling any whole fish, turning it can be tricky. We recommend using two metal spatulas held side by side to gently turn the pompano. The rich flavor of this fish is delicious served simply with a squeeze of fresh lemon, but it can also be enjoyed with a classic butter sauce flavored with tarragon (see our variation on page 256).

Charcoal-Grilled Whole Pompano
SERVES 4

Because some of its oil drips down into the coals during grilling, flare-ups do occur. When this happens, move the fish to a cooler part of the grill or spray the flames with water.

2	whole pompano (about 1½ pounds each), scaled, gutted, and skin slashed on both sides (see the illustrations on page 250)
2	tablespoons extra-virgin olive oil Salt and ground black pepper Vegetable oil for the cooking grate Lemon wedges for serving

1. Light a large chimney starter filled three-quarters full with hardwood charcoal (about 4½ quarts) and allow to burn until all the charcoal is covered with a layer of fine gray ash. Build a single-level fire by spreading the coals evenly over the bottom of the grill. Set the cooking grate in place, cover the grill with the lid, and let the grate heat up, about 10 minutes. Use a grill brush to scrape the cooking grate clean. The grill is ready when the coals are medium. (See how to gauge heat level on page 4.)

2. Rub the fish with the olive oil and season generously with salt and pepper on the outside as well as inside the cavity of each fish.

3. Lightly dip a small wad of paper towels in vegetable oil; holding the wad with long-handled tongs, wipe the cooking grate (see page 224). Place the fish on the grill. Grill, uncovered, until the side of the fish facing the charcoal is browned and crisp, 6 to 7 minutes. Gently turn the fish over using two metal spatulas and cook until the flesh is no longer translucent at the center and the skin on both sides of each fish is blistered and crisp, 6 to 7 minutes more. (To check for doneness, peek into the slashed flesh or into the interior through the opened bottom area of each fish to see that the flesh is no longer translucent.) Use the two metal spatulas to transfer the fish to a platter (see the illustration on page 251).

4. Fillet the fish according to the illustrations on page 251 and serve with the lemon wedges.

➤ VARIATIONS

Gas-Grilled Whole Pompano

Be sure to keep an eye on the grill while the pompano cooks. If large amounts of smoke are coming from the grill, flare-ups are probably occurring under the closed lid. When this happens, carefully move the fish to a cooler part of the grill or spray the flames with water to prevent the skin from charring.

1. Turn on all the burners to high, cover, and heat the grill until very hot, about 15 minutes. Use a grill brush to scrape the cooking grate clean. Turn all the burners down to medium-high.

2. Follow the recipe for Charcoal-Grilled Pompano from step 2, grilling the fish, covered, until the side of the fish facing the fire is browned and crisp, about 7 minutes. Gently turn the fish over using two metal spatulas and cook until the flesh is no longer translucent at the center and the skin on both sides of each fish is blistered and crisp, about 7 minutes more. (To check for doneness, peek into the slashed flesh or into the interior through the opened bottom area of each fish to see that the flesh is no longer translucent.) Use the two metal spatulas to transfer the fish to a platter (see the illustration on page 251). Fillet and serve as directed.

Grilled Whole Pompano with Tarragon Butter Sauce

Here, pompano is paired with a butter sauce flavored with white wine and tarragon.

I	cup dry white wine
2	large shallots, minced
I	tablespoon white wine vinegar
¼	cup heavy cream
I	recipe Charcoal-Grilled or Gas-Grilled Whole Pompano
4	tablespoons (½ stick) cold unsalted butter, cut into 4 pieces
I	teaspoon chopped fresh tarragon leaves Salt and ground black pepper

1. Combine the wine, shallots, and vinegar in a small saucepan. Bring to a boil over high heat; reduce the heat to medium-high and simmer until almost all the liquid has evaporated, 9 to 10

minutes. Add the heavy cream and bring to a boil. Cook for 1 minute. Remove the pan from the heat and set it aside.

2. Follow the recipe for Charcoal-Grilled or Gas-Grilled Whole Pompano; tent foil over the platter with the grilled fish to keep it warm.

3. Bring the white wine and cream mixture back to a boil over medium heat. Reduce the heat to low and whisk in the butter, one piece at a time, until all the pieces are incorporated into the sauce. Add the tarragon and season with salt and pepper to taste.

4. Place one fillet on each plate, and spoon some of the butter sauce over the top. Serve immediately.

WHOLE TROUT

AT THREE QUARTERS OF A POUND, FRESHWATER trout is an ideal fish for grilling. (Steelhead trout spend part of their life cycle in the ocean and taste and look more like salmon.) Freshwater trout have thin, delicate skin and fine flesh that is pinkish when raw and white when cooked.

We did not make any slits in the sides of this fish because each fish is small enough to cook through evenly without the slits and we didn't want to encourage any tearing of the trout's thin skin. Trout is not terribly oily, so flare-ups are not really a concern. The small size of the trout means that the flesh will cook through without any charring of the skin. Because each person is served a whole fish, there's no need to fillet the fish after grilling.

➤⊱

Charcoal-Grilled Whole Freshwater Trout

SERVES 4

This recipe is designed for freshwater trout, such as rainbow, golden, lake, or brook trout. If you find steelhead trout or arctic char, refer to the section on grilled salmon fillets. Freshwater trout is delicious grilled; the skin becomes thin and crispy, and the fine flesh is full-flavored but not fishy. If you find the presence of fish heads on a serving platter or dinner plate to be disturbing, simply cut the heads off before grilling or have your fishmonger do it.

4   whole freshwater trout (each about ¾ pound),
     scaled and gutted (see the illustrations on
     page 250)
3   tablespoons extra-virgin olive oil
     Salt and ground black pepper
     Vegetable oil for the cooking grate
     Lemon wedges for serving

1. Light a large chimney starter filled with hardwood charcoal (about 6 quarts) and allow to burn until all the charcoal is covered in a layer of fine gray ash. Build a single-level fire by spreading the coals evenly over the bottom of the grill. Set the cooking grate in place, cover the grill with the lid, and let the grate heat up, about 10 minutes. Use a grill brush to scrape the cooking grate clean. The grill is ready when the coals are medium-hot. (See how to gauge heat level on page 4.)

2. Rub the fish with the olive oil and season generously with salt and pepper on the outside as well as the inside of each fish.

3. Lightly dip a small wad of paper towels in vegetable oil; holding the wad with long-handled tongs, wipe the cooking grate (see page 224). Place the fish on the grill. Grill, uncovered, until the side of the fish facing the charcoal is browned and crisp, about 4 minutes. Gently turn the fish over using two metal spatulas and cook until the flesh is no longer translucent at the center and the skin on both sides of each fish is blistered and crisp, 4 to 5 minutes more. (To check for doneness, peek into the interior through the opened bottom area of each fish to see that the flesh is no longer translucent.) Use the two metal spatulas to transfer the fish to a platter (see the illustration on page 251). Serve immediately with the lemon wedges.

➤   VARIATIONS

Gas-Grilled Whole Freshwater Trout
Turn on all the burners to high, cover, and heat the grill until very hot, about 15 minutes. Use a grill brush to scrape the cooking grate clean. Leave all the burners on high. Follow the recipe for Charcoal-Grilled Freshwater Trout from step 2, grilling the fish covered.

Grilled Whole Freshwater Trout with Bacon and Horseradish-Peppercorn Sauce
You will need a large fish basket for this recipe to keep the bacon from falling off the trout during grilling. Make sure to oil the basket well and remove the fish promptly after grilling so they don't stick. If you do not have a fish basket, you can always grill the trout according to the directions in the preceding recipes and cook the bacon separately, crumbling and sprinkling it over the grilled fish just before serving.

SAUCE
¾   cup sour cream
3   tablespoons milk
3   tablespoons minced chives
2   teaspoons prepared horseradish
1   teaspoon juice from 1 lemon
¾   teaspoon coarsely ground black peppercorns
½   teaspoon salt

FISH
4   whole freshwater trout (each about ¾ pound),
     scaled and gutted (see the illustrations on
     page 250)
3   tablespoons vegetable oil
     Ground black pepper
8   slices (about 8 ounces) bacon
     Nonstick cooking spray for oiling the fish
     basket

1. Mix the sour cream, milk, chives, horseradish, lemon juice, peppercorns, and salt together in a medium bowl. Cover and refrigerate the sauce for up to 1 day.

2. Rub the fish with the oil and season generously with pepper on the outside as well as the inside of each fish. Lay one slice of bacon over the length of each side of each fish and place all the trout in an oiled fish basket.

3. Grill the trout as directed in the recipe for Charcoal-Grilled or Gas-Grilled Whole Freshwater Trout. Remove the basket from the grill and carefully transfer the fish to four plates. Serve immediately, passing the sauce separately.

WHAT ABOUT WHOLE SALMON?

A WHOLE SALMON IS TOO LARGE TO GRILL over direct heat (the skin burns before the fish is cooked through), but we thought we would be able to devise a method for grill-roasting this favorite fish. (See page 3 for definitions of grill-roasting and barbecuing.) Despite visions of crispy, crackling skin and smoky, juicy, flavorful flesh, our attempts to make a well-seasoned, smoky, whole grill-roasted salmon proved unsuccessful. In fact, after several efforts, we concluded instead that barbecuing an entire side (see page 237) produces better results with less hassle and effort.

While flavorful on its own, salmon benefits greatly from being properly seasoned and browned. When cooked whole, it is especially hard to season the meat of the fish. We tried seasoning the outside of the fish, as well as the interior cavity, but to no avail; except for the skin and the small area of flesh that surrounds the cavity of the fish, the fish remained largely unseasoned and bland. Brining also seemed out of the question with such a large fish (the smallest salmon available during testing was 7 pounds) in such an odd elongated shape. There simply was no practical container in which to brine it.

Because a side of salmon contains no bones, it can be bent to fit into a large, round container for brining. Alternatively, the meat can be seasoned directly with salt and pepper, unlike the meat of the whole salmon, which is surrounded with skin. The meat on a side of salmon gains additional flavor through browning and caramelization. Unfortunately, because virtually no meat on a whole salmon is exposed during cooking, only the surrounding skin gets browned and crisp; the flavor is more like smoky poached salmon, not the roasted, rich flavor one expects.

We were surprised to find that the texture of the whole grill-roasted fish, while moist, was also unpleasantly mushy and spongy. The barbecued side of salmon, on the other hand, remained moist, but it also developed an appealing firmness and structure that the whole grill-roasted salmon lacked. Another bonus of the side of salmon was the crust that developed on the surface of the meat, making for a nice contrast with the softer texture of the interior.

Finally, we find that a whole salmon is a lot of fish to be moving on and off a grill; it has a high risk of being broken or dropped. It takes two people and a lot of effort to remove this large a fish from the grill intact, and the results are less than worth the effort. While it also takes a bit of effort to lift a side of salmon off the grill without having it stick or break, we believe that in this case it is worth the extra effort.

7

SHELLFISH

SHELLFISH

CHARCOAL-GRILLED SHRIMP 262
    Gas-Grilled Shrimp
    Grilled Shrimp with Spicy Garlic Paste
    Grilled Shrimp with Lemon, Garlic, and Oregano Paste
    Grilled Shrimp with Southwestern Flavors
    New Orleans–Style Grilled Shrimp
    Grilled Thai-Style Shrimp with Pineapple

CHARCOAL-GRILLED SCALLOPS 266
    Gas-Grilled Scallops
    Grilled Scallops with Mustard, Sherry, and Cream
    Grilled Scallops with Orange-Chili Vinaigrette

CHARCOAL-GRILLED CLAMS, MUSSELS, OR OYSTERS 269
    Gas-Grilled Clams, Mussels, or Oysters
    Grilled Clams, Mussels, or Oysters with Spicy Lemon Butter
    Grilled Clams, Mussels, or Oysters with Tangy Soy-Citrus Sauce
    Grilled Clams, Mussels, or Oysters with Mignonette Sauce

CHARCOAL-GRILLED LOBSTERS 273
    Gas-Grilled Lobsters
    Grilled Lobsters with Tarragon-Chive Butter
    Grilled Lobsters with Chili Butter

CHARCOAL-GRILLED SOFT-SHELL CRABS 276
    Gas-Grilled Soft-Shell Crabs
    Grilled Soft-Shell Crabs with Spicy Butter
    Grilled Soft-Shell Crabs with Tartar Sauce

THIS CHAPTER COVERS THE MOST COMMONLY available shellfish, all of which are suitable for grilling. This includes shrimp, scallops, clams, mussels, oysters, lobsters, and soft-shell crabs. Even though shellfish cooks in a matter of minutes on the grill, it does pick up some smoky flavor that nicely complements its inherent richness and briny character.

It goes without saying that shellfish must be purchased from a trusted source. Many shellfish are sold alive. This means lobsters should be moving around in the tank, and oysters, clams, and mussels should be tightly shut. If the shellfish doesn't smell fresh or look fresh, it probably isn't. Given the perishability of shellfish, we suggest shopping and cooking on the same day.

SHRIMP

ONCE SHRIMP ARE PURCHASED, THEY NEED to be prepared before being cooked. Should they be peeled? Should the vein that runs down the back of each shrimp be removed?

After some initial tests, we concluded that shrimp destined for the grill should not be peeled. The shell shields the meat from the intense heat and helps to keep the shrimp moist and tender. Try as we might, we found it impossible to grill peeled shrimp without overcooking them and making the meat dry and tough, especially the exterior layers. The only method for peeled shrimp that worked was to intentionally undercook them, but that left the inside a little gooey, something that almost no one enjoyed.

To make it easier to eat grilled shrimp, we found it useful to slit open the shells with a pair of manicure scissors. The shells still protect the meat as the shrimp cook, but they come right off at the table.

In addition to peeling, the issue of deveining generates much controversy, even among experts. Although some people won't eat shrimp that have not been deveined, others believe that the "vein"—actually the animal's intestinal tract—contributes flavor and insist on leaving it in. In our tests, we could not detect an effect on flavor (either positive or negative) when we left the vein in. The vein is generally so tiny in most medium-sized shrimp that it virtually disappears after cooking. Out of laziness, we leave it in. In very large shrimp, the vein is usually larger as well. Very large veins are unsightly and can detract from the overall texture of the shrimp, so they are best removed before cooking.

SHRIMP SIZES

Shrimp are sold by size (small, medium, large, and extra-large) as well as by the number needed to make a pound, usually given in a range. Choosing shrimp by the numerical rating is more accurate than choosing by a size label, which varies from store to store. Here's how the two sizing systems generally line up.

SMALL
51 TO 60 SHRIMP
PER POUND

MEDIUM
40 TO 50 SHRIMP
PER POUND

LARGE
31 TO 40 SHRIMP
PER POUND

EXTRA-LARGE
21 TO 25 SHRIMP
PER POUND

Once you've bought and prepared your shrimp, the hard part is over. Grilling is simple; as soon as the shrimp turn pink, they are done. That said, we did find it advisable to add one more step to preparation to keep the shrimp from drying out, as they tend to do over intense dry heat. We discovered that brining—soaking the shrimp in a salt solution before cooking—which works so well with poultry, also works with shrimp. Brining causes shrimp to become especially firm and plump (we found that they may gain as much as 10 percent in water weight).

The science is fairly simple. The salt causes protein strands in the shrimp to unwind, allowing them to trap and hold onto more moisture when cooked. At its most successful, brining gives mushy shrimp the firm yet tender texture of a lobster tail. Even top-quality shrimp are improved by this process.

Once the shrimp have been brined, they can be threaded onto skewers and grilled. We found that shrimp should be cooked quickly to prevent them from toughening. This means using a very hot fire.

When grilling, we like to coat shrimp with a paste or marinade before cooking. The flavorings adhere to the shell beautifully. When you peel the shrimp at the table, the seasonings stick to your fingers and are in turn transferred directly to the meat as you eat it. Licking your fingers also helps.

Charcoal-Grilled Shrimp
SERVES 4 TO 6

We recommend that you brine the shrimp before grilling to make them especially plump and juicy. To use kosher salt in the brine, see page 172 for conversion information. To keep the shrimp from dropping through the cooking grate onto the hot coals, thread them on skewers. Use tongs to turn the skewered shrimp.

2 tablespoons table salt (see note)
2 pounds extra-large shrimp (21 to 25 per pound)
2 tablespoons extra-virgin olive oil
Lemon wedges for serving

1. Dissolve the salt in 1 quart of cold water in a gallon-size zipper-lock bag. Add the shrimp, press out as much air as possible from the bag, and seal. Let stand 20 to 25 minutes. Drain and rinse the shrimp thoroughly under cold running water. Open the back of the shells with manicure scissors and devein if desired (see the illustrations below). Toss the shrimp and oil in a medium bowl to coat.

2. Meanwhile, light a large chimney starter filled with hardwood charcoal (about 6 quarts) and allow to burn until all the charcoal is covered with a layer of fine gray ash. Build a single-level fire by spreading the coals evenly over the bottom of the grill. Set the cooking grate in place, cover the grill with the lid, and let the grate heat up, about 5 minutes. Use

PREPARING SHRIMP FOR GRILLING

1. When grilling shrimp, we find it best to keep them in their shells. The shells hold in moisture as well as flavor while the shrimp cook. However, eating shrimp cooked in the shell can be a challenge. As a compromise, we found it helpful to slit the back of the shell with a pair of manicure or other small scissors with a fine point. When ready to eat, each person can quickly and easily peel away the shell.

2. Slitting the back of the shell makes it easy to devein the shrimp as well. In our testing, we found that deveining is beneficial only in cases where the vein is especially dark and thick. If you choose to devein shrimp, slit open the back of the shell as in step 1. Invariably, you will cut a little into the meat and expose the vein as you do this. Use the tip of the scissors to lift up the vein and then grab it with your fingers and discard.

a grill brush to scrape the cooking grate clean. The grill is ready when the coals are medium-hot. (See how to gauge heat level on page 4.)

3. Following the illustrations on page 264, thread the shrimp on skewers. Grill the shrimp, uncovered, turning the skewers once, until the shells are barely charred and bright pink, 4 to 6 minutes. Serve hot or at room temperature with the lemon wedges.

➤ VARIATIONS
Gas-Grilled Shrimp
Note that the grilling times are slightly longer when using a gas grill.

Follow step 1 of the recipe for Charcoal-Grilled Shrimp. Turn on all the burners to high, close the lid, and heat the grill until very hot, about 15 minutes. Use a grill brush to scrape the cooking grate clean. Leave the burners on high. Continue with the recipe from step 3, grilling the shrimp covered, and increasing the grilling time to 5 to 7 minutes.

Grilled Shrimp with Spicy Garlic Paste
The garlic paste adheres perfectly and will coat your fingers as you peel and eat the grilled shrimp.

Mince 1 large garlic clove with 1 teaspoon salt to form a smooth paste (see the illustrations at right). Combine the garlic paste with 2 tablespoons extra-virgin olive oil, 2 teaspoons lemon juice, 1 teaspoon sweet paprika, and ½ teaspoon cayenne pepper in a medium bowl. Follow the recipe for Charcoal-Grilled or Gas-Grilled Shrimp, tossing the brined and drained shrimp with the garlic mixture instead of the oil to coat well. Thread the shrimp on skewers and grill as directed.

Grilled Shrimp with Lemon, Garlic, and Oregano Paste
The fresh oregano in this recipe can be replaced with other fresh herbs, including chives, tarragon, parsley, or basil.

Mince 1 large garlic clove with 1 teaspoon salt to form a smooth paste (see the illustrations at right). Combine the garlic paste with 2 tablespoons extra-virgin olive oil, 2 teaspoons lemon juice, and 2 teaspoons chopped fresh oregano leaves in a medium bowl. Follow the recipe for Charcoal-Grilled or Gas-Grilled Shrimp, tossing

BARBECUE 911

Chunky, Rather than Smooth, Garlic Paste

There are times when you want minced garlic to be absolutely smooth. A garlic press yields a smooth paste easily, but not everyone owns one of these gadgets. You can obtain the same effect with a chef's knife and some salt.

1. Mince the garlic as you normally would on a cutting board. Sprinkle the minced garlic with a pinch of salt. If possible, use kosher or coarse salt; the larger crystals do a better job of breaking down the garlic than fine table salt.

2. Drag the side of the chef's knife over the garlic-salt mixture to form a fine paste. Continue to mince and drag the knife as necessary until the paste is smooth.

the brined and drained shrimp with the garlic mixture instead of the oil to coat well. Thread the shrimp on skewers and grill as directed.

Grilled Shrimp with Southwestern Flavors
Serve these shrimp with warm cornbread (page 371).

Heat 2 tablespoons extra-virgin olive oil in a small skillet over medium heat. Add 2 garlic cloves, minced or pressed through a garlic press, 2 teaspoons chili powder, and 1 teaspoon ground cumin and sauté until the garlic is fragrant, 30 to 45 seconds. Scrape the mixture into a heatproof bowl and cool to room temperature. Mix in 2½ tablespoons lime juice and 2 tablespoons minced fresh cilantro leaves. Follow the recipe for Charcoal-Grilled or Gas-Grilled Shrimp, tossing the brined and drained shrimp with the garlic mixture instead of the oil to coat well. Thread the shrimp on skewers and grill as directed. Serve with lime wedges instead of the lemon wedges.

New Orleans–Style Grilled Shrimp

These shrimp are tossed with a spicy paste, grilled, and drizzled with a rich butter-garlic mixture.

I	teaspoon dried thyme
I	teaspoon dried oregano
I	teaspoon sweet paprika

SKEWERING SHRIMP

1. Thread shrimp on skewers by passing the skewer through the body near the tail, folding the shrimp over, and passing the skewer through the body again near the head. Threading each shrimp twice keeps it in place (it won't spin around) and makes it easier to cook the shrimp on both sides by turning the skewer just once.

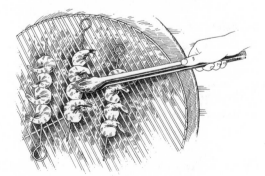

2. Long-handled tongs make it easy to turn hot skewers on the grill. Lightly grasp a single shrimp to turn the entire skewer.

I	teaspoon garlic powder
½	teaspoon salt
	Pinch cayenne pepper
4	tablespoons (½ stick) unsalted butter
2	medium garlic cloves, minced or pressed through a garlic press (about 2 teaspoons)
I	recipe Charcoal-Grilled or Gas-Grilled Shrimp (without the olive oil)
I½	tablespoons vegetable oil

1. Mix the thyme, oregano, paprika, garlic powder, salt, and cayenne together in a small bowl.

2. Melt the butter in a small saucepan over medium heat. When the butter begins to sizzle, add the garlic and cook for 30 seconds. Remove the pan from the heat, cover, and keep warm.

3. Follow the recipe for Charcoal-Grilled or Gas-Grilled Shrimp, tossing the brined and drained shrimp with the vegetable oil and spice mixture instead of the olive oil. Grill the shrimp as directed, then arrange the skewers on a platter. Drizzle with the butter mixture and serve with the lemon wedges.

Grilled Thai-Style Shrimp with Pineapple

Although a red Thai chile is authentic, any small, hot fresh chile can be used in this recipe. To save time, buy peeled and cored pineapple at the supermarket. If you prepare the pineapple yourself, reserve half a large pineapple for this recipe.

3	tablespoons water
2	tablespoons fish sauce
2	tablespoons juice from 2 limes, plus I lime cut into wedges
2	tablespoons chopped fresh basil leaves
I	tablespoon sugar
I	tablespoon rice vinegar
I	red Thai chile, stemmed, seeded, and minced (about ½ teaspoon)
I	recipe Charcoal-Grilled or Gas-Grilled Shrimp (without the lemon wedges)
2	cups fresh pineapple cut into I-inch chunks

1. Mix the water, fish sauce, lime juice, basil, sugar, vinegar, and chile in a small bowl. Set aside.

2. Follow the recipe for Charcoal-Grilled or Gas-Grilled Shrimp with the following change: Thread the shrimp and pineapple onto the skewers, following the illustration below. Grill as directed. Serve the shrimp and pineapple immediately, passing the dipping sauce and the lime wedges.

SCALLOPS

SCALLOPS OFFER SEVERAL CHOICES FOR THE cook, both when shopping and when cooking. There are three main varieties of scallops: sea, bay, and calico. Sea scallops are available year-round throughout the country. Like all scallops, the product sold at the market is the dense, disk-shaped muscle that propels the live scallop in its shell through the water. The guts and roe are usually jettisoned at sea because they are so perishable. Ivory-colored sea scallops are usually at least an inch in diameter (and often much bigger) and look like squat marshmallows. Sometimes they are sold cut up, but we found that they can lose moisture when handled this way and are best purchased whole.

Small, cork-shaped bay scallops (about one-half inch in diameter) are harvested in a small area between Cape Cod and Long Island. Bay scallops are seasonal—available from late fall through midwinter—and are very expensive, up to $20 a

SKEWERING SHRIMP WITH PINEAPPLE

Thread the tail of a shrimp, then a chunk of pineapple, and finally the head of the shrimp onto a skewer, so that the shrimp forms a half-circle around the pineapple.

pound. They are delicious but nearly impossible to find outside of top restaurants.

Calico scallops are a small species (less than ½ inch across and taller than they are wide) harvested in the southern United States and around the world. They are inexpensive (often priced at just a few dollars per pound) but generally not terribly good. Unlike sea and bay scallops, which are harvested by hand, calicos are shucked by machine steaming. This steaming partially cooks the scallops and gives them an opaque look. Calicos are often sold as "bays," but they are not the same thing. In our kitchen tests, we found that calicos are easy to overcook and often end up with a rubbery, eraser-like texture.

We tested all three kinds of scallops on the grill. Sea scallops were the hands-down winner. Because they are much larger than bay or calico scallops, sea scallops can remain on the grill long enough to pick up some smoky flavor and caramelization. Smaller scallops overcook before they pick up any grill flavor and won't brown in the minute or two it takes for them to cook through.

In addition to choosing the right species, you should inquire about processing when purchasing scallops. Most scallops (by some estimates up to 90 percent of the retail supply) are dipped in a phosphate and water mixture that may also contain citric and sorbic acids. Processing extends shelf life but harms the flavor and texture of scallops. Their naturally delicate, sweet flavor can be masked by the bitter-tasting chemicals. Even worse, during processing scallops absorb water. Besides the obvious objections (why pay for water weight or processing that detracts from their natural flavor?), processed scallops are more difficult to cook. They contain so much water that they "steam" on the grill, so it's nearly impossible to get them to brown well. A caramelized exterior greatly enhances the natural sweetness of the scallop and provides a nice crisp contrast with the tender interior. It is a must.

By law, processed scallops must be identified as such at the wholesale level, so ask your fishmonger. Also, look at the scallops. Scallops are naturally ivory or pinkish tan; processing turns them bright white. Processed scallops are slippery and swollen and are usually sitting in milky white liquid at the store. Unprocessed scallops (also called dry scallops) are sticky and flabby. If they are surrounded by any liquid (and often they are not), the juices are clear, not white.

To preserve the creamy texture of the flesh, we like to cook scallops to medium-rare, which means the scallop is hot all the way through but the center still retains some translucence. As a scallop cooks, the soft flesh firms and you can see an opaqueness that starts at the bottom of the scallop, where it touches the grill, and slowly creeps up toward the center. The scallop is medium-rare when the sides have firmed up and all but the middle third of the scallop has turned opaque.

We tried grilling plain scallops, scallops that had been blanched (a technique advocated by several sources), scallops tossed with melted butter, and scallops tossed with oil. The plain scallops browned a bit but were dry around the edges. The blanched scallops did not caramelize at all and were terrible. The scallops tossed with melted butter or oil before being cooked browned better and tasted better than plain scallops. The edges were crisp but not dry, as was the case with plain scallops.

In most cases (and in all of the recipes that follow), we prefer the sweet, nutty flavor of butter with scallops. However, oil makes sense with certain seasonings, especially Asian ingredients.

Despite being coated with fat, scallops can still stick to the grill. Make sure the grill is extremely hot (a hot grill will promote fast browning, too) and perfectly clean. As an added precaution, wipe a wad of oiled paper towels over the grate just before cooking the scallops.

Charcoal-Grilled Scallops
SERVES 4

Ask for "dry" scallops, which haven't been treated with chemicals to extend shelf life. Dry scallops are far sweeter and less watery, so they caramelize better on the grill. To ensure that the scallops do not stick to the cooking grate, oil the grate before starting to cook.

1½   pounds large sea scallops, tough tendons removed (see illustration 1 below)
1½   tablespoons unsalted butter, melted and cooled
      Salt and ground black pepper
      Vegetable oil for the cooking grate
      Lemon wedges for serving

1. Light a large chimney starter filled with hardwood charcoal (about 6 quarts) and allow to burn until all the charcoal is covered with a layer of fine gray ash. Spread the coals evenly over the bottom of the grill. Set the cooking grate in place, cover the grill with the lid, and let the grate heat

PREPARING SCALLOPS FOR THE GRILL

1. The small, rough-textured, crescent-shaped tendon that attaches the scallop to the shell is not always removed during processing. You can readily remove any tendons that are still attached. If you don't, they will toughen slightly during cooking and are not very appealing to eat.

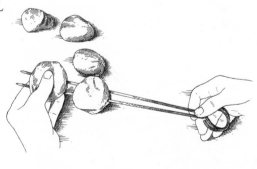

2. Thread the scallops onto doubled skewers so that the flat sides of each scallop will directly touch the cooking grate. This promotes better browning on each scallop. To turn the skewers, gently grasp one scallop with a pair of tongs and flip. (This method is the same as the one used for shrimp. See the illustration on page 264.)

up, about 5 minutes. Use a grill brush to scrape the cooking grate clean.

2. Meanwhile, toss the scallops and butter together in a medium bowl. Season with salt and pepper to taste. Thread the scallops onto doubled skewers (see illustration 2 on the facing page) so that the flat sides of the scallops will directly touch the cooking grate. The grill is ready when the coals are medium-hot. (See how to gauge heat level on page 4.)

3. Lightly dip a small wad of paper towels in vegetable oil; holding the wad with long-handled tongs, wipe the cooking grate (see page 224). Grill the scallops, uncovered, turning the skewers once (see illustration 2 on page 264), until richly caramelized on each side and medium-rare (the sides of the scallops will be firm and all but the middle third of each scallop will be opaque), 5 to 7 minutes. Serve hot or at room temperature with the lemon wedges.

➤ VARIATIONS
Gas-Grilled Scallops
Get the gas grill as hot as possible so that the scallops will brown. Also be sure to oil the cooking grate before starting to cook so that the scallops do not stick to the grate.

Turn on all the burners to high, close the lid, and heat the grill until very hot, about 15 minutes. Use a grill brush to scrape the cooking grate clean. Leave all the burners on high. Follow the recipe for Charcoal-Grilled Scallops from step 2, grilling the scallops, covered, turning the skewers once (see illustration 2 on page 264), until richly caramelized on each side and medium-rare (the sides of the scallops will be firm and all but the middle third of each scallop will be opaque), 6 to 8 minutes. Serve hot or at room temperature with the lemon wedges.

Grilled Scallops
with Mustard, Sherry, and Cream
A rich sherry cream sauce provides the perfect backdrop for sweet, grilled scallops. Whole-grain mustard and sherry vinegar add texture and brightness to the sauce.

1/2	cup dry sherry
2	medium shallots, minced
1/2	cup heavy cream
1	tablespoon whole-grain mustard
	Salt and ground black pepper
1	recipe Charcoal-Grilled or Gas-Grilled Scallops
1	teaspoon sherry vinegar
	Lemon wedges for serving

1. Follow the recipe for Charcoal-Grilled or Gas-Grilled Scallops through step 1, heating the grill as directed.

2. Meanwhile, place the sherry and shallots in a small saucepan and bring to a boil over high heat. Lower the heat to medium-high and simmer until the sherry has almost evaporated, about 7 minutes. Add the cream and mustard and simmer until slightly thickened, about 2 minutes. Season with salt and pepper to taste. Remove the pan from the heat and cover to keep warm.

3. Follow the recipe for Charcoal-Grilled or Gas-Grilled Scallops. Toss the scallops with the butter, salt, and pepper, thread on skewers, and grill as directed. Place the skewers with the grilled scallops on a platter.

4. Whisk the vinegar into the sauce, then drizzle the sauce over the grilled scallops. Serve immediately with the lemon wedges.

Grilled Scallops
with Orange-Chili Vinaigrette
For a composed salad, combine mixed greens, crumbled bacon, diced hard-cooked eggs, and thinly sliced red onion; top with the scallops. Make twice as much vinaigrette, using half for the scallops and half to toss with the salad greens.

3/4	cup orange juice
2	medium shallots, minced
1/2	teaspoon chili powder
1	tablespoon red wine vinegar
1	teaspoon honey
1/3	cup vegetable oil
2	tablespoons minced fresh cilantro leaves
	Salt and ground black pepper
1	recipe Charcoal-Grilled or Gas-Grilled Scallops

1. Follow the recipe for Charcoal-Grilled or Gas-Grilled Scallops through step 1, heating the grill as directed.

2. Meanwhile, combine the orange juice,

shallots, and chili powder in a small saucepan and bring to a boil over high heat. Lower the heat to medium-high and simmer until thick and syrupy, about 8 minutes. Transfer the mixture to a heatproof mixing bowl and cool to room temperature. Whisk in the vinegar and honey. Slowly whisk in the oil until the dressing is smooth. Stir in the cilantro and salt and pepper to taste.

3. Follow the recipe for Charcoal-Grilled or Gas-Grilled Scallops. Toss the scallops with the butter, salt, and pepper, thread on skewers, and grill as directed. Place the skewers with the grilled scallops on a platter.

4. Drizzle the dressing over the grilled scallops. Serve immediately with the lemon wedges.

CLAMS, MUSSELS, AND OYSTERS

CLAMS, MUSSELS, AND OYSTERS BELONG to the group of shellfish known as bivalves (scallops are also bivalves), and they can all be grilled in the same fashion. These two-shelled creatures are easy to cook; when they open, they are done. One of the biggest challenges when cooking bivalves is making sure they are clean. Even perfectly cooked clams and mussels can be made inedible by lingering sand. (Sand is not much of an issue with oysters as long as you scrub the shells well before cooking.)

After much trial and error in the test kitchen, we concluded that it is impossible to remove all the sand from dirty clams and mussels before cooking. We tried various soaking regimens—such as soaking in cold water for two hours, soaking in water with flour, soaking in water with cornmeal, and scrubbing and rinsing in five changes of water. None of these techniques worked.

During the course of this testing, we noticed that some varieties of clams and mussels were extremely clean and free of grit. A quick scrub of the shell exterior and these bivalves were ready for the grill. After talking to seafood experts around the country, we came to this conclusion: If you want to minimize your kitchen work and ensure that your clams and mussels are free of

grit, you must shop carefully.

Clams can be divided into two categories: hard-shell varieties (such as littlenecks and cherrystones) and soft-shell varieties (such as steamers and razor clams). Hard-shells grow along sandy beaches and bays; soft-shells in muddy tidal flats. A modest shift in location makes all the difference in the kitchen.

When harvested, hard-shells remain tightly closed. In our tests, we found that the meat inside was always free of sand. The exterior of each clam should be scrubbed under cold running water to remove any caked-on mud, but otherwise these clams can be cooked without further worry about grit.

Soft-shell clams gape when they are alive. We found that they almost always contain a lot of sand. While it's worthwhile to soak them in several batches of cold water to remove some of the sand, you can never get rid of it all. And sometimes you must rinse the cooked clams after shucking as well.

We ultimately concluded that hard-shell clams (that is, littlenecks or cherrystones) are worth the extra money at the market. Gritty clams, no matter how cheap, are inedible. Buying either littlenecks or cherrystones ensures that the clams will be clean.

DEBEARDING MUSSELS

Mussels often contain a weedy beard protruding from the crack between the two shells. It's fairly small and can be difficult to tug out of place. We have found the easiest way to perform this task is to trap the beard between the side of a small paring knife and your thumb and pull to remove it. The flat surface of the knife gives you some leverage to extract the pesky beard.

A similar distinction can be made with mussels based on how and where they are grown. Most mussels are now farmed, either on ropes or along seabeds. (You may also see "wild" mussels at the market. These mussels are caught the old-fashioned way—by dredging along the sea floor. In our tests, we found them extremely muddy and practically inedible.) Rope-cultured mussels can cost up to twice as much as wild or bottom-cultured mussels, but we found them to be free of grit. Since mussels are relatively inexpensive (no more than a few dollars per pound), we think clean mussels are worth the extra money. Look for tags, usually attached to the bags of mussels, indicating how and where the mussels were grown.

Sand is not an issue when buying oysters, but careful shopping is still very important. In general, we prefer oysters from cold northern waters, which tend to be briny and have a flavor that's more crisp than that of oysters from warmer southern waters.

When shopping, look for tightly closed clams, mussels, and oysters (avoid any that are gaping; they may be dying or dead). Clams need only be scrubbed. Mussels may need scrubbing as well as debearding. Simply grab onto the weedy protrusion and pull it out from between the shells and discard (see the illustration on the facing page). Don't debeard mussels until you are ready to cook them, as debearding can cause mussels to die. Mussels or clams kept in sealed plastic bags or under water will also die. Keep them in a bowl in the refrigerator and use them within a day or two for best results.

While steaming is the easiest way to cook clams and mussels (oysters are often eaten raw on the half shell), grilling these bivalves is an interesting option, especially for summer entertaining. If you are cooking outside and want to throw a few clams or mussels on the grill to serve as an appetizer, we think you will be pleased with the results.

We found that it is important not to move the shellfish around on the grill and to handle them carefully once they open. You want to preserve the natural juices, so when the clams or mussels open, transfer them with tongs to a platter, holding them steady so as not to spill any of the liquid.

Charcoal-Grilled Clams, Mussels, or Oysters

SERVES 4 TO 6 AS AN APPETIZER

We often like to throw clams or mussels on the grill and cook them just until they open. Don't move the shellfish around too much or you risk spilling the liquid out of the shells. This cooking method delivers pure clam, mussel, or oyster flavor. If you like, serve with lemon wedges, a bottle of Tabasco or other hot sauce, and some Fresh Tomato Salsa (see page 390).

24   clams or oysters, or 30 to 35 mussels (about 2 pounds), scrubbed and debearded (see the illustration on the facing page) if cooking mussels
Lemon wedges, hot sauce, and/or salsa (optional)

1. Light a large chimney starter filled with hardwood charcoal (about 6 quarts) and allow to burn until all the charcoal is covered with a layer of fine gray ash. Build a single-level fire by spreading the coals evenly over the bottom of the grill. Set the cooking grate in place, cover the grill with the lid, and let the grate heat up, about 5 minutes. Use a grill brush to scrape the cooking grate clean. The grill is ready when the coals are medium-hot. (See how to gauge heat level on page 4.)

2. Place the shellfish directly on the cooking grate. Grill, uncovered and without turning, until the shellfish open, 3 to 5 minutes for mussels and oysters or 6 to 10 minutes for clams.

3. With tongs, carefully transfer the opened shellfish to a flat serving platter, trying to preserve the juices. Discard the top shells and loosen the meat in the bottom shells before serving, if desired (see the illustration on page 270). Serve with the lemon wedges, hot sauce, and/or salsa passed separately.

➤ VARIATIONS

Gas-Grilled Clams, Mussels, or Oysters
The shellfish take slightly longer to cook on a gas grill.

Turn on all the burners to high, close the lid, and heat the grill until very hot, about 15 minutes. Use a grill brush to scrape the cooking grate clean. Leave the burners on high. Follow the recipe for

Charcoal-Grilled Clams, Mussels, or Oysters from step 2, grilling the shellfish, with the cover down, without turning, until the shellfish open, 4 to 6 minutes for mussels and oysters or 7 to 10 minutes for clams. Plate and serve as directed.

Grilled Clams, Mussels, or Oysters with Spicy Lemon Butter

Have your guests remove the meat of the shellfish with small forks and dip it into this tangy, spicy butter.

4	tablespoons (¹/₂ stick) unsalted butter
I	tablespoon hot sauce
I	teaspoon juice from I lemon
¹/₄	teaspoon salt
I	recipe Charcoal-Grilled or Gas-Grilled Clams, Mussels, or Oysters (without the hot sauce or salsa)

1. Melt the butter in a small saucepan over medium-low heat. Remove the pan from the heat and add the hot sauce, lemon juice, and salt. Keep the sauce warm.

2. Follow the recipe for Charcoal-Grilled or Gas-Grilled Clams, Mussels, or Oysters. Discard the top shells when the cooking is done. Pour the

SERVING CLAMS, MUSSELS, AND OYSTERS

The easiest way to serve grilled clams, mussels, or oysters is to divide them among small plates and give each person a small fork. However, if you want guests to eat them while milling about the grill, try the following method.

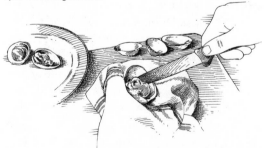

Holding each clam, mussel, or oyster in a kitchen towel as it comes off the grill, pull off and discard the top shell, then slide a paring knife under the meat to detach it from the bottom shell. By the time you have done this to each clam, mussel, or oyster, the shells should have cooled enough to permit everyone to pick them up and slurp the meat directly from the shells.

warm butter mixture into a small serving bowl. Serve the shellfish with the spicy lemon butter for dipping, as well as with the lemon wedges.

Grilled Clams, Mussels, or Oysters with Tangy Soy-Citrus Sauce

A combination of lemon and lime juices is added to light soy sauce to make a fresh, straightforward sauce for shellfish.

¹/₂	cup light soy sauce
I	tablespoon juice from I lemon
I	tablespoon juice from I lime
I	scallion, sliced thin
I	teaspoon grated fresh ginger
I	recipe Charcoal-Grilled or Gas-Grilled Clams, Mussels, or Oysters (without the lemon wedges, hot sauce, or salsa)

1. Combine the soy sauce, citrus juices, scallion, and ginger in a small bowl. Set the sauce aside.

2. Follow the recipe for Charcoal-Grilled or Gas-Grilled Clams, Mussels, or Oysters. Discard the top shells when the cooking is done. Drizzle the sauce over the shellfish and serve immediately.

Grilled Clams, Mussels, or Oysters with Mignonette Sauce

Bright and clean, mignonette sauce brings out the best in briny, fresh shellfish. One warning: Use this tangy sauce sparingly. A little goes a long way.

¹/₂	cup red wine vinegar
2	medium shallots, chopped fine, or ¹/₄ cup minced red onion
2	tablespoons juice from I lemon
I¹/₂	tablespoons minced fresh parsley leaves
I	recipe Charcoal-Grilled or Gas-Grilled Clams, Mussels, or Oysters (without the lemon wedges, hot sauce, or salsa)

1. Mix together the vinegar, shallots, lemon juice, and parsley in a small serving bowl. Set the sauce aside.

2. Follow the recipe for Charcoal-Grilled or Gas-Grilled Clams, Mussels, or Oysters. Discard the top shells when the cooking is done. Serve with mignonette sauce for dipping.

INGREDIENTS: Red Wine Vinegar

The source of that notable edge you taste when sampling any red wine vinegar is acetic acid, the chief flavor component in all vinegar and the byproduct of the bacterium *Acetobacter aceti,* which feeds on the alcohol in wine. The process of converting red wine to vinegar once took months, if not years, but now, with the help of an acetator (a machine that speeds the metabolism of the bacteria), red wine vinegar can be made in less than 24 hours.

Does this faster, cheaper method—the one used to make most supermarket brands—produce inferior red wine vinegar? Or is this a case in which modern technology trumps Old World craftsmanship, which is still employed by makers of the more expensive red wine vinegars? To find out, we included in our tasting vinegars made using the fast process (acetator) and the slow process (often called the Orleans method, after the city in France where it was developed).

We first tasted 10 nationally available supermarket brands in two ways: by dipping sugar cubes in each brand and sucking out the vinegar (to cut down on palate fatigue) and by making a simple vinaigrette with each and tasting it on iceberg lettuce. We then pitted the winners of the supermarket tasting against four high-end red wine vinegars.

Although no single grape variety is thought to make the best red wine vinegar, we were curious to find out if our tasters were unwittingly fond of vinegars made from the same grape. We sent the vinegars to a food lab for an anthocyanin pigment profile, a test that can detect the 10 common pigments found in red grapes. Although the lab was unable to distinguish specific grape varieties (Cabernet, Merlot, Pinot Noir, Zinfandel, and the like), it did provide us with an interesting piece of information: Some of the vinegars weren't made with wine grapes (known as *Vitus vinifera*), but with less expensive Concord-type grapes, the kind used to make Welch's grape juice.

Did the vinegars made with grape juice fare poorly, as might be expected? Far from it. The taste-test results were both shocking and unambiguous: Concord-type grapes not only do just fine when it comes to making vinegar, they may be a key element in the success of the top-rated brands in our tasting. Spectrum, our overall winner, is made from a mix of wine grapes and Concord grapes. Pompeian, which came in second among the supermarket brands, is made entirely of Concord-type grapes.

What else might contribute to the flavor of these vinegars?

One possibility, we thought, was the way in which the acetic acid is developed. Manufacturers that mass-produce vinegar generally prefer not to use the Orleans method because it's slow and expensive. Spectrum red wine vinegar is produced with the Orleans method, but Pompeian is made in an acetator in less than 24 hours.

What, then, can explain why Spectrum and Pompeian won the supermarket tasting and beat the other gourmet vinegars? Oddly enough, for a food that defines sourness, the answer seems to lie in its sweetness. It turns out that Americans like their vinegar sweet (think balsamic vinegar).

The production of Spectrum is outsourced to a small manufacturer in Modena, Italy, that makes generous use of the Trebbiano grape, the same grape used to make balsamic vinegar. The Trebbiano, which is a white wine grape, gives Spectrum the sweetness our tasters admired. Pompeian vinegar is finished with a touch of sherry vinegar, added to give the red vinegar a more fruity, well-rounded flavor. Also significant to our results may be that both Spectrum and Pompeian start with wines containing Concord grapes, which are sweet enough to be a common choice when making jams and jellies.

When pitted against gourmet vinegars, Spectrum and Pompeian still came out on top. Which red wine vinegar should you buy? The answer comes faster than it takes an acetator to convert red wine to vinegar: Skip the specialty shop and head to the supermarket.

THE BEST RED WINE VINEGARS
Spectrum and Pompeian vinegars are available in supermarkets and bested gourmet brands costing eight times as much.

LOBSTERS

THE IDEA OF GRILLING LOBSTERS IS CERTAINLY appealing. Smoke is an ideal complement to sweet, rich lobster meat. The problem is keeping the lobster on the grill long enough for the meat to pick up some grill flavor without drying out.

Lobsters must be split in half lengthwise before being grilled. If grilled whole, the shell will char a bit but the meat will steam and ultimately taste no different from a lobster cooked in a pot. The issue of splitting aside, we had many questions about the best way to grill a lobster. What size lobster is best for grilling? Should it be grilled plain or basted with butter or oil? Will the claws (which are not open) cook at the same rate as the exposed meat, or do they need some help?

Our initial tests clearly demonstrated the advantages of working with medium-large lobsters. Small lobsters spent so little time on the grill that they picked up almost no smoke flavor. Large lobsters were hard to position on the grill. In fact,

two split 3-pounders were hanging off the sides of our gas grill. The ideal lobster for grilling weighs between 1½ and 2 pounds—big enough to spend a decent amount of time on the grill but still small enough to fit on most grills.

We always remove the stomach sac and intestinal tract when cooking split lobsters. Grilling is no exception. We wondered if we should do something with the tomalley. When roasting lobsters, we often enrich the tomalley with bread crumbs and butter. The same idea worked beautifully on the grill, as long as we waited to add the tomalley mixture until the lobster had been flipped cut-side up.

As might be expected, we found that lobsters grilled without butter were dry. A liberal basting with butter helped keep the meat tender and added a delicious flavor.

The various recipes we consulted were split on the issue of turning the lobsters. Some said it was best to cook the lobsters cut-side down for maximum browning. Some said it was best to cook the

PREPARING LOBSTERS FOR GRILLING

1. With the blade of a chef's knife facing the head, kill the lobster by plunging the knife into the body at the point where the shell forms a "T." Move the blade down straight through the head.

2. Holding the upper body with one hand and positioning the knife blade so that it faces the tail end, cut through the body toward the tail, making sure to cut all the way through the shell. You should have two halves now.

3. Use a spoon to remove and discard the stomach sac.

4. Remove and discard the intestinal tract.

5. Scoop out the green tomalley and transfer to a medium bowl.

6. To accelerate cooking of the claws, which cook more slowly than the rest of the lobster, use the back of a chef's knife to whack one side of each claw to make a small opening.

lobsters cut-side up for maximum juice retention. Other sources argued for a middle ground.

We grilled lobsters cut-side up for the entire cooking time as well as cut-side down for the entire cooking time and found both methods to be problematic. The meat needs some browning for flavor, but cooking the lobsters cut-side down does promote the loss of juices and toughens the tail meat. As a compromise, we started the lobsters cut-side down, cooked them for just two minutes to keep moisture loss to a minimum, then flipped the lobsters cut-side up and continued grilling. This method also afforded us an opportunity to add the tomalley mixture and give it plenty of time to heat through.

This regimen worked fine for the tomalley, body, and tail, but the claws were a problem. Because they were not cut in half, as was the rest of the lobster, they took longer to cook. Several times we removed lobsters from the grill thinking they were perfectly cooked only to find that the claws were almost raw. Lobster sushi is an expensive mistake.

Jasper White, a consulting editor for *Cook's Illustrated* magazine and the author of *Lobster at Home* (Scribner, 1998), the definitive book on lobster cookery, suggested cracking one side of each claw to speed their cooking. (Cracking just one side of the claw minimizes the loss of juices.) He also suggested covering the claws with a disposable aluminum pie plate or roasting pan to ensure that they would be cooked through. We found that both tips worked beautifully.

Our final experiment revolved around the heat level of the grill. We wondered if there was any advantage to a medium or low fire. We found that there was not. We discovered that grilling over a medium-hot fire cooks the lobsters quickly, which lets them retain more moisture than when cooked over cooler fires. A split 1½-pound lobster can be done in as little as six minutes over a blazing fire.

~❧~

Charcoal-Grilled Lobsters

SERVES 2 AS A MAIN COURSE
OR 4 AS AN APPETIZER

Be sure not to overcook the lobster; like other shellfish, lobster meat gets tough when cooked for too long. The lobsters are done when the tomalley mixture is bubbling and

the tail meat has turned a creamy opaque white. Have all the garlic and parsley minced and the bread crumbs ready before you start the grill. For the bread crumbs, use bread that is a few days old, cut it into ½-inch cubes, and pulse the cubes in a food processor until they turn into fine crumbs. Don't halve the lobsters until the charcoal has been lit. You will need two disposable aluminum pie pans or small roasting pans for this recipe.

6	tablespoons (¾ stick) unsalted butter, melted
2	medium garlic cloves, minced or pressed through a garlic press (about 2 teaspoons)
2	live lobsters (each 1½ to 2 pounds)
¼	cup fresh bread crumbs
2	tablespoons minced fresh parsley leaves
	Salt and ground black pepper
	Vegetable oil for the cooking grate
	Lemon wedges for serving

1. Light a large chimney starter filled with hardwood charcoal (about 6 quarts) and allow to burn until all the charcoal is covered with a layer of fine gray ash. Build a single-level fire by spreading the coals evenly over the bottom of the grill. Set the cooking grate in place, cover the grill with the lid, and let the grate heat up, about 5 minutes. Use a grill brush to scrape the cooking grate clean. The grill is ready when the coals are medium-hot. (See how to gauge heat level on page 4.)

2. Meanwhile, mix together the butter and garlic in a small bowl. Split the lobsters in half lengthwise, according to the illustrations on the facing page, removing the stomach sac and intestinal tract. Scoop out the green tomalley and place it in a medium bowl. Using the back of a knife, whack one side of each claw, just to make an opening (this will help accelerate cooking). Add the bread crumbs, parsley, and 2 tablespoons of the melted garlic butter to the bowl with the tomalley. Use a fork to mix together, breaking up the tomalley at the same time. Season lightly with salt and pepper to taste.

3. Season the tail meat with salt and pepper to taste. Brush the lobster halves with some of the garlic butter. Take the lobsters to the grill on a large tray. Lightly dip a small wad of paper

towels in vegetable oil; holding the wad with long-handled tongs, wipe the cooking grate (see page 224).

4. Place the lobsters on the grill shell-side up. Grill, uncovered, for 2 minutes. Transfer the lobsters to the tray, turning them shell-side down. Spoon the tomalley mixture evenly into the open cavities of all four lobster halves. Place the lobsters back onto the grill, shell-side down. Baste the lobsters with the remaining garlic butter and cover the claws with disposable aluminum pie plates or roasting pans. Grill until the tail meat turns an opaque creamy white and the tomalley mixture is bubbly and has begun to brown on top, 4 to 6 minutes.

5. Serve the lobsters immediately with the lemon wedges. Use lobster picks to get the meat from inside the claws and knuckles.

➤ VARIATIONS
Gas-Grilled Lobsters
Even though the grill cover is down, you should still use two disposable aluminum pie plates or roasting pans to cover the claws as they cook.

1. Turn on all the burners to high, close the lid, and heat the grill until very hot, about 15 minutes. Use a grill brush to scrape the cooking grate clean. Leave the burners on high.

2. Follow steps 2 and 3 of the recipe for Charcoal-Grilled Lobsters. In step 4, grill the lobsters, covered, for 2 minutes. Transfer the lobsters to the tray, turning them shell-side down. Spoon the tomalley mixture evenly into the open cavities of all four lobster halves. Place the lobsters back onto the grill, shell-side down. Baste the lobsters with the remaining garlic butter and cover the claws with disposable aluminum pie plates or roasting pans. Close the grill lid and grill until the tail meat turns an opaque creamy white color and the tomalley mixture is bubbly and has begun to brown on top, 5 to 7 minutes. Proceed with step 5 of the recipe.

Grilled Lobsters with Tarragon-Chive Butter
Other fresh herbs, including chervil or cilantro, can be used to flavor the garlic butter.

Follow the recipe for Charcoal-Grilled or Gas-Grilled Lobsters, adding 2 teaspoons minced fresh chives and 1 teaspoon minced fresh tarragon leaves to the garlic butter. Replace the parsley in the bread-crumb mixture with 2 tablespoons minced fresh chives and 2 teaspoons minced fresh tarragon leaves.

MAKING FRESH BREAD CRUMBS
Fresh bread crumbs are far superior to bland, overly fine commercial crumbs. Any stray hunk of good-quality bread (preferably made without sweetener, seeds, or other extraneous ingredients) can be turned into fresh crumbs. Country white bread, plain Italian bread, and baguettes are ideal. Slightly stale bread is easier to cut, but crumbs can be made from fresh bread. You can use the crumbs as is or toast them in a dry skillet over medium heat until golden brown.

1. Slice off and discard the bottom crust of the bread if it is tough and overbaked.

2. Slice the bread into ³/₈-inch-thick pieces. Cut these slices into ³/₈-inch strips, then cut these into cubes and chop until you have small pieces about the size of lemon seeds.

3. To make the crumbs in a food processor, cut the trimmed loaf into 1-inch cubes, then pulse the cubes in a food processor to the desired crumb size.

Grilled Lobsters with Chili Butter

Serve with lime wedges instead of lemon.

Follow the recipe for Charcoal-Grilled or Gas-Grilled Lobsters, adding 1½ teaspoons chili powder and ¼ to ½ teaspoon cayenne pepper to the garlic butter. Serve the lobsters with lime wedges instead of the lemon wedges.

SOFT-SHELL CRABS

THERE ARE DOZENS OF SPECIES OF CRAB, BUT the blue crab, which is found in waters along the East Coast, is the most common variety. A soft-shell crab is a blue crab that has been taken out of the water just after shedding its shell. At this brief stage of its life, the whole crab, with its new, soft, gray skin, is almost completely edible and fabulously delicious.

For the cook, soft-shells are a wonderfully immediate experience; once cleaned, they demand to be cooked and eaten on the spot, so they offer a very direct taste of the sea. Because they must be cooked so quickly after they are killed and cleaned, home cooks have an advantage over restaurants. We're convinced that the best way to enjoy soft-shells is to cook them at home, where you can be sure to eat them within minutes of cleaning them.

The goal in preparing soft-shells is to get them crisp. The legs should crunch delicately, while the body should provide a contrast between its thin, crisp outer skin and the soft, rich interior that explodes juicily in the mouth. Frying delivers these results, but it is better suited to restaurants. Air pockets and water in the crab cause a lot of dangerous splattering. Grilling is a better choice for home cooks because it is safe and clean.

Grilling crabs is fairly straightforward. Since the crabs should be crisp, it's no surprise that high heat delivers the best results. We grilled plain crabs as well as crabs basted with melted butter and oil. The plain crabs did not crisp up as well as those basted with fat. In addition, the plain crabs stuck a bit to the grill. We felt that the flavor of melted butter tasted better with the crabs than oil. However, oil is fine for an Asian variation with a ginger and garlic sauce.

We tried soaking the crabs in milk before grilling (a tip advocated by some experts) and found that the crabs browned slightly better but that the difference was too slight to warrant the soaking time.

If you're serving crabs as a main course, count on two crabs per person. Serve one crab per person as an appetizer.

CLEANING SOFT-SHELL CRABS

1. Don't clean crabs until you are ready to cook them. Start by cutting off the crab's mouth with kitchen scissors; the mouth is the first part of the shell to harden. You can also cut off the eyes at the same time.

2. Next, lift the pointed side of the crab and cut out the spongy off-white gills underneath; the gills are fibrous, watery, and unpleasant to eat.

3. Finally, turn the crab on its back and cut off the triangular, or T-shaped, "apron flap."

Charcoal-Grilled Soft-Shell Crabs

SERVES 4 AS A MAIN COURSE
OR 8 AS AN APPETIZER

Grilling is a great way to prepare crab at home, highlighting the sweetness and freshness of the crab without the fuss or mess of frying. The secret to great soft-shells is to make sure that the thin shells become crisp and appealing. In this recipe, butter and cooking over a hot fire crisp the thin shell beautifully. If you like the flavor of garlic, add 1 clove, very finely minced, to the melted butter.

8   medium-to-large soft-shell crabs, cleaned (see the illustrations on page 275)

4   tablespoons (1/2 stick) unsalted butter, melted
    Salt
    Lemon wedges for serving

1. Light a large chimney starter filled with hardwood charcoal (about 6 quarts) and allow to burn until all the charcoal is covered with a layer of fine gray ash. Build a single-level fire by spreading the coals evenly over the bottom of the grill. Set the cooking grate in place, cover the grill with the lid, and let the grate heat up, about 5 minutes. Use a grill brush to scrape the cooking grate clean. The grill is ready when the coals are medium-hot. (To gauge heat level, see page 4.)

2. Brush both sides of the crabs with butter and season with salt to taste. Grill the crabs, uncovered, turning them every 2 minutes and brushing often with butter, until the shells turn orange and spotty brown and the crabs are cooked through, about 6 minutes for medium crabs, and up to 9 minutes for larger crabs. Serve immediately with the lemon wedges.

➤ VARIATIONS

Gas-Grilled Soft-Shell Crabs

1. Turn on all the burners to high, close the lid, and heat the grill until very hot, about 15 minutes.

Use a grill brush to scrape the cooking grate clean. Leave the burners on high.

2. Follow step 2 of the recipe for Charcoal-Grilled Soft-Shell Crabs, grilling the crabs, covered, turning them every few minutes and brushing often with butter, until the shells turn orange and spotty brown and the crabs are cooked through, about 7 minutes for medium crabs, and up to 10 minutes for larger crabs. Serve immediately with the lemon wedges.

Grilled Soft-Shell Crabs with Spicy Butter

Follow the recipe for Charcoal-Grilled or Gas-Grilled Soft-Shell Crabs, stirring 1 tablespoon hot sauce into the melted butter.

Grilled Soft-Shell Crabs with Tartar Sauce

Cornichons are tiny, intensely flavored pickles available jarred in most supermarkets and sold by the pound in delis. If you like, add 1 tablespoon minced fresh tarragon to give the tartar sauce a bright, anise flavor.

TARTAR SAUCE

3/4   cup mayonnaise

1 1/2 tablespoons minced cornichons (about 3 large), plus 1 teaspoon cornichon juice

1   tablespoon minced scallion

1   tablespoon minced red onion

1   tablespoon drained capers, minced

1   recipe Charcoal-Grilled or Gas-Grilled Soft-Shell Crabs

1. Mix together the mayonnaise, cornichons and juice, scallion, red onion, and capers in a medium bowl. Cover and refrigerate the tartar sauce until the flavors blend, at least 30 minutes or up to 2 days.

2. Follow the recipe for Charcoal-Grilled or Gas-Grilled Soft-Shell Crabs. Serve the grilled crabs with tartar sauce on the side.

CHICKEN ALLA DIAVOLA **PAGE 188**

GRILL-ROASTED WHOLE CHICKEN **PAGE 191**

THAI GRILLED CHICKEN BREASTS WITH SPICY, SWEET, AND SOUR DIPPING SAUCE **PAGE 177**

SPICE RUBS FOR GRILLED CHICKEN **PAGES 382–384**

GRILLED CHICKEN KEBABS WITH GARLIC AND HERB MARINADE **PAGE 163**

281

GRILLED CHICKEN BREAST WITH BARBECUE SAUCE AND SESAME-LEMON CUCUMBER SALAD **PAGES 170 AND 351**

GRILLED GLAZED SALMON FILLETS **PAGE 236**

SALSA VERDE **PAGE 397**

284

GRILLED SHRIMP WITH SOUTHWESTERN FLAVORS **PAGE 263**

GRILLED TUNA STEAKS WITH WATERCRESS, PARSLEY, AND SPICED VINAIGRETTE **PAGE 244**

BARBECUED SALMON **PAGE 239**

GRILLED PIZZA WITH FRESH TOMATOES AND BASIL **PAGE 335**

GRILLED POTATO AND ARUGULA SALAD WITH DIJON MUSTARD VINAIGRETTE **PAGE 320**

289

SPANISH-STYLE GRILLED BELL PEPPERS WITH GREEN OLIVES AND SHERRY VINEGAR **PAGE 316**

290

QUICK BARBECUE SAUCE **PAGE 387**

291

GRILLED CORN WITH SPICY CHILI BUTTER **PAGE 299**

292

8

VEGETABLES

VEGETABLES

GRILLED ASPARAGUS 296
    Grilled Asparagus with Grilled Lemon Vinaigrette
    Grilled Asparagus with Orange-Sesame Vinaigrette
    Grilled Asparagus with Peanut Sauce
    Grilled Asparagus with Rosemary and Goat Cheese
    Grilled Asparagus with Blue Cheese and Anchovy Dressing
    Grilled Asparagus with Almonds, Green Olives, and Sherry Vinaigrette

GRILLED CORN 299
    Grilled Corn with Spicy Chili Butter
    Grilled Corn with Soy-Honey Glaze
    Grilled Corn with Herb Butter
    Grilled Corn with Garlic Butter and Cheese

GRILLED EGGPLANT 301
    Grilled Eggplant with Basil Oil
    Grilled Eggplant with Cherry Tomato and Cilantro Vinaigrette
    Grilled Eggplant with Ginger and Soy
    Grilled Eggplant with Sweet Miso Glaze
    Grilled Curried Eggplant

BABA GHANOUSH 303
    Baba Ghanoush with Sautéed Onion

GRILLED BELGIAN ENDIVE 304
    Grilled Belgian Endive with Lemon-Garlic Butter
    Grilled Belgian Endive with Mustard Dressing and Parmesan
    Grilled Belgian Endive with Balsamic Dressing

GRILLED FENNEL 306
    Grilled Fennel with Grapefruit Vinaigrette
    Grilled Fennel with Mint and Tarragon Vinaigrette
    Grilled Fennel with Tarragon and Shallot
    Grilled Fennel with Citrus

GRILL-ROASTED GARLIC 309

GRILLED GREEN BEANS 309

GRILLED PORTOBELLOS 310
    Grilled Portobellos with Tarragon
    Grilled Portobellos with Garlic, Rosemary, and Balsamic Vinegar

GRILLED PORTOBELLO SANDWICHES
WITH BOURSIN CHEESE AND TOMATOES 312

GRILLED ONIONS 313
    Grilled Onions with Garlic and Thyme
    Grilled Red Onion and Tomato Salad
    Grilled Onion Relish

GRILL-ROASTED BELL PEPPERS 316

GRILLED BELL PEPPERS 316
    Grilled Bell Peppers with Mint and Feta
    Spanish-Style Grilled Bell Peppers with Green Olives and Sherry Vinegar
    Grilled Bell Peppers with Black Olives and Basil

BASTING OILS FOR VEGETABLES 317
    Garlic Basting Oil
    Lemon-Rosemary Basting Oil

GRILLED PLANTAINS 318
    Grilled Plantains with Lime and Mint

GRILLED POTATOES FOR SALAD 319
    Grilled Potato and Arugula Salad with Dijon Mustard Vinaigrette
    Spicy Grilled Potato Salad with Corn and Chiles
    German-Style Grilled Potato Salad

GRILL-ROASTED SWEET POTATOES 321
    Grill-Roasted Sweet Potatoes with Sweet Sesame and Soy Sauce

GRILLED ROUND OR PLUM TOMATOES 322

GRILLED CHERRY TOMATOES 322
    Grilled Cherry Tomatoes with Greek Flavors

GRILLED BUTTERNUT SQUASH 323
    Spicy Grilled Butternut Squash with Garlic and Rosemary

GRILLED ZUCCHINI OR SUMMER SQUASH 325
    Grilled Zucchini or Summer Squash with Tomatoes and Basil
    Grilled Zucchini or Summer Squash with Capers and Oregano

GLAZES AND SAUCES FOR GRILLED FRUIT 326
    Rum-Molasses Glaze
    Sour Orange Glaze
    Simplified Caramel Sauce
    Sweet and Spicy Hoisin Glaze

GRILLED VEGETABLES AND FRUITS MAKE GREAT accompaniments with plenty of bright, intense flavors. They are also quick and easy to prepare. In general, vegetables should be cut to expose the maximum surface area to the grill, which helps them cook quickly and thoroughly. Smaller vegetables, such as cherry tomatoes and button mushrooms, need to be skewered to keep them from falling through the grill, as do slices of some larger vegetables, like onions.

Once most vegetables and fruits are streaked with grill marks, they are done. Vegetables and fruits will pick up any off flavors from the grill, so make sure the cooking grate is clean.

Since vegetables and fruits are usually grilled along with something else, we have not given separate charcoal and gas variations in this chapter. Most likely you will be lighting a fire to grill fish, chicken, or meat, and the vegetables and fruit will need to work within the constraints of that fire. In any case, the timing for grilling vegetables and fruits is the same on both charcoal and gas; just remember to keep the lid down when cooking over gas and up when cooking over charcoal.

ASPARAGUS

ASPARAGUS PRESENTS ONLY ONE PREPARATION issue: Should the spears be peeled, or is it better to discard the tough, fibrous ends entirely? In our tests, we found that peeled asparagus have a silkier texture, but we preferred the contrast between the crisp peel and tender inner flesh of the unpeeled asparagus. Peeling is also a lot of work. We prefer to simply snap off the tough ends and proceed with cooking.

The intense dry heat of the grill concentrates the flavor of the asparagus, and the exterior caramelization makes the spears especially sweet. The result is asparagus with a heightened and, we think, delicious flavor.

Grilled Asparagus

SERVES 4

Thick spears will burn on the surface before they cook through. Use spears no thicker than ⅝ inch.

1½ pounds asparagus, tough ends snapped off (see the illustration below)
1 tablespoon extra-virgin olive oil
 Salt and ground black pepper

1. Toss the asparagus with the oil in a medium bowl or on a rimmed baking sheet.

2. Grill the asparagus over a medium-hot fire (see how to gauge heat level on page 4), turning once, until tender and streaked with light grill marks, 5 to 7 minutes. Transfer the grilled asparagus to a platter. Season to taste with salt and pepper. Serve hot, warm, or at room temperature.

➤ VARIATIONS

Grilled Asparagus with Grilled Lemon Vinaigrette
Grilling the lemon not only mellows its flavors but also helps to release its juices.

1 lemon, cut in half crosswise
6 tablespoons extra-virgin olive oil
1 medium shallot, minced
½ teaspoon minced fresh thyme leaves
 Salt and ground black pepper
1 recipe Grilled Asparagus

1. Place the lemon halves on the grill, cut-side down, and grill until tender and streaked with light grill marks, about 3 minutes. When the lemon is cool enough to handle, squeeze and strain the juice into a medium nonreactive bowl;

TRIMMING TOUGH ENDS FROM ASPARAGUS

In our tests, we found that the tough, woody part of the stem will break off in just the right place if you hold the spear the right way. With one hand, hold the asparagus about halfway down the stalk; with the thumb and index fingers of the other hand, hold the spear about an inch up from the bottom. Bend the stalk until it snaps.

you should have about 2 tablespoons. Whisk in the olive oil, shallot, and thyme. Season with salt and pepper to taste.

2. Arrange the grilled asparagus on a platter and drizzle with the dressing. Serve immediately.

Grilled Asparagus with Orange–Sesame Vinaigrette

If tahini is unavailable, increase the sesame seeds to 3 tablespoons and the sesame oil to 1 teaspoon; instead of whisking the ingredients together, pulse them in a food processor for 10 seconds.

6	tablespoons extra-virgin olive oil
I	tablespoon sesame seeds, toasted in a small dry skillet over medium heat until fragrant, about 4 minutes
I	tablespoon juice and I teaspoon grated zest from I orange
I	tablespoon rice vinegar
I	teaspoon soy sauce
I	teaspoon tahini
¹/₂	teaspoon minced fresh ginger
¹/₂	teaspoon toasted sesame oil
	Salt and ground black pepper
I	recipe Grilled Asparagus

1. Combine the olive oil, toasted sesame seeds, orange juice and zest, vinegar, soy sauce, tahini, ginger, and sesame oil in a medium bowl and whisk thoroughly to combine. Season with salt and pepper to taste.

2. Arrange the grilled asparagus on a serving platter and drizzle with the dressing. Serve immediately.

Grilled Asparagus with Peanut Sauce

The aggressive flavors in this Thai-style sauce work well with grilled asparagus.

I	tablespoon smooth peanut butter
I	tablespoon toasted sesame oil
I	tablespoon water
I¹/₂	teaspoons soy sauce
I¹/₂	teaspoons rice vinegar
I¹/₂	teaspoons minced fresh ginger
I	medium garlic clove, minced or pressed through a garlic press (about I teaspoon)

	Salt and ground black pepper
I¹/₂	pounds asparagus, tough ends snapped off (see the illustration on the facing page)
I	tablespoon minced fresh cilantro leaves

1. Whisk the peanut butter, oil, water, soy sauce, vinegar, ginger, garlic, and salt and pepper to taste together in a small bowl. Toss the asparagus with half of the peanut dressing in a medium bowl or on a rimmed baking sheet. Whisk the cilantro into the remaining dressing and set it aside.

2. Grill the asparagus over a medium-hot fire (see how to gauge heat level on page 4), turning once, until tender and streaked with light grill marks, 5 to 7 minutes.

3. Transfer the grilled asparagus to a platter. Toss the asparagus with the remaining dressing. Adjust the seasonings and serve hot, warm, or at room temperature.

Grilled Asparagus with Rosemary and Goat Cheese

The woodsy flavor of rosemary highlights the grilled flavor of the asparagus.

2	tablespoons extra-virgin olive oil
I	tablespoon juice from I lemon
I	medium garlic clove, minced or pressed through a garlic press (about I teaspoon)
¹/₂	teaspoon minced fresh rosemary
	Salt and ground black pepper
I¹/₂	pounds asparagus, tough ends snapped off (see the illustration the facing page)
I	ounce goat cheese, crumbled (about ¹/₄ cup)

1. Whisk the oil, lemon juice, garlic, rosemary, and salt and pepper to taste together in a small bowl. Toss the asparagus with 1 tablespoon of the dressing in a medium bowl or on a rimmed baking sheet.

2. Grill the asparagus over a medium-hot fire (see how to gauge heat level on page 4), turning once, until tender and streaked with light grill marks, 5 to 7 minutes.

3. Transfer the grilled asparagus to a platter. Toss the asparagus with the remaining dressing. Adjust the seasonings, sprinkle with the cheese, and serve hot, warm, or at room temperature.

Grilled Asparagus with Blue Cheese and Anchovy Dressing

A little blue cheese goes a long way in this dish. If you prefer, use feta cheese instead.

2	tablespoons extra-virgin olive oil
I	tablespoon juice from I lemon
2	anchovy fillets, minced
I	medium garlic clove, minced or pressed through a garlic press (about I teaspoon) Salt and ground black pepper
I¹/₂	pounds asparagus, tough ends snapped off (see the illustration on page 296)
I	ounce blue cheese, crumbled (about ¹/₄ cup)

1. Whisk the oil, lemon juice, anchovies, garlic, and salt and pepper to taste together in a small bowl. Toss the asparagus with 1 tablespoon of the dressing in a medium bowl or on a rimmed baking sheet.

2. Grill the asparagus over a medium-hot fire (see how to gauge heat level on page 4), turning once, until tender and streaked with light grill marks, 5 to 7 minutes.

3. Transfer the grilled asparagus to a platter. Toss the asparagus with the remaining dressing. Adjust the seasonings, sprinkle with the cheese, and serve hot, warm, or at room temperature.

Grilled Asparagus with Almonds, Green Olives, and Sherry Vinaigrette

Spanish flavors make this dish an excellent addition to an antipasto spread.

2	tablespoons extra-virgin olive oil
2	tablespoons minced onion
I	tablespoon sherry vinegar
I	medium garlic clove, minced or pressed through a garlic press (about I teaspoon)
¹/₂	teaspoon ground cumin Salt and ground black pepper
I¹/₂	pounds asparagus, tough ends snapped off (see the illustration on page 296)
¹/₄	cup sliced almonds, toasted in a small dry skillet over medium heat until fragrant, about 4 minutes
2	tablespoons pitted and chopped green olives

1. Whisk the oil, onion, vinegar, garlic, cumin, and salt and pepper to taste together in a small bowl. Toss the asparagus with 2 tablespoons of the dressing in a medium bowl or on a rimmed baking sheet.

2. Grill the asparagus over a medium-hot fire (see how to gauge heat level on page 4), turning once, until tender and streaked with light grill marks, 5 to 7 minutes.

3. Transfer the grilled asparagus to a platter. Toss the asparagus with the remaining dressing. Adjust the seasonings, sprinkle with the almonds and olives, and serve hot, warm, or at room temperature.

MINCING ANCHOVIES

Anchovies often stick to the side of a chef's knife, making it hard to cut them into small bits. Here are two better ways to mince them.

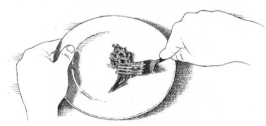

A. Use a dinner fork to mash delicate anchovy fillets into a paste. Mash the fillets on a small plate to catch any oil the anchovies give off.

B. A garlic press will turn anchovies into a fine puree. This method is especially handy when you have already dirtied the press with garlic.

CORN

WHILE GRILLING HUSK-ON CORN DELIVERS great pure corn flavor, it lacks the smokiness of the grill; essentially, the corn is steamed in its protective husk. Grilling with the husk off is too aggressive for most varieties of corn. We compromised by leaving only the innermost layer of husk in place and were rewarded with perfectly tender corn graced with the grill's flavor. Prepared in this way, the corn does not need basting with oil.

Grilled Corn

SERVES 8

See the illustration on page 300 for tips on judging when the corn is ready to come off the grill.

8 ears fresh corn, prepared according to the illustrations on page 300
   Salt and ground black pepper
   Unsalted butter (optional)

1. Grill the corn over a medium-hot fire (see how to gauge heat level on page 4), turning the ears every 1½ to 2 minutes, until the dark outlines of the kernels show through the husk and the husk is charred and beginning to peel away from the tip to expose some kernels, 8 to 10 minutes.

2. Transfer the corn to a platter. Carefully remove and discard the charred husks and silk. Season the corn with salt and pepper to taste. Serve immediately with butter, if desired.

➤ VARIATIONS

Grilled Corn with Spicy Chili Butter

Sautéing the spices with the butter and garlic brings out their flavor. Because salt does not dissolve readily in butter, it's best to serve the salt on the side.

6 tablespoons (¾ stick) unsalted butter
2 medium garlic cloves, minced or pressed through a garlic press (about 2 teaspoons)
1 teaspoon chili powder
½ teaspoon ground cumin
½ teaspoon paprika
⅛ teaspoon cayenne pepper
8 ears fresh corn, prepared according to the illustrations on page 300
1 lime, cut into 8 wedges
   Salt

1. Melt the butter in a 10-inch skillet over medium heat. When the foam subsides, add the

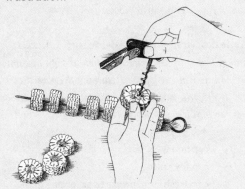

BARBECUE 911

Trouble Skewering Corn

Trying to poke a skewer through the thick center of a corn cob is often an exercise in frustration.

After cutting the cob into chunks, run a corkscrew through each piece, which will make it easy to run a skewer in. The coiled hole helps ensure a snug fit. See page 315 for instructions on grilling corn kebabs.

SCIENCE: Corn Storage

While the general rule of thumb is to buy and eat corn the same day it has been harvested (as soon as the corn is harvested, the sugars start converting to starches and the corn loses sweetness), most of us have been guilty of trying to break that rule for one reason or another. We tried a variety of methods for overnight storage using Silver Queen corn, one of the more perishable varieties. We found that the worst thing you can do to corn is to leave it sitting out on the counter. Throwing it into the refrigerator without any wrapping is nearly as bad. Storing in an airtight bag helps, but the hands-down winner entailed wrapping the corn (husks left on) in a wet paper bag and then in a plastic bag. After 24 hours of storage, we found the corn stored this way to be juicy and sweet.

garlic, chili powder, cumin, paprika, and cayenne and cook until fragrant, about 1 minute. Turn off the heat and set aside.

2. Grill the corn over a medium-hot fire (see how to gauge heat level on page 4), turning the

ears every 1½ to 2 minutes, until the dark outlines of the kernels show through the husk and the husk is charred and beginning to peel away from the tip to expose some kernels, 8 to 10 minutes.

3. Transfer the corn to a platter. Carefully remove and discard the charred husks and silk. Using tongs, take each ear of corn and roll it in the butter mixture. Serve immediately, with the lime wedges and salt to taste.

Grilled Corn with Soy-Honey Glaze

Corn grilled with soy sauce is a familiar sight at summer fairs and festivals in Japan. Returning the glazed ears of corn to the grill caramelizes the sugar in the sauce and gives the corn a deep, smoky flavor.

- ⅓ cup honey
- ⅓ cup soy sauce
- 8 ears fresh corn, prepared according to the illustrations below

1. Mix the honey and soy sauce together in a 10-inch skillet. Bring to a simmer over medium-high heat. Reduce the heat to medium and simmer until slightly syrupy and reduced to about ½ cup, about 5 minutes. Turn off the heat and set aside.

2. Grill the corn over a medium-hot fire (see how to gauge heat level on page 4), turning the ears every 1½ to 2 minutes, until the dark outlines of the kernels show through the husk and the husk is charred and beginning to peel away from the tip to expose some kernels, 8 to 10 minutes.

3. Transfer the corn to a platter. Carefully remove and discard the charred husks and silk.

Using tongs, take each ear of corn and roll it in the soy mixture. Return the glazed corn to the grill for an additional 1 to 2 minutes, turning once. Serve immediately.

Grilled Corn with Herb Butter

Brush with the herb butter just before serving.

Melt 6 tablespoons (¾ stick) unsalted butter in a small saucepan. Add 3 tablespoons minced fresh parsley, thyme, cilantro, basil, and/or other fresh herbs and salt and pepper to taste; keep the butter warm. Follow the recipe for Grilled Corn, brushing the herb butter over the grilled corn in step 2.

Grilled Corn with Garlic Butter and Cheese

The buttery, nutty flavor of Parmesan cheese works surprisingly well with the flavor of grilled corn.

JUDGING WHEN GRILLED CORN IS DONE

As soon as the husk picks up the dark silhouette of the kernels and begins to pull away from the tip of the ear, the corn is ready to come off the grill.

PREPARING CORN FOR GRILLING

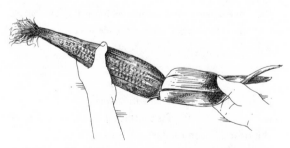

1. Remove all but the innermost layer of the husk. The kernels should be covered by, but visible through, the innermost layer.

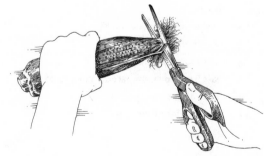

2. Use scissors to snip off the tassel, or long silk ends, at the tip of the ear.

Melt 6 tablespoons (¾ stick) unsalted butter in a small saucepan over medium heat until bubbling. Add 1 medium garlic clove, minced or pressed through a garlic press (about 1 teaspoon), and cook until fragrant, about 30 seconds. Remove the pan from the heat and stir in ¼ teaspoon salt. Follow the recipe for Grilled Corn, brushing the butter over the grilled corn in step 2. Sprinkle with ¼ cup grated Parmesan cheese and serve immediately.

EGGPLANT

THE BIGGEST CHALLENGE THAT CONFRONTS the cook when preparing eggplant is excess moisture. That's why grilling is such an ideal method for cooking eggplant. Under the broiler or in a hot pan, the eggplant steams in its own juices and becomes mushy. Eggplant is often salted before being cooked to draw out these juices.

On the grill, there's no need to draw out moisture from eggplant slices before grilling. The moisture will vaporize or fall harmlessly through the cooking grate. The eggplant browns beautifully and becomes crisp in spots. In our tests, we found that thinner slices can fall apart on the cooking grate. Thicker pieces, ideally ¾-inch-thick rounds, can withstand grilling.

Grilled Eggplant
SERVES 4

There's no need to salt eggplant destined for the grill. The intense grill heat will vaporize excess moisture.

- 3 tablespoons extra-virgin olive oil
- 2 medium garlic cloves, minced or pressed through a garlic press (about 2 teaspoons)
- 2 teaspoons minced fresh thyme or oregano leaves
  Salt and ground black pepper
- 1 large eggplant (about 1½ pounds), ends trimmed, cut crosswise into ¾-inch-thick rounds

1. Combine the oil, garlic, thyme, and salt and pepper to taste in a small bowl. Place the

eggplant on a platter and brush both sides with the oil mixture.

2. Grill the eggplant over a medium-hot fire (see how to gauge heat level on page 4), turning once, until both sides are streaked with dark grill marks, 8 to 10 minutes. Serve hot, warm, or at room temperature.

> VARIATIONS
Grilled Eggplant with Basil Oil
Make sure to cook the garlic until it is barely starting to sizzle. The oil will then be just hot enough to slightly wilt the basil when they are processed together.

- ¼ cup extra-virgin olive oil
- 1 medium garlic clove, minced or pressed through a garlic press (about 1 teaspoon)
- ½ cup packed fresh basil leaves
  Salt and ground black pepper
- 1 recipe Grilled Eggplant

1. Place the oil and garlic in a small skillet and turn the heat to medium. Cook until the garlic just starts to sizzle and becomes fragrant, about 2 minutes.

2. Place the basil in the workbowl of a food processor. Very carefully pour the hot oil over the basil. Process until the mixture is fragrant and almost smooth, about 30 seconds. Season with salt and pepper to taste.

3. Transfer the grilled eggplant to a platter and drizzle with the basil oil. Serve immediately.

Grilled Eggplant with Cherry Tomato and Cilantro Vinaigrette
Grape tomatoes can also be used in this recipe. Choose the ripest tomatoes for the best, most flavorful vinaigrette.

- ½ pint cherry tomatoes, each tomato quartered (about 1 cup)
- 6 tablespoons extra-virgin olive oil
- 1 medium shallot, minced
- 2 tablespoons minced fresh cilantro leaves
- 2 tablespoons juice from 2 limes
- ¼ teaspoon salt
  Pinch cayenne pepper
- 1 recipe Grilled Eggplant

1. Mix the tomatoes, oil, shallot, cilantro, lime juice, salt, and cayenne together in a medium bowl. Let stand at room temperature until juicy and seasoned, about 20 minutes.

2. Transfer the grilled eggplant to a platter. Pour the vinaigrette over the grilled eggplant and serve immediately.

Grilled Eggplant with Ginger and Soy

Honey gives the sauce a thick texture and gentle sweetness.

2	tablespoons soy sauce
1½	tablespoons honey
1	tablespoon rice vinegar
1	tablespoon water
1	teaspoon toasted sesame oil
3	tablespoons peanut oil
1	tablespoon minced fresh ginger
	Ground black pepper
1	large eggplant (about 1½ pounds), ends trimmed, cut crosswise into ¾-inch-thick rounds
2	medium scallions, sliced thin

1. Combine the soy sauce, honey, vinegar, and water in a small skillet. Bring to a boil over medium-high heat and simmer until slightly thickened, about 2 minutes. Remove the pan from the heat and stir in the sesame oil. Set this sauce aside.

2. Combine the peanut oil, ginger, and pepper to taste in a small bowl. Place the eggplant on a platter and brush both sides with the peanut oil mixture.

3. Grill the eggplant over a medium-hot fire (see how to gauge heat level on page 4), turning once, until streaked with dark grill marks, 8 to 10 minutes.

4. Transfer the grilled eggplant to a platter. Drizzle the thickened soy mixture over the eggplant and sprinkle with the scallions. Serve hot, warm, or at room temperature.

Grilled Eggplant with Sweet Miso Glaze

Miso, fermented soybean paste, is both salty and sweet. You can find it in Asian specialty food shops, natural food stores, and some supermarkets. In Japan, eggplant is traditionally grilled and then doused with this sweet glaze.

INGREDIENTS: Miso

Most miso pastes are made from a combination of fermented soybeans and white rice. Some miso may contain just soybeans, while others may replace the white rice with brown rice or barley. White miso (shiromiso) is the type commonly used to make miso soup. This and other types of miso and their flavor characteristics are described below.

White Miso (Shiromiso): White miso is the type Westerners are most likely to be familiar with. It is brownish yellow in color—not pure white, as its name may lead you to believe—and its flavor is mellow, with a light sweetness, a light saltiness, and a delicacy that can range from fruity to nutty, depending on the brand. White miso is the favorite in the test kitchen.

Brown or Red Miso (Akamiso): Brown or red miso has a darker color and a saltier, more assertive flavor that lacks the delicate sweetness of white miso. It has a meaty, roasted quality.

Brown Rice Miso (Genmaimiso): Like brown or red miso, brown rice miso is darker in color than white miso, and it lacks the subtleties of white miso. Brown rice miso has a strong saltiness, a soy sauce–like flavor, a hefty smokiness, and a few faint but detectable sour notes.

Barley Miso (Mugimiso): Barley miso resembles white miso in appearance, but its flavor is distinctly malty. Our tasters also identified sweet, nutty, and tea-like flavor characteristics.

7	tablespoons sugar
¼	cup white miso
3	tablespoons water
2	tablespoons mirin (sweet Japanese rice wine)
3	tablespoons peanut or vegetable oil
2	medium garlic cloves, minced or pressed through a garlic press (about 2 teaspoons)
	Salt and ground black pepper
1	large eggplant (about 1½ pounds), ends trimmed, cut crosswise into ¾-inch-thick rounds
2½	tablespoons sesame seeds, toasted in a small dry skillet over medium heat until fragrant, about 7 minutes

1. Mix the sugar, miso, water, and mirin together in a medium bowl. Set aside.

2. Combine the oil, garlic, and salt and pepper to taste in a small bowl. Place the eggplant on a platter and brush both sides with the oil mixture.

3. Grill the eggplant over a medium-hot fire (see how to gauge heat level on page 4), turning once, until streaked with grill marks, 6 to 8 minutes. Brush both sides with the miso glaze and grill until the glaze is hot and the eggplant is tender throughout, about 1 minute longer on each side.

4. Transfer the grilled eggplant to a platter. Adjust the seasonings and sprinkle with the sesame seeds. Serve hot, warm, or at room temperature.

Grilled Curried Eggplant

Grilled eggplant takes very well to the flavors of yogurt and spices. Serve with basmati rice.

- 1/2 cup plain yogurt
- 5 tablespoons vegetable oil
- 2 teaspoons sugar
- 1 teaspoon curry powder
- 2 medium garlic cloves, minced or pressed through a garlic press (about 2 teaspoons)
  Salt and ground black pepper
- 1 large eggplant (about 1 1/2 pounds), ends trimmed, cut crosswise into 3/4-inch-thick rounds

1. Mix the yogurt, 2 tablespoons of the oil, the sugar, and curry powder together in a medium bowl. Set aside.

2. Combine the remaining 3 tablespoons oil, the garlic, and salt and pepper to taste in a small bowl. Place the eggplant on a platter and brush both sides with the garlic and oil mixture.

3. Grill the eggplant over a medium-hot fire (see how to gauge heat level on page 4), turning once, until streaked with grill marks, 6 to 8 minutes. Brush both sides with the yogurt-curry mixture and grill until the glaze is hot and the eggplant is tender throughout, about 1 minute longer on each side.

4. Transfer the grilled eggplant to a platter. Adjust the seasonings and serve hot, warm, or at room temperature.

BABA GHANOUSH

THE TRADITIONAL METHOD FOR COOKING eggplant for baba ghanoush is to scorch it over a hot, smoky grill. There the purple fruit grows bruised, then black, until its insides almost slosh within their charred skin. The hot, soft interior is scooped out with a spoon and the outer ruins discarded. Baba ghanoush made with eggplant not cooked to this sloshy soft stage simply isn't as good. Undercooked eggplant, while misleadingly soft to the touch (eggplant has, after all, a yielding quality), will taste spongy-green and remain unmoved by additional seasonings. Don't bother discarding the seeds, but do use a gentle hand with the garlic, tahini, and lemon juice; too much of any of these ingredients can overwhelm the rich smokiness of the grilled eggplant.

Baba Ghanoush
MAKES ABOUT 2 CUPS

When buying eggplants, select those with shiny, taut, and unbruised skins and an even shape (eggplants with a bulbous shape won't cook evenly).

We prefer to serve baba ghanoush only lightly chilled. If yours is cold, let it stand at room temperature for about 20 minutes before serving. Baba ghanoush does not keep well, so plan to make it the day you want to serve it. Pita bread, black olives, tomato wedges, and cucumber slices are nice accompaniments.

- 2 pounds eggplant (about 2 large globe eggplants, 5 medium Italian eggplants, or 12 medium Japanese eggplants), each eggplant poked uniformly over the entire surface with a fork to prevent it from bursting
- 2 tablespoons tahini
- 1 tablespoon juice from 1 lemon
- 1 tablespoon extra-virgin olive oil, plus extra for serving
- 1 small garlic clove, minced or pressed through a garlic press (about 1/2 teaspoon)
  Salt and ground black pepper
- 2 teaspoons chopped fresh parsley leaves

1. Grill the eggplants over a hot fire (see how to gauge heat level on page 4) until the skins

darken and wrinkle on all sides and the eggplants are uniformly soft when pressed with tongs, about 25 minutes for large globe eggplants, 20 minutes for Italian eggplants, and 15 minutes for Japanese eggplants, turning the eggplants every 5 minutes. Transfer the eggplants to a rimmed baking sheet and cool 5 minutes.

2. Set a small colander over a bowl or in the sink. Trim the top and bottom off each eggplant. Slit the eggplants lengthwise. Use a spoon to scoop the hot pulp from the skins and place the pulp in the colander (you should have about 2 cups packed pulp); discard the skins. Let the pulp drain 3 minutes.

3. Transfer the pulp to the workbowl of a food processor. Add the tahini, lemon juice, oil, garlic, ¼ teaspoon salt, and ¼ teaspoon pepper and process until the mixture has a coarse, choppy texture, about eight 1-second pulses. Adjust the seasoning with salt and pepper to taste. Transfer to a serving bowl, cover with plastic wrap flush with the surface of the dip, and refrigerate until lightly chilled, 45 to 60 minutes. To serve, use a spoon to make a trough in the center of the dip and spoon a little olive oil into it. Sprinkle with the parsley and serve.

➤ VARIATION
Baba Ghanoush with Sautéed Onion
Sautéed onion gives the baba ghanoush a sweet, rich flavor.

Heat 1 tablespoon extra-virgin olive oil in small skillet over low heat until shimmering; add 1 small onion, chopped fine, and cook, stirring occasionally, until the edges are golden brown, about 10 minutes. Follow the recipe for Baba Ghanoush, stirring the onion into the dip after processing.

ENDIVE

ALTHOUGH WE GENERALLY THINK OF CRISP and crunchy Belgian endive in terms of salads, it grills beautifully. The texture softens, but the vegetable holds its shape. Best of all, the bitter flavor mellows a bit when exposed to intense heat.

We tried grilling endive whole, but it charred on the outside before the interior cooked through. We had far better results when we sliced each head in half lengthwise. With a piece of the core still attached, the layers of leaves stay together. Since the core is exposed, it softens quickly and is crisp-tender by the time the exterior is streaked with dark grill marks.

Grilled Belgian Endive
SERVES 6 TO 8
Delicate endive can fall apart easily if not handled gently. Move the halved endive on the grill by grasping the curved sides gently with tongs and supporting the cut sides with a spatula while lifting and turning.

8 medium heads Belgian endive (about 4 ounces each), wilted or bruised outer leaves discarded, root ends trimmed, and each head halved lengthwise (see the illustrations on the facing page)
3 tablespoons extra-virgin olive oil
Salt and ground black pepper

1. Toss the endive halves and oil in a large bowl until the endive is well coated with the oil. Season with salt and pepper to taste.

2. Grill the endive over a medium-hot fire (see how to gauge heat level on page 4), turning once, until dark grill marks appear and the center of each is crisp-tender, 5 to 7 minutes. Serve hot or at room temperature.

➤ VARIATIONS
Grilled Belgian Endive with Lemon-Garlic Butter
The lemon zest, garlic, and thyme only need to be cooked until they are fragrant. If the zest is overcooked, it will become bitter.

6 tablespoons (¾ stick) unsalted butter
1 medium garlic clove, minced or pressed through a garlic press (about 1 teaspoon)
1 teaspoon grated zest from 1 lemon
½ teaspoon minced fresh thyme leaves
1 recipe Grilled Belgian Endive
Salt and ground black pepper

Place the butter in a small skillet or saucepan over medium heat. When the butter has melted, add the garlic, zest, and thyme and cook until fragrant, about 2 minutes. Drizzle over the grilled endive and season the endive with salt and pepper to taste. Serve immediately.

Grilled Belgian Endive with Mustard Dressing and Parmesan

Mustard, anchovies, garlic, and capers join together to complement the bitter flavor of Belgian endive.

1	tablespoon Dijon mustard
2	anchovy fillets, minced
1	teaspoon red wine vinegar
1	medium garlic clove, minced or pressed through a garlic press (about 1 teaspoon)
1	teaspoon drained capers, chopped
1/3	cup extra-virgin olive oil
8	medium heads Belgian endive, prepared according to the illustrations below Grated Parmesan cheese

1. Whisk the mustard, anchovies, vinegar, garlic, and capers together in a large mixing bowl. Gradually whisk in the oil. Add the endive and toss to coat each piece; reserving the remaining dressing.

2. Grill the endive over a medium-hot fire (see how to gauge heat level on page 4), turning once, until dark grill marks appear and the center of each is crisp-tender, 5 to 7 minutes.

3. Transfer the grilled endive to a platter, drizzle with the reserved dressing, and sprinkle with Parmesan to taste. Serve hot.

Grilled Belgian Endive with Balsamic Dressing

See page 307 for the results from our tasting of inexpensive balsamic vinegars.

1/4	cup balsamic vinegar
1	tablespoon honey
1	medium garlic clove, minced or pressed through a garlic press (about 1 teaspoon)
1/3	cup extra-virgin olive oil
2	teaspoons chopped fresh thyme leaves Salt and ground black pepper
8	medium heads Belgian endive, prepared according to the illustrations below

1. Whisk the vinegar, honey, and garlic together in a large bowl. Gradually whisk in the oil. Stir in the thyme and salt and pepper to taste. Add the endive and toss to coat each piece; reserve the remaining dressing.

2. Grill the endive over a medium-hot fire (see how to gauge heat level on page 4), turning once, until dark grill marks appear and the center of each is crisp-tender, 5 to 7 minutes.

3. Transfer the grilled endive to a platter and drizzle with the reserved dressing. Serve hot or at room temperature.

PREPARING ENDIVE FOR GRILLING

1. With a knife, shave off the discolored end of the endive. Cut the thinnest slice possible—you want the layers of leaves to remain intact as the endive cooks.

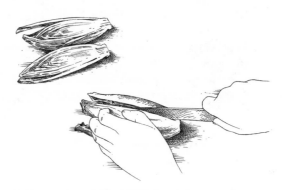

2. Cut the endive in half lengthwise through the core end.

FENNEL

GRILLING CAUSES THE NATURAL SUGARS IN fennel to caramelize, thereby enhancing its flavor. Like endive, fennel holds its shape well on the grill and softens to a creamy texture.

The biggest challenge when grilling fennel is slicing the bulb so that the pieces pick up as much flavor as possible without falling through the cooking grate. Thin strips of fennel must be cooked on a grill grid (see page 20). We had better luck when we sliced the bulb through the core end into fan-shaped pieces. With a piece of the core still attached, the various layers remained intact as a single piece. With two flat sides, fan-shaped pieces also have plenty of surface area, so they pick up a lot of grill flavor.

Grilled Fennel

SERVES 4

Fennel grills beautifully. Its anise flavor is complemented by the caramelization of natural sugars on the surface of the vegetable.

> 2   medium fennel bulbs (about 2 pounds), stems and fronds trimmed and discarded, base shaved off, tough or blemished outer layers removed, and cut vertically through the base into 1/4-inch-thick slices (see the illustrations below)
> 3   tablespoons extra-virgin olive oil
>   Salt and ground black pepper

1. Toss the fennel and oil together in a large bowl. Season to taste with salt and pepper.

2. Grill the fennel over a medium-hot fire (see how to gauge heat level on page 4), turning once, until tender and streaked with dark grill marks, 7 to 9 minutes. Transfer the grilled fennel to a platter. Serve hot, warm, or at room temperature.

> VARIATIONS

Grilled Fennel with Grapefruit Vinaigrette

If your grapefruit is especially tart, you may want to add more honey.

> 3/4 cup juice from 1 pink grapefruit
> 6   tablespoons extra-virgin olive oil
> 1   medium shallot, minced
> 1   teaspoon honey, or more to taste
> 1/4 teaspoon finely minced or grated fresh ginger
>   Salt and ground black pepper
> 1   recipe Grilled Fennel

1. Bring the grapefruit juice to a simmer in a 10-inch nonstick skillet over medium-high heat. Reduce the heat and simmer the juice gently, adjusting the heat as necessary, until the juice has reduced to a syrupy glaze (you should have about 2 tablespoons), about 15 minutes.

2. Whisk the reduced grapefruit juice, oil, shallot, honey, and ginger together in a small bowl. Season with salt and pepper to taste, and add more honey if necessary.

PREPARING FENNEL FOR GRILLING

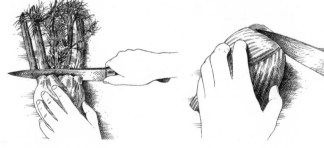

1. Cut off the stems and feathery fronds. (The fronds can be minced and used for garnishing.)

2. Trim a very thin slice from the base and remove any tough or blemished outer layers from the bulb.

3. Slice the bulb vertically through the base into 1/4-inch-thick pieces that resemble fans.

3. Arrange the grilled fennel on a platter and drizzle with the vinaigrette. Serve immediately.

Grilled Fennel with Mint and Tarragon Vinaigrette

The anise flavors of the tarragon and fennel are highlighted by the brightness of the mint.

- 6 tablespoons extra-virgin olive oil
- 2 tablespoons white wine vinegar
- 2 teaspoons minced fresh tarragon leaves
- 1½ teaspoons minced fresh mint leaves
  Salt and ground black pepper
- 1 recipe Grilled Fennel

1. Whisk the oil, vinegar, tarragon, and mint together in a small bowl. Season with salt and pepper to taste.

2. Arrange the grilled fennel on a platter and drizzle with the vinaigrette. Serve immediately.

INGREDIENTS: Balsamic Vinegar

There are balsamic vinegars you can buy for $2.50 and ones that nudge the $300 mark. The more expensive vinegars bear the title tradizionale or extra-vecchio tradizionale (traditional or extra-old traditional) aceto balsamico. According to Italian law, these traditional vinegars must come from the northern Italian provinces of Modena and Reggio Emilia and be created and aged in the time-honored fashion.

For hundreds of years, tradizionale balsamico vinegar has been made from Trebbiano grapes grown in the Modena and Reggio Emilia regions of northern Italy. The grapes are crushed and the must is slowly cooked over an open flame. The must begins mellowing in a large wooden barrel, where it ferments and turns to vinegar. The vinegar is then passed through a series of barrels made from a variety of woods. To be considered worthy of the tradizionale title, the vinegar must be moved from barrel to barrel for a minimum of 12 years. An extra-vecchio tradizionale vinegar must be aged for at least 25 years.

Because of its complex flavor and high production cost, tradizionale balsamic vinegar is used by those in the know as a condiment rather than an ingredient. The longer the vinegar ages, the thicker and more intense it becomes, maturing from a thin liquid into a spoon-coating, syrupy one—perfect for topping strawberries or cantaloupe. This is the aristocrat of balsamic vinegars.

The more common varieties, those with a price tag under $30, are categorized as commercial or industrial balsamic vinegars. These vinegars are the kind with which most Americans are familiar and are often used to complete a vinaigrette or flavor a sauce. The flavor profile of commercial balsamic vinegars ranges widely from mild, woody, and herbaceous to artificial and sour. Commercial balsamic vinegar may or may not be aged and may or may not contain artificial caramel color or flavor.

We wondered how bad—or good—inexpensive commercial balsamic vinegars would be when compared in a blind tasting. To level the playing field—and ease the burden on our budget—we limited the tasting to balsamic vinegars that cost $15 and under. We included samples of the many production styles, including some aged in the traditional fashion, some with added caramel color and flavor, and some made from a blend of aged red wine vinegar and grape must.

We found that a higher price tag did not correlate with a better vinegar. In addition, age seemed to play a less important role than we had expected. Across the board, tasters found balsamic vinegars containing caramel or artificial color or flavor "sour" and "uninteresting." The top brands from our tasting contain no artificial colors or flavors whatsoever. Our findings led us to believe that must is paramount to making a full-flavored balsamic vinegar. As the must ages, it becomes thick and sweet, contributing a character almost like sherry or port. Producers who substitute artificial color and flavor for must end up with a shallow product.

So how can consumers figure out what type of balsamic vinegar to buy? The easy answer is to check the label. If it discloses that artificial ingredients or sweeteners have been added, don't buy it.

THE BEST INEXPENSIVE BALSAMIC VINEGARS
Among the dozen vinegars tested, we preferred 365 Every Day Value (left), Masserie di Sant'Eramo (center), and Fiorucci Riserva (right).

Grilled Fennel with Tarragon and Shallot

Tarragon gives a boost to the mild anise flavor of fennel. Vinegar and shallots temper the sweetness of the vegetable.

- 1   medium shallot, minced
- 2   tablespoons red wine vinegar
- 1   teaspoon honey
      Salt and ground black pepper
- 1/4 cup extra-virgin olive oil
- 2   medium fennel bulbs (about 2 pounds), prepared according to the illustrations on page 306
- 1 1/2 tablespoons minced fresh tarragon leaves

1. Mix the shallot, vinegar, honey, and salt and pepper to taste together in a large bowl. Gradually whisk in the oil. Add the fennel and tarragon and toss to coat; reserve the remaining dressing.

2. Grill the fennel over a medium-hot fire (see how to gauge heat level on page 4), turning once, until tender and streaked with dark grill marks, 7 to 9 minutes.

3. Arrange the grilled fennel on a platter and drizzle with the reserved dressing. Serve hot, warm, or at room temperature.

Grilled Fennel with Citrus

A light dressing of citrus juices lends a subtle twist to grilled fennel. Serve with a mild, white-fleshed fish such as snapper.

- 1/4 cup orange juice
- 1   medium shallot, minced
- 1   tablespoon juice from 1 lemon
- 1   medium garlic clove, minced or pressed through a garlic press (about 1 teaspoon)
      Salt and ground black pepper
- 1/4 cup extra-virgin olive oil
- 2   medium fennel bulbs (about 2 pounds), prepared according to the illustrations on page 306
- 2   teaspoons minced fresh thyme leaves

1. Whisk the orange juice, shallot, lemon juice, garlic, and salt and pepper to taste together in large bowl. Gradually whisk in the oil. Add the fennel and thyme and toss to coat, reserving the remaining dressing.

2. Grill the fennel over a medium-hot fire (see how to gauge heat level on page 4), turning once, until tender and streaked with dark grill marks, 7 to 9 minutes.

3. Arrange the grilled fennel on a platter and drizzle with the reserved dressing. Serve hot, warm, or at room temperature.

GARLIC

IT IS POSSIBLE TO ROAST GARLIC ON THE grill if you adapt the classic oven-roasting technique, which involves cutting off the top of the head of garlic to expose the cloves, oiling the garlic, and then wrapping it in foil. We found that this method worked fine as long as we didn't grill the garlic over a hot fire. Even when wrapped

GRILL-ROASTING GARLIC

1. Before grilling, slice the top third (the side opposite the root) off the head of garlic, so that all the cloves are exposed. Discard the top.

2. Once grilled, push from the root end down to squeeze the cloves from their papery skins.

in a double layer of foil, garlic grilled over a hot fire scorched before the cloves had softened to a creamy consistency. Garlic must be grilled over a fairly cool fire. You have several options.

If you are grill-roasting (see page 3 for a definition of grill-roasting) or grilling over a two-level fire, simply place the garlic packet on the cooler side of the grill and cook, turning once, until the garlic gives a bit when gently squeezed. If you are grilling over a single-level fire, you must wait until the fire has died down. Only when the fire has cooled to medium can you place the garlic on the grill. To trap the remaining heat, grill the garlic with the grill cover on, whether you are using a gas or a charcoal grill. The foil protects the garlic from picking up any off flavors.

Grill-Roasted Garlic

MAKES ABOUT ½ CUP

Roasted garlic can be used simply as a spread on grilled bread or to flavor any number of foods, from mashed potatoes to salads and sauces. Mash herbs into the roasted garlic for a more interesting spread; chopped fresh thyme leaves or a small amount of chopped fresh rosemary work especially well this way.

3 medium heads of garlic, prepared according to illustration I on the facing page
1½ tablespoons extra-virgin olive oil
Salt and ground black pepper

1. Cut two 12-inch squares of aluminum foil. Lay one on top of the other to form a double layer of foil. Toss the cut heads of garlic with the oil in a medium bowl and season generously with salt and pepper to taste. Place the garlic in the center of the foil and wrap so that both sides of the packet are flat (you must cook both sides of the garlic on the grill).

2. If using a single- or two-level fire, grill over medium heat (see how to gauge heat level on page 4), covered, for 25 minutes, turning once. If grill-roasting, cook for 35 to 45 minutes, turning once. When done, the garlic will give a bit when lightly squeezed.

3. Remove the packet from the grill; let the

garlic rest, still wrapped, for 15 minutes, or until cool enough to handle. Remove the garlic from the foil and squeeze the cloves out of their papery skins (see illustration 2 on the facing page). The cloves should be soft enough to mash. (The garlic can be refrigerated in an airtight container overnight.)

GREEN BEANS

ALTHOUGH WE PROBABLY WOULDN'T GRILL thin, just-picked green beans, this cooking method works well with thicker, older beans. Tender beans are best boiled or steamed to preserve their delicate flavor, but thicker beans are often bland when prepared those ways. When grilled, they pick up a lightly caramelized flavor.

When simply oiled before being grilled, the green beans were a bit tough. We found that if we rinsed the beans first, then tossed them in oil without drying them, the beans were crisp-tender after about six minutes on the grill. The extra moisture clinging to the beans evaporated during the first minute or two of cooking and helped to "steam" them a bit.

Grilled Green Beans

SERVES 4

Green beans will not dry out on the grill if you rinse them and leave the excess water on the beans. They cook quickly

GRILLING GREEN BEANS

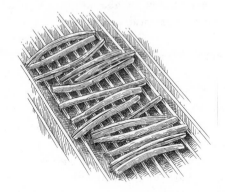

Place the beans perpendicular to the cooking grate rods so that they won't fall through the grate. If you prefer, use a grill grid, but the beans won't caramelize as well.

and retain a good crunch. Add a minced clove of garlic to the oil for more flavor, or serve with crumbled goat cheese.

1 ½   pounds green beans, rinsed (do not pat dry)
1 ½   tablespoons extra-virgin olive oil
       Salt and ground black pepper

1. Toss the moist beans with oil in a large bowl. Season with salt and pepper to taste.

2. Grill the beans over a medium-hot fire (see how to gauge heat level on page 4), with the green beans placed perpendicular to the cooking grate rods (see the illustration on page 309). Grill until the beans are lightly browned and crisp-tender, about 6 minutes. Serve hot, warm, or at room temperature.

PORTOBELLO MUSHROOMS

IN SOME CIRCLES, GRILLED PORTOBELLOS have become the new "burger." Although we are happy to use meaty grilled portobellos in sandwiches, they are also ideal as a side dish or as a salad ingredient. Unfortunately, many grilled portobellos are flaccid. Ideally, they should be plump, juicy, and slightly charred. With portobellos ranging from 4 to 6 inches in diameter, the first problem we encountered was how to develop an across-the-board grilling method for both smaller and larger mushrooms. This, we knew, would be difficult since we wanted to keep the grilling temperature relatively high. We wanted to be able to grill portobellos side by side with meat, which needs a hot fire. Grilling directly on the rack over the fire proved problematic because the larger portobellos were charred to a black crisp by the time they had cooked through. Seeking refuge, we elevated the mushrooms on a grill rack, but now they took eons to cook through. We suspected that if we found a way to shield the mushrooms from the fire, we could grill them until entirely cooked through and also infuse them with a pure, smoky flavor without the bitterness associated with the direct-grilling method. We called upon an old campfire friend—aluminum foil—and loosely

wrapped each mushroom in a handcrafted foil packet. We placed the portobellos gill-side up (through our endeavors we had learned that this method traps juices) on the grill. After about 10 minutes, the mushrooms were tender and juicy to the core, without sacrificing any of the grill's smoky attributes.

Grilled Portobellos
SERVES 4

We prefer large 5- to 6-inch portobellos for grilling because they are sold loose, not prepackaged, and are typically fresher. However, if you cannot find large ones, use six 4- to 5-inch portobellos, which are usually sold three to a package; decrease their grilling time, wrapped in foil, to about 9 minutes.

½   cup extra-virgin olive oil
3   tablespoons juice from 1 lemon
6   medium garlic cloves, minced or
     pressed through a garlic press
     (about 2 tablespoons)
¼   teaspoon salt
4   portobello mushrooms, each 5 to
     6 inches in diameter (or about 6 ounces
     each), stems removed and discarded,
     caps wiped clean

1. Combine the oil, lemon juice, garlic, and salt in a large zipper-lock plastic bag. Add the mushrooms, seal the bag, and gently shake to coat the mushrooms with the marinade. Let stand at room temperature for 1 hour. Meanwhile, cut four 12 by 12-inch pieces of foil (or six 9 by 9-inch pieces if using smaller mushrooms).

2. Remove the mushrooms from the marinade. Place a foil square on a work surface and set a mushroom on top, gill-side up. Fold the foil edges over to enclose the mushroom and seal the edges shut. Repeat with the remaining mushrooms. Grill the mushrooms over a medium-hot fire (see how to gauge heat level on page 4), with the sealed side of the foil packet facing up, until the mushrooms are juicy and tender, 10 to 12 minutes. Using tongs, unwrap the mushrooms and discard the foil. Return the unwrapped mushrooms to the grill,

gill-side up, and cook until grill marked, 30 to 60 seconds. Remove from the grill and serve hot or warm or use in one of the following recipes.

➤ VARIATIONS
Grilled Portobellos with Tarragon
This variation is great served with a grilled steak or a juicy hamburger.

1   tablespoon chopped fresh tarragon leaves
2   teaspoons rice vinegar

PREPARING WHITE BUTTON MUSHROOMS FOR GRILLING

In addition to large portobello mushrooms, you can grill white button, or cremini, mushrooms. Clean these small mushrooms and trim any dry ends from the stems. Skewer them through the cap and stem so that they are less likely to rotate when turned on the grill. Refer to "Grilling Vegetables at a Glance" on page 315 for grilling instructions.

1   medium garlic clove, minced or pressed through a garlic press (about 1 teaspoon)
1/4   teaspoon salt
2   teaspoons vegetable or canola oil
1   recipe Grilled Portobellos, cut into 1/2-inch cubes
    Ground black pepper

Combine the tarragon, vinegar, garlic, and salt in a medium bowl and then whisk in the oil. Add the mushrooms and pepper to taste and toss to coat. Serve immediately or cover with plastic wrap and let stand at room temperature up to 30 minutes.

Grilled Portobellos with Garlic, Rosemary, and Balsamic Vinegar
If you cannot find large portobellos, use six 4- to 5-inch portobellos. Decrease their grilling time, wrapped in foil, to about 9 minutes.

1/4   cup extra-virgin olive oil
2   tablespoons balsamic vinegar
2   medium garlic cloves, minced or pressed through a garlic press (about 2 teaspoons)
2   teaspoons minced fresh rosemary
    Salt and ground black pepper

SCIENCE: To Wash or Not to Wash Mushrooms

Common culinary wisdom dictates that mushrooms should never, ever be washed. Put these spongy fungi under the faucet or in a bowl with water, the dictum goes, and they will soak up the water like a sponge.

Like most cooks, we had always blindly followed this precept. But when we learned that mushrooms consist of more than 80 percent water, we began to question their ability to absorb yet more liquid. As we so often do in situations like this, we consulted the work of food scientist and author Harold McGee. Sure enough, in his book *The Curious Cook* (North Point Press, 1990) we found an experiment he had devised to test this very piece of accepted mushroom lore. We decided to duplicate McGee's work in our test kitchen.

We weighed out 6 ounces of white mushrooms and put them into a bowl, then added water to cover and let them sit. After five minutes we shook off the surface water and weighed the mushrooms again. Our results replicated McGee's—the total weight gain for all the mushrooms together was 1/4 ounce, which translates to about 1 1/2 teaspoons of water.

We suspected that this gain represented mostly surface moisture rather than absorption, so we repeated the experiment with 6 ounces of broccoli, which no one would claim is an absorbent vegetable. The weight gain after a five-minute soak was almost identical—1/5 of an ounce—suggesting that most of the moisture was clinging to the surface of the vegetables rather than being absorbed by them.

So, as it turns out, mushrooms can be cleaned in the same way that other vegetables are cleaned—rinsed under cold water. However, it's best to rinse them just before cooking and to avoid rinsing altogether if you are using them uncooked, since the surfaces of wet mushrooms turn dark and slimy when they're exposed to air for more than four or five minutes.

4   portobello mushrooms, each 5 to 6 inches
     in diameter (or about 6 ounces each), stems
     removed and discarded, caps wiped clean

1. Whisk the oil, vinegar, garlic, rosemary, ¼ teaspoon salt, and pepper to taste together in small bowl. Brush both sides of each mushroom cap with the oil mixture and season with additional salt and pepper to taste.

2. Cut four 12 by 12-inch pieces of foil (or six 9 by 9-inch pieces if using smaller mushrooms). Place a foil square on a work surface and set a mushroom on top, gill-side up. Fold the foil edges over to enclose the mushroom and seal the edges shut. Repeat with the remaining mushrooms.

3. Grill the mushrooms over a medium-hot fire (see how to gauge heat level on page 4), with the sealed side of the foil packet facing up, until the mushrooms are juicy and tender, 10 to 12 minutes. Using tongs, unwrap the mushrooms and discard the foil. Return the unwrapped mushrooms to the grill, gill-side up, and cook until grill marked, 30 to 60 seconds.

4. Slice the grilled mushrooms into wide strips (or leave whole) and serve hot.

Grilled Portobello Sandwiches with Boursin Cheese and Tomatoes

SERVES 4

If you cannot find large portobellos, use six 4- to 5-inch portobellos. Decrease their grilling time, wrapped in foil, to about 9 minutes.

Portobello mushrooms are delicious in sandwiches. Here they are paired with Boursin cheese (a soft cheese flavored with herbs and garlic) and tomatoes. If you cannot find Boursin cheese, simply mix ¼ cup cream cheese with ½ teaspoon thyme and ½ garlic clove, minced or pressed through a garlic press, and season with salt and pepper to taste. Use 1 tablespoon of the cream cheese spread on each sandwich.

4   portobello mushrooms, each 5 to 6 inches
     in diameter (or about 6 ounces each),
     stems removed and discarded, caps
     wiped clean

6   tablespoons extra-virgin olive oil
     Salt and ground black pepper
8   slices country bread, about 4 inches in
     diameter and ½ inch thick
8   teaspoons Boursin cheese
2   medium tomatoes, cored and cut crosswise
     into ¼-inch-thick slices
4   cups mesclun mix

1. Brush a total of 3 tablespoons of the oil on both sides of each mushroom cap and season with salt and pepper to taste.

2. Cut four 12 by 12-inch pieces of foil (or six

BARBECUE 911

Grilling in the Dark

You like to grill all year round, but as summer winds down and the days get shorter, you may find yourself grilling in the dark. If you don't have great outdoor lighting and think a flashlight is too cumbersome, here's a fun and easy alternative.

Simply put on a camping headlamp and you'll be ready to fire up the grill! This contraption not only allows you to point the light directly where you are looking, but also keeps your hands free for cooking purposes.

312

9 by 9-inch pieces if using smaller mushrooms). Place a foil square on a work surface and set a mushroom on top, gill-side up. Fold the foil edges over to enclose the mushroom and seal the edges shut. Repeat with the remaining mushrooms.

3. Grill the mushrooms over a medium-hot fire (see how to gauge heat level on page 4), with the sealed side of the foil packet facing up, until the mushrooms are juicy and tender, 10 to 12 minutes. Using tongs, unwrap the mushrooms and discard the foil. Return the unwrapped mushrooms to the grill, gill-side up, and cook until grill marked, 30 to 60 seconds. Cut the grilled mushrooms into ½-inch-thick slices.

4. Brush the remaining 3 tablespoons oil over both sides of each bread slice. Grill, turning once, until both sides of each slice are toasted and have dark grill marks, 1 to 2 minutes. Transfer the bread slices to a cutting board.

5. Spread 2 teaspoons Boursin cheese onto 4 slices of the bread. On the remaining slices, build the sandwich: Place mushroom slices on each of the 4 pieces of bread; cover with tomato slices and some mesclun mix. Place the bread with the cheese on top of the sandwich and serve immediately.

ONIONS

GRILLING ONIONS SOUNDS LIKE A GREAT idea. Ideally, the onions will caramelize on the grill and become crisp in spots. Slices expose the greatest surface area and make the most sense. However, as the slices cook, the rings separate and can easily fall down onto the coals as you try to flip or move the onions. To keep the slices from falling apart, we found that it is necessary to skewer each onion slice crosswise (from side to side) so that it will rest flat on the grill and can be easily turned. Thick slices are best for skewering—anything less than ½ inch thick will be difficult to work with. It's easier to work with large onions rather than smaller ones. In our tests, we particularly liked red, Vidalia, and Spanish, in part because it's easier to find oversized versions of these varieties. The Vidalias were particularly sweet, while the Spanish onions were heartier and not really sweet at all. The red onions were right in

between and appealed to tasters who wanted their grilled onions neither too sweet nor too savory.

❧

Grilled Onions
SERVES 4

These onions are wonderful on burgers or served with just about any grilled meat, game, or poultry. The onions sweeten and caramelize as they cook on the grill.

2   large onions, papery skins removed, cut crosswise into ½-inch-thick rounds
2   tablespoons extra-virgin olive oil
    Salt and ground black pepper

1. Place the onion slices on a baking sheet and brush with the oil. Season with salt and pepper to taste on both sides. Thread the onions onto skewers (see the illustration on page 314).

2. Grill the onions over a medium-hot fire (see how to gauge heat level on page 4), turning once, until streaked with dark grill marks, 10 to 12 minutes. Serve hot or at room temperature.

➤ VARIATIONS
Grilled Onions with Garlic and Thyme
Garlic and thyme add an extra flavor dimension to grilled onions. Other herbs, such as chives, parsley, tarragon, oregano, or rosemary, may be substituted for the thyme. If using rosemary, reduce the amount to ½ teaspoon.

1½   tablespoons extra-virgin olive oil
1   teaspoon chopped fresh thyme leaves
1   medium garlic clove, minced or pressed through a garlic press (about 1 teaspoon)
1   teaspoon white wine vinegar
2   large onions, papery skins removed, cut crosswise into ½-inch-thick rounds
    Salt and ground black pepper

1. Mix the oil, thyme, garlic, and vinegar together in a small bowl. Place the onion slices on a baking sheet and brush both sides of each slice with the oil mixture. Season with salt and pepper to taste. Thread the onions onto skewers (see the illustration on page 314).

2. Grill the onions over a medium-hot fire (see

how to gauge heat level on page 4), turning once, until streaked with dark grill marks, 10 to 12 minutes. Serve hot, warm, or at room temperature.

Grilled Red Onion and Tomato Salad

The sweetness of grilled onions is an excellent foil for the acidity of tomatoes. Try to use a high-quality, aged balsamic vinegar for this salad. Serve with steaks or burgers.

2   large red onions, papery skins removed, cut
      crosswise into 1/2-inch-thick rounds

3   tablespoons extra-virgin olive oil
      Salt and ground black pepper

3   small, ripe tomatoes (about 1 pound), cored
      and cut into 3/4-inch-thick wedges

10   large fresh basil leaves, chopped coarse

2   teaspoons balsamic vinegar

1. Place the onions on a baking sheet and brush both sides of each slice with a total of 2 tablespoons of the oil. Sprinkle generously with salt and pepper to taste. Thread the onions onto skewers (see the illustration at right).

2. Grill the onions over a medium-hot fire (see how to gauge heat level on page 4), turning once, until streaked with dark grill marks, 10 to 12 minutes.

3. Transfer the onions to a cutting board and cool slightly. Remove the skewers. Cut the onion slices in half, then place them in a serving bowl and toss gently to separate the layers.

4. Add the tomatoes, basil, and salt and pepper to taste to the bowl with the onions. Drizzle the remaining 1 tablespoon oil and the vinegar over the salad; toss gently. (The salad can be covered and set aside at room temperature for up to 1 hour.)

Grilled Onion Relish

Serve this relish with hamburgers, hot dogs, or any other grilled meat. You can also toss it with your favorite green salad. Use the same baking sheet to hold the onions before and after grilling.

2   large onions, papery skins removed, cut
      crosswise into 1/2-inch-thick rounds

2   tablespoons extra-virgin olive oil
      Salt and ground black pepper

BARBECUE 911

Onions that Fall through the Grate

How many times have you grilled onions only to have them slide off the skewers, through the grate, and onto the coals? Here's how to grill onions safely and easily.

Cut thick slices (at least 1/2 inch) from large red, Vidalia, or Spanish onions and impale them all the way through from side to side with a slender bamboo skewer (it should be about the same thickness as a toothpick or a thin metal skewer). If using longer skewers, thread two slices on each skewer. The skewered onion slices remain intact as they grill, so that no rings can fall onto the coals. As a plus, the onions are easily flipped with tongs.

1   large red bell pepper

2   medium Italian or Greek pepperoncini
      (pickled peppers), chopped fine

1/4   cup red wine vinegar

1   teaspoon sugar

1. Place the onion slices on a baking sheet and brush with the oil and season with salt and pepper to taste on both sides. Thread the onions onto skewers (see the illustration above).

2. Grill the onions over a medium-hot fire (see how to gauge heat level on page 4), turning once, until streaked with dark grill marks, 10 to 12 minutes. When the onions are done, transfer them to the baking sheet and cool for 10 minutes. While the onions are cooking, grill the bell pepper, turning it every 3 or 4 minutes, until all sides are blistered and charred, about 15 minutes. When the pepper is done, place it in a bowl and cover the bowl with

plastic wrap; allow to steam for 15 minutes.

3. Chop the grilled onions into ¼-inch dice and mix with the pepperoncini, vinegar, and sugar in a medium bowl. Using your fingers, peel the blackened skin from the bell pepper. Remove and discard the core and seeds. Chop the pepper into ¼-inch dice and mix the pepper with the onion mixture. Let stand at least 30 minutes to blend flavors. Serve warm or at room temperature.

BELL PEPPERS

THE ROASTING OF BELL PEPPERS HAS BECOME very popular, and for very good reasons. When roasted, sweet red bell peppers assume a complex, smoky flavor. They can be used on sandwiches or in sauces, or they can be served as part of an antipasto. Although the broiler is the best place to roast peppers, if you are grilling it is easy enough to roast peppers on the grill.

We found that you must take care not to over-roast the peppers. When the skin of a pepper puffs up and turns black, it has reached the point at which flavor is maximized and the texture of the flesh is soft but not mushy. After this point, continued exposure to heat results in darkened flesh that is thinner, flabbier-textured, and slightly bitter.

Roasted peppers need time to cool before being handled; steaming during this time makes it a bit easier to peel off the charred skin. The ideal steaming time is 15 minutes. The best method is to use a heat-resistant bowl (glass, ceramic, or metal) with a piece of plastic wrap secured over the top to trap the steam.

Don't be tempted to rinse the seeds away as you peel the peppers. Notice the rich oils that accumulate on your fingers as you work. It seems silly to rinse away those oils rather than savor them later with your meal.

Grilling Vegetables at a Glance

Use this chart as a guide to grilling the following vegetables. Lightly toss the vegetables or brush them on both sides with olive oil, preferably extra-virgin, before grilling. These vegetables should be cooked over a medium-hot fire.

VEGETABLE	PREPARATION	GRILLING DIRECTIONS
Asparagus	Snap off tough ends.	Grill, turning once, until tender and streaked with light grill marks, 5 to 7 minutes.
Corn	Remove all but last layer of husk.	Grill, turning every 1½ to 2 minutes, until husk chars and begins to peel away at tip, exposing some kernels, 8 to 10 minutes.
Corn Kebabs	Remove the husk and silk from the corn cobs. Cut crosswise into 1-inch rounds and skewer (see page 299).	Grill, turning every 1½ to 2 minutes, until corn is tender and lightly charred, 4 to 6 minutes.
Eggplant	Remove ends. Cut into ¾-inch-thick rounds or ¾-inch-thick strips.	Grill, turning once, until flesh is darkly colored, 8 to 10 minutes.
Endive	Cut in half lengthwise through stem end.	Grill, flat-side down, until streaked with dark grill marks, 5 to 7 minutes.
Fennel	Remove stalks and fronds. Slice vertically through base into ¼-inch-thick pieces.	Grill, turning once, until streaked with dark grill marks and quite soft, 7 to 9 minutes.
Mushrooms, white and cremini	Clean with a damp towel and trim thin slice from stems.	Grill on a vegetable grid, turning several times, until golden brown, 6 to 7 minutes.
Onions	Peel and cut into ½-inch-thick slices.	Grill, turning occasionally, until lightly charred, 10 to 12 minutes.
Peppers, bell	Core, seed, and cut into large wedges.	Grill, turning every two minutes, until streaked with dark grill marks, 8 to 10 minutes.
Tomatoes, cherry	Remove stems.	Grill on a grill grid or threaded onto skewers, turning several times, until streaked with dark grill marks, about 3 minutes.
Tomatoes, plum	Cut in half lengthwise and seed.	Grill, turning once, until streaked with dark grill marks, about 6 minutes.
Zucchini and Summer Squash	Remove ends. Slice lengthwise into ½-inch-thick strips.	Grill, turning once, until streaked with dark grill marks, 8 to 10 minutes.

The way peppers are treated after they are peeled will determine how long they keep. Simply wrapped in plastic wrap, peppers will keep their full, meaty texture for only about two days in the refrigerator. Drizzled with a generous amount of olive oil and placed in an airtight container, peppers will keep about one week without losing texture or flavor.

Although we love the silky texture of skinned roasted peppers, grilled bell peppers also can be served with their skins on, if desired. In that case, you need to oil the peppers quite well and to cook them less—just until lightly colored. The skins should wrinkle but not blister. Grilled peppers can be seasoned in numerous ways and make an excellent side dish.

Grill-Roasted Bell Peppers

MAKES 3 ROASTED PEPPERS

Although peppers are often roasted under a broiler or over an open gas burner in the kitchen, we find it practical and easy to do this job while grilling other foods. You'll find many uses for these peppers. They're great in sandwiches, on pizza, or as an omelet filling, to name a few.

    3   large bell peppers, preferably red, yellow, or
        orange
    2–3 tablespoons extra-virgin olive oil

1. Grill the whole peppers over a medium-hot fire (see how to gauge heat level on page 4), turning as the skin on each side blisters and chars (every 3 to 4 minutes), for a total of about 15 minutes.

2. Remove the peppers from the grill and transfer to a large bowl. Cover with plastic wrap and allow to steam for 15 minutes. With your fingers, scrape off the blackened skin from the peppers. Remove and discard the core and seeds. Place the peppers in an airtight container, drizzle with the olive oil, and refrigerate for up to 1 week.

Grilled Bell Peppers

SERVES 4 TO 6

Sweet bell peppers are especially tasty when grilled. Serve them as a side dish or as part of an antipasto platter with cold cuts, olives, and marinated mushrooms.

    3   large red, yellow, or orange bell peppers,
        prepared according to the illustrations
        on the facing page
    2   tablespoons extra-virgin olive oil
        Salt and ground black pepper

1. Toss the peppers and oil together in a large heat-resistant bowl. Season to taste with salt and pepper. Transfer the peppers to the grill, reserving the residual oil for the grilled peppers.

2. Grill the peppers over a medium-hot fire (see how to gauge heat level on page 4), turning every 2 minutes, until dark grill marks appear, the skins begin to wrinkle, and the peppers are crisp-tender, 8 to 10 minutes total.

3. Put the peppers back in the bowl and toss to coat with the residual oil. Allow the peppers to cool slightly and then cut them into thinner strips. Serve warm or at room temperature.

➤ VARIATIONS
Grilled Bell Peppers with Mint and Feta
The Greek flavors in this recipe go well with lamb.

    1½ tablespoons red wine vinegar
    1   tablespoon minced fresh mint leaves
    1   tablespoon minced fresh parsley leaves
    1   recipe Grilled Bell Peppers
    4   ounces feta cheese, crumbled
        (about ¼ cup)

Add the vinegar, mint, and parsley to the grilled pepper strips and toss to combine. Transfer the pepper mixture to a serving bowl. Sprinkle with the cheese and serve warm or at room temperature.

Spanish-Style Grilled Bell Peppers with Green Olives and Sherry Vinegar
Sherry vinegar adds a tangy, acidic edge to this dish. We suggest using red peppers in this recipe. Serve with other tapas (small dishes) for a Spanish-style appetizer spread.

    ¼   cup pitted Spanish green olives, sliced
    1½ tablespoons sherry vinegar
    1   tablespoon chopped fresh parsley leaves
    1   teaspoon capers, chopped
    1   recipe Grilled Bell Peppers

Toss the olives, vinegar, parsley, and capers with the grilled pepper strips. Serve warm or at room temperature.

Grilled Bell Peppers with Black Olives and Basil

Serve these peppers as a side dish with grilled fish or chicken, or use them as a sandwich filling.

1	recipe Grilled Bell Peppers
1/4	cup pitted black olives, sliced
1 1/2	tablespoons juice from 1 lemon
1 1/2	tablespoons thinly sliced fresh basil leaves
1	small garlic clove, minced or pressed through a garlic press (about 1/2 teaspoon)

Once the grilled peppers have cooled and been cut into thin strips, return them to the bowl. Toss the olives, lemon juice, basil, and garlic with the grilled pepper strips. Serve warm or at room temperature.

PREPARING BELL PEPPERS FOR THE GRILL

1. Cut each pepper in half lengthwise (through the stem end). Remove the core and seeds.

2. Cut the clean halves into thirds lengthwise.

BASTING OILS FOR VEGETABLES

THE BEST WAY TO SEASON VEGETABLES is to brush them with flavored oil just before grilling. Seasoning with salt and pepper both before and after grilling maximizes flavor.

Garlic Basting Oil

MAKES ABOUT 1/2 CUP

For extra flavor, use this basting oil, or the one that follows, instead of plain olive oil when cooking endive, fennel, or radicchio. These flavored oils work well with other vegetables, too, including peppers, onions, mushrooms, asparagus, and zucchini.

1/2	cup extra-virgin olive oil
1	small garlic clove, minced or pressed through a garlic press (about 1/2 teaspoon)

Combine the ingredients in a small bowl; let stand to allow the flavors to meld, about 10 minutes. Use while fresh and discard any unused oil.

Lemon-Rosemary Basting Oil

MAKES ABOUT 1/2 CUP

1/2	cup extra-virgin olive oil
1	teaspoon minced fresh rosemary
1	tablespoon juice plus 1 teaspoon grated zest from 1 lemon

Combine the ingredients in a small bowl; let stand to allow the flavors to meld, about 10 minutes. Use while fresh and discard any unused oil.

PLANTAINS

PLANTAINS ARE A STAPLE IN LATIN AMERICAN cuisine. They are widely available in many supermarkets and are always sold in Latino markets. You may also see them in some Asian food stores. Although plantains are technically a fruit rather than a vegetable (they closely resemble bananas in appearance), they are usually served as a side dish instead of dessert. They are starchier and less sweet than bananas. Also, if you look closely, you will notice that plantains are larger than most bananas, and their skins have more pronounced ridges that run from tip to tip. Finally, plantains are sold individually rather than in bunches.

Plantains are great grilled. Their sweet nature is complemented by the smokiness of the grill. We prefer ripe, black-skinned plantains for grilling. (Green plantains are most often fried to make a side dish called tostones.) Ripe plantains are also easier to peel than green ones and their flesh is a bit sweeter (although not really sugary like a banana).

We found that the plantains must be peeled and oiled before grilling or they will stick to the cooking grate. By the time the plantains are streaked with grill marks, they will be cooked through, tender, and ready to serve. Serve the plantains as a side dish to grilled chicken, fish, beef or pork.

Grilled Plantains

SERVES 4

Plantains absorb the flavors of the grill well and can be served with almost anything. Try these plantains with grilled chicken, fish, beef, or pork. For this recipe, the plantains are quartered, peeled, and then cut in half lengthwise.

2   large ripe plantains (10 to 12 ounces each)
2   tablespoons vegetable oil
    Salt

1. Trim the ends from the plantains and then cut the plantains crosswise into 4 pieces. With a paring knife, make a slit in the peel of each piece, from one end to the other end, and then peel away the skin with your fingers. Cut each piece of plantain in half lengthwise. Gently toss the plantains, oil, and salt to taste in a large bowl until the plantains are evenly coated with oil.

2. Grill the plantains over a medium-hot fire (see how to gauge heat level on page 4), turning once, until grill marks appear, 7 to 8 minutes. Serve immediately.

➤ VARIATION

Grilled Plantains with Lime and Mint
These grilled plantains are seasoned simply with a squeeze of lime and a sprinkling of mint.

1   recipe Grilled Plantains
2   tablespoons minced fresh mint leaves
1   lime, cut into 4 wedges

After removing the plantains from the grill, place them on a serving platter, sprinkle with the mint, and serve immediately with the lime wedges.

GRILLED POTATO SALAD

GRILLED POTATO SALAD IS THE PERFECT backyard-barbecue dish. But grilling potatoes can be a challenge, requiring a deft hand and a good dose of patience on the part of the grill master. If the fire is too hot, all you're going to get is a raw-on-the-inside, burnt-on-the-outside spud. But if you're nursing a modest, low-fire grill, your potatoes are more likely to be served alongside tomorrow's bacon and eggs than with your burger.

When researching different ways to grill potatoes, we were confronted time and time again with the method of blanching the potatoes in boiling water first and then transferring them to the grill just long enough to char slightly. The advantage to this is that the potatoes finish cooking on the grill in the same time it takes for the skin to color. We wondered if it would be possible to cook the potatoes entirely on the grill.

We grilled two different types of potatoes—russets and Yukon Golds, diced and then skewered, to allow us to rotate the potatoes for even browning. We used a medium-hot grill. After we took the potatoes off the grill, we immediately dressed each with a simple vinaigrette. To our dismay, all of the potatoes were starchy, mealy, and dry.

Maybe the potatoes did need to spend some time in boiling water first to prevent them from drying out on the grill. We dropped a platoon of cut potatoes into a pot of boiling water, cooking them until slightly underdone. Now we faced another problem: Many of the parboiled chunks split as we tried to thread them onto skewers. A test cook came up with a brilliant solution—skewer the potatoes first, boil them on the skewers, and then transfer them to the hot grill. So we threaded the raw potatoes onto skewers and submerged them in boiling water until they were just tender. With tongs, we easily transferred the skewers from pot to baking sheet to grill. About five minutes later, we had perfectly browned potatoes that were tender, moist, and really smoky. But they still needed a bit of spunk. For the next round, we brushed the skewered potatoes with some olive oil and sprinkled them with salt and pepper before putting them on the fire. When these potatoes came off the grill, we had to hide them from the rest of the kitchen staff if we wanted to save any for a salad—they were just too tempting to eat on their own as a snack.

Now that we had finally found a grilling method for the potatoes, we tried them in salad. Dressed with a simple vinaigrette, these potatoes retained their smoky flavor and had a wonderfully hearty texture not typically found in boiled potato salad.

Grilled Potatoes for Salad

SERVES 4 TO 6

When buying potatoes for these salads, the color is less important than the size; make sure they are no longer than 3 inches. You will need about fifteen 10-inch metal or wooden skewers. Prepare the other salad ingredients while the water heats so that the salad can be made with potatoes that are hot off the grill. Because the potatoes are precooked, they need only brown on the grill; you can grill them alongside your main dish over a grill fire of any intensity.

1½	teaspoons salt
1½	pounds new potatoes, 2 to 3 inches long, scrubbed and cut into eighths
2	tablespoons extra-virgin olive oil
¼	teaspoon ground black pepper

1. Bring 4 quarts of water to a boil in a Dutch oven or stockpot over high heat. Add 1 teaspoon of the salt.

2. Meanwhile, if using wooden skewers, trim them to lengths that can be submerged in the Dutch oven or stockpot. Skewer each piece of potato through the center with the skin facing out. Place 8 or 9 potato pieces on each skewer.

3. Drop the skewers into the boiling water and boil until a paring knife slips in and out of a potato easily, about 10 minutes.

4. While the potatoes boil, line a rimmed baking sheet with paper towels. With tongs, transfer the skewers to the baking sheet. Pat the potatoes dry with additional paper towels. Discard the paper towels. (The potatoes can be cooled to room temperature, covered with plastic wrap, and kept at room temperature for up to 2 hours.) Brush all sides of the potatoes with the oil and sprinkle with the remaining ½ teaspoon salt and the pepper.

5. Place the skewers on the hot grill. Cook, turning the skewers twice with tongs, until all sides are browned, 2 to 3 minutes per side over hot or medium-hot heat, or 4 to 5 minutes per side over medium or medium-low heat (see how to gauge heat level on page 4).

6. Slide the hot potatoes off the skewers and into a medium bowl. Use immediately in one of the following recipes.

SCRUBBING POTATOES

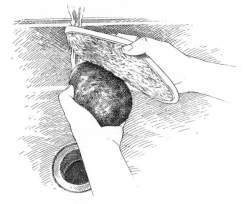

Buy a rough-textured bathing or exfoliating bath glove especially for use in the kitchen. The glove cleans dirt away from potatoes and other root vegetables, but it's relatively gentle and won't scrub away the skin.

➤ VARIATIONS

Grilled Potato and Arugula Salad with Dijon Mustard Vinaigrette

If you prefer, watercress can be substituted for the arugula.

I	recipe Grilled Potatoes for Salad
1½	teaspoons rice vinegar
	Salt
½	teaspoon ground black pepper
I	large bunch arugula, washed, dried, and stems trimmed (about 3 cups)
I	medium yellow bell pepper, cored, seeded, and cut into thin strips
3	tablespoons minced fresh chives
2	tablespoons extra-virgin olive oil
I	teaspoon Dijon mustard
I	small shallot, minced

1. Toss the hot potatoes with 1 teaspoon of the vinegar, ¼ teaspoon salt, and the pepper. Add the arugula, bell pepper, and chives and toss to combine.

2. Combine the oil, mustard, shallot, the remaining ½ teaspoon vinegar, and salt to taste in a small bowl. Pour the dressing over the potatoes and toss to combine. Serve immediately.

Spicy Grilled Potato Salad with Corn and Chiles

See page 299 for tips on grilling corn. Poblano chiles are relatively mild; to alter the spiciness in this salad, decrease or increase the quantity of jalapeños. You can roast the poblano chiles right on the grill.

I	recipe Grilled Potatoes for Salad
I	teaspoon white wine vinegar
	Salt
¼	teaspoon ground black pepper
I	cup cooked corn kernels cut from 2 ears grilled corn
2	medium poblano chiles, stemmed, roasted, peeled, seeded, and cut into ½-inch pieces
2	jalapeño chiles, stemmed, seeded, and minced
3	tablespoons juice from 3 limes
½	teaspoon sugar
4	tablespoons extra-virgin olive oil
3	medium scallions, white parts only, sliced thin
3	tablespoons minced fresh cilantro leaves

1. Toss the hot potatoes with the vinegar, ¼ teaspoon salt, and the pepper. Add the corn, poblanos, and jalapeños and toss to combine.

2. Whisk the lime juice and sugar together in a small bowl until the sugar dissolves. Whisk in the oil and salt to taste. Pour the dressing over the potatoes and add the scallions and cilantro. Toss to combine. Serve. (The salad can be covered with plastic wrap and kept at room temperature for up to 30 minutes; toss before serving.)

German-Style Grilled Potato Salad

For this recipe, toast the mustard seeds in a small dry skillet (with the cover on to keep the seeds in place) until lightly browned (this will take several minutes). Add the hot seeds to the vinegar and let them steep while you prepare the rest of the ingredients.

I	recipe Grilled Potatoes for Salad
3	tablespoons red wine vinegar
I	tablespoon yellow mustard seeds, toasted and added to the red wine vinegar (see note)
	Salt
½	teaspoon ground black pepper
4	ounces (about 4 slices) bacon, cut crosswise into ¼-inch strips
I	medium shallot, minced
⅓	cup low-sodium chicken broth
I	small celery rib, chopped fine (about ¼ cup)
2	tablespoons minced fresh parsley leaves

1. Toss the hot potatoes with 2 tablespoons of the vinegar (with all the mustard seeds), ¼ teaspoon salt, and the pepper.

2. Fry the bacon in a medium skillet over medium-high heat until brown and crisp, about 6 minutes. With a slotted spoon, transfer the bacon to the bowl with the potatoes. Reduce the heat to medium, add the shallot to the fat in the skillet, and cook, stirring occasionally, until softened, about 3 minutes. Add the broth and bring to a boil. Stir in the remaining 1 tablespoon vinegar. Pour the mixture over the potatoes and add the celery, parsley, and salt to taste; toss to combine. Serve. (The salad can be covered with plastic wrap and kept at room temperature for up to 30 minutes; toss before serving.)

SWEET POTATOES

BECAUSE OF THEIR CRUMBLY, STICKY TEXTURE, we find that sweet potatoes do not grill well when sliced. If you don't precook the slices, they don't cook through. If you do precook the slices, they become soft almost instantly and stick to the cooking grate.

However, it is possible to grill-roast whole sweet potatoes over indirect heat. (See page 3 for a definition of grill-roasting.) We found it best to lightly oil the skin for maximum crispness. When cooked alongside ribs or a whole chicken, the sweet potatoes absorb a fair amount of smoke flavor. For the best results, stick with medium-sized sweet potatoes. Mammoth sweet potatoes, which weigh a pound each, are too big for single servings and will char before they cook through properly.

Grill-roasted sweet potatoes can be served with butter and salt, but they are just as delicious with salsa, hot sauce, lime wedges, or the soy-sesame sauce at right.

Grill-Roasted Sweet Potatoes

SERVES 4

Sweet potatoes cooked whole on the grill are simple and phenomenally delicious. The skin crisps up and the flesh steams to fluffy perfection, ready to be eaten with butter and salt. We like to cook sweet potatoes this way when grill-roasting something else, such as poultry or ribs.

4	medium sweet potatoes (about 10 ounces each), scrubbed and blotted dry
	Vegetable oil for rubbing on the potato skin
	Salt
	Unsalted butter

1. Rub the sweet potatoes with a small amount of vegetable oil to barely coat the skin.

2. Grill the sweet potatoes, covered, over the cooler side of a two-level fire, turning every 10 to 12 minutes, until the sweet potatoes are tender, 45 minutes to 1 hour. (To check for doneness, stick the tip of a paring knife into the potato. It should offer no resistance, and the skin should be dark brown and crisp.) Remove the sweet potatoes from the grill.

3. Cut a slit along the top of each sweet potato and carefully squeeze to push up the flesh. Serve hot, in the style of baked potatoes, with salt and butter.

➤ VARIATION
Grill-Roasted Sweet Potatoes with Sweet Sesame and Soy Sauce

Soy sauce adds a salty contrast to the sweetness of the sweet potato and the added sugar. If you don't have black sesame seeds on hand, white sesame seeds are just as tasty.

1	recipe Grill-Roasted Sweet Potatoes
1/4	cup sugar
3	tablespoons soy sauce
4	teaspoons sake (Japanese rice wine)
1	tablespoon toasted sesame oil
2	teaspoons black sesame seeds, toasted in a small, dry skillet over medium heat until fragrant, about 4 minutes

While the sweet potatoes are cooking, combine the sugar, soy sauce, sake, and oil in a small saucepan set over medium heat. Cook, stirring often, just until the sugar has dissolved. Transfer the mixture to a small bowl. When the potatoes are done, cut a slit along the top of each sweet potato and carefully squeeze to push up the flesh. Drizzle a little of the soy-sesame mixture over each potato, then sprinkle with the sesame seeds. Serve immediately.

TOMATOES

ROUND, PLUM, AND CHERRY TOMATOES CAN all be grilled very briefly. Round and plum tomatoes should be halved and seeded, leaving behind just the meaty flesh. Cherry tomatoes should be skewered and grilled whole.

We found it best to grill the tomato halves skin-side up first, then skin-side down. Cooking the tomatoes skin-side up exposes their flesh to intense grill heat and caramelizes them lightly. Then, before the tomatoes become too soft, they are flipped so that they can continue grilling with their delicate flesh protected.

Grilled Round or Plum Tomatoes

SERVES 4

Grilling concentrates the flavor of tomatoes and intensifies their sweetness. Be sure to remove the seeds from the tomatoes before grilling; they can be quite bitter and watery. Serve the tomatoes as a side dish or use them as the basis for a smoky salsa or tomato sauce for pasta, pizza, or bruschetta.

4   small round tomatoes, cored, halved, and seeded, or 4 large plum tomatoes, cored, halved, and seeded (see the illustrations below)

2   tablespoons extra-virgin olive oil
     Salt and ground black pepper

1. Brush both sides of each tomato half with oil and season with salt and pepper to taste.

2. Grill the tomato halves, skin-side up, over a medium–hot fire (see how to gauge heat level on page 4) until the flesh has dark grill marks, about 4 minutes. Turn the tomato halves over and cook, skin-side down, until the skins have blistered and begun to pull away from the flesh, about 2 minutes. Serve the grilled tomatoes hot, warm, or at room temperature.

Grilled Cherry Tomatoes

SERVES 4

Cherry tomatoes are great for grilling. They cook up in minutes and make a tasty addition to pasta dishes or are delicious served on their own as a late-summer side dish. Fresh, thinly sliced basil goes especially well with these tomatoes.

1   pound cherry tomatoes, stems removed

2   tablespoons extra-virgin olive oil

1   medium garlic clove, minced or pressed through a garlic press (about 1 teaspoon)
     Salt and ground black pepper

1. Toss the tomatoes, oil, and garlic together in a medium bowl. Season with salt and pepper to taste. Thread the tomatoes onto skewers through the stem ends.

2. Grill the tomatoes over a medium–hot fire (see how to gauge heat level on page 4), turning once or twice, until dark grill marks appear and the skins begin to blister and wrinkle, about 3 minutes.

3. Remove the skewers from the grill and allow the tomatoes to cool slightly. Remove the tomatoes from the skewers (using a clean kitchen towel to hold the skewers) and serve immediately.

SEEDING TOMATOES

Seeding rids tomatoes of excess liquid and is an essential step before grilling them. Because of their different shapes, round and plum tomatoes are seeded differently.

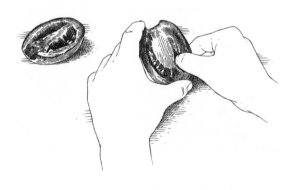

ROUND TOMATOES
Halve the cored tomato along its equator. If the tomato is ripe and juicy, gently give it a squeeze and shake out the seeds and gelatinous material. If not, scoop them out with your finger or a small spoon.

PLUM TOMATOES
Halve the cored tomato lengthwise, cutting through the core end. Break through the inner membrane with your finger and scoop out the seeds and gelatinous material.

➤ VARIATION
**Grilled Cherry Tomatoes
with Greek Flavors**
This marinade also works well with grilled plum or round tomatoes.

    2   tablespoons extra-virgin olive oil
    2   teaspoons red wine vinegar
    1   medium garlic clove, minced or pressed
        through a garlic press (about 1 teaspoon)
    1   teaspoon chopped fresh oregano leaves
  1/4   teaspoon sugar
    1   pound cherry tomatoes, stems removed
        Salt and ground black pepper

1. Mix the oil, vinegar, garlic, oregano, and sugar together in a medium bowl. Add the tomatoes and toss to coat. Season with salt and pepper to taste. Thread the tomatoes onto skewers through the stem ends.

2. Grill the tomatoes over a medium-hot fire (see how to gauge heat level on page 4), turning once or twice, until dark grill marks appear and the skins begin to blister and wrinkle, about 3 minutes.

3. Remove the skewers from the grill and allow the tomatoes to cool slightly. Remove the tomatoes from the skewers (using a clean kitchen towel to hold the skewers) and serve immediately.

CORING TOMATOES
Tomatoes are almost always cored—that is, the tough stem end is removed and discarded.

Place the tomato on its side on a work surface. Holding the tomato stable with one hand, insert the tip of a paring knife about 1 inch into the tomato at an angle just outside the core. Move the paring knife with a sawing motion, at the same time rotating the tomato toward you until the core is cut free.

WINTER SQUASH
WINTER SQUASH MAY NOT BE THE MOST obvious choice for grilling. However, in early fall, when grilling is still possible and squash fills markets, this dish makes good sense. Like potatoes, winter squash must be parboiled before being grilled. We find that butternut squash has the best texture and flavor among squash varieties.

Grilled Butternut Squash
SERVES 4 TO 6
This recipe calls for a lot of squash slices. Depending on the space between the bars on your cooking grate, you might want to cook them on a grill grid (see page 20) to prevent any slices from dropping down onto the fire.

    1   small butternut squash (about 2 pounds),
        peeled, seeded, and cut into 1/2-inch-thick
        slices (see the illustrations on page 324)
        Salt
    3   tablespoons extra-virgin olive oil
        Ground black pepper

1. Place the squash slices in a large pot. Cover with 2 quarts of cold water. Add 1 teaspoon salt and bring to a boil over high heat. Reduce the heat to medium and simmer until the squash is barely tender, about 3 minutes. Strain through a colander, being careful not to break up the squash slices. Transfer the squash to a large bowl; drizzle the oil over the top. Season with salt and pepper to taste, and gently turn the squash over to coat both sides of each slice with oil.

2. Grill the squash over a medium-hot fire (see how to gauge heat level on page 4), turning once, until dark brown caramelization occurs and the flesh becomes very tender, 8 to 10 minutes. Serve hot, warm, or at room temperature.

➤ VARIATION
**Spicy Grilled Butternut Squash
with Garlic and Rosemary**
Serve this squash in autumn with grilled meat.

    1   small butternut squash (about 2 pounds),
        peeled, seeded, and cut into 1/2-inch-thick
        slices (see the illustrations on page 324)

        Salt
4   tablespoons extra-virgin olive oil
2   tablespoons brown sugar
I   teaspoon chopped fresh rosemary
I   medium garlic clove, minced or pressed
        through a garlic press (about I teaspoon)
½   teaspoon red pepper flakes

1. Place the squash slices in a large pot. Cover with 2 quarts of cold water. Add 1 teaspoon salt and bring to a boil over high heat. Reduce the heat to medium and simmer until the squash is barely tender, about 3 minutes. Strain through a colander, being careful not to break up the slices. Transfer to a large bowl and drizzle the oil over the top. Sprinkle with the brown sugar, rosemary, garlic, red pepper flakes, and salt to taste. Gently turn the squash over to coat each slice with oil and seasonings.

2. Grill the squash over a medium-hot fire (see how to gauge heat level on page 4), turning once, until dark brown caramelization occurs and the flesh becomes very tender, 8 to 10 minutes. Serve hot, warm, or at room temperature.

ZUCCHINI AND SUMMER SQUASH

THE BIGGEST PROBLEM THAT CONFRONTS the cook when preparing zucchini and yellow summer squash is their wateriness. Both are about 95 percent water and will become soupy if just thrown into a hot pan. If they cook in their own juices, they won't brown. And since both are fairly mild, they really benefit from some browning.

That's why grilling is the easiest way to cook summer squash and zucchini. Cooked indoors, the squash must be shredded and squeezed dry or salted. Neither step is necessary when grilling. Simply cut the squash lengthwise into thick strips that are large enough to stay put on top of the grill rack.

The intense heat of the grill quickly expels excess moisture from the vegetables, and that moisture evaporates or drips down harmlessly onto the fire rather than sitting in a pan with the squash on the stovetop.

PREPARING BUTTERNUT SQUASH

1. Lay the squash on a cutting board. Cut off about ½ inch from both ends and discard. Cut the squash crosswise just above the bulbous base to create a long narrow section and a rounded section.

2. Stand the round section on its flat bottom. Use a sharp knife to cut down the sides of the squash, removing the tough outer skin.

3. Cut the squash straight down in half to expose the seeds. Scrape out the seeds using a metal spoon. Set each half, seed-side down, on the board, and cut into ½-inch-thick half circles.

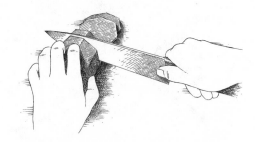

4. Stand the longer section of the squash on the cutting board and cut off the tough outer skin using the same technique described in step 2 (if this section is too tall, cut it in half crosswise first). Cut the peeled squash crosswise into ½-inch-thick rounds.

Grilled Zucchini or Summer Squash

SERVES 4

Excess moisture in zucchini and summer squash evaporates over the fire, making salting before cooking unnecessary.

- 4 medium zucchini or summer squash (about 1½ pounds), trimmed and sliced lengthwise (see the illustrations at right)
- 2 tablespoons extra-virgin olive oil
    Salt and ground black pepper

1. Lay the zucchini or squash on a large baking sheet and brush both sides of each slice with the oil. Sprinkle generously with salt and pepper.

2. Grill the zucchini or squash over a medium-hot fire (see how to gauge heat level on page 4), turning once, until streaked with dark grill marks, 8 to 10 minutes.

3. Transfer the zucchini or squash to a platter. Adjust the seasonings and serve hot, warm, or at room temperature.

➤ VARIATIONS

Grilled Zucchini or Summer Squash with Tomatoes and Basil

Grilled squash can also be marinated in a vinaigrette made with red wine vinegar. Substitute parsley, mint, cilantro, or tarragon leaves for the basil if desired.

- 1 tablespoon balsamic vinegar
    Salt and ground black pepper
- 2 tablespoons extra-virgin olive oil
- 1 large ripe tomato, cored and cut into thin wedges
- 2 tablespoons minced fresh basil leaves
- 1 recipe Grilled Zucchini or Summer Squash

1. Whisk the vinegar and salt and pepper to taste together in a large serving bowl. Whisk in the oil. Add the tomato and basil, toss gently, and set aside to marinate for at least 30 minutes and up to 1 hour.

2. Cool the grilled zucchini or squash and cut into 1-inch pieces.

3. Add the zucchini or squash to the bowl with the tomatoes and toss gently, adjusting the seasonings as needed. Serve warm or at room temperature.

Grilled Zucchini or Summer Squash with Capers and Oregano

Capers are pretty salty, so season the zucchini or squash sparingly.

- 1 tablespoon red wine vinegar
- 1 tablespoon capers, chopped
- 1 medium garlic clove, minced or pressed through a garlic press (about 1 teaspoon)
- 2 tablespoons extra-virgin olive oil
    Salt and ground black pepper

PREPARING ZUCCHINI OR SUMMER SQUASH FOR THE GRILL

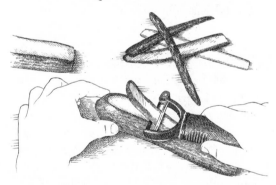

1. Cut a zucchini or summer squash in half lengthwise and run a cheese plane or Y-shaped vegetable peeler over the skinned side a couple of times. This exposes some flesh and flattens the squash slightly for stability on the cooking grate.

2. The extra exposed flesh allows for grill marks on both sides of each squash half.

1   recipe Grilled Zucchini or Summer Squash
1   tablespoon minced fresh oregano leaves

1. Whisk the vinegar, capers, and garlic together in a large serving bowl. Whisk in the oil and add salt and pepper to taste. Set the dressing aside.

2. Cool the grilled zucchini or squash and cut into 1-inch pieces.

3. Add the zucchini or squash to the bowl with the dressing and toss gently. Add the oregano and adjust the seasonings. Serve warm or at room temperature.

FRUIT

GRILLED FRUIT MAKES A SIMPLE SUMMERTIME dessert, or it can be used as an accompaniment to grilled pork, chicken, or fish. Grilling intensifies the sweetness of the fruit through caramelization.

In the chart on the facing page, we have included those fruits that we believe do best on the grill. Use smaller plums, peaches, apples, and pears when grilling, since larger fruit may burn on the outside before heating through to the center. All fruit to be grilled should be ripe, but still firm. Grill delicate fruits with their skins intact, as the skins keep the fruit from falling apart on the grill.

Grill over a medium–hot fire (see how to gauge heat level on page 4). Brush all prepared fruit lightly with vegetable oil before grilling. Fruit is done when it is marked on the exterior and just barely softened and heated through at the center.

GLAZES AND SAUCES FOR GRILLED FRUIT

THE FOLLOWING GLAZES, EXCEPT THE CARAMEL sauce, can be brushed on fruit during the last minute or so of cooking. (The caramel sauce is too sugary to use on the grill.) Keep the extra for drizzling onto fruit after grilling.

For a delicious dessert, top ice cream with grilled fruit and Simplified Caramel Sauce (see the facing page), Rum-Molasses Glaze (this page), or Sour Orange Glaze (this page). Sprinkle with toasted nuts of your choice.

Rum-Molasses Glaze
MAKES ABOUT 1/2 CUP

This glaze goes very well with bananas, pineapple, mangoes, pears, peaches, and apples. Use half of the mixture to brush onto the fruit during the last minute or two of cooking and the other half to drizzle over the fruit before serving. This recipe glazes 4 servings of fruit, with extra sauce to drizzle over the top of each serving.

1/4   cup plus 1/2 teaspoon dark rum
6   tablespoons molasses
1   tablespoon plus 1 teaspoon juice from 1 to 2 limes
3   tablespoons cold unsalted butter, cut into 1/4-inch pieces

1. Combine 1/4 cup of the rum, the molasses, and 1 tablespoon of the lime juice in a small, heavy-bottomed saucepan and bring to a boil over high heat. Reduce the heat to medium-high and cook until reduced to 1/3 cup, about 5 minutes.

2. Remove the pan from the heat and whisk in the butter until melted and incorporated. Stir in the remaining 1/2 teaspoon rum and 1 teaspoon lime juice. Use warm or at room temperature.

Sour Orange Glaze
MAKES ABOUT 1/2 CUP

As with the Rum-Molasses Glaze, this glaze can be brushed onto fruit during the last minutes of cooking. This recipe glazes 4 servings of fruit, with extra sauce to drizzle over the fruit before serving. This glaze goes well with all the fruit included in the chart.

1/2   cup orange juice
1/4   cup packed brown sugar
3   tablespoons juice from 3 limes
3   tablespoons cold unsalted butter, cut into 1/4-inch pieces.

1. Combine the orange juice, brown sugar, and 2½ tablespoons of the lime juice in a small saucepan and bring to a boil over high heat. Reduce the heat to medium-high and cook until reduced to 1/3 cup, about 7 minutes.

2. Remove the pan from the heat and whisk in the butter until melted and incorporated. Stir in the remaining ½ tablespoon lime juice. Use warm or at room temperature.

Simplified Caramel Sauce

MAKES ½ CUP

Use this sauce over ice cream and grilled fruit. This recipe makes enough for 4 desserts. Caramel sauce is especially good with grilled bananas, pears, apples, and peaches.

½	cup sugar
2½	tablespoons water
⅓	cup heavy cream
1	tablespoon rum or brandy

1. Combine the sugar and water in a medium, heavy-bottomed saucepan over medium-low heat. Stir until the sugar dissolves. Increase the heat to high and cook, swirling the pan occasionally but not stirring, until the caramel is uniformly golden amber in color, about 4 minutes.

2. Wearing oven mitts to protect your hands, remove the pan from the heat and slowly whisk in the cream, about one tablespoon at a time, making sure to keep the bubbling caramel away from your arms; stir until smooth. Stir in the rum. Set the caramel sauce aside to thicken and cool.

Sweet and Spicy Hoisin Glaze

MAKES A GENEROUS ¼ CUP

Fruit served with this glaze should be used as a side dish for the main meal. Use this glaze on stone fruit such as peaches or plums; it also goes well with grilled pineapple or mangoes. This recipe makes enough glaze to coat 4 servings of fruit.

2	tablespoons hoisin sauce
1	tablespoon soy sauce
1	tablespoon rice vinegar
1	tablespoon honey
½	teaspoon red pepper flakes

Mix all the ingredients together in a small bowl.

Grilling Fruit at a Glance

Use this chart as a guide to grilling the following fruits. Use a grill brush to scrape the cooking grate clean. Lightly brush the prepared fruit with vegetable oil. These fruits should be cooked over a medium-hot fire.

FRUIT	PREPARATION	GRILLING DIRECTIONS
Apple (small)	Cut in half through the core. Remove the core with a melon baller or sturdy teaspoon measure. Use a paring knife to cut out the stem.	Grill, skin-side up, for 5 to 6 minutes; turn and grill, skin-side down, for 5 to 6 minutes.
Banana	Leave the skin on; cut in half lengthwise using a sharp paring knife.	Grill, skin-side up, for 2 minutes; turn and grill, skin-side down, for another 2 minutes.
Mango	Peel, pit, and cut into 4 pieces (see the illustrations on page 328).	Grill larger pieces for 5 minutes, smaller pieces for 4 minutes, turning all the pieces once halfway through cooking time.
Peach (small)	Cut in half and remove the pit.	Grill, skin-side up, for 4 minutes; turn and grill, skin-side down, for 3 to 4 minutes.
Pear (small)	Cut in half lengthwise. Remove the core with a melon baller or sturdy teaspoon measure. Use a paring knife to cut out the stem.	Grill, skin-side up, for 5 minutes; turn and grill, skin-side down, for 5 minutes.
Pineapple	Cut into half circles (see the illustrations on page 328).	Grill for 6 minutes, turning once halfway through cooking time.
Plum (small)	Cut in half and remove the pit.	Grill, skin-side up, for 4 minutes; turn and grill, skin-side down, for another 2 minutes.

PREPARING A MANGO FOR GRILLING

1. A sharp paring knife makes it easy to peel a mango. Start by removing a thin slice from one end of the mango so that it sits flat on a work surface.

2. Hold the mango, cut side down, and remove the skin in thin strips with a paring knife, working from top to bottom.

3. Once the peel has been completely removed, cut down along the side of the flat pit to remove the flesh from one side of the mango. Do the same thing on the other side of the pit.

4. Trim around the pit to remove any remaining flesh.

PREPARING A PINEAPPLE FOR GRILLING

When preparing a pineapple for grilling, you need to cut pieces large enough so that they won't fall through the cooking grate.

1. Using a chef's knife, cut off ½ inch from the top and bottom of the pineapple, removing the leaves at the same time. Discard the top and bottom.

2. Set the flat bottom of the pineapple on the cutting board. Using a sharp knife, cut the outer ½ inch off the pineapple, running from the top to the bottom of the pineapple. Discard the outer portion.

3. Cut the peeled pineapple lengthwise through the center.

4. Cut each piece in half crosswise to yield a total of 4 equal pieces.

5. Remove the core of each piece, cutting at an angle to one side of the core and then cutting at an angle to the other side to meet the first cut, forming a V-cut. Remove core and discard.

6. Cut each cored quarter crosswise into ½-inch-thick slices. Each piece should resemble half a pineapple ring.

9

PIZZA AND BRUSCHETTA

PIZZA AND BRUSCHETTA

〜〜〜〜〜〜〜〜〜〜〜〜〜〜〜〜〜〜〜〜〜〜〜〜〜〜〜〜〜〜〜〜〜

GARLIC-HERB PIZZA DOUGH 332
    Hand-Kneaded Garlic-Herb Pizza Dough
    Garlic-Herb Pizza Dough Kneaded in a Standing Mixer

GRILLED PIZZA WITH OLIVE OIL AND SALT 334

GRILLED PIZZA WITH FRESH TOMATOES AND BASIL 335

GRILLED PIZZA WITH SHRIMP AND FETA CHEESE 335

GRILLED PIZZA WITH PORTOBELLO MUSHROOMS AND ONIONS 338

GRILLED PIZZA WITH GRILLED EGGPLANT AND GOAT CHEESE 338

GRILLED PIZZA WITH FENNEL, SUN-DRIED TOMATO, AND ASIAGO 340

GRILLED PIZZA WITH PROSCIUTTO, ARUGULA, AND
GORGONZOLA 340

GRILLED PIZZA WITH ASPARAGUS, CARAMELIZED ONIONS,
BLACK OLIVES, AND THYME 341

GRILLED PIZZA WITH BACON, CORN, AND CILANTRO 342

GRILLED BREAD FOR BRUSCHETTA 343

BRUSCHETTA WITH TOMATOES AND BASIL 343

BRUSCHETTA WITH SAUTÉED SPICY SHRIMP 343

BRUSCHETTA WITH FRESH HERBS 344

BRUSCHETTA WITH RED ONIONS, HERBS, AND PARMESAN 344

BRUSCHETTA WITH GRILLED PORTOBELLO MUSHROOMS 344

BRUSCHETTA WITH TAPENADE AND GOAT CHEESE 345

BRUSCHETTA WITH SAUTÉED SWEET PEPPERS 345

BRUSCHETTA WITH GRILLED EGGPLANT, ROSEMARY, AND
FETA CHEESE 345

BRUSCHETTA WITH ARUGULA, RED ONION, AND ROSEMARY–WHITE
BEAN SPREAD 346

IF YOU THINK GRILLED PIZZA SOUNDS
like one of those silly chef-inspired creations, think
again. Grilled flatbreads have a long history in Italy
and elsewhere. Our goal when developing these
pizza recipes was to stay faithful to the concept but
to streamline the process for American cooks.

Bruschetta is authentic Italian garlic bread.
Because it starts with a purchased loaf of bread,
it is much simpler to prepare than pizza. In fact,
making bruschetta is an excellent way to recycle
day-old bread. Thick slices of crusty country bread
are grilled, rubbed with garlic, then brushed with
quality olive oil. Toppings can be as simple as salt
or minced fresh herbs or slightly more involved,
such as grilled vegetables or diced fresh tomatoes.

As with vegetables and fruits, we often find
ourselves grilling pizza and bruschetta as part of
an entire meal from the grill. Since we generally
like to eat grilled pizza and bruschetta as appetizers, we suggest grilling them first, then cooking
the main course.

Bruschetta cooks so quickly that the fire will
still be plenty hot for grilling. In the case of pizza,
you may need to add more coals to grill the main
course, if using a charcoal grill. (See pages 336–
337 for tips on grilling pizza.)

Pizza Dough

THE TRICKIEST PART OF MAKING PIZZA AT
home lies in preparing the dough. While pizza
dough is nothing more than bread dough with oil
added for softness and suppleness, we found in our
testing that minor changes in the ingredient list
can yield dramatically different results.

Our goal in testing was threefold: We wanted
to develop a recipe that was simple to put
together; the dough had to be easy to shape and
stretch thin; and the crust needed to cook up crisp
and chewy, not tough and leathery.

After some initial tests, it was clear that
bread flour delivers the best texture. Bread
flour makes pizza crust that is chewy and crisp.
All-purpose flour can be used in a pinch, but
the resulting crust is less crisp. (See the box at
right for more information on the advantages of

INGREDIENTS: Bread Flour

When milling flour, a flour company must make a number of
choices that influence the way its product performs in recipes.
For starters, there is the essence of the flour, the wheat itself.
Bread flour is typically made from hard red winter wheat, which
has a protein content of about 13 percent. In comparison,
all-purpose flour is a blend of hard and soft wheats and has a
protein content of 10 or 11 percent. You can actually feel this
difference with your fingers; hard wheat flours tend to have a
subtle granular feel, while soft wheat flours feel fine but starchy,
much like cornstarch.

High-protein bread flours are generally recommended for
yeasted products and other baked goods that require a lot of
structural support. The reason is that the higher the protein level
in a flour, the greater the potential for the formation of gluten,
which is what supports the "lift" in yeasted baked products.
Gluten forms sheets that are elastic enough to move with the gas
released by yeast but are also sturdy enough to prevent that gas
from escaping, so that the dough doesn't deflate. Lower-protein
flours, on the other hand, are recommended for chemically leav-
ened baked goods such as cakes. This is because baking powder
and baking soda are quick leaveners. They lack the power and
endurance of yeast, which is able to force the naturally resistant
gluten sheets to expand. Gluten can overpower quick leaveners,
causing the final baked product to fall flat.

Because pizza is made with yeast, it came as little surprise to us
that bread flour made better pizza than all-purpose flour. The crust
was crispier. All-purpose flour makes a softer, chewier pizza crust.

using bread flour in pizza dough.)

The second key to perfect crust is water. We
found that using more water makes the dough
softer and more elastic. Soft dough stretches more
easily than a stiffer, harder dough with less water.

For combining the dry ingredients (flour and
salt) with the wet ingredients, the food processor
is our first choice. The liquid gets evenly incorporated into the dry ingredients, and the blade kneads
the dough in just 30 seconds. Of course, the dough
can also be kneaded by hand or with a standing
mixer. If making the dough by hand, resist the
temptation to add a lot of flour as you knead.

We use plastic wrap to cover the oiled bowl
that holds the rising dough. We found that the
tight seal offered by plastic wrap keeps the dough

EQUIPMENT: Food Processor

Spending several hundred dollars on a standing mixer is not an option for many cooks. They would rather use a food processor for grating, chopping, and shredding, as well as for kneading dough. (An inexpensive handheld mixer can handle [if not as well] most of the other tasks usually reserved for a standing mixer, including whipping cream and beating cake batter.)

So how to go about buying a food processor that can handle pesto as well as pizza dough? We evaluated eight food processors based on the results in five general categories: chopping and grinding, slicing, grating, pureeing, and kneading.

We found that most food processors chop, grind, slice, grate, and puree at least minimally well. Of course, there are differences in the performance of models, but they were not as dramatic as in the results of our kneading tests.

A food processor doesn't really knead bread dough fully, but it does bring the dry and wet ingredients together beautifully to form the dough. If a recipe calls for a smooth, satiny ball of dough, you will have to knead the dough by hand on the counter after processing; however, the kneading time should be just a few minutes. With pizza, hand kneading is not necessary because a satiny ball of dough is not really needed.

We found that successful kneading in a food processor was linked directly to large bowl size as well as to the weight of the base. The 11-cup machines performed best because they provided ample space for the ball of dough to move around. A heavy base provides stability, and the nods went to KitchenAid and Cuisinart, with their substantial, 10-pound-plus bases. Sturdy, sharp blades were also a plus.

moist and protects it from drafts better than the standard damp cloth. We reserve the damp cloth for use when the dough has been divided into balls and is waiting to be stretched.

To stretch dough to its maximum diameter, let it rest once or twice during the shaping process. Once you feel some resistance, cover the dough with a damp cloth and wait five minutes before going at it again. Fingertips and hands generally do a better job of stretching dough than a rolling pin, which presses air out of the risen dough and makes it tough. This low-tech method is also superior to flipping dough in the air and other frivolous techniques that may work in a pizza parlor but can lead to disaster at home. (For illustrations of shaping

pizza dough, see page 336.)

Even if you are grilling only a few individual pizzas, make a full dough recipe. After the dough has risen and been divided, place the extra pieces in an airtight container and freeze them for up to 1 month. Defrost and stretch the dough when desired.

Garlic-Herb Pizza Dough
MAKES ENOUGH FOR 8 INDIVIDUAL PIZZAS

The food processor is our favorite tool for making pizza dough because it works so quickly. However, you can knead this dough by hand or in a standing mixer (see the directions on the facing page). This dough requires 1 to 1½ hours of rising time. You can omit the garlic and herbs from this recipe to make a plain dough, but with grilled pizzas, which are so lightly topped, the crust should be as flavorful as possible. In fact, when brushed with oil and grilled, this dough is good enough to eat on its own as well as an accompaniment to meals.

2	tablespoons extra-virgin olive oil
4	medium garlic cloves, minced or pressed through a garlic press (about 4 teaspoons)
1	teaspoon minced fresh rosemary, thyme leaves, or oregano leaves
4	cups (22 ounces) bread flour, plus extra for dusting hands and work surfaces
1	envelope (about 2¼ teaspoons) instant yeast
1½	teaspoons salt
1¾	cups warm water (110 degrees) Vegetable oil or spray for oiling the container or bowl

1. Heat the oil in a small skillet over medium heat. Add the garlic and rosemary and sauté until the garlic is golden, 2 to 3 minutes. Remove the pan from the heat and cool the mixture to room temperature.

2. Process the flour, yeast, salt, and sautéed garlic mixture in a large food processor, pulsing to combine. Continue pulsing while pouring 1½ cups of the water through the feed tube. If the dough does not readily form into a ball, gradually add the remaining ¼ cup water and continue to pulse until a ball forms. Process until the dough is smooth and elastic, about 30 seconds longer.

3. The dough will be a bit tacky, so use a rubber

spatula to turn it out onto a lightly floured work surface; knead by hand for a few strokes to form a smooth, round ball. Put the dough in an oiled, straight-sided plastic container or deep, oiled bowl and cover with plastic wrap. Let rise until doubled in size, 1 to 1½ hours. Press the dough down with your fist and turn it out onto a lightly floured work surface. Divide and shape the dough as directed on page 336.

➤ VARIATIONS
Hand-Kneaded
Garlic-Herb Pizza Dough
Follow the recipe for Garlic-Herb Pizza Dough through step 1. Combine half of the flour, the yeast, and the salt in a deep bowl. Add the water and the sautéed garlic mixture and use a wooden spoon to combine. Add the remaining flour, stirring until a cohesive mass forms. Turn the dough out onto a lightly floured work surface and knead until smooth and elastic, 7 to 8 minutes. Use as little dusting flour as possible while kneading. Form the dough into a ball, put it in an oiled, straight-sided plastic container or deep, oiled bowl, cover it with plastic wrap, and proceed with the recipe.

Garlic-Herb Pizza Dough
Kneaded in a Standing Mixer
Follow the recipe for Garlic-Herb Pizza Dough through step 1. Place the flour, yeast, and salt

in the deep bowl of a standing mixer. With the paddle attachment, briefly combine the dry ingredients on low speed. Slowly add the water and the sautéed garlic mixture and continue to mix on low speed until a cohesive mass forms. Stop the mixer and replace the paddle with the dough hook. Knead until the dough is smooth and elastic, about 5 minutes. Form the dough into a ball, place it in an oiled, straight-sided plastic container or deep, oiled bowl, cover it with plastic wrap, and proceed with the recipe.

GRILLED PIZZA

GETTING THE TOPPING HOT IS THE HARDEST challenge when grilling pizza. Toppings have only a few minutes to heat through (any longer and the bottom of the crust will burn), so they must be kept fairly light.

We found that heavy toppings or liquidy sauces make grilled pizza very soggy and should be avoided. In our tests, raw ingredients that need only be heated through (fresh tomatoes, cheese, sliced shrimp) and cooked ingredients that are fairly dry (sautéed onions, grilled mushrooms, eggplant) worked best as toppings for grilled pizzas.

Because grilled pizzas are flipped (the bottom of the dough round eventually becomes the top of the pizza), we do not dust peels or baking sheets with sandy semolina or cornmeal, as is done for oven-baked pizza. Flour keeps the dough from sticking yet does not make the crust gritty, as did the semolina and cornmeal in our tests.

We found that oil helps keep grilled pizza dough moist, prevents sticking to the grill, and promotes even browning. Keep a brush and a small bowl of olive oil nearby when grilling pizzas. We brush some oil on the dough before it is grilled and then again when it is flipped.

Although we prefer to top grilled pizzas on a baking sheet and not on the grill, you will still spend a fair amount of time near the fire. To keep your hands as far away from the grill as possible, use tongs with long, heat-resistant handles to maneuver the dough. For the results from our

NO-FUSS FLOURING

Hauling out a large container of flour can be a nuisance when all you have to do is dust a work surface. Fashioning your own flour shaker solves the problem. Set a funnel in an empty glass salt shaker and scoop a little flour into the funnel. When the shaker has been filled, seal it and store it in the pantry.

BARBECUE 911

Pizza Breaking Apart on the Grill

Once the toppings on a grilled pizza are heated through, it is important to remove the pizza from the grill swiftly to make sure that the crust does not burn. For many grill cooks, though, that is more easily said than done, as the pizza can be difficult to maneuver intact with tongs or a spatula.

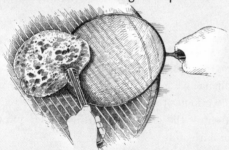

Use a splatter screen or rimless baking sheet as a pizza peel. Wear an oven mitt on one hand to hold the "peel" and use tongs or a spatula with the other hand to slide the pizza onto the peel.

testing of tongs, see page 19.

Once the dough has been flipped, it's time to add the toppings. We recommend that you use disposable aluminum pie plates to concentrate heat and to get the toppings hot by the time the bottom crust is nicely browned. If the toppings are not ready and the bottom crust is done, you can slide the pizzas onto a baking sheet and place them under the broiler.

In our testing, we found that large crusts are hard to flip, so we recommend making only small pizzas on the grill. This necessitates working in batches, so consider grilling pizzas for an informal meal when everyone is gathered in the backyard. Serve each pizza immediately as it comes off the grill. An extra pair of hands to top crusts while you tend the grill is helpful.

If you prefer not to be grilling pizzas to order, the crusts can be grilled until nicely browned

on both sides and then slid onto a baking sheet, cooled, covered, and kept at room temperature for several hours. When you are ready to serve the pizzas, brush the tops of the grilled pizza rounds with a little oil, add the toppings, and slide the crusts under a preheated broiler for several minutes. While the smoky grill flavor will not be as intense, this do-ahead method is much easier than the "grill, then top, then grill" method.

Most of the following grilled pizza recipes will serve four as a light summer meal (two small pizzas per person) or eight as a first course. We particularly like to serve grilled pizzas as a first course or hors d'oeuvre with drinks and then follow with something else from the grill.

Grilled Pizza with Olive Oil and Salt

MAKES 8 INDIVIDUAL PIZZAS

This basic pizza is flavored only with good olive oil and salt. Serve it with drinks or as an accompaniment to meals.

I   recipe Garlic-Herb Pizza Dough (page 332)
     Extra-virgin olive oil for brushing on the
     stretched dough
     Salt, preferably kosher

1. Prepare and shape the dough as directed. Light the grill. (See "Firing the Grill for Pizza" on page 336 for more instructions.)

2. When the grill is medium-hot, brush some oil over each stretched dough round and sprinkle with salt to taste.

3. Slide your hand under several dough rounds and gently flip them onto the grill, oiled-side down. Grill until dark brown grill marks appear, 1 to 2 minutes. Prick any bubbles that develop on the top surface with a fork. Brush the tops with more oil and flip the dough rounds. Grill until the pizza bottoms are crisp and browned, 2 to 3 minutes. Serve immediately and repeat the process with the remaining dough rounds.

Grilled Pizza with Fresh Tomatoes and Basil

MAKES 8 INDIVIDUAL PIZZAS

When tomatoes are at their best and all your cooking is outside on the grill, think of this light pizza.

I   recipe Garlic-Herb Pizza Dough (page 332)
     Extra-virgin olive oil for brushing on the
     stretched dough
     Salt
3   medium ripe tomatoes, cored and sliced
     crosswise into thin rounds
I   ounce grated Parmesan cheese (about $1/2$ cup)
     (optional)
I   cup lightly packed chopped fresh basil leaves
     Ground black pepper
$1/4$ cup pitted and quartered oil-cured black olives
     (optional)

1. Prepare and shape the dough as directed. Light the grill. (See "Firing the Grill for Pizza" on page 336, for more instructions.)

2. When the grill is medium-hot, brush some oil over each stretched dough round and sprinkle with salt to taste.

3. Slide your hand under several dough rounds and gently flip them onto the grill, oiled-side down. Grill until dark brown grill marks appear, 1 to 2 minutes. Prick any bubbles that develop on the top surface with a fork. Brush the tops with more oil and flip the dough rounds onto a clean baking sheet or peel, grilled-side up.

4. Brush the grilled dough surfaces with more oil. Arrange a portion of the tomatoes over each dough round, leaving a ½-inch border around the edges uncovered. Sprinkle with the Parmesan, if using, basil, and salt and pepper to taste. Drizzle with oil and dot with the olives, if using.

5. Slide the pizzas back onto the grill and cover each with a disposable aluminum pie plate. Grill until the pizza bottoms are crisp and browned, the tomatoes are hot, and the cheese (if using) melts, 2 to 3 minutes. Serve immediately and repeat the process with the remaining dough rounds.

Grilled Pizza with Shrimp and Feta Cheese

MAKES 8 INDIVIDUAL PIZZAS

This pizza is more moist than some of the others; serve it with a salad as a dinner for four.

I   recipe Garlic-Herb Pizza Dough (page 332)
$1/4$ cup extra-virgin olive oil, plus extra for
     brushing on the stretched dough
6   medium garlic cloves, minced or pressed
     through a garlic press (about 2 tablespoons)
4   teaspoons minced fresh oregano leaves
     Salt and ground black pepper
I   pound medium shrimp (40 to 50 per pound),
     peeled and halved lengthwise
8   ounces feta cheese, crumbled (about 2 cups)

1. Prepare and shape the dough as directed. Light the grill. (See "Firing the Grill for Pizza" on page 336 for more instructions.) Combine ¼ cup of the oil, the garlic, 2 teaspoons of the oregano, and salt and pepper to taste in a small bowl.

2. When the grill is medium-hot, brush some plain olive oil over each stretched dough round and sprinkle with salt to taste.

3. Slide your hand under several dough rounds and gently flip them onto the grill, oiled-side down. Grill until dark brown grill marks appear, 1 to 2 minutes. Prick any bubbles that develop on the top surface with a fork. Brush the tops with more plain olive oil and flip the dough rounds onto a clean baking sheet or peel, grilled-side up.

4. Arrange a portion of the shrimp over each dough round, leaving a ½-inch border around the edges uncovered. Brush some herb oil over each pizza, making sure the shrimp are lightly brushed with oil as well. Sprinkle the feta and the remaining 2 teaspoons oregano over the shrimp.

5. Slide the pizzas back onto the grill and cover each with a disposable aluminum pie plate. Grill until the pizza bottoms are crisp and browned, the shrimp are pink, and the cheese melts, 2 to 3 minutes. Serve immediately and repeat the process with the remaining dough rounds.

Grilled Pizza 101

Grilled pizza is an unexpected treat, with the fire imparting a light smoky flavor to the crust. Grilling is our favorite way to prepare pizza in the summer. We especially like grilled pizza as an appetizer, and suggest grilling it first, then cooking the main course.

FIRING THE GRILL FOR PIZZA

Whether you use a charcoal or gas grill, pizzas should always be cooked over a medium-hot, single-level fire (see how to gauge heat level on page 4).

☛ **For a charcoal grill:** Light a chimney starter filled with hardwood charcoal, and allow to burn until all the charcoal is covered with a layer of fine gray ash. Spread the lit coals in a single layer over the bottom of the grill. Set the cooking grate in place, place the cover on the grill, and let it heat up for 5 minutes. Use a grill brush to scrape the cooking grate clean. When the fire is medium-hot, you are ready to grill the pizzas.

☛ **For a gas grill:** The whole operation is quite simple. Just heat the grill by turning on all the burners to high and closing the lid, then turn the burners down to medium-high. Once you are done grilling the pizzas, you can adjust the burners as desired to create whatever kind of fire is needed.

The lid will be open (on both charcoal and gas) as you move pizzas on and off the grill, so you must heat toppings through by covering the pizzas with disposable pie plates. (It helps, too, if the toppings aren't ice cold when you put them on the pizza dough, so if they have been refrigerated, let them come to room temperature.) You will need to grill the pizzas in batches.

We like to serve grilled pizza as an appetizer. If cooking fish or steak for the main course, you will need to add more coals to the fire once the pizzas are done. With long-handled tongs, lift up the cooking grate and throw a handful or two of unlit coals onto the pile. Wait 10 minutes to make sure the coals are lit, then check for the appropriate heat level before grilling the main course.

SHAPING PIZZA DOUGH

1. Use a chef's knife or bench scraper to divide the risen and punched-down dough into eight pieces. A single dough recipe will make eight 8-inch pies.

2. Form each piece of dough into a smooth, round ball and cover them with a damp cloth. Let the dough relax for at least 5 minutes but no more than 30 minutes.

3. Working with one ball of dough at a time and keeping the others covered, flatten the dough ball into a disk using the palms of your hands.

4. Starting at the center of the disk and working outward, use your fingertips to press the dough into a round about ½ inch thick.

5. Use one hand to hold the dough in place and the other to stretch the dough outward. Rotate the dough a quarter turn and stretch it again. Continue turning and stretching until the dough will not stretch any further. Let the dough relax for 5 minutes, then continue stretching until it reaches a diameter of 8 inches. The dough should be about ¼ inch thick.

6. Use your palm to press down and flatten the thick edge of the dough. Transfer the dough rounds to baking sheets or metal peels that have been lightly dusted with flour; cover with a cloth until ready to use.

KEEPING PIZZA TOPPINGS ON HAND

Don't limit yourself to just the toppings in the recipes on pages 334–342. Whenever you are grilling or cooking something that would make a good pizza topping, reserve a little bit in a clean, plastic container, label it, and refrigerate or freeze it. When you're ready to make pizza, your toppings will be at hand.

SLICING MOZZARELLA FOR PIZZA

You want even slices of cheese on pizza, so that it melts at the same rate, but fresh mozzarella is quite soft, making it difficult to slice neatly with a knife. Simply place a piece of mozzarella in an egg slicer. Close the egg slicer to cut through the cheese. Remove the cheese from the egg slicer and separate into individual slices.

MAKING GRILLED PIZZA

1. Carefully lift the dough rounds and transfer them to a rimless metal baking sheet or pizza peel dusted with flour.

2. When the fire is ready, brush the tops of the dough rounds with oil and sprinkle them with salt. Slide your hand under each dough round and gently flip the dough onto the grill, oiled-side down. Cook them until dark grill marks appear, 1 to 2 minutes.

3. Use a fork to prick any bubbles that develop on the top surface of the dough rounds.

4. Brush the tops with more oil, then use long-handled tongs to flip the dough, grilled-side up, onto the (clean) baking sheet or pizza peel. (We find that topping the pizzas right on the grill can be difficult, given the intense heat, and so prefer this method.)

5. Brush the grilled surfaces with more oil.

6. Quickly arrange the toppings over the grilled surfaces, leaving a ½-inch border around the edges uncovered.

7. Slide the pizzas back onto the grill. Cover the pizzas with disposable aluminum pie plates and grill until the pizza bottoms are crisp and browned, 2 to 3 minutes.

Grilled Pizza with Portobello Mushrooms and Onions

MAKES 8 INDIVIDUAL PIZZAS

You can sauté the onions well in advance, but because you grill the mushrooms, it makes sense to cook them right before grilling the pizzas.

I	recipe Garlic-Herb Pizza Dough (page 332)
4	tablespoons extra-virgin olive oil, plus extra for brushing on the stretched dough
2	medium onions, halved and sliced thin
2	tablespoons balsamic vinegar
I	teaspoon minced fresh oregano or thyme leaves
	Salt and ground black pepper
4	medium portobello mushrooms (about I pound), stems removed and discarded and caps wiped clean
I	ounce grated Parmesan cheese (about ½ cup)

1. Prepare the dough as directed, but do not shape. Light the grill. (See "Firing the Grill for Pizza" on page 336 for more instructions.)

2. Heat 2 tablespoons of the oil in a large skillet over medium heat. Add the onions and sauté until golden, about 8 minutes. Stir in the vinegar and cook until the liquid has evaporated, about 1 minute. Stir in the oregano and salt and pepper to taste. Set the onions aside.

3. Brush the mushrooms with 2 tablespoons of the oil and season with salt and pepper to taste. Grill over a medium-hot fire (see how to gauge heat level on page 4), turning once, until the caps are streaked with dark grill marks, 8 to 10 minutes. Remove the mushrooms from the grill and cut into ¼-inch strips. Set the mushrooms aside.

4. Stretch the dough as directed in the illustrations on page 336. Check to make sure the grill is medium-hot. Brush some oil over each stretched dough round and sprinkle with salt to taste.

5. Slide your hand under several dough rounds and gently flip them onto the grill, oiled-side down. Grill until dark brown grill marks appear, 1 to 2 minutes. Prick any bubbles that develop on the top surface with a fork. Brush the tops with more oil and flip the dough rounds onto a clean

baking sheet or peel, grilled-side up.

6. Arrange a portion of the onions and mushrooms over each dough round, leaving a ½-inch border around the edges uncovered. Sprinkle with some of the cheese.

7. Slide the pizzas back onto the grill and cover each pizza with a disposable aluminum pie plate. Grill until the pizza bottoms are crisp and browned, the vegetables are hot, and the cheese melts, 2 to 3 minutes. Serve immediately and repeat the process with the remaining dough rounds.

Grilled Pizza with Grilled Eggplant and Goat Cheese

MAKES 8 INDIVIDUAL PIZZAS

Thin rounds of eggplant are brushed with a garlicky basil oil, grilled, then layered over grilled crusts and sprinkled with goat cheese.

I	recipe Garlic-Herb Pizza Dough (page 332)
¼	cup extra-virgin olive oil, plus extra for brushing on the stretched dough
6	medium garlic cloves, minced or pressed through a garlic press (about 2 tablespoons)
4	tablespoons minced fresh basil leaves
	Salt and ground black pepper
I	large eggplant (about I ½ pounds), ends trimmed, cut crosswise into ¼-inch-thick rounds
8	ounces goat cheese, crumbled (about 2 cups)

1. Prepare the dough as directed, but do not shape. Light the grill. (See "Firing the Grill for Pizza" on page 336 for more instructions.)

2. Combine ¼ cup of the oil, the garlic, 2 tablespoons of the basil, and salt and pepper to taste in small bowl.

3. Brush both sides of the eggplant slices with half of the herb oil. Grill over a medium-hot fire (see how to gauge heat level on page 4), turning once, until the flesh is darkly colored, 8 to 10 minutes. Set the eggplant aside.

4. Stretch the dough as directed in the illustrations on page 336. Check to make sure the grill is medium-hot. Brush some plain olive oil over each stretched dough round and sprinkle with salt to taste.

5. Slide your hand under several dough rounds and gently flip them onto the grill, oiled-side down. Grill until dark brown grill marks appear, 1 to 2 minutes. Prick any bubbles that develop on the top surface with a fork. Brush the tops with more plain olive oil and flip the dough rounds onto a clean baking sheet or peel, grilled-side up.

6. Brush the grilled dough surfaces with the remaining herb oil. Arrange a portion of the eggplant slices over each dough round, leaving a ½-inch border around the edges uncovered. Sprinkle with some of the goat cheese and the remaining 2 tablespoons basil.

7. Slide the pizzas back onto the grill and cover each pizza with a disposable aluminum pie plate. Grill until the pizza bottoms are crisp and browned, the eggplant is hot, and the cheese melts, 2 to 3 minutes. Serve immediately and repeat the process with the remaining dough rounds.

EQUIPMENT: Pizza Cutters

Homemade pizza can be the most rewarding of comfort foods, but all too often you end up with uneven, half-cut slices because you don't have a knife big enough to cut through the thick crust and extra cheese. Purchasing a pizza cutter is a natural solution, but our local kitchen store offered more pizza cutter models than Domino's has toppings. A shoddy pizza cutter drags melted cheese and toppings out of place, sprays hot grease, and fails to cut through crispy crust cleanly, leaving you to finish the job by tearing loose a slice by hand. A good pizza cutter gets the job done quickly, cleanly, and safely (and also makes an excellent tool for trimming the edges of rolled-out pastry dough). But with so many different options, how do you know which brand to choose? We decided to line up 10 different models ranging from double-wheeled pizza cutters to straight-edged pizza choppers to see which would stand supreme.

The basic wheel cutter is the most common variety, with dozens of models to choose from, priced from $3 to $25. Pre-testing eliminated the flimsiest models from further consideration, leaving eight sturdy wheels to test on thin- and thick-crust pizzas, evaluating them on price, cutting ability, ease of use, and safety. All of the pizza wheels cut through crisp thin-crust pies without a problem, but thick-crust, deep-dish pizzas overloaded with gooey cheese and toppings quickly thinned the pack. Cutters with large, 4-inch-diameter wheels were able to plow through the pies without a problem, while those with smaller wheels were quickly mired in the mess and left us with greasy knuckles. Of the large-wheel cutters, the clear winner was the Oxo Good Grips 4-inch ($10). Testers liked its rubberized, non-slip handle, protective thumb guard, and angled neck, which made cutting easier on the wrist. The large KitchenAid cutter ($15) also performed well and was the only cutter to come with a protective sheath, but it was heavy (almost 1 pound) and testers with smaller hands found it hard to grip the oversized handle, which was made from hard plastic and tended to get slippery.

Instead of a wheel cutter, professional pizzerias often employ a large rocking knife to cut clean through the pie in one stroke without dragging any hot cheese out of place. A few home versions of these knives are available, though usually by mail order. VillaWare's 14-inch Stainless Pizza Chopper ($14) cuts cleanly through crusts both thick and thin, but its size makes it doubly awkward: It's a bit too short to cut through a larger diameter pizza, but still too large for easy storage. LamsonSharp makes a similar size rocker ($25), but its wooden handles are trouble in the dishwasher, and its ultra-sharp edge curves up toward the grips, posing a serious hazard to exposed pinkies. Although these models managed to cleave the pizzas with relative ease, their oversized, machete-like blades seemed a bit over the top—not only difficult to store but just flat-out dangerous.

As the tests concluded, the superior performance of the pizza wheel means that we can finally have handsome homemade pizza. So save your money (and your fingers) and go with our champion—the Oxo Good Grips.

THE BEST PIZZA CUTTER
OXO GOOD GRIPS 4-INCH PIZZA WHEEL
The large wheel and comfortable handle on this cutter took home the trophy. It plowed through thin-crust and deep-dish pies alike.

Grilled Pizza with Fennel, Sun-Dried Tomato, and Asiago

MAKES 8 INDIVIDUAL PIZZAS

The sautéed fennel and onion topping can be prepared a day in advance. Bring to room temperature before topping the pizza.

I	recipe Garlic-Herb Pizza Dough (page 332)
3	tablespoons extra-virgin olive oil, plus extra for brushing on the stretched dough
I	large Spanish onion, halved and sliced thin
I	medium fennel bulb, stems and fronds discarded; bulb halved, cored, and sliced very thin
4	large garlic cloves, minced or pressed through a garlic press (about 2 tablespoons)
I	tablespoon fresh thyme leaves
I	teaspoon fennel seeds
¼	teaspoon red pepper flakes
	Salt
½	cup drained and slivered sun-dried tomatoes
I	ounce grated Asiago cheese (about ½ cup)

1. Prepare and shape the dough as directed. Light the grill. (See "Firing the Grill for Pizza" on page 336 for more instructions.)

2. While preparing the dough, heat 3 tablespoons of the oil in a large skillet over medium-high heat. Add the onion and fennel and cook, stirring often, until the vegetables soften, about 8 minutes. Add the garlic and continue cooking for 2 minutes. Stir in the thyme, fennel seeds, and red pepper flakes. Season with salt to taste. Set the onion-fennel mixture aside.

3. Check to make sure the grill is medium-hot. (See how to gauge heat level on page 4.) Brush some oil over each stretched dough round and sprinkle with salt to taste.

4. Slide your hand under several dough rounds and gently flip them onto the grill, oiled-side down. Grill until dark brown grill marks appear, 1 to 2 minutes. Prick any bubbles that develop on the top surface with a fork. Brush the tops with more oil and flip the dough rounds onto a clean baking sheet or peel, grilled-side up.

5. Brush the grilled dough surfaces with more oil. Arrange a portion of the onion-fennel mixture

BARBECUE 911

Grilled Pizza with Cold Toppings

Grilled pizza is delicious, but often the crust starts to burn on the bottom before the toppings are hot. It's important to top grilled pizzas very lightly and use ingredients that will cook quickly. Here's a good way to ensure that the toppings get nice and hot.

Once the toppings have been applied, invert a disposable aluminum pie plate over the pizza. The pie plate traps heat, creating an oven-like effect.

over each dough round, leaving a ½-inch border around the edges uncovered. Sprinkle some tomatoes and Asiago over the vegetables.

6. Slide the pizzas back onto the grill and cover each pizza with a disposable aluminum pie plate. Grill until the pizza bottoms are crisp and browned, the vegetables are hot, and the cheese melts, 2 to 3 minutes. Serve immediately and repeat the process with the remaining dough rounds.

Grilled Pizza with Prosciutto, Arugula, and Gorgonzola

MAKES 8 INDIVIDUAL PIZZAS

In this recipe, cheese pizzas are layered with prosciutto and arugula salad when they come off the grill. The residual heat from the pizzas softens the prosciutto and wilts the greens. Don't dress the arugula until you are ready to start grilling. If you prefer, replace the Gorgonzola with the same amount of fresh goat cheese or fresh mozzarella.

1. recipe Garlic-Herb Pizza Dough (page 332)
1. medium bunch arugula, washed, dried, and stemmed (about 4 cups loosely packed)
2. tablespoons extra-virgin olive oil, plus extra for brushing on the stretched dough
Salt and ground black pepper
4. ounces crumbled Gorgonzola cheese (about 1 cup)
1. ounce grated Parmesan cheese (about ½ cup)
¼. pound thinly sliced prosciutto

1. Prepare and shape the dough as directed. Light the grill. (See "Firing the Grill for Pizza" on page 336 for more instructions.)

2. While the grill heats up, place the arugula in a medium bowl. Drizzle 2 tablespoons of the oil over the arugula and sprinkle with salt and pepper to taste. Toss and set the salad aside.

3. When the grill is medium-hot (see how to gauge heat level on page 4), brush some oil over each stretched dough round and sprinkle with salt to taste.

4. Slide your hand under several dough rounds and gently flip them onto the grill, oiled-side down. Grill until dark brown grill marks appear, 1 to 2 minutes. Prick any bubbles that develop on the top surface with a fork. Brush the tops with more oil and flip the dough rounds onto a clean baking sheet or peel, grilled-side up.

5. Brush the grilled dough surfaces with more oil. Dot each round with some Gorgonzola and Parmesan, leaving a ½-inch border around the edges uncovered.

6. Slide the pizzas back onto the grill and cover each pizza with a disposable aluminum pie plate. Grill until the pizza bottoms are crisp and browned and the cheeses melt, 2 to 3 minutes.

7. When the pizzas come off the grill, cover each with a layer of prosciutto and some arugula. Serve immediately and repeat the process with the remaining dough rounds.

Grilled Pizza with Asparagus, Caramelized Onions, Black Olives, and Thyme

MAKES 8 INDIVIDUAL PIZZAS

To save preparation time, prepare the onions the day before and bring them to room temperature before topping the pizza.

1. recipe Garlic-Herb Pizza Dough (page 332)
3. tablespoons extra-virgin olive oil, plus extra for brushing on the stretched dough
2. medium yellow onions, halved and sliced thin
Salt
1. teaspoon fresh thyme leaves
Ground black pepper
1. pound asparagus, tough ends snapped off
½. cup pitted and quartered kalamata olives
1. ounce grated Parmesan cheese (about ½ cup)

1. Prepare and shape the dough as directed. Light the grill. (See "Firing the Grill for Pizza" on page 336 for more instructions.)

2. While preparing the dough, heat 2 tablespoons of the oil in a large skillet over medium-high heat. Add the onions and sprinkle with ¼ teaspoon salt. Sauté until softened, about 5 to 7 minutes. Reduce the heat to medium-low and continue cooking until the onions are very soft and caramelized, 12 to 15 minutes longer. Stir in the thyme and season with pepper to taste.

3. Toss the asparagus with 1 tablespoon oil and salt and pepper to taste in a medium bowl. Grill over a medium-hot fire (see how to gauge heat level on page 4), turning once, until browned and barely tender, about 6 minutes. Remove the asparagus from the grill and cut each piece in half. Set the asparagus aside.

4. Check to make sure the grill is medium-hot. Brush some oil over each stretched dough round and sprinkle with salt to taste.

5. Slide your hand under several dough rounds and gently flip them onto the grill, oiled-side down. Grill until dark brown grill marks appear, 1 to 2 minutes. Prick any bubbles that develop on the top surface with a fork. Brush the tops with more oil and flip the dough rounds onto a clean baking sheet or peel, grilled-side up.

6. Brush the grilled dough surfaces with more oil. Arrange a portion of the onion mixture and the asparagus over each dough round, leaving a ½-inch border around the edges uncovered. Sprinkle some olives and cheese over the vegetables.

7. Slide the pizzas back onto the grill and cover each pizza with a disposable aluminum pie plate. Grill until the pizza bottoms are crisp and browned, the vegetables are hot, and the cheese melts, 2 to 3 minutes. Serve immediately and repeat the process with the remaining dough rounds.

Grilled Pizza with Bacon, Corn, and Cilantro

MAKES 8 INDIVIDUAL PIZZAS

This southwestern-style pizza is delicious, if unusual.

I	recipe Garlic-Herb Pizza Dough (page 332)
12	ounces (about 12 slices) bacon, cut crosswise into ¼-inch pieces
	Extra-virgin olive oil for brushing on the stretched dough
	Salt
2	ears corn, husks and silk removed, kernels cut off the cob
8	ounces Pepper Jack cheese, grated (about 2½ cups)
½	cup minced fresh cilantro leaves

1. Prepare and shape the dough as directed. Light the grill. (See "Firing the Grill for Pizza" on page 336 for more instructions.)

2. While preparing the dough, place the bacon in a large skillet over medium heat. Cook until crisp and brown, about 8 minutes. Use a slotted spoon to transfer the bacon to a paper towel–lined plate.

3. When the grill is medium-hot (see how to gauge heat level on page 4), brush some oil over each stretched dough round and sprinkle with salt to taste.

4. Slide your hand under several dough rounds and gently flip them onto the grill, oiled-side down. Grill until dark brown grill marks appear, 1 to 2 minutes. Prick any bubbles that develop on

BARBECUE 911

Burned Toast

Unevenly sliced bread poses a problem when grilling; thinner slices will burn before thicker slices are done. Getting slices of consistent thickness, unfortunately, isn't always easy, especially with artisanal loaves of bread, whose crusts are thick and difficult to cut cleanly. Use this technique to cut even slices so that each slice grills at the same rate.

Turn the loaf on its side and cut through the top and bottom crust simultaneously. The crust on the side of the bread, which is now facing down, is often thinner and easier to slice. Don't forget to use a bread knife, which is long and serrated, and cuts bread more easily than other types of knives. And don't step away from the grill when grilling bread—it can turn from perfectly grilled to perfectly burnt, very quickly.

the top surface with a fork. Brush the tops with more oil and flip the dough rounds onto a clean baking sheet or peel, grilled-side up.

5. Brush the grilled dough surfaces with more oil. Arrange a portion of the bacon, corn, and cheese over each dough round, leaving a ½-inch border around the edges uncovered.

6. Slide the pizzas back onto the grill and cover each pizza with a disposable aluminum pie plate. Grill until the pizza bottoms are crisp and browned, the corn is hot, and the cheese melts, 2 to 3 minutes. Sprinkle each pizza with a little cilantro and serve immediately. Repeat the process with the remaining dough rounds.

Bruschetta

AUTHENTIC ITALIAN GARLIC BREAD, CALLED bruschetta, is never squishy or soft. Crisp, toasted slices of country bread are brushed with extra-virgin olive oil (never butter), rubbed with raw garlic, and then slathered with various ingredients. Toppings can be as simple as salt and pepper or fresh herbs. Ripe tomatoes, grilled mushrooms, or sautéed onions make more substantial toppings.

We found that narrow loaves of Italian bread are not suitable for bruschetta. We prefer crusty country loaves that yield larger slices. Oblong loaves that measure about five inches across are best, but round loaves will work. As for thickness, we found that about one inch provides enough heft to support weighty toppings and gives a good chew.

Oil can be drizzled over the toast or brushed on for more even coverage. Grilling the bread creates little jagged edges that pull off tiny bits of garlic when the raw clove is rubbed over the bread. For more garlic flavor, rub vigorously. One large piece of toast is enough for a single appetizer serving. Two or three slices make a good lunch when accompanied by a salad.

Because bread toasts so quickly on the grill (it takes just a minute or two), it's easy enough to grill bruschetta before making the main course. Although bread is best grilled over a medium fire, you can toast it over a hot fire as long as you watch it vigilantly. For instance, this may be necessary if you want to serve bruschetta before grilling steak, since the latter requires a hot fire.

Grilled Bread for Bruschetta

MAKES 8 TO 10 SLICES

Garlic bread, Italian style. Serve this simple grilled bread as an accompaniment to meals or use as part of an hors d'oeuvre spread with cheese, meats, and vegetables.

I	loaf country bread (about 12 by 5 inches) cut crosswise into I-inch-thick slices, ends discarded
3	tablespoons extra-virgin olive oil
I	large garlic clove, peeled and halved

Grill the bread over a medium fire (see how to gauge heat level on page 4), turning once, until golden brown on both sides, 1 to 1½ minutes. Remove the bread from the grill, brush both sides of each slice with the oil, and rub with the cut garlic clove.

Bruschetta with Tomatoes and Basil

MAKES 8 TO 10 SLICES

This is the classic bruschetta, although you can substitute other herbs. Decrease the quantity of stronger herbs, such as thyme or oregano.

4	medium ripe tomatoes, cored, seeded, and cut into ½-inch dice
⅓	cup shredded fresh basil leaves
	Salt and ground black pepper
I	recipe Grilled Bread for Bruschetta

1. Mix the tomatoes, basil, and salt and pepper to taste together in a medium bowl. Set aside.

2. Use a slotted spoon to divide the tomato mixture among the grilled bread slices. Serve immediately.

Bruschetta with Sautéed Spicy Shrimp

MAKES 8 TO 10 SLICES

The cream in this recipe is optional. If you have it on hand, it adds a little extra richness to the shrimp. Be sure to serve the shrimp mixture warm on the grilled bread; once the mixture cools down, it loses its appeal.

2	tablespoons unsalted butter
I	medium garlic clove, minced or pressed through a garlic press (about I teaspoon)
½	teaspoon red pepper flakes
1¼	pounds shrimp, peeled and cut into ¼- to ⅜-inch pieces
2	tablespoons heavy cream (optional)
	Salt and ground black pepper
1½	teaspoons juice from I lemon
2	tablespoons minced fresh parsley leaves
I	recipe Grilled Bread for Bruschetta

1. Melt the butter in a large skillet over medium-high heat. Once the foam begins to subside, add the garlic and red pepper flakes and sauté until fragrant but not brown, about 30 seconds. Add the shrimp and cook until pink, about 1 minute. Add the heavy cream, if using, season with salt and pepper to taste, and cook until the shrimp are bright pink and opaque at the center, 1 minute longer. Stir in the lemon juice and parsley. Cover and keep warm.

2. Top each grilled bread slice with a portion of the warm shrimp mixture and serve immediately.

Bruschetta with Fresh Herbs

MAKES 8 TO 10 SLICES

This is ideal as an accompaniment to meals or as an antipasto.

5	tablespoons extra-virgin olive oil
1½	tablespoons minced fresh parsley leaves
1	tablespoon minced fresh oregano or thyme leaves
1	tablespoon minced fresh sage leaves
	Salt and ground black pepper
1	recipe Grilled Bread for Bruschetta (page 343), without the oil

1. Mix the oil, herbs, and salt and pepper to taste together in a small bowl. Set aside.

2. Brush the grilled bread with the herb oil and serve immediately.

Bruschetta with Red Onions, Herbs, and Parmesan

MAKES 8 TO 10 SLICES

The sautéed onions may be prepared in advance and the toasts assembled at the last minute. Bring the prepared onions to room temperature before serving.

3	tablespoons extra-virgin olive oil
4	medium red onions, halved lengthwise and sliced thin
4	teaspoons sugar
2	tablespoons balsamic vinegar
1½	tablespoons minced fresh herbs such as parsley, basil, or chives
	Salt and ground black pepper

1	recipe Grilled Bread for Bruschetta (page 343)
3	tablespoons grated Parmesan cheese

1. Heat the oil in a large skillet over medium-high heat. Add the onions and sugar and sauté, stirring often, until softened, 7 to 8 minutes. Reduce the heat to medium-low. Continue to cook, stirring often, until the onions are sweet and tender, 7 to 8 minutes longer. Stir in the vinegar and herbs and season to taste with salt and pepper. Set the onion mixture aside. (It can be covered and refrigerated for several days.)

2. Divide the onion mixture among the grilled bread slices and sprinkle with the Parmesan. Serve immediately.

Bruschetta with Grilled Portobello Mushrooms

MAKES 8 TO 10 SLICES

To serve, flip the mushrooms onto the toast so that their juices seep down into the bread.

4	large portobello mushrooms, stems removed and discarded, caps wiped clean
3	tablespoons extra-virgin olive oil
1	tablespoon minced fresh rosemary
	Salt and ground black pepper
1	recipe Grilled Bread for Bruschetta (page 343)

MAKING PARMESAN SHAVINGS

Thin shavings of Parmesan can be used to garnish a variety of dishes. Simply run a sharp vegetable peeler along the length of a piece of cheese to remove paper-thin curls.

1. Place the mushroom caps on a large baking sheet. Mix the oil with the rosemary and salt and pepper to taste in a small bowl. Brush the oil mixture over both sides of the mushrooms.

2. Grill the mushrooms over a medium fire (see how to gauge heat level on page 4), turning once, until the caps are cooked through and streaked with dark grill marks, 8 to 10 minutes. Transfer to a cutting board when done.

3. Halve the grilled mushrooms. Place one half, gill-side down, over each slice of grilled bread. Serve immediately.

Bruschetta with Tapenade and Goat Cheese

MAKES 8 TO 10 SLICES

Tapenade is an intensely flavored olive spread that goes beautifully with bruschetta and goat cheese.

1	cup kalamata olives, pitted and halved (about 20 large)
2	medium garlic cloves, roughly chopped
4	anchovy fillets, roughly chopped
2	teaspoons drained capers
6	tablespoons extra-virgin olive oil
1	recipe Grilled Bread for Bruschetta (page 343), without the oil
4	ounces fresh goat cheese, crumbled (about 1 cup)

1. Place the olives, chopped garlic, anchovies, capers, and oil in a food processor. Process until the mixture becomes a slightly chunky paste (do not overprocess). Set aside.

2. Spread about 2 tablespoons of the olive mixture over each slice of grilled bread. Sprinkle with the goat cheese and serve immediately.

Bruschetta with Sautéed Sweet Peppers

MAKES 8 TO 10 SLICES

3	tablespoons plus 1 teaspoon extra-virgin olive oil
4	large red bell peppers, cored, seeded, and cut into 3- by ¼-inch strips
2	medium onions, halved and sliced thin
¾	teaspoon salt
3	medium garlic cloves, minced or pressed through garlic press (about 1 tablespoon)
¼	teaspoon red pepper flakes
1	(14.5-ounce) can diced tomatoes, drained, ¼ cup juice reserved
1½	teaspoons chopped fresh thyme leaves
4	teaspoons sherry vinegar
1	recipe Grilled Bread for Bruschetta (page 343)
2	ounces Parmesan cheese, shaved with a vegetable peeler (½ to 1 cup shavings)

1. Heat 3 tablespoons of the oil, the bell peppers, onions, and ½ teaspoon of the salt in a 12-inch skillet over medium-high heat; cook, stirring occasionally, until the vegetables are softened and browned around the edges, 10 to 12 minutes. Reduce the heat to medium, push the vegetables to the sides of the skillet, and add the remaining 1 teaspoon oil, the garlic, and red pepper flakes to the cleared center. Cook the garlic, mashing it with a wooden spoon, until fragrant, about 30 seconds, then stir the garlic into the vegetables. Reduce the heat to low and stir in the tomatoes, reserved juice, and thyme. Cover and cook, stirring occasionally, until the moisture has evaporated, 15 to 18 minutes. Off the heat, stir in the vinegar and remaining ¼ teaspoon salt.

2. Divide the pepper mixture evenly among the grilled bread slices, top with the shaved Parmesan, and serve.

Bruschetta with Grilled Eggplant, Rosemary, and Feta Cheese

MAKES 8 TO 10 SLICES

If desired, the eggplant can be grilled ahead of time, refrigerated, and brought back to room temperature before serving on bruschetta. You can substitute an equal amount of ricotta salata (a firm, salted cheese) or goat cheese for the feta cheese if you choose.

4	tablespoons extra-virgin olive oil
1½	tablespoons balsamic vinegar
1	medium garlic clove, minced or pressed through a garlic press (about 1 teaspoon)

I   teaspoon chopped fresh rosemary
I   large eggplant (about 1 1/2 pounds),
ends trimmed, cut crosswise into
3/4-inch-thick slices
Salt and ground black pepper
I   recipe Grilled Bread for Bruschetta (page 343)
3   ounces feta cheese, crumbled (about 3/4 cup)

1. Mix the oil, vinegar, garlic, and rosemary together in a small bowl. Lay the eggplant slices on a baking sheet and brush both sides of each slice with the vinegar-oil mixture. Sprinkle with salt and pepper to taste.

2. Grill the eggplant over a medium-hot fire (see how to gauge heat level on page 4), turning once, until streaked with dark grill marks, about 8 to 10 minutes. Remove the eggplant from the grill and cut crosswise into 1-inch strips.

3. Top each slice of grilled bread with a portion of the eggplant slices and crumbled feta. Serve immediately.

Bruschetta with Arugula, Red Onion, and Rosemary–White Bean Spread

MAKES 8 TO 10 SLICES

In a recent taste test, we preferred Westbrae Natural Organic great northern beans and Progresso cannellini beans—by far—to the other brands sampled.

I   (19-ounce) can cannellini or great Northern beans, rinsed and drained
3   tablespoons extra-virgin olive oil
2   tablespoons water
I   tablespoon juice from I lemon
I   small garlic clove, crushed
3/4   teaspoon salt
1/4   teaspoon ground black pepper
1/4   teaspoon chopped fresh rosemary
I   tablespoon balsamic vinegar
1/4   medium red onion, sliced thin (about 1/4 cup)
I   recipe Grilled Bread for Bruschetta (page 343)

I   small bunch arugula, washed, dried, and cut into 1/2-inch strips (about 3 cups)

1. In a food processor, process two thirds of the beans, 2 tablespoons of the oil, the water, lemon juice, garlic, 1/2 teaspoon of the salt, and 1/8 teaspoon of the pepper until smooth, about 10 seconds. Add the remaining beans and the rosemary; pulse until incorporated but not smooth, about five 1-second pulses.

2. Whisk the remaining 1 tablespoon oil, the vinegar, the remaining 1/4 teaspoon salt, and the remaining 1/8 teaspoon pepper together in a medium bowl; add the onion slices and toss.

3. Divide the bean spread evenly among the grilled bread slices. Toss the arugula with the onion until coated. Top each bread slice with a portion of the arugula mixture. Serve immediately.

TASTING: Canned White Beans

We sampled four canned white beans in our search for the best canned beans. Because so few brands of canned cannellini beans are distributed nationwide, we broadened our taste test to include alternative white beans with widespread distribution. We tasted each contender twice: straight from the can (after being drained and rinsed) and prepared in a recipe. Here are the two that came out on top:

THE BEST CANNED WHITE BEANS

WESTBRAE NATURAL
Great Northern Beans

Tasters liked the "earthy" flavor and "creamy" texture of these beans.

PROGRESSO
Cannellini Beans

Tasters praised their "sweet, slightly salty" flavor.

10

SALADS AND SIDE DISHES

SALADS AND SIDE DISHES

YOGURT-MINT CUCUMBER SALAD 351

CREAMY DILL CUCUMBER SALAD 351

SESAME-LEMON CUCUMBER SALAD 351

TOMATO SALAD WITH ARUGULA AND SHAVED PARMESAN 352

ISRAELI TOMATO AND CUCUMBER SALAD 352

TOMATO SALAD WITH FETA AND CUMIN-YOGURT DRESSING 352

TOMATO, MOZZARELLA, AND BASIL SALAD (INSALATA CAPRESE) 353

CREAMY COLESLAW... 354

SWEET-AND-SOUR COLESLAW 355
    Curried Coleslaw with Apples and Raisins

FOOLPROOF HARD-COOKED EGGS 355

AMERICAN POTATO SALAD WITH HARD-COOKED EGGS AND SWEET PICKLES .. 357

FRENCH POTATO SALAD 359
    French Potato Salad with Arugula, Roquefort, and Walnuts
    French Potato Salad with Radishes, Cornichons, and Capers
    French Potato Salad with Hard Salami and Gruyère

GERMAN POTATO SALAD 360

MACARONI SALAD 362
    Macaroni Salad with Curried Apples
    Macaroni Salad with Chipotles and Cilantro

PASTA SALAD WITH BROCCOLI AND OLIVES 363

PASTA SALAD WITH EGGPLANT, TOMATOES, AND BASIL 364

PASTA SALAD WITH ARUGULA AND SUN-DRIED TOMATO VINAIGRETTE 364

BREAD SALAD WITH TOMATOES, HERBS, AND RED ONIONS 365

BREAD SALAD WITH ROASTED PEPPERS AND OLIVES 365

PITA BREAD SALAD WITH OLIVES, FETA, AND MINT 366

TABBOULEH 367

BOSTON BAKED BEANS 369
    Barbecued Baked Beans

ALL-PURPOSE CORNBREAD 371
    Spicy Jalapeño-Cheddar Cornbread

SIDE DISHES, SUCH AS POTATO SALAD, coleslaw, and baked beans are as synonymous with "cookouts" as the grilled steak, hamburger, or ribs they're served alongside. Slices of fresh cornbread are also a welcome addition to the barbecue table. This chapter encompasses all our favorite sides for foods cooked on the grill. Also, see the grilled vegetable recipes in chapter 8 for more side dish options.

CUCUMBER SALADS

COOL CUCUMBER SALADS GO WELL WITH many grilled foods, especially those that are spicy. But, more often than not, by the time you eat a cucumber salad, the cucumbers have gone soft and watery, losing their appealing texture and diluting the dressing to near tastelessness. This made the primary goal of our testing simple: Maximize the crunch.

The standard recommendation for ridding watery vegetables such as cucumbers, zucchini, and eggplant of unwanted moisture is to salt them. The salt creates a higher concentration of ions (tiny, charged particles) at the surface of the vegetable than exists deep within its cells. To equalize the concentration levels, the water within the cells is drawn out through permeable cell walls. In the case of cucumbers, this leaves them wilted, yet very crunchy. Of course, some culinary questions remain: How much salt should be used? Should the cucumber slices be weighted,

or pressed, to squeeze out the liquid? How long should they drain?

To find out if pressing salted cucumbers really squeezes out more liquid, we trimmed and seeded six cucumbers to a weight of 8 ounces each, sliced them on the bias, and tossed each batch with 1 teaspoon of salt in its own colander set over a bowl. Three batches had zipper-lock freezer bags filled with water placed on top; no additional weight was added to the other three. Then we left them all to drain, measuring the liquid each had released after 30 minutes and after one, two, three, and 12 hours. At each time point, the weighted cucumbers had released about 1 tablespoon more liquid than the unweighted cucumbers; 3 versus 2 tablespoons after 30 minutes, 4 versus 3 after one hour, and so on. Interestingly, the weighted cukes gave off no more liquid after 12 hours than they had after three hours (7 tablespoons at both points). So weighting the cucumbers is worthwhile, but forget about draining the cucumbers overnight; it's not necessary.

At the one-hour mark, we could not detect an appreciable difference in flavor or texture between weighted and unweighted cukes. But we wanted to see how they would perform in salads with different types of dressings. We mixed one batch each of the weighted and unweighted cucumbers with three types of sauces—creamy, oil-based, and water-based—and allowed each to sit at room temperature for one hour. This is where the true value of better-drained cucumbers became obvious; every single taster preferred the salads made

SALTING CUCUMBERS

1. Peel and halve each cucumber lengthwise. Use a small spoon to remove the seeds and surrounding liquid from each cucumber half.

2. Lay the cucumber halves flat-side down on a work surface and slice them on the diagonal into ¼-inch-thick pieces. Toss the cucumbers and salt (1 teaspoon for each cucumber) in a colander set in a bowl.

3. Place a gallon-size zipper-lock plastic bag filled with water on top of the cucumbers to weigh them down and force out the liquid. Drain for at least 1 hour and up to 3 hours.

with pressed cucumbers for their superior crunch and less diluted dressings.

As for the amount of salt, some cooks recommend simply using the quantity with which you would normally season the cucumber, while others say you should use more, up to 2 tablespoons per cucumber, and then rinse off the excess before further use. We tried a few cucumbers prepared exactly as those described in the first test except with 2 tablespoons of salt. The cucumbers tossed with 2 tablespoons of salt did give up about 1 tablespoon more liquid within the first hour than those tossed with 1 teaspoon had, but they also required rinsing and blotting dry with paper towels. And despite this extra hassle, they still tasted much too salty in the salads. We decided to forgo the extra salt.

Yogurt–Mint Cucumber Salad

SERVES 4

Known as raita, this creamy salad is traditionally served as a cooling contrast to curry dishes. It is a natural pairing with grilled lamb.

3	medium cucumbers, peeled, seeded, sliced, salted, and drained, as shown on the facing page
	Salt
1	cup plain low-fat yogurt
1/4	cup minced fresh mint leaves
2	tablespoons extra-virgin olive oil
1	medium garlic clove, minced or pressed through a garlic press (about 1 teaspoon)
	Ground black pepper

Let the salted cucumbers drain, weighted, in the colander for at least 1 hour and up to 3 hours. Whisk the yogurt, mint, oil, garlic, and salt and pepper to taste in a medium bowl. Add the drained cucumbers; toss to coat. Serve chilled, adjusting seasonings if necessary.

Creamy Dill Cucumber Salad

SERVES 4

Salting and draining the onion along with the cucumbers in this recipe removes the sharp sting of raw onion. The flavors in this salad work well with grilled chicken or fish.

3	medium cucumbers, peeled, seeded, sliced, salted, and drained, as shown on the facing page
1/2	medium red onion, sliced very thin, salted and drained with the cucumbers
	Salt
1	cup sour cream
1/4	cup minced fresh dill
3	tablespoons cider vinegar
1	teaspoon sugar
	Ground black pepper

Let the salted cucumbers and onion drain, weighted, in the colander for at least 1 hour and up to 3 hours. Whisk the sour cream, dill, vinegar, sugar, and salt and pepper to taste in a medium bowl. Add the drained cucumbers and onion; toss to coat. Serve chilled, adjusting seasonings if necessary.

Sesame–Lemon Cucumber Salad

SERVES 4

Mild rice vinegar works well in this Asian-inspired dressing.

3	medium cucumbers, peeled, seeded, sliced, salted, and drained, as shown on the facing page
	Salt
1/4	cup rice vinegar
2	tablespoons toasted sesame oil
1	tablespoon juice from 1 lemon
1	tablespoon sesame seeds, toasted in a small dry skillet over medium heat until fragrant, about 4 minutes
2	teaspoons sugar
1/8	teaspoon red pepper flakes, plus more to taste

Let the salted cucumbers drain, weighted, in the colander for at least 1 hour and up to 3 hours. Whisk all of the ingredients except the cucumbers in a medium bowl. Add the drained cucumbers; toss to coat. Serve chilled or at room temperature.

TOMATO SALADS

TOMATOES ARE THE BASIS FOR COUNTLESS summer salads. A bonus of summer tomato salads is that the mildly acidic juices from the tomatoes themselves provide a delicious base for a dressing, so little additional acid is needed. To make this work, you need to extract a little of the juice from the tomatoes before you make the salad. This is easily done. Simply cutting the tomatoes into wedges and letting them sit for 15 minutes allows them to exude their juices. Salting the cut tomatoes helps this process and seasons the tomatoes and their juices at the same time.

Some cooks recommend peeling the tomatoes, but we find the skin on local vine-ripened tomatoes to be thin and unobtrusive. If home-grown or locally grown tomatoes are unavailable, substitute halved cherry tomatoes.

Tomato Salad with Arugula and Shaved Parmesan

SERVES 4 TO 6

Use a vegetable peeler to remove thin shavings from the chunk of cheese. (See the illustration on page 344.) Serve this salad with grilled steak or chicken.

4–5	medium ripe tomatoes
1/2	teaspoon salt
2	tablespoons extra-virgin olive oil
1	tablespoon balsamic vinegar
1	small garlic clove, minced or pressed through a garlic press (about 1/2 teaspoon) Ground black pepper
1	small bunch arugula, washed, dried, stemmed, and chopped coarse (about 1 cup loosely packed)
24	shavings Parmesan cheese

1. Core and halve the tomatoes lengthwise, then cut each half into 4 or 5 wedges. Toss the wedges with the salt in a large bowl; let rest until a small pool of liquid accumulates, 15 to 20 minutes.

2. Meanwhile, whisk the oil, vinegar, garlic, and pepper to taste in a small bowl. Pour the mixture over the tomatoes and their accumulated liquid; toss to coat. Set aside to blend flavors, about 5 minutes.

3. Add the arugula and Parmesan; toss to combine. Adjust the seasonings and serve immediately.

Israeli Tomato and Cucumber Salad

SERVES 4 TO 6

Try serving this salad with grilled fish, such as salmon.

2	medium cucumbers Salt
4–5	large ripe tomatoes
1/4	cup finely chopped red onion
1/4	cup chopped fresh mint leaves
3	tablespoons extra-virgin olive oil
3	tablespoons juice from 1 lemon Ground black pepper

1. Peel the cucumbers, halve lengthwise, and remove the seeds (see illustration 1 on page 350); cut halves in half lengthwise, then cut crosswise into 1/4-inch-thick pieces (see illustration 2). Toss the cucumbers with 2 teaspoons salt in a colander and place a gallon-size plastic bag filled with water on top of the cucumbers to weigh them down and force out the liquid (see illustration 3). Let drain for at least 1 hour and up to 3 hours; discard liquid.

2. Core and halve the tomatoes, then cut each half into 4 or 5 wedges. Toss the wedges with 1/2 teaspoon salt in a large bowl; let rest until a small pool of liquid accumulates, 15 to 20 minutes.

3. Meanwhile, whisk the red onion, mint, oil, lemon juice, and pepper to taste in a small bowl. Pour the mixture over the tomatoes and their accumulated liquid and toss to coat. Let rest to blend flavors, about 5 minutes.

4. Add the drained cucumber pieces; toss to combine. Adjust seasonings and serve immediately.

Tomato Salad with Feta and Cumin-Yogurt Dressing

SERVES 4 TO 6

Draining the yogurt in a fine sieve gives it a creamier, denser texture, which is better suited to use in a dressing. This salad is particularly good with grilled chicken.

4–5 large ripe tomatoes

1/2 teaspoon salt

1/4 cup plain yogurt, drained in a fine sieve for
about 30 minutes (discard the liquid)

3 small scallions, sliced thin

1 tablespoon extra-virgin olive oil

1 tablespoon juice from 1 lemon

1 teaspoon ground cumin

1 tablespoon chopped fresh oregano leaves

1 small garlic clove, minced or pressed through a
garlic press (about 1/2 teaspoon)
Ground black pepper

1 small chunk feta cheese (about 3 ounces)

1. Core and halve the tomatoes, then cut each half into 4 or 5 wedges. Toss the wedges with the salt in a large bowl; let rest until a small pool of liquid accumulates, 15 to 20 minutes.

2. Meanwhile, whisk the drained yogurt, scallions, oil, lemon juice, cumin, oregano, garlic, and pepper to taste in a small bowl. Pour the mixture over the tomatoes and their accumulated liquid; toss to coat. Set aside to blend flavors, about 5 minutes.

3. Crumble the feta over the tomatoes; toss to combine. Adjust seasonings and serve immediately.

❧

Tomato, Mozzarella, and Basil Salad (Insalata Caprese)

SERVES 4 TO 6

It is not necessary to salt the tomatoes for this salad. For best presentation, discard the first and last slice from each tomato. Serve this salad with Grilled Tuscan Steak (page 40) for an Italian-inspired meal.

4 medium, very ripe tomatoes, cored and cut
into 1/4-inch-thick slices

16 ounces fresh mozzarella, cut into
1/4-inch-thick slices

2 tablespoons roughly chopped fresh basil leaves

1/4 teaspoon kosher salt or sea salt

1/8 teaspoon ground black pepper

1/4 cup extra-virgin olive oil

Layer the tomatoes and mozzarella alternately and in concentric circles on a medium platter.

Sprinkle the tomatoes and cheese with the basil, salt, and pepper. Drizzle the oil over the platter and allow the flavors to meld for 5 to 10 minutes. Serve immediately.

~~~~~~

COLESLAW

DESPITE ITS SIMPLICITY, COLESLAW HAS always bothered us for two reasons: the pool of watery dressing that appears at the bottom of the bowl after a few hours, and the salad's sharp flavor, no matter what kind or quantity of vinegar is used. Our slaw always seemed to taste better when we tried it again the next day, but by then the dressing was the consistency of skim milk.

While most recipes instruct the cook to toss the shredded cabbage with the dressing immediately, a few add an extra step. Either the shredded (or merely quartered) cabbage is soaked in ice water for crisping and refreshing, or it is salted, drained, and allowed to wilt.

Cabbage soaked in ice water was crisp, plump, and fresh. If looks were all that mattered, this cabbage would have scored high next to the limp, salted cabbage in the neighboring colander. But its good looks were deceiving. Even though we drained the cabbage and dried it thoroughly, the dressing didn't adhere. Furthermore, within minutes, the cabbage shreds started to lose their recently acquired water, creating a large puddle of water that was diluting the creamy dressing. The stiff cabbage shreds were strawlike, making them difficult to fork and even more difficult to get into the mouth without leaving a creamy trail.

Quite unlike the ice-water cabbage, the salted shreds lost most of their liquid while sitting in the salt; this left them wilted but pickle-crisp. Because the cabbage had already lost most of its liquid, little was left to be drawn out by the salt in the dressing. We had found the solution to the problem of watery dressing. In addition, we found that this cabbage, having less water in it, took on more of the dressing's flavors and that, unlike the stiff shreds of ice-water cabbage, this limp cabbage was also easier to eat.

We did discover that the salting process leaves the cabbage a bit too salty, but a quick rinse washes away the excess salt. After the cabbage has been rinsed, just pat it dry with paper towels and refrigerate until you are ready to combine it with the dressing. If the coleslaw is to be eaten immediately, rinse it quickly in ice water rather than tap water, then pat it dry. Coleslaw, at least the creamy kind, should be served cold.

Having figured out how to keep the cabbage from watering down the dressing, we were ready to tackle the problem of acidity in the dressing. We found a few creamy coleslaw recipes in which the cabbage was tossed with sour cream only or with a combination of mayonnaise and sour cream—no vinegar. Although we were looking for ways to tone down the tang, a mix of sour cream and mayonnaise proved too mild for our taste. Other recipes called for lemon juice rather than vinegar. Although the lemon juice gave the coleslaw a pleasantly tart flavor, it lacked the depth that vinegar could offer. We decided to give low-acidity rice vinegar a try. We drizzled a bit of rice vinegar over the mayonnaise-tossed cabbage and found its mild acidity to be just right.

Although there are several styles of coleslaw, the two that follow are classics—one mild and creamy, the other sweet and sour. Adjust either recipe to your taste. If sour cream is a must for you in creamy slaw, then substitute it for some or all of the mayonnaise. Also, try adding green pepper, celery, red onions, or apples.

Creamy Coleslaw
SERVES 4

If you like caraway or celery seed in your coleslaw, you can add ¼ teaspoon of either with the mayonnaise and vinegar. You can shred, salt, rinse, and pat the cabbage dry a day ahead, but dress it close to serving time.

½	medium head (1 pound) red or green cabbage, shredded (see the illustrations below)
1	large carrot, peeled and grated
1	teaspoon salt
½	cup mayonnaise
¼	cup minced onion
2	tablespoons rice vinegar
	Ground black pepper

1. Toss the cabbage and carrot with the salt in a colander or large mesh strainer set over a medium bowl. Let stand until the cabbage wilts, at least 1 hour and up to 4 hours.

2. Dump the wilted cabbage and carrot into the bowl and rinse thoroughly in cold water (use ice water if serving slaw immediately). Pour the vegetables back into the colander, pressing, but not squeezing, to drain. Pat dry with paper towels. (The vegetables can be stored in a zipper-lock bag and refrigerated overnight.)

3. Pour the cabbage and carrot back into the bowl. Add the mayonnaise, onion, and vinegar; toss to coat. Season with pepper to taste. Cover and refrigerate until ready to serve.

SHREDDING CABBAGE

1. Cut a whole head of cabbage into quarters. Cut away the hard piece of the core attached to each quarter.

2. Separate the cored cabbage quarters into stacks of leaves that flatten when pressed lightly.

3. Use a chef's knife to cut each stack of cabbage diagonally into long, thin pieces. Alternatively, roll the stacked leaves crosswise to fit them into the feed tube of a food processor fitted with the shredding disk.

Sweet-and-Sour Coleslaw

SERVES 4

Because rice vinegar tends to mellow, you may want to use cider vinegar if making the slaw a day ahead. The presence of the sugar in this recipe keeps you from having to rinse off salt from the cabbage, as is ordinarily the case.

½ medium head (1 pound) red or green cabbage, shredded (see the illustrations on the facing page)

1 large carrot, peeled and grated

½ cup sugar

1 teaspoon salt

¼ teaspoon celery seed

6 tablespoons vegetable oil

¼ cup rice wine vinegar

Ground black pepper

1. Toss the cabbage and carrot with the sugar, salt, and celery seed in a colander or large mesh strainer set over a medium bowl. Let stand until the cabbage wilts, at least 1 hour and up to 4 hours.

2. Pour the draining liquid from the bowl; rinse and dry the bowl. Transfer the wilted cabbage and carrot to the bowl.

3. Add the oil and vinegar; toss to coat. Season with pepper to taste. Cover and refrigerate until ready to serve. (The slaw can be refrigerated for up to 2 days.)

➤ VARIATION

Curried Coleslaw with Apples and Raisins

SERVES 6

With the addition of apple and raisins, this variation makes 2 more servings. This slaw is particularly good served with grilled pork.

Follow the recipe for Sweet-and-Sour Coleslaw, adding 1 teaspoon curry powder, 1 medium apple, peeled and cut into small dice, and ¼ cup raisins with the oil and vinegar.

AMERICAN POTATO SALAD

WHAT'S A SUMMER PICNIC OR BACKYARD barbecue without potato salad? This dish should be easy to make well, but all too often the potatoes are bland, and they fall apart under the weight of the dressing.

Foolproof Hard-Cooked Eggs

MAKES 3

You can double or triple this recipe as long as you use a pot large enough to hold the eggs in a single layer, covered by an inch of water.

3 large eggs

1. Place the eggs in a medium saucepan, cover with 1 inch of water, and bring to a boil over high heat. Remove the pan from the heat, cover, and let sit for 10 minutes. Meanwhile, fill a medium bowl with 1 quart of water and 1 tray of ice cubes (or the equivalent).

2. Transfer the eggs to the ice bath with a slotted spoon and let sit 5 minutes. Peel the eggs according to the illustrations below.

PEELING HARD-COOKED EGGS

1. Tap the egg all over against the counter surface and then roll it gently back and forth a few times on the counter to crack the shell all over.

2. Begin peeling from the air pocket (the wider end of the egg). The shell should come off in spiral strips attached to a thin membrane.

We decided to focus on a simple mayonnaise-based salad with hard-cooked eggs, pickles, and celery. We first wanted to know what type of potato to use and how to cook it. Recipe writers seemed split down the middle between starchy potatoes (like russets) and waxy potatoes (like Red Bliss), with starchy praised for being more absorbent and waxy admired for their sturdiness. When making potato salad, we have always just boiled potatoes with the skin on, but steaming, microwaving, roasting, and baking were all options worth trying.

Next, should the potatoes be peeled? If so, when? Some recipes called for cooking potatoes with the skin on, then peeling and seasoning them immediately, working on the assumption that hot potatoes absorb more flavor than cold ones. We also wondered if the extra step of seasoning the cooked potatoes with vinegar, salt, and pepper

first made any difference. Could we instead just toss all the ingredients together at the same time?

After boiling, steaming, baking/roasting, and microwaving four different varieties of potatoes—Red Bliss, russets, all-purpose, and Yukon Golds—we found Red Bliss to be the potato of choice and boiling to be the cooking method of choice. Higher-starch potatoes—all-purpose and Yukon Golds as well as russets—are not sturdy enough for salad. They fall apart when cut, making for a sloppy-looking salad.

Next, we wanted to see if we could boost flavor at the cooking stage by boiling the potatoes in chicken broth or in water heavily seasoned with bay leaves and garlic cloves. The chicken broth might just as well have been water—there wasn't a hint of evidence that the potatoes had been cooked in broth. The bay leaves and garlic smelled wonderful as the potatoes cooked, but the potatoes were still bland.

INGREDIENTS: Mayonnaise

Although we love homemade mayonnaise on occasion, we realize that it's not always convenient to whip up a batch, so we set up a tasting of seven nationally available brands of commercially prepared mayonnaise along with Kraft Miracle Whip. Even though the U.S. Food and Drug Administration does not recognize Miracle Whip as a real mayonnaise, we included it in our tasting because of its resounding popularity. Why is Miracle Whip considered a salad dressing and not a mayonnaise? The FDA defines mayonnaise as an emulsified semisolid food that is at least 65 percent vegetable oil by weight, is at least 2.5 percent acidifying ingredient (vinegar and/or lemon juice) by weight, and contains whole eggs or egg yolks. Miracle Whip, which is also sweeter than regular mayo, weighs in with only 40 percent soybean oil. (Water makes up the difference.)

A good mayonnaise will have a clear egg flavor and a touch of acidity to offset the significant amount of fat from the oil. Our tasters liked Hellmann's Real Mayonnaise for having that balance, and Kraft Real Mayonnaise was thought to be "flavorful but not overpowering." Which one should you buy? We recommend Hellmann's, but the difference between the two contenders is not overwhelming.

Finally, is it possible for a light mayo to be as flavorful as the full-fat original? We put five brands to the test: Kraft Light Mayonnaise, Hellmann's Light Mayonnaise, Miracle Whip Light Salad Dressing, Spectrum Light Canola Mayonnaise, and

Nayonaise (a soy-based sandwich spread), all with a fat content of 3 to 5 grams per serving. To see if our tasters could tell the difference, we also threw the winner of the full-fat tasting into the mix (Hellmann's Real Mayonnaise, 11 grams of fat per serving).

The results? Last place went to Nayonaise. Tasters were unanimous in thinking it bore no resemblance to mayonnaise. Miracle Whip and Spectrum didn't fare much better. Tasters thought Kraft was too sweet. Hellmann's Light came in second place, very nearly beating out the winner, Hellmann's Real Mayonnaise. Although the light version had a pastier texture than regular Hellmann's, the bright, balanced flavors were similar.

THE BEST COMMERCIAL MAYONNAISE
Hellmann's (left), which is known as Best Foods west of the Rockies, took top honors in our tasting. Among the five brands of reduced-fat mayonnaise tested, Hellmann's Light (right) was the clear winner and rated nearly as well as its full-fat cousin.

The fact that nothing seemed to penetrate the potatoes got us wondering: Does the potato skin act as a barrier? We performed an experiment by cooking two batches of unpeeled potatoes, the first in heavily salted water and the second in unsalted water. We rinsed them quickly under cold running water and tasted. Sure enough, both batches of potatoes tasted exactly the same. We tried boiling peeled potatoes, but they were waterlogged compared with their unpeeled counterparts.

We found the paper-thin skin of the boiled red potato not unpleasant to taste and certainly pleasant

to look at in what is often a monochromatic salad. Although this saved the peeling step, we found the skin tended to rip when the potato was cut. Because the skin was particularly susceptible to ripping when the potatoes were very hot, we solved the problem in two ways. First, we cut the potatoes with a serrated knife, which minimized ripping, and second, we let them cool before cutting them.

Now, it was on to our last step. To find out if the now-cool potatoes would have the capacity to absorb seasoning, we made two salads, letting one cool completely before dressing with vinegar, salt and pepper, and mayonnaise and letting the other cool just until warm and preseasoning it with vinegar and salt and pepper well before adding the mayonnaise. (We found the potatoes could still be cut cleanly as long as they were warm but not hot.) The results were clear. The salad made with potatoes seasoned when still warm was zesty and delicious. The other salad was bland in comparison.

SCIENCE: Keeping Potato Salad Safe

Mayonnaise has gotten a bad reputation, being blamed for spoiled potato salads and upset stomachs after many summer picnics and barbecues. You may think that switching from a mayonnaise-based dressing to a vinaigrette will protect your potato salad (and your family) from food poisoning. Think again.

The main ingredients in mayonnaise are raw eggs, vegetable oil, and an acid (usually vinegar or lemon juice). The eggs used in commercially made mayonnaise have been pasteurized to kill salmonella and other bacteria. The acid is another safeguard; because bacteria do not fare well in acidic environments, the lemon juice or vinegar inhibits bacterial growth. Mayonnaise, even when homemade, is rarely the problem. It's the potatoes that are more likely to go bad.

The bacteria usually responsible for spoiled potato salad are *Bacillus cereus* and *Staphylococcus aureus* (commonly known as staph). Both are found in soil and dust, and they thrive on starchy foods like rice, pasta, and potatoes. If they find their way to your potato salad via unwashed vegetables, an unwashed cutting board, or contaminated hands, they can wreak havoc on your digestive system.

Most food-borne bacteria grow well at temperatures between 40 and 140 degrees Fahrenheit. This is known as the temperature danger zone, and if contaminated food remains in this zone for too long, the bacteria can produce enough toxins to make you sick. The U.S. Food and Drug Administration recommends refrigerating food within two hours of its preparation, or one hour if the room temperature is above 90 degrees.

Even with our German Potato Salad (page 360), which contains 1/2 cup of vinegar, we think it's best to play it safe and follow the FDA's guidelines. Don't leave any potato salad out for more than two hours, and promptly refrigerate any leftovers in a covered container.

American Potato Salad with Hard-Cooked Eggs and Sweet Pickles

SERVES 4 TO 6

Use sweet pickles, not relish, for the best results. Like creamy coleslaw, potato salad can be served with just about any grilled meat, poultry, or fish.

2	pounds red potatoes (about 6 medium or 18 small), scrubbed
1/4	cup red wine vinegar
	Salt and ground black pepper
3	Hard-Cooked Eggs (page 355), peeled and cut into 1/2-inch dice
1/2	cup mayonnaise
1	medium celery rib, minced (about 1/2 cup)
1/4	cup sweet pickles, minced
2	tablespoons minced fresh parsley leaves
2	tablespoons minced red onion
2	teaspoons Dijon mustard

1. Cover the potatoes with 1 inch of water in a stockpot or Dutch oven. Bring to a simmer over medium-high heat. Reduce the heat to medium and simmer, stirring once or twice to ensure even

cooking, until the potatoes are tender (a thin-bladed paring knife can be slipped into and out of the center of the potatoes with no resistance), 25 to 30 minutes for medium potatoes or 15 to 20 minutes for small potatoes.

2. Drain the potatoes. Cool the potatoes slightly and peel if you like. Cut the potatoes into ¾-inch cubes (use a serrated knife if they have skins) while still warm, rinsing the knife occasionally in warm water to remove the starch.

3. Place the warm potato cubes in a large bowl. Add the vinegar, ½ teaspoon salt, and ¼ teaspoon pepper and toss gently. Cover the bowl with plastic wrap and refrigerate until cool, about 20 minutes.

4. When the potatoes are cool, toss with the remaining ingredients and season with salt and pepper to taste. Serve immediately or cover and refrigerate for up to 1 day.

FRENCH POTATO SALAD

HAVING LITTLE IN COMMON WITH ITS American counterpart, French potato salad is served warm or at room temperature and is composed of sliced potatoes glistening with olive oil, white wine vinegar, and plenty of fresh herbs. We knew we wanted to go the traditional route and use red potatoes for our salad. Cut into slices, the red potatoes don't crumble and are therefore more aesthetically pleasing for a composed salad. We expected quick success with this seemingly simple recipe—how hard could it be to boil a few potatoes and toss them in vinaigrette? We sliced the potatoes, dressed them while they were still warm (warm potatoes are more absorbent than cool ones), and served them up. Our confidence plummeted as taster after taster remarked on how dull and bland our salad was.

We shifted our focus toward the vinaigrette ingredients—all traditional components of French potato salad: olive oil, white wine vinegar, herbs, mustard, minced onion, chicken stock, and white wine. We decided to experiment with each component until we found a surefire way to pump up the flavor. The first improvement came by using slightly more vinegar than is called for in the test kitchen's standard formula for vinaigrette, 4 parts oil to 1 part vinegar. These bland potatoes could handle extra acid. We loved the sharp flavor notes added by champagne vinegar but found that white wine vinegar worked well, too. As for the olive oil, extra-virgin or pure olive oil made an equally good base for the dressing; tasters found little distinction between the two (the former being more flavorful than the latter), presumably because of the other potent ingredients in the vinaigrette. However, expensive fruity olive oils were rejected for their overpowering nature.

We liked the extra moisture and layer of complexity that chicken stock (or broth) and wine added (salads made strictly with oil and vinegar were a tad dry), but it seemed wasteful to uncork a bottle or open a can to use only a few tablespoons. We found a solution to this problem and a revelation when we consulted Julia Child's *The Way to Cook* (Knopf, 1989). She suggests adding some of the potato cooking water to the vinaigrette, a quick and frugal solution that also added plenty of potato flavor and a nice touch of saltiness. Two teaspoons of Dijon mustard and a sprinkle of ground black pepper perked things up, while the gentle assertiveness of minced shallot and a partially blanched garlic clove (raw garlic was too harsh) added even more depth. As for the fresh herbs, we made salads with all manner of them, including chives, dill, basil, parsley, tarragon, and chervil. But an inherently French fines herbes mixture seemed appropriate in theory and was heavenly in reality. Chives, parsley, tarragon, and chervil make up this classic quartet, with its anise undertones.

The last but not least fine point: How to toss the cooked, warm potatoes with the vinaigrette without damaging the slices? The solution was simple. We carefully laid the potatoes in a single layer on a rimmed baking sheet, then poured the vinaigrette over them. Spreading out the potatoes in this way also allowed them to cool off a bit, preventing residual cooking and potential mushiness. While we let the vinaigrette soak into the potatoes, we had just enough time to chop the herbs and shallot before sprinkling them on the finished salad.

French Potato Salad

SERVES 4 TO 6

If fresh chervil isn't available, substitute an additional ½ tablespoon of minced parsley and an additional ½ teaspoon of minced tarragon. For best flavor, serve the salad warm, but to make ahead, follow the recipe through step 2, cover with plastic wrap, and refrigerate. Before serving, bring the salad to room temperature, then add the shallot and herbs. A little more refined than other potato salads, this salad's delicate flavors go particularly well with grilled chicken or fish.

2	pounds (about 6 medium or 18 small) red potatoes, scrubbed and cut into ¼-inch-thick slices
2	tablespoons salt
1	medium garlic clove, peeled and threaded on a skewer
¼	cup olive oil
1½	tablespoons champagne vinegar or white wine vinegar
2	teaspoons Dijon mustard
½	teaspoon ground black pepper
1	small shallot, minced (about 2 tablespoons)
1	tablespoon minced fresh chervil leaves
1	tablespoon minced fresh parsley leaves
1	tablespoon minced fresh chives
1	teaspoon minced fresh tarragon leaves

1. Place the potatoes, 6 cups of cold water, and the salt in a large saucepan. Bring to a boil over high heat, then reduce the heat to medium. Lower the skewered garlic into the simmering water and partially blanch, about 45 seconds. Immediately run the garlic under cold running water to stop the cooking process; remove the garlic from the skewer and set aside. Simmer the potatoes, uncovered, until tender but still firm (a thin-bladed paring knife can be slipped into and out of the center of a potato slice with no resistance), about 5 minutes. Drain the potatoes, reserving ¼ cup cooking water. Arrange the hot potatoes close together in a single layer on a rimmed baking sheet.

2. Press the garlic through a garlic press or mince by hand. Whisk the garlic, reserved potato cooking water, oil, vinegar, mustard, and pepper together in a small bowl until combined. Drizzle the dressing evenly over the warm potato slices; let stand 10 minutes.

3. Meanwhile, toss the shallot and herbs gently together in a small bowl. Transfer the potatoes to a large serving bowl. Add the shallot-herb mixture and mix lightly with a rubber spatula to combine. Serve immediately.

VARIATIONS

French Potato Salad with Arugula, Roquefort, and Walnuts

Follow the recipe for French Potato Salad, omitting the herbs and tossing the dressed potatoes with ½ cup walnuts, toasted and chopped coarse, 4 ounces Roquefort cheese, crumbled, and 1 small bunch arugula, washed, dried, stemmed, and torn into bite-size pieces (about 3 cups), along with the minced shallot in step 3.

French Potato Salad with Radishes, Cornichons, and Capers

Follow the recipe for French Potato Salad, omitting the herbs and substituting 2 tablespoons minced red onion for the shallot. Toss the dressed potatoes with 2 medium red radishes, thinly sliced (about ⅓ cup), ¼ cup capers, rinsed and drained, and ¼ cup cornichons, thinly sliced, along with the red onion in step 3.

French Potato Salad with Hard Salami and Gruyère

Follow the recipe for French Potato Salad, omitting the herbs and substituting 2 teaspoons whole-grain mustard for the Dijon mustard and 2 tablespoons minced red onion for the shallot. Toss the dressed potatoes with 3 ounces hard salami, cut into ¼-inch matchsticks, 2 ounces Gruyère, very thinly sliced or shaved with a vegetable peeler, and 1 tablespoon minced fresh thyme leaves along with the red onion in step 3.

GERMAN POTATO SALAD

SERVED HOT OR WARM, PUNGENTLY TANGY from its vinegar dressing, and chock-full of bacon flavor, German potato salad should be a welcome change from the cold comfort of American-style potato salad. But a recent tasting of German potato salad recipes brought about quite different results. These were the comments, across the board: tasteless, broken-down potatoes; unbalanced, flavorless vinaigrettes; and greasy. It was time to take this recipe into the 21st century.

Starting with the potatoes, we chose low-starch red. We decided to cut the potatoes before boiling, thus dramatically reducing their cooking time. Using salted water ensured that the potatoes were also well seasoned.

The beauty of the dressing for this potato salad is the foundation of rendered bacon fat (vegetable and olive oils were tested and flatly rejected). However, we knew that we wanted to eschew the usual overly greasy vinaigrette. We fried up pounds of bacon, increasing the amount of bacon fat (and crumbled bacon pieces) until tasters were satisfied. Half a pound of bacon was the right amount for 2 pounds of potatoes, with plenty of bacon to bite into. It also produced a hefty ⅓ cup of bacon fat for the dressing. Tasty? Yes. Light? No way. This heavy dressing was just what we were trying to avoid. Part of the solution to the greasiness problem was to spoon off some excess bacon fat; 2 pounds of potatoes required a dressing with just ¼ cup. Any more and the salad was just too fatty.

Choosing the right vinegar to balance the bacon fat was also key. Along with cider vinegar (the usual choice in most recipes), we tested white wine, red wine, distilled white, and rice vinegars. Surprisingly, tasters preferred the distilled white vinegar, which is often the last choice in the test kitchen owing to its bland flavor. But in this case, that was exactly what we needed—clean acidity without much personality of its own to mask the flavor of the bacon. One cup of vinegar made the right quantity of dressing (the hot potatoes soaked up an amazing amount), but now tasters' palates were assaulted with a harsh, unbalanced dressing. We diluted the acidity with some of the potato cooking water, a trick we picked up when researching our French Potato Salad (page 359).

Sautéed onion was a must (raw onion was too harsh), and after trying red, white, and yellow, we found that you really can't go wrong with any of them. Mustard appears in some German potato salad recipes, but certainly not all. After starting out with salads made with no mustard, tasters were receptive to its addition. We first tried Dijon (both smooth and cracked varieties), but tasters weren't crazy about the wine flavor that it added. Brown mustard was neither here nor there. Whole-grain German-style mustard (of course) proved the best bet. Dotted with flecks of whole mustard seeds, the salad now had both the right flavor and a rustic appearance. A half teaspoon of sugar offset the tartness of the vinegar and mustard, and some chopped parsley added freshness.

Mixing the dressing and potatoes in a big serving bowl is typically how the salad is combined. We found, though, that the potatoes lost most of their heat that way. Instead, we dumped the potatoes right into the skillet where the vinaigrette was waiting, giving them a quick toss right in the hot pan before piling the whole thing into a serving dish. Nice and warm, tangy and full of flavor, this was German potato salad at its very best.

German Potato Salad
SERVES 4 TO 6
Unlike a nonstick skillet, a traditional skillet will allow the bacon to form caramelized bits on the pan bottom. This will result in a richer-tasting dressing and a more flavorful salad. The rich flavors in this salad complement grilled beef, pork, or an oily fish, such as salmon.

2 pounds red potatoes (about 6 medium or 18 small), scrubbed and halved if small or quartered if medium
Salt
8 ounces (about 8 slices) bacon, cut crosswise into ½-inch pieces
1 medium onion, chopped fine
½ teaspoon sugar
½ cup distilled white vinegar
1 tablespoon whole-grain German-style mustard
¼ teaspoon ground black pepper
¼ cup loosely packed chopped fresh parsley leaves

1. Place the potatoes, 1 tablespoon salt, and water to cover in a large saucepan or Dutch oven; bring to a boil over high heat, then reduce the heat to medium and simmer until the potatoes are tender (a thin-bladed paring knife can be slipped into and out of the potatoes with little resistance), about 10 minutes. Reserve ½ cup potato cooking water, then drain the potatoes; return the potatoes to the pot and cover to keep warm.

2. While the potatoes are cooking, fry the bacon in a large skillet over medium heat, stirring occasionally, until browned and crisp, about 5 minutes. With a slotted spoon, transfer the bacon to a paper towel–lined plate; pour off all but ¼ cup bacon grease. Add the onion to the skillet and cook, stirring occasionally, over medium heat until softened and beginning to brown, about 4 minutes. Stir in the sugar until dissolved, about 30 seconds. Add the vinegar and reserved potato cooking water; bring to a simmer and cook until the mixture is reduced to about 1 cup, about 3 minutes. Off the heat, whisk in the mustard and pepper. Add the potatoes, parsley, and bacon to the skillet and toss to combine; adjust the seasonings with salt to taste. Transfer to a bowl and serve immediately, while still warm.

MACARONI SALAD

MACARONI SALAD IS AN AMERICAN DELI staple. For many people, it's hard to imagine a picnic or summer barbecue without this salad of tender elbow noodles and creamy dressing. Although relatively easy to make, it is also easy to make badly. Few dishes are less appetizing than a bowl of underseasoned, overcooked noodles accompanied by flavorless, limp celery, killer-sweet pickle relish, and an excess of mayonnaise. Good macaroni salad, however, is dreamy when made with perfectly cooked, well-seasoned noodles and crisp vegetables dressed lightly in mayonnaise.

To start, we focused on the noodles. We tried cooking them al dente, and although we prefer a slightly resistant texture in hot noodles, we found them overly toothsome and stiff when cold. Thoroughly cooked noodles, which offered no resistance when eaten hot, took on a pleasantly yielding and bouncy texture when cool and were also able to maintain their shape without becoming mushy. Noodles that were overcooked even just slightly tasted mushy and slimy and tore into pieces when tossed with the other ingredients. We also found that adding more salt than usual to the cooking water made for a more evenly seasoned salad. While the noodles will taste a little salty on their own, they will be perfectly seasoned when mixed with the other ingredients and served cold. We found that 2 tablespoons of table salt to 4 quarts of water was just right to season 1 pound of macaroni.

Another trick we picked up was how to turn the hot noodles into a cold salad quickly. When the hot noodles were allowed to cool on their own, they

DRYING MACARONI

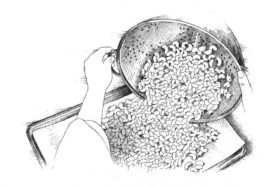

1. Shake the macaroni dry in the colander and spread it in an even layer on a rimmed baking sheet lined with paper towels. Let the macaroni dry for 3 minutes.

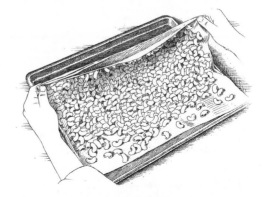

2. Roll the macaroni in paper towels to blot any remaining moisture, then transfer to a large bowl.

clumped together into a starchy mass and began to overcook from their own residual heat. Going against all we have learned about how to cook pasta, we rinsed the hot noodles under cold water, which both stopped them from cooking any further and washed away some of the extra starch. (When serving pasta hot with sauce, this starch is a good thing, because it helps the sauce cling to the pasta.) We then spread out the noodles on paper towels to help drain off this extra water (see the illustrations on page 361). If we skipped this step, water was caught in the curves of the macaroni and turned the dressing watery.

We found the noodles were best mixed with the classic assortment of fresh vegetables and seasonings: celery, red onion, hard-cooked eggs, and sweet pickles. Fresh parsley added a clean, herbal flavor and a little mustard provided some kick. Wary of burying this fresh-tasting mixture with too much mayonnaise, we started off using only ½ cup per pound of noodles but found that they readily soaked up mayonnaise until we hit 1 cup. Although many recipes call for vinegar, we preferred the light, fresh acidity of lemon juice. The salad tastes best when allowed to cool for at least one hour in the refrigerator. The seasonings mellow substantially, so use a liberal hand with salt and pepper.

Macaroni Salad

SERVES 8 TO 10

See the illustrations on page 361 for drying the cooked macaroni.

	Salt
I	pound elbow macaroni
I	medium celery rib, minced
¼	small red onion, minced
3	Hard-Cooked Eggs (page 355), peeled and diced small
¼	cup minced sweet pickles
¼	cup minced fresh parsley leaves
¼	cup juice from 2 lemons
I	cup mayonnaise
2	teaspoons Dijon mustard
	Ground black pepper

1. Bring 4 quarts of water to a boil in a large pot and add 2 tablespoons salt. Stir in the macaroni and cook until thoroughly done, 10 to 12 minutes. Drain the macaroni into a colander and rinse with cold water until cool. Shake the macaroni dry in the colander and then spread it in an even layer on a rimmed baking sheet lined with paper towels. Let the macaroni dry for 3 minutes.

2. Roll the macaroni in paper towels to blot any remaining moisture and transfer the drained macaroni to a large bowl. Toss with the remaining ingredients and season liberally with salt and pepper to taste. Refrigerate the macaroni salad for at least 1 hour or up to 1 day.

➤ VARIATIONS

Macaroni Salad with Curried Apples
Follow the recipe for Macaroni Salad, replacing the hard-cooked eggs, sweet pickles, parsley, and mustard with 1 medium Granny Smith apple, cored and cut into ¼-inch dice (about 1½ cups), and ¼ cup minced fresh basil leaves. Mix 1 tablespoon curry powder into the mayonnaise and proceed as directed.

Macaroni Salad with Chipotles and Cilantro
Toast 1½ cups frozen corn kernels and 2 medium unpeeled garlic cloves in a nonstick skillet set over high heat until the corn turns spotty brown, about 5 minutes; peel and mince the garlic. Follow the recipe for Macaroni Salad, replacing the hard-cooked eggs, sweet pickles, parsley, and mustard with the corn and garlic, 3 scallions, minced (about ¼ cup), 1 cup cherry tomatoes, quartered, and ¼ cup minced fresh cilantro leaves. Mix 1 tablespoon minced chipotle chiles in adobo sauce into the mayonnaise and proceed as directed.

PASTA SALAD

BECAUSE PASTA SALADS MAKE THE MOST sense as a side dish for a summer meal, we've always found it odd that many recipes are heavy and creamy. A good pasta salad should be light and refreshing, with a fair amount of vegetables. (We find little bits of salami a greasy and distressing addition to deli pasta salads.) The dressing should help convey flavors and keep the pasta moist, not weigh it down. Vinaigrette, not mayonnaise, is the obvious choice.

Almost every deli in America sells a pasta salad dressed with vinaigrette. Often made with fusilli (tricolor fusilli in trendier markets), this salad invariably looks unappetizing. The pasta is so mushy that you can see it falling apart through the glass deli case. And the vegetables are tired and sad. The broccoli has faded to drab olive green and the shredded carrots that most markets add have wilted. And as for the flavor—these unattractive salads usually look better than they taste.

The problem with most of these pasta salads is that the acid causes the pasta to soften and dulls the color and flavor of many vegetables, especially green ones. But leave out the lemon juice or vinegar and the salad tastes flat. We wanted to develop a light, vinaigrette-dressed vegetable pasta salad that looked good and tasted even better.

We started by making salads with four very simple vinaigrettes. Each contained a different acidic liquid, along with olive oil, salt, and pepper. Each was used to dress a simple pasta salad with blanched and cooled broccoli. The salad made with white wine vinegar looked fine but tasted too acidic. The salad made with lemon juice was clearly the best. It had a nice bright flavor but was neither "puckery" nor sour. After half an hour, we noticed that the broccoli in the three salads with vinegar was turning olive green and starting to fall apart. But even after several hours, the broccoli in the salad with lemon juice was green and crunchy.

With lemon juice now our choice of acid, we focused on the sequence of assembling the dish. Would hot vegetables absorb more dressing and taste better? Should we run the vegetables under cold water after cooking to set their color? Neither idea panned out. We found that green vegetables like broccoli are most susceptible to the effects of acid when they are hot. Letting them cool to room temperature helped stem any color loss, but unfortunately you can't speed up the process by running them under cold water. No matter how well we drained them, the vegetables tasted waterlogged after being rinsed in cold water. The best method is to let the vegetables rest in the colander for at least 20 minutes, or until barely warm to the touch, before tossing them with the pasta and dressing.

At this point, we had a master recipe that we liked pretty well, but it needed some other flavors. An herb—we chose basil, but almost anything will work—perked things up. Olives (or sundried tomatoes) made everything more lively by adding some acidity and saltiness to a dish that was otherwise a bit bland. And for our variation with arugula and sun-dried tomatoes, we preferred the more robust flavor of a red wine vinaigrette to a dressing made with lemon juice.

Pasta Salad
with Broccoli and Olives

SERVES 6 TO 8

If you prefer, increase the red pepper flakes or replace them with a few grindings of black pepper.

	Salt
2	pounds broccoli (about 2 small heads), florets cut into bite-size pieces (about 7 cups)
1/4	cup juice and 1/2 teaspoon grated zest from 2 lemons
I	medium garlic clove, minced or pressed through a garlic press (about 1 teaspoon)
1/2	teaspoon red pepper flakes
1/2	cup extra-virgin olive oil
I	pound short, bite-size pasta, such as fusilli, farfalle, or orecchiette
20	large black olives, such as kalamata or another brine-cured variety, pitted and chopped
15	large fresh basil leaves, shredded

1. Bring 4 quarts of water to a boil in a large pot over high heat. Bring several quarts of water to a boil in a large saucepan. Add salt to taste and broccoli to the saucepan and cook until crisp-tender, about 2 minutes. Drain and cool to room temperature.

2. Meanwhile, whisk the lemon juice and zest, garlic, ¾ teaspoon salt, and the red pepper flakes in a large bowl; whisk in the oil in a slow, steady stream until smooth.

3. Add pasta and 1 tablespoon salt to the boiling water. Cook until the pasta is al dente and drain. Whisk the dressing again to blend; add the hot

pasta, cooled broccoli, olives, and basil; toss to mix thoroughly. Cool to room temperature, adjust seasonings, and serve. (The pasta salad can be covered with plastic wrap and refrigerated for 1 day; return to room temperature before serving.)

Pasta Salad with Eggplant, Tomatoes, and Basil
SERVES 6 TO 8

The eggplants can be broiled until golden brown if you prefer not to grill them.

2	medium eggplants (about 1 pound total), cut into 1/2-inch-thick rounds
1/2	cup extra-virgin olive oil, plus extra for brushing on the eggplant
	Salt and ground black pepper
1/4	cup juice and 1/2 teaspoon grated zest from 2 lemons
1	medium garlic clove, minced or pressed through a garlic press (about 1 teaspoon)
1/2	teaspoon red pepper flakes
1	pound short, bite-size pasta, such as fusilli, farfalle, or orecchiette
2	large ripe tomatoes, cored, seeded, and cut into 1/2-inch dice
15	large fresh basil leaves, shredded

1. Light the grill. Bring 4 quarts of water to a boil in a large pot over high heat.

2. Lightly brush the eggplant with oil and sprinkle with salt and pepper to taste. Grill, turning once, until marked with dark stripes, about 10 minutes. Cool and cut into bite-size pieces.

3. Meanwhile, whisk the lemon juice and zest, garlic, 3/4 teaspoon salt, and the red pepper flakes in a large bowl; whisk in the oil in a slow, steady stream until smooth.

4. Add the pasta and 1 tablespoon salt to the boiling water. Cook until the pasta is al dente and drain. Whisk the dressing again to blend; add the hot pasta, cooled eggplant, tomatoes, and basil; toss to mix thoroughly. Cool to room temperature, adjust seasonings, and serve. (The pasta salad can be covered with plastic wrap and refrigerated for 1 day; return to room temperature before serving.)

Pasta Salad with Arugula and Sun-Dried Tomato Vinaigrette
SERVES 6 TO 8

	Salt
1	pound fusilli or another short, bite-size pasta
1	tablespoon extra-virgin olive oil
1	(8-ounce) jar sun-dried tomatoes packed in olive oil
2	tablespoons red wine vinegar
1	large garlic clove, minced to a paste (about 1 1/2 teaspoons)
1/8	teaspoon ground black pepper
1	medium bunch arugula, washed, dried, stemmed, and torn into bite-size pieces (about 4 cups loosely packed)
1/2	cup green olives, pitted and sliced
6	ounces fresh mozzarella cheese, cut into 1/2-inch cubes

1. Bring 4 quarts of water to a boil in a large pot over high heat. Add 1 tablespoon salt and the pasta to the boiling water. Cook until al dente. Drain, rinsing the pasta well with cold water. Drain the cold pasta well, transfer it to a large mixing bowl, and toss it with the olive oil. Set aside.

2. Drain the tomatoes, reserving the oil. (You should have 1/3 cup reserved oil. If necessary, make up the difference with extra-virgin olive oil.) Coarsely chop the tomatoes. Whisk the reserved oil from the tomatoes with the vinegar, garlic, 1/4 teaspoon salt, and the pepper in a small bowl.

3. Add the arugula, olives, mozzarella, and chopped tomatoes to the bowl with the pasta. Pour the tomato vinaigrette over the pasta, toss gently, and serve immediately.

BREAD SALAD

TO THE ITALIANS, BREAD IS HOLY; IT IS almost unthinkable to throw it away. It is not surprising, then, that there are so many uses for bread throughout Italy. One of the most delightful and perhaps surprising dishes that evolved in this part of the world is what amounts to a stale bread salad.

Such thrifty salads are superb dishes because they allow flavorful and fresh tomatoes to be fully experienced, along with fragrant mint, parsley, and fresh cilantro. Another crucial ingredient is high-quality extra-virgin olive oil. Because the dry bread so readily absorbs moisture, much of the flavor of the dish is derived from the dressing.

Last but not least, fundamental to the success of these salads is the quality of the bread. Sliced white bread or airy supermarket bread that is highly refined and becomes rock-hard within a few days simply won't do. Ideally, the bread used in bread salads should not contain sugar or sweeteners of any kind, because this would conflict with the savory nature of the other ingredients; nor should it include such ingredients as raisins or nuts. What the bread should have is a sturdy texture and a good wheaty flavor.

Depending on how stale the bread is, it may need to be dampened with a little water. The extent of dampening is determined by the dryness of the bread; if the bread is made too damp, it will collapse into a soggy mess when the dressing is added. Therefore, it's best to assemble the salad, see how much the bread softens, and then adjust the texture by sprinkling lightly with water.

Because the bread becomes soggy fairly quickly, neither of these salads should be made much in advance of serving. The best approach is to prepare all of the salad ingredients, then combine them just before serving.

Bread Salad with Tomatoes, Herbs, and Red Onions

SERVES 4 TO 6

Use coarse peasant bread or any sturdy Italian-style bread in this classic Italian recipe. This salad pairs well with grilled steak or poultry.

1	pound day-old sturdy Italian-style bread, crusts removed, cut or torn into 1-inch cubes (about 6 cups)
1/2	cup extra-virgin olive oil
3	tablespoons red wine vinegar

2	large ripe tomatoes, cored, seeded, and cut into medium dice
1/2	red onion, sliced very thin
2	tablespoons torn fresh basil or mint leaves
1	tablespoon minced fresh parsley leaves
2	teaspoons whole fresh oregano leaves
1/2	teaspoon salt
1/4	teaspoon ground black pepper

Place the bread cubes in a shallow bowl. Mix the oil, vinegar, tomatoes, onion, and half of the herbs in a medium bowl. Let stand to allow the flavors to develop, about 10 minutes, then add to the bread, along with the remaining herbs, and toss well. Season with the salt and pepper. If the bread still seems dry, sprinkle with 1 or 2 tablespoons of water to rehydrate it a bit. Serve. (If the bread used is quite sturdy, the salad can be covered and set aside up to 2 hours.)

Bread Salad with Roasted Peppers and Olives

SERVES 4 TO 6

Sourdough or a sturdy peasant bread is needed for this salad. Airy, unsubstantial bread will become soggy quickly. This salad pairs well with grilled steak or salmon.

1	pound day-old sturdy Italian-style bread, crusts removed, cut or torn into 1-inch cubes (about 6 cups)
2	medium bell peppers, 1 red and 1 yellow, grill-roasted (see page 316), cored, seeded, and cut into 1/2-inch strips
1/2	cup extra-virgin olive oil
1/4	cup cider vinegar
1	small red or white onion, quartered and sliced thin
1	medium scallion, sliced thin, including 2 inches of the green part
3	tablespoons pitted and sliced green olives
1	tablespoon minced fresh oregano leaves
1/2	teaspoon salt
1/4	teaspoon ground black pepper

1. Mix the bread cubes and pepper strips in a large bowl; set aside.

2. Mix the oil, vinegar, onion, scallion, olives, oregano, salt, and pepper in a medium bowl; let stand to allow the flavors to develop, about 10 minutes. Add the dressing to the bread and peppers; toss to combine. If the bread still seems dry, sprinkle with 1 or 2 tablespoons of water to rehydrate it a bit. Serve. (If the bread used is quite sturdy, the salad can be covered and set aside up to 2 hours.)

PITA BREAD SALAD

TRADITIONALLY, FATTOUSH CONSISTS OF small bites of pita bread mixed with cucumbers and tomatoes and dressed with lemon juice and a fruity olive oil. But after making several of these traditional Middle Eastern salads, we noticed a few minor flaws. While the salads we tested were tasty, they lacked body and texture.

Wanting to create a more substantial salad—one that could be eaten as a light entrée—we decided that cheese would be a key ingredient. Feta cheese naturally came to mind, as it is one of the more popular cheeses consumed in countries in the eastern Mediterranean. Feta's bright, fresh flavor would also meld well in the salad without making it too heavy.

Continuing our ingredient search, we wanted to select items that would lend crispness to the salad without adding excess moisture. Romaine lettuce was perfect. It added crunch without making the other ingredients soggy, and it contributed body as well. We wanted to avoid tomatoes, but tasters missed their sweetness, so we tried several varieties with less moisture than traditional vine-ripened tomatoes. We found that halved cherry tomatoes contributed deep tomato flavor with less liquid. Some briny kalamata olives and thinly sliced red onion rounded out our ingredient list.

To finish our pita bread salad, we needed a dressing. We knew we wanted to stay with the traditional trio of olive oil, lemon, and mint, but we found that our normal ratio of 4 parts oil to 1 part acid resulted in a boring salad, short on brightness. So we played with the ratio until settling on 2 parts oil to 1 part acid. While this seemed extreme, it gave the salad a tartness that tasters preferred.

Finally, we added chopped mint. The only problem with the mint was that with one bite you might get intense mint flavor, and with the next you might not get any. For some reason, the mint was not evenly distributed throughout the chunky salad. To solve this problem, we threw all of the dressing ingredients in a blender and processed them until the mint was finely chopped. The salad made with this dressing was just right; the mint flavor was evenly distributed and complemented the other ingredients without overpowering them.

Pita Bread Salad with Olives, Feta, and Mint
SERVES 6

Let the onions sit in the dressing for 5 minutes to remove some of their sting. Serve this salad with shish kebab.

4	(8-inch) pita breads, torn into ¹/₂-inch pieces
¹/₂	cup extra-virgin olive oil
¹/₄	cup packed fresh mint leaves, torn into small pieces
¹/₄	cup juice from 2 lemons
¹/₂	small red onion, sliced thin
I	small head romaine lettuce, cut or torn into I-inch pieces (about 6 cups loosely packed)
20	cherry tomatoes, halved
¹/₂	cup kalamata olives, pitted and sliced
6	ounces feta cheese, crumbled (about I ¹/₂ cups)

1. Adjust an oven rack to the middle position and heat the oven to 375 degrees. Place the bread on a rimmed baking sheet and bake until crisp but not brown, 7 to 10 minutes. Remove the bread from the oven and cool to room temperature.

2. Meanwhile, process the oil, mint, and lemon juice in a blender until the mint is finely chopped, using a rubber spatula to scrape the sides of the blender as necessary, about twenty 1-second pulses. Combine the dressing and onion in a large bowl, toss to coat, and let stand for 5 minutes.

3. Add the pita, romaine, tomatoes, and olives to the bowl with the onion and toss to coat. Arrange the salad on a large serving platter or individual plates, sprinkle with the feta, and serve immediately.

TABBOULEH

PERHAPS THE BEST-KNOWN ARAB DISH IN THE United States is tabbouleh. However, the tabbouleh typically served here is very different from the original. In its Middle Eastern home, this dish is basically a parsley salad with bulgur rather than a bulgur salad with parsley—what is frequently found here.

In addition to finely minced parsley, a perfect tabbouleh includes morsels of bulgur—crushed, parboiled wheat—tossed in a penetrating, minty lemon dressing with bits of ripe tomato. While these principal ingredients remain the same, a variety of preparation techniques exist, each Arab cook being convinced that his or her method produces the finest version.

We tried processing the bulgur in the five most commonly used ways. First we rinsed the grain, combined it with the minced tomato, and set it aside to absorb the tomato juices. With this method, the bulgur remained unacceptably crunchy. Next we marinated the bulgur in a lemon juice and olive oil dressing. This approach produced bulgur that was tasty but still crunchy. The third method, soaking the grain in water until fluffy and then squeezing out the excess moisture, produced an acceptable but somewhat bland-flavored wheat. Next we soaked the wheat in water for about five minutes, then drained the liquid and replaced it with the lemon–olive oil dressing. We discovered that the wheat's texture was good and the flavor much improved.

But the all-out winner came as a surprise. We first rinsed the bulgur, then mixed it with fresh lemon juice. We then set the mixture aside to allow the juice to be absorbed. When treated in this way, bulgur acquires a fresh and intense flavor even better than our last method.

Once the remaining ingredients—parsley, finely chopped scallions, fresh mint, and tomatoes—and the dressing were added to the wheat, we found it best to let the mixture sit for an hour or so to blend the flavors; after five or six hours, though, the scallions became too strong and overpowered the other flavors.

The final question to answer concerned the proportion of parsley to bulgur. Although some

local Lebanese restaurateurs favor a 9:1 ratio of parsley to bulgur, we found that the wholesome goodness of the wheat was lost. We recommend a more balanced proportion of 5 parts parsley to 3 or 4 parts wheat.

Tabbouleh
SERVES 4 TO 6

Middle Eastern cooks frequently serve this salad with crisp inner leaves of romaine lettuce, using them as spoons to scoop the salad from the serving dish. Fine-grain bulgur is best in this recipe, but medium-grain will work; avoid coarse-grain bulgur, which must be cooked. Try this salad with grilled fish or lamb.

½   cup fine-grain bulgur wheat, rinsed under running water and drained
⅓   cup juice from 2 or 3 lemons
⅓   cup extra-virgin olive oil
    Salt
⅛   teaspoon Middle Eastern red pepper or cayenne pepper (optional)
2   cups minced fresh parsley leaves
2   medium ripe tomatoes, halved, cored, seeded, and cut into very small dice
4   medium scallions, green and white parts, minced
2   tablespoons minced fresh mint leaves

1. Mix the bulgur with ¼ cup of the lemon juice in a medium bowl; set aside until the grains are tender and fluffy, 20 to 40 minutes, depending on the age and type of the bulgur.

2. Mix the remaining lemon juice, the olive oil, salt to taste, and red pepper (if using) together in a small bowl. In a large bowl, combine the bulgur, parsley, tomatoes, scallions, and mint; add the dressing and toss to combine. Cover and refrigerate to let the flavors blend, 1 to 2 hours. Serve.

BOSTON BAKED BEANS

BAKED BEANS ARE A NATURAL WITH PULLED pork, barbecued ribs, and even barbecued chicken. Heady with smoky pork and bittersweet molasses,

367

authentic Boston baked beans are both sweet and savory, a unique combination of the simplest ingredients, unified and refined during a long simmer—a fine example of the whole being greater than the sum of its parts.

A close reading of recipes—and there are thousands out there—made it clear that authentic Boston baked beans are not about fancy seasonings. They are about developing intense flavor by means of the judicious employment of canonical ingredients (beans, pork, molasses, mustard, and sometimes onion) and slow cooking. Tasters quickly rejected recipes with lengthy lists of nontraditional ingredients and short cooking times.

The most important item on the shopping list is, of course, the beans, the classic choice being standard dried white beans in one of three sizes: small white beans, midsize navy or pea beans, or large great northern beans. While the latter two choices were adequate, tasters preferred the small white beans for their dense, creamy texture and their ability to remain firm and intact over the course of a long simmer. (The two larger sizes tended to split.) Consistent with the test kitchen's previous findings, we found that there was no need to soak the beans before cooking, so we gladly skipped that step. We did test canned white beans and were not impressed by their lackluster performance. Within two hours of baking, they turned to mush, and they lacked the full flavor of the dried beans.

Next came the meat. Some type of cured pork is essential for depth of flavor and lush texture, though its flavor should never dominate. Although traditionalists swear by salt pork, we first tried pork brisket, which is a meatier version of salt pork. Its flavor was enjoyable, but tasters felt the beans lacked richness—the brisket was too lean. Not surprisingly, salt pork scored high with tasters, although some felt the flavor was too mild. Bacon, a more modern choice, was deemed "too smoky and overwhelming" for most, though the heartier pork flavor was appreciated. On a whim, we put both salt pork and bacon into the pot and found the perfect solution. The bacon brought the desired depth to the beans, and the salt pork muted the bacon's hickory tang. Twice as much salt pork as bacon proved the right balance.

In traditional recipes, the salt pork is cast raw into the beans (often as a large piece) and melts into the sauce, but during tests it failed to render completely. Gelatinous chunks of fatty pork bobbing among the beans left even the most carnivorous taster cold. We first diced the pork into smaller bits, but this was only a partial remedy; unmelted fat remained. Next we browned it in the Dutch oven prior to adding the beans, and the results were surprising. This simple step (not recommended in any of the recipes we'd found) made the flavor of the beans significantly fuller and better than anything we had yet tasted. Apparently, the melted fat more readily flavored the cooking liquid, and the browned bits of meat tasted richer.

While yellow onion is a controversial ingredient in classic recipes, we sensed its flavor could be important, and our intuition proved right. Tasters loved the sweetness and full flavor that it gave to the beans, especially once sautéed in the rendered pork fat. Tasters favored a fine dice so that the onion all but disappeared by the time the beans were ready.

Next we tackled the final two ingredients: mustard and molasses. Dried mustard, the standard choice, had worked fine up until now, but we felt home cooks were more likely to have prepared mustard on hand. And it provides a nice perk—vinegar—to cut the beans' sweetness. We tested several varieties, including Dijon, German whole grain, yellow, and brown. They all brought a unique angle to the beans, but brown mustard—Gulden's brown mustard, in particular—was best, imparting a pleasant sharpness without calling attention to itself. Even with the mustard's tang, though, we found it necessary to add vinegar for acidity. Most classic recipes that include cider vinegar add it at the start of the cooking time, but we found the acidity stayed sharper when added to the beans once finished. A scant teaspoon proved enough to cut the sweetness of the molasses and to accent the other flavors.

The molasses, we discovered, would take some finessing, as its brutish flavor and intense sweetness dominated the beans when added carelessly. After tasting batches made with mild, full-flavored (also known as "robust"), and blackstrap varieties, most tasters preferred the subtler tones of the mild variety. We settled on just ½ cup molasses baked with the beans for a balance of moderate sweetness and palate-cleansing bitterness. A tablespoon added after cooking gently reemphasized its character.

All that was left to do now was tweak the cooking time. For testing purposes, we had been cooking the beans at 250 degrees for six to seven hours. While pleased with the results, we were curious to see what other temperatures might accomplish. We knew that to a certain extent, flavor and texture were in opposition. The longer the beans cooked, the better the sauce's flavor, but past a certain crucial moment of equilibrium, time worked against the beans, turning them to mush.

We tested cooking temperatures in increments of 25 degrees between 200 and 350 degrees and met with interesting results. At 200 degrees, the beans took upward of eight hours to cook and were still on the crunchy side. At 350 degrees, the beans percolated vigorously and exploded. Midpoints of 275 and 300 degrees were more successful. The beans were creamy textured and the sauce full flavored. With little difference in the outcome when either temperature was used, we chose 300 degrees, which made the beans cook faster, finishing in just about five hours—less time than we had thought possible.

While pleased with the texture and flavor, we still wanted a thicker sauce—soupy beans were not acceptable. We discovered that it was not simply a matter of reducing the volume of water, however, as this led to unevenly cooked beans. We had been cooking the beans from start to finish covered with a lid, which had prevented the cooking liquid from reducing effectively. When we removed the lid for the last hour in the oven, we got the results we were seeking—the sauce was reduced to a syrupy, intensified state that perfectly coated the beans.

Boston Baked Beans

SERVES 4 TO 6

If you prefer a stronger molasses flavor, substitute dark or "robust" molasses for the mild. For the richest flavor, look for chunks of salt pork with a high fat-to-meat ratio.

- 4 ounces salt pork, trimmed of rind and cut into ½-inch cubes
- 2 ounces (about 2 slices) bacon, chopped fine
- 1 medium onion, minced
- ½ cup plus 1 tablespoon mild molasses
- 1½ tablespoons prepared brown mustard, such as Gulden's
- 1 pound (about 2½ cups) dried small white beans, rinsed and picked over
  Salt
- 9 cups water
- 1 teaspoon cider vinegar
  Ground black pepper

Adjust an oven rack to the lower-middle position and heat the oven to 300 degrees. Cook the salt pork and bacon in a large Dutch oven over medium heat, stirring occasionally, until it is lightly browned and most of the fat is rendered, about 7 minutes. Add the onion and cook until softened and beginning to brown, about 8 minutes. Add ½ cup of the molasses, the mustard, beans, 1¼ teaspoons salt, and the water; increase the heat to medium-high and bring to a boil. Cover the pot and set in the oven. Bake until the beans are tender, about 4 hours, stirring once after 2 hours. Remove the lid and continue to bake until the liquid has thickened to a syrupy consistency, 1 to 1½ hours longer. Remove the beans from the oven; stir in the remaining 1 tablespoon molasses and the vinegar. Season to taste with salt and pepper. Serve.

➤ VARIATION
Barbecued Baked Beans

Barbecued baked beans are slow-simmered, oven-cooked beans that are similar to Boston baked beans. Barbecued baked beans are a bit brasher in flavor, however, so they stand up even better to the big flavors of grilled and barbecued foods. Black coffee is not such a strange companion to beans. It often appears in chili recipes, "cowboy" cooking, and barbecue sauce recipes. If you do not have time to make freshly brewed coffee, instant will do.

4   ounces (about 4 slices) bacon, chopped fine
1   medium onion, minced
4   medium garlic cloves, minced or pressed through a garlic press (about 4 teaspoons)
1   pound (about 2½ cups) dried small white beans, rinsed and picked over
1   cup strong black coffee
½   cup plus 1 tablespoon barbecue sauce
¼   cup packed dark brown sugar
1   tablespoon mild molasses
1½ tablespoons prepared brown mustard, such as Gulden's
½   teaspoon hot pepper sauce
    Salt
8   cups water
    Ground black pepper

Adjust an oven rack to the lower-middle position and heat the oven to 300 degrees. Cook the bacon in a large Dutch oven over medium heat, stirring occasionally, until it is lightly browned and most of the fat is rendered, about 7 minutes. Add the onion and cook until softened and beginning to brown, about 8 minutes. Add the garlic and cook until fragrant, about 30 seconds. Add the beans, coffee, ½ cup of the barbecue sauce, the brown sugar, molasses, mustard, hot sauce, 2 teaspoons salt, and the water; increase the heat to medium-high and bring to a boil. Cover the pot and set in the oven. Bake until the beans are tender, about 4 hours, stirring once after 2 hours. Remove the lid and continue to bake until the liquid has thickened to a syrupy consistency, 1 to 1½ hours longer. Remove from the oven and stir in the remaining 1 tablespoon barbecue sauce. Season to taste with salt and pepper.

CORNBREAD

CORNBREAD IS OFTEN SERVED WITH OUR favorite barbecued foods, like ribs and pulled pork. Cornbread can also be dunked into baked beans or served alongside grill-roasted turkey.

Deeply rooted in American culture, cornbread has been around long enough to take on a distinctly different character depending on where it is made. In the South, it has become a squat, savory skillet bread. In cooler northern regions, where it has become more cake than bread, it is light, tender, and generously sweetened. Despite these regional variations in texture and appearance, however, cornbread has remained unfortunately constant in one respect: It lacks convincing corn flavor.

Wanting to avoid a regional food fight, we figured that everyone—north and south of the Mason-Dixon line—could agree on one simple notion: Cornbread ought to be rich with the flavor of corn. A deeply browned crust also seemed far from controversial, and, when it came to texture, we attempted a reasonable regional compromise: moist and somewhat fluffy but neither cakey nor heavy.

We started out with a northern-style recipe calling for equal amounts of flour and cornmeal. (It is customary for southern-style recipes to minimize or eliminate the flour altogether.) Our first tests involved the cornmeal. The different brands ran the gamut from fine and powdery to coarse and uneven, yielding wild variations in texture, from dry and cottony to downright crunchy, but not one produced very much corn flavor. We quickly came to the conclusion that our recipe, like it or not, would have to call for a national brand of cornmeal to avoid these huge textural swings. The obvious option was Quaker yellow cornmeal, which is available in every supermarket from New Orleans to Portland, Maine. Although our choice may rightfully be considered heretical by many cornbread mavens, it was the only way we could be sure our recipe would deliver consistent results.

Reliable though it is, Quaker cornmeal is degerminated—robbed of the germ (the heart of the kernel) during processing. It is thus also robbed of flavor. (In whole-grain cornmeal, the germ is left intact.) By using degerminated cornmeal, we were now taking a step backward in our quest to build more corn flavor. Increasing the amount of cornmeal to compensate caused the cornbread to lose its lightness. And tasters didn't care for the abundance of hard, crunchy grains. Our next move was to soak the cornmeal in boiling water before mixing it with the other ingredients (a common recipe directive), reasoning that this would both soften the cornmeal and extract more of its flavor. But the added moisture made the cornbread even heavier and slightly rubbery, while contributing not a bit of extra corn flavor. Relenting, we reduced the cornmeal (we now had more flour than cornmeal), which produced the best texture thus far and alleviated any grittiness or heaviness.

To boost corn flavor, a few recipes added fresh corn to the batter. While appreciating the sweet corn taste, tasters objected to the tough, chewy kernels. Chopping the corn by hand was time-consuming. Pureeing the corn in the food processor was much quicker and broke down the kernels more efficiently. With pureed corn, our recipe was finally starting to develop a fuller flavor.

The dairy component up until now had been whole milk. To compensate for the extra liquid exuded by the pureed corn, we reduced the amount, but this just made the cornbread bland. We tried substituting a modest amount of buttermilk, which produced both a lighter texture and a tangier flavor. The sweetener also had an effect on texture; honey and maple syrup added nice flavor accents, but they also added moisture. Granulated and light brown sugars made for a better texture, but the light brown sugar did more to accentuate the corn flavor. Two eggs worked well in this bread, offering structure without cakiness. A modest amount of baking powder boosted by a bit of baking soda (to react with the acidic buttermilk) yielded the best rise.

The fat used in cornbread can vary from bacon drippings to melted butter or vegetable oil. Cooking bacon for this relatively quick recipe seemed an unnecessary step, and butter indisputably added more flavor and color than vegetable oil. Because we were already using the food processor for the corn, we decided to avoid

dirtying another bowl and added all of the wet ingredients together. We even added the light brown sugar to the wet mix to eliminate the pesky lumps it had been forming in the flour mixture. Then we noticed that some recipes added the melted butter last. This created subtle streaks of unmixed butter in the batter, but, as the bread baked, the butter rose to the surface and created a more deeply browned top crust and a stronger butter flavor. Now our recipe, too, would add the butter last. For the best flavor and texture, our recipe would also add a lot more butter than many others—a whole stick.

Although the increase in butter and the adjustment to the mixing method improved the browning, the bread was still missing a thick and crunchy crust. Southern cornbreads, which usually showcase such a crust, are baked in fat-coated, piping-hot cast-iron skillets. Because some cooks don't own a cast-iron (or any other ovenproof) skillet, we tried an 8-inch-square baking dish. Heating it in the oven or on the stovetop before adding the batter was not only awkward but dangerous (especially with Pyrex, which can shatter if handled this way), so we abandoned this idea. Most recipes that call for a baking dish use a moderate oven temperature of 350 degrees. A hotter oven—the kind used in many Southern recipes with a skillet—was better. Baked at 400 degrees, the crust was both crunchy and full of buttery, toasted corn flavor.

All-Purpose Cornbread

MAKES ONE 8-INCH SQUARE

Before preparing the baking dish or any of the other ingredients, measure out the frozen corn kernels and let them stand at room temperature until thawed. When corn is in season, fresh cooked kernels can be substituted for the frozen corn. This recipe was developed with Quaker yellow cornmeal; a stone-ground whole-grain cornmeal will work but will yield a drier and less tender cornbread. We prefer a Pyrex glass baking dish because it yields a nice golden-brown crust, but a metal baking dish (nonstick or traditional) will also work. The cornbread is best served warm; leftovers can be wrapped in foil and reheated in a 350-degree oven for 10 to 15 minutes.

1½   cups (7½ ounces) unbleached all-purpose flour
1   cup (5½ ounces) yellow cornmeal (see note)
2   teaspoons baking powder
¾   teaspoon salt
¼   teaspoon baking soda
1   cup buttermilk
¾   cup frozen corn kernels, thawed
¼   cup packed light brown sugar
2   large eggs
8   tablespoons (1 stick) unsalted butter, melted and cooled slightly

1. Adjust an oven rack to the middle position; heat the oven to 400 degrees. Spray an 8-inch square baking dish with nonstick cooking spray. Whisk the flour, cornmeal, baking powder, salt, and baking soda in a medium bowl until combined; set aside.

SHREDDING SEMISOFT CHEESE NEATLY

Use nonstick cooking spray to lightly coat the coarse side of a box grater, then shred the cheese as usual. The cooking spray will keep cheese from sticking to the surface of the grater.

2. In a food processor or blender, process the buttermilk, thawed corn kernels, and brown sugar until combined, about 5 seconds. Add the eggs and process until well combined (the corn lumps will remain), about 5 seconds longer.

3. Using a rubber spatula, make a well in the center of the dry ingredients; pour the wet ingredients into the well. Begin folding the dry ingredients into the wet, giving the mixture only a few turns to barely combine; add the melted butter and continue folding until the dry ingredients are just moistened. Pour the batter into the prepared baking dish; smooth the surface with a rubber spatula. Bake until deep golden brown and a toothpick inserted in the center comes out clean, 25 to 35 minutes. Cool on a wire rack 10 minutes; invert the cornbread onto a wire rack, then turn right-side up and continue to cool until warm, about 10 minutes longer. Cut into pieces and serve.

➤   VARIATION

Spicy Jalapeño–Cheddar Cornbread
Shred 4 ounces sharp cheddar cheese (you should have about 1⅓ cups). Follow the recipe for All-Purpose Cornbread, reducing the salt to ½ teaspoon; add ⅜ teaspoon cayenne, 1 medium jalapeño chile, stemmed, seeded, and chopped fine, and half of the shredded cheddar to the flour mixture in step 1 and toss well to combine. Reduce the sugar to 2 tablespoons and sprinkle the remaining cheddar over the batter in the baking dish just before baking.

11

RUBS AND SAUCES

RUBS AND SAUCES

RUBS AND PASTES FOR MEAT 376
    Dry Rub for Barbecue
    Simple Barbecue Rub
    Simple Spice Rub for Beef or Lamb
    Mediterranean Herb and Garlic Paste for Meat

RUBS FOR PORK 377
    Basic Spice Rub for Pork
    Indian Spice Rub for Pork
    Herb Rub for Pork
    Chipotle and Ancho Rub for Pork
    Simple Spice Rub for Pork
    Orange, Sage, and Garlic Wet Rub for Pork
    Asian Wet Rub for Pork
    Mustard, Garlic, and Honey Wet Rub for Pork
    Caribbean Wet Rub for Pork

RUB FOR FISH 379
    Simple Spice Rub for Fish

RUBS AND PASTES FOR STEAK 380
    Chile-Cumin Spice Rub for Steak
    Cocoa-Cumin-Allspice Rub for Steak
    Tarragon–Mustard Seed Rub for Steak
    Star Anise and Coffee Bean Spice Rub for Steak
    Peppery Coriander and Dill Spice Rub for Steak
    Cracked Peppercorn Rub for Steak
    Rosemary-Garlic Paste for Steak

RUBS AND PASTES FOR POULTRY 382
    Cajun Spice Rub for Chicken Parts
    Tex-Mex Spice Rub for Chicken Parts
    Jamaican Spice Rub for Chicken Parts
    Aromatic Rub for Poultry
    Pantry Spice Rub for Chicken
    Citrus and Cilantro Spice Paste for Chicken Parts
    Indian Spice Rub for Poultry
    Asian Spice Paste for Chicken Parts
    Mediterranean Spice Paste for Chicken Parts

COMPOUND BUTTERS FOR GRILLED STEAK OR FISH 384
    Parsley Butter
    Parsley-Lemon Butter
    Tarragon-Lime Butter
    Tapenade Butter
    Rosemary-Parmesan Butter
    Roasted Red Pepper and Smoked Paprika Butter
    Roquefort Butter

BARBECUE SAUCES AND GLAZES. 386
    Classic Barbecue Sauce
    Barbecue Sauce with Mexican Flavors
    Barbecue Sauce with Asian Flavors
    Barbecue Sauce with Caribbean Flavors
    Quick Barbecue Sauce
    Sweet-Sour-Spicy Barbecue Sauce
    Eastern North Carolina Barbecue Sauce
    Mid–South Carolina Mustard Sauce
    Sweetened Soy Glaze
    Hoisin, Honey, and Ginger Glaze

SALSAS. 390
    Fresh Tomato Salsa
    Chunky Guacamole
    Spicy Yellow Pepper and Tomato Salsa
    Grilled Corn Salsa
    Black Bean and Mango Salsa
    Mango Salsa
    Pineapple Salsa
    Peach Salsa

RELISHES, CHUTNEYS, AND OTHER SAUCES 393
    Black Olive and Citrus Relish
    Avocado-Corn Relish
    Cranberry-Onion Relish
    Quick Onion and Parsley Relish
    Warm Cucumber and Red Onion Relish with Mint
    Onion, Black Olive, and Caper Relish
    Red Pepper–Jícama Relish
    Curried Fruit Chutney with Lime and Ginger
    Dried Peach and Apple Chutney
    Parsley Sauce with Cornichons and Capers
    Salsa Verde
    Chimichurri
    Chermoula
    Salmoriglio Sauce
    Romesco Sauce
    Cilantro-Parsley Sauce with Pickled Jalapeños
    Classic Pesto
    Mojo Sauce
    Pureed Red Pepper Sauce with Basil
    Tomatillo-Chile Sauce
    Spicy Peanut Dipping Sauce

RUBS AND PASTES

GRILLED FOODS HAVE GREAT FLAVOR ON THEIR
own, but sometimes we like a little variety, which
is when rubs and pastes come in handy. Rubs
(mixtures of dry spices) and pastes (spices and herbs
moistened with oil and/or other liquids) are often
used to coat foods before grilling. Rubs and pastes
encourage the formation of a deeply browned crust
filled with complex, concentrated flavors. Like
marinades, spice rubs and pastes add flavor to food
before it is cooked, but we think rubs and pastes
have several advantages over marinades.

Because rubs and pastes are composed almost
solely of spices and herbs, they provide a stronger
flavor than marinades. (Marinades consist mostly
of oil with an acidic liquid added, such as lemon
juice or vinegar.) Rubs and pastes also adhere to
foods better than marinades do—after all, they are
massaged directly into foods before grilling. The
better the adherence the better the flavor. Finally,
because of the oil in marinades, there can be flare-
ups. By contrast, spice rubs can be left on foods for
several hours without causing fires.

Spice rubs and herb pastes can be used on
just about any type of food you want to grill. In
general, you can freely mix and match rubs and
pastes with different foods. That said, it is still
worth observing a couple of useful guidelines.
First, consider matching the strength of the rub
or paste with the nature of the food being cooked.
For example, earthier spices are better with meat,
lighter spices and herbs with fish and chicken. Also
keep in mind that spices like cumin and paprika
are good "bulk" spices, while aromatic spices like
cinnamon and cloves should be used sparingly so
as not to overwhelm.

We find that bare hands—not brushes—are the
best tools for applying rubs. Use a bit of pressure to
make sure that the rub or paste actually adheres to
the food. Although rubs and pastes can be applied
right before cooking, we've discovered that the
flavor of the spices penetrates deeper into the food
if given time. Refrigerate rubbed meats for at least
a few hours to maximize the return.

Most dry rubs should keep for up to a month
when stored in an airtight container, unless
they contain brown sugar, in which case they
should be used sooner (within a week or two).
We don't recommend storing wet rubs.

Dry Rub for Barbecue
MAKES ABOUT 1 CUP

*You can adjust the proportions of spices in this all-purpose
rub or add or subtract a spice, as you wish. For instance, if
you don't like spicy foods, reduce the cayenne. Or, if you
are using hot chili powder, eliminate the cayenne entirely.
This rub works well with ribs and brisket as well as with
Boston butt for pulled pork (page 114).*

4	tablespoons sweet paprika
2	tablespoons chili powder
2	tablespoons ground cumin
2	tablespoons dark brown sugar
2	tablespoons salt
1	tablespoon dried oregano
1	tablespoon sugar
1	tablespoon ground black pepper
1	tablespoon ground white pepper
1–2	teaspoons cayenne pepper

Mix all of the ingredients together in a small
bowl.

Simple Barbecue Rub
MAKES ABOUT 1 CUP

*This rub is even simpler than the previous recipe and can
also be used with ribs, brisket, and Boston butt for pulled
pork. It's less peppery and not as sweet. A hint of cloves
makes this basic rub interesting.*

1/2	cup sweet paprika
2	tablespoons ground cumin
2	tablespoons mild chili powder
2	tablespoons ground black pepper
1	teaspoon cayenne pepper
1/2	teaspoon ground cloves

Mix all of the ingredients together in a small bowl.
(The rub can be stored in an airtight container at
room temperature for up to a month.)

Simple Spice Rub
for Beef or Lamb

MAKES ABOUT ¹/₄ CUP

This fragrant rub works well with most cuts of beef and lamb, especially flank steak, shoulder steak, lamb shoulder chops, and butterflied leg of lamb. See page 381 for the results from our tasting of black pepper brands.

1	tablespoon black peppercorns
1	tablespoon white peppercorns
1¹/₂	teaspoons coriander seeds
1¹/₂	teaspoons cumin seeds
¹/₂	teaspoon red pepper flakes
¹/₂	teaspoon ground cinnamon

1. Toast the black and white peppercorns and the coriander and cumin seeds in a small skillet over medium heat, shaking the pan occasionally to prevent burning, until the first wisps of smoke appear, 3 to 5 minutes. Remove the pan from the heat, cool the spices to room temperature, and then mix them with the pepper flakes and cinnamon.

2. Grind the spice mixture to a powder in a spice grinder or dedicated coffee grinder. (The rub can be stored in an airtight container at room temperature for up to a month.)

Mediterranean Herb
and Garlic Paste for Meat

MAKES ABOUT ¹/₂ CUP

You may omit one or two of the herbs in this recipe, but be sure to compensate with the other herbs so that the total amount equals a scant quarter cup. This all-purpose paste is great rubbed onto steaks and chops (veal, pork, or lamb) before grilling. Be sure to season them with salt and pepper as well (unless you are brining).

¹/₄	cup extra-virgin olive oil
3	medium garlic cloves, minced or pressed through a garlic press (about 1 tablespoon)
1	tablespoon chopped fresh parsley leaves
2	teaspoons chopped fresh sage leaves
2	teaspoons chopped fresh thyme leaves
2	teaspoons chopped fresh rosemary
2	teaspoons chopped fresh oregano leaves

Mix all of the ingredients together in a small bowl. Rub the paste onto the meat before grilling, making sure to season the meat with salt and pepper to taste.

Basic Spice Rub
for Pork

MAKES ENOUGH FOR 4 CHOPS
OR 2 TENDERLOINS

The sweet and spicy flavors in this rub are a nice complement to rich pork. Use hot chili powder for more heat.

1	tablespoon ground cumin
1	tablespoon chili powder
1	tablespoon curry powder
2	teaspoons brown sugar
1	teaspoon ground black pepper

Combine all of the ingredients in a small bowl.

Indian Spice Rub
for Pork

MAKES ENOUGH FOR 4 CHOPS
OR 2 TENDERLOINS

Serve this fragrant combination with either Pineapple Salsa (page 393) or Mango Salsa (page 392).

1	tablespoon fennel seeds
1	tablespoon ground cumin
2	teaspoons brown sugar
1	teaspoon ground coriander
1	teaspoon ground cardamom
1	teaspoon dry mustard
¹/₂	teaspoon ground cinnamon
¹/₄	teaspoon ground cloves

Grind the fennel seeds to a powder in a spice grinder or dedicated coffee grinder. Transfer to a small bowl and stir in the remaining ingredients.

Herb Rub for Pork

MAKES ENOUGH FOR 4 CHOPS
OR 2 TENDERLOINS

A little salt is added to this rub to help break the dried herbs down into a powder. Do not salt the meat if using this rub.

1½   teaspoons dried thyme
1½   teaspoons dried rosemary
1½   teaspoons black peppercorns
2   bay leaves, crumbled
2   whole cloves or allspice berries
½   teaspoon salt

Grind all of the ingredients to a powder in a spice grinder or dedicated coffee grinder. (The rub can be stored in an airtight container at room temperature for up to a month.)

Chipotle and Ancho Rub for Pork

MAKES ENOUGH FOR 4 CHOPS
OR 2 TENDERLOINS

A little of this potent rub goes a long way.

1   dried chipotle chile, stemmed, seeded, and cut into rough pieces
½   medium ancho chile, stemmed, seeded, and torn into rough pieces
2   teaspoons brown sugar
1   teaspoon dried oregano
¼   teaspoon garlic powder
¼   teaspoon salt

Grind both chiles to a powder in a spice grinder or dedicated coffee grinder. Transfer to a small bowl and stir in the remaining ingredients.

Simple Spice Rub for Pork

MAKES ENOUGH FOR 4 CHOPS OR 2 TENDERLOINS

If you want some heat, add cayenne pepper or red pepper flakes to the mix.

1½   tablespoons fennel seeds
1½   tablespoons cumin seeds
1½   tablespoons coriander seeds
2   teaspoons dry mustard
2   teaspoons brown sugar
1   teaspoon ground cinnamon

1. Toast the fennel, cumin, and coriander seeds in a small skillet over medium heat, shaking the pan occasionally to prevent burning, until the first wisps of smoke appear, 3 to 5 minutes. Remove the pan from the heat, cool the spices to room temperature, then mix with the mustard, brown sugar, and cinnamon.

2. Grind the spice mixture to a powder in a spice grinder or dedicated coffee grinder.

Orange, Sage, and Garlic Wet Rub for Pork

MAKES ABOUT ⅓ CUP,
ENOUGH FOR 2 TENDERLOINS

If you have no orange marmalade, substitute an equal amount of honey.

3   medium garlic cloves, minced or pressed through a garlic press (about 1 tablespoon)
1   tablespoon grated zest from 1 orange

EQUIPMENT: Coffee Grinder as Spice Grinder

The test kitchen standard for grinding spices is an inexpensive blade-type electric coffee grinder (which we use for spices only, reserving a separate unit to grind coffee). Coffee grinders are our first choice when grinding spices because of their effectiveness and ease of use. They are easy to control for texture of grind: Each coffee grinder we tested reduced mountains of cardamom seeds, toasted whole cumin and coriander seeds, and chipotle chiles to fine powders. (We chose these spices because of their varying hardnesses, densities, shapes, and oil content.) The only physical exertion required to use them is pressing a button. No stress, strain, or sore forearms, and they produced consistently strong results on all of the test spices. They are easy to brush or wipe clean (just mind the blade!) and no more expensive than manual grinders or mortars and pestles. The Krups Fast-Touch Coffee Mill (Model 203), Braun Aromatic Coffee Grinder (Model KSM 2B), Mr. Coffee Coffee Grinder (Model IDS55), and Capresso Cool Grind all did an equally good job with small and large amounts of spices.

1 tablespoon chopped fresh sage leaves
1 tablespoon orange marmalade
1 tablespoon extra-virgin olive oil
1/2 teaspoon ground black pepper
1/4 teaspoon salt

Combine all of the ingredients in a small bowl.

Asian Wet Rub for Pork

MAKES ABOUT 1/2 CUP,
ENOUGH FOR 2 TENDERLOINS

If you don't have hoisin sauce on hand, use an equal amount of soy sauce in its place.

2 tablespoons minced fresh ginger
2 medium scallions, minced
2 tablespoons light brown sugar
3 medium garlic cloves, minced or pressed through a garlic press (about 1 tablespoon)
1 tablespoon hoisin sauce
1 tablespoon toasted sesame oil
1/2 teaspoon red pepper flakes
1/4 teaspoon Chinese five-spice powder
1/4 teaspoon salt

Combine all of the ingredients in a small bowl.

Mustard, Garlic, and Honey Wet Rub for Pork

MAKES ABOUT 1/3 CUP,
ENOUGH FOR 2 TENDERLOINS

You can substitute 1 teaspoon dried rosemary for the fresh herb if desired.

3 medium garlic cloves, minced or pressed through a garlic press (about 1 tablespoon)
1 tablespoon extra-virgin olive oil
2 teaspoons honey
2 teaspoons Dijon mustard
2 teaspoons chopped fresh rosemary
1 teaspoon grated zest from 1 lemon
1/2 teaspoon black pepper
1/4 teaspoon salt

Combine all of the ingredients in a small bowl.

Caribbean Wet Rub for Pork

MAKES ABOUT 1/3 CUP,
ENOUGH FOR 2 TENDERLOINS

Scotch bonnet chiles are extremely hot, so be certain to wash your hands thoroughly with soap and hot water right after chopping it or, better yet, wear rubber gloves.

2 medium scallions, minced
1 tablespoon extra-virgin olive oil
1 tablespoon grated zest from 2 to 3 limes
1 tablespoon light brown sugar
1 tablespoon chopped fresh thyme leaves
1 large garlic clove, minced or pressed through a garlic press (about 1 1/2 teaspoons)
1 teaspoon dry mustard
1/2 medium Scotch Bonnet or habanero chile, stemmed, seeded, and minced (about 1 teaspoon)
Pinch ground allspice

Combine all of the ingredients in a small bowl.

Simple Spice Rub for Fish

MAKES ABOUT 1/4 CUP

Use this aromatic mixture on oily fish such as salmon, mackerel, or bluefish. It's delicious on our Barbecued Salmon (page 239), when used in place of the white pepper and paprika.

1 1/2 tablespoons fennel seeds
1 1/2 tablespoons coriander seeds
1 1/2 tablespoons white peppercorns
3 whole cloves
2 whole star anise

1. Toast the fennel, coriander, peppercorns, cloves, and star anise in a small skillet over medium heat, shaking the pan occasionally to prevent burning, until the first wisps of smoke appear, 3 to 5 minutes. Remove the pan from the heat and cool the spices to room temperature.

2. Grind the spice mixture to a powder in a spice grinder or dedicated coffee grinder. (The rub can be stored in an airtight container at room temperature for up to a month.)

Chile-Cumin Spice Rub for Steak

MAKES ABOUT ⅓ CUP

3 dried chipotle chiles, stemmed, seeded, and cut into rough pieces
2 dried ancho chiles, stemmed, seeded, and torn into rough pieces
1 tablespoon ground cumin
1 tablespoon salt
2 teaspoons sugar

Grind the chiles in a spice grinder or dedicated coffee grinder until powdery. Whisk together the ground chiles and the remaining ingredients in a small bowl until combined. (The rub can be stored in an airtight container at room temperature for up to a month.)

Cocoa-Cumin-Allspice Rub for Steak

MAKES ABOUT ⅓ CUP

4 teaspoons ground cumin
4 teaspoons black peppercorns
1 tablespoon unsweetened cocoa
2 teaspoons ground allspice
2 teaspoons salt

Grind all of the ingredients in a spice grinder or dedicated coffee grinder until no whole peppercorns remain. (The rub can be stored in an airtight container at room temperature for up to a month.)

Tarragon–Mustard Seed Rub for Steak

MAKES ABOUT ⅓ CUP

3 tablespoons dried tarragon
2 tablespoons yellow mustard seeds
1 tablespoon salt
2¼ teaspoons black peppercorns

Grind all of the ingredients in a spice grinder or dedicated coffee grinder until no whole peppercorns

remain. (The rub can be stored in an airtight container at room temperature for up to a month.)

Star Anise and Coffee Bean Spice Rub for Steak

MAKES ABOUT ⅓ CUP

6 pods star anise or 1 whole star anise
2 tablespoons whole coffee beans
1 tablespoon black peppercorns
2 teaspoons salt
1 teaspoon sugar

Grind all of the ingredients in a spice grinder or dedicated coffee grinder until no whole peppercorns remain. (The rub can be stored in an airtight container at room temperature for up to a month.)

Peppery Coriander and Dill Spice Rub for Steak

MAKES ABOUT ⅓ CUP

2 tablespoons black peppercorns
2 tablespoons coriander seeds
1 tablespoon dill seeds

AN IMPROVISED MORTAR AND PESTLE

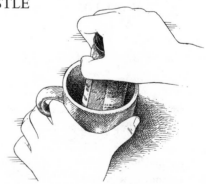

Stone, marble, wood, or porcelain mortars (bowls) and pestles (dowel-shaped grinding tools) are great for grinding peppercorns and other whole spices. Many modern kitchens do not have this tool. If you do not, you can improvise with a shallow, diner-style coffee cup and a heavy glass spice bottle. Place the peppercorns or other spices to be ground in the cup and then grind them to the desired consistency with the bottom of the spice bottle.

2½ teaspoons salt

1½ teaspoons red pepper flakes

2 tablespoons coarsely ground black pepper

1 tablespoon kosher or coarse sea salt

Grind all of the ingredients in a spice grinder or dedicated coffee grinder until no whole peppercorns remain. (The rub can be stored in an airtight container at room temperature for up to a month.)

Mix the pepper and salt together in a small bowl. Rub this mixture onto steaks before grilling, omitting the salt and pepper in the recipe. (The rub can be stored in an airtight container at room temperature for up to a month.)

Cracked Peppercorn Rub for Steak

MAKES ABOUT 3 TABLESPOONS,
ENOUGH FOR 4 SMALL OR 2 LARGE STEAKS

To coarsely grind the black peppercorns, use a spice grinder or dedicated coffee grinder, or crush them manually with a mortar and pestle. You can improvise with a coffee mug and glass spice bottle as directed on the facing page. This rub is especially good with mild-tasting filet mignon.

Rosemary-Garlic Paste for Steak

MAKES ABOUT ¼ CUP,
ENOUGH FOR 4 SMALL OR 2 LARGE STEAKS

This paste is best when left on the steak for at least 2 hours prior to grilling. If you don't have time to let the steaks sit, however, you will still get a good, though less pronounced, garlic and herb flavor. Try this zesty paste with mild-tasting filet mignon.

INGREDIENTS: Black Pepper

For a spice that we use just about every day, and with a wide variety of foods, it's hard not to wonder if we take pepper too much for granted. Although most of us tend to think that one jar of black pepper is the same as another, several varieties exist. The most readily available include Vietnamese pepper, Lampong (from the island of Sumatra), and Malabar and Tellicherry (both from India). Among spice experts, each has gained a reputation for its particular attributes.

We wondered if we should be seeking out black pepper from a particular region of a particular country. Or, at the other end of the spectrum, perhaps all this fuss over grinding fresh whole peppercorns is nonsense, not really providing any improved flavor. We decided to hold a blind tasting to sort it all out. We included in our tasting the two preeminent national supermarket brands as well as the above-mentioned varieties, which were ordered from specialty spice and gourmet stores.

Tasters had the option of trying each pepper by itself or on plain white rice. Overall, our tasting confirmed that freshly ground pepper is far superior to pepper purchased already ground. The latter carried minimal aroma and tended to taste sharp and one-dimensional, lacking in complexity. Whole peppercorns that were ground just before the tasting contained bold as well as subtle flavors, and aromas that were both lively and complex.

As for differences between the varieties of freshly ground

peppercorns, we found them to be distinct yet subtle. All were appreciated for their particular characteristics, receiving high scores within a close range of one another. Based on these results, we concluded that what is important is not so much which variety of pepper you buy but how you buy it.

Why did we find the most noticeable differences in pepper to be between fresh-ground whole pepper and commercially ground pepper? When a peppercorn is cracked, the volatile chemical components that give pepper its bold aroma as well as its subtle characteristics immediately begin to disperse. These more subtle flavors often include pine and citrus. So with time (and cracking), what remains is the predominant nonvolatile compound in black pepper, piperine. Piperine is the source of black pepper's renowned pungency and is what gives it its characteristic hot, sharp, and stinging qualities. It is also said to stimulate saliva and gastric juices, creating the sensation of hunger.

THE BEST BLACK PEPPER

McCormick Whole Black Peppercorns beat out the rest of the supermarket competition as well as several mail-order brands. Note that this "premium" product, sold in glass bottles, also fared better than McCormick peppercorns sold in plastic bottles. This brand is sold under the Schilling label on the West Coast.

4 medium garlic cloves, minced with a pinch of kosher or coarse sea salt into a fine paste (see the illustrations on page 263)

2 tablespoons extra-virgin olive oil

1½ teaspoons chopped fresh rosemary

Mix all of the ingredients together in a small bowl. Rub the paste onto the steaks, cover, and refrigerate the steaks for at least 2 hours and up to 1 day. Season the steaks with salt and pepper to taste as directed in the appropriate recipe.

Cajun Spice Rub for Chicken Parts

MAKES ABOUT ½ CUP,
ENOUGH TO SEASON A SINGLE RECIPE OF
EITHER DARK OR WHITE MEAT PARTS

¼ cup sweet paprika

1 tablespoon kosher salt

1 tablespoon garlic powder

1½ teaspoons dried thyme

1 teaspoon ground celery seeds

1 teaspoon ground black pepper

1 teaspoon cayenne pepper

Combine all of the ingredients in a small bowl. (The rub can be stored in an airtight container at room temperature for up to a month.)

Tex-Mex Spice Rub for Chicken Parts

MAKES ABOUT ½ CUP,
ENOUGH TO SEASON A SINGLE RECIPE OF
EITHER DARK OR WHITE MEAT PARTS

2 tablespoons ground cumin

1 tablespoon chili powder

1 tablespoon ground coriander

1 tablespoon dried oregano

1 tablespoon garlic powder

2 teaspoons kosher salt

1 teaspoon unsweetened cocoa

½ teaspoon cayenne pepper

Combine all of the ingredients in a small bowl. (The rub can be stored in an airtight container at room temperature for up to a month.)

Jamaican Spice Rub for Chicken Parts

MAKES ABOUT ½ CUP,
ENOUGH TO SEASON A SINGLE RECIPE OF
EITHER DARK OR WHITE MEAT PARTS

2 tablespoons brown sugar

1½ tablespoons kosher salt

1½ tablespoons ground coriander

1 tablespoon ground ginger

1 tablespoon garlic powder

1½ teaspoons ground allspice

1½ teaspoons ground black pepper

1 teaspoon cayenne pepper

1 teaspoon ground nutmeg

¾ teaspoon ground cinnamon

Combine all of the ingredients in a small bowl.

Aromatic Rub for Poultry

MAKES ABOUT ½ CUP

This rub (and the one that follows) is less potent and peppery than the Dry Rub for Barbecue (page 376), making it well suited to poultry. A single recipe will coat a turkey, two chickens, two ducks, or four Cornish hens.

1½ tablespoons ground cardamom

1½ tablespoons ground ginger

1½ tablespoons ground black pepper

1 tablespoon ground turmeric

1 tablespoon ground cumin

1 tablespoon ground coriander

1½ teaspoons ground allspice

½ teaspoon ground cloves

Mix all of the ingredients together in a small bowl. (The rub can be stored in an airtight container at room temperature for up to a month.)

Many of our spice rub recipes call for toasting whole spices in a warm pan and then grinding them in a coffee mill or spice grinder. Why not just start with ground spices? In some cases, ground spices are just fine. However, when we want a particularly fragrant or aromatic rub, toasting whole spices produces better results. When whole spices are toasted, the heat releases oils and chemicals in the spices that break down and reform into new tastes and aromas. You want to heat the spices long enough to release as much flavor as possible. However, you don't want to burn the spices. At the first signs of smoke, remove the pan from the heat. Also, make sure to toast the spices over medium heat; higher heat can cause the spices to burn.

STORING SPICES EFFICIENTLY

1. Using stick-on dots, write the name and purchase date on the lids of spice jars when you bring them home from the market.

2. It is easy to locate and extract the spice you want and to know when a spice is past its prime and should be replaced. Dried spices should be discarded after one year.

Pantry Spice Rub for Chicken

MAKES ABOUT $1/2$ CUP, ENOUGH TO SEASON A SINGLE RECIPE OF WHOLE CHICKEN OR EITHER DARK OR WHITE MEAT PARTS

2   tablespoons ground cumin
2   tablespoons curry powder
2   tablespoons chili powder
1   tablespoon ground allspice
1   tablespoon ground black pepper
1   teaspoon ground cinnamon

Combine all of the ingredients in a small bowl. Rub the mixture over the brined and dried chicken parts before grilling. (The rub can be stored in an airtight container at room temperature for up to a month.)

Citrus and Cilantro Spice Paste for Chicken Parts

MAKES ABOUT $1/3$ CUP, ENOUGH TO SEASON A SINGLE RECIPE OF EITHER DARK OR WHITE MEAT PARTS

2   tablespoons juice from 1 orange
2   tablespoons fresh cilantro leaves
1   tablespoon juice from 1 lime
1   tablespoon olive oil
1   teaspoon ground cumin
1   teaspoon chili powder
1   teaspoon sweet paprika
1   teaspoon ground coriander
1   garlic clove, peeled

Puree all of the ingredients in a food processor or blender until smooth. Rub the paste over the brined and dried chicken parts before grilling.

Indian Spice Rub for Poultry

MAKES ABOUT $1/2$ CUP

This rub gets a lot of flavor from four robust spices. A single recipe will coat a turkey, two chickens, two ducks, or four Cornish hens.

3 tablespoons curry powder

3 tablespoons chili powder

1½ tablespoons ground allspice

1½ teaspoons ground cinnamon

Mix all of the ingredients together in a small bowl. (The rub can be stored in an airtight container at room temperature for up to a month.)

Asian Spice Paste for Chicken Parts

MAKES ABOUT ⅓ CUP, ENOUGH TO SEASON A SINGLE RECIPE OF EITHER DARK OR WHITE MEAT PARTS

2 tablespoons soy sauce

2 tablespoons peanut oil

2 tablespoons fresh cilantro leaves

1 tablespoon stemmed, seeded, and minced jalapeño or other fresh chile

1 tablespoon chopped fresh ginger

1 garlic clove, peeled

Puree all of the ingredients in a food processor or blender until smooth. Rub the paste over the brined and dried chicken parts before grilling.

Mediterranean Spice Paste for Chicken Parts

MAKES ABOUT ½ CUP, ENOUGH TO SEASON A SINGLE RECIPE OF EITHER DARK OR WHITE MEAT PARTS

¼ cup packed fresh parsley leaves

¼ cup extra-virgin olive oil

2 tablespoons grated zest from 1 lemon

4 medium garlic cloves, peeled

1 tablespoon fresh thyme leaves

1 tablespoon fresh rosemary

1 tablespoon fresh sage leaves

½ teaspoon salt

Puree all of the ingredients in a food processor or blender until smooth. Rub the paste over the brined and dried chicken parts before grilling.

COMPOUND BUTTERS FOR GRILLED STEAK OR FISH

WHILE WE GENERALLY SEASON STEAKS AND FISH with just salt and pepper before cooking, we sometimes serve them with a dollop of seasoned butter, called a compound butter.

Parsley Butter

ENOUGH FOR 4 SERVINGS

The butter moistens the meat and improves its mouthfeel, especially if you are grilling steaks that are not well marbled. If you are making a large batch of compound butter, use a standing mixer to combine the ingredients evenly. You can double or triple any of these recipes and store the extra butter in the freezer.

4 tablespoons (½ stick) unsalted butter, softened

2 tablespoons minced fresh parsley leaves

2 tablespoons minced shallot (optional)

⅛ teaspoon salt

Pinch ground black pepper

1. Beat the butter with a large fork in a medium bowl until light and fluffy. Add the remaining ingredients and mix to combine.

2. Following the illustration below, roll the butter into a log about 3 inches long and 1½ inches

ROLLING THE COMPOUND BUTTER

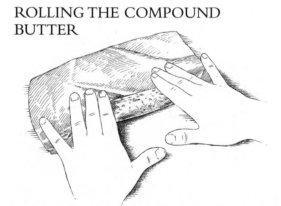

Once the ingredients have been combined, place the butter mixture in the center of a piece of plastic wrap. Fold one edge of the plastic wrap over the butter. Glide your hands back and forth over the butter to shape it into a cylinder. Twist the ends of the plastic wrap shut and refrigerate until firm.

in diameter. Refrigerate until firm, at least 2 hours and up to 3 days. (The butter can be frozen for 2 months. When ready to use, let soften just until it can be cut, about 15 minutes.)

3. When ready to use, remove the butter from the refrigerator and slice it into 4 pieces just before grilling the steak or fish. After grilling, place one piece of butter on each portion. Let them rest for 2 minutes before serving.

➤ VARIATIONS
Parsley-Lemon Butter
Follow the recipe for Parsley Butter, substituting 2 teaspoons grated lemon zest for the shallot.

Tarragon-Lime Butter

- 4 tablespoons ($\frac{1}{2}$ stick) unsalted butter, softened
- 2 tablespoons minced scallion
- 1 tablespoon minced fresh tarragon leaves
- 2 teaspoons juice from 1 lime
- $\frac{1}{8}$ teaspoon salt
  Pinch ground black pepper

Beat the butter with a large fork in a medium bowl until light and fluffy. Add the remaining ingredients and mix to combine. Follow steps 2 and 3 of the Parsley Butter recipe.

Tapenade Butter

- 4 tablespoons ($\frac{1}{2}$ stick) unsalted butter, softened
- 10 pitted and finely chopped oil-cured black olives (about 2 tablespoons)
- $1\frac{1}{2}$ teaspoons brandy
- 1 teaspoon minced fresh thyme leaves
- 1 small garlic clove, minced or pressed through a garlic press (about $\frac{1}{2}$ teaspoon)
- $\frac{1}{2}$ anchovy fillet, minced
- $\frac{1}{8}$ teaspoon grated orange zest
- $\frac{1}{8}$ teaspoon salt
  Pinch ground black pepper

Beat the butter with a large fork in a medium bowl until light and fluffy. Add the remaining ingredients and mix to combine. Follow steps 2 and 3 of the Parsley Butter recipe.

Rosemary-Parmesan Butter

- 4 tablespoons ($\frac{1}{2}$ stick) unsalted butter, softened
- 3 tablespoons grated Parmesan cheese
- 2 teaspoons chopped fresh rosemary
- 1 small garlic clove, minced or pressed through a garlic press (about $\frac{1}{2}$ teaspoon)
- $\frac{1}{8}$ teaspoon red pepper flakes
- $\frac{1}{8}$ teaspoon salt

Beat the butter with a large fork in a medium bowl until light and fluffy. Add the remaining ingredients and mix to combine. Follow steps 2 and 3 of the Parsley Butter recipe.

Roasted Red Pepper and Smoked Paprika Butter

- 4 tablespoons ($\frac{1}{2}$ stick) unsalted butter, softened
- 2 tablespoons very finely minced jarred roasted red bell peppers (about 1 ounce)
- 1 tablespoon minced fresh thyme leaves
- $\frac{3}{4}$ teaspoon smoked paprika
- $\frac{1}{2}$ teaspoon salt
  Ground black pepper

Beat the butter with a large fork in a medium bowl until light and fluffy. Add the remaining ingredients and mix to combine. Follow steps 2 and 3 of the Parsley Butter recipe.

Roquefort Butter

- 4 tablespoons ($\frac{1}{2}$ stick) unsalted butter, softened
- 3 tablespoons crumbled Roquefort cheese
- 1 medium shallot, minced
- 2 teaspoons port
- 2 teaspoons minced fresh sage leaves
- 1 teaspoon minced fresh parsley leaves
- $\frac{1}{8}$ teaspoon salt
  Pinch ground black pepper

Beat the butter with a large fork in a medium bowl until light and fluffy. Add the remaining ingredients and mix to combine. Follow steps 2 and 3 of the Parsley Butter recipe.

BARBECUE SAUCES AND GLAZES

OF ALL THE SAUCES AND GLAZES USED FOR barbecuing, those based on tomatoes and some sort of sweetener are the most common. The problem with these ingredients, however, is that they cause the sauce to burn if left on grilled foods for any length of time. For this reason, these sauces are usually brushed on grilled foods during the last few minutes of cooking and are also served at the table.

Classic barbecue sauce, we discovered, is relatively easy to make. The combination of tomato sauce and whole tomatoes in juice cooks down to a thick, glossy texture. Vinegar, brown sugar, and molasses add the sour and sweet notes, while spices (paprika, chili powder, black pepper, and salt) round out the flavors. For some brightness, we added a little fresh orange juice as well. The only downside to this sauce is that it takes at least two hours of gentle simmering for the flavors to come together and for the tomatoes to break down into a sauce of the proper consistency.

Was there a way to shorten the cooking time? The answer was yes. The first thing we had to do for quick barbecue sauce was abandon the canned whole tomatoes—they took too long to cook down. So we tried all tomato sauce (and no fresh tomatoes), which made a sauce that seemed more appropriate for pasta. We then tried ketchup and had better luck because it is already sweet, tart, and thick.

The only other major obstacle we encountered when developing our quick rendition of barbecue sauce was the onion. After two hours of simmering in our classic barbecue sauce, the onion became, not surprisingly, very soft. In our quick-cooked version, though, it remained crunchy. We tried pureeing the quick sauce after it had cooked, as we did with our classic sauce, but the quick sauce lost its glossy texture and became grainy. One of our test cooks then suggested using onion juice—made by pureeing raw onion with water—to give the sauce some onion flavor without texture. This worked liked a charm.

At this point, it was only a matter of adding flavors. Worcestershire sauce and Dijon mustard contributed instant depth. The usual spices—chili powder, cayenne, black pepper—provided more flavor and heat.

In the event classic or quick barbecue sauce is not for you, several specialized barbecue sauces, with distinct flavor profiles, are also included in the following pages.

Classic Barbecue Sauce
MAKES 3 GENEROUS CUPS

Brush this sauce onto chicken parts during the last minute or two of grilling or serve at the table with ribs, brisket, or pulled pork.

2	tablespoons vegetable oil
I	medium onion, minced
I	(28-ounce) can whole tomatoes with juice
I	(8-ounce) can tomato sauce
³/₄	cup distilled white vinegar
¹/₄	cup packed dark brown sugar
¹/₄	cup orange juice
2	tablespoons molasses
I	tablespoon sweet paprika
I	tablespoon chili powder
2	teaspoons liquid smoke (optional)
2	teaspoons ground black pepper
I	teaspoon salt

1. Heat the oil in a large, heavy-bottomed saucepan over medium heat until hot and shimmering (but not smoking). Add the onion and cook, stirring occasionally, until golden brown, 7 to 10 minutes. Add the remaining ingredients. Bring to a boil, then reduce the heat to the lowest possible setting and simmer, uncovered and stirring occasionally, until thickened, 2 to 2½ hours.

2. Puree the sauce, in batches, if necessary, in a blender or food processor. Transfer the sauce to a bowl and use immediately or let it cool, then store in an airtight container. (The sauce can be refrigerated for 2 weeks or frozen for several months.)

➤ VARIATIONS
Barbecue Sauce with Mexican Flavors
A few ingredients added to basic barbecue sauce give this recipe a south-of-the-border flavor.

Follow the recipe for Classic Barbecue Sauce, stirring 6 tablespoons juice from 6 limes, 3 tablespoons chopped fresh cilantro leaves, 1½ teaspoons ground cumin, and 1½ teaspoons chili powder into the finished sauce.

Barbecue Sauce with Asian Flavors

Soy sauce, ginger, and sesame oil give this tomato-based sauce an Asian flavor.

Follow the recipe for Classic Barbecue Sauce, stirring 6 tablespoons soy sauce, 6 tablespoons rice vinegar, 3 tablespoons sugar, 1½ tablespoons toasted sesame oil, and 1 tablespoon minced fresh ginger into the finished sauce.

Barbecue Sauce with Caribbean Flavors

When you brush foods with this sauce, serve Black Bean and Mango Salsa (page 392) on the side.

Follow the recipe for Classic Barbecue Sauce, stirring 2 tablespoons pineapple juice, 2 tablespoons dark rum, 1 tablespoon Caribbean hot sauce, 2 teaspoons sugar, and a pinch of ground allspice into the finished sauce.

Quick Barbecue Sauce

MAKES ABOUT 1½ CUPS

Classic barbecue sauce must simmer for a long time for the whole tomatoes in it to break down. However, we found that starting with ketchup can shorten the process. Use this sauce as you would any other barbecue sauce—either brushed on foods during the last minutes of grilling or served at the table as a dipping sauce with ribs or brisket.

1	medium onion, peeled and quartered
¼	cup water
1	cup ketchup
5	tablespoons molasses
2	tablespoons cider vinegar
2	tablespoons Worcestershire sauce
2	tablespoons Dijon mustard
1½	teaspoons liquid smoke (optional)
1	teaspoon hot pepper sauce, such as Tabasco
¼	teaspoon ground black pepper
2	tablespoons vegetable oil
1	medium garlic clove, minced or pressed through a garlic press (about 1 teaspoon)

1	teaspoon chili powder
¼	teaspoon cayenne pepper

1. Process the onion with the water in a food processor until pureed and the mixture resembles slush, about 30 seconds. Strain the mixture through a fine-mesh strainer into a liquid measuring cup, pressing on the solids with a rubber spatula to obtain ½ cup juice. Discard the solids.

2. Whisk the onion juice, ketchup, molasses, vinegar, Worcestershire, mustard, liquid smoke (if using), hot pepper sauce, and black pepper together in a medium bowl.

3. Heat the oil in a large nonreactive saucepan over medium heat until shimmering but not smoking. Add the garlic, chili powder, and cayenne; cook until fragrant, about 30 seconds. Whisk in the ketchup mixture and bring to a boil; reduce the heat to medium-low and simmer gently, uncovered, until the flavors meld and the sauce is thickened, about 25 minutes. Cool the sauce to room temperature before using. (The sauce can be refrigerated in an airtight container for up to 1 week.)

Sweet-Sour-Spicy Barbecue Sauce

MAKES ABOUT 1½ CUPS

We developed this highly acidic sauce for beef ribs. The vinegar, tomato paste, and spices balance the richness of the beef. It is quite strong, so brush only a little bit of it on the ribs to start. If you like your sauce especially spicy, add another ½ teaspoon cayenne.

1	cup distilled white vinegar
½	cup sugar
¼	cup tomato paste
2	tablespoons salt
2	tablespoons sweet paprika
2	teaspoons dried mustard
2	teaspoons ground black pepper
½	teaspoon cayenne pepper
½	teaspoon onion powder
½	teaspoon garlic powder
½	teaspoon chili powder
4	tablespoons vegetable oil

BARBECUE 911

Sticky, Smelly Basting Brushes

It can be very difficult to clean a basting brush that has been dipped in oil or sauce. As a result, the bristles often remain sticky and sometimes even get smelly as the brush sits in a drawer between uses. Here's a better way to care for your brushes.

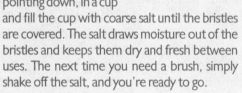

Wash the dirty brushes thoroughly with liquid dish soap and very hot water, then rinse well and shake dry. Place the brushes, bristles pointing down, in a cup and fill the cup with coarse salt until the bristles are covered. The salt draws moisture out of the bristles and keeps them dry and fresh between uses. The next time you need a brush, simply shake off the salt, and you're ready to go.

1. Mix the vinegar, sugar, tomato paste, and salt together in a medium bowl. In another bowl, combine the paprika, dried mustard, black pepper, cayenne, onion powder, garlic powder, and chili powder.

2. Heat the oil in a small saucepan over medium heat. Add the spice mixture and cook until sizzling and fragrant, 30 to 45 seconds. Stir in the vinegar mixture and increase the heat to high. Bring to a boil, reduce the heat to low, and simmer for 5 minutes. Remove the pan from the heat and cool to room temperature. (The sauce can be refrigerated in an airtight container for up to 1 week.)

Eastern North Carolina Barbecue Sauce

MAKES ABOUT 2 CUPS

This sauce contains no tomato but is rich with heat and vinegar. It is traditionally served with Pulled Pork (page 114) but can also be brushed onto ribs or brisket.

I	cup distilled white vinegar
I	cup cider vinegar
I	tablespoon sugar
I	tablespoon red pepper flakes
I	tablespoon hot pepper sauce, such as Tabasco
	Salt and ground black pepper

Mix all of the ingredients, including salt and pepper to taste, together in a medium bowl. (The sauce can be refrigerated in an airtight container for several days.)

Mid–South Carolina Mustard Sauce

MAKES ABOUT 2 1/2 CUPS

Here is another classic sauce for Pulled Pork (page 114) that works well with other cuts of grilled pork, too.

I	cup cider vinegar
I	cup vegetable oil
6	tablespoons Dijon mustard
2	tablespoons maple syrup or honey
4	teaspoons Worcestershire sauce
2	teaspoons salt
I	teaspoon hot pepper sauce, such as Tabasco
	Ground black pepper

Mix all of the ingredients, including black pepper to taste, together in a medium bowl. (The sauce can be refrigerated in an airtight container for several days.)

Sweetened Soy Glaze

MAKES I GENEROUS CUP

This Asian sauce is more traditional than Barbecue Sauce with Asian Flavors (page 387) because it does not contain any tomato. It is great on beef ribs.

1/2	cup soy sauce
1/4	cup water
1/4	cup sugar
I	tablespoon rice vinegar
2	teaspoons minced fresh ginger
I	medium garlic clove, minced or pressed through a garlic press (about I teaspoon)

2 teaspoons cornstarch dissolved in
1 tablespoon cold water
1 medium scallion, sliced thin
1 teaspoon toasted sesame oil

1. Bring the soy sauce, water, sugar, vinegar, ginger, and garlic to a boil in a medium saucepan over medium heat. Whisk in the cornstarch mixture and cook for 1 minute.

2. Remove the pan from the heat and whisk in the scallion and sesame oil. (The glaze can be refrigerated in an airtight container for a day or two.)

Hoisin, Honey, and Ginger Glaze

MAKES ABOUT 1 1/2 CUPS

This sweet and thick glaze is great on spareribs or any other cut of pork.

1/2 cup soy sauce
1/4 cup ketchup
1/4 cup honey
2 tablespoons brown sugar
2 tablespoons juice from 1 lemon
1 1/2 tablespoons hoisin sauce
2 teaspoons vegetable oil
2 medium garlic cloves, minced or pressed through a garlic press (about 2 teaspoons)
1 teaspoon minced fresh ginger

1. Mix the soy sauce, ketchup, honey, brown sugar, lemon juice, and hoisin sauce together in a medium bowl.

2. Heat the oil in a small saucepan over medium-high heat until shimmering. Add the garlic and ginger and cook until fragrant but not browned, about 30 seconds. Add the soy mixture and bring to a boil. Cook for 1 minute and remove the pan from the heat. Cool to room temperature. (The glaze may be refrigerated in an airtight container for up to 1 week.)

SALSAS, RELISHES, CHUTNEYS, AND OTHER SAUCES

THE CONDIMENT-LIKE SALSAS, RELISHES, AND sauces in this section can be served at the table with grilled meat, poultry, or fish. Many are made with raw ingredients; the rest are lightly cooked. Most can be made in advance and refrigerated for several days and brought to room temperature before serving.

The terms "salsa," and "relish" can be used interchangeably, although salsas are usually made with Latin ingredients or flavors. "Chutney" usually refers to a cooked sauce with a jam-like consistency.

CUTTING TOMATOES FOR SALSA

1. Cut each cored tomato in half through the equator.

2. Cut each half into 3/8-inch-thick slices.

3. Stack two slices, cut them into 3/8-inch strips, and then cut them into 3/8-inch dice.

Fresh Tomato Salsa
MAKES ABOUT 3 CUPS

Most of a chile's heat resides in the ribs. If you prefer more heat, we suggest mincing the ribs along with the seeds and adding them to the recipe to taste; if you prefer less heat, discard the seeds and ribs. The amount of sugar and lime juice to use depends on the ripeness of the tomatoes. The salsa can be made 2 to 3 hours in advance, but hold off adding the salt, lime juice, and sugar until just before serving. In addition to being a great dip for tortilla chips, this salsa is a nice accompaniment to grilled steaks, chicken, and fish.

1½	pounds firm, ripe tomatoes, cut into ⅜-inch dice (about 3 cups)
1	jalapeño chile, seeds and ribs removed and set aside (see note), then minced
½	cup minced red onion
1	small garlic clove, minced or pressed through a garlic press (about ½ teaspoon)
¼	cup chopped fresh cilantro leaves
½	teaspoon salt
	Pinch ground black pepper
2–6	teaspoons juice from 1 to 2 limes
	Sugar to taste (up to 1 teaspoon)

1. Set a large colander in a large bowl. Place the tomatoes in the colander and let drain 30 minutes. As the tomatoes drain, layer the jalapeño, onion, garlic, and cilantro on top. Shake the colander to drain off the excess tomato juice. Discard the juice; wipe out the bowl.

2. Transfer the contents of the colander to the now-empty bowl. Add the salt, pepper, and 2 teaspoons lime juice; toss to combine. Taste and add the minced jalapeño ribs and seeds, if using, sugar, and additional lime juice to taste.

Chunky Guacamole
MAKES 2½ TO 3 CUPS

Guacamole is an essential accompaniment to fajitas with grilled flank steak. To minimize discoloration, prepare the minced ingredients first so that they are ready to mix with the avocados as soon as they are cut. Ripe avocados are a must. To test for ripeness, flick the small stem off the end of the avocado. If it comes off easily and you can see green underneath it, the avocado is ripe. If it does not come off or if you see brown underneath, the avocado is not ripe. The guacamole can be covered with plastic wrap, pressed directly onto the surface of the mixture, and refrigerated for 1 day. Return the guacamole to room temperature, removing the plastic wrap just before serving.

3	ripe medium avocados (preferably pebbly-skinned Hass)
¼	cup minced fresh cilantro leaves
2	tablespoons minced onion
1	small jalapeño chile, seeds and ribs removed, then minced
1	medium garlic clove, minced or pressed through a garlic press (about 1 teaspoon)

PITTING AN AVOCADO
Digging out the pit with a spoon can mar the soft flesh and is generally a messy proposition. Use this method instead.

1. Start by slicing around the pit and through both end with a chef's knife. With your hands, twist the avocado to separate the two halves.

2. Stick the blade of the chef's knife sharply into the pit. Lift the knife, twisting the blade to loosen and remove the pit.

3. Don't pull the pit off the knife with your hands. Instead, use a large wooden spoon to pry the pit safely off the knife.

½   teaspoon ground cumin (optional)

¼   teaspoon salt

2   tablespoons juice from 2 limes

1. Halve 1 avocado, remove the pit (see the illustrations on the facing page), and scoop the flesh into a medium bowl. Use a fork to mash the flesh lightly with the cilantro, onion, chile, garlic, cumin (if using), and salt until just combined.

2. Halve and pit the remaining 2 avocados. Make ½-inch crosshatch incisions in the flesh of each avocado half with a dinner knife, cutting down to but not through the skin (see illustration 1 below). Separate the diced flesh from the skin using a spoon inserted between the skin and flesh, gently scooping out the avocado cubes (see illustration 2 below). Add the cubes to the bowl with the mashed avocado mixture.

3. Sprinkle the lime juice over the diced avocado and mix the entire contents of the bowl lightly with a fork until combined but still chunky. Adjust the seasonings with salt to taste, if necessary, and serve.

~≪≫~

Spicy Yellow Pepper and Tomato Salsa

MAKES ABOUT 2 CUPS

Most of a chile's heat resides in the ribs. If you prefer more heat, we suggest mincing the ribs along with the seeds and

adding them to the recipe to taste; if you prefer less heat, discard the seeds and ribs. This salsa is perfect with grilled fish.

2   small tomatoes (about ½ pound), cored and cut into ¼-inch dice

½   medium yellow bell pepper, cored, seeded, and cut into ¼-inch dice (about ½ cup)

¼   cup finely chopped red onion

I   jalapeño chile, seeds and ribs removed and set aside (see note), then minced

I   tablespoon juice from I lime

I   tablespoon chopped fresh cilantro leaves

I   medium garlic clove, minced or pressed through a garlic press (about I teaspoon)

½   teaspoon bottled hot sauce (optional)

½   teaspoon salt

¼   teaspoon sugar

Mix all of the ingredients together in a medium bowl. Cover and refrigerate to blend the flavors, at least 1 hour but preferably overnight. (The salsa can be refrigerated in an airtight container for several days.)

~≪≫~

Grilled Corn Salsa

MAKES ABOUT 2 CUPS

This is a great use for leftover grilled corn that has not been buttered. Serve this salsa with tortilla chips or as a condiment for grilled seafood or chicken.

DICING AN AVOCADO

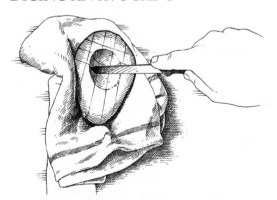

1. Use a dish towel to hold the avocado steady. Make ½-inch crosshatch incisions in the flesh of each avocado half with a dinner knife, cutting down to but not through the skin.

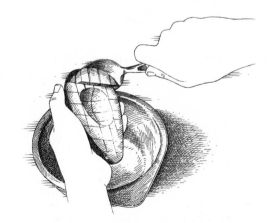

2. Separate the diced flesh from the skin using a spoon inserted between the skin and flesh, gently scooping out the avocado cubes.

2 ears grilled corn (see page 299), kernels cut from the cobs (about 1 cup)
1 medium red bell pepper, cored, seeded, and diced small
1 medium scallion, sliced thin
1½ tablespoons corn or vegetable oil
1½ tablespoons juice from 1 to 2 limes
1 tablespoon chopped fresh cilantro leaves
½ medium jalapeño chile, seeds and ribs removed, then minced
1 small garlic clove, minced or pressed through a garlic press (½ teaspoon)
1 teaspoon ground cumin
Salt

Place all of the ingredients, including salt to taste, in a medium bowl. Toss and adjust the seasonings. (The salsa can be refrigerated in an airtight container for 1 day.)

Black Bean and Mango Salsa
MAKES ABOUT 2½ CUPS
This Caribbean-inspired mixture is great with grilled pork.

1 medium mango, peeled, pitted, and cut into ¼-inch dice (see the illustrations on page 328)
½ cup cooked black beans
¼ medium red bell pepper, cored, seeded, and diced small
¼ medium green bell pepper, cored, seeded, and diced small
¼ medium red onion, diced small

6 tablespoons pineapple juice
¼ cup juice from 4 limes
¼ cup chopped fresh cilantro leaves
1 tablespoon ground cumin
½ jalapeño chile, seeds and ribs removed, then minced
Salt and ground black pepper

Mix all of the ingredients, including salt and pepper to taste, together in a medium bowl. Refrigerate the salsa in an airtight container to blend the flavors at least 1 hour or up to 4 days.

Mango Salsa
MAKES ABOUT 2 CUPS
This salsa goes especially well with pork.

2 medium mangoes, peeled, pitted, and cut into ¼-inch dice (see the illustrations on page 328)
½ medium red onion, minced
2 scallions, sliced thin
½ medium jalapeño chile, seeds and ribs removed, then minced
2 tablespoons minced fresh cilantro leaves
1 tablespoon juice from 1 lime
Salt and ground black pepper

Mix all of the ingredients, including salt and pepper to taste, together in a medium bowl. (The salsa can be refrigerated in an airtight container for several days.)

PREPARING A PINEAPPLE

1. Start by trimming the ends of the pineapple so that it will sit flat on a work surface. Cut the pineapple through the ends into quarters.

2. Place each quarter, cut-side up, on the work surface, and slide the knife between the skin and flesh to remove the skin.

3. Stand each quarter on end and slice off the tough, light-colored core attached to the inside of each piece. Discard the core. The peeled and cored pineapple can be diced or sliced, as desired.

Pineapple Salsa

MAKES ABOUT 2 1/2 CUPS

This sweet and spicy salsa works well with pork.

1/4   small pineapple, peeled, cored, and cut into 1/2-inch dice (about 1 1/4 cups)

1   small barely ripe banana, peeled and cut into 1/2-inch dice

1/2   cup seedless green grapes, halved or quartered

1/2   firm avocado, peeled, pitted, and cut into 1/2-inch dice (see the illustrations on page 391)

1   jalapeño chile, seeds and ribs removed, then minced

4   teaspoons juice from 1 to 2 limes

1   teaspoon minced fresh oregano leaves
      Salt

Combine all of the ingredients, including salt to taste, in a medium bowl. Let the salsa stand at room temperature for 30 minutes. (The banana and avocado will darken if the salsa is prepared much further in advance.)

Peach Salsa

MAKES ABOUT 2 1/2 CUPS

Nectarines can be substituted for the peaches. This salsa works well with pork or lamb.

2   ripe but still firm peaches, pitted and chopped coarse

1   small red bell pepper, cored, seeded, and diced

1   small red onion, diced

6   tablespoons juice from 6 limes

1/4   cup chopped fresh parsley leaves

1/4   cup pineapple juice

1   jalapeño chile, seeds and ribs removed, then minced

1   medium garlic clove, minced or pressed through a garlic press (about 1 teaspoon)
      Salt

Mix all of the ingredients, including salt to taste, together in a medium bowl. Cover the salsa and refrigerate to blend the flavors at least 1 hour or up to 4 days.

Black Olive and Citrus Relish

MAKES ABOUT 1 1/2 CUPS

Use only the segmented fruit in the relish, not the juices, which will water down the flavor and texture. This relish pairs well with a firm, white fish.

2   medium oranges, segmented (pith and membrane removed) and cut into 1/2-inch pieces

1   medium pink grapefruit, segmented (pith and membrane removed) and cut into 1/2-inch pieces

10   kalamata olives, pitted and chopped (about 1/4 cup)

2   tablespoons minced fresh parsley leaves

1/2   teaspoon ground cumin

1/2   teaspoon paprika
      Cayenne pepper
      Salt

Mix all of the ingredients, including cayenne and salt to taste, together in a medium bowl. Serve the relish at room temperature with grilled fish. (The relish can be covered and set aside up to 1 hour.)

Avocado-Corn Relish

MAKES ABOUT 2 CUPS

Serve this chunky relish with fish or chicken.

1   ear corn, husked and cut in half

1   ripe but firm avocado, peeled, pitted, and diced large (see the illustrations on page 391)

1/2   small red onion, diced small

1/2   small red bell pepper, cored, seeded, and diced small

2 1/2   tablespoons juice from 2 to 3 limes

2   tablespoons extra-virgin olive oil

1 1/2   tablespoons red wine vinegar

1 1/2   tablespoons chopped fresh oregano leaves

1   medium garlic clove, minced or pressed through a garlic press (about 1 teaspoon)

1   teaspoon ground cumin

1/4   teaspoon chili powder
      Dash hot red pepper sauce, or to taste
      Salt and ground black pepper

1. Bring about 1 quart of water to a boil in a medium saucepan. Add the corn and boil until just cooked, 3 to 5 minutes. Drain and rinse the corn under cold running water. Cut the kernels from each half of the cob.

2. Mix the corn with the remaining ingredients, including salt and pepper to taste, in a medium bowl. (The relish can be refrigerated in an airtight container for 1 day.)

Cranberry–Onion Relish

MAKES ABOUT 1 1/2 CUPS

This sweet-sour condiment goes very well with pork, although a little goes a long way.

3	tablespoons unsalted butter
2	large onions, halved and sliced thin
1/4	cup sugar

1	cup whole cranberries, picked through
1/2	cup red wine
2	tablespoons red wine vinegar
1 1/2	tablespoons grenadine (optional)
1/2	teaspoon salt

1. Melt the butter in a large sauté pan over medium-low heat. Add the onions and cook until they are very soft, about 25 minutes. Increase the heat to medium-high and add the sugar; cook, stirring frequently, until the onions are golden brown and caramelized, 10 to 12 minutes longer.

2. Add the cranberries, wine, vinegar, grenadine (if using), and salt and bring the mixture to a boil. Reduce the heat and simmer, partially covered, until most of the liquid has evaporated and the mixture has a jam-like consistency, about 20 minutes. Serve warm or at room temperature. (The relish can be refrigerated in an airtight container for up to 1 week. Bring to room temperature before serving.)

JUICING LEMONS

Everyone seems to have a trick for juicing lemons. We find that this one extracts the most juice possible from lemons as well as limes.

1. Roll the lemon on a hard surface, pressing down firmly with the palm of your hand to break the membranes inside the fruit.

2. Cut the lemon in half. Use a wooden reamer (preferably one with sharp ridges and a pointed tip) to extract the juice into a bowl. To catch the seeds and pulp, place a mesh strainer over the bowl.

Quick Onion and Parsley Relish

MAKES A GENEROUS 3/4 CUP

Serve with lamb or beef.

1/2	medium red onion, diced small
1/2	cup chopped fresh parsley leaves
1/4	cup extra-virgin olive oil
1/4	cup juice from 2 lemons
	Salt and ground black pepper

Mix the onion, parsley, oil, and lemon juice together in a small bowl. Season with salt and pepper to taste. (The relish can be covered and set aside at room temperature for several hours.)

Warm Cucumber and Red Onion Relish with Mint

MAKES ABOUT 2 CUPS

This relish is perfect with salmon but works with most fish.

5	tablespoons extra-virgin olive oil
2	medium cucumbers, peeled, halved lengthwise, seeded, and sliced thin

1　medium red onion, halved and sliced thin
　　Salt and ground black pepper
2　tablespoons red wine vinegar
2　tablespoons chopped fresh mint leaves

1. Heat 2 tablespoons of the oil in a large skillet over medium-high heat. Add the cucumbers and sauté until lightly colored, about 2 minutes. Add the onion and salt and pepper to taste. Cook just until the vegetables turn translucent, about 2 minutes longer.

2. Turn the cucumber mixture into a medium bowl. Stir in the vinegar, mint, and remaining 3 tablespoons oil. Adjust the seasonings. Serve warm.

Onion, Black Olive, and Caper Relish

MAKES ABOUT 2 CUPS

This intensely flavored, highly acidic relish complements fish, especially bluefish and tuna.

8　tablespoons extra-virgin olive oil
2　medium onions, halved and sliced thin
6　medium garlic cloves, sliced thin
1/2　cup black olives, such as kalamatas, pitted and chopped coarse
1/4　cup drained capers
1/4　cup balsamic vinegar
2　anchovy fillets, minced
2　tablespoons minced fresh parsley leaves
1　teaspoon minced fresh marjoram or oregano leaves
　　Salt and ground black pepper

1. Heat 2 tablespoons of the oil in a large skillet. Add the onions and sauté over medium heat until softened, about 5 minutes. Add the garlic and sauté until fragrant, about 1 minute longer.

2. Turn the onion mixture into a medium bowl. Stir in the remaining 6 tablespoons oil and the remaining ingredients, including salt (use sparingly) and pepper to taste. Serve warm or at room temperature. (The relish can be covered and set aside at room temperature for several hours.)

Red Pepper–Jícama Relish

MAKES ABOUT 3 1/2 CUPS

This crunchy, refreshing, slaw-like relish is mildly sweet, making it a nice foil for spicy foods. This relish is especially good served with pork.

3　tablespoons vegetable oil
1 1/2　tablespoons juice from 1 to 2 limes
2　teaspoons honey
1/4　teaspoon ground cumin
1/4　teaspoon chili powder
1/4　teaspoon salt
　　Ground black pepper
1　medium red bell pepper, cored, seeded, and cut into thin strips
1/2　small jícama (8 ounces), tough outer skin removed, cut into matchsticks (see the illustrations below)
1　medium Granny Smith apple, cored, quartered, and cut into 1/4-inch dice
2　small scallions, sliced thin

PREPARING JÍCAMA

1. Slice the jícama in half through its equator.

2. Use a paring knife to peel the brown outer skin.

3. Place each half flat-side down on the cutting board and slice into half circles 1/8 inch thick.

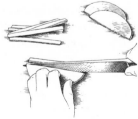

4. Stack the half circles and slice lengthwise into matchsticks.

1. Whisk the oil, lime juice, honey, cumin, chili powder, salt, and pepper to taste together in a small bowl.

2. Place the red pepper, jícama, apple, and scallions in a large bowl and pour the dressing over the top; toss to coat. Adjust the seasonings. (The relish can be refrigerated in an airtight container for several hours.)

Curried Fruit Chutney with Lime and Ginger
MAKES ABOUT 4 CUPS

Beef is a good choice with curried fruits. Unlike most chutneys, this one is only lightly cooked, so the fruits remain distinct. We also like this chutney with grilled squab.

I	tablespoon olive oil
I	small onion, halved and sliced very thin
I	tablespoon minced fresh ginger
I	large garlic clove, minced or pressed through a garlic press (about 1 1/2 teaspoons)
1/2	medium mango, peeled, pitted, and cut into 1/4-inch dice (see page 328)
I	medium peach, peeled, pitted, and quartered
I	medium plum, peeled, pitted and quartered
I	medium apricot, peeled, pitted, and quartered
I	medium nectarine, peeled, pitted, and quartered
2	tablespoons juice from 2 limes
I	tablespoon orange juice
1 1/2	teaspoons ground coriander
I	teaspoon curry powder
1/2	teaspoon ground cinnamon
1/2	teaspoon red pepper flakes
	Salt and ground black pepper

1. Heat the oil in a large saucepan over medium-high heat until shimmering. Add the onion and sauté until lightly browned, 4 to 5 minutes. Add the ginger and garlic and sauté until fragrant, about 1 minute.

2. Lower the heat to medium and add the remaining ingredients, including salt and pepper to taste. Cook until the fruits start to soften but have not fallen apart, about 5 minutes. Adjust the seasonings. (The chutney can be refrigerated in an airtight container for several days.)

Dried Peach and Apple Chutney
MAKES ABOUT 4 CUPS

Dried apricots, plums, or nectarines can be substituted for the dried peaches in this uncooked chutney. The flavors in this chutney are a perfect match with pork. Also, try serving this chutney with any mild-flavored fish, such as snapper or mahi-mahi. Toast the almonds in a dry skillet over medium heat until fragrant, about 5 minutes.

6	ounces dried peaches, cut into 1/4-inch strips (about 2 cups)
1/4	cup dry red wine
1/4	cup warm water
2	small tart apples, cored, quartered, and sliced thin
1/4	cup blanched, slivered almonds, toasted (see note)
2	tablespoons brown sugar
1 1/2	teaspoons minced fresh ginger
1/2	teaspoon ground coriander
1/2	teaspoon ground cumin
1/4	teaspoon cayenne pepper
2	tablespoons juice from 2 limes
2	tablespoons orange juice
2	tablespoons minced fresh cilantro leaves
	Salt and ground black pepper

1. Soak the peaches in a medium bowl with the wine and water until tender, about 15 minutes.

2. Mix the apples, almonds, brown sugar, ginger, coriander, cumin, and cayenne together in a medium bowl. Stir in the peaches and their liquid, along with the lime juice, orange juice, cilantro, and salt and pepper to taste. (The chutney can be refrigerated in an airtight container for several hours.)

Parsley Sauce with Cornichons and Capers
MAKES ABOUT 1 1/4 CUPS

This sauce pairs perfectly with beef, especially tenderloin.

3/4	cup minced fresh parsley leaves
1/2	cup extra-virgin olive oil
12	cornichons, minced (about 6 tablespoons), plus 1 teaspoon cornichon juice

¼ cup drained capers, chopped coarse

2 medium scallions, white and light green parts, minced

¼ teaspoon ground black pepper

Pinch salt

Mix all of the ingredients together in a medium bowl. (The sauce can be covered and set aside at room temperature for several hours.)

Salsa Verde

MAKES A GENEROUS ¾ CUP

A slice of sandwich bread pureed into the sauce keeps the flavors balanced and gives the sauce body. Toasting the bread rids it of excess moisture that might otherwise make for a gummy sauce. Salsa verde is excellent with grilled meats, especially Grill-Roasted Beef Tenderloin (page 73). It is best served immediately after it is made, but can be refrigerated in an airtight container for up to 2 days. Bring the sauce to room temperature and stir to recombine it before serving.

1 large slice white bread

½ cup extra-virgin olive oil

2 tablespoons juice from 1 lemon

2 cups lightly packed fresh parsley leaves, preferably flat-leaf parsley

2 medium anchovy fillets

2 tablespoons drained capers

1 small garlic clove, minced or pressed through a garlic press (about ½ teaspoon)

⅛ teaspoon salt

1. Toast the bread in a toaster at the lowest setting until the surface is dry but not browned, about 15 seconds. Remove the crust and cut the bread into rough ½-inch pieces (you should have about ½ cup).

2. Process the bread pieces, oil, and lemon juice in a food processor until smooth, about 10 seconds. Add the parsley, anchovies, capers, garlic, and salt. Pulse until the mixture is finely chopped (the mixture should not be smooth), about five 1-second pulses, scraping down the bowl with a rubber spatula after 3 pulses. Transfer the mixture to a small bowl and serve.

Chimichurri

MAKES 1 GENEROUS CUP

Like a loose, fresh salsa in consistency, this mixture is a common accompaniment to grilled meats in South America. For best results, use flat-leaf parsley. This sauce works well with beef, especially mild filet mignon or tenderloin. Although this sauce tastes best the day it is made, any that is left over can be refrigerated for several days.

1 cup packed fresh parsley leaves, preferably flat-leaf parsley

5 medium garlic cloves, peeled

½ cup extra-virgin olive oil

¼ cup finely minced red onion

¼ cup red wine vinegar

2 tablespoons water

1 teaspoon salt

¼ teaspoon red pepper flakes

Process the parsley and garlic in a food processor, stopping as necessary to scrape down the sides of the bowl with a rubber spatula, until the garlic and parsley are chopped fine (about twenty 1-second pulses); transfer to a medium bowl. Whisk in the remaining ingredients until thoroughly blended. Let stand for 30 minutes to allow the flavors to develop before serving.

Chermoula

Spoon a little of this North African–style sauce over grilled tuna or swordfish.

¾ cup packed fresh cilantro leaves

½ cup extra-virgin olive oil

3 tablespoons juice from 1 lemon

4 medium garlic cloves, peeled

1 teaspoon ground cumin

1 teaspoon paprika

¼ teaspoon cayenne pepper

Salt

Place the cilantro, olive oil, lemon juice, garlic, cumin, paprika, cayenne, and ¼ teaspoon salt in a food processor. Process, stopping to scrape down the sides of the bowl several times, until smooth, 10 to 15 seconds. Transfer the mixture to a small bowl and serve.

Salmoriglio Sauce

MAKES ABOUT ³/₄ CUP

Considered one of the essential sauces of Sicilian cookery, salmoriglio is the traditional accompaniment to grilled fish, especially swordfish. Try serving salmoriglio sauce with other firm white fish as well as grilled chicken.

3	tablespoons packed fresh oregano leaves
2	tablespoons juice from 1 lemon
1	medium garlic clove, chopped coarse
¼	teaspoon salt
¼	teaspoon coarsely ground black pepper
½	cup extra-virgin olive oil

Place the oregano, lemon juice, garlic, salt, and pepper in a food processor. Process, scraping down the sides of the bowl as necessary, until the garlic and oregano are finely chopped, about 30 seconds. With the motor running, pour the oil through the feed tube in a slow, steady stream and process until the sauce is thoroughly combined, about 30 seconds. Transfer the mixture to a small bowl and serve.

INGREDIENTS:
Jarred Roasted Red Peppers

Jarred peppers are convenient, but are all brands created equal? To find out, we collected six brands from local supermarkets. The top two brands, Divina and Greek Gourmet, were preferred for their "soft and tender texture" (the Divina) and "refreshing," "piquant," "smoky" flavor (the Greek Gourmet). The other brands were marked down for their lack of "roasty flavor" and for the unpleasantly overpowering flavor of the brines. These peppers tasted as if they'd been "buried under brine and acid," or they had a "pepperoncini-like sourness" or a "sweet and acidic aftertaste." The conclusion? Tasters preferred peppers with a full, smoky, roasted flavor, a brine that was spicy and not too sweet, and a tender texture.

THE BEST JARRED ROASTED RED PEPPERS

Divina peppers (left) were the top choice of tasters. Greek Gourmet peppers (right) came in a close second.

Romesco Sauce

MAKES ABOUT 2 CUPS

Serve this flavorful sauce with beef, chicken, or fish.

1–2	slices white sandwich bread
3	tablespoons slivered almonds, toasted in a small dry skillet over medium heat until beginning to brown, about 4 minutes
1	(12-ounce) jar roasted red peppers, drained (about 1³/₄ cups)
1	small ripe tomato, cored, seeded, and chopped medium
2	tablespoons extra-virgin olive oil
1½	tablespoons sherry vinegar
1	large garlic clove, minced or pressed through a garlic press (about 1½ teaspoons)
¼	teaspoon cayenne pepper
	Salt

1. Toast the bread in a toaster at the lowest setting until the surface is dry but not browned, about 15 seconds. Remove the crusts and cut the bread into rough ½-inch pieces (you should have about ½ cup).

2. Process the bread and almonds in a food processor until the nuts are finely ground, 10 to 15 seconds. Add the red peppers, tomato, oil, vinegar, garlic, cayenne, and ½ teaspoon salt. Pulse, scraping down the bowl as necessary, until the mixture is similar in texture to mayonnaise, 20 to 30 seconds. Adjust the seasoning with salt to taste; transfer the mixture to a bowl and serve. (The sauce can be refrigerated in an airtight container for up to 2 days; return it to room temperature before serving.)

Cilantro-Parsley Sauce with Pickled Jalapeños

MAKES 2½ GENEROUS CUPS

This sauce will discolor if left to sit for too long; it's best served within 4 hours. Serve with beef.

2–3	slices white sandwich bread
1	cup extra-virgin olive oil
¼	cup juice from 2 lemons

2 cups lightly packed fresh cilantro leaves

2 cups lightly packed fresh parsley leaves, preferably flat-leaf parsley

¼ cup drained pickled jalapeño slices, chopped medium

1 large garlic clove, minced or pressed through garlic press (about 1½ teaspoons)

Salt

1. Toast the bread in a toaster at the lowest setting until the surface is dry but not browned, about 15 seconds. Remove the crusts and cut the bread into rough ½-inch pieces (you should have about 1 cup).

2. Process the bread, oil, and lemon juice in a food processor until smooth, 10 to 15 seconds. Add the cilantro, parsley, jalapeños, garlic, and ¼ teaspoon salt. Pulse until finely chopped (the mixture should not be smooth), about ten 1-second pulses, scraping down the bowl as necessary. Adjust the seasoning with salt to taste; transfer to a bowl and serve.

Classic Pesto

MAKES 1 GENEROUS CUP

We coat our Grilled Butterflied Chicken (page 185) with this pesto, but you could also spread it on Garlic-Herb Pizza Dough (page 332) after it comes off the grill for a flavor boost, or try a spoonful on fish.

¼ cup pine nuts, walnuts, or almonds

3 medium garlic cloves, unpeeled

2 cups packed fresh basil leaves

2 tablespoons fresh parsley leaves (optional)

7 tablespoons extra-virgin olive oil

Salt

¼ cup grated Parmesan cheese

1. Toast the nuts in a small, dry skillet over medium heat, stirring frequently, until just golden and fragrant, 4 to 5 minutes. Transfer the nuts to a plate.

2. Add the garlic to the empty skillet. Toast, shaking the pan occasionally, until fragrant and the color of the cloves deepens slightly, about 7 minutes. Let the garlic cool, then peel and chop.

3. Combine the basil and parsley (if using) in a heavy-duty gallon-size zipper-lock plastic bag.

Pound the bag with the flat side of a meat pounder or rolling pin until all the leaves are bruised (see the illustration below).

4. Place the nuts, garlic, pounded herb(s), oil, and ½ teaspoon salt in a food processor. Process until smooth, stopping as necessary to scrape down the sides of the bowl. Transfer the mixture to a small bowl, stir in the Parmesan, and adjust the salt to taste. (The surface of the pesto can be covered with a sheet of plastic wrap or a thin film of oil and refrigerated for up to 3 days.)

Mojo Sauce

MAKES 1 GENEROUS CUP

This Cuban citrus sauce is delicious with pork.

½ cup extra-virgin olive oil

6 medium garlic cloves, minced or pressed through a garlic press (about 2 tablespoons)

½ teaspoon ground cumin

½ cup orange juice

¼ cup juice from 4 limes

1 teaspoon salt

½ teaspoon ground black pepper

1. Heat the oil in a small, deep saucepan over medium heat until shimmering. Add the garlic and cumin and cook until fragrant but not browned, 30 to 45 seconds.

2. Remove the pan from the heat and add the

BRUISING HERB LEAVES

Bruising herb leaves, especially basil, in a zipper-lock plastic bag with a meat pounder (or rolling pin) is a quick but effective substitute for hand pounding with a mortar and pestle, and it helps release the herbs' flavor.

orange juice, lime juice, salt, and pepper carefully, as the mixture may splatter. Place the pan back on the heat, bring to a simmer, and cook for 1 minute. Remove the pan from the heat and cool the sauce to room temperature. (The sauce can be refrigerated in an airtight container for up to 3 days.)

Pureed Red Pepper Sauce with Basil

MAKES ABOUT 1 CUP

Most pureed bell pepper sauces call for roasted, peeled peppers. In this recipe, diced raw peppers are sweated in a covered pan until very tender and then pureed to create a rich, thick sauce. Serve with pork, chicken, or white-fleshed fish such as snapper.

1½	tablespoons extra-virgin olive oil
1	small onion, chopped
1	large red bell pepper, cored, seeded, and diced
½	cup low-sodium chicken broth
1	medium garlic clove, minced or pressed through a garlic press (about 1 teaspoon)
2	tablespoons minced fresh basil leaves
1–2	teaspoons balsamic vinegar
	Salt and ground black pepper

1. Heat the oil in a small saucepan over medium heat. Add the onion and sauté until softened, about 3 minutes. Reduce the heat to low. Add the red pepper, cover, and cook, stirring frequently, until very tender, 15 to 20 minutes.

2. Transfer the mixture to a blender or food processor. Add the broth and process until smooth.

3. Return the mixture to a clean saucepan. Add the garlic and simmer to blend flavors, about 5 minutes. Stir in the basil and season with vinegar, salt, and pepper to taste. Serve immediately. (The sauce can be refrigerated in an airtight container for several days. When ready to serve, reheat the sauce gently.)

Tomatillo-Chile Sauce

MAKES ABOUT 1 CUP

Serve this tart, fragrant sauce with seafood, beef, or even chicken. Vary the amount of chiles as desired.

½	pound fresh tomatillos, husked and washed
1–2	medium jalapeño or serrano chiles, seeds and ribs removed
2	tablespoons chopped fresh cilantro leaves
½	small onion, chopped
1	small garlic clove, chopped
1½	teaspoons vegetable oil
½	cup low-sodium chicken broth
	Salt

1. Place the tomatillos and chiles in a medium saucepan and add water to cover. Bring to a boil, cover, and simmer until barely tender, about 8 minutes. Drain and transfer the tomatillos and chiles to a blender or food processor. Add the cilantro, onion, and garlic and pulse to a coarse puree.

2. Heat the oil in a medium skillet over medium-high heat until shimmering. Add the tomatillo puree all at once and cook, stirring often, until the mixture darkens and thickens, about 5 minutes. Reduce the heat to medium, add the broth, and simmer, stirring occasionally, until the mixture thickens, 10 to 15 minutes. Season with salt to taste. (The sauce can be refrigerated in an airtight container for up to 2 days.)

Spicy Peanut Dipping Sauce

MAKES ABOUT 1¼ CUPS

This sauce can be made a day in advance and refrigerated. Bring the sauce to room temperature before serving. Serve with our Beef Satay (page 60) or Thai Chicken Satay (page 164), or with shrimp.

½	cup creamy peanut butter
¼	cup hot water
2	tablespoons juice from 2 limes
2	tablespoons Asian chili sauce
1	tablespoon soy sauce
1	tablespoon dark brown sugar
1	tablespoon chopped fresh cilantro leaves
1	medium garlic clove, minced or pressed through a garlic press (about 1 teaspoon)
2	scallions, sliced thin

Whisk the peanut butter and hot water together in a medium bowl. Stir in the remaining ingredients. Transfer to a small serving bowl.

INDEX

NOTE: PAGE NUMBERS IN *ITALICS* REFER TO COLOR PHOTOGRAPHS.

A

Alder wood, 10
Allspice-Cocoa-Cumin Rub for
    Steak, 380
Almonds, Green Olives, and Sherry
    Vinaigrette, Grilled Asparagus
    with, 298
Ancho and Chipotle Rub for Pork,
    378
Anchovy(ies):
    Dressing, 298
    mincing, 298
Apple(s):
    Chutney, 96–97
    Curried, Macaroni Salad with, 362
    and Dried Peach Chutney, 396
    grilling, 327
    preparing for skewering, 162
    and Raisins, Curried Coleslaw
        with, 355
Arugula:
    a Bed of, Grilled Veal Chops on,
        77, *124*
    and Grilled Potato Salad with Dijon
        Mustard Vinaigrette, *290,* 320
    Prosciutto, and Gorgonzola,
        Grilled Pizza with, 340–41
    Red Onion, and Rosemary–
        White Bean Spread,
        Bruschetta with, 346
    Roquefort, and Walnuts, French
        Potato Salad with, 359
    and Shaved Parmesan, Tomato
        Salad with, 352
    and Sun-Dried Tomato Vinaigrette,
        Pasta Salad with, 364
Asiago, Fennel, and Sun-Dried Tomato,
    Grilled Pizza with, 340
Asparagus:
    Grilled, *118,* 296
        with Almonds, Green Olives,
            and Sherry Vinaigrette, 298
        with Blue Cheese and Anchovy
            Dressing, 298
        Caramelized Onions, Black
            Olives, and Thyme, Grilled
            Pizza with, 341–42
        with Grilled Lemon Vinaigrette,
            296–97
        with Orange-Sesame
            Vinaigrette, 297

Asparagus *(cont.)*
    with Peanut Sauce, 297
    with Rosemary and Goat
        Cheese, 297
    grilling, at a glance, 315
    snapping off tough ends, 296
Avocado(es):
    Chunky Guacamole, 390–91
    -Corn Relish, 393–94
    dicing, 391
    removing pit from, 390

B

Baba Ghanoush, 303–4
    with Sautéed Onion, 304
Bacon:
    Corn, and Cilantro, Grilled Pizza
        with, 342
    and Horseradish-Peppercorn
        Sauce, Grilled Whole
        Freshwater Trout with, 257
Bags, brown paper, 24
Baking sheets, rimless, 334, 337
Balsamic (vinegar):
    Dressing, 305
    taste tests on, 307
    Vinaigrette, 94–95
Bananas, grilling, 327
Barbecue sauces:
    applying, 3, 11, 171
    with Asian Flavors, 387
    bottled, taste tests on, 192
    with Caribbean Flavors, 387
    Classic, 386
    cooking times, 386
    Eastern North Carolina, 388
    ingredients in, 386
    with Mexican Flavors, 386–87
    Mid–South Carolina Mustard, 388
    Quick, *289,* 387
    Sweet-Sour-Spicy, 387–88
    for Texas-Style Beef Ribs, 81
Barbecuing:
    baby back ribs, 110–11
    beef brisket, 85–86, 87
    best fire for, 78
    on charcoal grill, basics of, 8
    cooking temperatures for, 3
    description of, 3

Barbecuing *(cont.)*
    on gas grill, basics of, 9
    pulled pork, 113–14
    salmon fillets, 237–38
    spareribs, 107–8
    spice rubs for, 376
    Texas-style ribs, 79–80
    wood chips and chunks for, 8, 9,
        10, 109
Basil:
    Bruschetta with Tomatoes and, 343
    Classic Pesto, 399
    Grilled Bell Peppers with Black
        Olives and, 317
    Grilled Pizza with Fresh Tomatoes
        and, *288,* 335
    Grilled Zucchini or Summer
        Squash with Tomatoes and,
        325
    Oil, 301
    Pasta Salad with Eggplant,
        Tomatoes, and, 364
    Pureed Red Pepper Sauce with, 400
    Tomato, and Mozzarella Salad
        (Insalata Caprese), 353
    -Tomato Relish, Fresh, 255
Baskets, fish, 21, 224–25
Bean(s):
    baked
        Barbecued, 369–70
        best beans for, 368
        Boston, 369
        cooking method, 369
        ingredients in, 368–69
    Black, and Mango Salsa, 392
    Green, Grilled, 309–10
    white
        canned, taste tests on, 346
        -Rosemary Spread, Arugula,
            and Red Onion, Bruschetta
            with, 346
Beef, 28–88
    aging, 68
    brisket, 85–88
        Barbecued, on a Charcoal
            Grill, 86
        Barbecued, on a Gas Grill, 87–88
        barbecuing, key steps to, 87
        barbecuing method for, 85–86
        carving, 87
        flat versus point cut, 86

Beef *(cont.)*
    internal temperature of, 85
    location of, 30, 86
  cuts of, primal, 30
  grilling, three rules for, 35–36
  hamburgers, 61–65
    beef for, buying or grinding,
      61–62
    Charcoal-Grilled, 63–64, *121*
    Gas-Grilled, 64
    Grilled, with Cognac, Mustard,
      and Chives, 64–65
    Grilled, with Garlic, Chipotles,
      and Scallions, 64
    Grilled, with Porcini
      Mushrooms and Thyme, 65
    Grilled Cheeseburgers, 64
    Grilled Ultimate, 65
    grilling method for, 63
    seasoning and shaping, 62–63
  kebabs, 55–59
    with Asian Flavors, 59
    Charcoal-Grilled, 58, *122*
    cutting beef for, 56, 57
    Gas-Grilled, 58–59
    grilling method for, 57–58
    marinating, 56–57
    preparing onions for, 57
    Southwestern, 59
    testing beef steaks for, 55–56
    top blade steak for, 32, 56
    vegetables and fruits for, 57
  optimum internal temperatures
    for, 35
  primal cuts of, 30
  prime rib, 66–69
    aging, 68
    buying, 65
    carving, 66
    Grill-Roasted, on a Charcoal
      Grill, 67
    Grill-Roasted, on a Gas Grill,
      67–69
    Grill-Roasted, with Garlic and
      Rosemary Crust, 69
    grill-roasting method, 66
    internal temperature of, 66
    location of, 30
    trimming, 66
    tying up, 66, 67
  satay
    best beef steaks for, 59
    Charcoal-Grilled, with Spicy
      Peanut Dipping Sauce, 60
    Gas-Grilled, with Spicy Peanut
      Dipping Sauce, 61
    marinating, 59–60
    preparing sauce for, 60
    slicing meat for, 59, 60

Beef *(cont.)*
  short ribs
    Charcoal-Grilled, 83–84
    English-style, preparing, 82–83
    flanken-style, about, 82, 83
    Gas-Grilled, 84
    Grilled, Korean Style, 84
    Grilled, with Chipotle and
      Citrus Marinade, 84
    grilling method for, 83
  Spice Rub for, Simple, 377
  steaks. *See* Steaks (beef)
  tenderloin, 69–74
    buying, 69–70, 72
    Grill-Roasted, on a Charcoal
      Grill, 73
    Grill-Roasted, on a Gas Grill,
      73–74
    Grill-Roasted, with Garlic and
      Rosemary, 74
    Grill-Roasted, with Mixed
      Peppercorn Crust, 74
    grill-roasting method for, 72–73
    location of, 30
    resting after cooking, 73
    salting, 71
    shaping and tying up, 69, 74
    smoke flavors for, 73
    steak cuts from, about, 32
    taste tests on, 72
    trimming, 70–71, 74
  Texas-style ribs, 77–81
    Barbecued, 80–81, *119*
    Barbecued, on a Gas Grill, 81
    Barbecue Sauce for, 81
    barbecuing method for, 79–80
    buying ribs for, 77, 79
    membrane on, 77–78
    rubs for, 78
    smoke flavors for, 79
  USDA grades of, 34
Belgian endive. *See* Endive, Belgian
Blue cheese:
  and Anchovy Dressing, Grilled
    Asparagus with, 298
  Butter, 42
  Dressing, 182
  French Potato Salad with Arugula,
    Roquefort, and Walnuts, 359
  Grilled Pizza with Prosciutto,
    Arugula, and Gorgonzola,
    340–41
  Roquefort Butter, 385
Bluefish:
  fillets
    Charcoal-Grilled, 225–26
    Cumin-Crusted, with Avocado-
      Corn Relish, 226
    Gas-Grilled, 226

Bluefish *(cont.)*
    grilling method for, 225
    substituting, for flavor variations,
      242
  whole, 249–52
    buying, 249
    Charcoal-Grilled, 249
    Gas-Grilled, 249–52
Bok Choy, Grilled, and Tuna Steaks
    with Soy-Ginger Glaze, 244
Boursin Cheese and Tomatoes,
    Grilled Portobello
    Sandwiches with, 312–13
Bread:
  cornbread
    All-Purpose, 371–72
    baking, 371
    ingredients in, 370–71
    Jalapeño-Cheddar, Spicy, 372
  crumbs, preparing, 274
  flour, 331
  salad
    Pita, with Olives, Feta, and
      Mint, 366
    preparing, 364–65
    with Roasted Peppers and
      Olives, 365–66
    with Tomatoes, Herbs, and Red
      Onions, 365
  slicing, tip for, 342
  see also Bruschetta; Pizza
Bread flour, about, 331
Brining:
  chicken, 172–73
    bone-in parts, 167–68
    cutlets, 158–59
    Thai-grilled, 175
    whole, 191
    wings, 183
  mahi-mahi, 228
  pork
    baby back ribs, 111
    chops, 92
    loin, 102
    tenderloin, 106
  poultry, 172–73
  salmon fillets, 238
  salt for, 172
  shrimp, 262
  turkey, 172–73
    breast, 203
    whole, 200, 204
Briquettes, charcoal, 2, 6, 112
Broccoli and Olives, Pasta Salad
    with, 363–64
Brown paper bags, 24
Bruschetta, 343–46
  with Fresh Herbs, 344
  Grilled Bread for, 343

Bruschetta *(cont.)*
  with Grilled Eggplant, Rosemary,
    and Feta Cheese, 345–46
  with Grilled Portobello
    Mushrooms, 344–45
  with Red Onions, Herbs, and
    Parmesan, 344
  with Sautéed Spicy Shrimp, 343–44
  with Sautéed Sweet Peppers, 345
  with Tapenade and Goat Cheese,
    345
  with Tomatoes and Basil, 343
Brushes:
  grill, for cleaning, 18–19
  small, for basting, 23, 388
Bulgur wheat, in Tabbouleh, 367
Burgers:
  hamburgers, 61–65
    beef for, buying or grinding,
      61–62
    Charcoal-Grilled, 63–64, *121*
    Gas-Grilled, 64
    Grilled, Ultimate, 65
    Grilled, with Cognac, Mustard,
      and Chives, 64–65
    Grilled, with Garlic, Chipotles,
      and Scallions, 64
    Grilled, with Porcini
      Mushrooms and Thyme, 65
    Grilled Cheeseburgers, 64
    grilling method for, 63
    seasoning and shaping, 62–63
  salmon
    Charcoal-Grilled, 245–46
    Gas-Grilled, 246
    preparing, 245, 246
    sauces for, 248
  tuna
    Charcoal-Grilled, 246–47
    Gas-Grilled, 247
    preparing, 245
    sauces for, 248
  turkey
    best ground turkey for, 197–98
    Charcoal-Grilled, *131*, 198–99
    flavorings and fillers for, 198
    Gas-Grilled, 199
    grilling method for, 198
    internal temperature for, 198
    with Miso, 199
    with Porcini Mushrooms, 199
    Ultimate, 199
Butter:
  Blue Cheese, 42
  Chili, 275
  Chili, Spicy, 299–300
  compound
    Chipotle-Lime, 227–28
    Parsley, 384–85

Butter *(cont.)*
  Parsley-Lemon, 385
  Roasted Red Pepper and
    Smoked Paprika, 385
  rolling, technique for, 384
  Roquefort, 385
  Rosemary-Parmesan, 385
  Tapenade, 385
  Tarragon-Lime, 385
  Garlic, 300–301
  Herb, 300
  Lemon, Spicy, 270
  Lemon-Garlic, 304–5
  Sauce, Tarragon, 256
  Tarragon-Chive, 274
Buttermilk, Sweet Curry Marinade
  with, 142
Butternut squash:
  Grilled, 323
  Grilled, Spicy, with Garlic and
    Rosemary, 323–24
  preparing for grilling, 324

C

Cabbage:
  coleslaw
    Creamy, 354
    Curried, with Apples and
      Raisins, 355
    Sweet-and-Sour, 355
  Napa, Slaw, 170
  salting, 353–54
  shredding, 354
Caper(s):
  French Potato Salad with Radishes,
    Cornichons, and, 359
  Grilled Zucchini or Summer
    Squash with Oregano and,
    325–26
  Onion, and Black Olive Relish, 395
  Parsley Sauce with Cornichons
    and, 396–97
Caramel Sauce, Simplified, 327
Charcoal:
  adding to lit fire, 6
  brands, testing of, 6
  briquettes, 2, 6, 112
  effect on food flavor, 6
  hardwood, 2, 6
  for indirect cooking, 8
  lighting, 5
  measuring, 6
  types of, 6
Charcoal grills:
  arranging coals in, 4
  barbecuing on, basics of, 8
  buying, guidelines for, 14–15

Charcoal grills *(cont.)*
  chimney starters for, 5
  cleaning grate of, 250
  compared with gas grills, 12
  electric starters for, 18
  equipment and tools for, 18–24
  features of, 14–15
  grilling on, basics of, 4–5
  grilling on, four tips for, 5
  grill-roasting on, basics of, 8
  judging fire intensity in, 4
  lighting fire in, 5
  lit, adding more charcoal to, 6
  modified two-level fire for, 2, 4
  oiling grate of, 224
  preheating, 11
  removing ashes from, 115
  rib racks for, 111
  single-level fire for, 2, 4
  two-level fire for, 2, 4
  V-racks for, 111, 200, 205
  wood chips and chunks for, 8,
    10, 109
  see also Charcoal
Cheddar-Jalapeño Cornbread, Spicy,
  372
Cheese:
  Asiago, Grilled Pizza with Fennel,
    Sun-Dried Tomato, and, 340
  blue
    and Anchovy Dressing, Grilled
      Asparagus with, 298
    Butter, 42
    Dressing, 182
    French Potato Salad with
      Arugula, Roquefort, and
      Walnuts, 359
    Grilled Pizza with Prosciutto,
      Arugula, and Gorgonzola,
      340–41
    Roquefort Butter, 385
  Boursin, and Tomatoes, Grilled
    Portobello Sandwiches with,
    312–13
  Cheddar-Jalapeño Cornbread,
    Spicy, 372
  Cheeseburgers, Grilled, 64
  feta
    Grilled Eggplant, and Rosemary,
      Bruschetta with, 345–46
    Olives, and Mint, Pita Bread
      Salad with, 366
    and Shrimp, Grilled Pizza with,
      335
    Tomato Salad with, and Cumin-
      Yogurt Dressing, 352–53
  goat
    Bruschetta with Tapenade and,
      345

Cheese (cont.)
  Grilled Asparagus with
    Rosemary and, 297
  Grilled Pizza with Grilled
    Eggplant and, 338–39
  Gruyère, French Potato Salad with
    Hard Salami and, 359
  mozzarella
    slicing, 337
    Tomato, and Basil Salad
      (Insalata Caprese), 353
  Parmesan
    Bruschetta with Red Onions,
      Herbs, and, 344
    Grilled Corn with Garlic
      Butter and Cheese, 300–301
    -Rosemary Butter, 385
    Shaved, and Arugula, Tomato
      Salad with, 352
    shavings, creating, 344
  semisoft, shredding, 372
Chermoula, 397
Cherry-Port Sauce, 218
Cherry wood, 10
Chicken, 154–94
  boneless breasts. See Chicken—
    cutlets
  boneless thighs. See Chicken—
    kebabs
  brining, 172–73
  butterflied, 184–89
    alla Diavola, preparing, 188
    alla Diavola on a Charcoal Grill,
      188–89, 278
    alla Diavola on a Gas Grill, 189
    with Barbecue Sauce, 187
    butterflying technique, 185
    carving, 186
    Charcoal-Grilled, 185–86
    with Chipotle, Honey, and
      Lime, 187
    Gas-Grilled, 186
    with Green Olive Tapenade, 187
    grilling method for, 184–85
    with Lemon and Rosemary, 187
    with Pesto, 186
    seasoning, 184
    weighting down, 184
  cutlets, 156–61
    brining, 158–59
    buying, 158
    Charcoal-Grilled, 159
    Gas-Grilled, 160
    Grilled, Salad with Sesame-
      Miso Dressing, 160–61
    grilling method for, 156–58
    pounding, 159
    removing tenderloin from, 159
    rubs and pastes for, 158

Chicken (cont.)
  taste tests on, 158
  trimming, 159
  internal temperature of,
    measuring, 190
  kebabs, 161–65
    Charcoal-Grilled, 163–64, 281
    checking for doneness, 163
    Curried, and Cucumber Salad
      with Yogurt and Mint, 164
    Gas-Grilled, 164
    Grilled Caribbean, with Black
      Bean and Mango Salsa, 164
    grilling method for, 163
    marinades for, 165
    marinating, 161–62
    Satay, Thai, with Spicy Peanut
      Sauce, 164
    seasoning, 161–62
    skewering, 163, 164
    Southwestern, with Red
      Pepper–Jícama Relish, 164
    vegetables and fruits for, 162–63
  parts, bone-in (breasts)
    brining, 168
    Charcoal-Grilled, 170–71, 282
    Charcoal-Grilled Mixed Parts,
      179–80
    flavoring, 168
    Gas-Grilled, 171
    Gas-Grilled Mixed Parts, 180
    grilling method for, 168
    rubs and pastes for, 280, 382–84
    serving with barbecue sauce, 168
    tandoori-style, preparing, 174
    Tandoori-Style Charcoal-
      Grilled, with Raita, 174–75
    Tandoori-Style Gas-Grilled,
      with Raita, 175
    Thai grilled, brining, 175
    Thai Grilled, on a Gas Grill, 179
    Thai grilled, preparing, 175–77
    Thai Grilled, with Spicy, Sweet,
      and Sour Dipping Sauce,
      177–79, 277
    whole breasts, splitting, 170
  parts, bone-in (thighs or legs)
    brining, 167–68
    Charcoal-Grilled Mixed Parts,
      179–80
    Charcoal-Grilled Thighs or
      Legs, 169
    flavoring, 167
    Gas-Grilled Mixed Parts, 180
    Gas-Grilled Thighs or Legs, 169
    Grilled Legs, Hoisin-Glazed,
      with Napa Cabbage Slaw, 170
    grilling method for, 166–68
    rubs and pastes for, 280, 382–84

Chicken (cont.)
  serving with barbecue sauce,
    168
  raw, handling, 157
  whole, 191–94
    brining, 172–73, 191
    buying, 156
    cutting up, 157
    Grill-Roasted, on a Charcoal
      Grill, 191–92, 279
    Grill-Roasted, on a Gas Grill,
      192–93
    Grill-Roasted, with Barbecue
      Sauce, 193
    Grill-Roasted Beer Can, 194
    grill-roasted beer can,
      preparing, 193–94
    grill-roasting method for, 190–91
    rubs for, 280, 382, 383
    taste tests, 156
  wings, 181–84
    brining, 183
    Charcoal-Grilled, 183
    cutting up, 181
    Gas-Grilled, 183–84
    grilling method for, 181–83
    sauces for, 182
Chile(s):
  Ancho and Chipotle Rub for
    Pork, 378
  and Corn, Spicy Grilled Potato
    Salad with, 320
  -Cumin Spice Rub for Steak, 380
  Habanero-Peach Chutney, 215
  jalapeño
    -Cheddar Cornbread, Spicy,
      372
    Pickled, Cilantro-Parsley Sauce
      with, 398–99
  -Orange Vinaigrette, 267–68
  poblano
    Roasted, Charcoal-Grilled Skirt
      Steak Tacos with, 53–54
    Roasted, Gas-Grilled Skirt
      Steak Tacos with, 54
  -Tomatillo Sauce, 400
  see also Chipotle(s)
Chili:
  Butter, 275
  Butter, Spicy, 299–300
  -Lime Glaze, 217
Chimichurri, 397
Chimney starters, 5, 18
Chipotle(s):
  and Ancho Rub for Pork, 378
  Chile-Cumin Spice Rub for
    Steak, 380
  and Cilantro, Macaroni Salad with,
    362

Chipotle(s) *(cont.)*
  and Citrus Marinade, 84
  -Lime Butter, 227–28
  Lime Sauce, Creamy, 248
  -Maple Glaze, 237
  Sauce, Sweet-and-Sour, 50–51
Chive-Tarragon Butter, 274
Chops, lamb. *See* Lamb—chops
Chops, pork. *See* Pork—chops
Chops, veal. *See* Veal—chops
Chutneys:
  Apple, 96–97
  Curried Fruit, with Lime and
    Ginger, 396
  description of, 389
  Dried Peach and Apple, 396
  Peach-Habanero, 215
Cilantro:
  Chermoula, 397
  and Cherry Tomato Vinaigrette,
    301–2
  and Chipotles, Macaroni Salad
    with, 362
  and Citrus Spice Paste for
    Chicken Parts, 383
  and Garlic Marinade with Garam
    Masala, 142
  Ginger Sauce, Creamy, 248
  Grilled Pizza with Bacon, Corn,
    and, 342
  Orange, and Lime Vinaigrette, 254
  -Parsley Sauce with Pickled
    Jalapeños, 398–99
Citrus:
  and Black Olive Relish, 393
  and Chipotle Marinade, 84
  and Cilantro Spice Paste for
    Chicken Parts, 383
  Grilled Fennel with, 308
  Mojo Sauce, 399–400
  -Soy Sauce, Tangy, 270
  see also specific citrus fruits
Clams:
  buying, 269
  cleaning, 268
  grilled
    Charcoal-, 269
    Gas-, 269–70
    with Mignonette Sauce, 270
    with Spicy Lemon Butter, 270
    with Tangy Soy-Citrus Sauce,
      270
  serving, 270
  storing, 269
  varieties of, 268
Cocoa-Cumin-Allspice Rub for
  Steak, 380
Coffee Bean and Star Anise Spice
  Rub for Steak, 380

Coleslaw:
  Creamy, 354
  Curried, with Apples and Raisins,
    355
  dressings for, 354
  preparing cabbage for, 353–54
  Sweet-and-Sour, 355
Compound butter. *See* Butter—
  compound
Coriander and Dill Spice Rub,
  Peppery, for Steak, 380–81
Corn, 298–301
  -Avocado Relish, 393–94
  Bacon, and Cilantro, Grilled Pizza
    with, 342
  and Chiles, Spicy Grilled Potato
    Salad with, 320
  Grilled, *123,* 299
    with Garlic Butter and Cheese,
      300–301
    with Herb Butter, 300
    Salsa, 391–92
    with Soy-Honey Glaze, 300
    with Spicy Chili Butter, *292,*
      299–300
  grilling, at a glance, 315
  judging when done, 300
  preparing for grilling, 300
  skewering, tip for, 299
  storing, 299
Cornbread:
  All-Purpose, 371–72
  baking, 371
  ingredients in, 370–71
  Jalapeño-Cheddar, Spicy, 372
Cornichons:
  and Capers, Parsley Sauce with,
    396–97
  Radishes, and Capers, French
    Potato Salad with, 359
Cornish hens:
  grill-roasted
    on a Charcoal Grill, 209
    on a Gas Grill, 209–10
  grill-roasting, method for, 208
  preparing, 208
  rubs for, 382, 383
  size of, 209
Crabs, soft-shell:
  cleaning, 275
  grilled
    Charcoal-, 276
    Gas-, 276
    with Spicy Butter, 276
    with Tartar Sauce, 276
  grilling method for, 275
Cranberry:
  -Onion Relish, 394
  –Red Pepper Relish, 203

Cucumber(s):
  and Mango Relish with Yogurt, 160
  peeling and seeding, 350
  and Red Onion Relish with
    Mint, Warm, 394–95
  salad
    Creamy Dill, 351
    Israeli Tomato and, 352
    Sesame-Lemon, *282,* 351
    Yogurt-Mint, 351
  salting and draining, 350–51
Cumin:
  -Chile Spice Rub for Steak, 380
  -Cocoa-Allspice Rub for Steak, 380
  -Crusted Bluefish with Avocado-
    Corn Relish, 226
  Spice Rub, 208
  -Yogurt Dressing, 352–53
Curry(ied):
  Apples, Macaroni Salad with, 362
  Chicken Kebabs and Cucumber
    Salad with Yogurt and Mint,
    164
  Coleslaw with Apples and Raisins,
    355
  Fruit Chutney with Lime and
    Ginger, 396
  Grilled Duck Breasts, 215
  Grilled Eggplant, 303
  Marinade, Sweet, with Buttermilk,
    142
Cutting boards, 176

D
Dill:
  and Coriander Spice Rub,
    Peppery, for Steak, 380–81
  Cucumber Salad, Creamy, 351
  -Mustard Sauce, 240
Dough, pizza. *See* Pizza—dough
Dressings:
  Anchovy, 298
  Balsamic, 305
  Blue Cheese, 182
  Cumin-Yogurt, 352–53
  Mustard, 305
  preparing, for German potato
    salad, 360
  Sesame-Miso, 160–61
  see also Vinaigrettes
Duck, 210–16
  breasts, 213–16
    Charcoal-Grilled, 214–15
    Gas-Grilled, 215
    Grilled, Curried, 215
    Grilled, with Peach-Habanero
      Chutney, 215

Duck *(cont.)*
    Grilled, with Pickled Ginger
        Relish, 215
    Grilled, with Tapenade, 216
    grilling method for, 213–14
    internal temperature of, 213
    preparing, 214
    resting, after cooking, 214
    types of, 212
    whole, 210–13
        Grill-Roasted, on a Charcoal
          Grill, 211–12
        Grill-Roasted, on a Gas Grill,
          212–13
        Grill-Roasted Five-Spice, with
          Soy Glaze, 213
        grill-roasting, method for,
          210–11
        rubs for, 382, 383

E

Eggplant, 301–4
    Grilled, 301
        Baba Ghanoush, 303–4
        Baba Ghanoush with Sautéed
          Onion, 304
        with Basil Oil, 301
        with Cherry Tomato and
          Cilantro Vinaigrette, 301–2
        Curried, 303
        with Ginger and Soy, 302
        and Goat Cheese, Grilled Pizza
          with, 338–39
        Rosemary, and Feta Cheese,
          Bruschetta with, 345–46
        with Sweet Miso Glaze, 302–3
    grilling, at a glance, 315
    Tomatoes, and Basil, Pasta Salad
        with, 364
Eggs:
    Hard-Cooked, and Sweet Pickles,
        American Potato Salad with,
        357–58
    Hard-Cooked, Foolproof, 355
    hard-cooked, peeling, 355
Electric starters, 18
Endive, Belgian:
    Grilled, 304
        with Balsamic Dressing, 305
        with Lemon-Garlic Butter,
          304–5
        with Mustard Dressing and
          Parmesan, 305
    grilling, at a glance, 315
    preparing for grilling, 305
Equipment:
    boning knives, 144

Equipment *(cont.)*
    for brining poultry, 173
    brown paper bags, 24
    brushes, grill, 18–19
    brushes, small, 23, 388
    charcoal ash scooper, 115
    chef's knives, 116
    chimney starters, 5, 18
    cutting boards, 176
    electric starters, 18
    fish baskets, 21, 224–25
    flour shaker, improvised, 333
    foil, heavy-duty, 23–24
    foil-lined platters, 152
    foil pans, 23
    food processors, 62, 332
    food storage containers, 24–25
    garlic presses, 178, 179
    grill grids, 20–21
    kitchen shears, 187
    mortars and pestles, improvised,
        380
    paper towels, 24
    pizza cutters, 339
    plastic wrap, 24
    rimless baking sheets, 334, 337
    santoku knives, 88
    spatulas, 20
    spice grinders, 380
    sprayer/misters, 21
    stain removers, 25–26
    steak knives, 34
    thermometers, grill, 21
    thermometers, instant-read, 21–22,
        38
    timer/thermometers, 22–23
    tongs, 19–20
    V-racks, 111, 200, 205
    see also Charcoal; Charcoal grills;
        Gas grills; Skewers and
        skewering methods

F

Fajitas, Classic, 51–52, *123*
Fennel:
    Grilled, 306
        with Citrus, 308
        with Grapefruit Vinaigrette,
          306–7
        with Mint and Tarragon
          Vinaigrette, 307
        and Orange Vinaigrette, 234–35
        with Tarragon and Shallot, 308
    grilling, at a glance, 315
    preparing for grilling, 306
    Sun-Dried Tomato, and Asiago,
        Grilled Pizza with, 340

Feta cheese:
    Grilled Eggplant, and Rosemary,
        Bruschetta with, 345–46
    Olives, and Mint, Pita Bread Salad
        with, 366
    and Shrimp, Grilled Pizza with, 335
    Tomato Salad with, and Cumin-
        Yogurt Dressing, 352–53
Fig and Lamb Kebabs with Garlic-
    Parsley Marinade, 141
Fish, 222–58
    burgers
        Salmon, Charcoal-Grilled,
          245–46
        Salmon, Gas-Grilled, 246
        salmon, preparing, 245, 246
        sauces for, 248
        Tuna, Charcoal-Grilled, 246–47
        Tuna, Gas-Grilled, 247
        tuna, preparing, 245
    buying, 224, 251
    compound butters for, 384–85
    fillets
        bluefish, 225–26
        grilling method for, 224–25
        mahi-mahi, 228–29
        red snapper, 229–30
        salmon, 233–40
        turning, 228
    kebabs, swordfish
        Charcoal-Grilled, 232
        Gas-Grilled, 232
        Grilled, with Salmoriglio Sauce,
          233
        grilling method for, 232
        Southeast Asian–Style, 232–33
    raw, foil-lined platters for, 152
    Spice Rub for, Simple, 379
    steaks
        grilling method for, 224–25
        halibut, 226–28
        swordfish, 230–31
        tuna, 240–44
        turning, 228
    sticking to grill, preventing, 224,
        250
    storing, 251
    substituting, for flavor variations,
        242
    whole, 249–58
        bluefish, 249–52
        filleting after cooking, 251
        flare-ups, avoiding, 250
        grilling method for, 250–51
        mackerel, 252–53
        pompano, 255–56
        red snapper, 253–55
        salmon, 258
        scaling and gutting, 250

Fish *(cont.)*
    slashing skin of, 250
    striped bass, 253–55
    troubleshooting, 250
    trout, 256–57
    turning and lifting, 250, 251
    see also specific fish types
Fish baskets, 21, 224–25
Fish sauce, taste tests on, 177
Flare-ups:
    on gas grills, tests on, 17
    handling, 21, 50, 250
Flour shaker, homemade, 333
Foil, heavy-duty, 23–24
Foil-lined platters, 152
Foil pans, 23
Food processors, 62, 332
Food safety practices, 11, 152, 157, 176
Food storage containers, 24–25
Fruit:
    for chicken kebabs, 162–63
    Chutney, Curried, with Lime and Ginger, 396
    glazes and sauces for, 326–27
    grilling chart for, 327
    see also specific fruits
Fuel. *See* Charcoal
Fuel tanks, checking level in, 7

G

Garam masala, 141
    Garlic and Cilantro Marinade with, 142
Garlic:
    Basting Oil, 317
    bread. *See* Bruschetta
    Butter, 300–301
        Lemon, 304–5
    Ginger, and Soy Marinade, 48
    Grill-Roasted, 309
    grill-roasting method for, 308
    -Herb Pizza Dough, 332–33
        Hand-Kneaded, 333
        Kneaded in a Standing Mixer, 333
    marinade
        Cilantro and, with Garam Masala, 142
        Herb and, 165
        Parsley, 141
        Rosemary, 137, 150
    paste
        Herb and, for Meat, Mediterranean, 377
        Herb and, Mediterranean, 139
        Lemon and Oregano, 263
        preparing, 263

Garlic *(cont.)*
        Rosemary, for Steak, 381–82
        Spicy, 263
    peeling, 143
    rub, wet
        Mustard, and Honey, for Pork, 379
        Orange, and Sage, for Pork, 378–79
Garlic presses, 178, 179
Gas grills:
    barbecuing on, basics of, 9
    buying, guidelines for, 16–17
    checking fuel level in tank, 7
    cleaning grates of, 250
    compared with charcoal grills, 12
    covering control panel on, 7
    equipment and tools for, 18–24
    features of, 7, 16–17
    grilling on, basics of, 7
    grilling on, three tips for, 7
    grill-roasting on, basics of, 9
    judging fire intensity in, 4
    lighting, 7
    modified two-level fire for, 3–7
    oiling grate of, 224
    portable models, 17–18
    preheating, 11
    regulating heat on, 7
    rib racks for, 111
    single-level fire for, 3, 7
    two-level fire for, 3, 7
    V-racks for, 111, 200, 205
    wood chips and chunks for, 9, 10, 109
Ginger:
    Cilantro Sauce, Creamy, 248
    Curried Fruit Chutney with Lime and, 396
    Garlic, and Soy Marinade, 48
    Hoisin, and Honey Glaze, 389
    peeling and mincing, 247
    Pickled, Relish, 215
    -Soy Glaze, 244
    Warm-Spiced Parsley Marinade with, 142
Glazes:
    Chili-Lime, 217
    for grilled fruit, 326–27
    Hoisin, Honey, and Ginger, 389
    Hoisin, Sweet and Spicy, 327
    Honey-Mustard, 237
    Maple-Chipotle, 237
    Maple-Mustard, 104
    Maple-Soy, 237
    Miso, Sweet, 302–3
    Rum-Molasses, 326
    for salmon fillets, 237
    Sour Orange, 326–27

Glazes *(cont.)*
    Soy, Sweetened, 388–89
    Soy-Ginger, 244
    Soy-Honey, 300
Goat cheese:
    Bruschetta with Tapenade and, 345
    Grilled Asparagus with Rosemary and, 297
    Grilled Pizza with Grilled Eggplant and, 338–39
Gorgonzola, Prosciutto, and Arugula, Grilled Pizza with, 340–41
Grapefruit Vinaigrette, 306–7
Green Beans, Grilled, 309–10
Green oak wood, 79
Grill grids, 20–21
Grilling:
    on charcoal grills, basics of, 4–5
    in the dark, tip for, 312
    definition of, 2
    equipment and tools for, 14–26
    on gas grills, basics of, 7
    indirect, basics of, 3, 8–9
    top ten mistakes in, 11
    see also Barbecuing; Grill-roasting
Grill-roasting:
    beef tenderloin, 72–73
    on charcoal grill, basics of, 8
    cooking temperatures for, 3
    Cornish hens, 208
    description of, 3
    duck, 210–11
    garlic, 308
    on gas grill, basics of, 9
    peppers, bell, 316
    pork loin, 102
    prime rib, 66
    turkey breast, 206
    whole chicken, 190–91, 193–94
    whole turkey, 200–201
    wood chips and chunks for, 8, 9, 10
Grills:
    cleaning grate of, 224, 250
    oiling grate of, 224
    rib racks for, 111
    V-racks for, 111, 200, 205
    see also Charcoal grills; Gas grills
Grill-smoking pork chops, 95–96, 97
Gruyère, French Potato Salad with Hard Salami and, 359
Guacamole, Chunky, 390–91

H

Habanero-Peach Chutney, 215
Halibut steaks:
    grilled
        Charcoal-, 227

Halibut steaks (cont.)
    with Chipotle-Lime Butter,
        227–28
    Gas-, 227
    grilling method for, 226–27
    removing bone from, 226
    substituting, for flavor variations, 242
Hamburgers, 61–65
    beef for, buying or grinding, 61–62
    grilled
        Charcoal-, 63–64, 121
        Cheeseburgers, 64
        with Cognac, Mustard, and
            Chives, 64–65
        with Garlic, Chipotles, and
            Scallions, 64
        Gas-, 64
        with Porcini Mushrooms and
            Thyme, 65
        Ultimate, 65
    grilling method for, 63
    seasoning and shaping, 62–63
Hardwood charcoal, 2, 6
Herb(s):
    Butter, 300
    Fresh, Bruschetta with, 344
    and Garlic Marinade, 165
    -Garlic Pizza Dough, 332–33
        Hand-Kneaded, 333
        Kneaded in a Standing Mixer,
            333
    -Infused Oil, 243
    leaves, bruising, 399
    Lemon Sauce, Creamy, 248
    paste
        Garlic and, for Meat,
            Mediterranean, 377
        Garlic and, Mediterranean, 139
        Mediterranean, 76
    Red Onions, and Parmesan,
        Bruschetta with, 344
    Rub for Pork, 377–78
    Tomatoes, and Red Onions, Bread
        Salad with, 365
    see also specific herbs
Hickory wood, 10, 79
Hoisin:
    Glaze, Sweet and Spicy, 327
    -Glazed Grilled Chicken Legs with
        Napa Cabbage Slaw, 170
    Honey, and Ginger Glaze, 389
    -Sesame Sauce, 182
Honey:
    Hoisin, and Ginger Glaze, 389
    measuring, 50
    Mustard, and Garlic Wet Rub for
        Pork, 379
    -Mustard Glaze, 237
    -Soy Glaze, 300

Honey (cont.)
    -Soy Marinade with Thyme, 150
Horseradish:
    Cream Sauce, 240
    -Peppercorn Sauce, 257

I

Indirect cooking:
    on charcoal grill, 8
    description of, 3
    equipment and tools for, 14–26
    on gas grill, 9
    see also Barbecuing; Grill-roasting
Ingredients:
    barbecue sauce, bottled, 192
    beans, canned white, 346
    beef tenderloin, 72
    bread flour, 331
    chicken cutlets, 158
    Cornish hens, 209
    duck, 212
    fish sauce, 177
    flat steaks, 49
    garam masala, 141
    ketchup, 64
    lamb legs, 135
    lamb shoulder chops, 136
    mayonnaise, 356
    miso, 302
    olive oils, extra-virgin, 40
    peanut oil, 160
    pepper, black, 381
    peppers, red roasted, jarred, 398
    pork, enhanced versus
        unenhanced, 107
    pork, modern versus
        old-fashioned, 92
    pork sausage, smoked, 101
    poussins, 209
    rib roasts, 65
    soy sauce, 46
    steak tips, 45
    turkey breast, 206
    veal, milk-fed versus natural, 75
    vinegar, balsamic, 307
    vinegar, red wine, 271

J

Jalapeño(s):
    -Cheddar Cornbread, Spicy, 372
    Pickled, Cilantro-Parsley Sauce
        with, 398–99
Jícama:
    preparing, 395
    -Red Pepper Relish, 395–96

K

Kebabs:
    beef, 55–59
        with Asian Flavors, 59
        Charcoal-Grilled, 58, 122
        cutting beef for, 56, 57
        Gas-Grilled, 58–59
        grilling method for, 57–58
        marinating, 56–57
        preparing onions for, 57
        Southwestern, 59
        testing beef steaks for, 55–56
        top blade steak for, 32, 56
        vegetables and fruits for, 57
    chicken, 161–65
        Charcoal-Grilled, 163–64, 281
        checking for doneness, 163
        Curried, and Cucumber Salad
            with Yogurt and Mint, 164
        Gas-Grilled, 164
        Grilled Caribbean, with Black
            Bean and Mango Salsa, 164
        grilling method for, 163
        marinades for, 165
        marinating, 161–62
        seasoning, 161–62
        skewering, 163, 164
        Southwestern, with Red
            Pepper–Jícama Relish, 164
        vegetables and fruits for, 162–63
    lamb (shish kebab)
        best lamb cuts for, 140
        best vegetables for, 140
        Charcoal-Grilled, 129, 141
        and Fig, with Garlic-Parsley
            Marinade, 141
        Gas-Grilled, 141
        marinades for, 142
        marinating, 140
        preparing lamb for, 140
    pork, 97–100
        best pork cuts for, 97–98
        butterflying pork for, 98
        Charcoal-Grilled, 98–99
        Gas-Grilled, 99
        Grilled, with Southeast Asian
            Flavors, 99–100
        Grilled, with West Indian
            Flavors, 99
        grilling method for, 98
        marinating, 98
    swordfish
        Charcoal-Grilled, 232
        Gas-Grilled, 232
        Grilled, with Salmoriglio Sauce,
            233
        grilling method for, 232
        Southeast Asian–Style, 232–33
    see also Satay

Ketchup, taste tests on, 64
Kitchen shears, 187
Knives:
    boning, 144
    chef's, 116
    santoku, 88
    steak, 34

L

Lamb, 134–52
    chops, 136–40
        blade, about, 136
        buying, 136
        grilling method for, 136
        location of, 135
        Loin or Rib, Charcoal-Grilled, 138–39
        loin or rib, frenching, 138
        Loin or Rib, Gas-Grilled, 139
        Loin or Rib, Grilled, and Zucchini with Mint Sauce, 139
        Loin or Rib, Grilled, with Mediterranean Herb and Garlic Paste, 139
        loin or rib, texture and flavor, 136, 138
        round-bone, about, 136
        Shoulder, Charcoal-Grilled, 136–37
        Shoulder, Gas-Grilled, 137
        Shoulder, Grilled, with Garlic-Rosemary Marinade, 137
        Shoulder, Grilled, with Near East Red Pepper Paste, 138
        Shoulder, Grilled, with Soy-Shallot Marinade, 137
        Shoulder, Grilled Spiced, with Quick Onion and Parsley Relish, 137
        shoulder, taste tests on, 136
    cuts of, primal, 135
    grilling, three rules for, 35–36
    internal temperature of, 135
    leg of
        boning, 146, 149
        buying, 146
        location of, 135
        skeletal structure of, 146
        taste tests on, 135
    leg of, butterflied, 146–52
        butterflying techniques, 147–48, 151
        buying, 147
        carving, 148
        Charcoal-Grilled, 148
        Gas-Grilled, 151–52

Lamb (cont.)
    grilling method for, 146, 148
    marinades for, 150
    resting after cooking, 148
    optimum internal temperatures for, 35
    primal cuts of, 135
    rack of, 143–46
        Charcoal-Grilled, 145
        frenched, 143
        Gas-Grilled, 145–46
        Grilled, with Garlic and Herbs, 146
        Grilled, with Turkish Spice Rub, 146
        grilling method for, 143–44
        internal temperature of, 144
        removing silver skin from, 145
        seasoning, 144
        trimming, 143, 145
    shish kebab
        best lamb cuts for, 140
        best vegetables for, 140
        Charcoal-Grilled, 129, 141
        and Fig, with Garlic-Parsley Marinade, 141
        Gas-Grilled, 141
        marinades for, 142
        marinating, 140
        preparing lamb for, 140
    Spice Rub for, Simple, 377
Lemon(s):
    butter
        Garlic, 304–5
        Parsley, 385
        Spicy, 270
    Garlic, and Oregano Paste, 263
    Grilled, Vinaigrette, 296–97
    juicing, 189, 394
    Marinade with Greek Flavorings, 150
    -Rosemary Basting Oil for Vegetables, 317
    Sauce
        Creamy Herb, 248
        Parsley, 231
Lighter fluid, 6
Lime:
    -Chili Glaze, 217
    -Chipotle Butter, 227–28
    Chipotle Sauce, Creamy, 248
    and Ginger, Curried Fruit Chutney with, 396
    Orange, and Cilantro Vinaigrette, 254
    -Tarragon Butter, 385
Lobsters, 272–75
    grilled
        Charcoal-, 273–74

Lobsters (cont.)
    with Chili Butter, 275
    Gas-, 274
    with Tarragon-Chive Butter, 274
    grilling method for, 272–73
    preparing for grilling, 272

M

Macaroni:
    cooked, drying, 361
    Salad, 362
        with Chipotles and Cilantro, 362
        with Curried Apples, 362
        preparing, 361–62
Mackerel, whole:
    Charcoal-Grilled, 252
    Gas-Grilled, 252–53
    Grilled, with Garlic, Ginger, and Sesame Oil, Spicy, 253
Mahi-mahi fillets:
    brining, 228
    grilled
        Charcoal-, 228–29
        Gas-, 229
        with Shallots, Lime, and Cilantro, 229
    grilling method for, 228
    substituting, for flavor variations, 242
Mango(es):
    and Black Bean Salsa, 392
    and Cucumber Relish with Yogurt, 160
    grilling, 327
    preparing for grilling, 328
    Salsa, 392
Maple:
    -Chipotle Glaze, 237
    -Mustard Glaze, 104
    -Soy Glaze, 237
Marinades:
    Asian, 165
    for beef
        ribs, 84
        steak tips, 47–48
    Caribbean, 165
    for chicken kebabs, 165
    Chipotle and Citrus, 84
    Curry, 165
    Curry, Sweet, with Buttermilk, 142
    Garlic
        and Cilantro, with Garam Masala, 142
        Ginger, and Soy, 48
        and Herb, 165
        -Rosemary, 137, 150
    for lamb
        butterflied leg of, 150

Marinades *(cont.)*
  chops, 137
  shish kebab, 142
  Lemon, with Greek Flavorings, 150
  Middle Eastern, 165
  Parsley, Warm-Spiced, with
    Ginger, 142
  Rosemary-Mint, with Garlic and
    Lemon, 142
  Southwestern, 47, 165
  Soy-Honey, with Thyme, 150
  Soy-Shallot, 137
  Tandoori, 150
Mayonnaise:
  jarred, taste tests on, 356
  Wasabi, 248
Meat:
  grilling, three rules for, 35–36
  Mediterranean Herb and Garlic
    Paste for, 377
  optimum internal temperatures
    for, 35
  raw, foil-lined platters for, 152
  resting after cooking, 103
  roasts, keeping crust crispy, 104
  rubs and pastes for, 376–77
  salting, 71
  slicing, 103
  see also Beef; Lamb; Pork; Veal
Mesquite wood, 10, 79
Mignonette Sauce, 270
Mint:
  Pita Bread Salad with Olives, Feta,
    and, 366
  -Rosemary Marinade with Garlic
    and Lemon, 142
  Sauce, 139, 152
  and Tarragon Vinaigrette, 307
  Warm Cucumber and Red Onion
    Relish with, 394–95
  -Yogurt Cucumber Salad, 351
Miso:
  Glaze, Sweet, 302–3
  -Sesame Dressing, 160–61
  Turkey Burgers with, 199
  types of, 302
Modified two-level fire, 2, 3, 4, 7
Mojo Sauce, 399–400
Molasses-Rum Glaze, 326
Mortars and pestles, improvising, 380
Mozzarella:
  slicing, 337
  Tomato, and Basil Salad (Insalata
    Caprese), 353
Mushroom(s):
  button (cremini)
    grilling, 315
    preparing for grilling, 311
    preparing for skewering, 162

Mushroom(s) *(cont.)*
  cleaning, 311
  porcini
    dried, rehydrating, 65
    -Rubbed Grilled Veal Chops, 76
    and Thyme, Grilled
      Hamburgers with, 65
    Turkey Burgers with, 199
  portobello, 310–13
    Charcoal-Grilled Free-Form
      Beef Wellington with Port
      Syrup, 43–44
    Gas-Grilled Free-Form Beef
      Wellington with Port Syrup, 44
    Grilled, 310–11
    Grilled, Bruschetta with, 344–45
    Grilled, Sandwiches with
      Boursin Cheese and
      Tomatoes, 312–13
    Grilled, with Garlic, Rosemary,
      and Balsamic Vinegar, 311–12
    Grilled, with Tarragon, 311
    and Onions, Grilled Pizza with,
      338
  Shiitake, Grilled, Asian-Style Grilled
    Squab on Salad with, 219–20
Mussels:
  buying, 269
  cleaning, 268
  debearding, 268, 269
  grilled
    Charcoal-, 269
    Gas-, 269–70
    with Mignonette Sauce, 270
    with Spicy Lemon Butter, 270
    with Tangy Soy-Citrus Sauce,
      270
  serving, 270
  storing, 269
Mustard:
  Dijon, Vinaigrette, 320
  -Dill Sauce, 240
  Dressing, 305
  Garlic, and Honey Wet Rub for
    Pork, 379
  -Honey Glaze, 237
  -Maple Glaze, 104
  Sauce, Mid–South Carolina, 388
  Seed–Tarragon Rub for Steak, 380
  Sherry, and Cream Sauce, 267

O

Oak wood, 10
Oil:
  applying to grill rack, 224
  olive
    Basil, 301

Oil *(cont.)*
  Basting, Garlic, 317
  Basting, Lemon-Rosemary, for
    Vegetables, 317
  Herb-Infused, 243
  and Salt, Grilled Pizza with, 334
  taste tests on, 40
  peanut, taste tests on, 160
Olive oil:
  Basil, 301
  Basting, Garlic, 317
  Basting, Lemon-Rosemary, for
    Vegetables, 317
  Herb-Infused, 243
  and Salt, Grilled Pizza with, 334
  taste tests on, 40
Olive(s):
  black
    Asparagus, Caramelized Onions,
      and Thyme, Grilled Pizza
      with, 341–42
    and Basil, Grilled Bell Peppers
      with, 317
    and Citrus Relish, 393
    Feta, and Mint, Pita Bread Salad
      with, 366
    Onion, and Caper Relish, 395
    Pasta Salad with Broccoli and,
      363–64
    Tapenade, 216, 345
    Tapenade Butter, 385
  green
    Almonds, and Sherry Vinaigrette,
      Grilled Asparagus with, 298
    Bread Salad with Roasted
      Peppers and, 365–66
    and Sherry Vinegar, Spanish-
      Style Grilled Bell Peppers
      with, *291,* 316–17
    Tapenade, 187
Onion(s):
  Black Olive, and Caper Relish, 395
  Caramelized, Asparagus, Black
    Olives, and Thyme, Grilled
    Pizza with, 341–42
  -Cranberry Relish, 394
  Grilled, 313
    with Garlic and Thyme, 313–14
    Red, and Flank Steak with
      Chimichurri Sauce, 51
    Red, and Tomato Salad, 314
    Relish, 314–15
    serving, with grilled sausages, 100
  Grilled Pizza with Portobello
    Mushrooms and, 338
  grilling, at a glance, 315
  for lamb shish kebab, 140
  and Parsley Relish, Quick, 394
  preparing, for skewering, 57, 162

Onion(s) *(cont.)*
  red
    Arugula, and Rosemary–White
      Bean Spread, Bruschetta
      with, 346
    and Cucumber Relish with
      Mint, Warm, 394–95
    and Flank Steak, Grilled, with
      Chimichurri Sauce, 51
    Grilled, and Tomato Salad, 314
    Herbs, and Parmesan,
      Bruschetta with, 344
    Tomatoes, and Herbs, Bread
      Salad with, 365
    Sautéed, Baba Ghanoush with,
      304
    slices, thick, skewering, 314
Orange(s):
  Black Olive and Citrus Relish, 393
  -Chile Vinaigrette, 267–68
  Glaze, Sour, 326–27
  and Grilled Fennel Vinaigrette,
    234–35
  Lime, and Cilantro Vinaigrette, 254
  Mojo Sauce, 399–400
  Sage, and Garlic Wet Rub for
    Pork, 378–79
  -Sesame Vinaigrette, 297
Oregano:
  Lemon, and Garlic Paste, 263
  Salmoriglio Sauce, 398
Oysters:
  buying, 269
  grilled
    Charcoal-, 269
    Gas-, 269–70
    with Mignonette Sauce, 270
    with Spicy Lemon Butter, 270
    with Tangy Soy-Citrus Sauce,
      270
  serving, 270

P
Paper bags, brown, 24
Paper towels, 24
Parmesan:
  Bruschetta with Red Onions,
    Herbs, and, 344
  Grilled Corn with Garlic Butter
    and Cheese, 300–301
  -Rosemary Butter, 385
  Shaved, and Arugula, Tomato Salad
    with, 352
  shavings, creating, 344
Parsley:
  Butter, 384–85
    Lemon, 385

Parsley *(cont.)*
  marinade
    Garlic, 141
    Warm-Spiced, with Ginger, 142
  and Onion Relish, Quick, 394
  sauce
    Chimichurri, 397
    Cilantro, with Pickled Jalapeños,
      398–99
    with Cornichons and Capers,
      396–97
    Lemon, 231
    Salsa Verde, *286,* 397
  Tabbouleh, 367
  Watercress, and Spiced Vinaigrette,
    Grilled Tuna Steaks with,
    244, *284*
Pasta:
  macaroni, drying, 361
  Macaroni Salad, 362
    with Chipotles and Cilantro, 362
    with Curried Apples, 362
    preparing, 361–62
  salad
    with Arugula and Sun-Dried
      Tomato Vinaigrette, 364
    with Broccoli and Olives, 363–64
    with Eggplant, Tomatoes, and
      Basil, 364
    preparing vinaigrette for, 363
Pastes:
  applying to foods, 376
  Asian Spice, for Chicken Parts, 384
  for beef steaks, 381–82
  for chicken, 384
  Citrus and Cilantro Spice, for
    Chicken Parts, 383
  Garlic, Spicy, 263
  guidelines for using, 376
  Lemon, Garlic, and Oregano, 263
  Mediterranean Herb, 76
  Mediterranean Herb and Garlic,
    139
  Mediterranean Herb and Garlic,
    for Meat, 377
  Mediterranean Spice, for Chicken
    Parts, 384
  Red Pepper, Near East, 138
  Rosemary Garlic, for Steak, 381–82
Peach(es):
  Dried, and Apple Chutney, 396
  grilling, 327
  -Habanero Chutney, 215
  preparing for grilling, 327
  preparing for skewering, 162
  Radicchio, and Balsamic
    Vinaigrette, Grilled Pork
    Chops with, 94–95
  Salsa, 393

Peanut (butter):
  Dipping Sauce, Spicy, 400
  Sauce, 297
Peanut oil, taste tests on, 160
Pears:
  grilling, 327
  preparing for skewering, 162
Peppercorn(s):
  Cracked, Rub for Steak, 381
  Crust, Grilled Tuna Steaks with,
    243
  grinding or crushing, 189, 380
  -Horseradish Sauce, 257
  Peppery Coriander and Dill Spice
    Rub for Steak, 380–81
  taste tests on, 381
Pepper(s), bell:
  for beef kebabs, 57
  cutting, 51, 317
  Grilled, 316
    with Black Olives and Basil, 317
    with Mint and Feta, 316
    serving, with grilled sausages, 100
    Spanish-Style, with Green
      Olives and Sherry Vinegar,
      291, 316–17
  grilling, at a glance, 315
  grilling method for, 316
  Grill-Roasted, 316
  for lamb shish kebab, 140
  preparing for skewering, 162
  preparing for the grill, 51, 317
  red
    -Cranberry Relish, 203
    -Jícama Relish, 395–96
    Paste, Near East, 138
    Pureed, Sauce with Basil, 400
    Roasted, and Smoked Paprika
      Butter, 385
    roasted, jarred, taste tests on, 398
    Romesco Sauce, 398
    Sautéed Sweet, Bruschetta with,
      345
  roasted
    jarred, taste tests on, 398
    and Olives, Bread Salad with,
      365–66
    peeling, 315
    Red, and Smoked Paprika
      Butter, 385
    roasting method for, 315
    Romesco Sauce, 398
    storing, 316
  seeding, 317
  Yellow, and Tomato Salsa, Spicy, 391
Peppers, chile. *See* Chile(s);
  Chipotle(s)
Pesto, Classic, 399
Pickled Ginger Relish, 215

Pickles, Sweet, and Hard-Cooked
    Eggs, American Potato Salad
    with, 357–58
Pineapple:
    Grilled Thai-Style Shrimp with,
        264–65
    grilling, 327
    preparing for grilling, 328
    preparing for salsa, 392
    Salsa, 393
    Salsa, Tomatillo and, Spicy, 160
    skewering, with shrimp, 265
Pita Bread Salad with Olives, Feta,
    and Mint, 366
Pizza, 330–42
    broiling, to finish cooking, 334
    cutting, tools for, 339
    dough
        bread flour for, 331
        food processor for, 332
        freezing, 332
        Garlic-Herb, 332–33
        Garlic-Herb, Hand-Kneaded,
            333
        Garlic-Herb, Kneaded in a
            Standing Mixer, 333
        kneading, 331, 332
        rising, 331–32
        shaping, 333, 336
    firing the grill for, 336
    grilled, 333–42
        with Asparagus, Caramelized
            Onions, Black Olives, and
            Thyme, 341–42
        with Bacon, Corn, and Cilantro,
            342
        with Fennel, Sun-Dried
            Tomato, and Asiago, 340
        with Fresh Tomatoes and Basil,
            288, 335
        with Grilled Eggplant and Goat
            Cheese, 338–39
        with Olive Oil and Salt, 334
        with Portobello Mushrooms
            and Onions, 338
        with Prosciutto, Arugula, and
            Gorgonzola, 340–41
        with Shrimp and Feta Cheese,
            335
    grilling method for, 333–34, 337
    preparing ahead, 334
    removing from grill, 334
    rimless baking sheet for, 334, 337
    slicing mozzarella for, 337
    toppings, tips for, 333, 337, 340
Pizza cutters, 339
Plantains, Grilled, 318
    with Lime and Mint, 318
Plastic wrap, 24

Plums, grilling, 327
Poblanos, roasted:
    Charcoal-Grilled Skirt Steak Tacos
        with, 53–54
    Gas-Grilled Skirt Steak Tacos
        with, 54
Pompano, whole:
    buying, 255
    grilled
        Charcoal-, 255
        Gas-, 256
        with Tarragon Butter Sauce, 256
Porcini mushroom(s):
    dried, rehydrating, 65
    -Rubbed Grilled Veal Chops, 76
    and Thyme, Grilled Hamburgers
        with, 65
    Turkey Burgers with, 199
Pork, 90–116
    baby back ribs, 109–12
        Barbecued, on a Charcoal Grill,
            111–12, 125
        Barbecued, on a Gas Grill, 112
        barbecuing method for, 110–11
        brining, 111
        buying, 110
        rib racks for, 111
        skin-like membrane on, 110
    chops, 91–97
        best cuts, for grilling, 91–92, 94
        blade, about, 94
        brining, 92
        buying, 96
        center-cut, about, 94
        Charcoal-Grilled, 93–94, 127
        Gas-Grilled, 94
        Gas Grill–Smoked, with Apple
            Chutney, 97
        Grilled, with Peaches,
            Radicchio, and Balsamic
            Vinaigrette, 94–95
        grilling method for, 92–93
        Grill-Smoked, with Apple
            Chutney, 96–97
        grill-smoking method for,
            95–96, 97
        internal temperature of, 93,
            95, 96
        location of, 91, 94
        marinating, 92
        rib, about, 94
        rubs for, 92
        sirloin, about, 94
        smoke flavors for, 95
        see also Pork—kebabs
    country-style ribs, about, 110
    cuts of, primal, 91
    grilling, three rules for, 35–36
    kebabs, 97–100

Pork (cont.)
    best pork chops for, 97–98
    butterflying pork for, 98
    Charcoal-Grilled, 98–99
    Gas-Grilled, 99
    Grilled, with Southeast Asian
        Flavors, 99–100
    Grilled, with West Indian
        Flavors, 99
    grilling method for, 98
    marinating, 98
leanness of, 91, 92
loin
    brining, 102
    Grill-Roasted, on a Charcoal
        Grill, 102–3
    Grill-Roasted, on a Gas Grill,
        103–4
    Grill-Roasted, with Barbecue
        Rub and Fruit Salsa, 104
    Grill-Roasted, with Garlic and
        Rosemary, 104
    Grill-Roasted, with Maple-
        Mustard Glaze, 104
    grill-roasting method for, 102
    internal temperature of, 102
    location of, 91
    seasoning, 102
    tying up, 101–2, 104
optimum internal temperatures
    for, 35
primal cuts of, 91
pulled, 113–16
    Barbecued, Cuban-Style, with
        Mojo Sauce, 115–16
    Barbecued, on a Charcoal Grill,
        114–15, 128
    Barbecued, on a Gas Grill, 115
    barbecuing, key steps to, 113
    barbecuing method for, 113–14
    best pork roasts for, 113–14
    resting after cooking, 114
    rubs for, 114
rubs for, 377–79
sausages
    accompaniments to, 100
    Charcoal-Grilled Italian, 101
    coiled, grilling, 100
    Gas-Grilled Italian, 101
    grilling method for, 100–101
    smoked, grilling method for, 101
spareribs
    Barbecued, on a Charcoal Grill,
        108
    Barbecued, on a Gas Grill, 108–9
    Barbecued, with Hoisin, Honey,
        and Ginger Glaze, 109
    Barbecued, with Mexican
        Flavors, 109

Pork *(cont.)*
  barbecuing method for, 107–8
  judging when done, 108
  location of, 91, 110
  resting after cooking, 108
  taste tests on, 92, 107
  tenderloin
    brining, 106
    Charcoal-Grilled, 106–7, *126*
    Gas-Grilled, 107
    grilling method for, 105–6
    internal temperature of, 105
    leanness of, 105
    location of, 91
    removing silver skin from, 106
    spice rubs for, 106
Port-Cherry Sauce, 218
Portobello(s), 310–13
  Charcoal-Grilled Free-Form Beef
    Wellington with Port Syrup,
    43–44
  Gas-Grilled Free-Form Beef
    Wellington with Port Syrup,
    44
  Grilled, 310–11
  Grilled, Bruschetta with, 344–45
  Grilled, Sandwiches with Boursin
    Cheese and Tomatoes, 312–13
  Grilled, with Garlic, Rosemary,
    and Balsamic Vinegar, 311–12
  Grilled, with Tarragon, 311
  and Onions, Grilled Pizza with,
    338
Potatoes:
  and Grilled Premium Steak with
    Blue Cheese Butter, 42
  scrubbing, 319
  Sweet, Grill-Roasted, 321
    with Sweet Sesame and Soy
    Sauce, 321
  see also Potato salad
Potato salad:
  American
    best potatoes for, 356
    cutting potatoes for, 357
    with Hard-Cooked Eggs and
      Sweet Pickles, 357–58
    hard-cooking eggs for, 355
    keeping safe, 357
    seasonings for, 356–57
  French, 359
    with Arugula, Roquefort, and
      Walnuts, 359
    with Hard Salami and Gruyère,
      359
    preparing vinaigrette for, 358
    with Radishes, Cornichons, and
      Capers, 359
  German, 360–61

Potato salad *(cont.)*
  grilled
    and Arugula with Dijon
      Mustard Vinaigrette, *290,* 320
    with Corn and Chiles, Spicy, 320
    German-Style, 320
    grilling potatoes for, 318–19
    Potatoes for, 319
Poultry:
  brining, 172–73
  raw, foil-lined platters for, 152
  rubs for, 382, 383
  sausages
    Charcoal-Grilled, 166
    Gas-Grilled, 166
    grilling method for, 165–66
  see also Chicken; Cornish Hens;
    Duck; Quail; Squab; Turkey
Poussins, about, 209
Prosciutto, Arugula, and Gorgonzola,
  Grilled Pizza with, 340–41

Q

Quail:
  grilled
    Charcoal-, *132,* 216–17
    with Cherry-Port Sauce, 218
    with Chili-Lime Glaze, 217
    Gas-, 217
    with Sage, Mustard, and Honey,
      217
  grilling method for, 216
  internal temperature of, 216
  preparing, 216, 217

R

Radicchio:
  Peaches, and Balsamic Vinaigrette,
    Grilled Pork Chops with,
    94–95
  preparing for grilling, 94
Radishes, Capers, and Cornichons,
  French Potato Salad with, 359
Raita, 174–75
Red snapper:
  fillets
    Charcoal-Grilled, 230
    Gas-Grilled, 230
    Grilled, with Spicy Yellow
      Pepper and Tomato Salsa, 230
    grilling method for, 229–30
    substituting, for flavor
      variations, 242
  whole
    Charcoal-Grilled, 253–54

Red snapper *(cont.)*
  flavor of, 253
  Gas-Grilled, 254
  Grilled, with Fresh Tomato-
    Basil Relish, 255
  Grilled, with Orange, Lime, and
    Cilantro Vinaigrette, 254
  Grilled, with Parsley-Lemon
    Butter, 254
Red wine vinegar, taste tests on, 271
Relishes:
  Avocado-Corn, 393–94
  Black Olive and Citrus, 393
  Cranberry-Onion, 394
  Cranberry–Red Pepper, 203
  Cucumber and Mango, with
    Yogurt, 160
  Cucumber and Red Onion, with
    Mint, Warm, 394–95
  description of, 389
  Grilled Onion, 314–15
  Onion, Black Olive, and Caper, 395
  Onion and Parsley, Quick, 394
  Pickled Ginger, 215
  Red Pepper–Jícama, 395–96
  Tomato-Basil, Fresh, 255
Ribs, beef. *See* Beef—short ribs;
    Beef—Texas-style ribs
Ribs, pork. *See* Pork—baby back
    ribs; Pork—spareribs
Romesco Sauce, 398
Roquefort:
  Arugula, and Walnuts, French
    Potato Salad with, 359
  Butter, 385
Rosemary:
  Garlic Marinade, 137, 150
  Garlic Paste for Steak, 381–82
  Grilled Asparagus with Goat
    Cheese and, 297
  -Lemon Basting Oil for Vegetables,
    317
  -Mint Marinade with Garlic and
    Lemon, 142
  -Parmesan Butter, 385
Rubs:
  applying to foods, 376
  Aromatic, for Poultry, 382
  Asian Wet, for Pork, 379
  Barbecue, Simple, 376
  for Barbecue, Dry, 376
  Basic Spice, for Pork, 377
  for beef and steaks, 377, 380–82
  Cajun Spice, for Chicken Parts,
    280, 382
  Caribbean Wet, for Pork, 379
  for chicken, *280,* 382–83
  Chile-Cumin Spice, for Steak, 380
  Chipotle and Ancho, for Pork, 378

Rubs (cont.)
    Cocoa-Cumin-Allspice, for Steak,
        380
    Cracked Peppercorn, for Steak, 381
    Cumin Spice, 208
    for fish, 379
    guidelines for using, 376
    Herb, for Pork, 377–78
    Indian Spice, for Pork, 377
    Indian Spice, for Poultry, 383–84
    Jamaican Spice, for Chicken Parts,
        280, 382
    for lamb, 377
    Mustard, Garlic, and Honey Wet,
        for Pork, 379
    Orange, Sage, and Garlic Wet, for
        Pork, 378–79
    Pantry Spice, for Chicken, 383
    Peppery Coriander and Dill Spice,
        for Steak, 380–81
    for pork, 377–79
    for poultry, 382–83
    Simple Spice, for Beef or Lamb, 377
    Simple Spice, for Fish, 379
    Simple Spice, for Pork, 378
    Star Anise and Coffee Bean Spice,
        for Steak, 380
    storing, 376
    Tarragon–Mustard Seed, for Steak,
        380
    Tex-Mex Spice, for Chicken Parts,
        280, 382
    Turkish Spice, 146
    see also Tapenade
Rum-Molasses Glaze, 326

S

Safety, food, 11, 152, 157, 176
Sage, Orange, and Garlic Wet Rub
    for Pork, 378–79
Salad dressings. See Dressings;
    Vinaigrettes
Salads:
    bread
        Pita, with Olives, Feta, and
            Mint, 366
        preparing, 364–65
        with Roasted Peppers and
            Olives, 365–66
        with Tomatoes, Herbs, and Red
            Onions, 365
    Chicken, Grilled, with Sesame-
        Miso Dressing, 160–61
    coleslaw
        Creamy, 354
        Curried, with Apples and
            Raisins, 355

Salads (cont.)
    preparing cabbage for, 353–54
    Sweet-and-Sour, 355
    cucumber
        Creamy Dill, 351
        preparing, 350–51
        Sesame-Lemon, 282, 351
        Yogurt-Mint, 351
    Macaroni, 362
        with Chipotles and Cilantro, 362
        with Curried Apples, 362
        preparing, 361–62
    Napa Cabbage Slaw, 170
    pasta
        with Arugula and Sun-Dried
            Tomato Vinaigrette, 364
        with Broccoli and Olives, 363–64
        with Eggplant, Tomatoes, and
            Basil, 364
        preparing vinaigrette for, 363
    potato salad
        American, with Hard-Cooked
            Eggs and Sweet Pickles, 357–58
        French, 359
        French, with Arugula,
            Roquefort, and Walnuts, 359
        French, with Hard Salami and
            Gruyère, 359
        French, with Radishes,
            Cornichons, and Capers, 359
        German, 360–61
        Grilled, and Arugula with Dijon
            Mustard Vinaigrette, 290, 320
        Grilled, German-Style, 320
        Grilled, with Corn and Chiles,
            Spicy, 320
        Grilled Potatoes for, 319
    Red Onion, Grilled, and Tomato,
        314
    Squab, Asian-Style Grilled,
        on, with Grilled Shiitake
        Mushrooms, 219–20
    Tabbouleh, 367
    tomato
        with Arugula and Shaved
            Parmesan, 352
        and Cucumber, Israeli, 352
        with Feta and Cumin-Yogurt
            Dressing, 352–53
        Mozzarella and Basil (Insalata
            Caprese), 353
    Salami, Hard, and Gruyère, French
        Potato Salad with, 359
    Salmon:
        burgers
            Charcoal-Grilled, 245–46
            Gas-Grilled, 246
            preparing, 245, 246
            sauces for, 248

Salmon (cont.)
    fillets, 233–40
        Barbecued, on a Charcoal-Grill,
            239, 287
        Barbecued, on a Gas-Grill,
            239–40
        barbecued, sauces for, 240
        barbecuing, key steps for, 238
        barbecuing method for, 237–38
        brining, 238
        buying, 233
        Charcoal-Grilled, 234
        cold-smoked, about, 238
        Gas-Grilled, 234
        Grilled, with Aromatic Spice
            Rub, 235
        Grilled, with Grilled Fennel and
            Orange Vinaigrette, 234–35
        grilled glazed, glazes for, 237
        Grilled Glazed, on a Charcoal
            Grill, 236, 283
        Grilled Glazed, on a Gas Grill,
            237
        grilled glazed, preparing, 235–36
        grilling method for, 233
        judging when done, 233
        marinating, 235
        removing pinbones from, 239,
            246
        substituting, for flavor
            variations, 242
    whole, cooking, 258
Salmoriglio Sauce, 398
Salsas:
    Black Bean and Mango, 392
    Chunky Guacamole, 390–91
    Corn, Grilled, 391–92
    cutting tomatoes for, 389
    description of, 389
    Mango, 392
    Peach, 393
    Pineapple, 393
    Tomatillo and Pineapple, Spicy, 160
    Tomato, Fresh, 390
    Verde, 286, 397
    Yellow Pepper and Tomato, Spicy,
        391
Salsa Verde, 286, 397
Salt, for brining, 172
Sandwiches, Grilled Portobello,
    with Boursin Cheese and
    Tomatoes, 312–13
Satay:
    beef
        best beef steaks for, 59
        Charcoal-Grilled, with Spicy
            Peanut Dipping Sauce, 60
        Gas-Grilled, with Spicy Peanut
            Dipping Sauce, 61

Satay *(cont.)*
  marinating, 59–60
  preparing sauce for, 60
  slicing meat for, 59, 60
  Chicken, Thai, with Spicy Peanut
    Sauce, 164
Sauces:
  Blue Cheese Dressing, 182
  for Buffalo Wings, Spicy, 182
  Caramel, Simplified, 327
  Chermoula, 397
  Cherry-Port, 218
  for chicken wings, 182
  Chimichurri, 397
  Chipotle, Sweet-and-Sour, 50–51
  Chipotle-Lime, Creamy, 248
  Cilantro-Parsley, with Pickled
    Jalapeños, 398–99
  Classic Pesto, 399
  for fish burgers, 248
  Ginger-Cilantro, Creamy, 248
  for grilled fruit, 327
  Hoisin-Sesame, 182
  Horseradish Cream, 240
  Horseradish-Peppercorn, 257
  Lemon Herb, Creamy, 248
  Lemon-Parsley, 231
  Mignonette, 270
  Mint, 139, 152
  Mojo, 399–400
  Mustard, Sherry, and Cream, 267
  Mustard-Dill, 240
  Parsley, with Cornichons and
    Capers, 396–97
  Peanut, 297
  Peanut Dipping, Spicy, 400
  Red Pepper, Pureed, with Basil,
    400
  Romesco, 398
  Salmoriglio, 398
  Salsa Verde, *286,* 397
  Soy-Citrus, Tangy, 270
  Spicy, Sweet, and Sour Dipping,
    177–79, *277*
  Tarragon Butter, 256
  Tartar, 276
  Tomatillo-Chile, 400
  Wasabi Mayonnaise, 248
  see also Barbecue Sauces; Butter—
    compound; Chutneys;
    Dressings; Glazes; Relishes;
    Salsas; Vinaigrettes
Sausages:
  pork
    accompaniments to, 100
    Charcoal-Grilled Italian, 101
    coiled, grilling, 100
    Gas-Grilled Italian, 101
    grilling method for, 100–101

Sausages *(cont.)*
  smoked, grilling method for, 101
  poultry
    Charcoal-Grilled, 166
    Gas-Grilled, 166
    grilling method for, 165–66
Scallops, 265–68
  grilled
    Charcoal-, 266–67
    Gas-, 267
    with Mustard, Sherry, and
      Cream, 267
    with Orange-Chile Vinaigrette,
      267–68
  grilling method for, 266
  judging when done, 266
  preparing for the grill, 266
  processed versus dry, 265–66
  removing tendons from, 266
  skewering, 266
  varieties of, 265
Science of cooking:
  beef, aging, 68
  best fire for barbecue, 78
  corn, storing, 299
  cutting boards and bacteria, 176
  meat, salting, 71
  mushrooms, cleaning, 311
  potato salad safety, 357
  spices, toasting, 383
Sesame:
  -Lemon Cucumber Salad, *282,*
    351
  -Miso Dressing, 160–61
  -Orange Vinaigrette, 297
Shallot(s):
  mincing, 42
  preparing for skewering, 162
  -Soy Marinade, 137
Shellfish, 260–76
  buying, 261
  see also Clams; Crabs; Lobsters;
    Mussels; Oysters; Scallops;
    Shrimp
Sherry, Mustard, and Cream Sauce,
  267
Sherry Vinaigrette, 298
Shiitake Mushrooms, Grilled, Asian-
  Style Grilled Squab on Salad
  with, 219–20
Shish kebab. *See* Lamb—shish kebab
Shrimp, 261–65
  brining, 262
  deveining, 261, 262
  and Feta Cheese, Grilled Pizza
    with, 335
  grilled
    Charcoal-, 262–63
    Gas-, 263

Shrimp *(cont.)*
  with Lemon, Garlic, and
    Oregano Paste, 263
  New Orleans–Style, 264
  with Southwestern Flavors,
    263–64, *285*
  with Spicy Garlic Paste, 263
  Thai-Style, with Pineapple, 264–65
  peeling, 261, 262
  preparing for grilling, 262
  Sautéed Spicy, Bruschetta with,
    343–44
  sizes of, 261
  skewering, 264, 265
Side dishes, 348–72
  baked beans
    Barbecued, 369–70
    Boston, 369
  bread salad
    Pita, with Olives, Feta, and
      Mint, 366
    with Roasted Peppers and
      Olives, 365–66
    with Tomatoes, Herbs, and Red
      Onions, 365
  coleslaw
    Creamy, 354
    Curried, with Apples and
      Raisins, 355
    Sweet-and-Sour, 355
  cornbread
    All-Purpose, 371–72
    Jalapeño-Cheddar, Spicy, 372
  cucumber salad
    Creamy Dill, 351
    Sesame-Lemon, *282,* 351
    Yogurt-Mint, 351
  Grilled Red Onion and Tomato
    Salad, 314
  Macaroni Salad, 362
    with Chipotles and Cilantro, 362
    with Curried Apples, 362
  Napa Cabbage Slaw, 170
  pasta salad
    with Arugula and Sun-Dried
      Tomato Vinaigrette, 364
    with Broccoli and Olives, 363–64
    with Eggplant, Tomatoes, and
      Basil, 364
  potato. *See* Potato salad
  Tabbouleh, 367
  tomato salad
    with Arugula and Shaved
      Parmesan, 352
    Cucumber and, Israeli, 352
    with Feta and Cumin-Yogurt
      Dressing, 352–53
    Mozzarella and Basil (Insalata
      Caprese), 353

Single-level fire, 2, 3, 4, 7
Skewers and skewering methods:
    for apples, 162
    for chicken kebabs, 163, 164
    for corn on the cob, 299
    metal, about, 21
    for mushrooms, 162
    for onions, 57, 162, 314
    for peaches, 162
    for pears, 162
    for peppers, 162
    for pineapple, 162
    for scallops, 266
    for shallots, 162
    for shrimp, 264
    wood, about, 21
    for zucchini, 162
Slaws:
    Coleslaw, Curried, with Apples
        and Raisins, 355
    Creamy Coleslaw, 354
    description of, 389
    Napa Cabbage, 170
    Sweet-and-Sour Coleslaw, 355
Smoke flavors:
    adding, method for, 10
    for barbecuing foods, 3
    from charcoal grills, 12
    from gas grills, 12
    for Texas-style beef ribs, 79
    see also Wood chips and chunks
Soy (sauce):
    -Citrus Sauce, Tangy, 270
    Garlic, and Ginger Marinade, 48
    -Ginger Glaze, 244
    -Honey Glaze, 300
    -Honey Marinade with Thyme,
        150
    -Maple Glaze, 237
    -Shallot Marinade, 137
    taste tests on, 46
Spatulas, 20
Spices:
    grinding, tools for, 380
    storing, tip for, 383
    toasting, 383
    see also Rubs; specific spices
Sprayer/misters, 21
Squab:
    grilled
        Asian-Style, on Salad with
            Grilled Shiitake Mushrooms,
            219–20
        Charcoal-, 218–19
        Gas-, 219
        with Greek Flavors, 220
    grilling method for, 218
    internal temperature of, 218
    preparing, 220

Squash:
    butternut
        Grilled, 323
        Grilled, Spicy, with Garlic and
            Rosemary, 323–24
        preparing for grilling, 324
    summer
        Grilled, 325
        Grilled, with Capers and
            Oregano, 325–26
        Grilled, with Tomatoes and
            Basil, 325
        grilling, 315
        preparing for the grill, 325
    zucchini
        Grilled, 325
        Grilled, with Capers and
            Oregano, 325–26
        Grilled, with Tomatoes and
            Basil, 325
        and Grilled Loin or Rib Lamb
            Chops with Mint Sauce, 139
        grilling, 315
        preparing for the grill, 325
        skewering, 162
Stain removers, 25–26
Star Anise and Coffee Bean Spice
    Rub for Steak, 380
Steaks, fish. See Fish—steaks
Steaks (beef), 31–55
    buying, guidelines for, 31–34
    compound butters for, 384–85
    filets mignons, 41–44
        about, 32
        Beef Wellington, Charcoal-
            Grilled Free-Form, with Port
            Syrup, 43–44
        Beef Wellington, Gas-Grilled
            Free-Form, with Port Syrup,
            44
        beef Wellington, preparing,
            42–43
        Charcoal-Grilled, 41, 118
        Gas-Grilled, 41
        Grilled Premium Steak and
            Potatoes with Blue Cheese
            Butter, 42
        reshaping and tying, 41
    flank, 48–52
        about, 33
        Charcoal-Grilled, 49
        Classic Fajitas, 51–52, 123
        Gas-Grilled, 50
        Grilled, and Red Onions with
            Chimichurri Sauce, 51
        Grilled, Rubbed with Latin
            Spices, 50
        Grilled, with Sweet-and-Sour
            Chipotle Sauce, 50–51

Steaks (beef) (cont.)
        grilling method for, 48
        resting after cooking, 48–49
        spice rubs for, 48
        steaks similar to, 49
        see also Beef—satay
    flap meat sirloin, about, 33
    flat, taste tests on, 49
    hanger, about, 33, 49
    internal temperature, checking, 38
    London broil
        buying steaks for, 32, 54
        Charcoal-Grilled, 55
        Gas-Grilled, 55
    porterhouse
        about, 33
        carving, 39
        Charcoal-Grilled, 38–39
        Gas-Grilled, 39
        Grilled Premium Steak and
            Potatoes with Blue Cheese
            Butter, 42
        Grilled Tuscan Steak with Olive
            Oil and Lemon, 40–41, 117
        grilling method for, 36–37
        resting after cooking, 37
        seasoning, 37
    premium
        Grilled, and Potatoes with Blue
            Cheese Butter, 42
        grilling method for, 36–37
        resting after cooking, 37
        seasoning, 37
        types of, 36
    rib
        about, 32
        Charcoal-Grilled, 37–38
        Gas-Grilled, 38
        Grilled Premium Steak and
            Potatoes with Blue Cheese
            Butter, 42
        grilling method for, 36–37
    rib-eye, about, 32
    round-bone, about, 33
    rubs and pastes for, 380–82
    shoulder, about, 32, 54
    skirt
        about, 33, 49
        Charcoal-Grilled, Tacos with
            Roasted Poblanos, 53–54
        Gas-Grilled, Tacos with
            Roasted Poblanos, 54
        grilling method for, 52
        marinating, 52–53
        slicing, 53
    strip
        about, 32
        Charcoal-Grilled, 37–38
        Gas-Grilled, 38

Steaks (beef) *(cont.)*
    Grilled Premium Steak and
       Potatoes with Blue Cheese
       Butter, 42
    grilling method for, 36–37
    T-bone
       about, 32
       carving, 39
       Charcoal-Grilled, 38–39
       Gas-Grilled, 39
       Grilled Premium Steak and
         Potatoes with Blue Cheese
         Butter, 42
       Grilled Tuscan Steak with Olive
         Oil and Lemon, 40–41, *117*
       grilling method for, 36–37
       resting after cooking, 37
       seasoning, 37
    tenderloin, about, 32
    tips, 44–48
       best beef cuts for, 33, 44, 45
       buying, 45
       Charcoal-Grilled, 47, *120*
       Gas-Grilled, 47
       grilling method for, 46–47
       marinades for, 47–48
       marinating, 45–46
       resting after cooking, 47
    top blade. *See* Beef—kebabs
    top loin, about, 32
    top sirloin, about, 33
Storage containers, for food, 24–25
Striped bass, whole:
    flavor of, 253
    grilled
       Charcoal-, 253–54
       with Fresh Tomato-Basil Relish,
         255
       Gas-, 254
       with Orange, Lime, and
         Cilantro Vinaigrette, 254
       with Parsley-Lemon Butter, 254
Summer squash:
    Grilled, 325
       with Capers and Oregano,
         325–26
       with Tomatoes and Basil, 325
    grilling, at a glance, 315
    preparing for the grill, 325
Sweet Potatoes, Grill-Roasted, 321
    with Sweet Sesame and Soy
       Sauce, 321
Swordfish, 230–33
    kebabs
       Charcoal-Grilled, 232
       Gas-Grilled, 232
       Grilled, with Salmoriglio Sauce,
         233
       grilling method for, 232

Swordfish *(cont.)*
    Southeast Asian–Style, 232–33
    steaks
       Charcoal-Grilled, 231
       Gas-Grilled, 231
       Grilled, with Chermoula, 231
       Grilled, with Lemon-Parsley
         Sauce, 231
       Grilled, with Salsa Verde, 231
       grilling method for, 230
       substituting, for flavor
         variations, 242

T

Tabbouleh, 367
Tacos, skirt steak:
    Charcoal-Grilled, with Roasted
       Poblanos, 53–54
    Gas-Grilled, with Roasted
       Poblanos, 54
Tandoori Marinade, 150
Tapenade, 216, 345
    Butter, 385
    Green Olive, 187
Tarragon:
    Butter Sauce, 256
    -Chive Butter, 274
    -Lime Butter, 385
    and Mint Vinaigrette, 307
    –Mustard Seed Rub for Steak, 380
Tartar Sauce, 276
Tenderloin, beef. *See* Beef—
    tenderloin
Tenderloin, pork. *See* Pork—
    tenderloin
Thermometers:
    grill, 21
    instant-read, 21–22, 38
    timer/thermometers, 22–23
Timer/thermometers, 22–23
Tomatillo:
    -Chile Sauce, 400
    and Pineapple Salsa, Spicy, 160
Tomato(es):
    and Basil, Bruschetta with, 343
    and Basil, Grilled Zucchini or
       Summer Squash with, 325
    -Basil Relish, Fresh, 255
    and Boursin Cheese, Grilled
       Portobello Sandwiches with,
       312–13
    Cherry, and Cilantro Vinaigrette,
       301–2
    cooking, for barbecue sauce, 386
    coring, 323
    Eggplant, and Basil, Pasta Salad
       with, 364

Tomato(es) *(cont.)*
    Fresh, and Basil, Grilled Pizza
       with, *288,* 335
    grilled
       Cherry, 322
       Cherry, with Greek Flavors, 323
       Round or Plum, 322
    and Grilled Red Onion Salad, 314
    grilling, at a glance, 315
    Herbs, and Red Onions, Bread
       Salad with, 365
    salad
       with Arugula and Shaved
         Parmesan, 352
       Cucumber and, Israeli, 352
       with Feta and Cumin-Yogurt
         Dressing, 352–53
       Mozzarella and Basil (Insalata
         Caprese), 353
    salsa
       cutting tomatoes for, 389
       Fresh, 390
       Spicy Yellow Pepper and, 391
    seeding, 322
    sun-dried
       Fennel, and Asiago, Grilled
         Pizza with, 340
       Vinaigrette, 364
Tongs, 19–20
Trout, whole freshwater:
    Charcoal-Grilled, 256–57
    Gas-Grilled, 257
    Grilled, with Bacon and
       Horseradish-Peppercorn
       Sauce, 257
Tuna, 240–48
    burgers
       Charcoal-Grilled, 246–47
       Gas-Grilled, 247
       preparing, 245
       sauces for, 248
    steaks, 240–44
       Charcoal-Grilled, 241
       Gas-Grilled, 242
       Grilled, and Bok Choy with
         Soy-Ginger Glaze, 244
       Grilled, Thin-Cut, 242–43
       Grilled, with Herb-Infused
         Oil, 243
       Grilled, with Peppercorn Crust,
         243
       Grilled, with Tarragon-Lime
         Butter or Tapenade Butter,
         244
       Grilled, with Watercress, Parsley,
         and Spiced Vinaigrette, 244,
         284
       Grilled Rare, with Soy, Ginger,
         and Wasabi, 243–44

Tuna *(cont.)*
    grilling method for, 240–41
    marinating, 241
    substituting, for flavor
        variations, 242
Turkey, 196–208
    breast, 203–7
        brining, 203
        buying, 203, 206
        Grill-Roasted, on a Charcoal
            Grill, 206–7
        Grill-Roasted, on a Gas Grill,
            207
        Grill-Roasted, with Cumin
            Spice Rub, 208
        grill-roasting method for, 206
        internal temperature of, 203,
            204
        preparing for grilling, 207
    burgers
        best ground turkey for, 197–98
        Charcoal-Grilled, *131,* 198–99
        flavorings and fillers for, 198
        Gas-Grilled, 199
        grilling method for, 198
        internal temperature of, 198
        with Miso, 199
        with Porcini Mushrooms, 199
        Ultimate, 199
    whole, 200–205
        brining, 172–73, 200, 204
        buying, 204
        carving, 205
        frozen, defrosting, 205
        Grill-Roasted, on a Charcoal
            Grill, *130,* 201–2
        Grill-Roasted, on a Gas Grill,
            202–3
        Grill-Roasted, with Cranberry–
            Red Pepper Relish, 203
        Grill-Roasted, with Spice Rub,
            203
        grill-roasting method for,
            200–201
        internal temperature of, 204
        protecting wings of, 204
        rubs for, 382, 383
        trussing, 200
        V-racks for, 200, 205
Two-level fire, 2, 3, 4, 7
Two-level fire, modified, 2, 3, 4, 7

V

Veal:
    chops
        best types of, 75
        Charcoal-Grilled, 76
        Gas-Grilled, 76
        Grilled, on a Bed of Arugula,
            77, *124*
        Grilled, Porcini-Rubbed, 76
        Grilled, with Mediterranean
            Herb Paste, 76
        grilling, three rules for, 35–36
        grilling method for, 75
        optimum internal temperatures
            for, 35
        taste tests on, 75
    milk-fed versus natural, 75
Vegetables, 294–326
    basting oils for, 317
    for beef kebabs, 57
    for chicken kebabs, 162–63
    grilling chart for, 315
    for lamb shish kebab, 140
    see also specific vegetables
Vinaigrettes:
    Balsamic, 94–95
    Cherry Tomato and Cilantro,
        301–2
    Dijon Mustard, 320
    Fennel, Grilled, and Orange,
        234–35
    Grapefruit, 306–7
    Lemon, Grilled, 296–97
    Mint and Tarragon, 307
    Orange, Lime, and Cilantro, 254
    Orange-Chile, 267–68
    Orange-Sesame, 297
    preparing, for French potato salad,
        358
    preparing, for pasta salad, 363
    Sherry, 298
    Spiced, 244
    Sun-Dried Tomato, 364
Vinegar:
    balsamic
        Dressing, 305
        taste tests on, 307
        Vinaigrette, 94–95
    red wine, taste tests on, 271
    Sherry Vinaigrette, 298
V-racks, 111, 200, 205

W

Walnuts, Arugula, and Roquefort,
    French Potato Salad with,
    359
Wasabi Mayonnaise, 248
Watercress, Parsley, and Spiced
    Vinaigrette, Grilled Tuna
    Steaks with, 244, *284*
Weather conditions and grilling,
    11, 12
Wood chips and chunks:
    for charcoal grill, 8, 10
    for gas grill, 9, 10
    for grill roasting, 8, 9, 10
    soaking, 10, 109
    wood types in, 10
    wrapping in foil, 10

Y

Yogurt:
    Cucumber and Mango Relish
        with, 160
    -Cumin Dressing, 352–53
    -Mint Cucumber Salad, 351
    Raita, 174–75
    Tandoori Marinade, 150

Z

Zucchini:
    Grilled, 325
        with Capers and Oregano,
            325–26
        with Tomatoes and Basil, 325
    and Grilled Loin or Rib Lamb
        Chops with Mint Sauce, 139
    grilling, at a glance, 315
    preparing for the grill, 325
    skewering, 162